METAHEURISTICS

METAHEURISTICS

FROM DESIGN TO IMPLEMENTATION

El-Ghazali Talbi
University of Lille – CNRS – INRIA

WILEY
A JOHN WILEY & SONS, INC., PUBLICATION

Published by John Wiley & Sons, Inc., Hoboken, New Jersey
Published simultaneously in Canada.

For general information on our other products and services or for technical support, please contact our Customer Care Department within the United States at (800) 762-2974, outside the United States at (317) 572-3993 or fax (317) 572-4002.

Wiley also publishes its books in a variety of electronic formats. Some content that appears in print may not be available in electronic formats. For more information about Wiley products, visit our web site at www.wiley.com.

Library of Congress Cataloging-in-Publication Data:

Talbi, El-Ghazali, 1965-
Metaheuristics : from design to implementation / El-ghazali Talbi.
p. cm.
Includes bibliographical references and index.
ISBN 978-0-470-27858-1 (cloth)
1. Mathematical optimization. 2. Heuristic programming. 3. Problem solving–Data processing. 4. Computer algorithms. I. Title.
QA402.5.T39 2009
519.6–dc22

2009017331

10 9 8 7 6 5 4 3 2

To my wife Keltoum, my daughter Besma, my parents and sisters.

CONTENTS

PREFACE

IMPORTANCE OF THIS BOOK

Applications of optimization are countless. Every process has a potential to be optimized. There is no company that is not involved in solving optimization problems. Indeed, many challenging applications in science and industry can be formulated as optimization problems. Optimization occurs in the minimization of time, cost, and risk or the maximization of profit, quality, and efficiency. For instance, there are many possible ways to design a network to optimize the cost and the quality of service; there are many ways to schedule a production to optimize the time; there are many ways to predict a 3D structure of a protein to optimize the potential energy, and so on.

A large number of real-life optimization problems in science, engineering, economics, and business are complex and difficult to solve. They cannot be solved in an exact manner within a reasonable amount of time. Using approximate algorithms is the main alternative to solve this class of problems.

Approximate algorithms can further be decomposed into two classes: specific heuristics and metaheuristics. Specific heuristics are problem dependent; they are designed and applicable to a particular problem. This book deals with metaheuristics that represent more general approximate algorithms applicable to a large variety of optimization problems. They can be tailored to solve any optimization problem. Metaheuristics solve instances of problems that are believed to be hard in general, by exploring the usually large solution search space of these instances. These algorithms achieve this by reducing the effective size of the space and by exploring that space efficiently. Metaheuristics serve three main purposes: solving problems faster, solving large problems, and obtaining robust algorithms. Moreover, they are simple to design and implement, and are very flexible.

Metaheuristics are a branch of optimization in computer science and applied mathematics that are related to algorithms and computational complexity theory. The past 20 years have witnessed the development of numerous metaheuristics in various communities that sit at the intersection of several fields, including artificial intelligence, computational intelligence, soft computing, mathematical programming, and operations research. Most of the metaheuristics mimic natural metaphors to solve complex optimization problems (e.g., evolution of species, annealing process, ant colony, particle swarm, immune system, bee colony, and wasp swarm).

Metaheuristics are more and more popular in different research areas and industries. One of the indicators of this situation is the huge number of sessions, workshops, and conferences dealing with the design and application of metaheuristics. For example, in the biannual EMO conference on evolutionary multiobjective optimization, there one more or less 100 papers and 200 participants. This is a subset family of metaheuristics (evolutionary algorithms) applied to a subset class of problems (multiobjective problems)! In practice, metaheuristics are raising a large interest in diverse technologies, industries, and services since they proved to be efficient algorithms in solving a wide range of complex real-life optimization problems in different domains: logistics, bioinformatics and computational biology, engineering design, networking, environment, transportation, data mining, finance, business, and so on. For instance, companies are faced with an increasingly complex environment, an economic pressure, and customer demands. Optimization plays an important role in the imperative cost reduction and fast product development.

PURPOSE OF THIS BOOK

The main goal of this book is to provide a unified view of metaheuristics. It presents the main design questions and search components for all families of metaheuristics. Not only the design aspect of metaheuristics but also their implementation using a software framework are presented. This will encourage the reuse of both the design and the code of existing search components with a high level of transparency regarding the target applications and architectures.

The book provides a complete background that enables readers to design and implement powerful metaheuristics to solve complex optimization problems in a diverse range of application domains. Readers learn to solve large-scale problems quickly and efficiently. Numerous real-world examples of problems and solutions demonstrate how metaheuristics are applied in such fields as telecommunication, logistics and transportation, bioinformatics, engineering design, scheduling, and so on. In this book, the key search components of metaheuristics are considered as a toolbox for

- Designing efficient metaheuristics for optimization problems (e.g., combinatorial optimization, continuous optimization).
- Designing efficient metaheuristics for multiobjective optimization problems.
- Designing hybrid, parallel, and distributed metaheuristics.
- Implementing metaheuristics on sequential and parallel machines.

AUDIENCE

For a practicing engineer, a researcher, or a student, this book provides not only the materiel for all metaheuristics but also the guidance and practical tools for solving complex optimization problems.

One of the main audience of this book is **advanced undergraduate and graduate students** in computer science, operations research, applied mathematics, control, business and management, engineering, and so on. Many undergraduate courses on optimization throughout the world would be interested in the contents thanks to the introductory part of the book and the additional information on Internet resources.

In addition, the **postgraduate** courses related to optimization and complex problem solving will be a direct target of the book. Metaheuristics are present in more and more postgraduate studies (computer science, business and management, mathematical programming, engineering, control, etc.).

The intended audience is also **researchers** in different disciplines. Researchers in computer science and operations research are developing new optimization algorithms. Many researchers in different application domains are also concerned with the use of metaheuristics to solve their problems.

Many **engineers** are also dealing with optimization in their problem solving. The purpose of the book is to help engineers to use metaheuristics for solving real-world optimization problems in various domains of application. The application part of the book will deal with many important and strategic domains such as computational biology, telecommunication, engineering design, data mining and machine learning, transportation and logistics, production systems, and so on.

The prerequisite knowledge the readers need to have is a basic background in algorithms. For the implementation part, basic background in programming with C++ will be a plus.

OUTLINE

The book is organized in the following six different chapters (Fig. P.1):

- **Common concepts for metaheuristics:** First, this chapter justifies the existence of the book. The main concepts of optimization models, complexity of

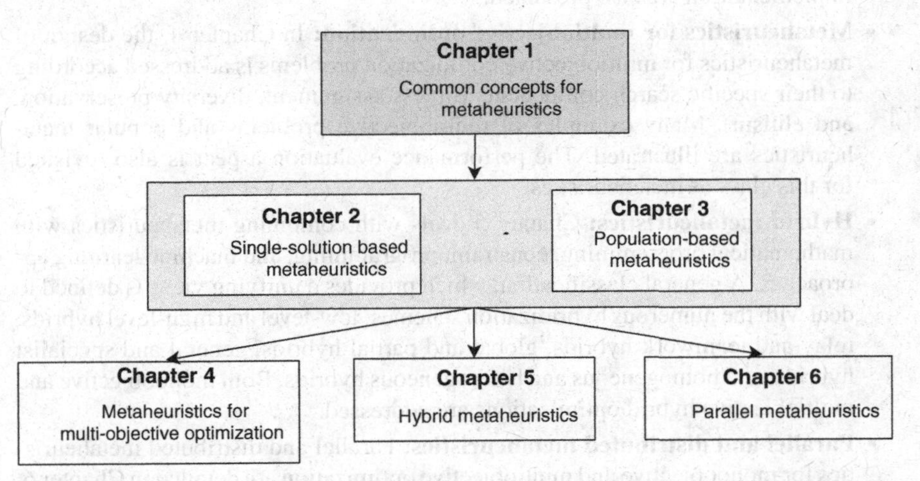

FIGURE P.1 Relationship between the different chapters of the book. The graph presents the dependencies between the chapters.

algorithms, and optimization methods are outlined. Then, the chapter exposes the common and basic concepts for metaheuristics (e.g., representation, objective function, and constraint handling). These concepts are used in designing *any* metaheuristic. The encoding (or representation) of a solution and its associated objective function are one of the most important features in metaheuristics. They will define the structure of the problem in which metaheuristics will search "good" solutions. Other important common issues of metaheuristics are detailed: performance evaluation and parameter tuning. Finally, the software engineering aspect dealing with frameworks for metaheuristics is presented.

- **Single-solution based metaheuristics:** In chapter 2, the focus is on the design and implementation of single-solution based metaheuristics such as local search, tabu search, simulated annealing, threshold accepting, variable neighborhood search, iterated local search, guided local search, GRASP, and so on. The common concepts of this class of metaheuristics are outlined (e.g., neighborhood, initial solution, and incremental evaluation). For each metaheuristic, the specific design and implementation of its search components are exposed. The parameters of each metaheuristic are analyzed and the relationship between different algorithms is addressed. Moreover, the convergence aspect of the introduced metaheuristics and many illustrative examples of their implementation are presented.
- **Population-based metaheuristics:** Chapter 3 concerns the design and implementation of population-based metaheuristics such as evolutionary algorithms (genetic algorithms, evolution strategies, genetic programming, evolutionary programming, estimation of distribution algorithms, differential evolution, and coevolutionary algorithms), swarm intelligence-based methods (e.g., ant colonies, particle swarm optimization), scatter search, bee colony, artificial immune systems, and so on. The common and specific search concepts of this class of metaheuristics are outlined. Many illustrative examples for their design and implementation are also presented.
- **Metaheuristics for multiobjective optimization:** In Chapter 4, the design of metaheuristics for multiobjective optimization problems is addressed according to their specific search components (fitness assignment, diversity preservation, and elitism). Many examples of multiobjective problems and popular metaheuristics are illustrated. The performance evaluation aspect is also revisited for this class of metaheuristics.
- **Hybrid metaheuristics:** Chapter 5 deals with combining metaheuristics with mathematical programming, constraint programming, and machine learning approaches. A general classification, which provides a unifying view, is defined to deal with the numerous hybridization schemes: low-level and high-level hybrids, relay and teamwork hybrids, global and partial hybrids, general and specialist hybrids, and homogeneous and heterogeneous hybrids. Both monoobjective and multiobjective hybrid optimizations are addressed.
- **Parallel and distributed metaheuristics:** Parallel and distributed metaheuristics for monoobjective and multiobjective optimization are detailed in Chapter 6.

The unified parallel models for mataheuristics (algorithmic level, iteration level, solution level) are analyzed in terms of design. The main concepts of parallel architectures and parallel programming paradigms, which interfere with the implementation of parallel metaheuristics, are also outlined.

Each chapter ends with a summary of the most important points. The evolving web site `http://paradiseo.gforge.inria.fr` contains the main material (tutorials, practical exercises, and problem-solving environment for some optimization problems).

Many search concepts are illustrated in this book: more than 170 examples and 169 exercises are provided. Appendix introduces the main concepts of the UML (Unified Modeling Language) notations and C++ concepts for an easy understanding and use of the ParadisEO framework for metaheuristics.

ACKNOWLEDGMENTS

Thanks go to

- My former and actual PhD students: V. Bachelet, M. Basseur, J.-C. Boisson, H. Bouziri, J. Brongniart, S. Cahon, Z. Hafidi, L. Jourdan, N. Jozefowiez, D. Kebbal, M. Khabzaoui, A. Khanafer, J. Lemesre, A. Liefooghe, T.-V. Luong, M. Mehdi, H. Meunier, M. Mezmaz, A. Tantar, E. Tantar, and B. Weinberg.
- Former and actual members of my research team OPAC and the INRIA DOLPHIN team project: C. Canape, F. Clautiaux, B. Derbel, C. Dhaenens, G. Even, M. Fatene, J. Humeau, T. Legrand, N. Melab, O. Schütze, and J. Tavares. A special thank to C. Dhaenens and N. Melab for their patience in reading some chapters of this book.
- Former and current collaborators: E. Alba, P. Bessière, P. Bouvry, D. Duvivier, C. Fonlupt, J.-M. Geib, K. Mellouli, T. Muntean, A.J. Nebro, P. Preux, M. Rahoual, D. Robillard, O. Roux, F. Semet, and A. Zomaya.

This book was written during my world scientific tour! This has influenced my inspiration. In fact, it was written during numerous international visits I made to attend seminars, training courses, and conferences in the past 2 years: Madrid, Algiers, Sydney, Dresden, Qatar, Saragossa, Tokyo, Dagstuhl, Gran Canaria, Amsterdam, Luxembourg, Barcelona, Pragua, Vienna, Hawaii, Porto, Montreal, Tunis, Dubai, Orlando, Rio de Janeiro, Warsaw, Hong Kong, Auckland, Singapour, Los Angeles, Tampa, Miami, Boston, Malaga, and (I will not forget it) Lille in France!

Finally, I would like to thank the team at John Wiley & Sons who gave me excellent support throughout this project.

GLOSSARY

ACO	Ant colony optimization
ADA	Annealed demon algorithm
aiNET	Artificial immune network
AIS	Artificial immune system
AMS	Adaptive multistart
ARMA	Autoregression moving average
ART	Adaptive reasoning technique
A-Teams	Asynchronous teams algorithm
BA	Bee algorithm
B&B	Branch and bound algorithm
BC	Bee colony
BDA	Bounded demon algorithm
BOA	Bayesian optimization algorithm
BOCTP	Biobjective covering tour problem
BOFSP	Biobjective flow-shop scheduling problem
CA	Cultural algorithms
CC-UMA	Cache coherent uniform memory access machine
CC-NUMA	Cache coherent nonuniform memory access machine
CEA	Coevolutionary algorithms
CIGAR	Case-injected genetic algorithm
CLONALG	Clonal selection algorithm
CLUMPS	Cluster of SMP machines
CMA	Covariance matrix adaptation
CMA-ES	CMA-evolution strategy
CMST	Capacitated minimum spanning tree problem
COSEARCH	Cooperative search algorithm
COW	Cluster of workstations
CP	Constraint programming
CPP	Clique partitioning problem
CSP	Constraint satisfaction problem
CTP	Covering tour problem

CTSP	Colorful traveling salesman problem
CVRP	Capacitated vehicle routing problem
CX	Cycle crossover
DA	Demon algorithm
DACE	Design and analysis of computer experiments
DE	Differential algorithm
DM	Data mining
DOE	Design of experiments
DP	Dynamic programming
EA	Evolutionary algorithm
EC	Evolutionary computation
EDA	Estimation of distribution algorithm
EMNA	Estimation of multivariate normal algorithm
EMO	Evolutionary multicriterion optimization
EO	Evolving objects
EP	Evolutionary programming
ES	Evolution strategy
FDC	Fitness distance correlation
FPGA	Field programming gate arrays
FPTAS	Fully polynomial-time approximation scheme
FSP	Flow-shop scheduling problem
GA	Genetic algorithms
GAP	Generalized assignment problem
GBP	Graph bipartitioning problem
GCP	Graph coloring problem
GDA	Great deluge algorithm
GLS	Guided local search algorithm
GP	Genetic programming
GPP	Graph partitioning problem
GPS	Global positioning system
GPSO	Geometric particle swarm optimization
GPU	Graphical processing unit
GRASP	Greedy adaptive search procedure
GVNS	General variable neighborhood search
HMSTP	Hop-constrained minimum spanning tree problem
HTC	High-throughput computing
HPC	High-performance computing
HRH	High-level relay hybrid

HTH	High-level teamwork hybrid
IBEA	Indicator-based evolutionary algorithm
ILP	Integer linear programming
ILS	Iterative local search
IP	Integer program
JSP	Job-shop scheduling problem
LAN	Local area network
LOP	Linear ordering problem
LP	Linear programming
LRH	Low-level relay hybrid
LS	Local search
LTH	Low-level teamwork hybrid
MBO	Marriage in honeybees optimization
MCDM	Multicriteria decision making
MDO	Multidisciplinary design optimization
MIMD	Multiple instruction streams—multiple data stream
MIP	Mixed integer programming
MISD	Multiple instruction streams—single data stream
MLS	Multistart local search
MLST	Minimum label spanning tree problem
MO	Moving objects
MOEO	Multiobjective evolving objects
MOEA	Multiobjective evolutionary algorithm
MOGA	Multiobjective genetic algorithm
MOP	Multiobjective optimization
MOSA	Multiobjective simulated annealing algorithm
MOTS	Multiobjective tabu search
MP	Mathematical programming
MPI	Message passing interface
MPP	Massively parallel processing machine
MSTP	Minimum spanning Tree Problem
NFL	No free lunch theorem
NLP	Nonlinear continuous optimization problem
NM	Noisy method
NOW	Network of workstations
NSA	Negative selection algorithm
NSGA	Nondominated sorting genetic algorithm
OBA	Old bachelor accepting algorithm

OX	Order crossover
PAES	Pareto archived evolution strategy
ParadisEO	Parallel and distributed evolving objects
PBIL	Population-based incremental learning algorithm
PCS	Parent centric crossover
PEO	Parallel Evolving objects
P-metaheuristic	Population-based metaheuristic
PMX	Partially mapped crossover
POPMUSIC	Partial optimization metaheuristic under special intensification conditions
PR	Path relinking
PSO	Particle swarm optimization
PTAS	Polynomial-time approximation scheme
PVM	Parallel virtual machine
QAP	Quadratic assignment problem
RADA	Randomized annealed demon algorithm
RBDA	Randomized bounded demon algorithm
RCL	Restricted candidate list
RMI	Remote method invocation
RPC	Remote procedural call
RRT	Record-to-record travel algorithm
SA	Simulated annealing
SAL	Smoothing algorithm
SAT	Satisfiability problems
SCP	Set covering problem
SCS	Shortest common supersequence problem
SDMCCP	Subset disjoint minimum cost cycle problem
SIMD	Single instruction stream—multiple data stream
SISD	Single instruction stream—single data stream
SM	Smoothing method
S-metaheuristic	Single-solution based metaheuristic
SMP	Symmetric multiprocessors
SMTWTP	Single-machine total-weighted tardiness problem
SPEA	Strength Pareto evolutionary algorithm
SPX	Simplex crossover
SS	Scatter search
SUS	Stochastic universal sampling
SVNS	Skewed variable neighborhood search
TA	Threshold accepting

TAPAS	Target aiming Pareto search
TS	Tabu search
TSP	Traveling salesman problem
UMDA	Univariate marginal distribution algorithm
UNDX	Unimodal normal distribution crossover
VEGA	Vector evaluated genetic algorithm
VIP	Vote-inherit-promote protocol
VND	Variable neighborhood descent
VNDS	Variable neighborhood decomposition search
VNS	Variable neighborhood search
VRP	Vehicle routing problem
WAN	Wide area network

CHAPTER 1

Common Concepts for Metaheuristics

Computing optimal solutions is intractable for many optimization problems of industrial and scientific importance. In practice, we are usually satisfied with "good" solutions, which are obtained by heuristic or metaheuristic algorithms. Metaheuristics represent a family of approximate[1] optimization techniques that gained a lot of popularity in the past two decades. They are among the most promising and successful techniques. Metaheuristics provide "acceptable" solutions in a reasonable time for solving hard and complex problems in science and engineering. This explains the significant growth of interest in metaheuristic domain. Unlike exact optimization algorithms, metaheuristics do not guarantee the optimality of the obtained solutions. Instead of approximation algorithms, metaheuristics do not define how close are the obtained solutions from the optimal ones.

The word *heuristic* has its origin in the old Greek word *heuriskein*, which means the art of discovering new strategies (rules) to solve problems. The suffix *meta*, also a Greek word, means "upper level methodology." The term *metaheuristic* was introduced by F. Glover in the paper [322]. Metaheuristic search methods can be defined as upper level general methodologies (templates) that can be used as guiding strategies in designing underlying heuristics to solve specific optimization problems.

This chapter is organized as follows. Section 1.1 discusses the diverse classical optimization models that can be used to formulate and solve optimization problems. It also introduces the basic concepts of algorithm and problem complexities. Some illustrative easy and hard optimization problems are given. Section 1.2 presents other models for optimization that are not static and deterministic. Those problems are characterized by dynamicity, uncertainty, or multiperiodicity. Then, Section 1.3 outlines the main families of optimization methods: exact versus approximate algorithms, metaheuristic versus approximation algorithms, iterative versus greedy algorithms, single-solution based metaheuristics versus population-based metaheuristics. Finally, an important question one might ask is answered: "when use metaheuristics?" Once the basic material for optimization problems and algorithms are presented, important common concepts of metaheuristics are introduced in Section 1.4, such as the

[1]There is a difference between approximate algorithms and approximation algorithms (see Section 1.3.2).

Metaheuristics: From Design to Implementation, by El-Ghazali Talbi

representation of solutions and the guiding objective function. Then, Sections 1.5, 1.6, and 1.7 present successively three important topics common to all metaheuristics: constraint handling, parameter tuning, and performance evaluation. Finally in Section 1.8, the software framework aspect of metaheuristics is discussed and the ParadisEO framework, which is used to implement the designed metaheuristics, is detailed.

1.1 OPTIMIZATION MODELS

As scientists, engineers, and managers, we always have to take decisions. Decision making is everywhere. As the world becomes more and more complex and competitive, decision making must be tackled in a rational and optimal way. Decision making consists in the following steps (Fig. 1.1):

- **Formulate the problem:** In this first step, a decision problem is identified. Then, an initial statement of the problem is made. This formulation may be imprecise. The internal and external factors and the objective(s) of the problem are outlined. Many decision makers may be involved in formulating the problem.
- **Model the problem:** In this important step, an abstract mathematical model is built for the problem. The modeler can be inspired by similar models in the literature. This will reduce the problem to well-studied optimization models. Usually, models we are solving are simplifications of the reality. They involve approximations and sometimes they skip processes that are complex to represent in a mathematical model. An interesting question may occur: why solve exactly real-life optimization problems that are fuzzy by nature?
- **Optimize the problem:** Once the problem is modeled, the solving procedure generates a "good" solution for the problem. The solution may be optimal or suboptimal. Let us notice that we are finding a solution for an abstract model of the problem and not for the originally formulated real-life problem. Therefore, the obtained solution performances are indicative when the model is an accurate one. The algorithm designer can reuse state-of-the-art algorithms on

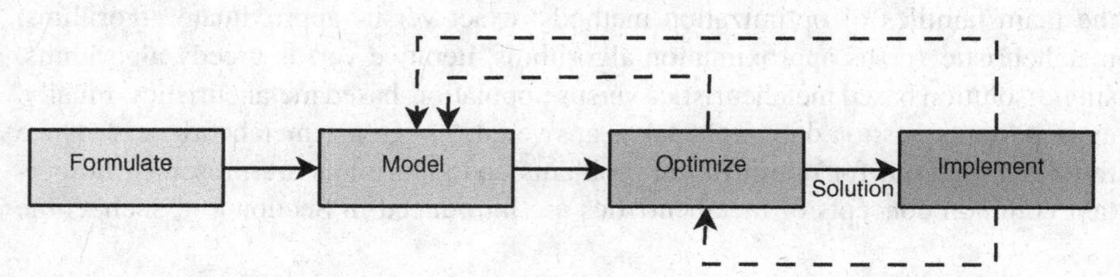

FIGURE 1.1 The classical process in decision making: formulate, model, solve, and implement. In practice, this process may be iterated to improve the optimization model or algorithm until an acceptable solution is found. Like life cycles in software engineering, the life cycle of optimization models and algorithms may be linear, spiral, or cascade.

similar problems or integrate the knowledge of this specific application into the algorithm.

- **Implement a solution:** The obtained solution is tested practically by the decision maker and is implemented if it is "acceptable." Some practical knowledge may be introduced in the solution to be implemented. If the solution is unacceptable, the model and/or the optimization algorithm has to be improved and the decision-making process is repeated.

1.1.1 Classical Optimization Models

As mentioned, optimization problems are encountered in many domains: science, engineering, management, and business. An optimization problem may be defined by the couple (S, f), where S represents the set of feasible solutions[2], and $f : S \longrightarrow \mathbb{R}$ the objective function[3] to optimize. The objective function assigns to every solution $s \in S$ of the search space a real number indicating its worth. The objective function f allows to define a total order relation between any pair of solutions in the search space.

Definition 1.1 Global optimum. *A solution $s^* \in S$ is a global optimum if it has a better objective function*[4] *than all solutions of the search space, that is,* $\forall s \in S, f(s^*) \leq f(s)$.

Hence, the main goal in solving an optimization problem is to find a global optimal solution s^*. Many global optimal solutions may exist for a given problem. Hence, to get more alternatives, the problem may also be defined as finding all global optimal solutions.

Different families of optimization models are used in practice to formulate and solve decision-making problems (Fig. 1.2). The most successful models are based on *mathematical programming* and *constraint programming*.

A commonly used model in mathematical programming is *linear programming* (LP), which can be formulated as follows:

$$\text{Min } c \cdot x$$

subject to

$$A \cdot x \geq b$$

$$x \geq 0$$

[2] A solution is also referred to as a configuration or a state. The set S is named search space, configuration space, or state space.

[3] Sometimes named cost, utility, or fitness function.

[4] We suppose without loss of generality a minimization problem. Maximizing an objective function f is equivalent to minimizing $-f$.

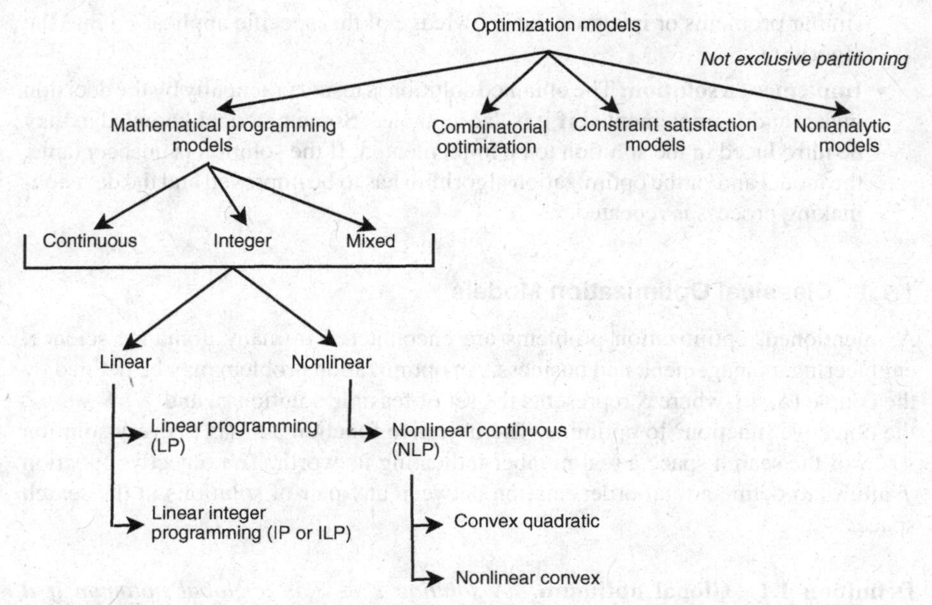

FIGURE 1.2 Classical optimization models. The different classes are possibly overlapping.

where x is a vector of continuous decision variables, and c and b (resp. A) are constant vectors (resp. matrix) of coefficients.

In a linear programming optimization problem, both the objective function $c \cdot x$ to be optimized and the constraints $A \cdot x \leq b$ are linear functions. Linear programming is one of the most satisfactory models of solving optimization problems[5]. Indeed, for continuous linear optimization problems[6], efficient exact algorithms such as the simplex-type method [174] or interior point methods exist [444]. The efficiency of the algorithms is due to the fact that the feasible region of the problem is a convex set and the objective function is a convex function. Then, the global optimum solution is necessarily a node of the polytope representing the feasible region (see Fig. 1.3). Moreover, any local optima[7] solution is a global optimum. In general, there is no reason to use metaheuristics to solve LP continuous problems.

Example 1.1 Linear programming model in decision making. A given company synthesizes two products Prod_1 and Prod_2 based on two kinds of raw materials M_1 and M_2. The objective consists in finding the most profitable product mix. Table 1.1 presents the daily available raw materials for M_1 and M_2, and for each product Prod_i the used amount of raw materials and the profit. The decision variables are x_1 and x_2 that

[5]LP models were developed during the second world war to solve logistic problems. Their use was kept secret until 1947.

[6]The decision variables are real values.

[7]See Definition 2.4 for the concept of local optimality.

TABLE 1.1 Data Associated with the Production Problem

	Usage for $Prod_1$	Usage for $Prod_2$	Material Availability
M_1	6	4	24
M_2	1	2	6
Profit per unit	€ 5	€ 4	

represent, respectively, the amounts of $Prod_1$ and $Prod_2$. The objective function consists in maximizing the profit.

The model of this problem may be formulated as an LP mathematical program:

$$\text{Max profit} = 5x_1 + 4x_2$$

subject to the constraints

$$6x_1 + 4x_2 \leq 24$$
$$1x_1 + 2x_2 \leq 6$$
$$x_1, x_2 \geq 0$$

Figure 1.3 illustrates the graphical interpretation of the model. Each constraint can be represented by a line. The objective function is an infinity of parallel lines. The optimum solution will always lie at an extreme point. The optimal solution is ($x_1 = 3$, $x_2 = 1.5$) with a profit of € 21.

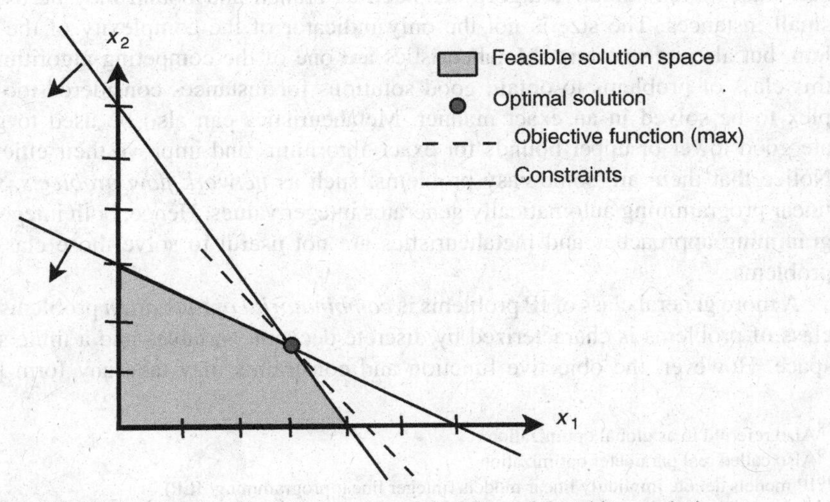

FIGURE 1.3 Graphical illustration of the LP model and its resolution.

Nonlinear programming models (NLP)[8] deal with mathematical programming problems where the objective function and/or the constraints are nonlinear [72]. A continuous nonlinear optimization problem consists in minimizing a function $f : S \subset \mathbb{R}^n \longrightarrow \mathbb{R}$ in a continuous domain. Nonlinear continuous models are, however, much more difficult to solve, even if there are many modeling possibilities that may be used to linearize a model: linearizing a product of variables [321], logical conditions, ordered set of variables, and so on [31]. Linearization techniques introduce in general extra variables and constraints in the model and in some cases some degree of approximation [319].

For NLP optimization models, specific simplex-inspired heuristics such as the Nelder and Mead algorithm may be used [578]. For quadratic and convex continuous problems, some efficient exact algorithms can be used to solve small or moderate problems [583]. Unfortunately, some problem properties such as high dimensionality, multimodality, epistasis (parameter interaction), and nondifferentiability render those traditional approaches impotent. Metaheuristics are good candidates for this class of problems to solve moderate and large instances.

Continuous optimization[9] theory in terms of optimization algorithms is more developed than discrete optimization. However, there are many real-life applications that must be modeled with discrete variables. Continuous models are inappropriate for those problems. Indeed, in many practical optimization problems, the resources are indivisible (machines, people, etc.). In an *integer program* (IP)[10] optimization model, the decision variables are discrete [579].

When the decision variables are both discrete and continuous, we are dealing with *mixed integer programming problems* (MIP). Hence, MIP models generalize LP and IP models. Solving MIP problems has improved dramatically of late with the use of advanced optimization techniques such as relaxations and decomposition approaches, and cutting plane algorithms (see Section 5.2.1). For IP and MIP models, enumerative algorithms such as branch and bound may be used for small instances. The size is not the only indicator of the complexity of the problem, but also its structure. Metaheuristics are one of the competing algorithms for this class of problems to obtain good solutions for instances considered too complex to be solved in an exact manner. Metaheuristics can also be used to generate good lower or upper bounds for exact algorithms and improve their efficiency. Notice that there are some easy problems, such as *network flow problems*, where linear programming automatically generates integer values. Hence, both integer programming approaches and metaheuristics are not useful to solve those classes of problems.

A more general class of IP problems is *combinatorial optimization* problems. This class of problems is characterized by discrete decision variables and a finite search space. However, the objective function and constraints may take any form [597].

[8] Also referred to as global optimization.
[9] Also called real parameter optimization.
[10] IP models denote implicitly linear models (integer linear programming: ILP).

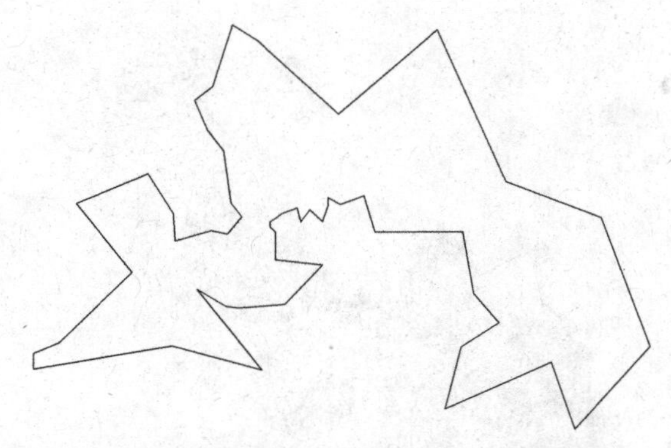

FIGURE 1.4 TSP instance with 52 cities.

The popularity of combinatorial optimization problems stems from the fact that in many real-world problems, the objective function and constraints are of different nature (nonlinear, nonanalytic, black box, etc.) whereas the search space is finite.

Example 1.2 Traveling salesman problem. Perhaps the most popular combinatorial optimization problem is the traveling salesman problem (TSP). It can be formulated as follows: given n cities and a distance matrix $d_{n,n}$, where each element d_{ij} represents the distance between the cities i and j, find a tour that minimizes the total distance. A tour visits each city exactly once (Hamiltonian cycle) (Figs. 1.4 and 1.5). The size of the search space is $n!$ Table 1.2 shows the combinatorial explosion of the number of solutions regarding the number of cities. Unfortunately, enumerating exhaustively all possible solutions is impractical for moderate and large instances.

Another common approach to model decision and optimization problems is *constraint programming* (CP), a programming paradigm that integrates richer modeling tools than the linear expressions of MIP models. A model is composed of a set of variables. Every variable has a finite domain of values. In the model, symbolic and

TABLE 1.2 Effect of the Number of Cities on the Size of the Search Space

Number of Cities n	Size of the Search Space
5	120
10	3, 628, 800
75	2.5×10^{109}

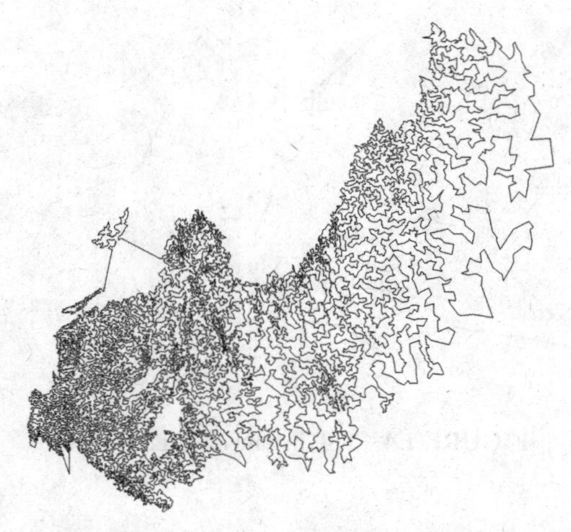

FIGURE 1.5 TSP instance with 24,978 cities.

mathematical constraints related to variables may be expressed. Global constraints represent constraints that refer to a set of variables. Hence, the CP paradigm models the properties of the desired solution. The declarative models in CP are flexible and are in general more compact than in MIP models.

Example 1.3 Assignment problem within constraint programming. The goal is to assign n objects $\{o_1, o_2, \ldots, o_n\}$ to n locations $\{l_1, l_2, \ldots, l_n\}$ where each object is placed on a different location. Using constraint programming techniques, the model will be the following:

$$\texttt{all\_different}(y_1, y_2, \ldots, y_n)$$

where y_i represents the index of the location to which the object o_i is assigned. The global constraint $\texttt{all\_different}(y_1, y_2, \ldots, y_n)$ specifies that all variables must be different. If this problem is modeled using an IP model, one has to introduce the following decision variables:

$$x_{ij} = \begin{cases} 1 & \text{if object } o_i \text{ is assigned to location } l_j \\ 0 & \text{otherwise} \end{cases}$$

Hence, much more variables (n^2 instead of n) are declared.

However, it does not mean that solving the problem will be more efficient within constraint programming than using mathematical programming. Solving the problem is another story. The advantage of MIP solvers is that they use relaxations of the problem to prune the search tree, while in CP they use constraint propagation techniques to reduce the variable domains (see Section 5.3.1). The efficiency of the solvers depends mainly on the structure of the target problem and its associated model. The modeling step of the problem is then very important. In general, CP techniques are less suitable for problems with a large number of feasible solutions, such as the assignment problem shown in the previous example. They are usually used for "tight" constrained problems such as timetabling and scheduling problems.

There are often many ways to formulate mathematically an optimization problem. The efficiency obtained in solving a given model may depend on the formulation used. This is why a lot of research is directed on the reformulation of optimization problems. It is sometimes interesting to increase the number of integer variables and constraints. For a more comprehensive study of mathematical programming approaches (resp. constraint programming techniques), the reader may refer to Refs [37,300,686] (resp. [34,287,664]).

For many problems arising in practical applications, one cannot expect the availability of analytical optimization models. For instance, in some applications one has to resort to simulation or physical models to evaluate the objective function. Mathematical programming and constraint programming approaches require an explicit mathematical formulation that is impossible to derive in problems where simulation is relevant [288].

1.1.2 Complexity Theory

This section deals with some results on intractability of problem solving. Our focus is the complexity of decidable problems. *Undecidable* problems[11] could never have any algorithm to solve them even with unlimited time and space resources [730]. A popular example of undecidable problems is the *halting problem* [782].

1.1.2.1 Complexity of Algorithms An algorithm needs two important resources to solve a problem: time and space. The time complexity of an algorithm is the number of steps required to solve a problem of size n. The complexity is generally defined in terms of the worst-case analysis.

The goal in the determination of the computational complexity of an algorithm is not to obtain an exact step count but an asymptotic bound on the step count. The Big-O notation makes use of asymptotic analysis. It is one of the most popular notations in the analysis of algorithms.

Definition 1.2 Big-O notation. *An algorithm has a complexity $f(n) = O(g(n))$ if there exist positive constants n_0 and c such that $\forall n > n_0,\ f(n) \leq c \cdot g(n)$.*

In this case, the function $f(n)$ is upper bounded by the function $g(n)$. The Big-O notation can be used to compute the time or the space complexity of an algorithm.

[11] Also called *noncomputable problems*.

Definition 1.3 Polynomial-time algorithm. *An algorithm is a polynomial-time algorithm if its complexity is $O(p(n))$, where $p(n)$ is a polynomial function of n.*

A polynomial function of degree k can be defined as follows:

$$p(n) = a_k \cdot n^k + \cdots + a_j \cdot n^j + \cdots + a_1 \cdot n + a_0$$

where $a_k > 0$ and $a_j \geq 0, \forall 1 \leq j \leq k-1$. The corresponding algorithm has a polynomial complexity of $O(n^k)$.

Example 1.4 Complexity of shortest path algorithms. Given a connected graph $G = (V, E)$, where V represents the set of nodes and E the set of edges. Let $D = (d_{ij})$ be a distance matrix where d_{ij} is the distance between the nodes i and j (we assume $d_{ij} = d_{ji} > 0$). The shortest path problem consists in finding the path from a source node i to a destination node j. A path $\pi(i, j)$ from i to j can be defined as a sequence $(i, i_1, i_2, \ldots, i_k, j)$, such that $(i, i_1) \in E$, $(i_k, j) \in E$, $(i_l, i_{l+1}) \in E, \forall 1 \leq l \leq k-1$. The length of a path $\pi(i, j)$ is the sum of the weights of its edges:

$$\text{length}(\pi(i, j)) = d_{ii_1} + d_{i_k j} + \sum_{l=1}^{k-1} d_{i_l i_{l+1}}$$

Let us consider the well-known Dijkstra algorithm to compute the shortest path between two nodes i and j [211]. It works by constructing a shortest path tree from the initial node to every other node in the graph. For each node of the graph, we have to consider all its neighbors. In the worst-case analysis, the number of neighbors for a node is in the order of n. The Dijkstra algorithm requires $O(n^2)$ running time where n represents the number of nodes of the graph. Then, the algorithm requires no more than a quadratic number of steps to find the shortest path. It is a polynomial-time algorithm.

Definition 1.4 Exponential-time algorithm. *An algorithm is an exponential-time algorithm if its complexity is $O(c^n)$, where c is a real constant strictly superior to* 1.

Table 1.3 illustrates how the search time of an algorithm grows with the size of the problem using different time complexities of an optimization algorithm. The table shows clearly the combinatorial explosion of exponential complexities compared to polynomial ones. In practice, one cannot wait some centuries to solve a problem. The problem shown in the last line of the table needs the age of universe to solve it in an exact manner using exhaustive search.

Two other notations are used to analyze algorithms: the Big-Ω and the Big-Θ notations.

Definition 1.5 Big-Ω notation. *An algorithm has a complexity $f(n) = \Omega(g(n))$ if there exist positive constants n_0 and c such that $\forall n > n_0, f(n) \geq c \cdot g(n)$. The complexity of the algorithm $f(n)$ is lower bounded by the function $g(n)$.*

TABLE 1.3 Search Time of an Algorithm as a Function of the Problem Size Using Different Complexities (from [299])

Complexity	Size = 10	Size = 20	Size = 30	Size = 40	Size = 50
$O(x)$	0.00001 s	0.00002 s	0.00003 s	0.00004 s	0.00005 s
$O(x^2)$	0.0001 s	0.0004 s	0.0009 s	0.0016 s	0.0025 s
$O(x^5)$	0.1 s	0.32 s	24.3 s	1.7 mn	5.2 mn
$O(2^x)$	0.001 s	1.0 s	17.9 mn	12.7 days	35.7 years
$O(3^x)$	0.059 s	58.0 mn	6.5 years	3855 centuries	2×10^8 centuries

Definition 1.6 Big-Θ notation. *An algorithm has a complexity $f(n) = \Theta(g(n))$ if there exist positive constants n_0, c_1, and c_2 such that $\forall n > n_0, c_1 \cdot g(n) \le f(n) \le c_2 \cdot g(n)$. The complexity of the algorithm $f(n)$ is lower bounded by the function $g(n)$.*

It is easier to find first the Big-O complexity of an algorithm, then derive successively the Big-Ω and Big-Θ complexities. The Big-Θ notation defines the exact bound (lower and upper) on the time complexity of an algorithm.

The asymptotic analysis of algorithms characterizes the growth rate of their time complexity as a function of the problem size (scalability issues). It allows a theoretical comparison of different algorithms in terms of the worst-case complexity. It does not specify the practical run time of the algorithm for a given instance of the problem. Indeed, the run time of an algorithm depends on the input data. For a more complete analysis, one can also derive the average-case complexities, which is a more difficult task.

1.1.2.2 Complexity of Problems The complexity of a problem is equivalent to the complexity of the best algorithm solving that problem. A problem is *tractable* (or easy) if there exists a polynomial-time algorithm to solve it. A problem is *intractable* (or difficult) if no polynomial-time algorithm exists to solve the problem.

The complexity theory of problems deals with *decision problems*. A decision problem always has a yes or no answer.

Example 1.5 Prime number decision problem. A popular decision problem consists in answering the following question: is a given number Q a prime number? It will return yes if the number Q is a prime one, otherwise the no answer is returned.

An optimization problem can always be reduced to a decision problem.

Example 1.6 Optimization versus decision problem. The optimization problem associated with the traveling salesman problem is "find the optimal Hamiltonian tour that optimizes the total distance," whereas the decision problem is "given an integer D, is there a Hamiltonian tour with a distance less than or equal to D?"

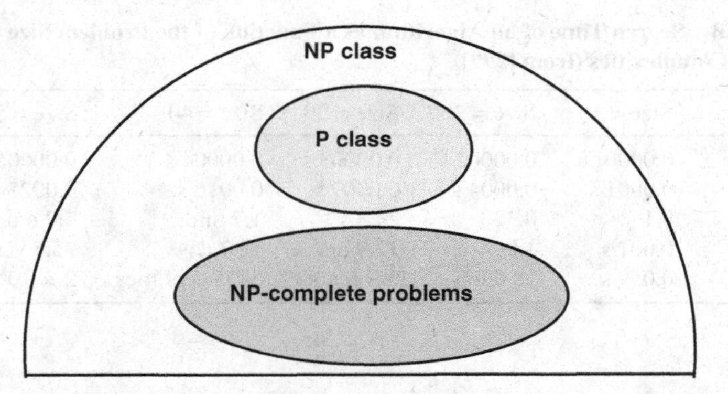

FIGURE 1.6 Complexity classes of decision problems.

An important aspect of computational theory is to categorize problems into complexity classes. A complexity class represents the set of all problems that can be solved using a given amount of computational resources. There are two important classes of problems: P and NP (Fig. 1.6).

The complexity class P represents the set of all decision problems that can be solved by a deterministic machine in polynomial time. A (deterministic) algorithm is polynomial for a decision problem A if its *worst*[12] complexity is bounded by a polynomial function $p(n)$ where n represents the size of the input instance I. Hence, the class P represents the family of problems where a known polynomial-time algorithm exists to solve the problem. Problems belonging to the class P are then relatively "easy" to solve.

Example 1.7 Some problems of class P. Some classical problems belonging to class P are minimum spanning tree, shortest path problems, maximum flow network, maximum bipartite matching, and linear programming continuous models[13]. In the book of Garey and Johnson, a more exhaustive list of easy and hard class P problems can be found [299].

The complexity class NP represents the set of all decision problems that can be solved by a nondeterministic algorithm[14] in polynomial time. A nondeterministic algorithm contains one or more choice points in which multiple different continuations are possible without any specification of which one will be taken. It uses the primitives: `choice` that proposes a solution (oracle), `check` that verifies in polynomial time if a solution proposal (certificate) gives a positive or negative answer, `success` when the algorithm answers yes after the check application, and `fail` when the algorithm

[12]We take into account the worst-case performance and not the average one.

[13]Linear programming continuous problems belong to class P, whereas one of the most efficient algorithms to solve LP programs, the simplex algorithm, has an exponential complexity.

[14]In computer science, the term algorithm stands for a deterministic algorithm.

does not respond "yes." Then, if the `choice` primitive proposes a solution that gives a "yes" answer and the oracle has the capacity to do it, then the computing complexity is polynomial.

Example 1.8 Nondeterministic algorithm for the 0–1 knapsack problem. The 0–1 knapsack decision problem can be defined as follows. Given a set of *N* objects. Each object *O* has a specified weight and a specified value. Given a capacity, which is the maximum total weight of the knapsack, and a quota, which is the minimum total value that one wants to get. The 0–1 knapsack decision problem consists in finding a subset of the objects whose total weight is at most equal to the capacity and whose total value is at least equal to the specified quota.

Let us consider the following nondeterministic algorithm to solve the knapsack decision problem:

Algorithm 1.1 Nondeterministic algorithm for the knapsack problem.

```
Input OS : set of objects ; QUOTA : number ; CAPACITY : number.
Output S : set of objects ; FOUND : boolean.
  S = empty ; total_value = 0 ; total_weight = 0 ; FOUND = false ;
  Pick an order L over the objects ;
  Loop
    Choose an object O in L ; Add O to S ;
    total_value = total_value + O.value ;
    total_weight = total_weight + O.weight ;
    If total_weight > CAPACITY Then fail
    Else If total_value ≥ QUOTA
          FOUND = true ;
          succeed ;
    Endif Endif
    Delete all objects up to O from L ;
  Endloop
```

The question whether P = NP[15] is one of the most important open questions due to the wide impact the answer would have on computational complexity theory. Obviously, for each problem in P we have a nondeterministic algorithm solving it. Then, $P \subseteq NP$ (Fig. 1.6). However, the following conjecture $P \subset NP$ is still an open question.

A decision problem *A* is *reduced polynomially* to a decision problem *B* if, for all input instances I_A for *A*, one can always construct an input instance I_B for *B* in polynomial-time function to the size $L(I_A)$ of the input I_A, such that I_A is a positive instance of *A* if and only if I_B is a positive instance of *B*.

[15] The question is one of the millennium problems with a prize of US$ 1,000,000 for a first-found solution.

A decision problem $A \in$ NP is *NP-complete* if *all* other problems of class NP are reduced polynomially to the problem A. Figure 1.6 shows the relationship between P, NP, and NP-complete problems. If a polynomial deterministic algorithm exists to solve an NP-complete problem, then all problems of class NP may be solved in polynomial time.

NP-hard problems are optimization problems whose associated decision problems are NP-complete. Most of the real-world optimization problems are NP-hard for which provably efficient algorithms do not exist. They require exponential time (unless P = NP) to be solved in optimality. Metaheuristics constitute an important alternative to solve this class of problems.

Example 1.9 Some NP-hard problems. Cook (1971) was the first to prove that the satisfiability problem (SAT) is NP-complete. The other NP-complete problems are at least as hard as the SAT problem. Many academic popular problems are NP-hard among them:

- Sequencing and scheduling problems such as flow-shop scheduling, job-shop scheduling, or open-shop scheduling.
- Assignment and location problems such as quadratic assignment problem (QAP), generalized assignment problem (GAP), location facility, and the p-median problem.
- Grouping problems such as data clustering, graph partitioning, and graph coloring.
- Routing and covering problems such as vehicle routing problems (VRP), set covering problem (SCP), Steiner tree problem, and covering tour problem (CTP).
- Knapsack and packing/cutting problems, and so on.

Many of those optimization problems (and others) will be introduced in the book in a progressive manner to illustrate the design of search components of metaheuristics. Those optimization problems are canonical models that can be applied to different real-life applications. Integer programming models belong in general to the NP-complete class. Unlike LP models, IP problems are difficult to solve because the feasible region is not a convex set.

Example 1.10 Still open problems. Some problems have not yet been proved to be NP-hard. A popular example is the graph isomorphism problem that determines if two graphs are isomorphic. Whether the problem is in P or NP-complete is an open question. More examples may be found in Ref. [299].

1.2 OTHER MODELS FOR OPTIMIZATION

The rest of the book focuses mainly on solving static and deterministic problems. Demand is growing to solve real-world optimization problems where the data are noisy or the objective function is changing dynamically. Finding robust solutions for some design problems is another important challenge in optimization. A transformation to deterministic and static problems is often proposed to solve such problems. Moreover, some adaptations may be proposed for metaheuristics in terms of intensification and diversification of the search to tackle this class of problems [414]. Chapter 4 deals with another class of optimization problems characterized by multiple objectives: the multiobjective optimization problems (MOP) class.

1.2.1 Optimization Under Uncertainty

In many concrete optimization problems, the input data are subject to noise. There are various sources of noise. For instance, the use of a stochastic simulator or an inherently noisy measurement device such as sensors will introduce an additive noise in the objective function. For a given solution x in the search space, a noisy objective function can be defined mathematically as follows:

$$f_{\text{noisy}}(x) = \int_{-\infty}^{+\infty} [f(x) + z]p(z)\mathrm{d}z$$

where $p(z)$ represents the probability distribution of the additive noise z. The additive noise z is mostly assumed to be normally distributed $N(0, \sigma)$ with zero mean and a σ variance [414]. Non-Gaussian noise can also be considered, such as the Cauchy distribution. For the same solution x, different values of the objective function f_{noisy} may be obtained by multiple evaluations. Unlike dynamic optimization, the function f_{noisy} is time invariant.

In practice, the objective function f_{noisy} is often approximated by the function f'_{noisy}, which is defined by the mean value on a given number of samples:

$$f'_{\text{noisy}}(x) = \frac{\sum_{i=1}^{N} [f(x) + z_i]}{N}$$

where z_i represents the noise associated with the sample i and N is the number of samples.

Example 1.11 Uncertainty in routing and scheduling problems. Uncertainty may be present in different components of routing problems. In vehicle routing problems, stochastic demands or stochastic transportation times between locations may be considered as sources of uncertainty. In scheduling problems, uncertainty can occur from many sources such as variable processing and release times or due date variations.

The simplest approach to handle uncertainty is to estimate the mean value of each parameter and solve a deterministic problem. The domain of *stochastic programming* has the goal to solve some limited range of optimization problems under uncertainty [442,674]. Hence, metaheuristics for solving deterministic optimization problems can help solve problems with uncertainty.

1.2.2 Dynamic Optimization

Dynamic Optimization problems represent an important challenge in many real-life applications. The input elements of the problem change over time. In dynamic optimization problems, the objective function is deterministic at a given time but varies over the time [414]:

$$f_{\text{dynamic}}(x) = f_t(x)$$

where t represents the time at which the objective function is evaluated. In that case, the optimal solution of the problem changes as well. Unlike optimization with uncertainty, the function f is deterministic. At a given time, the multiple evaluations of the objective function always give the same values.

Example 1.12 Dynamic routing problems. In many routing problems such as traveling salesman and vehicle routing problems, the properties of the input graph can change over time concurrently with the search process. For the TSP, some cities may be added or deleted during the tour. For the VRP, one can expect a new demand (new customer) to be handled in the problem. A solution might be regarded as a global optimal solution at a given time and may not be optimal in the next time.

The main issues in solving dynamic optimization problems are [91,564]

- Detect the change in the environment when it occurs. For most of real-life problems, the change is smooth rather than radical.
- Respond to the change in the environment to track the new global optimal solution. Hence, the search process must adapt quickly to the change of the objective function. The goal is to track dynamically the changing optimal solution as close as possible. The main challenge is to reuse information on previous searches to adapt to the problem change instead of re-solving the problem from scratch. Some forecasting strategies may also be used to predict the future scenarios.

The main question in designing a metaheuristic for dynamic optimization problems is what information during the search must be memorized and how this information will be used to guide the search and maintain adaptability to changes [91].

1.2.2.1 Multiperiodic Optimization In multiperiodic problems, the input data change periodically. It is a class of dynamic optimization problems where the change is known *a priori*. So, one has to take into account the planning horizon in optimizing those models. In general, static models taking into account the whole horizon are used to tackle this class of problems.

Example 1.13 Multiperiodic planning problem. An example of multiperiodic problems may be the planning of mobile telecommunication networks. One can design the network by taking into account all the periods. For instance, each period is characterized by a given traffic or new incoming technology. In designing the network at a given period, the telecommunication operator must take into account the future evolutions to make the implemented solution more flexible for the future periods. Optimizing the static models in sequence for each period may produce a solution that is not optimal over the whole planning horizon. For instance, the optimal planning for a period i may not be well adapted to a future period $i + k$ with a higher traffic in a given region. A multiperiodic model must integrate all the data associated with all periods to find the sequence of optimal solutions over the successive periods.

1.2.3 Robust Optimization

In many optimization problems, the decision variables or the environmental variables are perturbed or subject to change after a final solution has been obtained and implemented for the problem. Hence, in solving the problem we have to take into account that a solution should be acceptable with respect to slight changes of the decision variable values. The term *robust* qualifies those solutions. Robust optimization may be seen as a specific kind of problem with uncertainties.

Example 1.14 Robustness in multidisciplinary design optimization and engineering design. Robust optimization is of great importance in many domains such as in engineering design. The growing interest is driven by engineering demands to produce extremely robust solutions. Indeed, in this class of problems, the implemented solution must be insensitive to small variation in the design parameters. This variation may be caused by production tolerances, or parameter drifts during operation [74]. Another important application of robust optimization is in multidisciplinary design optimization, where multiple teams associated with different disciplines design a complex system by independently optimizing subsystems. For complexity reasons (time and/or cost), each team will optimize its own subsystem without a full and precise information on the output of other subsystems.

There are many possible ways to deal with robustness. The most used measure is to optimize the expected objective function given a probability distribution of the variation. The expected objective function to optimize in searching robust solutions may be formulated as follows:

$$f_{\text{robust}}(x) = \int_{-\infty}^{+\infty} f(x+\delta)p(\delta)\mathrm{d}\delta$$

where $p(\delta)$ represents the probability distribution of the decision variable disturbance. In general, the distribution takes a normal distribution. Usually, this effective objective function is not available. Hence, it is approximated, for instance, by a Monte Carlo

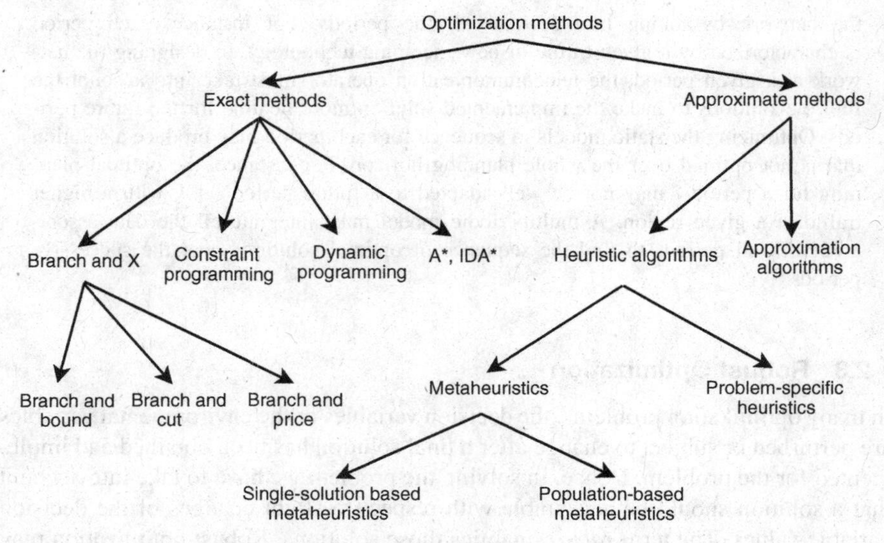

FIGURE 1.7 Classical optimization methods.

integration:

$$f'_{\text{robust}}(x) = \frac{\sum_{i=1}^{N} f(x + \delta_i)}{N}$$

Robust optimization has to find a trade-off between the quality of solutions and their robustness in terms of decision variable disturbance. This problem may be formulated as a multiobjective optimization problem (see Chapter 4) [415]. Unlike optimization under uncertainty, the objective function in robust optimization is considered as deterministic.

The introduced different variants of optimization models are not exclusive. For instance, many practical optimization problems include uncertainty as well as robustness and/or multiperiodicity. Thus, uncertainty, robustness, and dynamic issues must be jointly considered to solve this class of problems.

1.3 OPTIMIZATION METHODS

Following the complexity of the problem, it may be solved by an exact method or an approximate method (Fig. 1.7). Exact methods[16] obtain optimal solutions and guarantee their optimality. For NP-complete problems, exact algorithms are nonpolynomial-time algorithms (unless P = NP). Approximate (or heuristic) methods generate high-quality solutions in a reasonable time for practical use, but there is no guarantee of finding a global optimal solution.

[16] In the artificial intelligence community, those algorithms are also named *complete* algorithms.

1.3.1 Exact Methods

In the class of exact methods one can find the following classical algorithms: dynamic programming, branch and X family of algorithms (branch and bound, branch and cut, branch and price) developed in the operations research community, constraint programming, and A* family of search algorithms (A*, IDA*—iterative deepening algorithms) [473] developed in the artificial intelligence community [673]. Those enumerative methods may be viewed as tree search algorithms. The search is carried out over the whole interesting search space, and the problem is solved by subdividing it into simpler problems.

Dynamic programming is based on the recursive division of a problem into simpler subproblems. This procedure is based on the *Bellman's principle* that says that "the subpolicy of an optimal policy is itself optimal" [68]. This stagewise optimization method is the result of a sequence of partial decisions. The procedure avoids a total enumeration of the search space by pruning partial decision sequences that cannot lead to the optimal solution.

The *branch and bound* algorithm and *A** are based on an implicit enumeration of all solutions of the considered optimization problem. The search space is explored by dynamically building a tree whose root node represents the problem being solved and its whole associated search space. The leaf nodes are the potential solutions and the internal nodes are subproblems of the total solution space. The pruning of the search tree is based on a bounding function that prunes subtrees that do not contain any optimal solution. A more detailed description of dynamic programming and branch and bound algorithms may be found in Section 5.2.1.

Constraint programming is a language built around concepts of tree search and logical implications. Optimization problems in constraint programming are modeled by means of a set of variables linked by a set of constraints. The variables take their values on a finite domain of integers. The constraints may have mathematical or symbolic forms. A more detailed description of constraint programming techniques may be found in Section 5.3.1.

Exact methods can be applied to small instances of difficult problems. Table 1.4 shows for some popular NP-hard optimization problems the order of magnitude of the maximal size of instances that state-of-the-art exact methods can solve to optimality. Some of the exact algorithms used are implemented on large networks of workstations

TABLE 1.4 Order of Magnitude of the Maximal Size of Instances that State-of-the-Art Exact Methods can Solve to Optimality

Optimization Problems	Quadratic Assignment	Flow-Shop Scheduling (FSP)	Graph Coloring	Capacitated Vehicle Routing
Size of the instances	30 objects	100 jobs 20 machines	100 nodes	60 clients

For some practical problems, this maximum size may be negligible. For the TSP problem, an instance of size 13,509 has been solved to optimality [32].

TABLE 1.5 The Impact of the Structure on the Size of Instances (i.e., Number of Nodes for SOP and GC, Number of Objects for QAP) that State-of-the-Art Exact Methods can Solve to Optimality (SOP: Sequential Ordering Problem; QAP: Quadratic Assignment Problem; GC: Graph Coloring)

Optimization Problem	SOP	QAP	GC
Size of some unsolved instances	53	30	125
Size of some solved instances	70	36	561

(grid computing platforms) composed of more than 2000 processors with more than 2 months of computing time [546]!

The size of the instance is not the unique indicator that describes the difficulty of a problem, but also its structure. For a given problem, some small instances cannot be solved by an exact algorithm while some large instances may be solved exactly by the same algorithm. Table 1.5 shows for some popular optimization problems (e.g., SOP[17]: sequential ordering problem; QAP[18]: quadratic assignment problem; GC[19]: graph coloring) small instances that are not solved exactly and large instances solved exactly by state-of-the-art exact optimization methods.

Example 1.15 Phase transition. In many NP-hard optimization problems, a phase transition occurs in terms of the easiness/hardness of the problem; that is, the difficulty to solve the problem increases until a given size n, and beyond this value the problem is easier to solve [126]. Then, the hardest problems tend to be in the phase transition boundary. Let us consider the number partitioning problem, a widely cited NP-hard problem. Given a bag S of N positive integers $\{a_1, a_2, \ldots, a_n\}$, find a partition of the numbers into two equally disjoint bags S_1 and S_2 of cardinality $n/2$ that minimizes the absolute value of the difference of their sums:

$$f = \left| \sum_{i \in S_1} a_i - \sum_{i \in S_2} a_i \right|$$

For the number partitioning problem, the phase transition has been identified around the problem size of $n = 35$ [310,474].

Phase transition phenomena have also been identified in various problems such as graph coloring [126], SAT (propositional satisfiability) [558], CSP (constraint satisfaction problems) [706], traveling salesman problems [312], independent set problems [311], and Hamiltonian circuits [126].

In solving SAT problems, instances before the phase transition are easy to solve and those after the phase transition are mostly unsatisfiable [151]. The phase transition is formulated by the ratio between the number of clauses l and the number

[17]See http://www.iwr.uni-heidelberg.de/groups/comopt/software/TSPLIB95/.
[18]See http://www.seas.upenn.edu/qaplib/inst.html.
[19]See http://mat.gsia.cmu.edu/COLOR/instances.html.

of variables n. In a problem with k variables per clause, the phase transition can be estimated as [311]

$$\frac{l}{n} \approx \frac{\ln(2)}{\ln(1 - \frac{1}{2^k})}$$

For instance, for 3-SAT problems, the phase transition has been found experimentally around 4.3 [151].

1.3.2 Approximate Algorithms

In the class of approximate methods, two subclasses of algorithms may be distinguished: approximation algorithms and heuristic algorithms. Unlike heuristics, which usually find reasonably "good" solutions in a reasonable time, approximation algorithms provide provable solution quality and provable run-time bounds.

Heuristics find "good" solutions on large-size problem instances. They allow to obtain acceptable performance at acceptable costs in a wide range of problems. In general, heuristics do not have an approximation guarantee on the obtained solutions. They may be classified into two families: *specific heuristics* and *metaheuristics*. Specific heuristics are tailored and designed to solve a specific problem and/or instance. Metaheuristics are general-purpose algorithms that can be applied to solve almost any optimization problem. They may be viewed as upper level general methodologies that can be used as a guiding strategy in designing underlying heuristics to solve specific optimization problems.

1.3.2.1 Approximation Algorithms

In approximation algorithms, there is a guarantee on the bound of the obtained solution from the global optimum [380]. An ϵ-approximation algorithm generates an approximate solution a not less than a factor ϵ times the optimum solution s [793].

Definition 1.7 ϵ-Approximation algorithms. *An algorithm has an approximation factor ϵ if its time complexity is polynomial and for any input instance it produces a solution a such that*[20]

$$a \leq \epsilon \cdot s \quad \text{if } \epsilon > 1$$

$$\epsilon \cdot s \leq a \quad \text{if } \epsilon < 1$$

where s is the global optimal solution, and the factor ϵ defines the relative performance guarantee. The ϵ factor can be a constant or a function of the size of the input instance.

[20] In a minimization context.

An ϵ-approximation algorithm generates an *absolute performance guarantee*[21] ϵ, if the following property is proven:

$$(s - \epsilon) \leq a \leq (s + \epsilon)$$

Example 1.16 ϵ-Approximation for the bin packing problem. The bin packing problem is an NP-hard combinatorial optimization problem. Given a set of objects of different size and a finite number of bins of a given capacity. The problem consists in packing the set of objects so as to minimize the number of used bins. Approximation algorithms are generally greedy heuristics using the principle "hardest first, easiest last." The first fit greedy heuristic places each item into the first bin in which it will fit. The complexity of the first fit algorithm is $\Theta(n \cdot \log(n))$. An example of a good approximation algorithm for the bin packing problem is obtained by the first fit descending heuristic (FFD), which first sorts the objects into decreasing order by size:

$$\frac{11}{9}\text{opt} + 1$$

where opt is the number of bins given by the optimal solution. Without the sorting procedure, a worst bound is obtained within less computational time:

$$\frac{17}{10}\text{opt} + 2$$

NP-hard problems differ in their approximability. A well-known family of approximation problems is the PTAS class, where the problem can be approximated within any factor greater than 1.

Definition 1.8 PTAS (polynomial-time approximation scheme). *A problem is in the PTAS class if it has polynomial-time* $(1 + \epsilon)$*-approximation algorithm for any fixed* $\epsilon > 0$.

Definition 1.9 FPTAS (fully polynomial-time approximation scheme). *A problem is in the FPTAS class if it has polynomial-time* $(1 + \epsilon)$*-approximation algorithm in terms of both the input size and* $1/\epsilon$ *for any fixed* $\epsilon > 0$.

Some NP-hard problems are impossible to approximate within any constant factor (or even polynomial, unless P = NP)[22].

Example 1.17 PTAS for the 0–1 knapsack problem. Some problems such as Euclidean TSP, knapsack, and some scheduling problems are in the PTAS class. The

[21] Also referred to as bounded error.

[22] At `http://www.nada.kth.se/~viggo/wwwcompendium/`, there is a continuously updated catalog of approximability results for NP optimization problems.

0–1 knapsack problem has an FPTAS with a time complexity of $O(n^3/\epsilon)$. Problems such as the Max-SAT and vertex cover are much harder and are not members of the PTAS class.

The goal in designing an approximation algorithm for a problem is to find tight worst-case bounds. The study of approximation algorithms gives more knowledge on the difficulty of the problem and can help designing efficient heuristics. However, approximation algorithms are *specific* to the target optimization problem (problem dependent). This characteristic limits their applicability. Moreover, in practice, attainable approximations are too far from the global optimal solution, making those algorithms not very useful for many real-life applications.

1.3.3 Metaheuristics

Unlike exact methods, metaheuristics allow to tackle large-size problem instances by delivering satisfactory solutions in a reasonable time. There is no guarantee to find global optimal solutions or even bounded solutions. Metaheuristics have received more and more popularity in the past 20 years. Their use in many applications shows their efficiency and effectiveness to solve large and complex problems. Application of metaheuristics falls into a large number of areas; some them are

- Engineering design, topology optimization and structural optimization in electronics and VLSI, aerodynamics, fluid dynamics, telecommunications, automotive, and robotics.
- Machine learning and data mining in bioinformatics and computational biology, and finance.
- System modeling, simulation and identification in chemistry, physics, and biology; control, signal, and image processing.
- Planning in routing problems, robot planning, scheduling and production problems, logistics and transportation, supply chain management, environment, and so on.

Optimization is everywhere; optimization problems are often complex; then metaheuristics are everywhere. Even in the research community, the number of sessions, workshops, and conferences dealing with metaheuristics is growing significantly!

Figure 1.8 shows the genealogy of the numerous metaheuristics. The heuristic concept in solving optimization problems was introduced by Polya in 1945 [619]. The simplex algorithm, created by G. Dantzig in 1947, can be seen as a local search algorithm for linear programming problems. J. Edmonds was first to present the greedy heuristic in the combinatorial optimization literature in 1971 [237]. The original references of the following metaheuristics are based on their application to optimization and/or machine learning problems: ACO (ant colonies optimization) [215], AIS (artificial immune systems) [70,253], BC (bee colony) [689,835], CA (cultural algorithms) [652], CEA (coevolutionary algorithms) [375,397], CMA-ES (covariance matrix

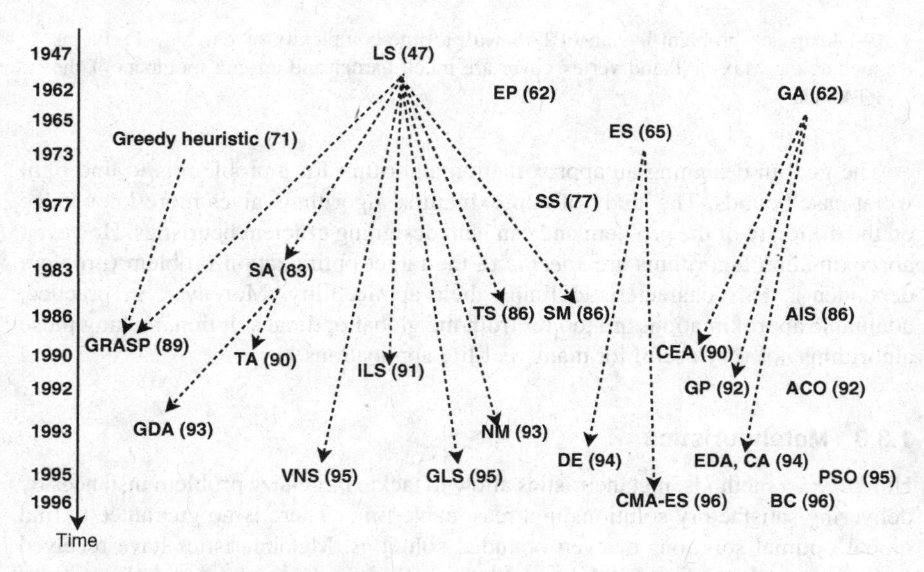

FIGURE 1.8 Genealogy of metaheuristics. The application to optimization and/or machine learning is taken into account as the original date.

adaptation evolution strategy) [363], DE (differential evolution) [626,724], EDA (estimation of distribution algorithms) [47], EP (evolutionary programming) [272], ES (evolution strategies) [642,687], GA (genetic algorithms) [383,384], GDA (great deluge) [229], GLS (guided local search) [805,807], GP (genetic programming) [480], GRASP (greedy adaptive search procedure) [255], ILS (iterated local search) [531], NM (noisy method) [124], PSO (particle swarm optimization) [457], SA (simulated annealing) [114,464], SM (smoothing method) [326], SS (scatter search) [320], TA (threshold accepting) [228], TS (tabu search) [322,364], and VNS (variable neighborhood search) [561].

In designing a metaheuristic, two contradictory criteria must be taken into account: exploration of the search space (diversification) and exploitation of the best solutions found (intensification) (Fig. 1.9). Promising regions are determined by the obtained "good" solutions. In intensification, the promising regions are explored more thoroughly in the hope to find better solutions. In diversification, nonexplored regions

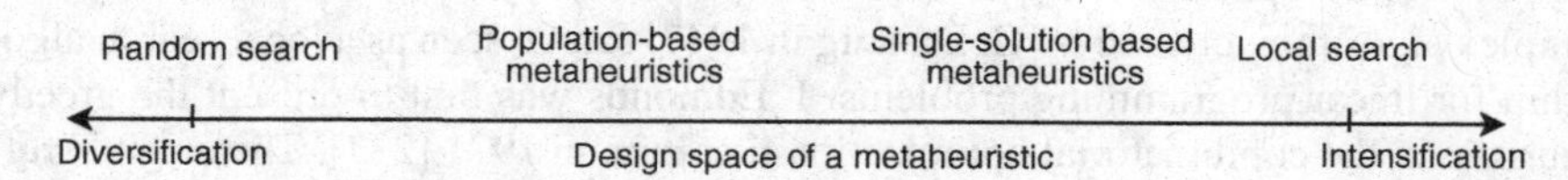

FIGURE 1.9 Two conflicting criteria in designing a metaheuristic: exploration (diversification) versus exploitation (intensification). In general, basic single-solution based metaheuristics are more exploitation oriented whereas basic population-based metaheuristics are more exploration oriented.

must be visited to be sure that all regions of the search space are evenly explored and that the search is not confined to only a reduced number of regions. In this design space, the extreme search algorithms in terms of the exploration (resp. exploitation) are random search (resp. iterative improvement local search). In random search, at each iteration, one generates a random solution in the search space. No search memory is used. In the basic steepest local search algorithm, at each iteration one selects the best neighboring solution that improves the current solution.

Many classification criteria may be used for metaheuristics:

- **Nature inspired versus nonnature inspired:** Many metaheuristics are inspired by natural processes: evolutionary algorithms and artificial immune systems from biology; ants, bees colonies, and particle swarm optimization from swarm intelligence into different species (social sciences); and simulated annealing from physics.
- **Memory usage versus memoryless methods:** Some metaheuristic algorithms are memoryless; that is, no information extracted dynamically is used during the search. Some representatives of this class are local search, GRASP, and simulated annealing. While other metaheuristics use a memory that contains some information extracted online during the search. For instance, short-term and long-term memories in tabu search.
- **Deterministic versus stochastic:** A deterministic metaheuristic solves an optimization problem by making deterministic decisions (e.g., local search, tabu search). In stochastic metaheuristics, some random rules are applied during the search (e.g., simulated annealing, evolutionary algorithms). In deterministic algorithms, using the same initial solution will lead to the same final solution, whereas in stochastic metaheuristics, different final solutions may be obtained from the same initial solution. This characteristic must be taken into account in the performance evaluation of metaheuristic algorithms.
- **Population-based search versus single-solution based search:** Single-solution based algorithms (e.g., local search, simulated annealing) manipulate and transform a single solution during the search while in population-based algorithms (e.g., particle swarm, evolutionary algorithms) a whole population of solutions is evolved. These two families have complementary characteristics: single-solution based metaheuristics are exploitation oriented; they have the power to intensify the search in local regions. Population-based metaheuristics are exploration oriented; they allow a better diversification in the whole search space. In the next chapters of this book, we have mainly used this classification. In fact, the algorithms belonging to each family of metaheuristics share many search mechanisms.
- **Iterative versus greedy:** In iterative algorithms, we start with a complete solution (or population of solutions) and transform it at each iteration using some search operators. Greedy algorithms start from an empty solution, and at each step a decision variable of the problem is assigned until a complete solution is obtained. Most of the metaheuristics are iterative algorithms.

1.3.4 Greedy Algorithms

In greedy or constructive algorithms[23], we start from scratch (empty solution) and construct a solution by assigning values to one decision variable at a time, until a complete solution is generated.

In an optimization problem, where a solution can be defined by the presence/absence of a finite set of elements $E = \{e_1, e_2, \ldots, e_n\}$, the objective function may be defined as $f : 2^E \to \mathbb{R}$, and the search space is defined as $F \subset 2^E$. A partial solution s may be seen as a subset $\{e_1, e_2, \ldots, e_k\}$ of elements e_i from the set of all elements E. The set defining the initial solution is empty. At each step, a local heuristic is used to select the new element to be included in the set. Once an element e_i is selected to be part of the solution, it is never replaced by another element. There is no backtracking of the already taken decisions. Typically, greedy heuristics are deterministic algorithms. Algorithm 1.2 shows the template of a greedy algorithm.

Algorithm 1.2 Template of a greedy algorithm.

> $s = \{\}$; /* Initial solution (null) */
> **Repeat**
> e_i = Local-Heuristic($E \backslash \{e/e \in s\}$) ;
>   /* next element selected from the set E minus already selected elements */
>   **If** $s \cup e_i \in F$ **Then** /* test the feasibility of the solution */
> $s = s \cup e_i$;
> **Until** Complete solution found

Greedy algorithms are popular techniques as they are simple to design. Moreover, greedy algorithms have in general a reduced complexity compared to iterative algorithms. However, in most of optimization problems, the local view of greedy heuristics decreases their performance compared to iterative algorithms.

The main design questions of a greedy method are the following:

- **The definition of the set of elements:** For a given problem, one has to identify a solution as a set of elements. So, the manipulated partial solutions may be viewed as subsets of elements.
- **The element selection heuristic:** At each step, a heuristic is used to select the next element to be part of the solution. In general, this heuristic chooses the best element from the current list in terms of its contribution in minimizing locally the objective function. So, the heuristic will calculate the *profit* for each element. Local optimality does not implicate a global optimality. The heuristic may be static or dynamic. In static heuristics, the profits associated with the elements do not change, whereas in dynamic heuristics, the profits are updated at each step.

[23] Also referred to as successive augmentation algorithms.

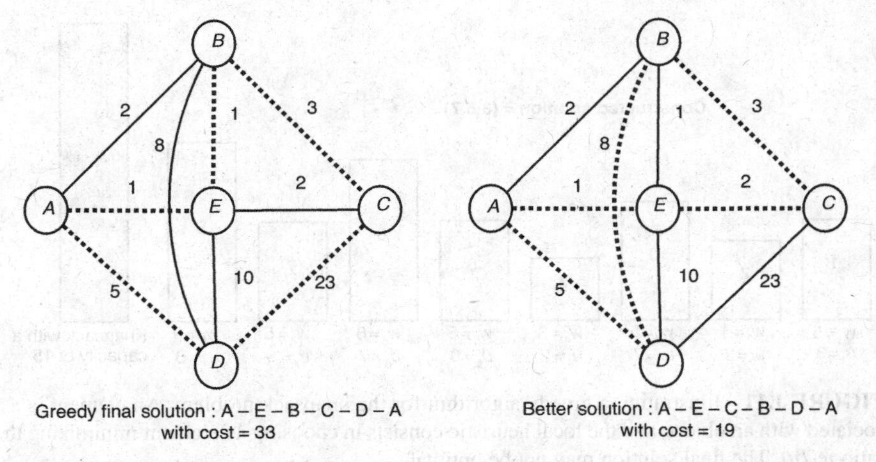

FIGURE 1.10 Illustrating a greedy algorithm for the TSP using a static heuristic. An element is associated with an edge of the graph, and the local heuristic consists in choosing the nearest neighbor. The obtained solution is $(A - E - B - C - D - A)$ with a total cost of 33, whereas a better solution with a cost of 19 is given (right).

Example 1.18 Static greedy algorithm for the TSP. In the TSP problem, the set E is defined by the set of edges. The set F of feasible solutions is defined by the subsets of 2^E that forms Hamiltonian cycles. Hence, a solution can be considered as a set of edges. A heuristic that can be used to select the next edge may be based on the distance. One possible local heuristic is to select the nearest neighbor. Figure 1.10 (left) illustrates the application of the nearest-neighbor greedy heuristic on the graph beginning from the node A. The local heuristic used is static; that is, the distances of the edges are not updated during the constructive process.

Greedy heuristics can be designed in a natural manner for many problems. Below are given some examples of well-known problems.

Example 1.19 Greedy algorithm for the knapsack problem. In the knapsack problem, the set E is defined by the set of objects to be packed. The set F represents all subsets of E that are feasible solutions. A local heuristic that can be used to solve the problem consists in choosing the object minimizing the ratio w_i/u_i where w_i (resp. u_i) represents the weight (resp. utility) of the object i. Figure 1.11 illustrates this greedy heuristic for a given instance of the knapsack problem.

Example 1.20 Greedy algorithm for the minimum spanning tree problem. There is a well-known optimal greedy algorithm for the spanning tree problem, the Kruskal algorithm. The minimum spanning tree problem belongs to class P, in terms of complexity. Given a connected graph $G = (V, E)$. With each edge $e \in E$ is associated a cost c_e. The problem is to find a spanning tree $T = (V, T)$ in graph G that minimizes the total cost $f(T) = \sum_{e \in T} c_e$. For this problem, set E is defined by the edges and set F is defined by all subsets of E that are trees. The local heuristic used consists in choosing first the least costly edges. In case of equality, an edge is randomly

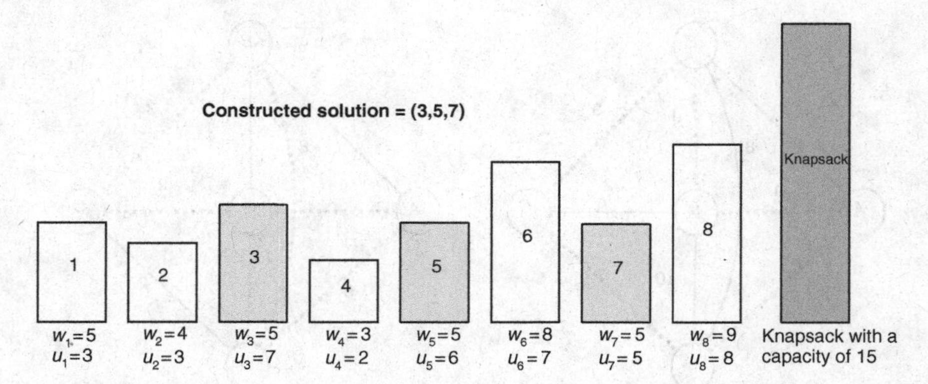

FIGURE 1.11 Illustrating a greedy algorithm for the knapsack problem. An element is associated with an object, and the local heuristic consists in choosing an element minimizing the ratio w_i/u_i. The final solution may not be optimal.

picked. Figure 1.12 illustrates this greedy heuristic for a given instance of the spanning tree problem. This algorithm always generates optimal solutions. Its time complexity is $O(m \cdot \log(m))$ where m represents the number of edges of the graph.

Greedy heuristics are in general myopic in their construction of a solution. Some greedy heuristics (e.g., pilot method) include look-ahead features where the future consequences of the selected element are estimated [38,803].

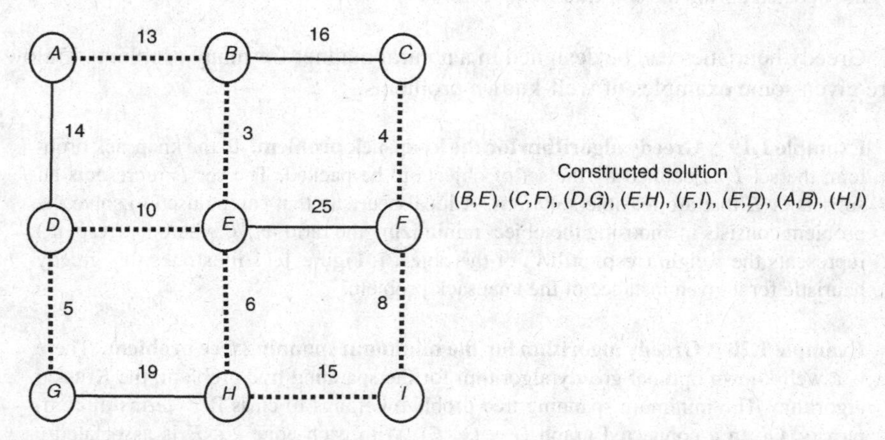

FIGURE 1.12 Illustrating a greedy algorithm for the spanning tree problem. The edge (*A*, *D*) has not been selected even if it is less costly than the edge (*H*, *I*) because it generates a nonfeasible solution (a cycle).

1.3.5 When Using Metaheuristics?

This section addresses the legitimate in using metaheuristics to solve an optimization problem. The complexity of a problem gives an indication on the hardness of the problem. It is also important to know the *size* of input instances the algorithm is supposed to solve. Even if a problem is NP-hard, small instances may be solved by an exact approach. Moreover, the *structure* of the instances plays an important role. Some medium- or even large-size instances with a specific structure may be solved in optimality by exact algorithms. Finally, the required search time to solve a given problem is an important issue in the selection of an optimization algorithm.

It is unwise to use metaheuristics to solve problems where efficient exact algorithms are available. An example of this class of problems is the P class of optimization problems. In the case where those exact algorithms give "acceptable" search time to solve the target instances, metaheuristics are useless. For instance, one should not use a metaheuristic to find a minimum spanning tree or a shortest path in a graph. Known polynomial-time exact algorithms exist for those problems.

Hence for easy optimization problems, metaheuristics are seldom used. Unfortunately, one can see many engineers and even researchers solving polynomial optimization problems with metaheuristics! So the first guideline in solving a problem is to analyze first its complexity. If the problem can be reduced to a classical or an already solved problem in the literature, then get a look at the state-of-the art best known optimization algorithms solving the problem. Otherwise, if there are related problems, the same methodology must be applied.

Example 1.21 Metaheuristics and LP continuous models. Polynomial-time problems such as linear programming models are very easy to solve with actual commercial (e.g., CPLEX, Lindo, XPRESS-MP, OSL) or free solvers (e.g., LP-solver) that are based on the simplex or interior methods. Some large-scale linear continuous problems having hundreds of thousands variables can be solved by those solvers using advanced algorithms such as the efficient manipulation of sparse matrices. However, for some very large polynomial problems or some specific problem structures, we may need the use of heuristics even if the complexity of this class of problems is polynomial. In an LP model, the number of vertices (extreme points) of the polytope representing the feasible region may be very large. Let us consider the $n \times n$ assignment problem, which includes $2n$ linear constraints and n^2 nonnegativity constraints. The polytope is composed of $n!$ vertices!

Even for polynomial problems, it is possible that the power of the polynomial function representing the complexity of the algorithm is so large that real-life instances cannot be solved in a reasonable time (e.g., a complexity of $O(n^{5000})$). In addition to the complexity of the problem, the required search time to solve the problem is another important parameter to take into account. Indeed, even if the problem is polynomial, the need of using metaheuristic may be justified for real-time search constraints.

Example 1.22 Real-time metaheuristics for polynomial dynamic problems. As an example of justifying the use of metaheuristics for polynomial problems, let us consider the shortest path in a graph of a real-life application that consists in finding a path between any two locations using GPS (Global Positioning System) technology. This graph has a huge number of nodes, and the search time is constrained as the customer has to obtain an answer in real time. In practice, even if this problem is polynomial, softwares in GPS systems are actually using heuristics to solve this problem. For those large instances, the use of polynomial algorithms such as the Dijkstra algorithm will be time consuming.

Many combinatorial optimization problems belong to the NP-hard class of problems. This high-dimensional and complex optimization class of problems arises in many areas of industrial concern: telecommunication, computational biology, transportation and logistics, planning and manufacturing, engineering design, and so on. Moreover, most of the classical optimization problems are NP-hard in their general formulation: traveling salesman, set covering, vehicle routing, graph partitioning, graph coloring, and so on [299].

For an NP-hard problem where state-of-the-art exact algorithms cannot solve the handled instances (size, structure) within the required search time, the use of metaheuristics is justified. For this class of problems, exact algorithms require (in the worst case) exponential time. The notion of "required time" depends on the target optimization problem. For some problems, an "acceptable" time may be equivalent to some seconds whereas for other problems it is equal to some months (production versus design problems). The fact that a problem is not in the P class does not imply that all large instances of the problem are hard or even that most of them are. The NP-completeness of a problem does not imply anything about the complexity of a particular class of instances that has to be solved.

Metaheuristics and IP/MIP problems: Despite the advances in reformulating IP and MIP models, and the development of new efficient procedures such as cutting planes and column generation, IP and MIP problems remain difficult to solve for moderate and large instances in a reasonable time. Let us notice that moderate and even large instances of some *structured* IP problems may be solved optimally.

Metaheuristics and CP: As for MIP models, constraint programming techniques enable to solve small instances of CP models in an optimal manner within a reasonable period of time. For very "tight" constrained problems, those strategies may solve moderate instances.

For nonlinear continuous (NLP) optimization, metaheuristics should be applied, if derivative-based methods, for example quasi-Newton method or conjugate gradient, fail due to a rugged search landscape (e.g., discontinuous, nonlinear, ill-conditioned, noisy, multimodal, nonsmooth, and nonseparable). The function f must be at least of moderate dimensionality (considerably greater than three variables). Those properties characterize many real-world problems. For easy problems, such as purely convex-quadratic functions, quasi-Newton method is typically faster by a factor of about 10 (in terms of computation time to attain a target value for the objective function) over one of the most efficient metaheuristics.

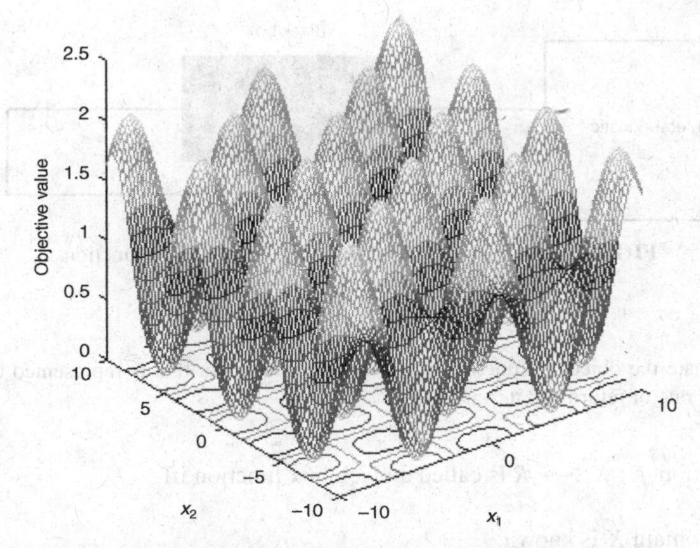

FIGURE 1.13 The Griewangk multimodal continuous function.

Example 1.23 Griewangk multimodal continuous function. This example shows a multimodal function to minimize the *Griewangk* function [774]:

$$f(\vec{x}) = 1 + \sum_{i=1}^{n} \frac{x_i^2}{4000} - \prod_{i=1}^{n} \cos\left(\frac{x_i}{\sqrt{i}}\right) \tag{1.1}$$

where $\vec{x} = \{x_1, x_2, \ldots, x_N\}$, with $x_i \in (-600, 600)$. Figure 1.13 illustrates the landscape associated with the function. The optimal solution for this function is the null vector $x^* = (0, \ldots, 0)$ with $f(x^*) = 0$.

Unlike mathematical programming, the main advantage of using metaheuristics is a restrictive assumption in formulating the model. Some optimization problems cannot be formulated with an unambiguous analytical mathematical notation. Indeed, the objective function may be a *black box* [448]. In a black box optimization, no analytical formulation of the objective exists (Fig. 1.14). Typical examples of optimization problems involving a black box scenario are shape optimization, model calibration (physical or biological), and parameter calibration.

Example 1.24 Optimization by simulation. Many problems in engineering such as in logistics, production, telecommunications, finance, or computational biology (e.g., structure prediction of proteins, molecular docking) are based on simulation to evaluate the quality of solutions. For instance, in risk analysis, Monte Carlo simulations are used

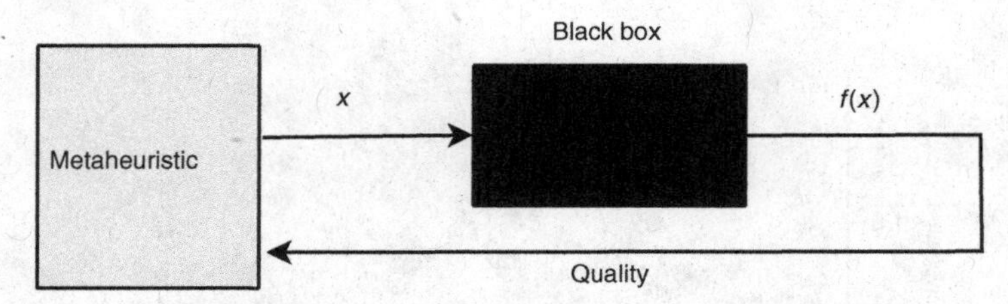

FIGURE 1.14 Black box scenario for the objective function.

to estimate the objective function of a portfolio investment that is represented by the average rate of return and its variance.

A function $f : X \longrightarrow R$ is called a black box function iff

- the domain X is known,
- it is possible to know f for each point of X according to a simulation, and
- no other information is available for the function f.

Very expensive experiments in terms of time and cost are associated with those problems. In general, a simulation must hold to evaluate the solution.

Another example of nonanalytical models of optimization is interactive optimization[24] that involves a human interaction to evaluate a solution. Usually, human evaluation is necessary when the form of the objective function is not known. Interactive optimization can concurrently accept evaluations from many users. Many real-life examples fit into the class of interactive optimization problems where the result should fit particular user preferences:

- Visual appeal or attractiveness [104,183].
- Taste of coffee [372] or color set of the user interface.
- Evolving images [705], 3D animated forms, music composition, various artistic designs, and forms to fit user aesthetic preferences [476,789].

Metaheuristics will gain more and more popularity in the future as optimization problems are increasing in size and in complexity. Indeed, complex problem models are needed to develop more accurate models for real-life problems in engineering and science (e.g., engineering design, computational biology, finance engineering, logistics, and transportation).

Let us summarize the main characteristics of optimization problems justifying the use of metaheuristics:

[24] Aesthetic selection in evolutionary algorithms.

- An easy problem (P class) with very large instances. In this case, exact polynomial-time algorithms are known but are too expensive due to the size of instances.
- An easy problem (P class) with hard real-time constraints (online algorithms). In real-time optimization problems, metaheuristics are widely used. Indeed, in this class of problems, we have to find a "good solution" online. Even if efficient exact algorithms are available to solve the problem, metaheuristics are used to reduce the search time. Dynamic optimization problems represent another example of such problems.
- A difficult problem (NP-hard class) with moderate size and/or difficult structures of the input instances.
- Optimization problems with time-consuming objective function(s) and/or constraints. Some real-life optimization problems are characterized by a huge computational cost of the objective function(s).
- Nonanalytic models of optimization problems that cannot be solved in an exhaustive manner. Many practical problems are defined by a black box scenario of the objective function.
- Moreover, those conditions may be amplified by nondeterministic models of optimization: problems with uncertainty and robust optimization. For some noisy problems, uncertainty and robustness cannot be modeled analytically. Some complex simulations (e.g., Monte Carlo) must be carried out that justify the use of metaheuristics. The ambiguity of the model does not encourage attempting to solve it with exact algorithms. As the data are fuzzy, this class of problems does not necessarily need the optimal solution to be found.

Example 1.25 Design versus control problems. The relative importance of the two main performance measures, quality of solutions and search time, depends on the characteristics of the target optimization problem. Two extreme problems may be considered here:

- **Design problems:** Design problems are generally solved once. They need a very good quality of solutions whereas the time available to solve the problem is important (e.g., several hours, days, months). In this class of problems, one can find the *strategic* problems (long-term problems), such as telecommunication network design and processor design. These problems involve an important financial investment; any imperfection will have a long-time impact on the solution. Hence, the critical aspect is the quality of solutions rather than the search time (Fig. 1.15). If possible, exact optimization algorithms must be used.
- **Control problems:** Control problems represent the other extreme where the problem must be solved frequently in real time. This class of *operational* problems involves short-term decisions (e.g., fractions of a second), such as routing messages in a computer network and traffic management in a city. For operational decision problems, very fast heuristics are needed; the quality of the solutions is less critical.

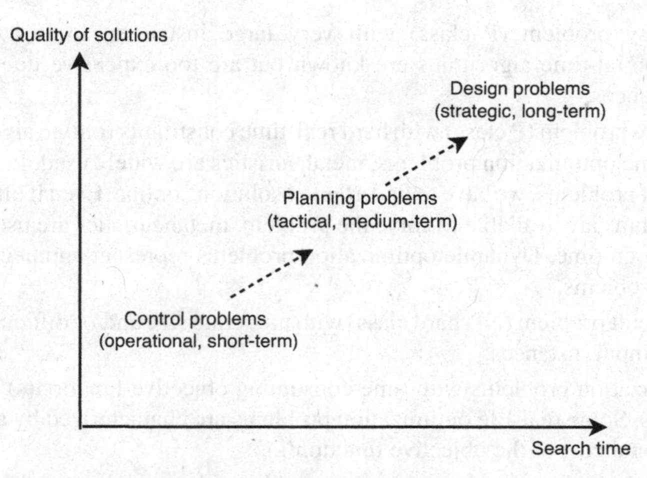

FIGURE 1.15 Different classes of problems in terms of the trade-off between quality of solutions and search time: design (strategic, long-term), planning (tactical, medium-term), control (operational, short-term).

Between these extremes, one can find an intermediate class of problems represented by planning problems and tactical problems (medium-term problems). In this class of problems, a trade-off between the quality of solution and the search time must be optimized. In general, exact optimization algorithms cannot be used to solve such problems.

The *development cost* of solving an optimization problem is also an important issue. Indeed, metaheuristics are easy to design and implement. Open-source and free software frameworks such as ParadisEO allow the efficient design and implementation of metaheuristics for monoobjective and multiobjective optimization problems, hybrid metaheuristics, and parallel metaheuristics. Reusing existing designs and codes will contribute to reducing the development cost.

1.4 MAIN COMMON CONCEPTS FOR METAHEURISTICS

There are two common design questions related to all iterative metaheuristics: the representation of solutions handled by algorithms and the definition of the objective function that will guide the search.

1.4.1 Representation

Designing any iterative metaheuristic needs an encoding (representation) of a solution[25]. It is a fundamental design question in the development of metaheuristics. The encoding plays a major role in the efficiency and effectiveness of any metaheuristic

[25] In the evolutionary computation community, the genotype defines the representation of a solution. A solution is defined as the phenotype.

and constitutes an essential step in designing a metaheuristic. The encoding must be suitable and relevant to the tackled optimization problem. Moreover, the efficiency of a representation is also related to the search operators applied on this representation (neighborhood, recombination, etc.). In fact, when defining a representation, one has to bear in mind how the solution will be evaluated and how the search operators will operate.

Many alternative representations may exist for a given problem. A representation must have the following characteristics:

- **Completeness:** One of the main characteristics of a representation is its completeness; that is, all solutions associated with the problem must be represented.
- **Connexity:** The connexity characteristic is very important in designing any search algorithm. A search path must exist between any two solutions of the search space. Any solution of the search space, especially the global optimum solution, can be attained.
- **Efficiency:** The representation must be easy to manipulate by the search operators. The time and space complexities of the operators dealing with the representation must be reduced.

Many straightforward encodings may be applied for some traditional families of optimization problems (Fig. 1.16). There are some classical representations that

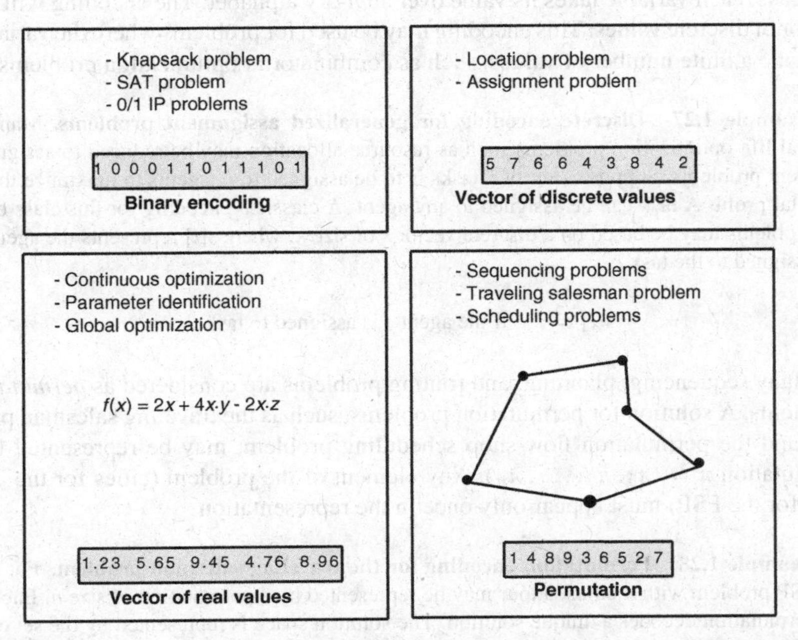

FIGURE 1.16 Some classical encodings: vector of binary values, vector of discrete values, vector of real values, and permutation.

are commonly used to solve a large variety of optimization problems. Those representations may be combined or underlying new representations. According to their structure, there are two main classes of representations: linear and nonlinear.

1.4.1.1 Linear Representations Linear representations may be viewed as strings of symbols of a given alphabet.

In many classical optimization problems, where the decision variables denote the presence or absence of an element or a yes/no decision, a *binary encoding* may be used. For instance, satisfiability problems and {0, 1}-linear programs are representative of such problems. The binary encoding consists in associating a binary value for each decision variable. A solution will be encoded by a vector of binary variables.

Example 1.26 Binary encoding for knapsack problems. For a 0/1-knapsack problem of n objects, a vector s of binary variables of size n may be used to represent a solution:

$$\forall i, s_i = \begin{cases} 1 & \text{if object } i \text{ is in the knapsack} \\ 0 & \text{otherwise} \end{cases}$$

The binary encoding uses a binary alphabet consisting in two different symbols. It may be generalized to any *discrete values* based encoding using an n-ary alphabet. In this case, each variable takes its value over an n-ary alphabet. The encoding will be a vector of discrete values. This encoding may be used for problems where the variables can take a finite number of values, such as combinatorial optimization problems.

Example 1.27 Discrete encoding for generalized assignment problems. Many real-life optimization problems such as resource allocation may be reduced to assignment problems. Suppose a set of k tasks is to be assigned to m agents to maximize the total profit. A task can be assigned to any agent. A classical encoding for this class of problems may be based on a discrete vector s of size k, where $s[i]$ represents the agent assigned to the task i.

$$s[i] = j \quad \text{if the agent } j \text{ is assigned to task } i$$

Many sequencing, planning, and routing problems are considered as *permutation* problems. A solution for permutation problems, such as the traveling salesman problem and the permutation flow-shop scheduling problem, may be represented by a permutation $\pi = (\pi_1, \pi_2, \ldots, \pi_n)$. Any element of the problem (cities for the TSP, jobs for the FSP) must appear only once in the representation.

Example 1.28 Permutation encoding for the traveling salesman problem. For a TSP problem with n cities, a tour may be represented by a permutation of size n. Each permutation decodes a unique solution. The solution space is represented by the set of all permutations. Its size is $|S| = (n-1)!$ if the first city of the tour is fixed.

Example 1.29 Reducing the representation space. In this example, we will see how a given problem can be made simpler by choosing a suitable representation. The N-Queens puzzle is the problem of putting N chess queens on an $N \times N$ chessboard such that none of them is able to capture any other using the standard chess queens moves. Any queen is assumed to be able to attack any other. The 8-Queens problem was originally defined by the chess player Max Bezzel in 1848.

A solution for this problem represents an assignment of the eight queens on the chessboard. First, let us encode a solution by a vector of eight Cartesian positions $x = (p_1, p_2, \ldots, p_8)$ where $p_i = (x_i, y_i)$ represents the Cartesian position of the queen i. The number of possibilities (size of the search space) is 64^8 that is over 4 billion solutions. If we prohibit more than one queen per row, so that each queen is assigned to a separate row, the search space will have 8^8 solutions that is over 16 million possibilities. Finally, if we forbid two queens to be both in the same column or row, the encoding will be reduced to a permutation of the n queens. This encoding will reduce the space to $n!$ solutions, which is only 40,320 possibilities for the 8-Queens problem. Figure 1.17 shows a solution for a 8-Queens problem. This example shows how the representation plays a major role in defining the space a given metaheuristic will have to explore.

For continuous optimization problems, the natural encoding is based on *real values*. For instance, this encoding is commonly used for nonlinear continuous optimization problems, where the most usual encoding is based on vectors of real values.

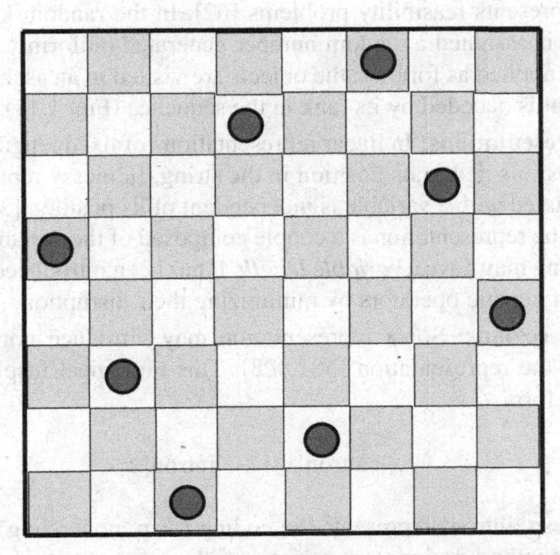

FIGURE 1.17 A solution for the 8-Queens problem represented by the permutation (6,4,7,1,8,2,5,3).

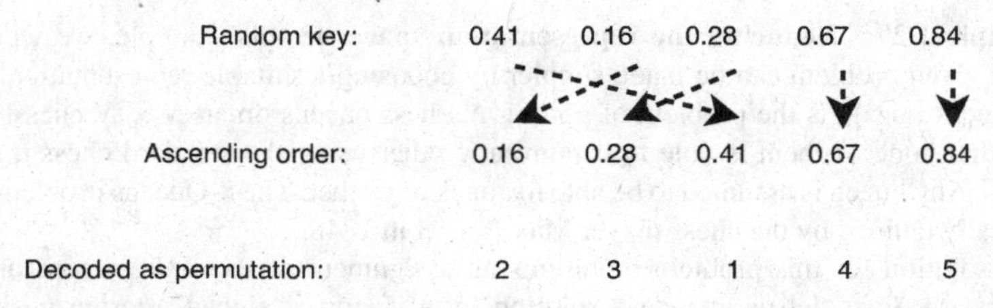

FIGURE 1.18 Random-key encoding and decoding.

Example 1.30 Mixed encodings in parameter optimization. Many optimization problems in engineering sciences consist in finding the best parameters in designing a given component. This class of problems is known as parameter optimization problems. Some parameters may be associated with real values while others are associated with discrete ones. Hence, a solution may be represented by a vector x of mixed values, where $x[i]$ represents the real or discrete value of parameter i. The size of the vector is equal to the number of parameters of the system.

Other "nontraditional" linear representations may be used. Some of them have been defined in the evolutionary computation community:

- **Random-key encoding:** The random-key representation uses real-valued encoding to represent permutations. Random-key encoding is useful for permutation-based representations, where the application of classical variation operators (e.g., crossover) presents feasibility problems [62]. In the random-key encoding, to each object is assigned a random number generated uniformly from [0,1[. The decoding is applied as follows: the objects are visited in an ascending order and each element is decoded by its rank in the sequence (Fig. 1.18).
- **Messy representations:** In linear representations of fixed length, the semantics of the values[26] is tied to its position in the string. In messy representations, the value associated with a variable is independent of its position [329]. Then, each element of the representation is a couple composed of the variable and its value. This encoding may have a *variable length*. It has been introduced to improve the efficiency of genetic operators by minimizing their disruption.
- **Noncoding regions:** Some representation may introduce noncoding regions (introns) in the representation [501,828]. This biological inspired representation has the form

$$x_1|\text{intron}|x_2|\cdots|\text{intron}|x_n$$

where x_i (resp. intron) represents the coding (resp. noncoding) part of the encoding. Noncoding regions are regions of the representation that provide no

[26]In evolutionary algorithms, the value is defined as an allele.

contribution to the objective (quality) of the solution. As in messy representations, this encoding has an impact on recombination search operators.

- **Diploid representations:** Diploid representations include multiple values for each position of the encoding. This representation requires a decoding procedure to determine which value will be associated with a given position. This encoding was first introduced for a quicker adaptation of solutions in solving dynamic cyclic problems [332].
- **Quantum representations:** In quantum computing systems, the smallest unit of information is the *qubit*. Unlike the classical bit, the qubit can be in the superposition of the two values at the same time. The state of a qubit can be represented as

$$|\Psi\rangle = \alpha|0\rangle + \beta|1\rangle$$

where $|\Psi\rangle$ denotes a function wave in Hilbert space, $|0\rangle$ and $|1\rangle$ represent, respectively, the classical bit values 0 and 1, and α and β are complex numbers that satisfy the probability amplitudes of the corresponding states[27]. If a superposition is measured with respect to the basis $\{|0\rangle, |1\rangle\}$, the probability to measure $|0\rangle$ is α^2 and the probability to measure $|1\rangle$ is β^2 [818].
A quantum encoding of n qubits can represent 2^n states at the same time. This means that one can represent an exponential amount of information. Using this probabilistic binary-based representation, one needs to design a decoder to generate and evaluate solutions [356].

Solutions in some optimization problems are encoded by *mixed representations*. The most popular mixed representation is the continuous/integer one, to solve MIP problems. Here, a solution is represented by a vector of mixed values (reals, binary values, and integers).

In *control problems*, decision variables represent values that are control variables taken in time (or frequency). In general, a discretization of time domain is realized. The representation generally used is $x = (c(t_1), \ldots, c(t_i), \ldots)$, where $c(t_i)$ represents the value of the control variable x at time t. If the sequence of values is monotonic, the following incremental representation may be used:

$$x_1 = c(t_1), x_i = (c(t_i) - c(t_{i-1}))$$

1.4.1.2 Nonlinear Representations

Nonlinear encodings are in general more complex structures. They are mostly based on graph structures. Among the traditional nonlinear representations, trees are the most used.

The tree encoding is used mainly for hierarchical structured optimization problems. In tree encoding, a solution is represented by a tree of some objects. For instance,

[27] $\alpha^2 + \beta^2 = 1$.

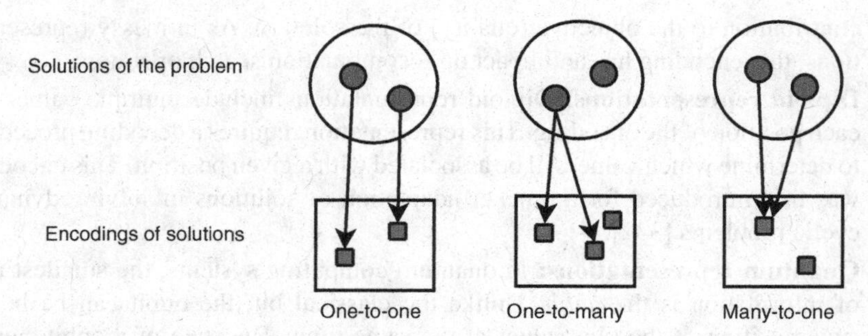

FIGURE 1.19 Mapping between the space of solutions and the space of encodings.

this structure is used in genetic programming. The tree may encode an arithmetic expression, a first-order predicate logic formula, or a program.

Example 1.31 Tree encoding for regression problems. Given some input and output values, regression problems consist in finding the function that will give the best (closest) output to all inputs. Any *S*-expression can be drawn as a tree of functions and terminals. These functions and terminals may be defined in various manners. For instance, the functions may be add, sub, sine, cosine, and so on. The terminals (leaves) represent constants or variables.

Other nonlinear representations can be used such as finite-state machines and graphs.

1.4.1.3 Representation-Solution Mapping

The representation-solution mapping function transforms the encoding (genotype) to a problem solution (phenotype). The mapping between the solution space and the encoding space involves three possibilities [251] (Fig. 1.19):

- **One-to-one:** This is the traditional class of representation. Here, a solution is represented by a single encoding and each encoding represents a single solution. There is no redundancy and no reduction of the original search space. For some constrained optimization problems, it is difficult to design such one-to-one mapping.
- **One-to-many:** In the one-to-many mapping, one solution may be represented by several encodings. The redundancy of the encoding will enlarge the size of the search space and may have an impact on the effectiveness of metaheuristics.

Example 1.32 Symmetry in partitioning problems. Partitioning problems, or clustering or grouping problems, represent an important class of problems. Problems such as clustering in data mining, graph partitioning problems (GPP), graph

TABLE 1.6 Partitioning Problems with Their Associated Constraints and Objective Functions

Problem	Constraint	Objective
Graph coloring	Adjacent nodes do not have the same color	Min. number of colors
Bin packing	Sum of elements sizes in any group is less than C	Min. number of groups
Data clustering	Fixed number of clusters	Max. intercluster distance
Graph partitioning	Groups of equal size	Min. number of edges between partitions
Assembly line balancing	Cycle time	Min. number of workstations

All of them are NP-hard problems.

coloring problem (GCP), and bin packing are well-known examples of grouping problems [251]. Grouping problems consist in partitioning a set S of elements into mutually disjoint subsets s_i, where $\cup s_i = S$ and $s_i \cap s_j = \emptyset$. The different grouping problems differ in their associated constraints and the objective function to optimize (see Table 1.6).

A straightforward representation associates with each element its group. For instance, the encoding $BAAB$ assigns the first element to group B, the second to group A, the third element to group A, and the last one to group B. The first and the last elements (resp. second and third) are then assigned to the same group. The encoding $ABBA$ represents the same solution. Hence, this representation belongs to the one-to-many class of encodings and is highly redundant. The number of different representations encoding the same solution grows exponentially with the number of partitions.

- **Many-to-one:** In this class, several solutions are represented by the same encoding. In general, those encodings are characterized by a lack of details in the encoding; some information on the solution is not explicitly represented. This will reduce the size of the original search space. In some cases, this will improve the efficiency of metaheuristics. This class of representation is also referred to as *indirect encoding*.

1.4.1.4 Direct Versus Indirect Encodings

When using an indirect representation, the encoding is not a complete solution for the problem. A *decoder* is required to express the solution given by the encoding. According to the information that is present in the indirect encoding, the decoder has more or less work to be able to derive a complete solution. The decoder may be *nondeterministic*. Indirect encodings are popular in optimization problems dealing with many constraints such as scheduling problems. For instance, the constraints associated with the optimization problem are handled by the decoder and will guarantee the validity of the solution that is derived.

Example 1.33 Indirect encodings for the job-shop scheduling problem (JSP). The simple job-shop scheduling problem may be defined as follows. Given a set of j jobs. Each job is composed of M operations to be realized on M machines. Each operation must be realized on a single machine. Each job has an operation that has to be performed on each machine. A schedule indicates at each time slot and on each machine, the operation being processed. The objective function to minimize is the *makespan* (total completion time). Let us denote $E_m(x)$ as the completion time of the last operation performed on machine m according to the schedule x. Then, the makespan can be defined as $C_{\max}(x) = \max_{1 \leq m \leq M} E_m(x)$. The following constraints must be fulfilled: a machine can perform only one operation at a time, the operations should be performed in a predefined order (the operations of a job cannot be executed concurrently on two different machines), and there is only one machine that is able to perform any operation.

A solution should represent a feasible schedule of occupation of the machines that indicates for each time slot of any machine if it is free or which operation of which job is being performed. A direct representation may be defined as the list of machines and the time slots that are used to perform the operations (Fig. 1.20a). For instance, the job i is composed of the operations Op7 and Op3. The operation Op7 is executed on machine m2 from time 1 to 3. The operation Op3 is performed on machine m3 from time 13 to 17, and so on. The assignment of an operation consists in the association of a machine and time slot taking in consideration precedence constraints. The order of execution of operations is defined at the level of operations.

Various indirect representations may be designed for the JSP problem. Such an indirect representation may be simply a permutation of j jobs (Fig. 1.20b). The search space is limited to the set of permutations of j integers, that is, of size $j!$. An encoding mechanism is used to transform the permutation into a complete and feasible schedule. The decoder has a very limited set of information and shall derive much more to obtain valid schedules. Various decoders may be imagined, with a variable degree of stochasticity. A very simple one would consider the permutation as a priority list and would derive a schedule that always gives priority to operations belonging to the highest priority jobs.

A second more rich indirect encoding is an array of $J \times M$ entries. Each job is assigned a class of markers, all associated with one job having the same tag (job number). The markers are then shuffled in the array. Figure 1.20c illustrates such an

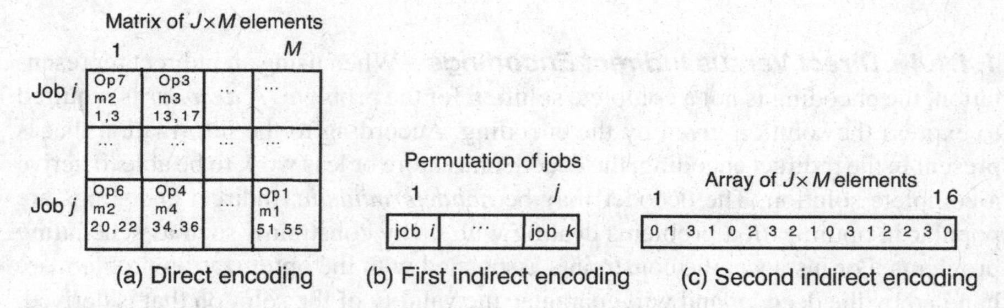

FIGURE 1.20 Direct and indirect encodings for the job-shop scheduling problem.

encoding for a 4×4 JSP. The decoder considers this array from the "left to the right." For each entry, it then schedules as soon as possible the next not-yet scheduled operation of the job associated with the marker that has been found.

Let us notice that the representation has an interaction with search operators and the objective function. Then, finding a suitable representation cannot be completely done without the specification of the search operators and the objective function. For instance, in the relationship between the representation and the search operators, an ideal encoding should have the *proximity* property: similar solutions in terms of their representations (genotypes) must be similar in the phenotype space. The similarity is defined relatively to the performed search operators.

Example 1.34 Encoding of real numbers. Let us consider an encoding for real numbers based on binary vectors. In many evolutionary algorithms such as genetic algorithms, this encoding is chosen to solve continuous optimization problems. Let us consider two consecutive integers, 15 and 16. Their binary representation is, respectively, 01111 and 10000. In the phenotype space, 15 is neighbor to 16, while in the genotype space, 5 bits must be flipped to obtain 16 from 15! Using variation operators based on the flip operator, this disparity between the genotype and the phenotype spaces may generate nonefficient metaheuristics. Gray code encoding solves this problem by mapping two neighbors in the genotype space (one-flip operation) to neighbors in the phenotype space. The main drawback of gray codes is still their ability to deal with dynamic ranges.

1.4.2 Objective Function

The objective function[28] f formulates the goal to achieve. It associates with each solution of the search space a real value that describes the quality or the fitness of the solution, $f : S \to \mathbb{R}$. Then, it represents an absolute value and allows a complete ordering of all solutions of the search space. As shown in the previous section, from the representation space of the solutions R, some decoding functions d may be applied, $d : R \to S$, to generate a solution that can be evaluated by the function f.

The objective function is an important element in designing a metaheuristic. It will guide the search toward "good" solutions of the search space. If the objective function is improperly defined, it can lead to nonacceptable solutions whatever metaheuristic is used.

1.4.2.1 *Self-Sufficient Objective Functions*

For some optimization problems, the definition of the objective function is straightforward. It specifies the originally formulated objective function.

Example 1.35 Straightforward guiding objective function. In many routing problems such as TSP and vehicle routing problems, the formulated objective is to minimize

[28] Also defined as the cost function, evaluation function, and utility function.

a given global distance. For instance, in the TSP, the objective corresponds to the total distance of the Hamiltonian tour:

$$f(s) = \sum_{i=1}^{n-1} d_{\pi(i),\pi(i+1)} + d_{\pi(n),\pi(1)}$$

where π represents a permutation encoding a tour and n the number of cities.

For continuous (linear and nonlinear) optimization problems, the guiding function to optimize by a metaheuristic is simply the target objective function. In those families of optimization problems, the guiding objective function used in the search algorithm is generally equal to the objective function that has been specified in the problem formulation.

1.4.2.2 Guiding Objective Functions For other problems, the definition of the objective function is a difficult task and constitutes a crucial question. The objective function has to be transformed for a better convergence of the metaheuristic. The new objective function will guide the search in a more efficient manner.

Example 1.36 Objective function to satisfiability problems. Let us formulate an objective function to solve satisfiability problems. SAT problems represent fundamental decision problems in artificial intelligence. The k-SAT problem can be defined as follows: given a function F of the propositional calculus in a conjunctive normal form (CNF). The function F is composed of m clauses C_i of k Boolean variables, where each clause C_i is a disjunction. The objective of the problem is to find an assignment of the k Boolean variables such as the value of the function F is true. Hence, all clauses must be satisfied.

$$F = (x_1 \vee \overline{x_4}) \wedge (\overline{x_1} \vee \overline{x_2} \vee x_3) \wedge (x_1 \vee x_3 \vee x_4) \wedge (\overline{x_1} \vee x_2) \wedge (x_1 \vee x_2 \vee x_4) \wedge (x_2 \vee \overline{x_4}) \wedge (\overline{x_2} \vee \overline{x_3})$$

A solution for the problem may be represented by a vector of k binary variables. A straightforward objective function is to use the original F function:

$$f = \begin{cases} 0 & \text{if is } F \text{ false} \\ 1 & \text{otherwise} \end{cases}$$

If one considers the two solutions $s_1 = (1, 0, 1, 1)$ and $s_2 = (1, 1, 1, 1)$, they will have the same objective function, that is, the 0 value, given that the function F is equal to *false*. The drawback of this objective function is that it has a poor differentiation between solutions. A more interesting objective function to solve the problem will be to count the number of satisfied clauses. Hence, the objective will be to maximize the number of satisfied clauses. This function is better in terms of guiding the search toward the optimal solution. In this case, the solution s_1 (resp. s_2) will have a value of 5 (resp. 6). This objective function leads to the MAX-SAT model.

1.4.2.3 Representation Decoding The design questions related to the definition of the representation and the objective function may be related. In some problems, the representation (genotype) is decoded to generate the best possible solution (phenotype). In this situation, the mapping between the representation and the objective function is not straightforward; that is, a decoder function must be specified to generate from a given representation the best solution according to the objective function.

Example 1.37 Let us illustrate the relationship between the representation and the objective function within the Steiner tree problem. It is a combinatorial optimization problem with many applications in telecommunication (network design) and biology (phylogenetics). Given a nonoriented weighted graph $G = (V, E)$ where V represents the nodes of the graph and E represents the edges of the graph. The weights associated with the edges are all positive. Let T be a subset of vertices identified as terminals. The goal is to find a minimum-weight connected subgraph that includes all the terminals. The resulting subgraph is obviously a tree. This problem is NP-hard whereas the minimum-weight spanning tree problem is polynomial; that is, the Kruskal or Prim algorithms are well-known efficient algorithms to solve the problem.

A solution of the Steiner tree problem may be characterized by the list of nonterminal nodes X. It is then represented by a vector of binary values. The size of the vector is the number of nonterminal nodes. The Steiner tree associated with a solution is equivalent to the minimum spanning tree of the set $T \cup X$. This is easily obtained by a polynomial algorithm such as the Kruskal algorithm. Figure 1.21 represents an example on an input graph instance, where the terminals are represented by $T = \{A, B, C, D\}$. The optimal solution is $s^* = \{1, 3, 5\}$, which is represented in Fig. 1.22.

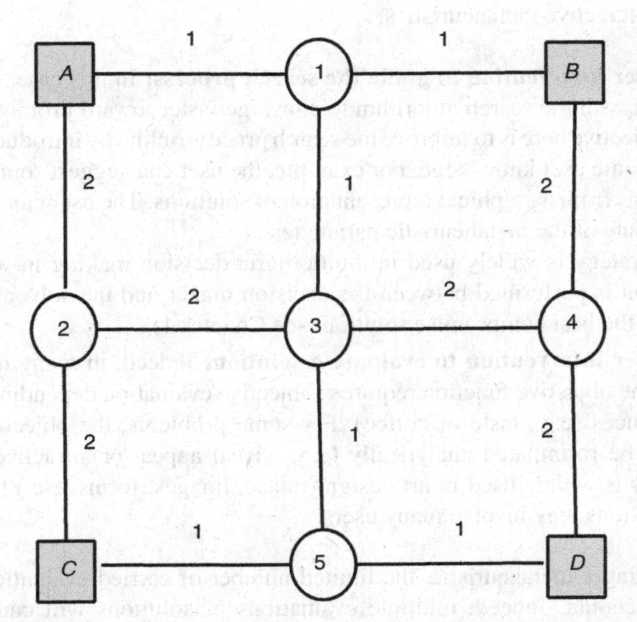

FIGURE 1.21 Instance for the Steiner tree problem: $T = \{A, B, C, D\}$.

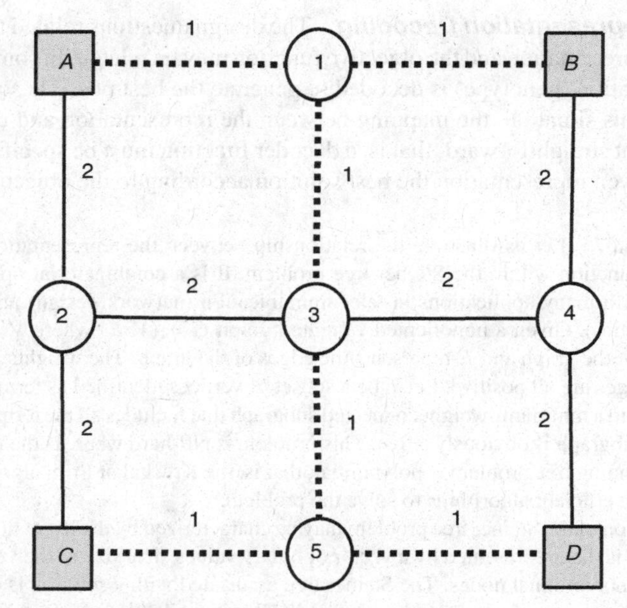

FIGURE 1.22 Optimal solution represented by the set {1, 3, 5}.

1.4.2.4 Interactive Optimization In interactive optimization, the user is involved online in the loop of a metaheuristic. There are two main motivations for designing interactive metaheuristics:

- **The user intervention to guide the search process:** In this case, the user can interact with the search algorithm to converge faster toward promising regions. The objective here is to improve the search process online by introducing dynamically some user knowledge. For example, the user can suggest some promising solutions from a graphical representation of solutions. The user can also suggest the update of the metaheuristic parameters.
  This strategy is widely used in multicriteria decision making in which an interaction is performed between the decision maker and the solver to converge toward the best compromise solution (see Chapter 4).
- **The user intervention to evaluate a solution:** Indeed, in many design problems, the objective function requires subjective evaluation depending on human preferences (e.g., taste of coffee). For some problems, the objective function cannot be formulated analytically (e.g., visual appeal or attractiveness). This strategy is widely used in art design (music, images, forms, etc.) [745]. Some applications may involve many users.

In designing a metaheuristic, the limited number of carried evaluations must be taken into account. Indeed, multiple evaluations of solutions will cause the user fatigue. Moreover, the evaluation by the user of a solution may be slow and expensive. Hence, the metaheuristic is supposed to converge toward a good solution in a limited number of iterations and using a limited size of population if a population-based metaheuristic is used.

1.4.2.5 Relative and Competitive Objective Functions

In some problems, it is impossible to have an objective function f that associates an absolute value with all solutions. For instance, those problems arise in game theory [175], cooperative or competitive coevolution [620], and learning classifier systems [821]. For instance, in a game the strategy A may be better than B, B better than C, and C better than A.

There are two alternatives to this class of problems: using relative or competitive objective functions. The relative fitness associates a rank with the individual in the population. In competitive fitness, a competition is applied over a subpopulation of solutions. Three different types of competition can be used: bipartite, tournament, and full. Bipartite competition compares two solutions s_1 and s_2 to determine the better one, whereas in case of full competition, all solutions are considered.

Population-based metaheuristics are well suited to this situation. In fact, in population-based metaheuristics, the selection strategies need only the relative or competitive fitness. Hence, the absolute quality of a solution is not necessary to evolve the population.

1.4.2.6 Meta-Modeling

It is well known that most of the time, in metaheuristics, the time-intensive part is the evaluation of the objective function. In many optimization problems, the objective function is quite costly to compute. The alternative to reduce this complexity is to approximate the objective function and then replace the original objective function by its approximation function. This approach is known as *meta-modeling*[29]. Moreover, for some problems, an analytical objective function is not available. In this case, the objective function may be approximated using a sample of solutions generated by physical experiments or simulations.

> **Example 1.38 Extremely expensive objective functions.** A classical example of extremely expensive objective function deals with structural design optimization [52,341]. For instance, in a three-dimensional aerodynamic design optimization, the evaluation of a structure consists in executing a costly CFD (computational fluid dynamics) simulation. A single simulation may take more than 1 day even on a parallel machine. In some problems such as telecommunication network design [752] or molecular docking [766], a time-consuming simulation must be used to evaluate the quality of the generated solutions. It is unimaginable to conduct physical

[29] Also known as surrogates or fitness approximation.

experiments for each potential solution. Moreover, meta-modeling is important in stochastic and robust optimization where additional objective function evaluations are necessary.

Many meta-modeling techniques may be employed for expensive objective functions. They are based on constructing an approximate model from a properly selected sample of solutions:

- **Neural networks:** Neural Network models such as multilayer perceptrons [644] and radial basis function [622] are the commonly used strategies.
- **Response surface methodologies:** This class is based on polynomial approximation of the objective function to create a response surface [571]. The most known methods belonging to this class are the least square method (quadratic polynomials) of Box and Wilson [90] and design of experiments (DOE) of Taguchi [668].
- Other candidate models in approximating objective functions are Kriging models [164], DACE (design and analysis of computer experiments) [679], Gaussian processes [316], and machine learning techniques such as SVM (support vector machines) [791].

The model selection problem is far from being a simple one [101]. There is a trade-off between the complexity of the model and its accuracy. To solve the classical bias and variance dilemma, the use of multiple models is encouraged. Constructing multiple local models instead of a global model can also be beneficial. The reader may refer to Ref. [413] for a more comprehensive survey.

Once the meta-model is constructed, it can be used in conjunction with the original objective function [413]. An alternative use of the original model and the approximated one can also be realized using different management strategies of meta-models[30] (Fig. 1.23) [208]. The trade-off here is the use of an expensive accurate evaluation versus a cheap erroneous evaluation of the objective function.

1.5 CONSTRAINT HANDLING

Dealing with constraints in optimization problems is another important topic for the efficient design of metaheuristics. Indeed, many continuous and discrete optimization problems are constrained, and it is not trivial to deal with those constraints. The constraints may be of any kind: linear or nonlinear and equality or inequality constraints. In this section, constraint handling strategies, which mainly act on the representation of solutions or the objective function, are presented. They can be classified as reject strategies, penalizing strategies, repairing strategies, decoding strategies, and preserving strategies. Other constraint handling approaches using search components

[30]Known as evolution control in evolutionary algorithms.

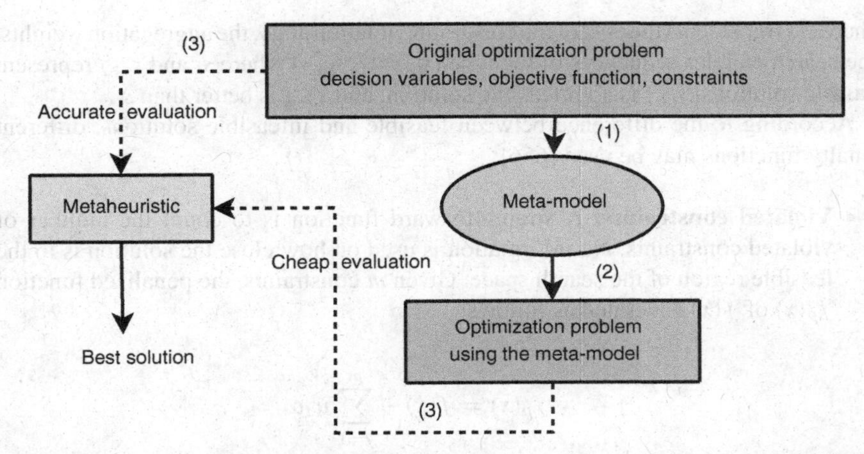

FIGURE 1.23 Optimization using a meta-model. Once the model is constructed (1), the metaheuristic can use either the meta-model (2) or the alternative between the two models (original and approximate) for a better compromise between accuracy and efficiency (3).

not directly related to the representation of solutions or the objective function may also be used, such as multiobjective optimization and coevolutionary models.

1.5.1 Reject Strategies

Reject strategies[31] represent a simple approach, where only feasible solutions are kept during the search and then infeasible solutions are automatically discarded.

This kind of strategies are conceivable if the portion of infeasible solutions of the search space is very small. Moreover, reject strategies do not exploit infeasible solutions. Indeed, it would be interesting to use some information on infeasible solutions to guide the search toward global optimum solutions that are in general on the boundary between feasible and infeasible solutions. In some optimization problems, feasible regions of the search space may be discontinuous. Hence, a path between two feasible solutions exists if it is composed of infeasible solutions.

1.5.2 Penalizing Strategies

In penalizing strategies, infeasible solutions are considered during the search process. The unconstrained objective function is extended by a penalty function that will penalize infeasible solutions. This is the most popular approach. Many alternatives may be used to define the penalties [304].

For instance, the objective function f may be penalized in a linear manner:

$$f'(s) = f(s) + \lambda c(s)$$

[31] Also named "death penalty."

where $c(s)$ represents the cost of the constraint violation and λ the aggregation weights. The search enables sequences of the type (s_t, s_{t+1}, s_{t+2}) where s_t and s_{t+2} represent feasible solutions, s_{t+1} is an infeasible solution, and s_{t+2} is better than s_t.

According to the difference between feasible and infeasible solutions, different penalty functions may be used [656]:

- **Violated constraints:** A straightforward function is to count the number of violated constraints. No information is used on how close the solution is to the feasible region of the search space. Given m constraints, the penalized function $f_p(x)$ of $f(x)$ is defined as follows:

$$f_p(x) = f(x) + \sum_{i=1}^{m} w_i \alpha_i$$

  where $\alpha_i = 1$ if constraint i is violated and $\alpha_i = 0$ otherwise, and w_i is the coefficient associated with each constraint i.
  For a problem with few and tight constraints, this strategy is useless.
- **Amount of infeasibility or repairing cost:** Information on how close a solution is to a feasible region is taken into account. This will give an idea about the cost of repairing the solution.
  For instance, more efficient approaches consist in including a distance to feasibility for each constraint. Considering q inequality constraints and $m - q$ equality constraints, the penalized function $f_p(x)$ will be formulated as follows:

$$f_p(x) = f(x) + \sum_{i=1}^{m} w_i d_i^k$$

  where d_i is a distance metric for the constraint i, $d_i = \alpha_i g_i(x)$ for $i = 1, \ldots, q$ and $d_i = |h_i(x)|$ for $i = q + 1, \ldots, m$. k is a user-defined constant (in general $k = 0, 1$), the constraints $1, \ldots, q$ are inequality constraints and the constraints $q + 1, \ldots, m$ are equality constraints.

When solving a constrained problem using a penalizing strategy, a good compromise for the initialization of the coefficient factors w_i must be found. Indeed, if w_i is too small, final solutions may be infeasible. If the coefficient factor w_i is too high, we may converge toward nonoptimal feasible solutions. The penalizing function used may be

- **Static:** In static strategies, a constant coefficient factor is defined for the whole search. The drawback of the static strategies is the determination of the coefficient factors w_i.

- **Dynamic:** In dynamic strategies, the coefficients factors w_i will change during the search. For instance, the severity of violating constraints may be increased with time. It means that when the search progresses, the penalties will be more strong, whereas in the beginning of the search highly infeasible solutions are admissible [423].

  Hence, a dynamic penalty function will take into account the time (e.g., number of iterations, generations, and number of generated solutions). Using a distance metric, the objective function may be formulated as follows:

$$f_p(x,t) = f(x) + \sum_{i=1}^{m} w_i(t) d_i^k$$

  where $w_i(t)$ is a decreasing monotonic function with t. More advanced functions such as annealing [547] or nonmonotonic functions (see Section 2.4.2) may be used.

  It is not simple to define a good dynamic penalty function. A good compromise for the initialization of the function $w_i(t)$ must be found. Indeed, if $w_i(t)$ is too slow decreasing, longer search is needed to find feasible solutions. Otherwise if $w_i(t)$ is too fast decreasing, we may converge quickly toward a nonoptimal feasible solution.

- **Adaptive:** The previously presented penalty functions (static and dynamic) do not exploit any information of the search process. In adaptive penalty functions, knowledge on the search process is included to improve the efficiency and the effectiveness of the search.

  The magnitude of the coefficient factors is updated according to the memory of the search [350]. The search memory may contain the best found solutions, last generated solutions, and so on. For instance, an adaptive strategy may consist in decreasing the coefficient factors when many feasible solutions are generated during the search, while increasing those factors if many infeasible solutions are generated.

Example 1.39 Adaptive penalization. Let us consider the capacitated vehicle routing problem (CVRP)[32]. An adaptive penalizing strategy may be applied to deal with the demand and duration constraints in a metaheuristic [308]:

$$f'(s) = f(s) + \alpha Q(s) + \beta D(s)$$

$Q(s)$ measures the total excess demand of all routes and $D(s)$ measures the excess duration of all routes. The parameters α and β are self-adjusting. Initially, the two parameters are initialized to 1. They are reduced (resp. increased) if the last μ visited

[32]The CVRP problem is defined in Exercise 1.11.

solutions are all feasible (resp. all infeasible), where μ is a user-defined parameter. The reduction (resp. increase) may consist in dividing (resp. multiplying) the actual value by 2, for example.

1.5.3 Repairing Strategies

Repairing strategies consist in heuristic algorithms transforming an infeasible solution into a feasible one. A repairing procedure is applied to infeasible solutions to generate feasible ones. For instance, those strategies are applied in the case where the search operators used by the optimization algorithms may generate infeasible solutions.

Example 1.40 Repairing strategy for the knapsack problem. In many combinatorial optimization problems, such as the knapsack problem, repairing strategies are used to handle the constraints. The knapsack problems represent an interesting class of problems with different applications. Moreover, many classical combinatorial optimization problems generate underlying knapsack problems. In the 0–1 knapsack problem, one have n different articles with weight w_i and utility u_i. A knapsack can hold a weight of at most w. The objective is to maximize the utility of the articles included in the knapsack satisfying the weight capacity of the knapsack. The decision variable x_j is defined as follows:

$$x_j = \begin{cases} 1 & \text{if the article is included} \\ 0 & \text{otherwise} \end{cases}$$

The problem consists in optimizing the objective function

$$\text{Max } f(x) = \sum_{j=1}^{n} x_j u_j$$

subject to the constraint

$$\sum_{j=1}^{n} w_j x_j \leq w$$

The following repairing procedure may be applied to infeasible solutions (see Algorithm 1.3). It consists in extracting from the knapsack some elements to satisfy the capacity constraint.

Algorithm 1.3 Repairing procedure for the knapsack.

Input: a nonfeasible solution s.
$s' = s$;
While s' nonfeasible (i.e., $\sum_{j=1}^{n} w_j x_j > w$) **Do**
Remove an item e_i from the knapsack: the element e_i maximizes the ratio $\frac{u_i}{w_i}$;
$s' = s' \setminus e_i$;
Endo
Output: a feasible solution s'.

The repairing heuristics are, of course, specific to the optimization problem at hand. Most of them are greedy heuristics. Then, the success of this strategy will depend on the availability of such efficient heuristics.

1.5.4 Decoding Strategies

A decoding procedure may be viewed as a function $R \rightarrow S$ that associates with each representation $r \in R$ a feasible solution $s \in S$ in the search space. This strategy consists in using indirect encodings (see Section 1.4.1.4). The topology of the search space is then transformed using the decoding function. The decoding function must have the following properties [179]:

- For each solution $r \in R$, corresponds a feasible solution $s \in S$.
- For each feasible solution $s \in S$, there is a representation $r \in R$ that corresponds to it.
- The computational complexity of the decoder must be reduced.
- The feasible solutions in S must have the same number of corresponding solutions in R.
- The representation space must have the locality property in the sense that distance between solutions in R must be positively correlated with the distance between feasible solutions in S.

1.5.5 Preserving Strategies

In preserving strategies for constraint handling, a specific representation and operators will ensure the generation of feasible solutions. They incorporate problem-specific knowledge into the representation and search operators to generate only feasible solutions and then preserve the feasibility of solutions.

This efficient class of strategies is tailored for specific problems. It cannot be generalized to handle constraints of all optimization problems. Moreover, for some problems such as the graph coloring problem, it is even difficult to find feasible initial solution or population of solutions to start the search.

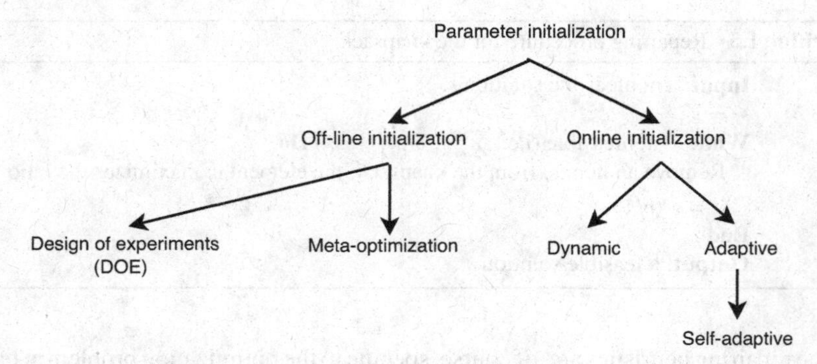

FIGURE 1.24 Parameter initialization strategies.

1.6 PARAMETER TUNING

Many parameters have to be tuned for any metaheuristic. Parameter tuning may allow a larger flexibility and robustness, but requires a careful initialization. Those parameters may have a great influence on the efficiency and effectiveness of the search. It is not obvious to define *a priori* which parameter setting should be used. The optimal values for the parameters depend mainly on the problem and even the instance to deal with and on the search time that the user wants to spend in solving the problem. A universally optimal parameter values set for a given metaheuristic does not exist.

There are two different strategies for parameter tuning: the *off-line*[33] parameter initialization (or meta-optimization) and the *online*[34] parameter tuning strategy (Fig. 1.24). In off-line parameter initialization, the values of different parameters are fixed before the execution of the metaheuristic, whereas in the online approach, the parameters are controlled and updated dynamically or adaptively during the execution of the metaheuristic.

1.6.1 Off-Line Parameter Initialization

As previously mentioned, metaheuristics have a major drawback; they need some parameter tuning that is not easy to perform in a thorough manner. Those parameters are not only numerical values but may also involve the use of search components.

Usually, metaheuristic designers tune one parameter at a time, and its optimal value is determined empirically. In this case, no interaction between parameters is studied. This sequential optimization strategy (i.e., one-by-one parameter) do not guarantee to find the optimal setting even if an exact optimization setting is performed.

[33] Also called endogenous strategy parameters [53].
[34] Also called exogenous strategy parameters.

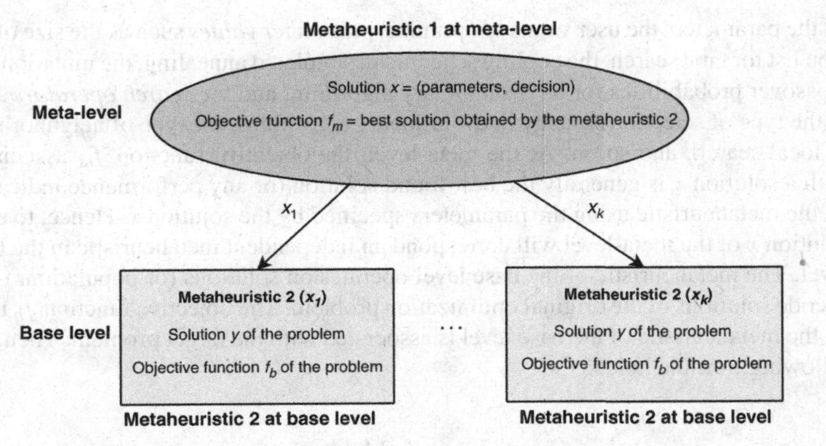

FIGURE 1.25 Meta-optimization using a meta-metaheuristic.

To overcome this problem, *experimental design*[35] is used [88]. Before using an experimental design approach, the following concepts must be defined:

- Factors[36] that represent the parameters to vary in the experiments.
- Levels that represent the different values of the parameters, which may be quantitative (e.g., mutation probability) or qualitative (e.g., neighborhood).

Let us consider n factors in which each factor has k levels, a full factorial design needs n^k experiments. Then, the "best" levels are identified for each factor. Hence, the main drawback of this approach is its high computational cost especially when the number of parameters (factors) and their domain values are large, that is, a very large number of experiments must be realized [683]. However, a small number of experiments may be performed by using *Latin hypercube* designs [536], sequential design, or *fractional design* [562].

Other approaches used in machine learning community such as *racing algorithms* [530] may be considered [76].

In off-line parameter initialization, the search for the best tuning of parameters of a metaheuristic in solving a given problem may be formulated as an optimization problem. Hence, this *meta-optimization* approach may be performed by any (meta)heuristic, leading to a meta-metaheuristic (or meta-algorithm) approach. Meta-optimization may be considered a hybrid scheme in metaheuristic design (see Section 5.1.1.2) (Fig. 1.25).

This approach is composed of two levels: the meta-level and the base level. At the meta-level, a metaheuristic operates on solutions (or populations) representing the parameters of the metaheuristic to optimize. A solution x at the meta-level will represent

[35] Also called *design of experiments* [266].

[36] Also named design variables, predictor variables, and input variables.

all the parameters the user wants to optimize: *parameter values* such as the size of the tabu list for tabu search, the cooling schedule in simulated annealing, the mutation and crossover probabilities for an evolutionary algorithm, and the *search operators* such as the type of selection strategy in evolutionary algorithms, the type of neighborhood in local search, and so on. At the meta-level, the objective function f_m associated with a solution x is generally the best found solution (or any performance indicator) by the metaheuristic using the parameters specified by the solution x. Hence, to each solution x of the meta-level will correspond an independent metaheuristic in the base level. The metaheuristic of the base level operates on solutions (or populations) that encode solutions of the original optimization problem. The objective function f_b used by the metaheuristic of the base level is associated with the target problem. Then, the following formula holds:

$$f_m(x) = f_b(\text{Meta}(x))$$

where Meta(x) represents the best solution returned by the metaheuristic using the parameters x.

1.6.2 Online Parameter Initialization

The drawback of the off-line approaches is their high computational cost, particularly if this approach is used for each input instance of the problem. Indeed, the optimal values of the parameters depend on the problem at hand and even on the various instances to solve. Then, to improve the effectiveness and the robustness of off-line approaches, they must be applied to any instance (or class of instances) of a given problem. Another alternative consists in using a parallel multistart approach that uses different parameter settings (see Chapter 6).

Another important drawback of off-line strategies is that the effectiveness of a parameter setting may change during the search; that is, at different moments of the search different optimal values are associated with a given parameter. Hence, online approaches that change the parameter values during the search must be designed. Online approaches may be classified as follows:

- **Dynamic update:** In a dynamic update, the change of the parameter value is performed without taking into account the search progress. A random or deterministic update of the parameter values is performed.
- **Adaptive update:** The adaptive approach changes the values according to the search progress. This is performed using the memory of the search.
  A subclass, referred to as *self-adaptive*[37] approach, consists in "evolving" the parameters during the search. Hence, the parameters are encoded into the representation and are subject to change as the solutions of the problem.

[37]Largely used in the evolutionary computation community.

In the rest of the book, many illustrative examples dealing with the off-line or online parameters initialization of each metaheuristic or search component are presented.

1.7 PERFORMANCE ANALYSIS OF METAHEURISTICS

Performance analysis of metaheuristics is a necessary task to perform and must be done on a fair basis. A theoretical approach is generally not sufficient to evaluate a metaheuristic [53]. This section addresses some guidelines of evaluating experimentally a metaheuristic and/or comparing metaheuristics in a rigorous way.

To evaluate the performance of a metaheuristic in a rigorous manner, the following three steps must be considered (Fig. 1.26):

- **Experimental design:** In the first step, the goals of the experiments, the selected instances, and factors have to be defined.
- **Measurement:** In the second step, the measures to compute are selected. After executing the different experiments, statistical analysis is applied to the obtained results. The performance analysis must be done with state-of-the-art optimization algorithms dedicated to the problem.
- **Reporting:** Finally, the results are presented in a comprehensive way, and an analysis is carried out following the defined goals. Another main issue here is to ensure the *reproducibility* of the computational experiments.

1.7.1 Experimental Design

In the computational experiment of a metaheuristic, the goals must be clearly defined. All the experiments, reported measures, and statistical analysis will depend on the purpose of designing the metaheuristic. Indeed, a contribution may be obtained for different criteria such as search time, quality of solutions, robustness in terms of the instances, solving large-scale problems, parallel scalability in terms of the number of processors, easiness of implementation, easiness to combine with other algorithms, flexibility to solve other problems or optimization models, innovation using new nature-inspired paradigms, automatic tuning of parameters, providing a tight approximation to the problem, and so on. Moreover, other purposes may be related to outline the contribution of a new search component in a given metaheuristic (representation, objective function, variation operators, diversification, intensification, hybrid models, parallel models, etc.).

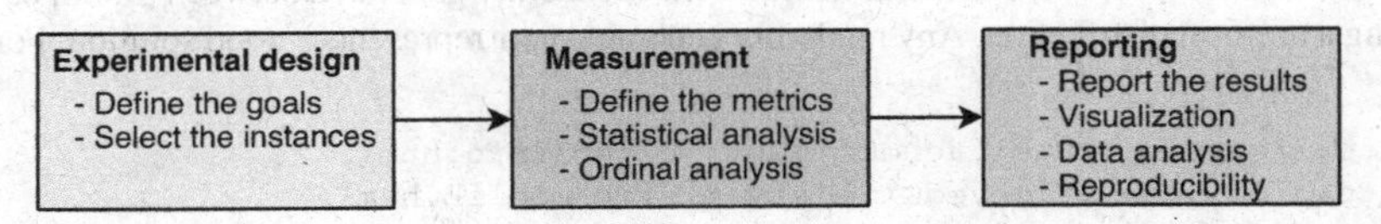

FIGURE 1.26 Different steps in the performance analysis of a metaheuristic: experimental design, measurement, and reporting.

Once the goals and factors are defined, methods from DOE can be suggested to conduct computational tests to ensure a rigorous statistical analysis [562]. It consists in selecting a set of combinations of values of factors to experiment (see Section 1.6.1). Then, the effect of a parameter (factor) p will be the change in the results obtained by the modification of the values of the parameter.

Once the goals are defined, the selection of the input instances to perform the evaluation must be carefully done. The structure associated with the input instances may influence significantly the performance of metaheuristics. Two types of instances exist:

- **Real-life instances:** They represent practical instances of the problem to be solved. If available, they constitute a good benchmark to carry out the performance evaluation of a metaheuristic.
  For some problems, it is difficult to obtain real-life instances for confidentiality reasons. In fact, most of the time, those data are proprietary and not public. For other problems, it is difficult to obtain a large number of real-life instances for financial reasons. For instance, in computational biology and bioinformatics, the generation of some genomic or proteomic data has a large cost. Also, collecting some real-life instances may be time consuming.
- **Constructed instances:** Many public libraries of "standard" instances are available on Internet [339]. They contain well-known instances for global optimization, combinatorial optimization, and mixed integer programs such as OR-Library[38], MIPLIB[39], DIMACS challenges[40], SATLIB for satisfiability problems, and the TSPLIB[41] (resp. QAPLIB) for the traveling salesman problem [646] (resp. the quadratic assignment problem).

  In addition to some real-life instances, those libraries contain in general *synthetic* or randomly generated instances. A disadvantage of *random* instances is that they are often too far from real-life problems to reflect their structure and important characteristics. The advantage of synthetic data is that they preserve the structure of real-life instances. Using a synthetic program, different instances in size and structure may be generated. Evaluating the performances of a given metaheuristic using only random instances may be controversial. For instance, the structure of uniformly generated random instances may be completely different from real-life instances of the problem, and then the effectiveness of the metaheuristic will be completely different in practice (see Section 2.2).

Example 1.41 Random instances may be controversial. Let us consider the symmetric TSP problem with n cities where the distance matrix is generated as follows: each element d_{ij}, $i \neq j$, of the distance matrix is independently generated between [0, 20] using a uniform distribution. Any randomly generated tour represents a good solution. For

[38] http://people.brunel.ac.uk/~mastjjb/jeb/info.html.
[39] http://www.caam.rice.edu/~bixby/miplib/miplib.html.
[40] http://dimacs.rutgers.edu/Challenges/.
[41] http://softlib.rice.edu/softlib/tsplib/.

TABLE 1.7 Some Classical Continuous Functions Used in Performance Evaluation of Metaheuristics

Function	Formulation
Sphere	$f(x) = \sum_{i=1}^{D} x_i^2$
Griewank	$f(x) = \frac{1}{4000} \sum_{i=1}^{D} x_i^2 - \prod_{i=1}^{D} \cos\left(\frac{x_i}{\sqrt{i}}\right) + 1$
Schaffer's f6	$f(x) = 0.5 - \frac{\left(\sin\sqrt{\left(x_1^2+x_2^2\right)}\right)^2 - 0.5}{\left(1+0.001\left(x_1^2+x_2^2\right)\right)^2}$
Rastrigin	$f(x) = \sum_{i=1}^{D} (x_i^2 - 10\cos(2\pi x_i) + 10)$
Rosenbrock	$f(x) = \sum_{i=1}^{D-1} (100(x_{i+1} - x_i^2)^2 + (x_i - 1)^2)$

D represents the number of dimensions associated with the problem.

example, for an instance of 5000 cities, it has been shown that the standard deviation is equal to 408 ($\sigma\sqrt{n}$) and the average cost is 50, 000 ($10 \cdot n$) [637]. According to the central limit theorem, almost any tour will have a good quality (i.e., cost of $\pm 3(408)$ of 50, 000). Hence, evaluating a metaheuristic on such instances is a pitfall to avoid. This is due to the independent random generation of the constants. Some correlation and internal consistency must be introduced for the constants.

Example 1.42 Continuous functions. In continuous optimization, some well-known functions are used to evaluate the performances of metaheuristics[42]: Schaffer, Griewank, Ackley, Rastrigin, Rosenbrock, and so on (see Table 1.7) [685]. These functions have different properties: for instance, the Sphere and Rastrigin are uncorrelated. The most studied dimensions are in the range [10–100]. Selected functions for metaheuristics must contain nonseparable, nonsymmetric, and nonlinear functions. Surprisingly, many used instances are separable, symmetric, or linear. Large dimensions are not always harder to solve. For instance, the Griewank function is easier to solve for large dimensions because the number of local optima decreases with the number of dimensions [815].

The selection of the input instances to evaluate a given metaheuristic may be chosen carefully. The set of instances must be diverse in terms of the size of the instances, their difficulties, and their structure. It must be divided into two subsets: the first subset will be used to tune the parameters of the metaheuristic and the second subset to evaluate the performance of the search algorithms. The calibration of the parameters of the metaheuristics is an important and tricky task. Most metaheuristics need the tuning of

[42]Test problems for global optimization may be found at `http://www2.imm.dtu.dk/~km/GlobOpt/testex/`.

various parameters that influence the quality of the obtained results. The values of the parameters associated with the used metaheuristics must be same for all instances. A single set of the parameter values is determined to solve all instances. No fine-tuning of the values is done for each instance unless the use of an automatic off-line or online initialization strategy (see Section 1.6). Indeed, this will cause an overfitting of the metaheuristic in solving known and specific instances. The parameter values will be excellent to solve the instances that serve to calibrate the parameters and very poor to tackle other instances. The robustness of the metaheuristic will be affected to solve unknown instances. Otherwise, the time to determine the parameter values of the metaheuristic to solve a given instance must be taken into account in the performance evaluation. Different parameter values may be adapted to different structures and sizes of the instances.

1.7.2 Measurement

In the second step, the performance measures and indicators to compute are selected. After executing the different experiments, some statistical analysis will be applied to the obtained results.

In exact optimization methods, the efficiency in terms of search time is the main indicator to evaluate the performances of the algorithms as they guarantee the global optimality of solutions. To evaluate the effectiveness of metaheuristic search methods, other indicators that are related to the quality of solutions have to be considered.

Performance indicators of a given metaheuristic may be classified into three groups [51]: solution quality, computational effort, and robustness. Other qualitative criteria such as the development cost, simplicity, ease of use, flexibility (wide applicability), and maintainability may be used.

1.7.2.1 Quality of Solutions Performance indicators for defining the quality of solutions in terms of precision are generally based on measuring the distance or the percent deviation of the obtained solution to one of the following solutions (Fig. 1.27):

- **Global optimal solution:** The use of global optimal solutions allows a more absolute performance evaluation of the different metaheuristics. The absolute

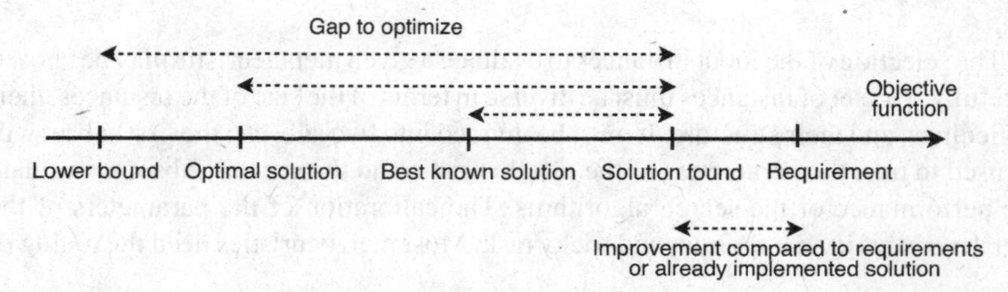

FIGURE 1.27 Performance assessment of the quality of the solutions. We suppose a minimization problem.

difference may be defined as $|f(s) - f(s^*)|$ or $|f(s) - f(s^*)|/f(s^*)$, where s is the obtained solution and s^* is the global optimal solution. Since those measures are not invariant under different scaling of the objective function, the following absolute approximation may be used: $|f(s) - f(s^*)|/|f_{\text{worst}} - f(s^*)|$ [838] or $|f(s) - f(s^*)|/|E_{\text{unif}}(f) - f(s^*)|$ [849], where f_{worst} represents the worst objective cost for the tackled instance[43], and $E_{\text{unif}}(f)$[44] denotes expectation with respect to the uniform distribution of solutions.

The global optimal solution may be found by an exact algorithm or may be available using "constructed" instances where the optimal solution is known *a priori* (by construction) [36]. Built-in optimal solutions have been considered for many academic problems [637]: traveling salesman problem [615], graph partitioning problem [483], Steiner tree problem [461], vertex packing, and maximum clique [677]. Also, for some problems, the optimal quality is known intrinsically. For example, in robot path planning, we have to optimize the distance between the actual position and the final one, and then the optimal solution has a null distance. Unfortunately, for many complex problems, global optimal solutions could not be available. There are also some statistical estimation techniques of optimal values in which a sample of solutions is used to predict the global optimal solution [209].

- **Lower/upper bound solution:** For optimization problems where the global optimal solution is not available, tight lower bounds[45] may be considered as an alternative to global optimal solutions. For some optimization problems, tight lower bounds are known and easy to obtain.

Example 1.43 Simple lower bound for the TSP. The Held–Karp (HK) 1-tree lower bound for the symmetric TSP problem is quick and easy to compute [371]. Given an instance (V, d) where V is the set of n cities and d the distance matrix. A node $v_0 \in V$ is selected. Let r be the total edge length of a minimum spanning tree over the $n-1$ cities ($v \in V - \{v_0\}$). The lower bound t is represented by the r value plus the two cheapest edges incident on v_0.

$$t = r + \min\{d(v_0, x) + d(v_0, y) : x, y \in V - \{v_0\}, x \neq y\}$$

Indeed, any TSP tour must use two edges e and f incident on the node v_0. Removing these two edges and the node v_0 from the tour yields a spanning tree of $V - \{v_0\}$. Typically, the lower bound t is 10% below the global optimal solution.

Different *relaxation* techniques may be used to find lower bounds such as the classical *continuous relaxation* and the *Lagrangian relaxation*. In continuous relaxation for IP problems, the variables are supposed to be real numbers instead

[43] For some problems, it is difficult to find the worst solution.

[44] This value can be efficiently computed for many problems. The expected error of a random solution is equal to 1.

[45] Lower bounds for minimization problems and upper bounds for maximization problems.

of integers. In Lagrangian relaxation, some constraints multiplied by Lagrange multipliers are incorporated into the objective function (see Section 5.2.1.2).

If the gap between the obtained solution and the lower bound is small, then the distance of the obtained solution to the optimal solution is smaller (see Fig. 1.27). In the case of null distance, the global optimality of the solution is proven. In the case of a large gap (e.g., > 20%), it can be due to the bad quality of the bound or the poor performance of the metaheuristic.

- **Best known solution:** For many classical problems, there exist libraries of standard instances available on the Web. For those instances, the best available solution is known and is updated each time an improvement is found.
- **Requirements or actual implemented solution:** For real-life problems, a decision maker may define a requirement on the quality of the solution to obtain. This solution may be the one that is currently implemented. These solutions may constitute the reference in terms of quality.

1.7.2.2 Computational Effort

The efficiency of a metaheuristic may be demonstrated using a theoretical analysis or an empirical one. In theoretical analysis, the worst-case complexity of the algorithm is generally computed (see Section 1.1.2). In general, reporting the asymptotic complexity is not sufficient and cannot tell the full story on computational performances of metaheuristics [419]. The average-case complexity, if it is possible to compute[46], is more practical [93].

In empirical analysis, measures related to the computation time of the metaheuristic used to solve a given instance are reported. The meaning of the computation time must be clearly specified: CPU time or wall clock time, with or without input/output and preprocessing/postprocessing time.

The main drawback of computation time measure is that it depends on the computer characteristics such as the hardware (e.g., processor, memories: RAM and cache, parallel architecture), operating systems, language, and compilers on which the metaheuristic is executed. Some indicators that are independent of the computer system may also be used, such as the number of objective function evaluations. It is an acceptable measure for time-intensive and constant objective functions. Using this metric may be problematic for problems where the evaluation cost is low compared to the rest of the metaheuristics or is not time constant in which it depends on the solution evaluated and time. This appears in some applications with variable length representations (genetic programming, robotics, etc.) and dynamic optimization problems.

Different stopping criteria may be used: time to obtain a given target solution, time to obtain a solution within a given percentage from a given solution (e.g., global optimal, lower bound, best known), number of iterations, and so on.

1.7.2.3 Robustness

There is no commonly acceptable definition of robustness. Different alternative definitions exist for robustness. In general, robustness is insensitivity against small deviations in the input instances (data) or the parameters of

[46] It needs a probability distribution of the input instances.

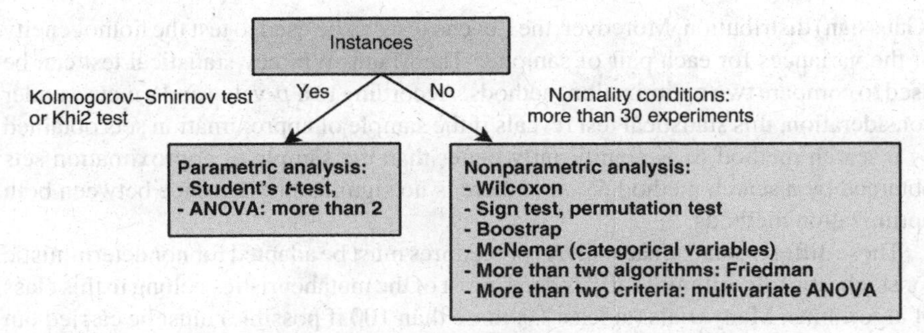

FIGURE 1.28 Statistical analysis of the obtained results.

the metaheuristic. The lower the variability of the obtained solutions the better the robustness [562].

In the metaheuristic community, robustness also measures the performance of the algorithms according to different types of input instances and/or problems. The metaheuristic should be able to perform well on a large variety of instances and/or problems using the same parameters. The parameters of the metaheuristic may be overfitted using the training set of instances and less efficient for other instances.

In stochastic algorithms, the robustness may also be related to the average/deviation behavior of the algorithm over different runs of the algorithm on the same instance.

1.7.2.4 Statistical Analysis Once the experimental results are obtained for different indicators, methods from statistical analysis[47] can be used to conduct the performance assessment of the designed metaheuristics [192]. While using any performance indicator (e.g., the quality of solutions c_i obtained by different metaheuristics M_i or their associated computational efforts t_i), some aggregation numbers that summarize the average and deviation tendencies must be considered. Then, different statistical tests may be carried out to analyze and compare the metaheuristics. The statistical tests are performed to estimate the confidence of the results to be scientifically valid (i.e., determining whether an obtained conclusion is due to a sampling error). The selection of a given statistical hypothesis testing tool is performed according to the characteristics of the data (e.g., variance, sample size) [562] (Fig. 1.28).

Under normality conditions, the most widely used test is the paired *t-test*. Otherwise, a nonparametric analysis may be realized such as the *Wilcoxon test* and the permutation test [337]. For a comparison of more than two algorithms, *ANOVA* models are well-established techniques to check the confidence of the results [146]. Multivariate ANOVA models allow simultaneous analysis of various performance measures (e.g., both the quality of solutions and the computation time). Kolmogorov–Smirnov test can be performed to check whether the obtained results follow a normal

[47] Many commercial (e.g., SAS, XPSS) and free softwares (e.g., R) are available to conduct such an analysis.

(Gaussian) distribution. Moreover, the Levene test can be used to test the homogeneity of the variances for each pair of samples. The Mann–Whitney statistical test can be used to compare two optimization methods. According to a p-value and a metric under consideration, this statistical test reveals if the sample of approximation sets obtained by a search method S_1 is significantly better than the sample of approximation sets obtained by a search method S_2, or if there is no significant difference between both optimization methods.

These different statistical analysis procedures must be adapted for nondeterministic (or stochastic) algorithms [740]. Indeed, most of the metaheuristics belong to this class of algorithms. Many trials (at least 10, more than 100 if possible) must be carried out to derive significant statistical results. From this set of trials, many measures may be computed: mean, median, minimum, maximum, standard deviation, the success rate that the reference solution (e.g., global optimum, best known, given goal) has been attained, and so on. The *success rate* represents the number of successful runs over the number of trials.

$$\text{success rate} = \frac{\text{number of successful runs}}{\text{total number of runs}}$$

The *performance rate* will take into account the computational effort by considering the number of objective function evaluations.

$$\text{performance rate} = \frac{\text{number of successful runs}}{\text{number of function evaluations} \times \text{total number of runs}}$$

When the number of trials n is important, the random variable associated with the average of the results found by a given metaheuristic over those trials tend to follow a Gaussian law of parameters m_0 and $\sigma_0/\sqrt{n}$, where m_0 (resp. σ_0) represents the average (resp. standard deviation) of the random variable associated with one experiment.

Confidence intervals (CI) can be used to indicate the reliability of the experiments. The confidence interval is an interval estimate of the set of experimental values. In practice, most confidence intervals are stated at the 95% level. It represents the probability that the experimental value is located in the interval $m - 1.96\sigma/\sqrt{n}$, $m + 1.96\sigma/\sqrt{n}$. A result with small CI is more reliable than results with a large CI.

1.7.2.5 Ordinal Data Analysis In comparing n metaheuristics for a given number of m experiments (instances, etc.), a set of ordinal values o_k $(1 \leq k \leq m)$ are generated for each method. For a given experiment, each ordinal value o_k denotes the rank of the metaheuristic compared to the other ones $(1 \leq o_k \leq n)$. Some ordinal data analysis methods may be applied to be able to compare the different metaheuristics. Those ordinal methods aggregate m linear orders O_k into a single linear order O so that the final order O summarizes the m orders O_k.

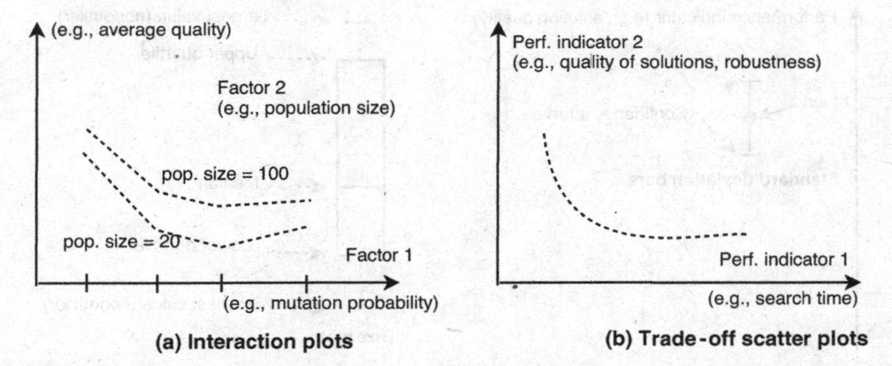

FIGURE 1.29 (a) Interaction plots analyze the effect of two factors (parameters, e.g., mutation probability, population size in evolutionary algorithms) on the obtained results (e.g., solution quality, time). (b) Scatter plots analyze the trade-off between the different performance indicators (e.g., quality of solutions, search time, robustness).

The commonly used ordinal aggregation methods are

- **Borda count voting method:** This method was proposed in 1770 by the French mathematician Jean-Charles de Borda. A method having a rank o_k is given o_k points. Given the m experiments, each method sums its points o_k to compute its total score. Then, the methods are classified according to their scores.
- **Copeland's method:** The Copeland method selects the method with the largest Copeland index. The Copeland index σ is the number of times a method beats other methods minus the number of times that method loses against other methods when the methods are considered in pairwise comparisons. For instance, let m and m' be two metaheuristics and $c_{mm'}$ the number of orders in which the metaheuristic m beats the metaheuristic m'. The Copelan index for the metaheuristic m will be $\sigma_m = \sum_{m'} c_{mm'} - c_{m'm}$. Then, the metaheuristics are ordered according to the decreasing values of the Copeland index σ.

1.7.3 Reporting

The interpretation of the results must be explicit and driven using the defined goals and considered performance measures. In general, it is not sufficient to present the large amount of data results using tables. Some visualization tools to analyze the data are welcome to complement the numerical results [780]. Indeed, graphical tools such as *deviation bars* (confidence intervals, box plots) and interaction plots allow a better understanding of the performance assessment of the obtained results.

Interaction plots represent the interaction between different factors and their effect on the obtained response (performance measure) (Fig. 1.29). *Box plots*[48] illustrate the

[48]Box plots were invented by the statistician John Tukey in 1977 [781].

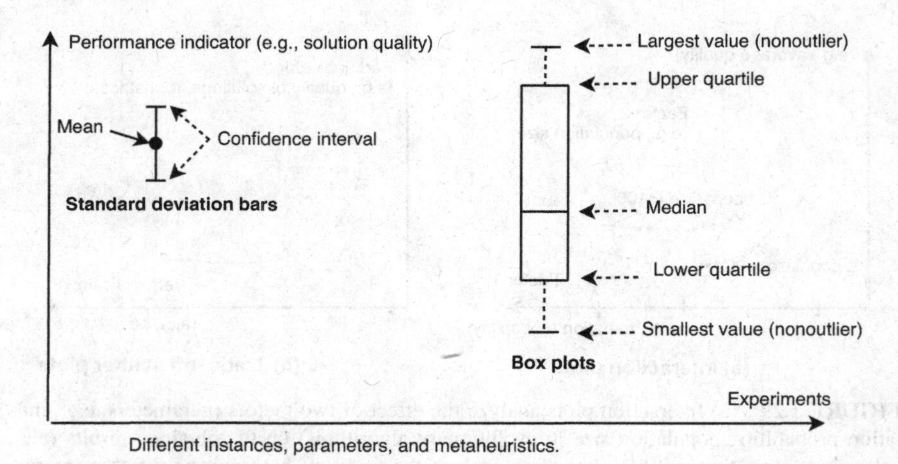

FIGURE 1.30 Some well-known visualization tools to report results: deviation bars, confidence intervals.

distribution of the results through their five-number summaries: the smallest value, lower quartile (Q1), median (Q2), upper quartile (Q3), and largest value (Fig. 1.30) [117]. They are useful in detecting outliers and indicating the dispersion and the skewness of the output data without any assumptions on the statistical distribution of the data.

Moreover, it is important to use *scatter plots* to illustrate the compromise between various performance indicators. For instance, the plots display quality of solutions versus time, or time versus robustness, or robustness versus quality (Fig. 1.29). Other plots measure the impact of a given factor on a performance indicator: time versus instance size and quality versus instance size. Indeed, analyzing the relationship between the quality of solution, the search time, the robustness, and the size/structure of instances must be performed in a comprehensive way. Other visualization tools may be used such as half-normal plots and histograms.

It would also be interesting to report negative results on applying a given metaheuristic or a search component to solve a given instance, problem, or class of problems. Indeed, most of the time only positive results are reported in the literature. From negative results, one may extract useful knowledge.

For a given experimental evaluation of a metaheuristic, *confidence intervals* may be plotted by a segment indicating the confidence interval at 95% level (Fig. 1.30). The middle of the segment shows the average of the experimental values.

More information on the behavior of a stochastic metaheuristic may be obtained by approximating the probability distribution for the time to a target solution value. To plot the empirical distribution for an algorithm and an instance, the i-smallest running time t_i may be associated with the probability $p_i = (i - (1/2))/n$, where n is the number of independent runs ($n \geq 100$), and plots the points $z_i = (t_i, p_i)$ for $i = [1, .., n]$.

A metaheuristic must be well documented to be reproduced. The program must be described in detail to allow its reproduction. If possible, making available the program, the instances, and the obtained results (complete solutions and the different measures) on the Web will be a plus. The different used parameters of the metaheuristic must be reported. Using different parameters in solving the different instances must also be reported. The use of software frameworks makes better the reproducibility, reusability, and extension of metaheuristics. In fact, if the competing metaheuristics are implemented using the same software framework, the performance metrics such as the search time are less biased to the programming skills and the computing system, and then the comparison is more fair and rigorous.

1.8 SOFTWARE FRAMEWORKS FOR METAHEURISTICS

In this section, the motivations for using a software framework for metaheuristics are outlined. Then, the main characteristics a framework should have are detailed. Finally, the ParadisEO framework that serves to design and implement various metaheuristics (e.g., S-metaheuristics, P-metaheuristics, hybrid, and parallel metaheuristics) in the whole book is presented.

1.8.1 Why a Software Framework for Metaheuristics?

Designing software frameworks for metaheuristics is primordial. In practice, there is a large diversity of optimization problems. Moreover, there is a continual evolution of the models associated with optimization problems. The problem may change or need further refinements. Some objectives and/or constraints may be added, deleted, or modified. In general, the efficient solving of a problem needs to experiment many solving methods, tuning the parameters of each metaheuristic, and so on. The metaheuristic domain in terms of new algorithms is also evolving. More and more increasingly complex metaheuristics are being developed (e.g., hybrid strategies, parallel models, etc.).

There is a clear need to provide a ready-to-use implementation of metaheuristics. It is important for application engineers to choose, implement, and apply the state-of-the art algorithms without in-depth programming knowledge and expertise in optimization. For optimization experts and developers, it is useful to evaluate and compare fairly different algorithms, transform ready-to-use algorithms, design new algorithms, and combine and parallelize algorithms.

Three major approaches are used for the development of metaheuristics:

- **From scratch or no reuse:** Nowadays, unfortunately this is the most popular approach. The basic idea behind the from scratch-oriented approach is the apparent simplicity of metaheuristic code. Programmers are tempted to develop themselves their codes. Therefore, they are faced with several problems: the development requires time and energy, and it is error prone and difficult to maintain and evolve.
  Numerous metaheuristics and their implementation (program codes) have been proposed, and are available on the Web. They can be reused and adapted to a

user problem. However, the user has to deeply examine the code and rewrite its problem-specific sections. This task is often tedious, error prone, takes a long time, and makes harder the produced code maintenance.

- **Only code reuse:** it consists of reusing third-party code available on the Web either as free individual programs or as libraries. Reusability may be defined as the ability of software components to build many different applications [262]. An old third-party code has usually application-dependent sections that must be extracted before the new application-dependent code can be inserted. Changing these sections is often time consuming and error prone.

  A better way to reuse the code of existing metaheuristics is through libraries [804]. The code reuse through libraries is obviously better because these libraries are often well tried, tested, and documented, thus more reliable. They allow a better maintainability and efficiency. Nowadays, it is recognized that the object-oriented paradigm is well-suited to develop reusable libraries. However, libraries allow code reuse but they do not permit the reuse of complete invariant part of algorithms. Libraries do not allow the reuse of design. Therefore, the coding effort using libraries remains important.

- **Both design and code reuse:** The objective of both code and design reuse approaches is to overcome this problem, that is, to redo as little code as possible each time a new optimization problem is dealt with. The basic idea is to capture into special components the recurring (or invariant) part of solution methods to standard problems belonging to a specific domain. These special components are called *design patterns* [293]. A pattern can be viewed as a programming language-independent description of a solution to a general design problem that must be adapted for its eventual use [523]. Useful design patterns related to a specific domain (e.g., metaheuristics) are in general implemented as *frameworks*. A framework approach is devoted to the design and code reuse of a metaheuristic [422]. A framework may be object oriented and defined as a set of classes that embody an abstract design for solutions to a family of related metaheuristics. Frameworks are well known in the software engineering literature. Frameworks can thus be viewed as programming language-dependent concrete realizations of patterns that facilitate direct reuse of design and code. They allow the reuse of the design and implementation of a whole metaheuristic. They are based on a strong conceptual separation of the invariant (generic) part of metaheuristics and their problem-specific part. Therefore, they allow the user to redo very little code, and it improves the quality and the maintainability of the metaheuristics.

Moreover, unlike libraries, frameworks are characterized by the inverse control mechanism for the interaction with the application code. In a framework, the provided code calls the user-defined one according to the Hollywood property "do not call us, we call you." Therefore, frameworks provide the full control structure of the invariant part of the algorithms, and the user has to supply only the problem-specific details. To meet this property, the design of a framework must be based on a clear conceptual separation between the solution methods and the problems they tackle.

This separation requires a solid understanding of the application domain. The domain analysis results in a model of the domain to be covered by reusable classes with some constant and variable aspects. The constant part is encapsulated in generic/abstract classes or skeletons that are implemented in the framework [22]. The variable part is problem specific, it is fixed in the framework but implemented by the user. This part consists of a set of holes or hot spots [624] that serve to fill the skeletons provided by the framework when building specific applications. It is recommended to use object-oriented composition rather than inheritance to perform this separation [660]. The reason is that classes are easier to reuse than individual methods. Another and completely different way to perform this separation may be used [81]. It provides a ready-to-use module for each part, and the two modules communicate through text files. This allows less flexibility than the object-oriented approach. Moreover, it induces an additional overhead, even if this is small. Nevertheless, this approach is multilanguage allowing more code reuse.

1.8.2 Main Characteristics of Software Frameworks

According to the openness criterion, two types of frameworks can be distinguished: *white* or glass box frameworks and *black box* (opaque) frameworks. In black box frameworks, one can reuse components by plugging them together through static parameterization and composition, and not worrying about how they accomplish their individual tasks [422]. In contrast, white box frameworks require an understanding of how the classes work so that correct subclasses (inheritance based) can be developed. Therefore, they allow more extendability. Frameworks often start as white box frameworks; these are primarily customized and reused through classes specialization. When the variable part has stabilized or been realized, it is often appropriate to evolve to black box frameworks [262].

Nowadays, the white box approach is more suited to metaheuristics. It is composed of adaptable software components intended to be reused to solve specific optimization problems. Unless the automatic or quasi-automatic design of a metaheuristic for a given problem is not solved, the designer must tailor a given metaheuristic to solve the problem. The source code level must be provided to the user to adapt his algorithm. The black box approach can be adapted to some families of optimization problems such as nonlinear continuous optimization problems where the same search components can be used (representation, search operators, etc.). In other families such as combinatorial optimization, the representation and search operators are always tailored to solve a problem using programming languages such as C++ or Java. For instance, the black box approach is used for linear programming optimization solvers (e.g., Cplex, Lindo, XPRESS-MP) that use a modeling language based on mathematical programming, such as the AMPL[49], GAMS,[50] or MPL[51] languages.

[49]www.ampl.com.
[50]www.gams.com.
[51]www.maximal-usa.com.

A framework is normally intended to be exploited by as many users as possible. Therefore, its exploitation could be successful only if some important user criteria are satisfied. The following are the major criteria of them and constitute the main objectives of the used framework in this book:

- **Maximum design and code reuse:** The framework must provide for the user a whole architecture design of his/her metaheuristic approach. Moreover, the programmer may redo as little code as possible. This objective requires a clear and maximal conceptual separation between the metaheuristics and the problems to be solved, and thus a deep domain analysis. The user might therefore develop only the minimal problem-specific code. It will simplify considerably the development of metaheuristics and reduce the development time.
- **Flexibility and adaptability:** It must be possible for the user to easily add new features/metaheuristics or change existing ones without implicating other components. Furthermore, as in practice existing problems evolve and new others arise, these have to be tackled by specializing/adapting the framework components.
- **Utility:** The framework must allow the user to cover a broad range of metaheuristics, problems, parallel distributed models, hybridization mechanisms, multi-objective optimization, and so on. To design optimization methods for hard problems, a lot of metaheuristics exist. Nevertheless, the scientist does not have necessarily the time and the capability to try all of them. Furthermore, to gain effective method, the parameters often need to be tuned. So a platform that can facilitate the design of optimization methods and their test is necessary to produce high-quality results.
- **Transparent and easy access to performance and robustness:** As the optimization applications are often time consuming, the performance issue is crucial. Parallelism and distribution are two important ways to achieve high-performance execution. To facilitate its use, it is implemented so that the user can deploy his/her parallel metaheuristic in a transparent manner. Moreover, the execution of the algorithms must be robust to guarantee the reliability and the quality of the results. The hybridization mechanism allows to obtain robust and better solutions.
- **Portability:** To satisfy a large number of users, the framework must support different material architectures (sequential, parallel, or distributed architecture) and their associated operating systems (Windows, Unix, MacOs).
- **Easy to use and efficiency:** The framework must be easy to use and does not incorporate an additional cost in terms of time or space complexity. The framework must preserve the efficiency of a special-purpose implementation. On the contrary, as the framework is normally developed by "professional" and knowledgeable software engineers and is largely tested by many users, it will be less error prone than ad-hoc special-purpose developed metaheuristics. Moreover, it is well known that the most intensive computational part in a metaheuristic is generally the evaluation of the objective function that is specified by the user to solve his specific problem.

Several frameworks for metaheuristics have been proposed in the literature. Most of them have the following limitations:

- **Metaheuristics:** most of the exiting frameworks focus only on a given metaheuristic or family of metaheuristics such as evolutionary algorithms (e.g., GAlib [809]), local search (e.g., EasyLocal++ [301], Localizer [550]), and scatter search (e.g., OPTQUEST). Only few frameworks are dedicated on the design of both families of metaheuristics. Indeed, a unified view of metaheuristics must be done to provide a generic framework.
- **Optimization problems:** most of the software frameworks are too narrow, that is, they have been designed for a given family of optimization problems: nonlinear continuous optimization (e.g., GenocopIII), combinatorial optimization (e.g., iOpt), monoobjective optimization (e.g., BEAGLE), multiobjective optimization (e.g., PISA [81]), and so on.
- **Parallel and hybrid metaheuristics:** Moreover, most of the existing frameworks either do not provide hybrid and parallel metaheuristics at all (Hotframe [262]) or supply just some parallel models: island model for evolutionary algorithms (e.g., DREAM [35], ECJ [819], JDEAL, distributed BEAGLE [291]), independent multistart and parallel evaluation of the neighborhood (e.g., TS [79]), or hybrid metaheuristics (iOpt [806]).
- **Architectures:** Finally, seldom a framework is found that can target many types of architectures: sequential and different types of parallel and distributed architectures, such as shared-memory (e.g., multicore, SMP), distributed-memory (e.g., clusters, network of workstations), and large-scale distributed architectures (e.g., desktop grids and high-performance grids). Some software frameworks are dedicated to a given type of parallel architectures (e.g., MALLBA [22], MAFRA [481], and TEMPLAR [426,427]).

Table 1.8 illustrates the characteristics of the main software frameworks for metaheuristics[52]. For a more detailed review of some software frameworks and libraries for metaheuristics, the reader may refer to Ref. [804].

1.8.3 ParadisEO Framework

In this book, we will use the ParadisEO[53] framework to illustrate the design and implementation of the different metaheuristics. The ParadisEO platform honors the criteria mentioned before, and it can be used both by no-specialists and by optimization method experts. It allows the design and implementation of

- Single-solution based and population-based metaheuristics in a unifying way (see Chapters 2 and 3).

[52]We do not claim an exhaustive comparison.

[53]ParadisEO is distributed under the CeCill license.

TABLE 1.8 Main Characteristics of Some Software Frameworks for Metaheuristics

Framework or Library	Metaheuristic	Optimization Problems	Parallel Models	Communication Systems
EasyLocal++	S-meta	Mono	-	-
Localizer++	S-meta	Mono	-	-
PISA	EA	Multi	-	-
MAFRA	LS, EA	Mono	-	-
iOpt	S-meta, GA, CP	Mono, COP	-	-
OptQuest	SS	Mono	-	-
GAlib	GA	Mono	Algo-level Ite-level	PVM
GenocopIII	EA	Mono, Cont	-	
DREAM	EA	Mono	Algo-level	Peer-to-peer sockets
MALLBA	LS EA	Mono	Algo-level Ite-level	MPI Netstream
Hotframe	S-meta, EA	Mono	-	-
TEMPLAR	LS, SA, GA	Mono, COP	Algo-level	MPI, threads
JDEAL	GA, ES	Mono	Ite-level	Sockets
ECJ	EA	Mono	Algo-level	Threads, sockets
Dist. BEAGLE	EA	Mono	Algo-level Ite-level	Sockets
ParadisEO	S-meta P-meta	Mono, Multi COP, Cont	Algo-level Ite-level Sol-level	MPI, threads Condor Globus

[S-meta: S-metaheuristics; P-meta: P-metaheuristics; COP: combinatorial optimization; Cont: continuous optimization; Mono: Monoobjective optimization; Multi: multiobjective optimization, LS: local search; ES: evolution strategy; SS: scatter search; EA: evolutionary algorithms; GA: genetic algorithms; Algo-level: algorithmic level of parallel model; Ite-level: iteration level of parallel models; Sol-level: solution level of parallel models. Unfortunately, only a few of them are maintained and used!.]

- Metaheuristics for monoobjective and multiobjective optimization problems (see Chapter 4).
- Metaheuristics for continuous and discrete optimization problems.
- Hybrid metaheuristics (see Chapter 5).
- Parallel and distributed metaheuristics (see Chapter 6).

ParadisEO is a white box object-oriented framework based on a clear conceptual separation of the metaheuristics from the problems they are intended to solve. This separation and the large variety of implemented optimization features allow a maximum code and design reuse. The separation is expressed at implementation level by splitting the classes into two categories: provided classes and required classes. The provided classes constitute a hierarchy of classes implementing the invariant part of the code. Expert users can extend the framework by inheritance/specialization. The required classes coding the problem-specific part are abstract classes that have to be specialized and implemented by the user.

The classes of the framework are fine-grained and instantiated as evolving objects embodying one and only one method. This is a particular design choice adopted in ParadisEO. The heavy use of these small-size classes allows more independence and thus a higher flexibility compared to other frameworks. Changing existing components and adding new ones can be easily done without impacting the rest of the application. Flexibility is enabled through the use of the object-oriented technology. Templates are used to model the metaheuristic features: coding structures, transformation operators, stopping criteria, and so on. These templates can be instantiated by the user according to his/her problem-dependent parameters. The object-oriented mechanisms such as inheritance, polymorphism, and so on are powerful ways to design new algorithms or evolve existing ones. Furthermore, ParadisEO integrates several services making it easier to use, including visualization facilities, online definition of parameters, application checkpointing, and so on.

ParadisEO is one of the rare frameworks that provides the most common parallel and distributed models. These models concern the three main parallel models: algorithmic level, iteration level, and solution level. They are portable on different types of architectures: distributed-memory machines and shared-memory multiprocessors as they are implemented using standard libraries such as message passing interface (MPI), multithreading (Pthreads), or grid middlewares (Condor or Globus). The models can be exploited in a transparent way, one has just to instantiate their associated ParadisEO components. The user has the possibility to choose by a simple instantiation for the communication layer. The models have been validated on academic and industrial problems. The experimental results demonstrate their efficiency. The experimentation also demonstrates the high reuse capabilities as the results show that the user redo little code. Furthermore, the framework provides the most common hybridization mechanisms. They can be exploited in a natural way to make cooperating metaheuristics belonging either to the same family or to different families.

ParadisEO is a C++ LGPL open-source framework (STL-Template)[54]. It is portable on Windows, Unix-like systems such as Linux and MacOS. It includes the following set of modules (Fig. 1.31):

- **Evolving objects (EO):** The EO library was developed initially for evolutionary algorithms (genetic algorithms, evolution strategies, evolutionary programming, genetic programming, and estimation distribution algorithms) [453]. It has been extended to population-based metaheuristics such as particle swarm optimization and ant colony[55] optimization.
- **Moving objects (MO):** It includes single-solution based metaheuristics such as local search, simulated annealing, tabu search, and iterated local search.

[54]Downloadable at `http://paradiseo.gforge.inria.fr`.

[55]The model implemented is inspired by the self-organization of *Pachycondyla apicalis* ant species.

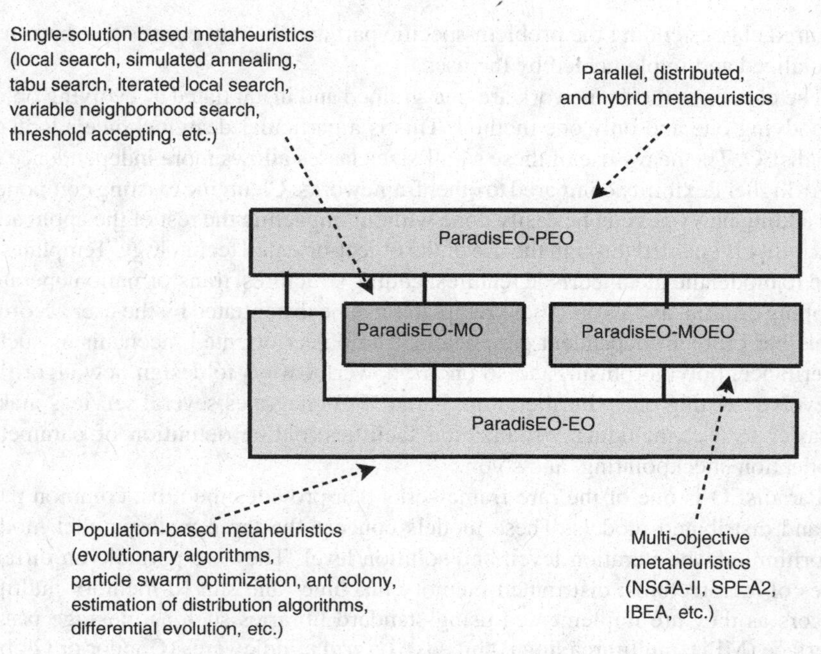

FIGURE 1.31 The different unified modules of the ParadisEO framework.

- **Multiobjective evolving objects (MOEO):** It includes the search mechanisms to solve multiobjective optimization problems such as fitness assignment, diversification, and elitism. From this set of mechanisms, classical algorithms such as NSGA-II, SPEA2, and IBEA have been implemented and are available.
- **Parallel evolving objects (PEO):** It includes the well-known parallel and distributed models for metaheuristics and their hybridization.

1.8.3.1 ParadisEO Architecture The architecture of ParadisEO is multilayered and modular allowing to achieve the objectives quoted above (Fig. 1.32).

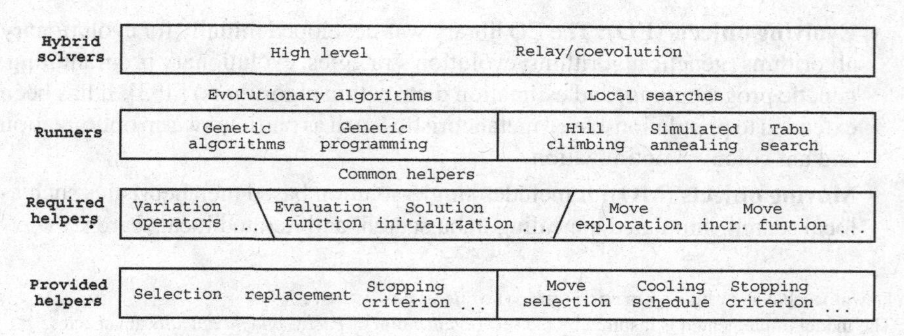

FIGURE 1.32 Architecture of the ParadisEO framework.

This allows particularly a high genericity, flexibility, and adaptability, an easy hybridization, and code and design reuse. The architecture has three layers identifying three major classes: *Solvers*, *Runners*, and *Helpers*.

- **Helpers:** Helpers are low-level classes that perform specific actions related to the search process. They are split into two categories: *population helpers* (PH) and *single-solution helpers* (SH). Population helpers include mainly the transformation, selection, and replacement operations, the evaluation function, and the stopping criterion. Solution helpers can be generic such as the neighborhood explorer class, or specific to the local search metaheuristic such as the tabu list manager class in the tabu search solution method. On the other hand, there are some special helpers dedicated to the management of parallel and distributed models, such as the communicators that embody the communication services. Helpers cooperate between them and interact with the components of the upper layer, that is, the runners. The runners invoke the helpers through function parameters. Indeed, helpers do not have not their own data, but they work on the internal data of the runners.
- **Runners:** The *Runners* layer contains a set of classes that implement the metaheuristics themselves. They perform the run of the metaheuristics from the initial state or population to the final one. One can distinguish the *population runners* (PR) such as genetic algorithms, evolution strategies, particle swarm, and so on and *single-solution runners* (SR) such as tabu search, simulated annealing, and hill climbing. Runners invoke the helpers to perform specific actions on their data. For instance, a PR may ask the fitness function evaluation helper to evaluate its population. An SR asks the movement helper to perform a given movement on the current state. Furthermore, runners can be serial or parallel distributed.
- **Solvers:** Solvers are devoted to control the search. They generate the initial state (solution or population) and define the strategy for combining and sequencing different metaheuristics. Two types of solvers can be distinguished: *single metaheuristic solvers* (SMS) and *multiple-metaheuristic solvers* (MMS). SMS are dedicated to the execution of a single metaheuristic. MMS are more complex as they control and sequence several metaheuristics that can be heterogeneous. They use different hybridization mechanisms. Solvers interact with the user by getting the input data and by delivering the output (best solution, statistics, etc.).

According to the generality of their embedded features, the classes of the architecture are split into two major categories: *provided* classes and *required* classes. Provided classes embody the factored out part of the metaheuristics. They are generic, implemented in the framework, and ensure the control at run time. Required classes are those that must be supplied by the user. They encapsulate the problem-specific aspects of the application. These classes are fixed but not implemented in ParadisEO. The programmer has the burden to develop them using the object-oriented specialization mechanism.

At each layer of the ParadisEO architecture, a set of classes is provided (Fig. 1.32). Some of them are devoted to the development of metaheuristics for monoobjective and multiobjective optimization, and others are devoted to manage transparently parallel and distributed models for metaheuristics and their hybridization.

There are two programming mechanisms to extend built-in classes: function substitution and subclassing. By providing some methods, any class accepts that the user specifies his own function as a parameter that will be used instead of the original function. This will avoid the use of subclassing, which is a more complex task. The user must at least provide the objective function associated with his problem.

1.9 CONCLUSIONS

When identifying a decision-making problem, the first issue deals with modeling the problem. Indeed, a mathematical model is built from the formulated problem. One can be inspired by similar models in the literature. This will reduce the problem to well-studied optimization models. One has also to be aware of the accuracy of the model. Usually, models we are solving are simplifications of the reality. They involve approximations and sometimes they skip processes that are complex to represent in a mathematical model.

Once the problem is modeled, the following roadmap may constitute a guideline in solving the problem (Fig.1.33).

First, whether it is legitimate to use metaheuristics for solving the problem must be addressed. The complexity and difficulty of the problem (e.g., NP-completeness, size, and structure of the input instances) and the requirements of the target optimization problem (e.g., search time, quality of the solutions, and robustness) must be taken into account. This step concerns the study of the intractability of the problem at hand. Moreover, a study of the state-of-the-art optimization algorithms (e.g., exact and heuristic algorithms) to solve the problem must be performed. For instance, the use of exact methods is preferable if the best known exact algorithm can solve in the required time the input instances of the target problem. Metaheuristic algorithms seek good solutions to optimization problems in circumstances where the complexity of the tackled problem or the search time available does not allow the use of exact optimization algorithms.

At the time the need to design a metaheuristic is identified, there are three common design questions related to all iterative metaheuristics:

- **Representation:** A traditional (e.g., linear/nonlinear, direct/indirect) or a specific encoding may be used to represent the solutions of the problem. Encoding plays a major role in the efficiency and effectiveness of any metaheuristic and constitutes an essential step in designing a metaheuristic. The representation must have some desired properties such as the completeness, connexity, and efficiency. The encoding must be suitable and relevant to the tackled optimization problem. Moreover, the efficiency of a representation is also related to the search

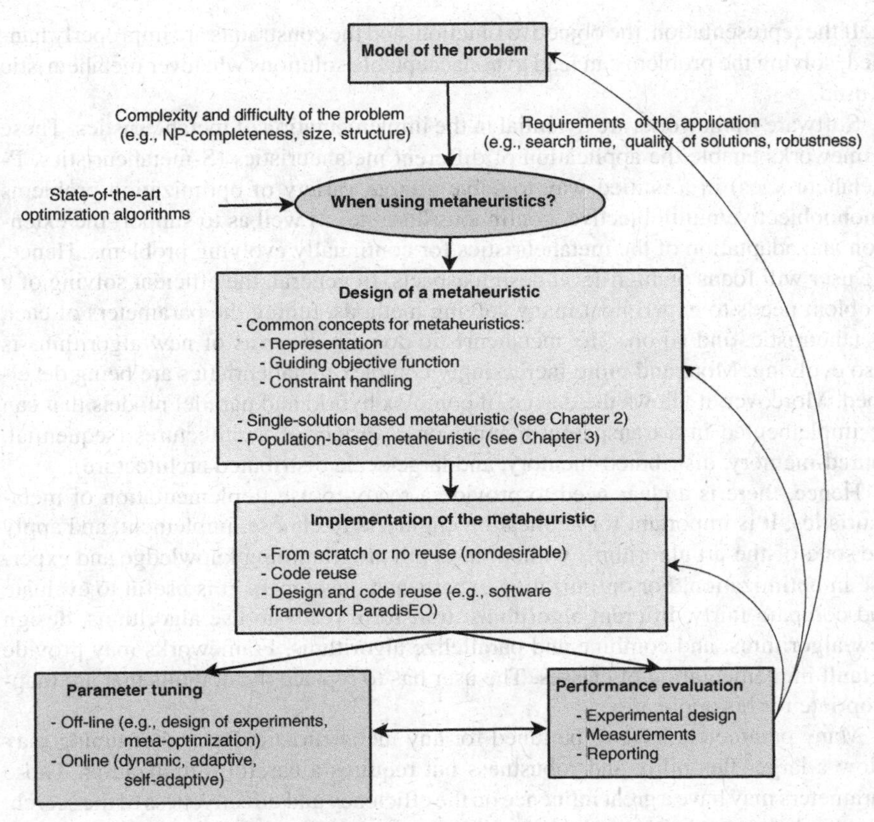

FIGURE 1.33 Guidelines for solving a given optimization problem.

operators applied to this representation (e.g., generation of the neighborhood, recombination of solutions). In fact, when defining a representation, one has to bear in mind how the solution will be evaluated and how the search operators will operate.

- **Objective function:** The objective function is an important element in designing a metaheuristic. It will guide the search toward "good" solutions of the search space. The guiding objective function is related to the goal to achieve. For efficiency and effectiveness reasons, the guiding function may be different from the objective function formulated by the model.
- **Constraint handling:** Dealing with constraints in optimization problems is another important aspect of the efficient design of metaheuristics. Indeed, many continuous and discrete optimization problems are constrained, and it is not trivial to deal with those constraints. Most of the constraint handling strategies act on the representation of solutions or the objective function (e.g., reject, penalizing, repairing, decoding, and preserving strategies).

If the representation, the objective function, and the constraints are improperly handled, solving the problem can lead to nonacceptable solutions whatever metaheuristic is used.

Software frameworks are essential in the implementation of metaheuristics. These frameworks enable the application of different metaheuristics (S-metaheuristics, P-metaheuristics) in a unified way to solve a large variety of optimization problems (monoobjective/multiobjective, continuous/discrete) as well as to support the extension and adaptation of the metaheuristics for continually evolving problems. Hence, the user will focus on high-level design aspects. In general, the efficient solving of a problem needs to experiment many solving methods, tuning the parameters of each metaheuristic, and so on. The metaheuristic domain in terms of new algorithms is also evolving. More and more increasingly complex metaheuristics are being developed. Moreover, it allows the design of complex hybrid and parallel models that can be implemented in a transparent manner on a variety of architectures (sequential, shared-memory, distributed-memory, and large-scale distributed architecture).

Hence, there is a clear need to provide a ready-to-use implementation of metaheuristics. It is important for application engineers to choose, implement, and apply the state-of-the-art algorithms without in-depth programming knowledge and expertise in optimization. For optimization experts and developers, it is useful to evaluate and compare fairly different algorithms, transform ready-to-use algorithms, design new algorithms, and combine and parallelize algorithms. Frameworks may provide default implementation of classes. The user has to replace the defaults that are inappropriate for his application.

Many parameters have to be tuned for any metaheuristic. Parameter tuning may allow a larger flexibility and robustness but requires a careful initialization. Those parameters may have a great influence on the efficiency and effectiveness of the search. It is not obvious to define *a priori* which parameter setting should be used. The optimal values for the parameters depend mainly on the problem and even the instance to deal with and on the search time that the user wants to spend in solving the problem. A universally optimal parameter values set for a given metaheuristic does not exist.

The performance evaluation of the developed metaheuristic is the last step of the roadmap. Worst-case and average-case theoretical analyses of metaheuristics present some insight into solving some traditional optimization models. In most of the cases, an experimental approach must be realized to evaluate a metaheuristic. Performance analysis of metaheuristics is a necessary task to perform and must be done on a fair basis. A theoretical approach is generally not sufficient to evaluate a metaheuristic. To evaluate the performance of a metaheuristic in a rigorous manner, the following three steps must be considered: experimental design (e.g., goals of the experiments, selected instances, and factors), measurement (e.g., quality of solutions, computational effort, and robustness), and reporting (e.g., box plots, interaction plots). The performance analysis must be done with the state-of-the-art optimization algorithms dedicated to the problem according to the defined goals. Another main issue here is to ensure the reproducibility of the computational experiments.

In the next two chapters, we will focus on the main search concepts for designing single-solution based metaheuristics and population-based metaheuristics. Each class of algorithms shares some common concepts that can be unified in the description and the design of a metaheuristic. This classification provides a clearer presentation of hybrid metaheuristics, parallel metaheuristics, and metaheuristics for multiobjective optimization.

1.10 EXERCISES

Exercise 1.1 Related problems to maximum clique. Given an undirected graph $G = (V, E)$. A clique Q of the graph G is a subset of V where any two vertices in Q are adjacent:

$$\forall i, j \in Q \times Q, (i, j) \in E$$

A maximum clique is a clique with the largest cardinality. The problem of finding the maximum clique is NP-hard. The clique number is the cardinality of the maximum clique. Given the following problems:

- The subset $I \subseteq V$ of maximum cardinality such as the set of edges of the subgraph induced by I is empty.
- Graph coloring.

Find the relationships between the formulated problems and the maximum clique problem. How these problems are identified in the literature?

Exercise 1.2 Easy versus hard optimization problem. Let us consider the set bipartitioning problem. Given a set X of n positive integers $e_1, e_2, \ldots, e_n$ where n is an even value. The problem consists in partitioning the set X into two subsets Y and Z of equal size. How many possible partitions of the set X exist?

Two optimization problems may be defined:

- Maximum set bipartitioning that consists in maximizing the difference between the sums of the two subsets Y and Z.
- Minimum set bipartitioning that consists in minimizing the difference between the sums of the two subsets Y and Z.

To which complexity class the two optimization problems belong? Let us consider the minimum set bipartitioning problem. Given the following greedy heuristic: sort the set X in decreasing order. For each element of $X[i]$ with $i = 1$ to n, assign it to the set with the smallest current sum. What is the time complexity of this heuristic?

Exercise 1.3 PTAS class of approximation. Can the maximum clique problem be approximated by any constant factor?

Exercise 1.4 Size of an instance versus its structure. The size of an instance is not the unique indicator that describes the difficulty of a problem, but also its structure. For a given problem, small instances cannot be solved to optimality while large instances may be solved exactly. Show for some classical optimization problems (e.g., satisfiability, knapsack, bin packing, vehicle routing, and set covering) that some small instances are not solved exactly while some large instances are solved to optimality by the state-of-the-art exact optimization methods.

Exercise 1.5 2-Approximation for the vertex covering problem. The vertex cover problem consists in finding the minimal vertex cover in a given graph. A vertex cover for an undirected graph $G = (V, E)$ is a subset S of its vertices such that each edge has at least one end point in S. For each edge (i, j) in E, one of i or j must be an element of S. Show that it is very easy to find a simple greedy heuristic that guarantees a 2-approximation factor. The complexity of the heuristic must be in the order of $O(m)$ where m is the number of edges.

Exercise 1.6 Specific heuristic. Let us consider the number partitioning problem presented in Example 1.15. Propose a *specific* heuristic to solve this problem. Consider the difference of number pairs in a decreasing order until only one number remains. For instance, if the input instance is (16, 13, 11, 10, 5), the first pair to consider will be (16, 13). Then, their difference is included in the input instance, that is, (3,11,10,5), where 3 represents the partition $\{16\}$ and $\{13\}$.

Exercise 1.7 Representation for constrained spanning tree problems. Given a connected graph $G = (V, E)$, a spanning tree is a minimum size connected and maximum size acyclic subgraph of G spanning all the vertices of V. The large numbers of applications have required the study of variants of the well-known minimum spanning tree problem (MSTP). Given a connected graph $G = (V, E)$, with $n = |V|$, $m = |E|$, a spanning tree is a connected and acyclic subgraph of G spanning all the vertices of V with $n - 1$ edges. Although the MSTP, the more studied problem involving spanning tree, can be solved in polynomial time, the outstanding importance of spanning trees in telecommunication or integrated circuit network design, biology, or computer science has required the development of more complex problems and often NP-hard variants. Indeed, adding some constraints (e.g., node degree, graph diameter) to the MSTP problem makes it NP-hard.

For instance, in the hop-constrained minimum spanning tree problem (HMSTP), the unique path from a specified root node, node 0, to any other node has no more than H hops (edges). Propose an encoding for the HMSTP problem.

Exercise 1.8 Indirect encoding for the bin packing problem. We consider in this exercise the bin packing problem (see Example 1.16). Let us consider an indirect encoding based on permutations. Propose a decoding function of permutations that generates feasible solutions to the bin packing problem. This representation belongs to the one-to-many class of encodings. Analyze the redundancy of this encoding. How the degree of redundancy grows with the number of bins?

Exercise 1.9 Encoding for the equal piles problem. Given a set of n one-dimensional objects of different sizes x_i ($i = 1, \ldots, n$), the objective is to distribute the objects into k piles G_l ($l = 1, \ldots, k$) such that the heights of the piles are as similar as possible:

$$f = \sum_{l=1}^{k} |s_l - S|$$

where $s_l = \sum_{j \in G_l} x_j$ is the sum of sizes for a given subset l and $S = \sum_{i=1}^{n} x_i / k$ is the average size of a subset. The problem is NP-hard even for $k = 2$. Propose a representation of solutions to tackle this problem.

Exercise 1.10 Greedy heuristic for the knapsack problem. In Example 1.40, a greedy heuristic for the 0–1 knapsack problem has been proposed. What will be the characteristic of the algorithm if the order of the elements when sorted by increasing weight is the same compared to their utilities when sorted by decreasing value?

Exercise 1.11 Greedy algorithms for vehicle routing problems. Vehicle routing problems represent very important applications in the area of logistics and transportation [775]. VRP are some of the most studied problems in the combinatorial optimization domain. The problem was introduced more than four decades ago by Dantzig and Ramser. The basic variant of the VRP is the capacitated vehicle routing problem. CVRP can be defined as follows: Let $G = (V, A)$ be a graph where V the set of vertices represents the customers. One vertex represents the depot with a fleet of m identical vehicles of capacity Q. We associate with each customer v_i a demand q_i and with each edge (v_i, v_j) of A a cost c_{ij} (Fig. 1.34). We have to find a set of routes where the objective is to minimize the total cost and satisfy the following constraints:

- For each vehicle, the total demand of the assigned customers does not exceed its capacity Q.

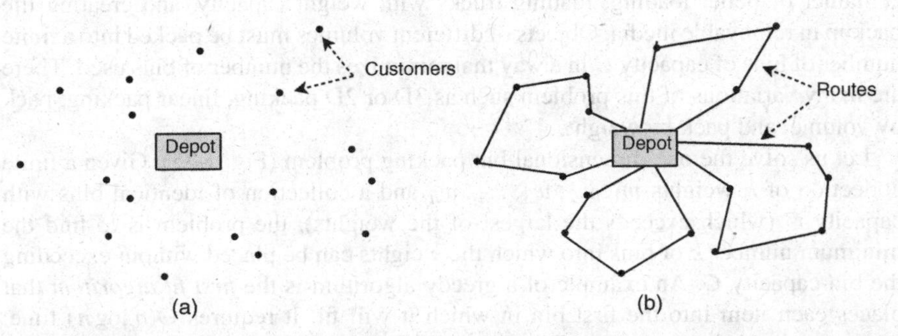

FIGURE 1.34 The capacitated vehicle routing problem. (a) From the depot, we serve a set of customers. (b) A given solution for the problem.

- Each route must begin and end at the depot node.
- Each customer is visited exactly once.

Define one or more greedy algorithms for the CVRP problem. Give some examples of constraints or more general models encountered in practice. For instance, one can propose

- Multiple depot VRP (MDVRP) where the customers get their deliveries from several depots.
- VRP with time windows (VRPTW), in case a time window (start time, end time, and service time) is associated with each customer.
- Periodic VRP (PVRP) in which a customer must be visited a prescribed number of times within the planning period. Each customer specifies a set of possible visit day combinations.
- Split delivery VRP (SDVRP) where several vehicles serve a customer.
- VRP with backhauls (VRPB) in which the vehicle must pick something up from the customer after all deliveries are carried out.
- VRP with pick ups and deliveries (VRPPS) if the vehicle picks something up and delivers it to the customer.

Exercise 1.12 Greedy algorithms for the Steiner tree problem. The goal of this exercise is to design a greedy heuristic for the Steiner tree problem. *Hints*: (a) Construct a graph where the nodes are terminals. The weight associated with an edge connecting two terminals represents the value of the shortest path between those terminals in the original graph. (b) Generate a spanning tree from this graph using the Kruskal algorithm. (c) From the edges obtained from the spanning tree, redesign the original graph using those selected edges and find the Steiner tree.

Exercise 1.13 Greedy algorithms for the bin packing problem. The bin packing problem is a well-known combinatorial problem with many applications such as container or pellet loading, loading trucks with weight capacity, and creating file backup in removable media. Objects of different volumes must be packed into a finite number of bins of capacity C in a way that minimizes the number of bins used. There are many variations of this problem such as 3D or 2D packing, linear packing, pack by volume, and pack by weight.

Let us solve the one-dimensional bin packing problem (Fig. 1.35). Given a finite collection of n weights $w_1, w_2, w_3, \ldots, w_n$ and a collection of identical bins with capacity C (which exceeds the largest of the weights), the problem is to find the minimum number k of bins into which the weights can be placed without exceeding the bin capacity C. An example of a greedy algorithm is the *first fit algorithm* that places each item into the first bin in which it will fit. It requires $\Theta(n \log n)$ time. Propose some improvements of this greedy algorithm. *Hint*: For example, a sorting of the elements may be done before the packing.

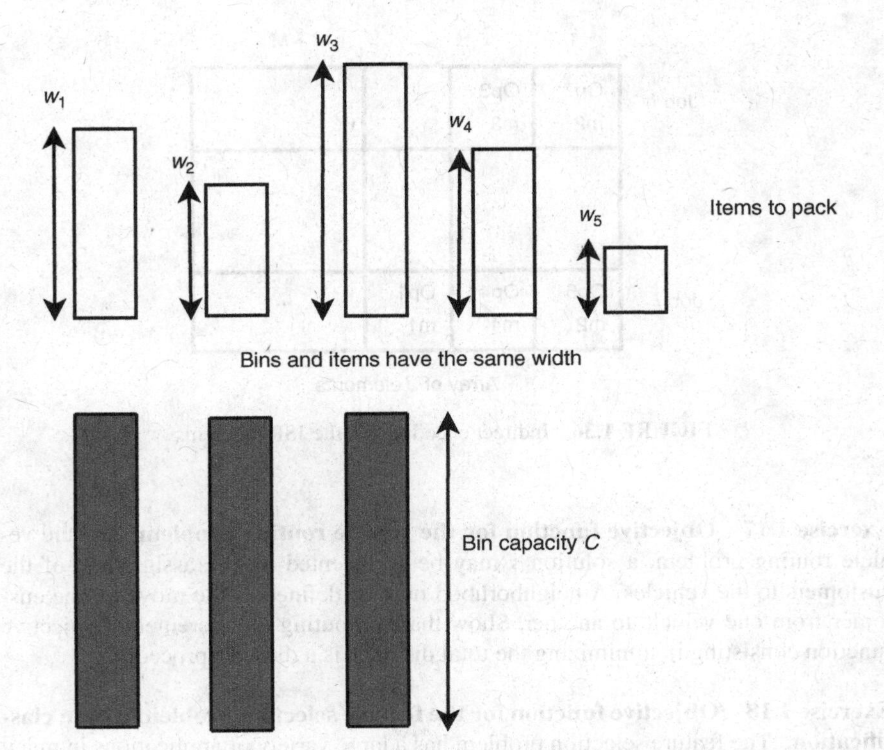

FIGURE 1.35 The one-dimensional bin packing problem.

Exercise 1.14 Random permutation. Design an efficient procedure for the generation of a random permutation.

Exercise 1.15 Generalized TSP problem. The generalized traveling salesman problem (GTSP) is a generalization of the well-known traveling salesman problem. Given an undirected complete graph $G = (V, E)$, where V represents the set of cities. In the GTSP, the set of nodes V is partitioned into m groups $W_1, W_2, \ldots, W_m$ where $0 < m \leq n$ and $W_1 \cup W_2 \cup \cdots \cup W_n = V$. Each city $v_i \in V$ belongs to one and only one group. The groups are disjoint, that is, $\forall i \neq j, W_i \cap W_j = \emptyset$. The objective is to find a minimum tour in terms of distance containing exactly one node from each group W_i. Propose a representation for the problem.

Exercise 1.16 Indirect encoding for the JSP. The job-shop scheduling problem has been defined in Example 1.33. Given the following indirect encoding: an array of j elements, each one being composed of a list of allocations of machines on which the operations are to be executed (Fig 1.36). Propose a decoder that generates a feasible schedule.

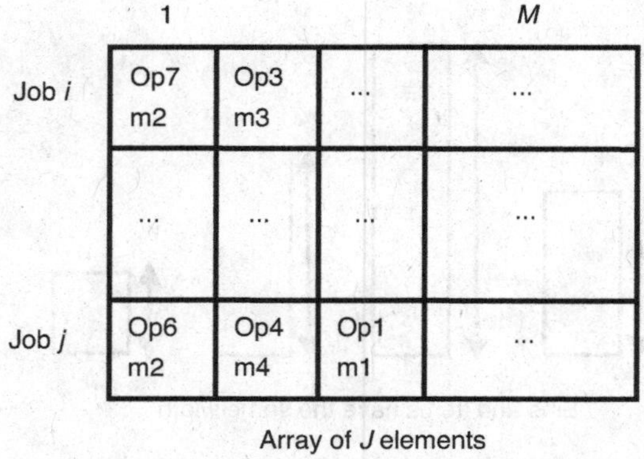

	1			M
Job i	Op7 m2	Op3 m3	...	...
	...	...	...	...
Job j	Op6 m2	Op4 m4	Op1 m1	...

Array of J elements

FIGURE 1.36 Indirect encoding for the JSP problem.

Exercise 1.17 Objective function for the vehicle routing problem. For the vehicle routing problem, a solution s may be represented by the assignment of the customers to the vehicles. A neighborhood may be defined as the move of one customer from one vehicle to another. Show that computing the incremental objective function consisting in minimizing the total distance is a difficult procedure.

Exercise 1.18 Objective function for the feature selection problem within classification. The feature selection problem has a large variety of applications in many domains such as data mining. In the feature selection problem, the objective is to find a subset of features such that a classification algorithm using only those selected feature provides the best performances. Any supervised classification algorithm may be used such as the support vector machines, decision trees, or naive Bayes. Given a set of instances I. Each instance is characterized by a large number of d features $F = \{f_1, f_2, \ldots, f_d\}$. Each instance is labeled with the class it belongs to. The problem consists in finding the optimal subset $S \subseteq F$. Propose an objective function for this problem.

Exercise 1.19 Domination analysis of metaheuristics. In combinatorial optimization problems, the domination analysis of a metaheuristic is defined by the number of solutions of the search space S that are dominated by the solution obtained by the metaheuristic. Suppose a metaheuristic H that generates the solution s_H from the search space S. The dominance associated with the metaheuristic H is the cardinality of the set $\{s \in S : f(s) \geq f(s_H)\}$. If the metaheuristic has obtained the global optimal solution s^*, the dominance $\text{dom}(H) = |S|$. Give a critical analysis of this performance indicator.

Exercise 1.20 Performance evaluation in dynamic optimization problems. To evaluate a metaheuristic in a dynamic problem, using classical measures such as the best found solution is not sufficient. Indeed, the concept of solution quality is changing over time. Propose a performance measure to deal with the quality of solutions in dynamic optimization problems with an *a priori* known time of the environment change $t_i, i \in [1, \ldots, n]$.

Exercise 1.21 Constraint handling. Given an objective function f to minimize and m constraints to satisfy. The new objective function f' that handles the constraints is defined as follows:

$$f'(x) = \begin{cases} f(x) & \text{if } x \text{ is a feasible solution} \\ K - \sum_{i=1}^{s} \frac{K}{m} & \text{otherwise} \end{cases}$$

where x is a solution to the problem, s is the number of satisfied constraints, and K is a very large constant value (e.g., $K = 10^9$). To which class of constraint handling strategies this approach belongs? Perform a critical analysis of this approach.

Exercise 1.22 Evaluation of metaheuristics as multiobjective optimization. Many quantitative and qualitative criteria can be considered to evaluate the performance of metaheuristics: efficiency, effectiveness, robustness, simplicity, flexibility, innovation, and so on. Let us consider only two quantitative criteria: efficiency and effectiveness. Figure 1.37 plots for two metaheuristics, Meta_1 and Meta_2, the evolution in time of the quality of best found solutions. According to each criterion, which

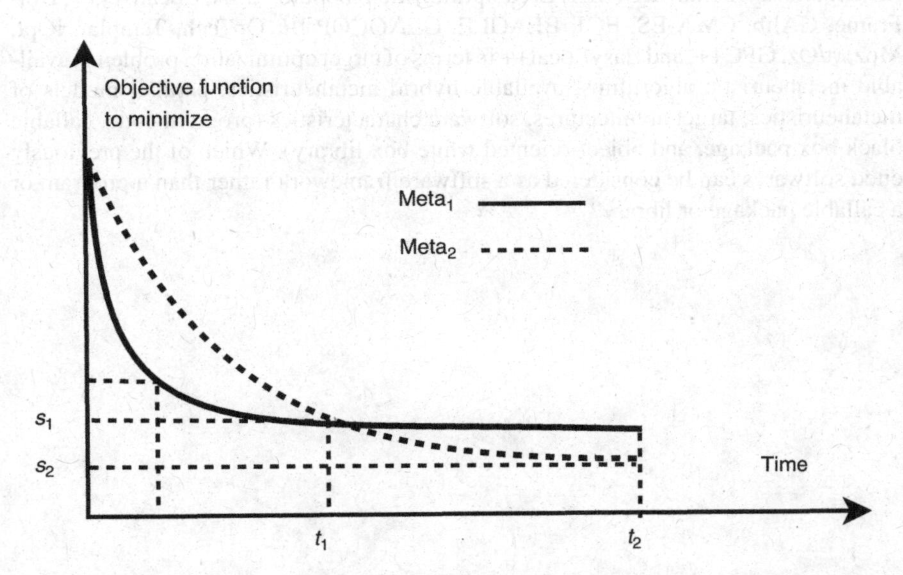

FIGURE 1.37 Efficiency versus effectiveness in the performance evaluation of metaheuristics. In terms of Pareto dominance optimality, no metaheuristic dominates the other one.

metaheuristic may be considered the best one? No metaheuristic dominates the other one for the two criteria. Propose some aggregations of the two criteria that generate a total ordering of metaheuristics. How can we deal with the qualitative criteria?

Exercise 1.23 Theoretical versus experimental evaluation. In comparing the theoretical and the experimental approach of the performance evaluation of a metaheuristic, one can make the following two statements:

- The theoretical approach gives more certain conclusions than the experimental approach.
- The experimental approach gives more certain conclusions than the theoretical approach.

Show that the two statements may be correct.

Exercise 1.24 Black box versus white box for metaheuristic software. Explain why the black box approach for software frameworks is not yet well suited for metaheuristics to solve general optimization problems. For which class of optimization problems, the black box approach may be appropriate for metaheuristics? Compare with the field of continuous linear programming (mathematical programming) and constraint programming.

Exercise 1.25 Software for metaheuristics. Analyze the following software for metaheuristics: ParadisEO, MATLAB optimization module, PISA, Localizer++, HotFrame, GAlib, CMA-ES, ECJ, BEAGLE, GENOCOP III, OpTech, Templar, iOpt, Mozart/Oz, GPC++, and EasyLocal++ in terms of target optimization problems, available metaheuristic algorithms, available hybrid metaheuristics, parallel models of metaheuristics, target architectures, software characteristics (program code, callable black box package, and object-oriented white box library). Which of the previously cited softwares can be considered as a software framework rather than a program or a callable package or library?

CHAPTER 2

Single-Solution Based Metaheuristics

While solving optimization problems, single-solution based metaheuristics (S-metaheuristics) improve a single solution. They could be viewed as "walks" through neighborhoods or search trajectories through the search space of the problem at hand [163]. The walks (or trajectories) are performed by iterative procedures that move from the current solution to another one in the search space. S-metaheuristics show their efficiency in tackling various optimization problems in different domains.

In this chapter, a unified view of the common search concepts for this class of metaheuristics is presented. Then, the main existing algorithms, both from the design and the implementation point of view, are detailed in an incremental way.

This chapter is organized as follows. After the high-level template of S-metaheuristics is presented, Section 2.1 details the common search components for S-metaheuristics: the definition of the neighborhood structure, the incremental evaluation function, and the determination of the initial solution. The concept of very large neighborhoods is also presented. Section 2.2 discusses the landscape analysis of optimization problems. Sections 2.3, 2.4, and 2.5 introduce, in an incremental manner, the well-known S-metaheuristics: local search, simulated annealing, and tabu search. Then, Sections 2.6, 2.7, and 2.8 present, respectively, the iterative local search, the variable neighborhood search, and the guided local search algorithms. In Section 2.9, other S-metaheuristics are dealt with, such as GRASP, the noisy and the smoothing methods. Finally, Section 2.10 presents the ParadisEO–MO (moving objects) module of the ParadisEO framework that is dedicated to the implementation of S-metaheuristics. Some design and implementations of S-metaheuristics such as local search, simulated annealing, tabu search, and iterated local search are illustrated.

2.1 COMMON CONCEPTS FOR SINGLE-SOLUTION BASED METAHEURISTICS

S-metaheuristics iteratively apply the generation and replacement procedures from the current single solution (Fig. 2.1). In the generation phase, a set of candidate solutions are generated from the current solution s. This set $C(s)$ is generally obtained by local

Metaheuristics: From Design to Implementation, by El-Ghazali Talbi

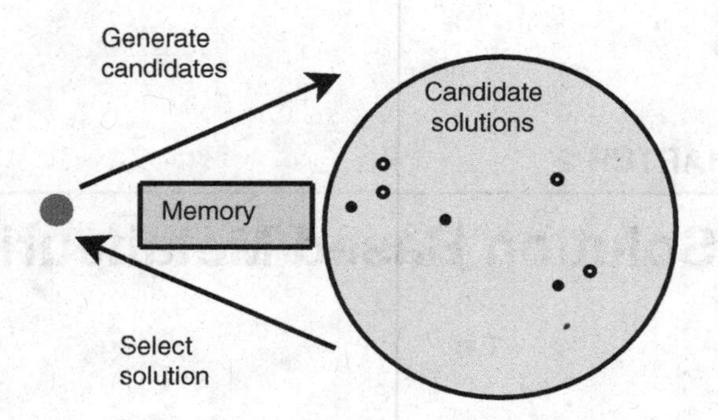

FIGURE 2.1 Main principles of single-based metaheuristics.

transformations of the solution. In the replacement phase,[1] a selection is performed from the candidate solution set $C(s)$ to replace the current solution; that is, a solution $s' \in C(s)$ is selected to be the new solution. This process iterates until a given stopping criteria. The generation and the replacement phases may be *memoryless*. In this case, the two procedures are based only on the current solution. Otherwise, some history of the search stored in a memory can be used in the generation of the candidate list of solutions and the selection of the new solution. Popular examples of such S-metaheuristics are local search, simulated annealing, and tabu search. Algorithm 2.1 illustrates the high-level template of S-metaheuristics.

Algorithm 2.1 High-level template of S-metaheuristics.

Input: Initial solution s_0.
$t = 0$;
Repeat
/* Generate candidate solutions (partial or complete neighborhood) from s_t */
Generate($C(s_t)$) ;
/* Select a solution from $C(s)$ to replace the current solution s_t */
$s_{t+1} =$ Select($C(s_t)$) ;
$t = t + 1$;
Until Stopping criteria satisfied
Output: Best solution found.

The common search concepts for *all* S-metaheuristics are the definition of the *neighborhood* structure and the determination of the *initial solution*.

2.1.1 Neighborhood

The definition of the neighborhood is a required common step for the design of any S-metaheuristic. The neighborhood structure plays a crucial role in the performance

[1] Also named transition rule, pivoting rule, and selection strategy.

of an S-metaheuristic. If the neighborhood structure is not adequate to the problem, any S-metaheuristic will fail to solve the problem.

Definition 2.1 Neighborhood. *A neighborhood function N is a mapping $N : S \rightarrow 2^S$ that assigns to each solution s of S a set of solutions $N(s) \subset S$.*

A solution s' in the neighborhood of s ($s' \in N(S)$) is called a *neighbor* of s. A neighbor is generated by the application of a *move* operator m that performs a small perturbation to the solution s. The main property that must characterize a neighborhood is *locality*. Locality is the effect on the solution when performing the move (perturbation) in the representation. When small changes are made in the representation, the solution must reveal small changes. In this case, the neighborhood is said to have a strong locality. Hence, a S-metaheuristic will perform a meaningful search in the landscape of the problem. Weak locality is characterized by a large effect on the solution when a small change is made in the representation. In the extreme case of weak locality, the search will converge toward a random search in the search space.

The structure of the neighborhood depends on the target optimization problem. It has been first defined in continuous optimization.

Definition 2.2 *The neighborhood $N(s)$ of a solution s in a continuous space is the ball with center s and radius equal to ϵ with $\epsilon > 0$.*

Hence, one have $N(s) = \{s' \in R^n / \|s' - s\| < \epsilon\}$. By using the Euclidean norm, we obtain $\|s' - s\| = \sqrt{(s'_1 - s_1)^2 + (s'_2 - s_2)^2 + \cdots + (s'_n - s_n)^2}$, which is the Euclidean distance between s' and s (Fig. 2.2).

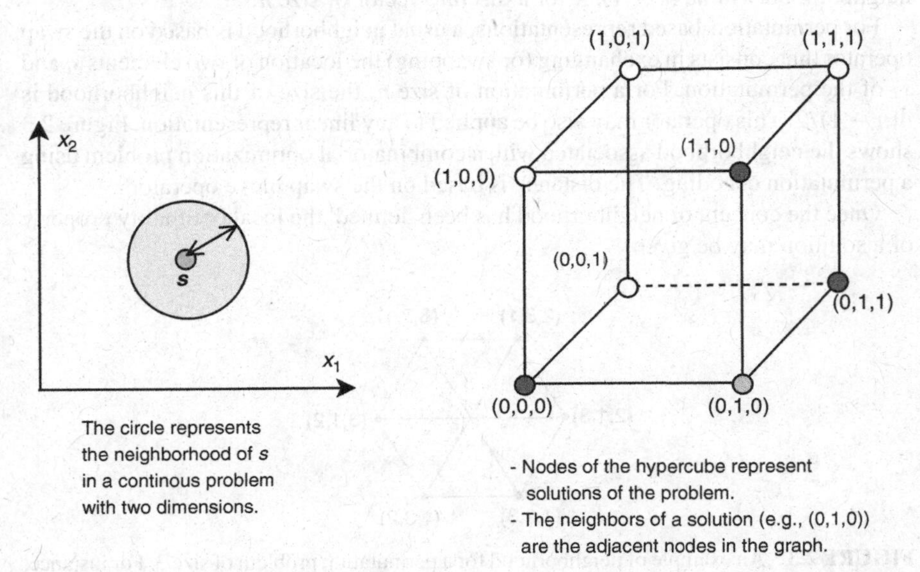
x_2
s
x_1
The circle represents the neighborhood of s in a continous problem with two dimensions.
(1,0,1)
(1,1,1)
(1,1,0)
(1,0,0)
(0,0,1)
(0,1,1)
(0,0,0)
(0,1,0)
- Nodes of the hypercube represent solutions of the problem.
- The neighbors of a solution (e.g., (0,1,0)) are the adjacent nodes in the graph.

FIGURE 2.2 Neighborhoods for a continuous problem and a discrete binary problem.

If the gradient (derivates of the objective function) can be calculated or approximated, a steepest descent (or ascent) indicating the direction to take can be applied. The main parameter in this first strategy is the length of the move in the selected direction. Otherwise, a random or deterministic generation of a subset of neighbors is carried out. In random generation of a neighbor, the normal variable $(0, \sigma_i)$ is added to the current value, where σ_i represents the main parameter in this second strategy.

The concept of neighborhood can be extended to discrete optimization.

Definition 2.3 *In a discrete optimization problem, the neighborhood $N(s)$ of a solution s is represented by the set $\{s'/d(s', s) \leq \epsilon\}$, where d represents a given distance that is related to the move operator.*

The neighborhood definition depends strongly on the representation associated with the problem at hand. Some usual neighborhoods are associated with traditional encodings.

The natural neighborhood for binary representations is based on the Hamming distance. In general, a distance equal to 1 is used. Then, the neighborhood of a solution s consists in flipping one bit of the solution. For a binary vector of size n, the size of the neighborhood will be n. Figure 2.2 shows the neighborhood for a continuous problem and a discrete binary problem. An Euclidean distance less than ϵ and a Hamming distance equal to 1 are used to define the neighborhood.

The Hamming neighborhood for binary encodings may be extended to any discrete vector representation using a given alphabet $\sum$. Indeed, the substitution can be generalized by replacing the discrete value of a vector element by any other character of the alphabet. If the cardinality of the alphabet $\sum$ is k, the size of the neighborhood will be $(k-1). n$ for a discrete vector of size n.

For permutation-based representations, a usual neighborhood is based on the swap operator that consists in exchanging (or swapping) the location of two elements s_i and s_j of the permutation. For a permutation of size n, the size of this neighborhood is $n(n-1)/2$. This operator may also be applied to any linear representation. Figure 2.3 shows the neighborhood associated with a combinatorial optimization problem using a permutation encoding. The distance is based on the swap move operator.

Once the concept of neighborhood has been defined, the local optimality property of a solution may be given.

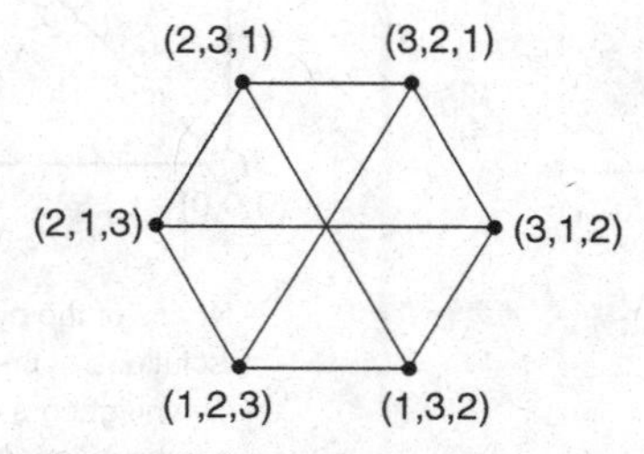

FIGURE 2.3 An example of neighborhood for a permutation problem of size 3. For instance, the neighbors of the solution (2, 3, 1) are (3, 2, 1), (2, 1, 3), and (1, 3, 2).

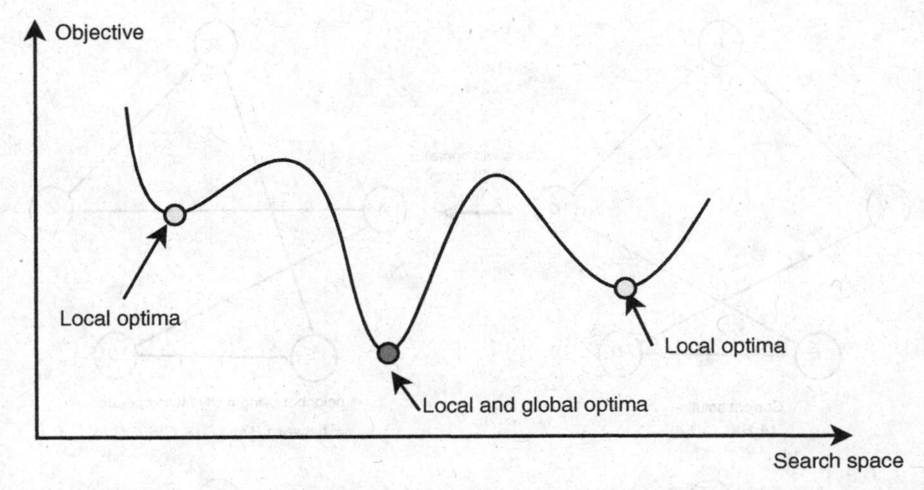

FIGURE 2.4 Local optimum and global optimum in a search space. A problem may have many global optimal solutions.

Definition 2.4 Local optimum. *Relatively to a given neighboring function N, a solution $s \in S$ is a local optimum if it has a better quality than all its neighbors; that is, $f(s) \leq f(s')$*[2] *for all $s' \in N(s)$ (Fig. 2.4).*

For the same optimization problem, a local optimum for a neighborhood N_1 may not be a local optimum for a different neighborhood N_2.

Example 2.1 k-distance neighborhood versus k-exchange neighborhood. For permutation problems, such as the TSP, the exchange operator (swap operator) may be used (Fig. 2.5). The size of this neighborhood is $n(n-1)/2$ where n represents the number of cities. Another widely used operator is the k-opt operator,[3] where k edges are removed from the solution and replaced with other k edges. Figure 2.5 (resp. Fig. 2.6) illustrates the application of the *2-opt operator* (resp. *3-opt operator*) on a tour. The neighborhood for the 2-opt operator is represented by all the permutations obtained by removing two edges. It replaces two directed edges (π_i, π_{i+1}) and (π_j, π_{j+1}) with (π_i, π_j) and (π_{i+1}, π_{j+1}), where $i \neq j-1, j, j+1$ $\forall i, j$. Formally, the neighbor solution is defined as

$$\pi'(k) = \pi(k) \quad \text{for } k \leq i \text{ or } k > j$$

$$\pi'(k) = \pi(i+j+1-k) \quad \text{for } i < k \leq j$$

The size of the neighborhood for the 2-opt operator is $[(n(n-1)/2) - n]$; all pairs of edges are concerned except the adjacent pairs.

[2]For a minimization problem.
[3]Also called k-exchange operator.

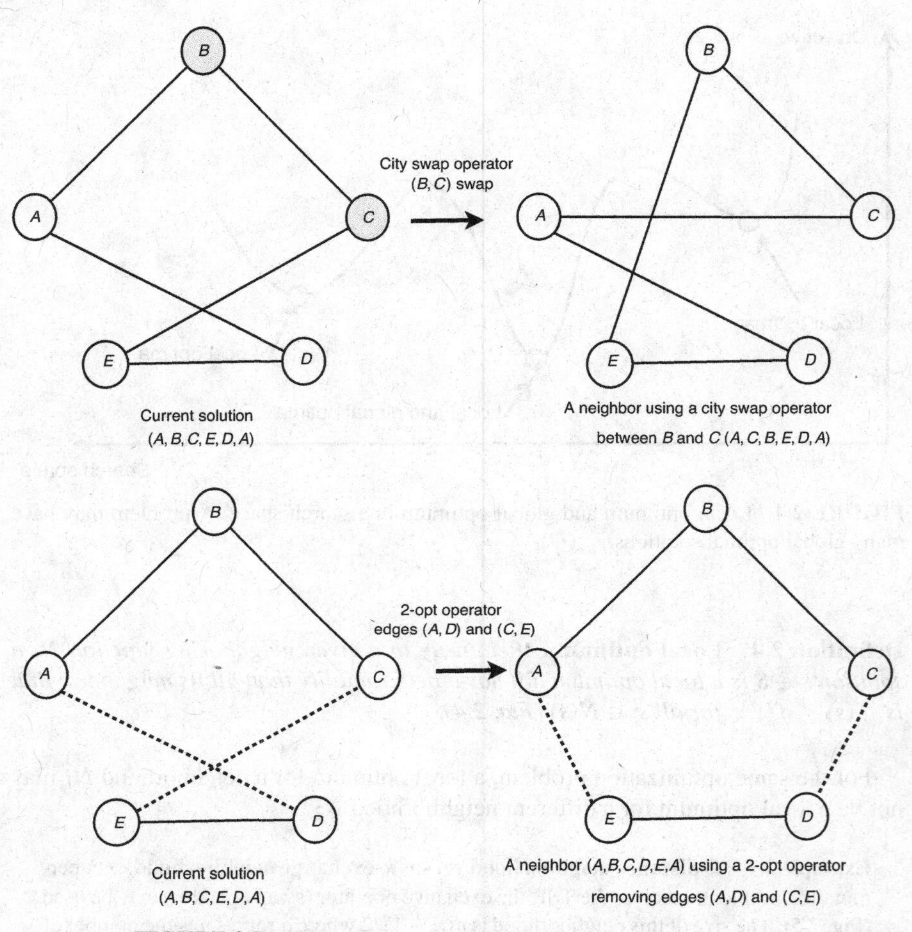

FIGURE 2.5 City swap operator and 2-opt operator for the TSP.

As mentioned, the efficiency of a neighborhood is related not only to the representation but also to the type of problems to solve. For instance, in scheduling problems, permutations represent a priority queue. Then, the relative order in the sequence is very important, whereas in the TSP it is the adjacency of the elements that is important. For scheduling problems, the 2-opt operator will generate a very large variation (weak locality), whereas for routing problems such as the TSP, it is a very efficient operator because the variation is much smaller (strong locality).

Example 2.2 Neighborhoods for permutation scheduling problems. For permutations representing sequencing and scheduling problems, the k-opt family of operators is not well suited. The following operators may be used:

- **Position-based neighborhood:** Figure 2.7 illustrates an example of a position-based operator, the *insertion operator*. In the insertion operator, an element at one

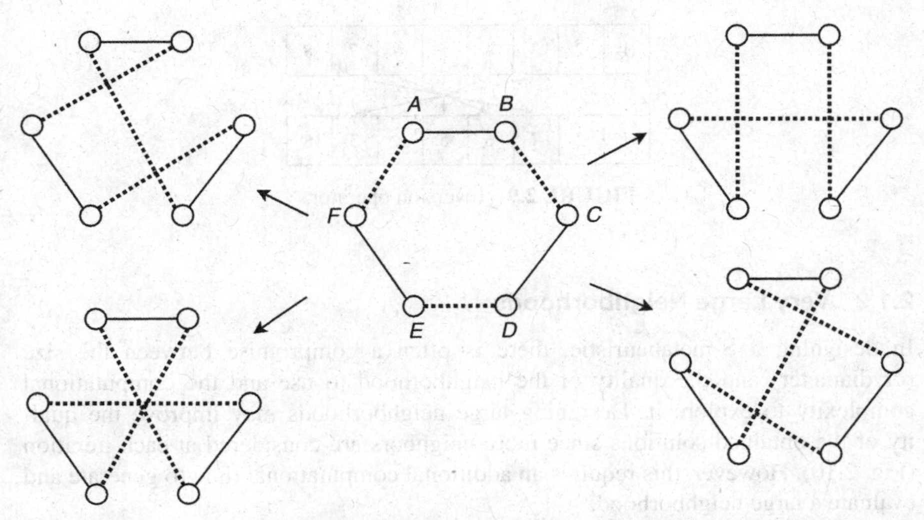

FIGURE 2.6 3-opt operator for the TSP. The neighbors of the solution (A,B,C,D,E,F) are (A,B,F,E,C,D), (A,B,D,C,F,E), (A,B,E,F,C,D), and (A,B,E,F,D,C).

position is removed and put at another position. The two positions are randomly selected.

- **Order-based neighborhood:** Many order-based operators can be used such as the exchange operator where arbitrarily selected two elements are swapped as shown in Fig. 2.8, and the inversion operator where two elements are randomly selected and the sequence of elements between these two elements are inverted as shown in Fig. 2.9.

Those operators are largely used in scheduling problems and seldom for routing problems such as the TSP for efficiency reasons.

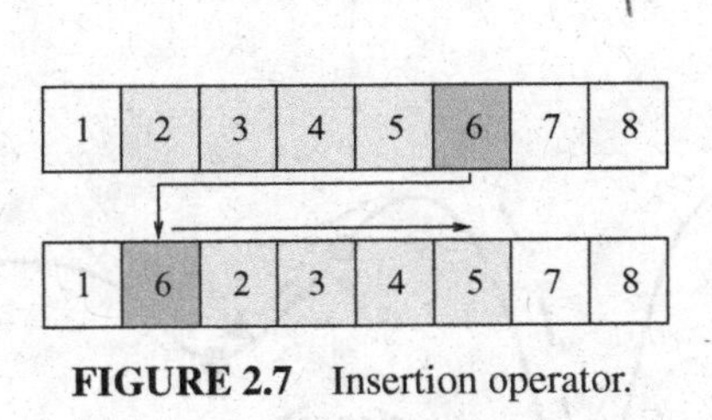

FIGURE 2.7 Insertion operator.

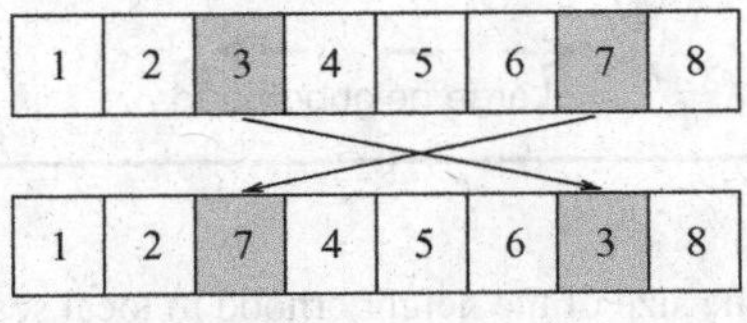

1	2	3	4	5	6	7	8
1	2	7	4	5	6	3	8

FIGURE 2.8 Exchange operator.

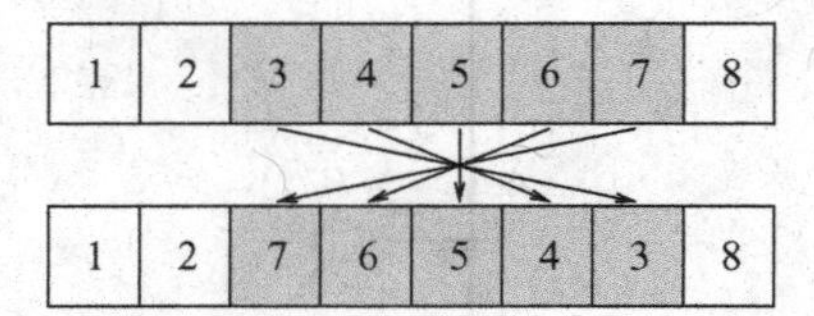

FIGURE 2.9 Inversion operator.

2.1.2 Very Large Neighborhoods

In designing a S-metaheuristic, there is often a compromise between the size (or diameter) and the quality of the neighborhood to use and the computational complexity to explore it. Designing large neighborhoods may improve the quality of the obtained solutions since more neighbors are considered at each iteration (Fig. 2.10). However, this requires an additional computational time to generate and evaluate a large neighborhood.

The size of the neighborhood for a solution s is the number of neighboring solutions of s. Most of the metaheuristics use small neighborhoods that is, in general, a polynomial function of the input instance size (e.g., linear or quadratic function). Some large neighborhoods may be high-order polynomial or exponential function of the size of the input instance. The neighborhood is *exponential* if its size grows exponentially with the size of the problem. Then, the complexity of the search will be much higher. So, the main issue here is to design efficient procedures to explore large neighborhoods. These efficient procedures identify improving neighbors or the best neighbor without the enumeration of the whole neighborhood (Fig. 2.11).

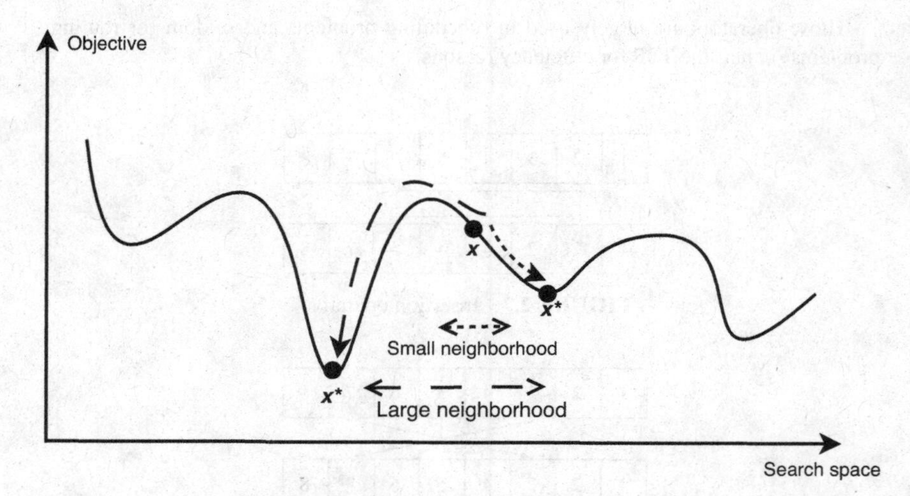

FIGURE 2.10 Impact of the size of the neighborhood in local search. Large neighborhoods improving the quality of the search with an expense of a higher computational time.

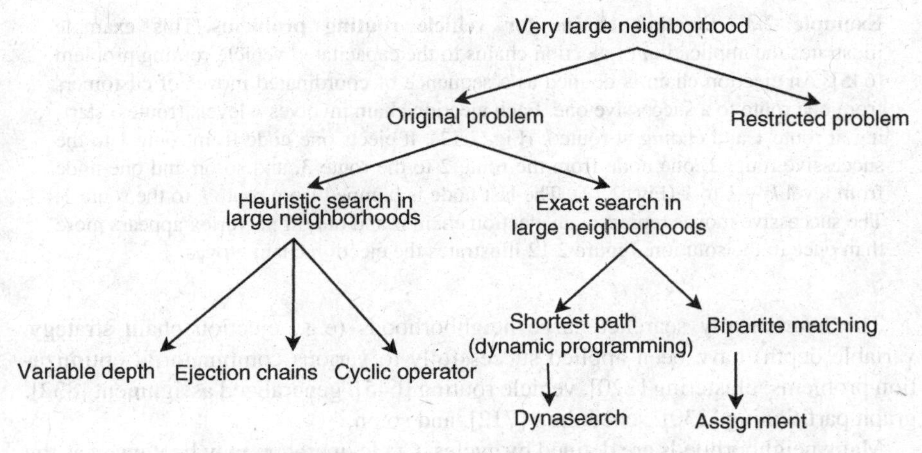

FIGURE 2.11 Very large neighborhood strategies.

A comprehensive survey of very large search neighborhoods may be found in Ref. [14].

2.1.2.1 *Heuristic Search in Large Neighborhoods* This approach consists in searching heuristically very large neighborhoods. A partial set of the large neighborhood is generated. Hence, finding the best neighbor (i.e., local optimum) is not guaranteed.

Let us consider a given neighborhood N defined by neighbors of distance $k = 1$ from a solution $s(N_1(s) = \{s' \in S/d(s, s') = 1\})$. In a similar way, a larger neighborhood $N_k(s)$ of distance k $(d = 2, 3, \ldots, n)$[4] is defined as the set

$$N_k(s) = N_{k-1}(s) \cup \{s''/\exists s' \in N_k(s) : s'' \in N_1(s')\}$$

Larger is the distance k, larger the neighborhood is. Since $N_n(s)$ is the whole search space, finding the best solution in this neighborhood is NP-hard if the original problem is NP-hard. Variable-depth search methods represent those strategies that explore partially the $N_k(s)$ neighborhoods. In general, a variable distance move (k-distance or k-exchange) with a distance of 2 or 3 may be appropriate.

This idea of variable-depth search methods has been first used in the classical Lin–Kernighan heuristic for the TSP [508] and the ejection chains. An *ejection chain* is a sequence of coordinated moves. Ejection chains were proposed first by Glover to solve the TSP problem [324]. They are based on alternating path methods, that is, alternating sequence of addition and deletion moves.

[4] n is related to the size of the problem (i.e., maximum distance between any two solutions).

Example 2.3 Ejection chains for vehicle routing problems. This example illustrates the application of ejection chains to the capacitated vehicle routing problem [645]. An ejection chain is defined as a sequence of coordinated moves of customers from one route to a successive one. Each ejection chain involves k levels (routes) starting at route 1 and ending at route k (Fig. 2.12). It ejects one node from route 1 to the successive route 2, one node from the route 2 to the route 3, and so on and one node from level $k-1$ to k (Fig. 2.12). The last node is bumped from route k to the route 1. The successive moves represent an ejection chain if and only if no vertex appears more than once in the solution. Figure 2.12 illustrates the ejection chain moves.

The heuristically searched large neighborhoods (e.g., ejection chain strategy, variable depth) have been applied successfully to various combinatorial optimization problems: clustering [220], vehicle routing [645], generalized assignment [832], graph partitioning [230], scheduling [712], and so on.

Many neighborhoods are defined by cycles. Cycle operators may be viewed as the generalization of the well-known 2-opt operator for the TSP problem, where more than two elements of the solution are involved to generate a neighbor.

Example 2.4 Cyclic exchange. A very large neighborhood based on cyclic exchange may be introduced into partitioning problems [15]. Let $E = \{e_1, e_2, \ldots, e_n\}$ be a set of elements to cluster into q subsets. A q-partition may be represented by the clustering $S = \{S_1, S_2, \ldots, S_q\}$. A 2-neighbor of the solution $S = \{S_1, S_2, \ldots, S_q\}$ is obtained by swapping two elements that belong to two different subsets. In its general form, the cyclic operator is based on swapping more than two elements and then involves more than two subsets (Fig. 2.13). A move involving k subsets S_i is represented by a cyclic permutation π of size k ($k \leq q$), where $\pi(i) = j$ represents the fact that the element e_i of the subset S_i is moved to the subset S_j. Hence, a solution $Q = \{Q_1, Q_2, \ldots, Q_q\}$ is a cyclic neighbor of the solution $S = \{S_1, S_2, \ldots, S_q\}$ if there exists a sequence $L = (o_1, \ldots, o_m)$ of size $m \leq k$ of moving single elements that generates Q from S. Let us notice that the first and the last move must concern the same partition (Fig. 2.13). The size of this neighborhood is $O(n^k)$. Using the cyclic operator, finding the best neighbor in the very large neighborhood has been reduced to the subset disjoint minimum cost cycle problem [769].

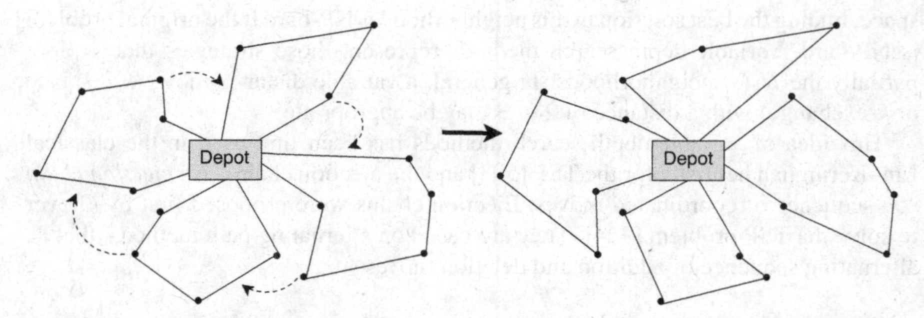

FIGURE 2.12 A four-level ejection chain for vehicle routing problems. Here, the ejection chain is based on a multinode insertion process.

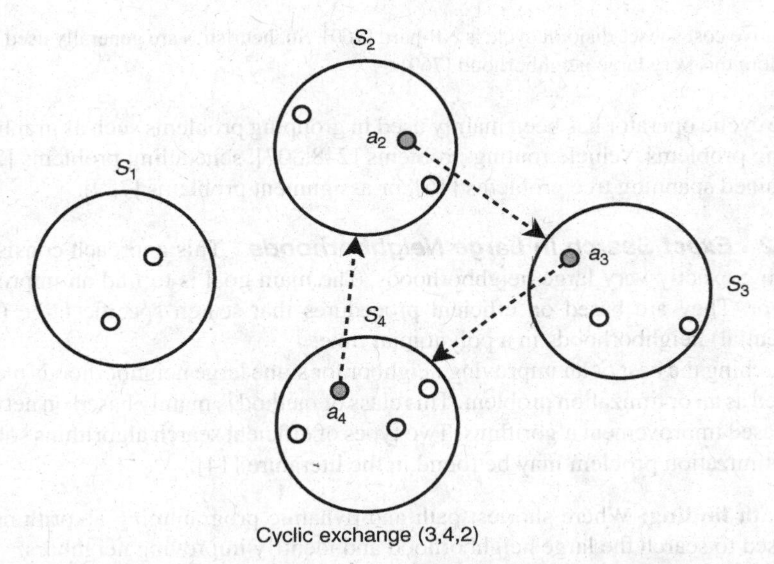

FIGURE 2.13 Very large neighborhood for partitioning problems: the cyclic exchange operator. Node a_2 is moved from subset S_2 to subset S_3, node a_3 is moved from subset S_3 to subset S_4, and node a_4 is moved from subset S_4 to subset S_2.

Indeed, finding an improving neighbor is based on the construction of the *improvement graph* [769]. Let $E = \{e_1, e_2, \ldots, e_n\}$ be the set of elements associated with the partitioning problem and let $x[i]$ be the subset containing the element e_i. The improvement graph $G = (V, E)$ is constructed as follows. The set $V = \{1, 2, \ldots, n\}$ of nodes is defined by the set of elements $(i = 1, \ldots, n)$ corresponding to the indices of the elements belonging to E. An edge $(i, j) \in E$ is associated with each move operation that transfers the element i from $x[i]$ to $x[j]$ and removes the element j from $x[j]$. Each edge (i, j) is weighted by a constant c_{ij}, which represents the cost increase of $x[j]$ when the element i is added to the set $x[i]$ and j is removed:

$$c_{ij} = d[\{i\} \cup x[j] - \{j\}] - d[x[j]]$$

Definition 2.5 Subset-disjoint cycle. *A cycle Z in a graph $G = (V, E)$ is subset disjoint if*

$$\forall i, j \in Z, x[i] \neq x[j]$$

that is, the nodes of Z are all in different subsets.

It is straightforward to see that there is a correspondence between cyclic exchange for the partitioning problem and subset-disjoint cycles in the improvement graph, that is, for every negative cost cyclic exchange, there is a negative cost subset-disjoint cycle in the improvement graph. The decision problem of whether there is a subset-disjoint cycle in the improvement graph is an NP-complete problem. Hence, the problem of finding a negative cost subset-disjoint cycle is NP-hard [769]. So, heuristics are generally used to explore this very large neighborhood [769].

The cyclic operator has been mainly used in grouping problems such as graph partitioning problems, vehicle routing problems [248,307], scheduling problems [283], constrained spanning tree problems [16], or assignment problems [759].

2.1.2.2 Exact Search in Large Neighborhoods This approach consists in searching exactly very large neighborhoods. The main goal is to find an improving neighbor. They are based on efficient procedures that search specific large (even exponential) neighborhoods in a polynomial time.

Searching the best or an improving neighbor for some large neighborhoods may be modeled as an optimization problem. This class of method is mainly based on network flow-based improvement algorithms. Two types of efficient search algorithms solving this optimization problem may be found in the literature [14]:

- **Path finding:** Where shortest path and dynamic programming algorithms are used to search the large neighborhood and identify improving neighbors.
- **Matching:** Where well-known polynomial-time matching algorithms are used to explore large neighborhoods for specific problems.

For instance, swap-based neighborhoods in permutations can be generalized by the use of multiple compounded swaps (e.g., dynasearch).

Definition 2.6 Independent swaps. *Given a permutation* $\pi = \{\pi_1, \pi_2, \ldots, \pi_n\}$, *a swap move* (i, j) *consists in exchanging the two elements* π_i *and* π_j *of the permutation* π. *Two swap moves* (i, j) *and* (k, l) *are independent if* $(max\{i, j\} < min\{k, l\})$ *or* $(min\{i, j\} > max\{k, l\})$.

A swap-based large neighborhood of a permutation can be defined by the union of an arbitrary number of independent swap moves.

Example 2.5 Dynasearch. Dynasearch is another classical large neighborhood approach that has been introduced for optimization problems where solutions are encoded by permutations (e.g., sequencing problems) [150]. The dynasearch two-exchange move is based on improving a Hamiltonian path between two elements $\pi(1)$ and $\pi(n)$ (see Fig. 2.14). The operator deletes the edges $(\pi(i), \pi(i+1))$, $(\pi(j), \pi(j+1))$, $(\pi(k), \pi(k+1))$, and $(\pi(l), \pi(l+1))$. The following conditions must

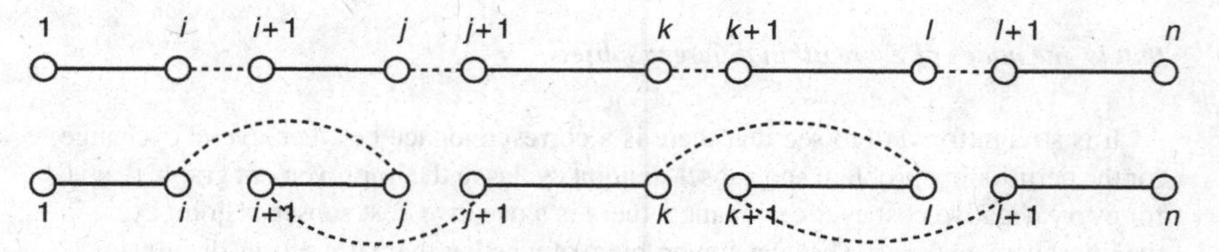

FIGURE 2.14 Dynasearch using two independent two-exchange moves: polynomial exploration of exponentially large neighborhoods.

hold: $1 < i + 1 < j \leq n$, $\pi(j + 1) \neq \pi(i)$, and $1 < k + 1 < l \leq n$, $\pi(l + 1) \neq \pi(k)$. The segments are independent if $j \leq k$ or $l < i$. Indeed, when this condition holds, the segments that are exchanged by the two moves do not share any edge.

The size of this exponential neighborhood is $O(2^{n-1})$. The problem of finding the best neighbor is reduced to the shortest path problem in the improvement graph. Then, it is explored in an efficient polynomial way by a dynamic programming algorithm in $O(n^2)$ for the TSP and in $O(n^3)$ for scheduling problems [94,396]. If the compounded swaps are limited to adjacent pairs, the time complexity of the algorithm is reduced to $O(n^2)$ in solving scheduling problems.

Another exponential neighborhood is defined by the *assignment neighborhood* [345]. It is based on the multiple application of the insertion operator. Let us consider the TSP problem. Giving a tour $S = (1, 2, \ldots, n, 1)$, where $d[i, j]$ represents the distance matrix. The assignment neighborhood consists in constructing the following bipartite improvement graph: select and eject k nodes $V = \{v_1, v_2, \ldots, v_k\}$ from the tour S, where $k = \lfloor n/2 \rfloor$. The set $U = \{u_1, u_2, \ldots, u_{n-k}\}$ represents the nonejected nodes of the tour S; that is, $U \cup V = S$. Then, a subtour $S' = (u_1, u_2, \ldots, u_{n-k}, u_1)$ is created. Finally, a complete bipartite graph $G = (N, V, E)$ is constructed, where $N = \{q_i : i = 1, \ldots, n - k\}$, q_i represents the edge (u_i, u_{i+1}) for $i = 1$ to $n - k - 1$,

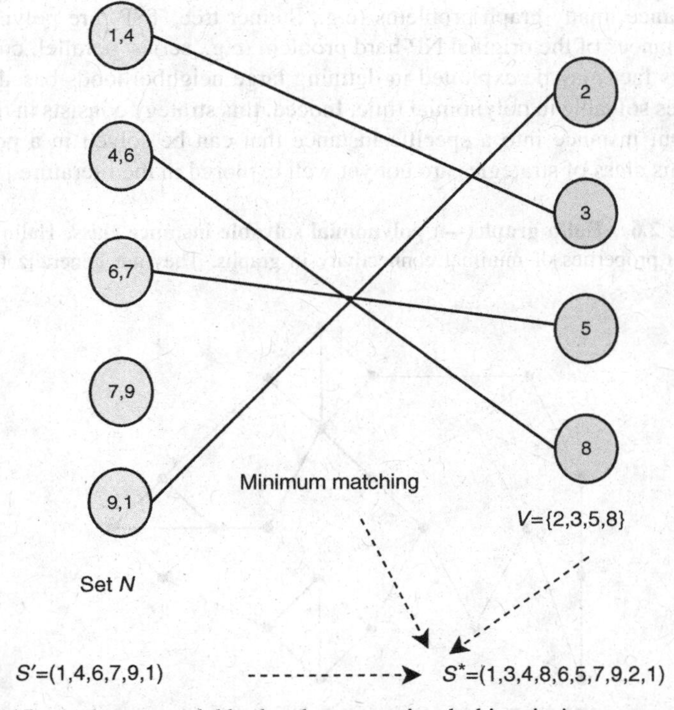

FIGURE 2.15 Assignment neighborhood: constructing the bipartite improvement graph and finding the optimal matching.

and $q_{n-k} = (u_{n-k}, u_1)$ (Fig. 2.15). The set of edges $E = (q_i, v_j)$ is weighted by $c[q_i, v_j] = d[u_i, v_j] + d[v_j', u_{i+1}] - d[u_i, u_{i+1}]$.

A neighbor S^* for the tour S is defined by inserting the nodes of V in the subtour S'. No more than one node is inserted between two adjacent nodes of the subtour S'. The problem of finding the best neighbor is then reduced to the minimum cost matching on a bipartite improvement graph. Figure 2.15 illustrates the construction of the improvement graph on the tour $S = (1, 2, \ldots, 9, 1)$ composed of nine nodes, where $V = \{2, 3, 5, 8\}$ and $U = \{1, 4, 6, 7, 9\}$. Hence, the subtour S' is defined as $(1, 4, 6, 7, 9, 1)$. For simplicity reasons, only the edges of the minimum cost matching are shown for the bipartite graph G. According to the optimal matching, the obtained tour is $(1, 3, 4, 8, 6, 5, 7, 9, 2, 1)$.

The generalization of the assignment operator for arbitrary k and n, and different inserting procedures (e.g., edges instead of nodes) in which the problem is reduced to a minimum weight matching problem is proposed [344].

Matching-based neighborhoods have been applied to many combinatorial optimization problems such as the TSP [347], quadratic assignment problem [203], and vehicle routing problems [225].

2.1.2.3 Polynomial-Specific Neighborhoods

Some NP-hard optimization problems may be solved in an efficient manner by restricting the input class instances or by adding/deleting constraints to the target optimization problem.

For instance, many graph problems (e.g., Steiner tree, TSP) are polynomial for *specific* instances of the original NP-hard problem (e.g., series–parallel, outerplanar, Halin). This fact may be exploited in defining large neighborhoods based on those special cases solvable in polynomial time. Indeed, this strategy consists in transforming the input instance into a specific instance that can be solved in a polynomial manner. This class of strategies are not yet well explored in the literature [14].

Example 2.6 Halin graphs—a polynomial solvable instance class. Halin graphs deal with properties of minimal connectivity in graphs. They are generalizations of

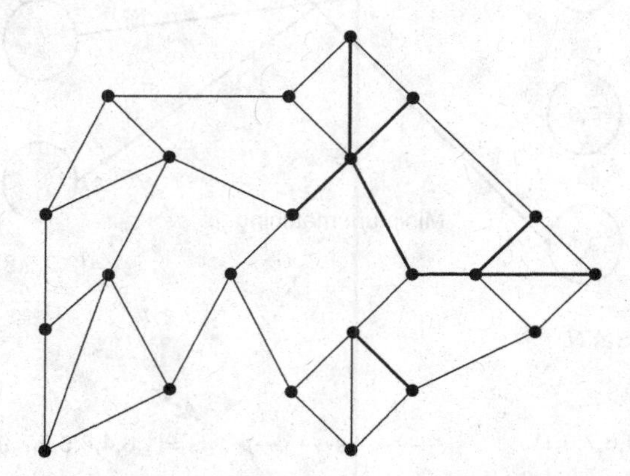

FIGURE 2.16 An example of a Halin graph [734].

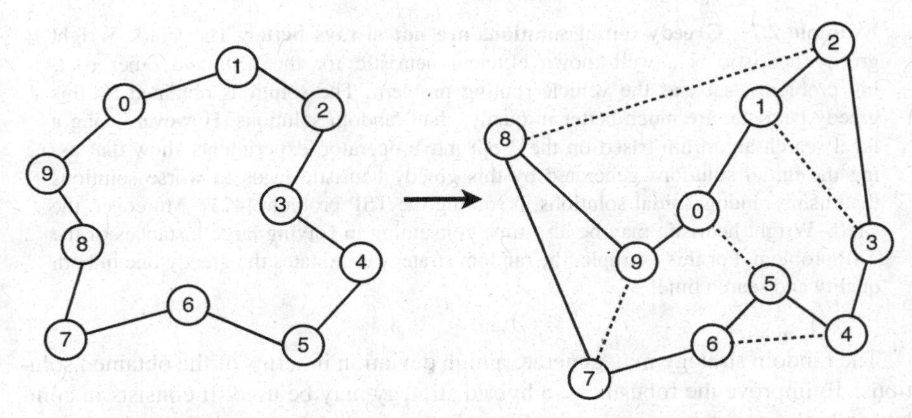

FIGURE 2.17 Extending a given input instance to a Halin graph.

tree and ring graphs. A graph is a Halin graph if it is formed by embedding a tree having no degree-2 vertices in the plane and connecting its leaves by a cycle that crosses none of its edges (Fig. 2.16). For this class of instances, a polynomial-time algorithm is known to solve the traveling salesman problem in $O(n)$ [157] and the Steiner tree problem [822]. Hence, Halin graphs may be used to construct large neighborhoods for the TSP as follows [14]: let π be the current tour. The solution π_{H} is a Halin extension of π if π_{H} is a Halin graph and π is a subgraph of π_{H} (Fig. 2.17). Suppose $HalinConstruct(\pi)$ is an efficient function that returns a Halin extension of the solution π. Then, the neighborhood $N(\pi)$ is constructed as $\{\pi' : \pi'$ is a tour in HalinConstruct$(\pi)\}$. Hence, finding the best tour in $N(\pi)$ is reduced to find the best tour in the solution $HalinConstruct(\pi)$.

2.1.3 Initial Solution

Two main strategies are used to generate the initial solution: a *random* and a *greedy* approach. There is always a trade-off between the use of random and greedy initial solutions in terms of the quality of solutions and the computational time. The best answer to this trade-off will depend mainly on the efficiency and effectiveness of the random and greedy algorithms at hand, and the S-metaheuristic properties. For instance, the larger is the neighborhood, the less is the sensitivity of the initial solution to the performance of the S-metaheuristics.

Generating a random initial solution is a quick operation, but the metaheuristic may take much larger number of iterations to converge. To speed up the search, a greedy heuristic may be used. Indeed, in most of the cases, greedy algorithms have a reduced polynomial-time complexity. Using greedy heuristics often leads to better quality local optima. Hence, the S-metaheuristic will require, in general, less iterations to converge toward a local optimum. Some approximation greedy algorithms may also be used to obtain a bound guarantee for the final solution. However, it does not mean that using better solutions as initial solutions will always lead to better local optima.

Example 2.7 Greedy initial solutions are not always better. The Clark–Wright greedy heuristic is a well-known efficient heuristic for the TSP and other routing problems, such as the vehicle routing problem. The solutions obtained by this greedy heuristic are much better in quality than random solutions. However, using a local search algorithm based on the 3-opt move operator, experiments show that using the initial solutions generated by this greedy heuristic leads to worse solutions than using random initial solutions in solving the TSP problem [421]. Moreover, the Clark–Wright heuristic may be also time consuming in solving large instances of the TSP problem. For this example, the random strategy dominates the greedy one in both quality and search time!

The random strategy may generate a high deviation in terms of the obtained solutions. To improve the robustness, a hybrid strategy may be used. It consists in combining both approaches: random and greedy. For instance, a pool of initial solutions can be composed of greedy solutions and randomly generated solutions. Moreover, different greedy strategies may be used in the initialization process. In fact, for some optimization problems, many greedy constructive algorithms exist and are easy to design and implement.

Example 2.8 A hybrid approach for the TSP. Given an instance with n cities, the following three algorithms can be used to generate a pool of initial solutions:

- An algorithm that generates a random permutation with uniform probability.
- A nearest-neighbor greedy algorithm that chooses a starting city i randomly. Then, among unsequenced cities, it chooses a city j that minimizes the length between i and j and iterates the same process on the city j until a complete tour is constructed. Using different starting cities allows to generate different final solutions. Hence, n different solutions may be obtained with this greedy procedure.
- Another greedy procedure, the cheapest insertion algorithm, first finds the minimum length path (i, j). Let C be the tour (i, j, i). Then, it chooses an unsequenced city that minimizes the length of the tour C and inserts it into C in the best possible way. This process is iterated until the tour C is composed of all the cities.

In some constrained optimization problems, it may be difficult to generate random solutions that are feasible. In this case, greedy algorithms are an alternative to generate feasible initial solutions.

For some specific real-life operational problems, the initial solution may be initialized (partially or completely) according to expertise or defined as the already implemented solution.

2.1.4 Incremental Evaluation of the Neighborhood

Often, the evaluation of the objective function is the most expensive part of a local search algorithm and more generally for any metaheuristic. A naive exploration of the neighborhood of a solution s is a *complete* evaluation of the objective function for every candidate neighbor s' of $N(s)$.

A more efficient way to evaluate the set of candidates is the *evaluation* $\Delta(s, m)$ of the objective function when it is possible to compute, where s is the current solution and m is the applied move. This is an important issue in terms of efficiency and must be taken into account in the design of an S-metaheuristic. It consists in evaluating only the transformation $\Delta(s, m)$ applied to a solution s rather than the complete evaluation of the neighbor solution $f(s') = f(s \oplus m)$. The definition of such an incremental evaluation and its complexity depends on the neighborhood used over the target optimization problem. It is a straightforward task for some problems and neighborhoods but may be very difficult for other problems and/or neighborhood structures.

Example 2.9 Incremental evaluation of the objective function. First, let us present an incremental evaluation for the 2-opt operator applied to the TSP. The incremental evaluation can be stated as follows:

$$\Delta f = c(\pi_i, \pi_j) + c(\pi_{i+1}, \pi_{j+1}) - c(\pi_i, \pi_{i+1}) - c(\pi_j, \pi_{j+1})$$

Let us consider the clique partitioning problem defined in Example 2.22. For any class C of the current solution s, $W(i, \emptyset) = 0$ and for $C \neq \emptyset$, $W(i, C) = \sum_{j \in C, j \neq i} w(i, j)$. The incremental evaluation of the objective function f in moving a node i from its class C_i to another one C will be $W(i, C) - W(i, C_i)$. Then, for an improving neighbor, we have $W(i, C) < W(i, C_i)$. The complexity of finding the best class C^* for a node i (i.e., $W(i, C^*)$ is minimum over all classes $C \neq C_i$) is $O(n)$.

The incremental evaluation function may also be approximated instead of having an exact value (e.g., *surrogate functions* [777]). This will reduce the computational complexity of the evaluation, but a less accuracy is achieved. This approach may be beneficial for very expensive incremental functions.

2.2 FITNESS LANDSCAPE ANALYSIS

The main point of interest in the domain of optimization must not be the design of the best algorithm for *all* optimization problems but the search for the most adapted algorithm to a given class of problems and/or instances. The question of whether a given optimization algorithm A is absolutely better than an optimization algorithm B is senseless. Indeed, the NFL theorem proves that, under certain assumptions, no optimization algorithm is superior to any other on *all* possible optimization problems; that is, if algorithm A performs better than B for a given problem, there is always another problem where B performs better than A [823]. No metaheuristic can be uniformly better than any other metaheuristic. The question of superiority of a given algorithm has a sense only in solving a given class of problems and/or instances. Many studies on the analysis of landscapes of different optimization problems have shown that not only different problems correspond to different structures but also different instances of the same problem correspond to different structures. In fact, no ideal metaheuristic, designed as a black box, may exist.

Example 2.10 Superiority of algorithms and problem classes. A comparison of two optimization methods may be carried out for a given class of problems and/or instances. For instance, there are problems where an evolutionary algorithm does not perform well, namely, on a simple unimodal function and on a random function. In a unimodal continuous function, local search algorithms such as quasi-Newton methods are much faster and efficient. In a random function or needle-in-a-haystack-type landscape (flat everywhere except at a single point), there is no structure that could be learned.

The analysis of landscapes of optimization problems[5] is an important aspect in designing a metaheuristic. The effectiveness of metaheuristics depends on the properties of the landscape (roughness, convexity, etc.) associated with the instance to solve. The study of the landscapes of an optimization problem provides a way of investigating the intrinsic natures and difficulties of its instances to integrate this knowledge about the problem structure in the design of a metaheuristic. The representation, neighborhood, and the objective function define the landscape in a complete manner and then influence on the search efficiency of a metaheuristic. Landscape analysis is performed in the hope to predict the behavior of different search components of a metaheuristic: representations, search operators, and objective function. Thus, analyzing the fitness landscape will help to design better representations, neighborhoods, and objective functions. Moreover, the landscape analysis affords a better understanding of the behavior of metaheuristics or any search component of a metaheuristic. One may explain why a given metaheuristic works or fails on a given problem and/or instance.

The notion of landscape has been first described by Wright in 1932 in biology [827]. In biology, the term fitness is derived from the term "survival of the fittest" in natural selection. The fitness corresponds to the relative ability of an organism to survive, to mate successfully, and to reproduce resulting in a new organism [451]. The fitness landscape has been used to study the dynamics of biological systems (species evolution) and understand evolutionary processes that are driven by specific operators such as mutation and crossover. Afterward, this concept has been used to analyze optimization problems [717,718,428].

Definition 2.7 Search space. *The search space*[6] *is defined by a directed graph* $G = (S, E)$*, where the set of vertices S corresponds to the solutions of the problem that are defined by the representation (encoding) used to solve the problem, and the set of edges E corresponds to the move operators used to generate new solutions (neighborhood in S-metaheuristics).*

[5] The fitness landscape analysis in not specific to S-metaheuristics. The same concepts may be reused in P-metaheuristics.

[6] Also named the configuration graph or state space.

There is an edge between solutions s_i and s_j if the solution s_j can be generated from the solution s_i using a move operator; that is, s_i and s_j are neighbors. Let us notice that using different neighboring relations generates different search spaces and landscapes and then produces, for instance, different numbers of local optima.

Definition 2.8 Fitness landscape. *The fitness landscape l may be defined by the tuple (G, f), where the graph G represents the search space and f represents the objective function that guides the search.*

A convenient way to describe a landscape consists in using some geographical terms. Then, considering the search space as the ground floor, we elevate each solution to an altitude equal to its quality. We obtain a landscape made of valleys, plains, peaks, canyon, cliffs, plateaus, basins, and so on (see Table 2.1). A S-metaheuristic may be seen as a trajectory or a walk in the landscape to find the lowest peak. Two successive solutions are always neighbors. The geographical metaphor provides a useful tool to represent the landscapes in one, two, or three dimensions. The problem lies in the difficulty to have a realistic view of the landscape for high-dimensional problems.

Example 2.11 NK-model for landscapes. The NK-model for landscapes, proposed by Kaufmann [452], defines a class of fitness landscapes that can be configured using two parameters N and K. The parameter N represents the dimension of the problem and the parameter K the degree of epistatic interactions between the decision variables of the fitness function. Each solution of the search space is supposed to be

TABLE 2.1 Some Representations of Landscapes in One Dimension Using the Geographical Metaphor

Flat, plain	
Basin, valley	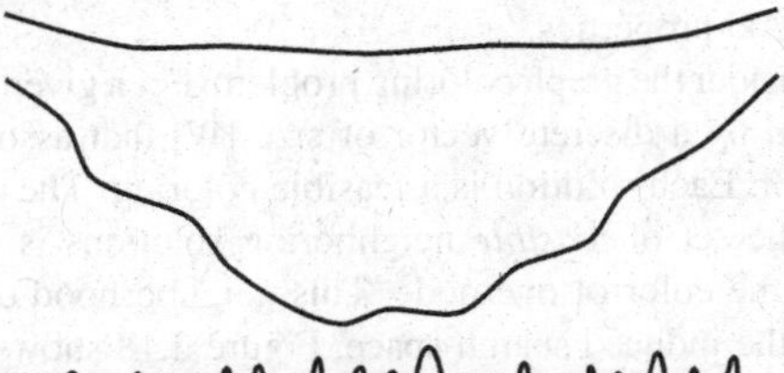
Rugged plain	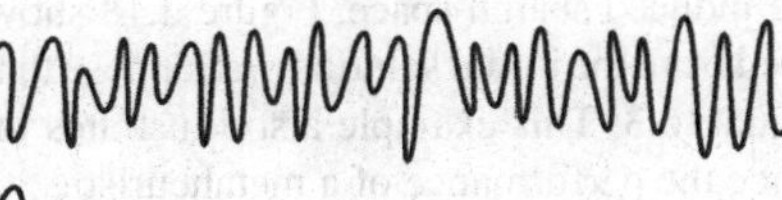
Rugged valley	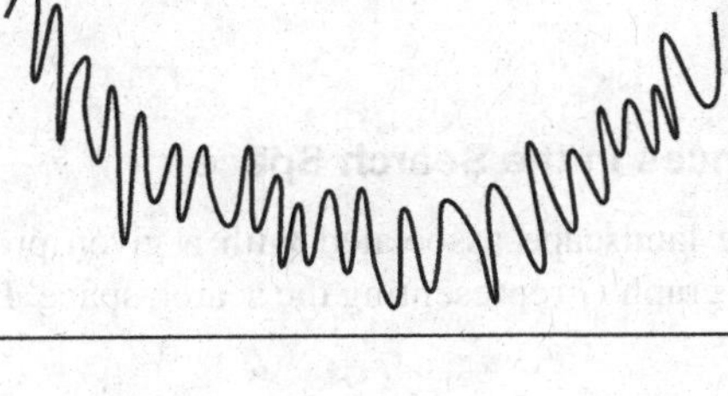

a binary vector of size N. Then, the search space may be viewed as an N-dimensional hypercube. The fitness function associated with a solution $x = (x_1, x_2, \ldots, x_N)$ is defined as follows:

$$f(x) = \frac{1}{N} \sum_{i=1}^{N} f_i(x_i, x_{i1}, x_{i2}, \ldots, x_{ik})$$

where the function f_i of the decision variable i depends on its value x_i and the values of k on other decision variables $x_{i1}, x_{i2}, \ldots, x_{ik}$. The decision variables $x_{i1}, x_{i2}, \ldots, x_{ik}$ are selected randomly from $[1, \ldots, N]$. For the 2^{K+1} different inputs, the function f_i assigns a uniformly distributed random number between 0 and 1.

For $K = 0$, the landscape has only one local optimal solution (i.e., global optimal), while for $K = N - 1$, the expected number of local optima is $(2^N/N + 1)$.

Furthermore, to be able to analyze the fitness landscape an important property has to be verified: connexity of the search space; that is, the landscape has to be *connected*. In other words, there exists a path in the search space graph G between any pair of vertices.

Example 2.12 Connexity of the search space. One of the most important properties of the search space G is its connexity. For any two solutions s_i and s_j (nodes of G), there should be a path from s_i to s_j. Hence, for any initial solution s_i there will be a path from s_i to the global optimal solution s^*.

Let us consider the quadratic assignment problem defined in Exercise 2.9. A solution is encoded by a permutation, and the neighborhood is based on the swapping between two elements. The search space (graph G) associated with this representation and neighborhood is connected. In fact, given any couple of permutations, there is always a path in G linking one permutation to another. Moreover, any swapping applied to any permutation of S always leads to an element of S. But, some search spaces do not offer those good properties.

Let us consider the graph coloring problem. For a given graph $H = (W, F)$, a solution is represented by a discrete vector of size $|W|$ that associates with each node of the graph its color. Each solution is a feasible coloring. The neighborhood $N(s)$ is defined as follows: the set of *feasible* neighboring solutions is obtained from the solution s by changing the color of one node. This neighborhood does not satisfy the connexity property for the induced search space. Figure 2.18 shows how the optimal coloring s^* cannot be reached from the initial solution s_1. Suppose that the maximal number of colors to be used is equal to 3. This example also illustrates that visiting infeasible solutions may help enhance the performance of a metaheuristic.

2.2.1 Distances in the Search Space

To analyze the landscape associated with a given problem, one needs to define a distance in the graph G representing the search space. In fact, the distance will define

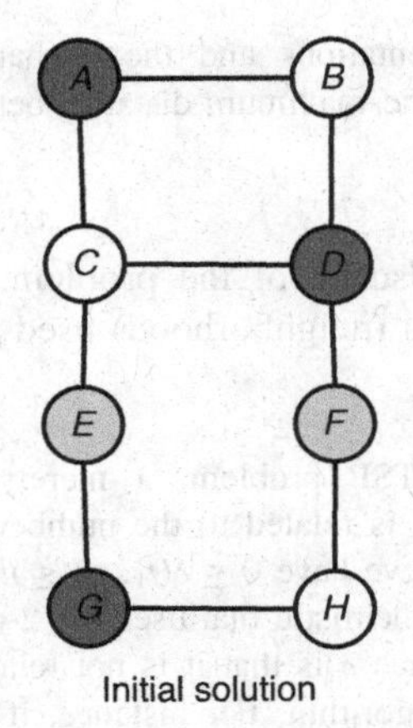

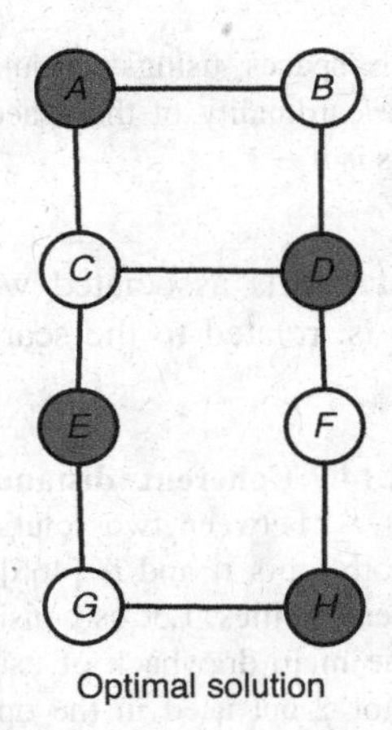

FIGURE 2.18 Connexity of the search space related to the graph coloring problem. The optimal solution cannot be reached from the given initial solution.

the spatial structure of the landscape. The concept of distance may also be useful in the design of some search mechanisms such as diversification and intensification procedures (e.g., path relinking, diversity measure).

Let $d(s_i, s_j)$ be the distance between solutions s_i and s_j in the search space. It is defined as the length of the shortest path in the graph G; that is, the minimum number of application of the move operator to obtain the solution s_j from the solution s_i. In topology, a distance must have the following properties:

Definition 2.9 *Let E be a set, a distance on E is any mapping:* $d : E \times E \rightarrow \mathbb{R}^+$, *such that*

- $d(x, y) = 0$ *if and only if* $x = y$ *(separative property);*
- $\forall x, y \in E \times E : d(x, y) = d(y, x)$ *(symmetrical property);*
- $\forall x, y, z \in E \times E \times E : d(x, y) + d(y, z) \geq d(x, z)$ *(triangular property).*

Example 2.13 Distances in some usual search spaces. In search spaces using binary representations and the flip move operator, the Hamming distance may be used:

$$d_{\mathrm{H}}(x, y) = \sum_{i=1}^{n} x_i \oplus y_i$$

It represents the number of different bit values between the two solutions. For a problem of size n, the size of the search space is 2^n and its diameter is equal to n.

In search spaces using permutation representations and the exchange move operator, the cardinality of the space is $n!$ and the maximum distance between two permutations is $n-1$.

As the distance is associated with the landscape of the problem, it must be *coherent*, that is, related to the search operators (neighborhood) used to solve the problem.

Example 2.14 Coherent distance. For the TSP problem, a merely intuitive distance $\delta(t_1, t_2)$ between two solutions t_1 and t_2 is related to the number of edges shared by both tours t_1 and t_2 [465]. Obviously, we have $0 \leq \delta(t_1, t_2) \leq n$, where n is the number of cities. Let us consider a S-metaheuristic that uses the 2-opt neighborhood. The main drawback of using the distance δ is that it is not related to the move operator 2-opt used in the optimization algorithm. For instance, if the 2-opt move is applied twice on a given solution, the generated solution may have 0, 3, or 4 edges not contained in the initial solution. Then, the coherent distance to use is $\Delta_{2-\text{opt}}(t_1, t_2)$ that denotes the minimum number of applications of the 2-opt move to obtain t_2 from t_1 [84]. However, there exists no polynomial algorithm to compute such a distance. This is why the distance dealing with the edges is always used in practice.

In some optimization problems and/or neighborhoods, computing a distance between solutions may be a complex task in terms of time complexity. Hence, for some problems computing the distance is an NP-complete problem or high-order polynomial problem.

2.2.2 Landscape Properties

Many indicators may be used to identify the fitness landscape properties: number of local optima, distribution of the local optima, ruggedness, structures of basins of attraction, presence of plateaus (neutral networks), distribution of the fitness (mean, variance), and so on. Most of them are based on statistical studies. Two types of indicators may be distinguished:

- **Global indicators:** Global approaches provide informations about the structure of the entire landscape [428,525,812]. They determine the structure of the landscape using the whole search space or its approximation. However, in optimization, the goal is to track "good" solutions. These good solutions represent a tiny part of the search space. Hence, the global approach is not sufficient to characterize a fitness landscape to be explored by a metaheuristic. Metaheuristics focus on good solutions that are handled as ordinary points by the global approach.
- **Local indicators:** The local approach consists in characterizing a local view of the landscape as explored by a metaheuristic. Indeed, metaheuristics have a

local view of the landscape, following some trajectories in the landscape and focusing on good solutions. Then it would be interesting to describe those good solutions and the regions where they are localized. The global approach does not answer those questions in the sense that it gives an average information on a large number of solutions that are not concerned with metaheuristics.

The two approaches are complementary. For instance, the local view of a landscape may be obtained by its exploration using a simple local search algorithm (steepest descent). During the search, the metaheuristic algorithm is used as a probe to extract some indicators that will characterize the landscape.

Example 2.15 Number of local optima. For some landscapes, the number of local optima may be computed theoretically or by enumeration. Let us consider the landscape of the number partitioning problem (see Example 1.15) where the neighborhood consists in moving a number a_i belonging to a partition S_1 to the other partition S_2. The number of local optima in this landscape is [260]

$$\sqrt{\frac{24}{\pi}}\frac{2^n}{n^{\frac{3}{2}}} \approx 2.764\frac{2^n}{n^{\frac{3}{2}}}$$

Notice that the size of the search space is 2^n. Thus, the number of local optima solutions is very large compared to the size of the search space. Indeed, the ratio of the local optima to the size of the search space is in the order of $O(n^{-1.5})$. Another representation or neighborhood must be designed for this problem to reduce the number of local optima.

In general, two different statistical measures are applied: *distribution measures* that study the topology of local optima solutions and the *correlation measures* that analyze the rugosity of the landscape and the correlation between the quality of solutions and their relative distance. In the rest of this section, the most important and commonly used indicators are outlined for each class.

2.2.2.1 Distribution Measures The objective of the distribution measures is the distribution analysis of the local optimal solutions in the landscape projected both in the search space G and in the objective space f. The commonly used measures are

- **Distribution in the search space:** For a population P, let us define the average distance $\text{dmm}\,(P)$ and the normalized average distance $\text{Dmm}\,(P)$:

$$\text{dmm}\,(P) = \frac{\sum_{s\in P}\sum_{t\in P, t\neq s}\text{dist}(s,t)}{|P|\cdot(|P|-1)} \qquad \text{Dmm}\,(P) = \frac{\text{dmm}\,(P)}{\text{diam}(S)}$$

The diameter of a population P of S is the maximal distance between elements of P:

$$\text{diam}(P) = \max_{s,t \in P} \text{dist}(s, t)$$

The normalized average distance characterizes the concentration of the population P in the search space. Notably, a weak distance indicates that the solutions belonging to the population P are clustered in a small region of the search space.

The indicator $\Delta_{\text{Dmm}} = (\text{Dmm}\,(U) - \text{Dmm}\,(O))/\text{Dmm}\,(U)$ represents the variation of the average distance between a uniform population U and a population of local optimal solutions O. The cardinality of the set O is chosen according to the complexity of the local search algorithm (e.g., $10^3 \leq |O| \leq 10^4$).

- **Entropy in the search space:** The entropy concept in information theory is related to the notion of diversity in optimization. It allows to measure the diversity of a given population in the search space. According to a given optimization problem, different mathematical formulations of the entropy can be applied to measure the dispersion of the population elements over the search space. A weak entropy reveals a concentration of solutions, whereas a high entropy shows an important dispersion of the solutions in the search space.

Example 2.16 Entropy for the quadratic assignment problem. For the quadratic assignment problem, the entropy may be based on the mapping of the objects over the different locations [269]:

$$\text{ent}\,(P) = \frac{-1}{n \log n} \sum_{i=1}^{n} \sum_{j=1}^{n} \left(\frac{n_{ij}}{\text{card}\,P} \log \frac{n_{ij}}{\text{card}\,P} \right) \qquad 0 \leq \text{ent}(P) \leq 1$$

where n_{ij} is the number of times an object i is assigned to location j in the population P.

The indicator $\Delta_{\text{ent}} = \text{ent}\,(U) - \text{ent}\,(O)/\text{ent}\,(U)$ represents the entropy variation between the starting population U and the final population of local optima O obtained after performing a local search algorithm on each solution of the population.

To evaluate the scatter of the solutions yielded by a metaheuristic (e.g., local search), a focus must be made on both their entropy and their distribution. The entropy gives an information about the scatter of the solutions but do not give information about the granularity of the concentrations. In fact, scattered concentrations or a single concentration may have the same low entropy. The mean distance gives a complementary information; it measures the concentration of the distribution (in a single region). In the analysis of the scatter of the local optima, the variations of the entropy and the mean distance between the initial population U and the final population O may be observed. Table 2.2 illustrates the fitness landscape structure according to the variation of the distance and the entropy.

TABLE 2.2 Use of the Entropy Variation and the Distance Variation to Analyze the Distribution of the Local Optima

Entropy Δ_{Ent}	Low variation	High variation	High variation
Distribution Δ_{Dmm}	Low variation	Low variation	High variation
Landscape	Uniform	Multimassif	One-Massif

A mathematical relationship between distribution-based measures and entropy-based measures shows that a low entropy is also a low distribution, but not vice versa [581]

- **Distribution in the objective space:** Many indicators can be used to analyze the distribution of solutions in the objective space. The *amplitude* Amp (P) of an arbitrary population P of solutions is the relative difference between the best quality of the population P and the worst one:

$$\mathrm{Amp}\,(P) = \frac{|P| \cdot (\max_{s \in P} f(s) - \min_{s \in P} f(s))}{\sum_{s \in P} f(s)}$$

The relative variation of the amplitude Δ_{Amp} between a starting random population U and the final population O is given by

$$\Delta_{\mathrm{Amp}} = \frac{\mathrm{Amp}\,(U) - \mathrm{Amp}\,(O)}{\mathrm{Amp}\,(U)}$$

The average Gap (O) of the relative gaps between the costs of the population O of local optima and the global optimal solution (or the best known solution) s^*

$$\mathrm{Gap}\,(O) = \frac{\sum_{s \in O} (f(s) - f(s^*))}{|O| \cdot f(s^*)}$$

A reduced gap indicates that the problem is relatively "easy" to solve.

2.2.2.2 *Correlation Measures* The objective of correlation measures is to estimate the ruggedness of the landscape along with the correlation between the quality of solutions and their distance to a global optimal solution. The landscape is described as rough (unsmooth) if it contains many local optimal solutions and is characterized by a low correlation between neighboring solutions. Many correlation indicators may be used:

- **Length of the walks:** The average length Lmm (P) of the descent walks relative to the population P can be defined as

$$\text{Lmm}(P) = \frac{\sum_{p \in P} l(p)}{|P|}$$

in which $l(p)$ is the length of the walk starting with the solution $p \in P$. In an intuitive way, the length of the walk gives some information about the ruggedness of the landscape. In a rugged landscape, the optima are numerous and the walks are short, whereas in a smooth landscape the number of optima is smaller and the walks are longer.

- **Autocorrelation function:** The autocorrelation function measures the ruggedness of a landscape, and the autocorrelation function proposed by Weinberger may be used [812]. The *autocorrelation function* $\rho(d)$ measures the correlation of solutions in the search space with distance d. It is approximated by using a large sample of solution pairs (n solutions with distance d):

$$\rho(d) = \frac{\sum_{s,t \in S \times S, \text{dist}(s,t)=d} (f(s) - \bar{f})(f(t) - \bar{f})}{n.\sigma_f^2}$$

This function corresponds to the usual understanding of the landscape ruggedness. The autocorrelation function provides a measure of the influence of the distance d on the variation of the fitnesses of solutions. The measure belongs to the interval $[-1, 1]$. The closer is the absolute value to 1, the larger is the correlation between the solutions.

The autocorrelation function $\rho(1)$ considers only neighboring solutions ($d = 1$). A low value ($\rho(1) \approx 0$) indicates that the variation of fitness between two neighbors is equal on average to the variation between any two solutions, so the landscape is rugged. On the contrary, a high value ($\rho(1) \approx 1$) indicates that two neighbors have a similar fitness value when both solutions are distant, and hence the landscape is smoother.

Another approach to approximate the autocorrelation function consists in analyzing the degree of correlation between solutions of distance s of the landscape by performing a random walk $\langle f(x_t) \rangle$ of size m. The *random walk correlation function* is defined as [812]

$$r(s) \approx \frac{1}{\sigma_f^2(m-s)} \sum_{t=1}^{m-s} (f(x_t) - \bar{f})(f(x_{t+s}) - \bar{f})$$

The idea is to generate a random walk in the search space via neighboring solutions. At each step, the fitness of the encountered solution is recorded. In this way, a *time series* of fitnesses $f_1, f_2, \ldots, f_n$ is generated.

Based on the autocorrelation function, the *correlation length* is the largest time lag (distance) for which the correlation between two solutions is statistically significant [719]. In other words, the correlation length measures the distance or time lag m between two configurations, at which the values of one configuration can still provide some information about the expected value of the other. Thus, the larger the correlation length is, the flatter and smoother the landscape is. The search in a smooth landscape is more easy. The smaller is the correlation length, the more rugged is the associated landscape and harder is the search.

The correlation length can be defined as

$$l = \frac{1}{\ln(|r(1)|)} = -\frac{1}{\ln(|\rho(1)|)}$$

This value can be normalized in the interval [0, 1] by using the diameter of the landscape

$$\xi = \frac{l}{\text{diam}(G)}$$

Higher the correlation is, closer the normalized correlation length is to 1. There is no correlation if the normalized correlation ξ is close to 0. In a rough landscape, the correlation length of an iterative random walk is low, and the length of an iterated local search Lmm (U) is low compared to the diameter of the search space. Lmm (U) is the average length of iterated local searches performed from the initial population U. For an arbitrary population P of solutions

$$\text{Lmm}(P) = 100 \times \frac{\text{lmm}(P)}{n}$$

where lmm (P) is the average of the length of local searches starting from the solutions of the population P.

A random walk in the landscape can be viewed as a time series. Once the time series of the fitnesses is obtained, a model can be built using the *Box–Jenkins approach*, and thus we can make forecast about future values or simulate process as the one that generated the original data [89]. An important assumption must be made here: the landscape has to be statistically isotropic; that is, the time series of the fitnesses forms a stationary random process. This means that the random walk is "representative" of the entire landscape, and thus the correlation structure of the time series can be regarded as the correlation structure of the whole landscape. For instance, one can find an ARMA[7] model that adequately represents the data generating process [387]. A search walk following an AR(1) model is in the form

$$y_t = c + \alpha_1 y_{t-1} + \epsilon_t$$

[7] The notation ARMA(p, q) refers to the model with p autoregressive terms and q moving average terms: $y_t = \epsilon_t + \sum_{i=1}^{p} \alpha_i y_{t-i} + \sum_{i=1}^{q} \theta_i \epsilon_{t-i}$.

This correlation structure given by the time series analysis implies that the fitness at a particular step in a random walk generated on this landscape totally depends on the fitness one step earlier. Knowing the fitness two steps earlier does not give any extra information on the expected value of fitness at the current step. Furthermore, the value of the parameter α_1 is the correlation coefficient between the fitness of two points one step apart in a random walk. Hence, for an AR(1) model, $r(d) = r(1)^d = e^{-d/l}$ where l is the correlation length. Table 2.3 shows some correlation lengths for different optimization problems. Those results have been obtained theoretically and confirmed experimentally [542,718].

The autocorrelation coefficient (or ruggedness) is a normalized measure of the autocorrelation function [29,30]:

$$\xi = \frac{1}{1 - \rho(1)}$$

This measure is based on the autocorrelation function of neighboring solutions $\rho(1)$. It evaluates globally the homogeneousness of the quality of the neighborhood. The larger the correlation, the flatter the landscape.

- **Fitness distance correlation:** Fitness distance correlation analysis measures how much the fitness of a solution correlates with the distance to the global optimum. The relationship between the fitness and the distance to a global optimum will have a strong effect on search difficulty [428,429]. To perform the fitness distance analysis, we need a sample of fitness values $F = \{f_1, f_2, \ldots, f_n\}$ and the corresponding set of distances to the global optimum $D = \{d_1, d_2, \ldots, d_n\}$. The correlation coefficient is given by

$$r = \frac{\text{cov}(F, D)}{\sigma_f \sigma_d}$$

TABLE 2.3 Correlation Lengths for Some Optimization Problems and Landscapes. TSP (Traveling Salesman Problem), QAP (Quadratic Assignment Problem), GBP (Graph Bipartitioning Problem), and NK-Model for Landscapes [542,718,719]

Problem	Move	Diameter	Neighborhood Size	Correlation Length
TSP	2-opt	$n-1$	$\frac{n(n-1)}{2}$	$\frac{n}{2}$
	Swap	$n-1$	$\frac{n(n-1)}{2}$	$\frac{n}{4}$
QAP	Swap	$n-1$	$\frac{n(n-1)}{2}$	$\approx\frac{n}{3}$
GBP	Swap	$\frac{n}{2}$	$\frac{n(n-1)}{2}$	$\approx\frac{n}{8}$
	Flip	n	$n-1$	$\approx\frac{n}{4}$
NK-model	Flip	n	$n-1$	$\frac{n}{k+1}$

where

$$\operatorname{cov}(F, D) = \frac{1}{n} \sum_{i=1}^{n} (f_i - \bar{f})(d_i - \bar{d})$$

$\bar{f}$ and σ_f represent the covariance and the standard deviation, respectively. FDC is founded on the following conjectures:

- **Straightforward:** Large positive correlations indicate that the problem is relatively easy to solve since as the fitness decreases, the distance to the global optimum also decreases. The existence of a search path in the landscape with improving fitnesses toward the global optimum seems likely.
- **Misleading:** Large negative correlations indicate that the problem is "misleading" and the move operator will guide the search away from the global optimum. A solution can be very close to the global optimal solution and has a poor quality.
- **Difficult:** Near-zero correlations indicate[8] that there is no correlation between fitness and distance.

A better way to analyze the FDC is to use the *fitness distance plot* that plots the fitness of the solutions against their distance to the global optimal solution (Fig. 2.19). In the case of the presence of many global optima in the problem, the computation of the distance takes the nearest global optimum. One major limitation of the FDC analysis for real-life problems is that its computation requires the knowledge of the global optima. This is not realistic for many optimization problems. In that case, the best known solution may be selected to represent the global optimum. Other critical potential limitations are the

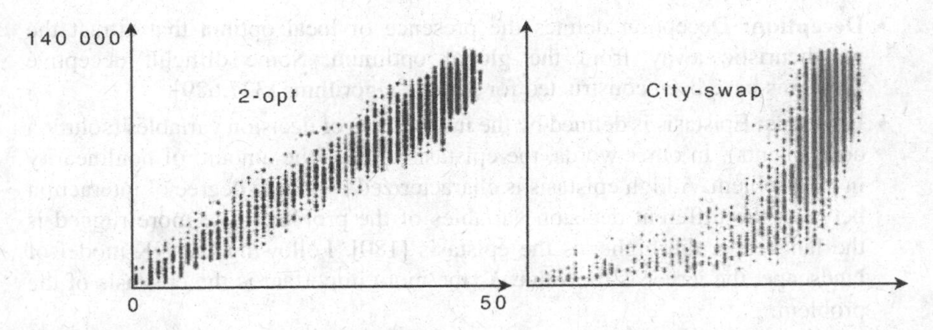

FIGURE 2.19 Using the FDC analysis, the figure shows the fitness distance plot of the instance *att48* of the TSP using the 2-opt and the city-swap neighborhood structures. The left figure for the 2-opt shows a high FDC (0.94) and the right figure shows a less important FDC for the city-swap operator (0.86). For the problem instance *tsp225*, the FDC is 0.99 for the 2-opt and 0.61 for the city swap.

[8]Empirical experiments propose an interval [−0.15, 0.15] [429].

generation of k-distant solutions and the computation of the distance between solutions.

Example 2.17 Landscape and neighborhoods. This example illustrates the importance of avoiding rugged multivalleys in a landscape. Let us consider the symmetric Euclidean TSP (2D or 3D) and analyze the landscape associated with two different neighborhoods: the *city swap* that consists in swapping two cities and the 2-opt that replaces two edges. The landscape associated with the 2-opt may be viewed as a "massif central,"[9] that is, a big deep valley where the local optimal solutions are gathered around the global optimal solution (low average distance to the global optimal solution and low entropy of the population of local optimal solutions) [750]. Indeed, the local optimal solutions are clustered in a reduced region of the search space; the distance between any local optima s_i and the global optimal solution s^* is reduced ($\delta(s_i, s^*) \leq n/3$, where n is the input size). The local optimal solutions share over 60% of their edges. Many studies reach the same conclusion [83,465]. One can reuse this knowledge to design an efficient hybrid metaheuristic [275]. In the 2-opt landscape, a simple local search algorithm allows to obtain relatively good results ($\text{Gap}(O) \leq 10\%$) [750].

This "massif central" structure is diluted when using the city-swap operator, which gives worst local optima compared to the 2-opt operator. The landscape associated with the city-swap operator has a rugged multivalley structure. The local optima are as uniform as random solutions. Moreover, the FDC coefficient and the correlation length are more important for the 2-opt landscape than the city-swap landscape for all instances of the TSPlib [646]. For the 2-opt operator, the FDC correlation is closer to 1; that is, more the solution is closer to the global optimal solution, better is the quality of the solution (Fig. 2.19).

Other measures may be used to characterize the difficulty of problems:

- **Deception:** Deception defines the presence of local optima that attract the metaheuristic away from the global optimum. Some difficult deceptive problems have been constructed for genetic algorithms [327,629].
- **Epistasis:** Epistasis is defined by the interactions of decision variables (solution components). In other words, the epistasis defines the amount of nonlinearity in the problem. A high epistasis is characterized by a high degree of interaction between the different decision variables of the problem. The more rugged is the landscape, the higher is the epistasis [180]. Following the NK-model of landscape, the larger is the value K, the more important is the epistasis of the problem.
- **Multimodality:** It defines the number of local optima in the search space.
- **Neutrality:** It defines the flatness of the landscape, that is, the existence of plateaus: regions with equal fitness.
- **Fractal:** When the variance of the difference in the fitness between two solutions of the search space scales as a *power law* with their distance from each other,

[9] Referred also as "big valley" structure.

the landscape is a fractal; that is,

$$\langle \| f(s) - f(t) \|^2 \rangle \propto d(s,t)^{2h}$$

where s and t represent any solutions of the search space s and t $(s \neq t)$ [813].

From a pragmatic point of view, the landscape of an easy instance is a valley (see Table 2.1); on the contrary, the landscape of a difficult instance is a rugged plain. Indeed, the metaheuristic methods easily manage to discover the bottom of a valley, and it is then enough to intensify the search in this area. With regard to the flat and rugged landscapes, there are a lot of places of good quality, but the latter are very dispersed and reaching the best is difficult; one can diversify much, but it is not sufficient for great spaces. For an intermediate landscape, the search algorithms should balance the intensification and the diversification, but this task is uneasy. According to this assumption, a promising approach consists in modifying the structure of the landscape to make it easier, that is, composed of a few deep valleys. The landscape can be modified by changing the neighborhood operator or the objective function.

Example 2.18 Landscape and instances structure. Let us consider the landscape analysis of the quadratic assignment problem where a known standard library exist: the QAPlib [96]. The landscape analysis shows that following the length of walks and the distribution of the local optima (entropy and distance), three different classes of instances may be defined (Fig. 2.20) [42,542]:

- **Nonstructured Landscape:** The instances of this type (type I) are almost all of a random uniform nature. The local optima are very scattered over the search space; the range of their quality is small and their average cost is rather good. So, a local search heuristic will "see" a flat rugged landscape with a good quality of solutions. In such a nonstructured landscape in which all regions have more or less the same quality, a local search will find quickly a good solution.
- **"Massif central":** This class (type II) includes only real or pseudoreal instances. It is characterized by a longer length of walks and a more clustered local optima (small entropy, small diameter), constituting a small number of concentrated "massifs." The landscape is composed of few deep valleys, where the best solutions are localized. In this landscape, an effective local search, such as tabu search, easily finds a promising valley and then exploits it.
- **"Multimassif":** This class (type III) comprises only large instances. The landscape contains multiple valleys more or less deep, in which the local optima are gathered (small entropy, medium diameter). For more efficiency, a metaheuristic has to both exploit the bottom of the valleys and explore the search space enough to ensure that the best valleys will be exploited. In fact, the exploitation of the bottom of a deep valley (as done by tabu search, for instance) is not needed if this valley is not the best one. However, the main difficulty in designing a metaheuristic is to

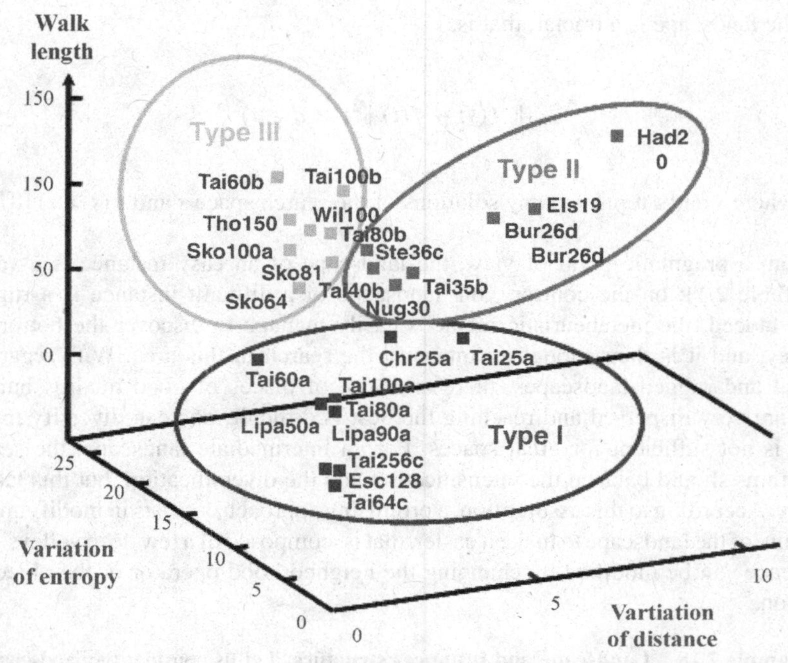

FIGURE 2.20 Correlation between the walk length and the distribution of the local optima (entropy and distance). We observe three different classes of instances.

balance the exploitation of valleys and the exploration of multiple valleys. As a result, the instances of type III are really more difficult to solve by a local search algorithm.

Example 2.19 Landscape and infeasible solutions. Let us consider the graph bipartitioning problem. Given an undirected graph $G = (V, E)$, the problem is to find a partition of the nodes in two equally sized groups G_1 and G_2, which minimizes the number of edges between nodes of different groups:

$$\text{Min}|(e(G_1, G_2))|$$

where $e(G_1, G_2) = \{(i, j) \in E / i \in G_1, j \in G_2\}$. A straightforward encoding is the binary representation in which each node of the graph is assigned to a group. Let us consider two move operators:

- Exchange operator that consists in swapping the position of a pair of nodes of the graph.
- Flip operator that consists in changing the location of a single node. This move operator may generate infeasible solutions. The search space is much larger than the first one. A penalty function is then integrated in the objective function [29].

The landscape analysis of the GBP shows that the landscape associated with the flip operator presents a higher correlation length and is more smoother than the exchange operator landscape [29]. Hence, the local search heuristic shows a better effectiveness in the flip landscape. This example illustrates that enlarging the search space to infeasible solutions may be more efficient.

2.2.3 Breaking Plateaus in a Flat Landscape

Many optimization problems are characterized by a flat landscape[10] in which there are many plateaus (i.e., many neighbors are equally fitted). The plateaus are tediously crossed by metaheuristics. Indeed, no information will guide the search toward better regions. Hence, it is important to break the plateaus of a landscape to make the optimization problem more easy to solve.

One such strategy consists in changing the objective function. The objective function is generally defined rather straightforward in problem solving: it is simply the value of the utility function to optimize. For some problems, embedding more information in the objective function leads to a significant improvement in the quality of the solutions that are reached.

Definition 2.10 Plateau. *Given a point s in the search space S and a v value taken in the range of values of the criterion f. Given $N(s)$, the set of points s' in the neighborhood of the solution s. Considering X a subset of $N(s)$ defined by $s'' \in X$ iff $f(s'') = v$, X is a plateau iff it contains at least two elements (i.e., $|X| \geq 2$).*

When the landscape is composed of several plateaus, the main objective function of the problem is not sufficient to discriminate neighbors of the current point. On each plateau, a metaheuristic has difficulties to be guided in the neighborhood of the current solution. In this situation, using other information to break those plateaus and guide the search can be useful.

A secondary criterion f' is useful if it can discriminate points that have the same value for the main criterion f and is correlated with the main objective of the problem. The "discrimination power" is thus an important characteristic of a criterion.

Definition 2.11 Discrimination power. *Let $\Phi \neq (f')$ be the number of different values that are taken by the criterion f' on a plateau of the main criterion f. The discrimination power of the criterion f', $\phi \neq (f')$, is the average number of $\Phi \neq (f')$ on a set of solutions.*

A discrimination criterion f' such that $\phi_{\neq}(f') \approx 1$ is not a good criterion since, on average, there is only one value of f' on each plateau of f. This means that f' cannot be used to guide the metaheuristic on the plateaus of f.

The new objective function can be defined as

$$f''(x) = k_1 \times f(x) + f'(x)$$

[10]Also referred as neutral.

where f is the main objective function of the problem, f' is the discrimination criterion, and k_1 is an upper bound for $f'(x)$ over all solutions of the search space. One needs to define the upper bound for the constant k_1 so that the main objective remains the most important.

Using extra information would help discriminate the solutions with the same value in the objective space but with a different value with regard to the decision space (search space). Generally, this approach does not require any additional work except the implementation of the discrimination criterion. The computational cost of the integrated secondary objectives must be taken into account. Obviously, this depends on the kind of onside properties that are used and the cost to compute them. Another application of this approach in P-metaheuristics would be to maintain the diversity of the population, a key point of a good search in P-metaheuristics.

Many real-life and academic optimization problems are characterized by plateaus in their landscape: scheduling problems using the makespan as the objective [232], satisfiability (SAT) problems using the number of nonsatisfied clauses as the objective [432], graph coloring problem using the number of colors as the objective, and so on.

Example 2.20 Breaking the plateaus of the job-shop scheduling problem. Let us consider here the job-shop scheduling problem presented in Example 1.33. The landscape of the problem using the makespan objective has many plateaus [232]. In addition to the discrimination power of a criterion, the correlation with the main objective must also be taken into account. Two secondary criteria may be integrated into the objective function f: H_2, and C_{op}. $H_2(x)$ can be defined as [374]

$$H_2(x) = \sum_{m=1}^{M} E_m^2(x)$$

where $E_m(x)$ is the completion time of the last operation performed on machine m according to the schedule x. $C_{op}(x)$ represents the number of critical operations of the schedule x. A critical operation is one that, if delayed, would increase the makespan of the schedule if reordering the operations is not allowed. It is commonly held that the less critical operations a schedule contains, the better the schedule is.

The new objective function can be defined as

$$f'(x) = k_1 \times k_2 \times C_{max}(x) + k_2 \times H_2(x) + C_{op}(x)$$

where C_{max} is the makespan, which is the main objective function of the problem

$$C_{max}(x) = \max_{1 \leq m \leq M}\{E_m(x)\}$$

k_1 is an upper bound for $H_2(x)$ over all the possible busy schedules,[11] and k_2 is an upper bound for the criterion $C_{op}(x)$ over all possible schedules. We need to define the upper bounds for the constants k_1 and k_2 so that the makespan remains the main

[11] A schedule x is a busy schedule if for each time slot t, where $0 \leq t \leq C_{max}(x)$, there is at least one operation running on a machine.

criterion. k_1 may be equal to $M \times D^2$, where D is the sum of the durations of all the operations of the instance. It is easy to see that the makespan of busy schedules is always smaller than this value. k_2 may be equal to $J \times M$, as there are $J \times M$ operations in the problem, so that there are no more than $J \times M$ critical operations.

Using the *same* metaheuristics, the new objective function f' provides better results in terms of the quality of the local optima that are found [232]. For this problem, this approach does not require a lot of implementation work and the computational cost is low.

The landscape analysis has some limitations. For instance, some measures require data that are difficult to obtain for complex real-life problems: global optimal solutions, number of local optima, distance definition, all solutions of distance d, and so on. However, approximations may be used to deal with those difficulties. As those approximations may lead to incorrect predictions, careful analysis must be carried out from those data [27,575]. Landscape analysis remains an interesting, valuable, and unavoidable tool for the analysis of the different search components of metaheuristics in solving complex optimization problems. The use of a set of different indicators is encouraged, rather than a single magic wand, to analyze the landscape of a problem and its difficulty.

2.3 LOCAL SEARCH

Local search[12] is likely the oldest and simplest metaheuristic method [3,598]. It starts at a given initial solution. At each iteration, the heuristic replaces the current solution by a neighbor that improves the objective function (Fig. 2.21). The search

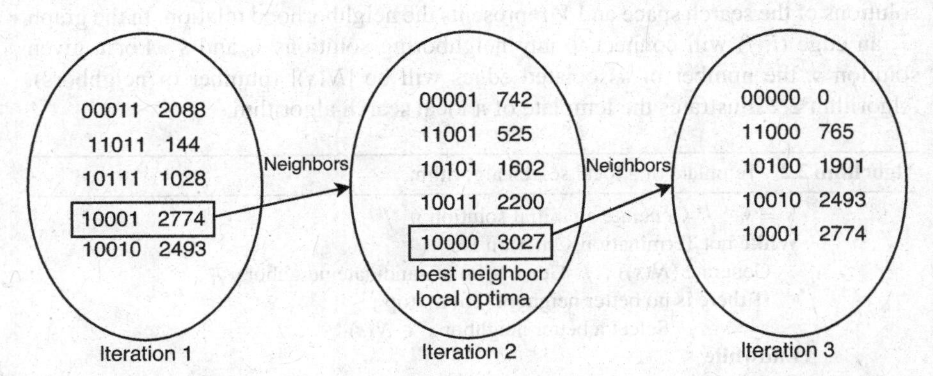

FIGURE 2.21 Local search process using a binary representation of solutions, a flip move operator, and the best neighbor selection strategy. The objective function to maximize is $x^3 - 60x^2 + 900x$. The global optimal solution is $f(01010) = f(10) = 4000$, while the final local optima found is $s = (10000)$, starting from the solution $s_0 = (10001)$.

[12] Also referred as hill climbing, descent, iterative improvement, and so on. In some literature, local search also refers to general S-metaheuristics.

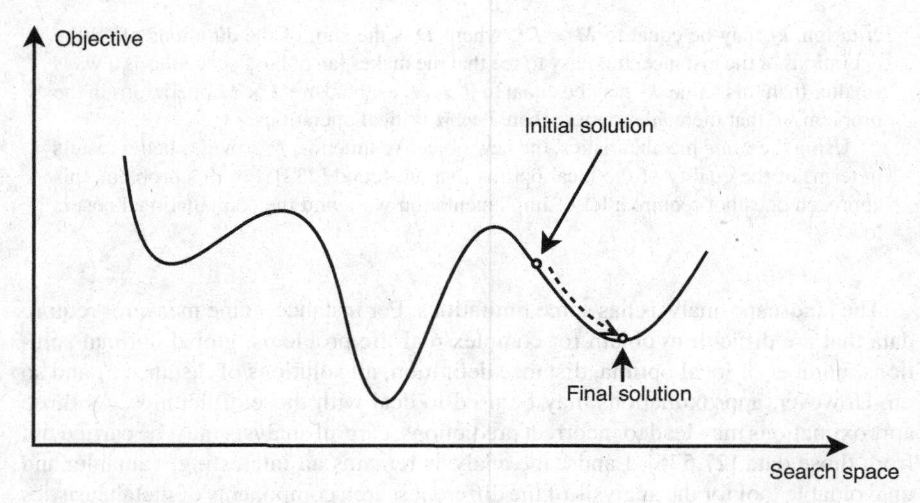

FIGURE 2.22 Local search (steepest descent) behavior in a given landscape.

stops when all candidate neighbors are worse than the current solution, meaning a local optimum is reached. For large neighborhoods, the candidate solutions may be a subset of the neighborhood. The main objective of this restricted neighborhood strategy is to speed up the search. Variants of LS may be distinguished according to the order in which the neighboring solutions are generated (deterministic/stochastic) and the selection strategy (selection of the neighboring solution) (Fig. 2.22).

LS may be seen as a descent walk in the graph representing the search space. This graph may be defined by $G = (S, V)$, where S represents the set of all feasible solutions of the search space and V represents the neighborhood relation. In the graph G, an edge (i, j) will connect to any neighboring solutions s_i and s_j. For a given solution s, the number of associated edges will be $|N(s)|$ (number of neighbors). Algorithm 2.2 illustrates the template of a local search algorithm.

Algorithm 2.2 Template of a local search algorithm.

$s = s_0$; /* Generate an initial solution s_0 */
While not Termination_Criterion **Do**
  Generate $(N(s))$; /* Generation of candidate neighbors */
  If there is no better neighbor **Then** Stop ;
  $s = s'$; /* Select a better neighbor $s' \in N(s)$ */
Endwhile
Output Final solution found (local optima).

From an initial solution s_0, the algorithm will generate a sequence $s_1, s_2, \ldots, s_k$ of solutions with the following characteristics (Fig. 1.32):

- The size of the sequence k is unknown a *priori*.
- $s_{i+1} \in N(s_i), \forall i \in [0, k-1]$.

- $f(s_{i+1}) < f(s_i), \forall i \in [0, k-1]$.[13]
- s_k is a local optimum: $f(s_k) \leq f(s), \forall s \in N(s_k)$.

In addition to the definition of the initial solution and the neighborhood, designing a local search algorithm has to address the selection strategy of the neighbor that will determine the next current solution.

2.3.1 Selection of the Neighbor

Many strategies can be applied in the selection of a better neighbor (Fig. 2.23):

- **Best improvement (steepest descent):** In this strategy, the best neighbor (i.e., neighbor that improves the most the cost function) is selected. The neighborhood is evaluated in a fully deterministic manner. Hence, the exploration of the neighborhood is *exhaustive*, and all possible moves are tried for a solution to select the best neighboring solution. This type of exploration may be time-consuming for large neighborhoods.
- **First improvement:** This strategy consists in choosing the first improving neighbor that is better than the current solution. Then, an improving neighbor is immediately selected to replace the current solution. This strategy involves a partial evaluation of the neighborhood. In a *cyclic* exploration, the neighborhood is evaluated in a deterministic way following a given order of generating the neighbors. In the worst case (i.e., when no improvement is found), a complete evaluation of the neighborhood is performed.
- **Random selection:** In this strategy, a random selection is applied to those neighbors improving the current solution.

A compromise in terms of quality of solutions and search time may consist in using the first improvement strategy when the initial solution is randomly generated

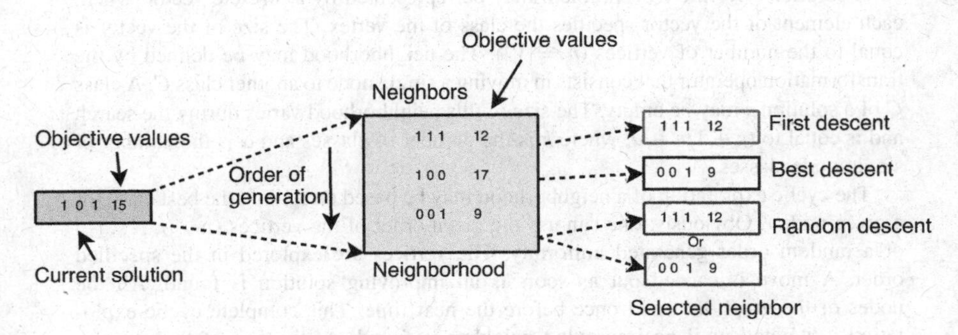

FIGURE 2.23 Selection strategies of improving neighbors.

[13]The problem is supposed to be a minimization problem.

and the best improvement strategy when the initial solution is generated using a greedy procedure. In practice, on many applications, it has been observed that the first improving strategy leads to the same quality of solutions as the best improving strategy while using a smaller computational time. Moreover, the probability of premature convergence to a local optima is less important in the first improvement strategy.

Example 2.21 Exhaustive versus cyclic exploration. Let us consider the neighborhood for the TSP that is based on the 2-opt move operator. A tour is represented by a permutation $(\pi_1, \pi_2, \ldots, \pi_n)$. In the exhaustive exploration, all 2-opt moves are applied. In a cyclic exploration, the order may be given as follows: apply successfully the 2-opt operator using the exchange of vertices (π_1, π_2) with (π_3, π_4), (π_4, π_5), and so on until an improving neighbor is found. In the worst case, the whole neighborhood is explored.

The order of application can be changed during the search. For instance, the initial parameter that determines the order may be chosen randomly. Instead of using always the edge (π_1, π_2), any edge (π_i, π_{i+1}) may represent the initial move.

Example 2.22 Cyclic exploration for a clique partitioning problem (CPP). Given a complete undirected graph $G = (V, E, w)$, where w represents positive or negative weights. To each edge (i, j) is associated a weight $w(i, j) = w(j, i)$. The objective of the CPP problem is to find a partition of the set of vertices V into k cliques $C_1, C_2, .., C_k$, minimizing the sum of the weights of the edges that have both end points in the same clique:

$$f(C_1, C_2, \ldots, C_k) = \frac{1}{2} \sum_{l=1}^{k} \sum_{(i,j) \in C_l \times C_l, i \neq j} w(i, j)$$

The number of cliques k is not fixed [125].

A solution s for the CPP problem may be represented by a discrete vector, where each element of the vector specifies the class of the vertex. The size of the vector is equal to the number of vertices ($n = |V|$). The neighborhood may be defined by the transformation operator that consists in moving a single node to another class C. A class C of a solution s may be empty. The size of this neighborhood varies during the search and is equal to $(k + 1)n - \alpha$, where k is the number of classes and α is the number of single-node classes.

The cyclic exploration of a neighborhood may be based on finding the best class for a given node i. Obviously, one can use the given order of the vertices $(v_1, v_2, \ldots, v_n)$ or a random order generated uniformly. The vertices are explored in the specified order. A move is carried out as soon as an improving solution is found. All the nodes of the graph are tried once before the next time. This complete cyclic exploration is iterated until no improving neighbor is found. At the end of the process, all the nodes are in their best classes (i.e., local optimum related to the given move operator).

2.3.2 Escaping from Local Optima

In general, local search is a very easy method to design and implement and gives fairly good solutions very quickly. This is why it is a widely used optimization method in practice. One of the main disadvantages of LS is that it converges toward local optima. Moreover, the algorithm can be very sensitive to the initial solution; that is, a large variability of the quality of solutions may be obtained for some problems. Moreover, there is no means to estimate the relative error from the global optimum and the number of iterations performed may not be known in advance. Even if the complexity, in practice, is acceptable, the worst case complexity of LS is exponential! Local search works well if there are not too many local optima in the search space or the quality of the different local optima is more or less similar. If the objective function is highly multimodal, which is the case for the majority of optimization problems, local search is usually not an effective method to use.

As the main disadvantage of local search algorithms is the convergence toward local optima, many alternatives algorithms have been proposed to avoid becoming stuck at local optima. These algorithms are become popular since the 1980s. Four different families of approaches can be used to avoid local optima (Fig. 2.24) :

- **Iterating from different initial solutions:** This strategy is applied in multistart local search, iterated local search, GRASP, and so forth.

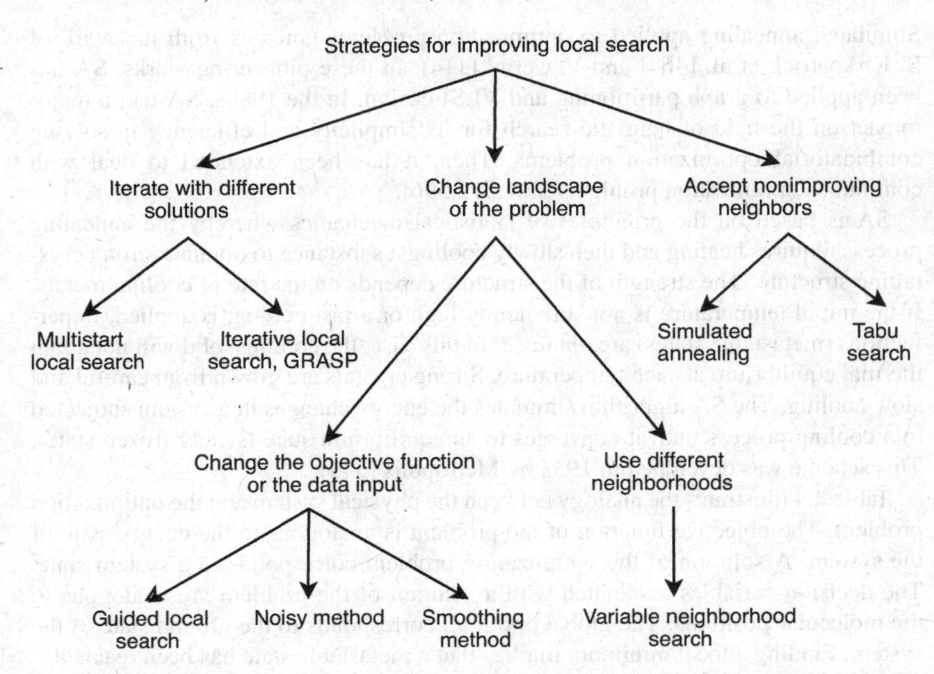

FIGURE 2.24 S-metaheuristic family of algorithms for improving local search and escaping from local optima.

- **Accepting nonimproving neighbors:** These approaches enable moves that degrade the current solution. It becomes possible to move out the basin of attraction of a given local optimum. Simulated annealing and tabu search are popular representative of this class of algorithms. Simulated annealing was the first algorithm addressing explicitly the question "why should we consider only downhill moves?"
- **Changing the neighborhood:** This class of approaches consists in changing the neighborhood structure during the search. For instance, this approach is used in variable neighborhood search strategies.
- **Changing the objective function or the input data of the problem:** In this class, the problem is transformed by perturbing the input data of the problem, the objective function or the constraints, in the hope to solve more efficiently the original problem. This approach has been implemented in the guided local search, the smoothing strategies, and the noising methods. The two last approaches may be viewed as approaches changing the landscape of the problem to solve.

2.4 SIMULATED ANNEALING

Simulated annealing applied to optimization problems emerges from the work of S. Kirkpatrick et al. [464] and V. Cerny [114]. In these pioneering works, SA has been applied to graph partitioning and VLSI design. In the 1980s, SA had a major impact on the field of heuristic search for its simplicity and efficiency in solving combinatorial optimization problems. Then, it has been extended to deal with continuous optimization problems [204,512,596].

SA is based on the principles of statistical mechanics whereby the annealing process requires heating and then slowly cooling a substance to obtain a strong crystalline structure. The strength of the structure depends on the rate of cooling metals. If the initial temperature is not sufficiently high or a fast cooling is applied, imperfections (metastable states) are obtained. In this case, the cooling solid will not attain thermal equilibrium at each temperature. Strong crystals are grown from careful and slow cooling. The SA algorithm simulates the energy changes in a system subjected to a cooling process until it converges to an equilibrium state (steady frozen state). This scheme was developed in 1953 by Metropolis [543].

Table 2.4 illustrates the analogy between the physical system and the optimization problem. The objective function of the problem is analogous to the energy state of the system. A solution of the optimization problem corresponds to a system state. The decision variables associated with a solution of the problem are analogous to the molecular positions. The global optimum corresponds to the ground state of the system. Finding a local minimum implies that a metastable state has been reached.

SA is a stochastic algorithm that enables under some conditions the degradation of a solution. The objective is to escape from local optima and so to delay the convergence. SA is a memoryless algorithm in the sense that the algorithm does not

TABLE 2.4 Analogy Between the Physical System and the Optimization Problem

Physical System	Optimization Problem
System state	Solution
Molecular positions	Decision variables
Energy	Objective function
Ground state	Global optimal solution
Metastable state	Local optimum
Rapid quenching	Local search
Temperature	Control parameter T
Careful annealing	Simulated annealing

use any information gathered during the search. From an initial solution, SA proceeds in several iterations. At each iteration, a random neighbor is generated. Moves that improve the cost function are always accepted. Otherwise, the neighbor is selected with a given probability that depends on the current temperature and the amount of degradation ΔE of the objective function. ΔE represents the difference in the objective value (energy) between the current solution and the generated neighboring solution. As the algorithm progresses, the probability that such moves are accepted decreases (Fig. 2.25). This probability follows, in general, the Boltzmann distribution:

$$P(\Delta E, T) = \mathrm{e}^{-\frac{f(s')-f(s)}{T}}$$

It uses a control parameter, called temperature, to determine the probability of accepting nonimproving solutions. At a particular level of temperature, many trials are explored. Once an equilibrium state is reached, the temperature is gradually decreased

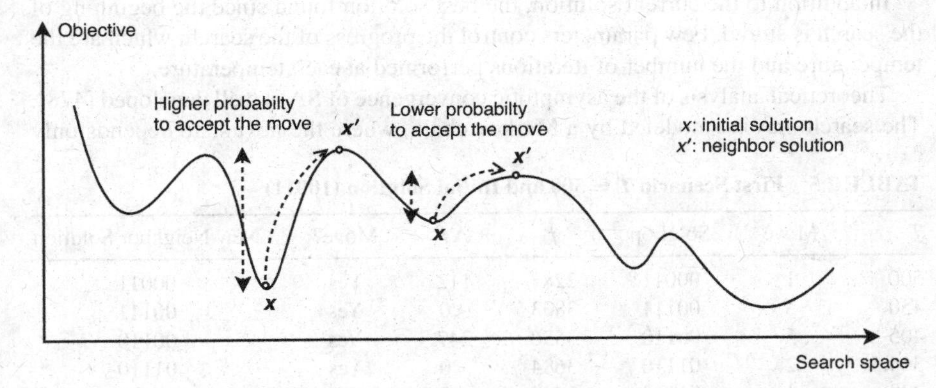

FIGURE 2.25 Simulated annealing escaping from local optima. The higher the temperature, the more significant the probability of accepting a worst move. At a given temperature, the lower the increase of the objective function, the more significant the probability of accepting the move. A better move is always accepted.

according to a cooling schedule such that few nonimproving solutions are accepted at the end of the search. Algorithm 2.3 describes the template of the SA algorithm.

Algorithm 2.3 Template of simulated annealing algorithm.

```
Input: Cooling schedule.
s = s0 ; /* Generation of the initial solution */
T = Tmax ; /* Starting temperature */
Repeat
  Repeat /* At a fixed temperature */
    Generate a random neighbor s' ;
    ΔE = f(s') − f(s) ;
    If ΔE ≤ 0 Then s = s' /* Accept the neighbor solution */
    Else Accept s' with a probability e^(−ΔE/T) ;
  Until Equilibrium condition
  /* e.g. a given number of iterations executed at each temperature T */
  T = g(T) ; /* Temperature update */
Until Stopping criteria satisfied /* e.g. T < Tmin */
Output: Best solution found.
```

Example 2.23 Illustration of the SA algorithm. Let us maximize the continuous function $f(x) = x^3 - 60x^2 + 900x + 100$. A solution x is represented as a string of 5 bits. The neighborhood consists in flipping randomly a bit. The global maximum of this function is 01010 ($x = 10$, $f(x) = 4100$). The first scenario starts from the solution 10011 ($x = 19$, $f(x) = 2399$) with an initial temperature T_0 equal to 500 (Table 2.5). The second scenario starts from the same solution 10011 with an initial temperature T_0 equal to 100 (Table 2.6). The initial temperature is not high enough and the algorithm gets stuck by local optima.

In addition to the current solution, the best solution found since the beginning of the search is stored. Few parameters control the progress of the search, which are the temperature and the number of iterations performed at each temperature.

Theoretical analysis of the asymptotic convergence of SA is well developed [478]. The search may be modeled by a Markov chain, where the next state depends only

TABLE 2.5 First Scenario $T = 500$ and Initial Solution (10011)

T	Move	Solution	f	Δf	Move?	New Neighbor Solution
500	1	00011	2287	112	Yes	00011
450	3	00111	3803	<0	Yes	00111
405	5	00110	3556	247	Yes	00110
364.5	2	01110	3684	<0	Yes	01110
328	4	01100	3998	<0	Yes	01100
295.2	3	01000	3972	16	Yes	01000
265.7	4	01010	**4100**	<0	Yes	01010
239.1	5	01011	4071	29	Yes	01011
215.2	1	11011	343	3728	No	01011

TABLE 2.6 Second Scenario: T = 100 and Initial Solution (10011). When Temperature is not High Enough, Algorithm Gets Stuck

T	Move	Solution	f	Δf	Move?	New Neighbor Solution
100	1	00011	2287	112	No	10011
90	3	10111	1227	1172	No	10011
81	5	10010	2692	<0	Yes	10010
72.9	2	11010	516	2176	No	10010
65.6	4	10000	**3236**	<0	Yes	10000
59	3	10100	2100	1136	Yes	10000

on the current state. There is a guarantee of convergence toward the optimal solution:

$$\Pr(s_M \in R) \rightarrow 1 \quad \text{as} \quad M \rightarrow \infty$$

where R represents the set of global optimal solutions and s_M the solution at iteration M under the following slow cooling schedule:

$$T_k = \frac{\Gamma}{\log k}$$

where Γ is a constant. In practice, such a cooling schedule is useless because it is an asymptotic convergence; that is, the convergence is obtained after an infinite number of iterations. However, much more work is needed in the analysis of finite time performance [267].

In addition to the common design issues for S-metaheuristics such as the definition of the neighborhood and the generation of the initial solution, the main design issues specific to SA are

- **The acceptance probability function:** It is the main element of SA that enables nonimproving neighbors to be selected.
- **The cooling schedule:** The cooling schedule defines the temperature at each step of the algorithm. It has an essential role in the efficiency and the effectiveness of the algorithm.

The following sections present a practical guideline in the definition of the acceptance probability function and the cooling schedule in SA.

2.4.1 Move Acceptance

The system can escape from local optima due to the probabilistic acceptance of a nonimproving neighbor. The probability of accepting a nonimproving neighbor is proportional to the temperature T and inversely proportional to the change of the objective function ΔE.

The law of thermodynamics states that at temperature T, the probability of an increase in energy of magnitude, ΔE, is given by $P(\Delta E, T) = \exp(-\Delta E/kt)$ where k is a constant known as Boltzmann's constant. So, the acceptance probability of a nonimproving move is

$$P(\Delta E, T) = \exp\left(\frac{-\delta E}{kt}\right) > R$$

where ΔE is the change in the evaluation function, T is the current temperature, and R is a uniform random number between 0 and 1.

At high temperatures, the probability of accepting worse moves is high. If $T = \infty$, all moves are accepted, which corresponds to a random local walk in the landscape. At low temperatures, the probability of accepting worse moves decreases. If $T = 0$, no worse moves are accepted and the search is equivalent to local search (i.e., hill climbing). Moreover, the probability of accepting a large deterioration in solution quality decreases exponentially toward 0 according to the Boltzmann distribution.

2.4.2 Cooling Schedule

The cooling schedule defines for each step of the algorithm i the temperature T_i. It has a great impact on the success of the SA optimization algorithm. Indeed, the performance of SA is very sensitive to the choice of the cooling schedule.

The parameters to consider in defining a cooling schedule are the starting temperature, the equilibrium state, a cooling function, and the final temperature that defines the stopping criteria. A guideline dealing with the initialization of each parameter is given next.

2.4.2.1 Initial Temperature If the starting temperature is very high, the search will be more or less a random local search. Otherwise, if the initial temperature is very low, the search will be more or less a first improving local search algorithm. Hence, we have to balance between these two extreme procedures. The starting temperature must not be too high to conduct a random search for a period of time but high enough to allow moves to almost neighborhood state.

There are three main strategies that can be used to deal with this parameter:

- **Accept all:** The starting temperature is set high enough to accept all neighbors during the initial phase of the algorithm [464]. The main drawback of this strategy is its high computational cost.
- **Acceptance deviation:** The starting temperature is computed by $k\sigma$ using preliminary experimentations, where σ represents the standard deviation of difference between values of objective functions and $k = -3/\ln(p)$ with the acceptance probability of p, which is greater than 3σ [392].

- **Acceptance ratio:** The starting temperature is defined so as to make the acceptance ratio of solutions greater than a predetermined value a_0

$$T_0 = \frac{\Delta^+}{\ln(m_1(a_0 - 1)/m_2 + a_0)}$$

where m_1 and m_2 are the numbers of solutions to be decreased and increased in preliminary experiments, respectively, and Δ^+ is the average of objective function values increased [2]. For instance, the initial temperature should be initialized in such a way that the acceptance rate is in the interval [40%, 50%].

2.4.2.2 *Equilibrium State* To reach an equilibrium state at each temperature, a number of sufficient transitions (moves) must be applied. Theory suggests that the number of iterations at each temperature might be exponential to the problem size, which is a difficult strategy to apply in practice. The number of iterations must be set according to the size of the problem instance and particularly proportional to the neighborhood size $|N(s)|$. The number of transitions visited may be as follows:

- **Static:** In a static strategy, the number of transitions is determined before the search starts. For instance, a given proportion y of the neighborhood $N(s)$ is explored. Hence, the number of generated neighbors from a solution s is $y \cdot |N(s)|$. The more significant the ratio y, the higher the computational cost and the better the results.
- **Adaptive:** The number of generated neighbors will depend on the characteristics of the search. For instance, it is not necessary to reach the equilibrium state at each temperature. Nonequilibrium simulated annealing algorithms may be used: the cooling schedule may be enforced as soon as an improving neighbor solution is generated. This feature may result in the reduction of the computational time without compromising the quality of the obtained solutions [107].

  Another adaptive approach using both the worst and the best solutions found in the inner loop of the algorithm may be used. Let f_l (resp. f_h) denote the smallest (resp. largest) objective function value in the current inner loop. The next number of transitions L is defined as follows:

$$L = L_B + \lfloor L_B \cdot F_- \rfloor$$

where $\lfloor x \rfloor$ is the largest integer smaller than x, $F_- = 1 - \exp(-(f_h - f_l)/f_h)$, and L_B is the initial value of the number of transitions [25].

2.4.2.3 *Cooling* In the SA algorithm, the temperature is decreased gradually such that

$$T_i > 0, \forall i$$

and

$$\lim_{i \longrightarrow \infty} T_i = 0$$

There is always a compromise between the quality of the obtained solutions and the speed of the cooling schedule. If the temperature is decreased slowly, better solutions are obtained but with a more significant computation time. The temperature T can be updated in different ways:

- **Linear:** In the trivial linear schedule, the temperature T is updated as follows: $T = T - \beta$, where β is a specified constant value. Hence, we have

$$T_i = T_0 - i \times \beta$$

  where T_i represents the temperature at iteration i.
- **Geometric:** In the geometric schedule, the temperature is updated using the formula

$$T = \alpha T$$

  where $\alpha \in]0, 1[$. It is the most popular cooling function. Experience has shown that α should be between 0.5 and 0.99.
- **Logarithmic:** The following formula is used:

$$T_i = \frac{T_0}{\log(i)}$$

  This schedule is too slow to be applied in practice but has the property of the convergence proof to a global optimum [303].
- **Very slow decrease:** The main trade-off in a cooling schedule is the use of a large number of iterations at a few temperatures or a small number of iterations at many temperatures. A very slow cooling schedule such as

$$T_{i+1} = \frac{T_i}{1 + \beta T_i}$$

  may be used [521], where $\beta = T_0 - T_F/(L-1)T_0T_F$ and T_F is the final temperature. Only one iteration is allowed at each temperature in this very slow decreasing function.
- **Nonmonotonic:** Typical cooling schedules use monotone temperatures. Some nonmonotone scheduling schemes where the temperature is increased again may be suggested [390]. This will encourage the diversification in the search space. For some types of search landscapes, the optimal schedule is nonmonotone [352].

- **Adaptive:** Most of the cooling schedules are static in the sense that the cooling schedule is defined completely *a priori*. In this case, the cooling schedule is "blind" to the characteristics of the search landscape. In an adaptive cooling schedule, the decreasing rate is dynamic and depends on some information obtained during the search [402]. A dynamic cooling schedule may be used where a small number of iterations are carried out at high temperatures and a large number of iterations at low temperatures.

2.4.2.4 Stopping Condition

Concerning the stopping condition, theory suggests a final temperature equal to 0. In practice, one can stop the search when the probability of accepting a move is negligible. The following stopping criteria may be used:

- Reaching a final temperature T_F is the most popular stopping criteria. This temperature must be low (e.g., $T_{\min} = 0.01$).
- Achieving a predetermined number of iterations without improvement of the best found solution [675].
- Achieving a predetermined number of times a percentage of neighbors at each temperature is accepted; that is, a counter increases by 1 each time a temperature is completed with the less percentage of accepted moves than a predetermined limit and is reset to 0 when a new best solution is found. If the counter reaches a predetermined limit R, the SA algorithm is stopped [420].

SA compared to local search is still simple and easy to implement. It gives good results for a wide spectrum of optimization problems: the historical ones such as TSP and VLSI design in different domains of application. A good survey on SA can be found in Refs [1,489,733].

2.4.3 Other Similar Methods

Other similar methods of simulated annealing have been proposed in the literature, such as threshold accepting, great deluge algorithm, record-to-record travel, and demon algorithms (Fig. 2.26). The main objective in the design of those SA-inspired algorithms is to speed up the search of the SA algorithm without sacrificing the quality of solutions.

2.4.3.1 Threshold Accepting

Threshold accepting may be viewed as the deterministic variant of simulated annealing [228]. TA escapes from local optima by accepting solutions that are not worse than the current solution by more than a given threshold Q. A deterministic acceptance function is defined as follows:

$$P_i(\Delta(s, s')) = \begin{cases} 1 & \text{if } Q_i \geq \Delta(s, s') \\ 0 & \text{otherwise} \end{cases}$$

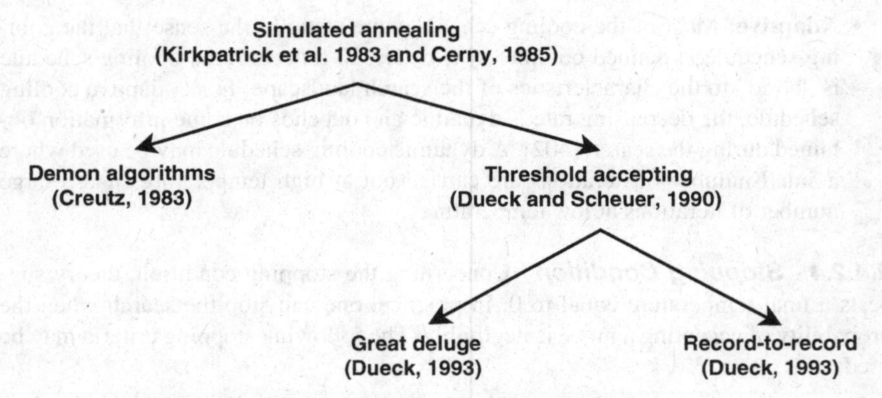

FIGURE 2.26 Genealogy of simulated annealing-based algorithms.

where Q_i is the threshold value at iteration i and $\Delta(s, s')$ is the change in the evaluation function between the current solution s and the neighbor solution s'. The threshold parameter in TA operates somewhat like the temperature in simulated annealing. Algorithm 2.4 describes the template of the TA algorithm. The number of generated neighbors at each iteration is fixed *a priori*. The threshold Q is updated following any annealing schedule.

Algorithm 2.4 Template of threshold accepting algorithm.

Input: Threshold annealing.
$s = s_0$; /* Generation of the initial solution */
$Q = Q_{max}$; /* Starting threshold */
Repeat
  Repeat /* At a fixed threshold */
    Generate a random neighbor $s' \in N(s)$;
    $\Delta E = f(s') - f(s)$;
    If $\Delta E \leq Q$ **Then** $s = s'$ /* Accept the neighbor solution */
  Until Equilibrium condition
  /* e.g. a given number of iterations executed at each threshold Q */
  $Q = g(Q)$; /* Threshold update */
Until Stopping criteria satisfied /* e.g. $Q \leq Q_{min}$ */
Output: Best solution found.

TA is a fast algorithm compared to SA because the generation of random number and exponential functions consume a significant amount of computational time. The literature reports some performance improvements compared to the simulated annealing algorithm in solving combinatorial optimization problems such as the traveling salesman problem [228,565].

In terms of asymptotic convergence, the theoretical properties of TA are similar to those of the SA algorithm [28].

The threshold Q is updated according to an annealing schedule. It must be set as a deterministic nonincreasing step function in the number of iterations i. The threshold decreases at each iteration and then reaches the value of 0 after a given number of iterations.

Example 2.24 Nonmonotone threshold schedule. This simple example will illustrate that the optimal threshold schedule to solve a given problem may be nonmonotone [390]. Let us consider the one-dimensional landscape of a problem shown in Fig. 2.27. The search space is composed of six solutions, and each solution has two neighbors. The number of iterations of the algorithm is fixed to M. The optimal schedule is defined as the one that maximizes the probability of finding the global optimum solution starting from any random initial solution. For many values of M, it has been shown that the optimal threshold schedule is nonmonotone with negative thresholds. For instance, for $M = 9$, the optimal schedule is $(0, -3, 3, -1, -3, 3, 3, -1)$ and the probability to find the global optimum is 0.8372.

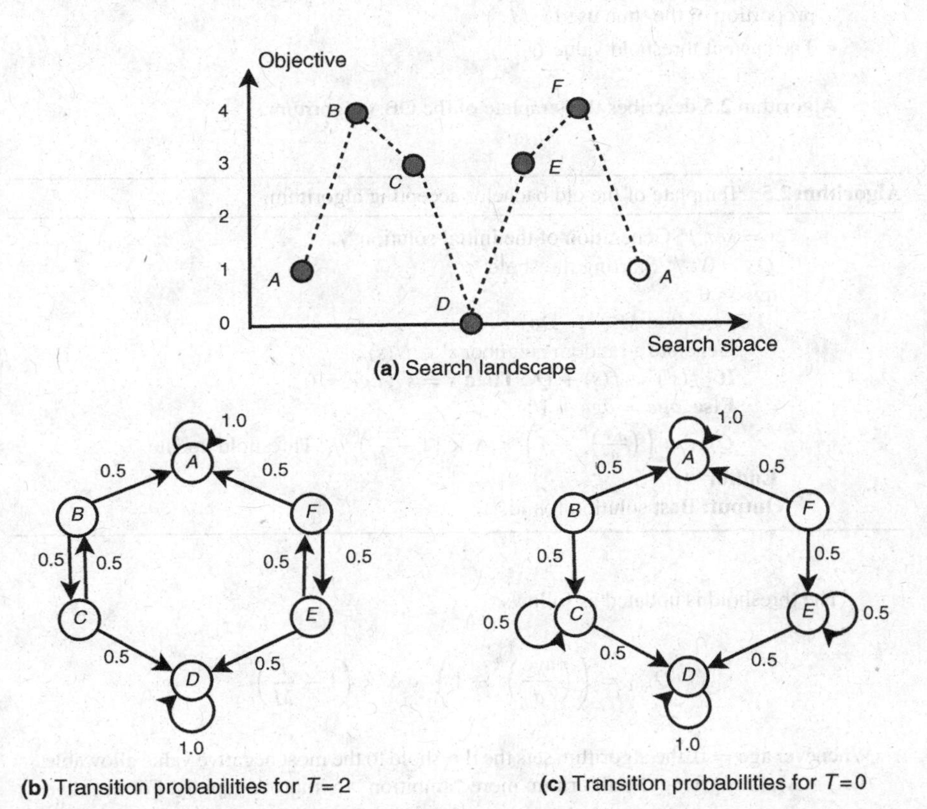

FIGURE 2.27 Nonmonotone optimal threshold schedule [390]. (a) Represents the search landscape of the problem. (b) (Resp. (c)) represents the transition probabilities for $T = 2 (T = 0)$.

Example 2.25 Adaptive nonmonotone threshold—the old bachelor acceptance. In the old bachelor acceptance algorithm, the threshold changes dynamically (up or down) based on the history of the search [390]. After each failure of accepting a new solution, the criterion for accepting is relaxed by slightly increasing the threshold Q_i[14]: $Q_{i+1} = Q_i + \text{incr}(Q_i)$. Hence, after many successive failures, the threshold will be large enough to escape from local optima. On the contrary, after each acceptance of a neighbor solution, the threshold is lowered so that the algorithm becomes more aggressive in moving toward a local optimum $Q_{i+1} = Q_i - \text{decr}(Q_i)$.
The decr and incr functions are based on the following factors:

- The neighborhood size $|N|$. This value has an impact on the "reachability" between solutions (i.e., the diameter and multiplicity of paths in the search space).
- The *age* of the current solution, which is the number of iterations since the last move acceptance. Larger values of the *age* implies greater likelihood that the current solution is a local optimum and that the threshold must increase.
- The amount of time remaining $M - i$, where M represents the total number of iterations and i the current iteration. The threshold update will depend on the proportion of the time used i/M.
- The current threshold value Q_i.

Algorithm 2.5 describes the template of the OBA algorithm.

Algorithm 2.5 Template of the old bachelor accepting algorithm.

$s = s_0$; /* Generation of the initial solution */
$Q_0 = 0$; /* Starting threshold */
$age = 0$;
For $i = 0$ to $M - 1$ **Do**
  Generate a random neighbor $s' \in N(s)$;
  If $f(s') < f(s) + Q_i$ **Then** $s = s'$; $age = 0$;
  Else $age = age + 1$;
  $Q_{i+1} = \left(\left(\frac{age}{a}\right)^b - 1\right) \times \Delta \times \left(1 - \frac{i}{M}\right)^c$ /* Threshold update */
Endfor
Output: Best solution found.

The threshold is updated as follows:

$$Q_{i+1} = \left(\left(\frac{\text{age}}{a}\right)^b - 1\right) \times \Delta \times \left(1 - \frac{i}{M}\right)^c$$

Whenever age $= 0$, the algorithm sets the threshold to the most negative value allowable (i.e., $-\Delta$), thus giving the algorithm more "ambition" to improve rapidly. For negative

[14]This is the motivation for the name "old bachelor acceptance."

values of the threshold, the algorithm may prefer a good improving move over a random improving move. The threshold then rises from this negative value until the next move acceptance occurs.

For age > 0, the update rule allows the threshold growth rate to increase with age. The parameters Δ, a, b, and c afford the ability to fine-tune the growth rate incr(Q_i) as follows: Δ represents the granularity of the update, a tunes the threshold growth by a multiplicative factor, b allows a power law growth rate, and c tunes a heuristic "dumping" factor $1 - (i/M)$ used to scale the magnitude of Q_i as $i \longrightarrow M$.

2.4.3.2 Record-to-Record Travel This algorithm is also a deterministic optimization algorithm inspired from simulated annealing [229]. The algorithm accepts a nonimproving neighbor solution with an objective value less than the RECORD minus a deviation D. RECORD represents the best objective value of the visited solutions during the search. The bound decreases with time as the objective value RECORD of the best found solution improves. Algorithm 2.6 describes the template of the RRT algorithm.

Algorithm 2.6 Template of the record-to-record travel algorithm.

Input: Deviation $D > 0$.
$s = s_0$; /* Generation of the initial solution */
$RECORD = f(s)$; /* Starting RECORD */
Repeat
  Generate a random neighbor s' ;
  If $f(s') < RECORD + D$ **Then** $s = s'$; /* Accept the neighbor solution */
  If $RECORD > f(s')$ **Then** $RECORD = f(s')$; /* RECORD update */
Until Stopping criteria satisfied
Output: Best solution found.

The RRT algorithm has the advantage to be dependent on only one parameter, the DEVIATION value. A small value for the deviation will produce poor results within a reduced search time. If the deviation is high, better results are produced after an important computational time.

2.4.3.3 Great Deluge Algorithm The great deluge algorithm was proposed by Dueck in 1993 [229]. The main difference with the SA algorithm is the deterministic acceptance function of neighboring solutions. The inspiration of the GDA algorithm comes from the analogy that the direction a hill climber would take in a great deluge to keep his feet dry. Finding the global optimum of an optimization problem[15] may be seen as finding the highest point in a landscape. As it rains incessantly without end, the level of the water increases. The algorithm never makes a move beyond the

[15]We suppose here a maximization problem.

water level. It will explore the uncovered area of the landscape to reach the global optimum.

Algorithm 2.7 describes the template of the GDA algorithm in a minimization context. A generated neighbor solution is accepted if the absolute value of the objective function is less than the current boundary value, named level. The initial value of the level is equal to the initial objective function. The level parameter in GDA operates somewhat like the temperature in SA. During the search, the value of the level is decreased monotonically. The decrement of the reduction is a parameter of the algorithm.

Algorithm 2.7 Template of the great deluge algorithm.

Input: Level L.
$s = s_0$; /* Generation of the initial solution */
Choose the rain speed UP ; /* $UP > 0$ */
Choose the initial water level $LEVEL$;
Repeat
    Generate a random neighbor s' ;
    If $f(s') < LEVEL$ **Then** $s = s'$ /* Accept the neighbor solution */
    $LEVEL = LEVEL - UP$; /* update the water level */
Until Stopping criteria satisfied
Output: Best solution found.

The great deluge algorithm needs the tuning of only one parameter, the UP value that represents the rain speed. The quality of the obtained results and the search time will depend only on this parameter. If the value of the UP parameter is high, the algorithm will be fast but will produce results of poor quality. Otherwise, if the UP value is small, the algorithm will generate relatively better results within a higher computational time. An example of a rule that can be used to define the value of the UP parameter may be the following [229]: a value smaller than 1% of the average gap between the quality of the current solution and the water level.

2.4.3.4 Demon Algorithms Since 1998 many S-metaheuristics based on the demon algorithm (DA) (see Ref. [165]) have been proposed [824]. The demon algorithm is another simulated annealing-based algorithm that uses computationally simpler acceptance functions.

Algorithm 2.8 describes the main demon algorithm. The acceptance function is based on the energy value of the demon (credit). The demon is initialized with a given value D. A nonimproved solution is accepted if the demon has more energy (credit) than the decrease of the objective value. When a DA algorithm accepts a solution of increased objective value, the change value of the objective is credited to the demon. In the same manner, when a DA algorithm accepts an improving solution, the decrease of the objective value is debited from the demon.

Algorithm 2.8 Template of the demon algorithm.

```
Input: Demon initial value D
s = s_0 ; /* Generation of the initial solution */
Repeat
    Generate a random neighbor s' ;
    ΔE = f(s') − f(s) ;
    If ΔE ≤ D Then
        s = s' ; /* Accept the neighbor solution */
        D = D − ΔE ; /* Demon value update */
Until Stopping criteria satisfied
Output: Best solution found.
```

The acceptance function of demon algorithms is computationally simpler than in SA. It requires a comparison and a subtraction, whereas in SA it requires an exponential function and a generation of a random number. Moreover, the demon values vary dynamically in the sense that the energy (credit) depends on the visited solutions (Markov chain) during the search, whereas in SA and TA the temperature (threshold) is not dynamically reduced. Indeed, the energy absorbed and released by the demon depends mainly on the accepted solutions.

Different variants of the DA algorithm can be found in the literature [610,824]. They differ by the annealing schedule of the acceptance function:

- **Bounded demon algorithm:** This algorithm imposes an upper bound D_0 for the credit of the demon. Hence, once the credit of the demon is greater than the upper bound, no credit is received even if improving solutions are generated.
- **Annealed demon algorithm:** In this algorithm, an annealing schedule similar to the simulated annealing one is used to decrease the credit of the demon. The credit of the demon will play the same role as the temperature in simulated annealing.
- **Randomized bounded demon algorithm:** A randomized search mechanism is introduced in the BDA algorithm. The credit of the demon is replaced with a normal Gaussian random variable, where the mean equals the credit of the demon (D_m), and a specified standard deviation D_{sd}. Hence, the energy associated with the demon will be $D = D_m +$ Gaussian noise.
- **Randomized annealed demon algorithm:** The same randomized search mechanism of the RBDA algorithm is introduced as in the ADA algorithm.

Table 2.7 illustrates the specificities of the different variants of the demon algorithms.

Compared to simulated annealing, the application of demon algorithms to academic and real-life problems show competitive quality of results within a reduced search time [610,824]. Moreover, they are very easy to design and implement and they need tuning of few parameters.

TABLE 2.7 Variants of Demon Algorithms and Their Specific Parts

Algorithm	Specificity
BDA	Initial demon value (upper bound): D_0 Demon value update: if $D > D_0$, then $D = D_0$
ADA	Demon value update: annealing schedule
RBDA and RADA	Initial demon value: mean $D_{\rm m}$ Acceptance function: $D = D_{\rm m}+$ Gaussian noise Demon value update: $D_{\rm m} = D_{\rm m} - \Delta E$

2.5 TABU SEARCH

Tabu search algorithm was proposed by Glover [323]. In 1986, he pointed out the controlled randomization in SA to escape from local optima and proposed a deterministic algorithm [322]. In a parallel work, a similar approach named "steepest ascent/mildest descent" has been proposed by Hansen [364]. In the 1990s, the tabu search algorithm became very popular in solving optimization problems in an approximate manner. Nowadays, it is one of the most widespread S-metaheuristics. The use of memory, which stores information related to the search process, represents the particular feature of tabu search.

TS behaves like a steepest LS algorithm, but it accepts nonimproving solutions to escape from local optima when all neighbors are nonimproving solutions. Usually, the whole neighborhood is explored in a deterministic manner, whereas in SA a random neighbor is selected. As in local search, when a better neighbor is found, it replaces the current solution. When a local optima is reached, the search carries on by selecting a candidate worse than the current solution. The best solution in the neighborhood is selected as the new current solution even if it is not improving the current solution. Tabu search may be viewed as a dynamic transformation of the neighborhood. This policy may generate cycles; that is, previous visited solutions could be selected again.

To avoid cycles, TS discards the neighbors that have been previously visited. It memorizes the recent search trajectory. Tabu search manages a memory of the solutions or moves recently applied, which is called the *tabu list*. This tabu list constitutes the short-term memory. At each iteration of TS, the short-term memory is updated. Storing all visited solutions is time and space consuming. Indeed, we have to check at each iteration if a generated solution does not belong to the list of all visited solutions. The tabu list usually contains a constant number of tabu moves. Usually, the attributes of the moves are stored in the tabu list.

By introducing the concept of solution features or move features in the tabu list, one may lose some information about the search memory. We can reject solutions that have not yet been generated. If a move is "good," but it is tabu, do we still reject it? The tabu list may be too restrictive; a nongenerated solution may be forbidden. Yet for some conditions, called *aspiration criteria*, tabu solutions may be accepted. The admissible neighbor solutions are those that are nontabu or hold the aspiration criteria.

In addition to the common design issues for S-metaheuristics such as the definition of the neighborhood and the generation of the initial solution, the main design issues that are specific to a simple TS are

- **Tabu list:** The goal of using the short-term memory is to prevent the search from revisiting previously visited solutions. As mentioned, storing the list of all visited solutions is not practical for efficiency issues.
- **Aspiration criterion:** A commonly used aspiration criteria consists in selecting a tabu move if it generates a solution that is better than the best found solution. Another aspiration criterion may be a tabu move that yields a better solution among the set of solutions possessing a given attribute.

Some advanced mechanisms are commonly introduced in tabu search to deal with the intensification and the diversification of the search:

- **Intensification (medium-term memory):** The medium-term memory stores the elite (e.g., best) solutions found during the search. The idea is to give priority to attributes of the set of elite solutions, usually in weighted probability manner. The search is biased by these attributes.
- **Diversification (long-term memory):** The long-term memory stores information on the visited solutions along the search. It explores the unvisited areas of the solution space. For instance, it will discourage the attributes of elite solutions in the generated solutions to diversify the search to other areas of the search space.

Algorithm 2.9 describes the template of the TS algorithm.

Algorithm 2.9 Template of tabu search algorithm.

```
s = s0 ; /* Initial solution */
Initialize the tabu list, medium-term and long-term memories ;
Repeat
    Find best admissible neighbor s' ; /* non tabu or aspiration criterion holds */
    s = s' ;
    Update tabu list, aspiration conditions, medium and long term memories ;
    If intensification_criterion holds Then intensification ;
    If diversification_criterion holds Then diversification ;
Until Stopping criteria satisfied
Output: Best solution found.
```

Theoretical studies carried out on tabu search algorithms are weaker than those established for simulated annealing. A simulated annealing execution lies within the convex hull of a set of tabu search executions [28]. Therefore, tabu search may inherit some nice theoretical properties of SA.

TABLE 2.8 The Different Search Memories of Tabu Search

Search Memory	Role	Popular Representation
Tabu list	Prevent cycling	Visited solutions, moves attributes Solution attributes
Medium-term memory	Intensification	Recency memory
Long-term memory	Diversification	Frequency memory

In addition to the search components of local search (hill climbing), such as the representation, neighborhood, initial solution, we have to define the following concepts that compose the search memory of TS: the tabu list (short-term memory), the medium-term memory, and the long-term memory (Table 2.8).

2.5.1 Short-Term Memory

The role of the short-term memory is to store the recent history of the search to prevent cycling. The naive straightforward representation consists in recording all visited solutions during the search. This representation ensures the lack of cycles but is seldom used as it produces a high complexity of data storage and computational time. For instance, checking the presence of all neighbor solutions in the tabu list will be prohibitive. The first improvement to reduce the complexity of the algorithm is to limit the size of the tabu list. If the tabu list contains the last k visited solutions, tabu search prevents a cycle of size at most k. Using hash codes may also reduce the complexity of the algorithms manipulating the list of visited solutions.

In general, attributes of the solutions or moves are used. This representation induces a less important data storage and computational time but skips some information on the history of the search. For instance, the absence of cycles is not ensured.

The most popular way to represent the tabu list is to record the move attributes. The tabu list will be composed of the reverse moves that are forbidden. This scheme is directly related to the neighborhood structure being used to solve the problem. If the move m is applied to the solution s_i to generate the solution s_j ($s_j = s_i \oplus m$), then the move m (or its reverse m^{-1} such that $(s_i \oplus m) \oplus m^{-1} = s_i$) is stored in the list. This move is forbidden for a given number of iterations, named the *tabu tenure* of the move. If the tabu list contains the last k moves, tabu search will not guarantee to prevent a cycle of size at most k.

Example 2.26 Tabu list based on move attributes. Let us consider a permutation optimization problem where the neighborhood is based on exchanging two elements of the permutation. Given a permutation π, a move is represented by two indices (i, j). This move generates the neighbor solution π' such that

$$\pi'(k) = \begin{cases} \pi(k) & \text{for } k \neq i \text{ and } k \neq j \\ \pi(j) & \text{for } k = i \\ \pi(i) & \text{for } k = j \end{cases}$$

The inverse move (j, i) may be stored in the tabu list and is forbidden. A stronger tabu representation may be related to the indices i and j. This will disallow any permutation involving the indices i and j.

In tabu search, many different tabu lists may be used in conjunction. For instance, some ingredients of the visited solutions and/or the moves are stored in multiple tabu lists. A move m is not tabu if the conditions for *all* tabu lists are satisfied. In many optimization problems, it is more and more popular to use simultaneously various move operators, and hence different neighborhoods are defined.

Example 2.27 Multiple tabu lists. Let us consider the maximum independent set problem. Given a graph $G = (V, E)$, the problem consists in finding a subset of vertices X of V, maximizing the cardinality of the set X, and satisfying the constraint that there is no edge $(i, j) \in E$ having its adjacent vertices in X. Tabu search may be applied to determine an independent set of size k [285]. The objective function consists in minimizing the number of edges having their adjacent vertices in X. The neighborhood is defined by the exchange of a vertex $v \in X$ with a vertex $w \in E - X$. The size of the neighborhood is $k(n - k) = O(nk)$, where n represents the number of vertices. Three different tabu lists may be used:

- The first tabu list T_1 stores the last generated solutions. A hashing technique may be used to speed up the test of tabu conditions [825].
- the second tabu list T_2 stores the last vertices introduced into X.
- the third tabu list T_3 stores the last vertices removed from X.

The size of the tabu list is a critical parameter that has a great impact on the performances of the tabu search algorithm. At each iteration, the last move is added in the tabu list, whereas the oldest move is removed from the list. The smaller is the value of the tabu list, the more significant is the probability of cycling. Larger values of the tabu list will provide many restrictions and encourage the diversification of the search as many moves are forbidden. A compromise must be found that depends on the landscape structure of the problem and its associated instances.

The tabu list size may take different forms:

- **Static:** In general, a static value is associated with the tabu list. It may depend on the size of the problem instance and particularly the size of the neighborhood. There is no optimal value of the tabu list for all problems or even all instances of a given problem. Moreover, the optimal value may vary during the search progress. To overcome this problem, a variable size of the tabu list may be used.
- **Dynamic:** The size of the tabu list may change during the search without using any information on the search memory.

Example 2.28 Robust tabu search. In this tabu search algorithm, a uniform random change of the tabu list size in a given interval $[T_{\min}, T_{\max}]$ is used [738].

- **Adaptive:** In the adaptive scheme, the size of the tabu list is updated according to the search memory. For instance, the size is updated upon the performance of the search in the last iterations [573].

Example 2.29 Reactive tabu search. In the reactive tabu search, the main idea is to increase the size of the tabu list when the short-term memory indicates that the search is revisiting solutions, that is, the presence of a cycle in the search [59]. Hence, the short-term memory stores the visited solutions and not the attributes of the solutions or moves. Hashing techniques are used to reduce the complexity of manipulating such short-term memories.

2.5.2 Medium-Term Memory

The role of the intensification is to exploit the information of the best found solutions (elite solutions) to guide the search in promising regions of the search space. This information is stored in a medium-term memory. The idea consists in extracting the (common) features of the elite solutions and then intensifying the search around solutions sharing those features. A popular approach consists in restarting the search with the best solution obtained and then fixing in this solution the most promising components extracted from the elite solutions.

The main representation used for the medium-term memory is the *recency memory*. First, the components associated with a solution have to be defined; this is a problem-specific task. The recency memory will memorize for each component the number of successive iterations the component is present in the visited solutions. The most commonly used event to start the intensification process is a given period or after a certain number of iterations without improvement.

Example 2.30 Recency memory in solving the GAP. Suppose one has to solve the generalized assignment problem where a solution is encoded by a discrete vector and the neighborhood is defined by the substitute operator. The recency memory may be represented by a symmetric matrix R where an element r_{ij} represents the number of successive iterations the object i has been assigned to the site j. The intensification will consist in starting the search from the best found solution s^*. The largest values r_{ij} are extracted from the recency matrix R. Then the associated elements i in the solution s^* are fixed to the sites j. The search will focus only on the other decision variables of the solution s^*.

The intensification of the search in a given region of the search space is not always useful. The effectiveness of the intensification depends on the landscape structure of the target optimization problem. For instance, if the landscape is composed of many basins of attraction and a simple TS without intensification component is effective to search in each basin of attraction, intensifying the search in each basin is useless.

2.5.3 Long-Term Memory

As mentioned many times, S-metaheuristics are more powerful search methods in terms of intensification. Long-term memory has been introduced in tabu search to encourage the diversification of the search. The role of the long-term memory is to force the search in nonexplored regions of the search space.

The main representation used for the long-term memory is the *frequency memory*. As in the recency memory, the components associated with a solution have first to be defined. The frequency memory will memorize for each component the number of times the component is present in all visited solutions.

Example 2.31 Frequency memory in solving the GAP. The frequency memory may be represented by a symmetric matrix F where an element f_{ij} represents the number of times the object i has been assigned to the site j from the beginning of the tabu search. The diversification may consist in starting the search from a new solution s^*. The elements i of the initial solution s^* are assigned to the sites j that are associated with smaller values of f_{ij}.

The diversification process can be applied periodically or after a given number of iterations without improvement. Three popular diversification strategies may be applied [306]:

- **Restart diversification:** This strategy consists in introducing in the current or best solution the least visited components. Then a new search is restarted from this new solution.
- **Continuous diversification:** This strategy introduces during a search a bias to encourage diversification. For example, the objective function can integrate the frequency occurrence of solution components in the evaluation of current solutions. Frequently applied moves or visited solutions are penalized.
- **Strategic oscillation:** Introduced by Glover in 1989, strategic oscillation allows to consider (and penalize) intermediate solutions that are infeasible. This strategy will guide the search toward infeasible solutions and then come back to a feasible solution.

Example 2.32 Tabu search for the TSP problem. Designing a TS for the TSP problem needs the definition of the tabu list (short-term memory), the medium- and long-term memories, and the aspiration criterion:

- The short-term memory maintains a list of t edges and prevents them from being selected for consideration of moves for a number of iterations l. After the given number of iterations (tabu tenure), these edges are released. One can use a 2D Boolean matrix to decide if an edge is tabu or not.
- The medium- and long-term memory maintains a list of t edges that have been considered in the last k best (worst) solutions. The process encourages (or discourages) their selection in future solutions using their frequency of

appearance in the set of elite solutions and the quality of solutions they have appeared.

- The usual aspiration criterion that accepts the tabu moves that generate better solutions than the best found one.

As for the intensification, the diversification of the search is not always useful. It depends on the landscape structure of the target optimization problem. For instance, if the landscape is a "massif central" where all good solutions are localized in the same region of the search space within a small distance, diversifying the search to other regions of the search space is useless. The search time assigned to the diversification and the intensification components of TS must be carefully tuned depending on the characteristics of the landscape structure associated with the problem.

TS has been successfully applied to many optimization problems. Compared to local search and simulated annealing, various search components of TS are problem specific and must be defined. The search space for TS design is much larger than for local search and simulated annealing. The degree of freedom in designing the different ingredients of TS is important. The representation associated with the tabu list, the medium-term memory, and the long-term memory must be designed according to the characteristics of the optimization problem at hand. This is not a straightforward task for some optimization problems. Moreover, TS may be very sensitive to some parameters such as the size of the tabu list.

2.6 ITERATED LOCAL SEARCH

The quality of the local optima obtained by a local search method depends on the initial solution. As we can generate local optima with high variability, iterated local search[16] may be used to improve the quality of successive local optima. This kind of strategy has been applied first in Ref. [531] and then generalized in Refs [518,726].

In *multistart local search*, the initial solution is always chosen randomly and then is unrelated to the generated local optima. ILS improves the classical multistart local search by perturbing the local optima and reconsidering them as initial solutions.

Example 2.33 Multistart local search fails for the graph bisection problem. It has been shown that many (i.e., several thousand) random initial solutions are necessary to afford stable solution quality for the graph bisection problem for instances of size $n = 500$ [420]. The number of restarts grows rapidly with the size of instances n (number of nodes) and becomes unreasonable for instances of size $n = 100{,}000$, which arises in real-life problems such as VLSI design problems.

The central limit phenomenon in the landscape of an optimization problem implies that when the size of the problem becomes very large, local optima obtained using

[16]Also known as iterated descent, large-step Markov chains, and chained local optimization.

different random initial solutions are more or less similar in terms of quality [60]. Hence, simple multistart generally fails for very large problem instances [684].

ILS is based on a simple principle that has been used in many specific heuristics such as the iterated Lin–Kernigham heuristic for the traveling salesman problem [418] and the adaptive tabu search for the quadratic assignment problem [751]. First, a local search is applied to an initial solution. Then, at each iteration, a *perturbation* of the obtained local optima is carried out. Finally, a local search is applied to the perturbed solution. The generated solution is accepted as the new current solution under some conditions. This process iterates until a given stopping criterion. Algorithm 2.10 describes the ILS algorithm.

Algorithm 2.10 Template of the iterated local search algorithm.

$s_* =$ local search(s_0) ; /* Apply a given local search algorithm */
Repeat
$s' =$ Perturb (s_*, search history) ; /* Perturb the obtained local optima */
$s'_* =$ Local search (s') ; /* Apply local search on the perturbed solution */
$s_* =$ Accept (s_*, s'_*, search memory) ; /* Accepting criteria */
Until Stopping criteria
Output: Best solution found.

Three basic elements compose an ILS (Fig. 2.28):

- **Local search:** Any S-metaheuristic (deterministic or stochastic) can be used in the ILS framework such as a simple descent algorithm, a tabu search, or simulated annealing. The search procedure is treated as a black box (Fig. 2.29). In the

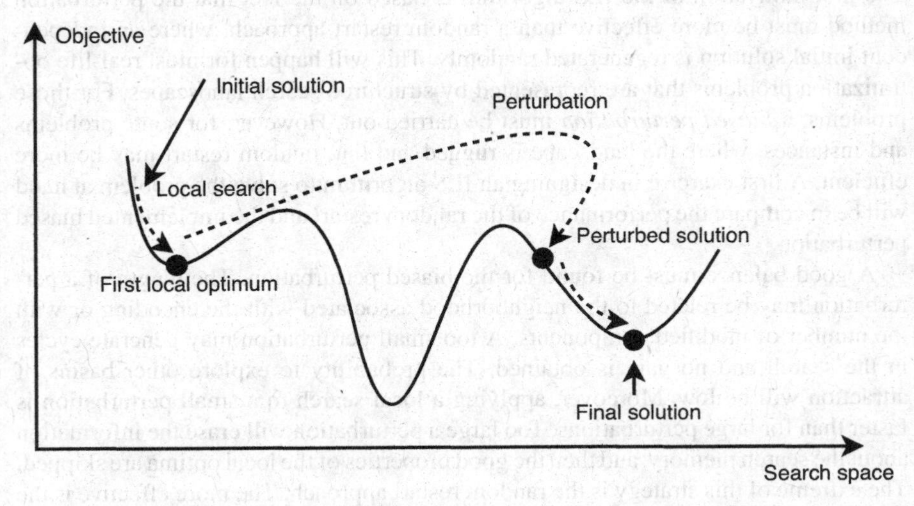

FIGURE 2.28 The principle of the iterated local search algorithm.

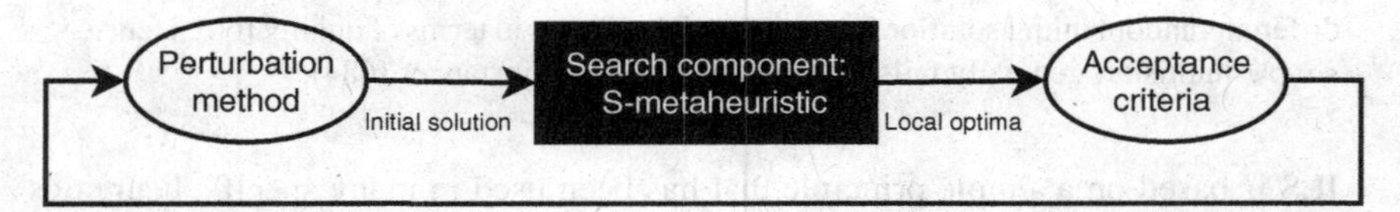

FIGURE 2.29 The search component is seen as a black box for the ILS algorithm.

literature, P-metaheuristics are not considered as candidates in the search procedure as they manipulate populations. However, some population-based metaheuristics integrate the concept of perturbation of the (sub)population to encourage the search diversification.

- **Perturbation Method.** The perturbation operator may be seen as a large random move of the current solution. The perturbation method should keep some part of the solution and perturb strongly another part of the solution to move hopefully to another basin of attraction.
- **Acceptance criteria.** The acceptance criterion defines the conditions the new local optima must satisfy to replace the current solution.

Once the S-metaheuristic involved in the ILS framework is specified, the design of ILS will depend mainly on the used perturbation method and the acceptance criterion. Many different designs may be defined according to various choices for implementing the perturbation method and the acceptance criterion.

2.6.1 Perturbation Method

The first motivation of the ILS algorithm is based on the fact that the perturbation method must be more effective than a random restart approach, where an independent initial solution is regenerated randomly. This will happen for most real-life optimization problems that are represented by structured search landscapes. For those problems, a *biased perturbation* must be carried out. However, for some problems and instances, where the landscape is rugged and flat, random restart may be more efficient. A first exercise in designing an ILS algorithm to solve the problem at hand will be to compare the performance of the random restart and the implemented biased perturbation.

A good balance must be found for the biased perturbation. The length of a perturbation may be related to the neighborhood associated with the encoding or with the number of modified components. A too small perturbation may generate cycles in the search and no gain is obtained. The probability to explore other basins of attraction will be low. Moreover, applying a local search to a small perturbation is faster than for large perturbations. Too large a perturbation will erase the information about the search memory, and then the good properties of the local optima are skipped. The extreme of this strategy is the random restart approach. The more effective is the

S-metaheuristic the larger the values of the perturbation must be. The optimal length depends mainly on the landscape structure of the optimization problem and must not exceed the correlation length (see Section 2.2.2). Even for a specific problem, it will depend on the instance at hand.

The move operator used in the perturbation may be of different nature from the neighborhood relation used in the local search procedure.

Many biased perturbation methods can be designed according to the following criteria:

- **Fixed or variable perturbations.** The length of the perturbations applied to a local optima may be defined as follows:
  - **Static.** The length is fixed *a priori* before the beginning of the ILS search.
  - **Dynamic.** The length of the perturbation is defined dynamically without taking into account the search memory.
  - **Adaptive.** In this strategy, the length of the perturbation is adapted during the search according to some informations about the search memory. Indeed, the optimal length will depend on the input instance and its structure. More information about the characteristics of the landscape may be extracted during the search.
- **Random or semideterministic perturbation.** The perturbation carried out on a solution may be a random one (memoryless) in which each move is generated randomly in the neighborhood. This leads to a Markovian chain. In semideterministic perturbations, the move is biased according to the memory of the search. For instance, the intensification and the diversification tasks of the tabu search algorithm using the medium-term memory and the long-term memory can be applied. The first approach is more popular in the literature, whereas the second approach needs more advanced and complex search mechanisms to be implemented.

2.6.2 Acceptance Criteria

The role of the acceptance criterion combined with the perturbation method is to control the classical trade-off between the intensification and the diversification tasks. The first extreme solution in terms of intensification is to accept only improving solutions in terms of the objective function (strong selection). The extreme solution in terms of diversification is to accept any solution without any regard to its quality (weak selection). Many acceptance criteria that balance the two goals may be applied:

- **Probabilistic acceptance criteria:** Many different probabilistic acceptance criteria can be found in the literature. For instance, the Boltzmann distribution of simulated annealing. In this case, a cooling schedule must be defined.

- **Deterministic acceptance criteria:** Some deterministic acceptance criteria may be inspired from the threshold accepting algorithms and the related algorithms, such as the great deluge and the record-to-record algorithms.

2.7 VARIABLE NEIGHBORHOOD SEARCH

Variable neighborhood search has been recently proposed by P. Hansen and N. Mladenovic [560]. The basic idea of VNS is to successively explore a set of predefined neighborhoods to provide a better solution. It explores either at random or systematically a set of neighborhoods to get different local optima and to escape from local optima. VNS exploits the fact that using various neighborhoods in local search may generate different local optima and that the global optima is a local optima for a given neighborhood (Fig. 2.30). Indeed, different neighborhoods generate different landscapes [428].

2.7.1 Variable Neighborhood Descent

The VNS algorithm is based on the variable neighborhood descent, which is a deterministic version of VNS. VND uses successive neighborhoods in descent to a local optimum. First, one has to define a set of neighborhood structures N_l ($l = 1, \ldots, l_{\max}$). Let N_1 be the first neighborhood to use and x the initial solution. If an improvement of the solution x in its current neighborhood $N_l(x)$ is not possible, the neighborhood structure is changed from N_l to N_{l+1}. If an improvement of the current solution x is found, the neighborhood structure returns to the first one $N_1(x)$ to restart the search (Fig. 2.31). This strategy will be effective if the different neighborhoods used are complementary in the sense that a local optima for a neighborhood N_i will not be a local optima in the neighborhood N_j. Algorithm 2.11 shows the VND algorithm.

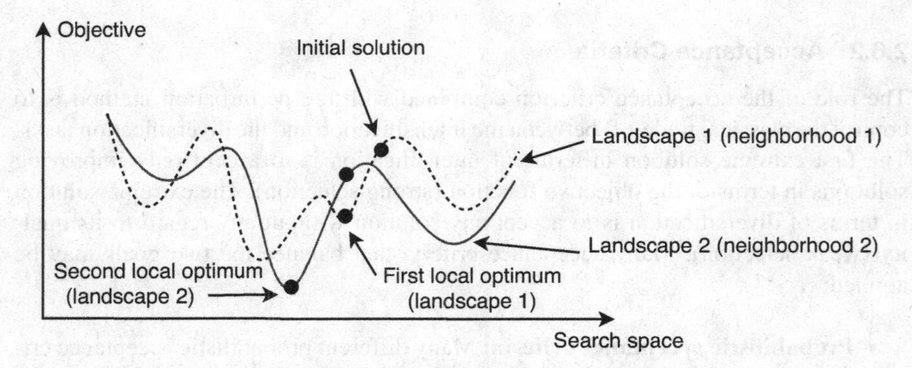

FIGURE 2.30 Variable neighborhood search using two neighborhoods. The first local optimum is obtained according to the neighborhood 1. According to the neighborhood 2, the second local optimum is obtained from the first local optimum.

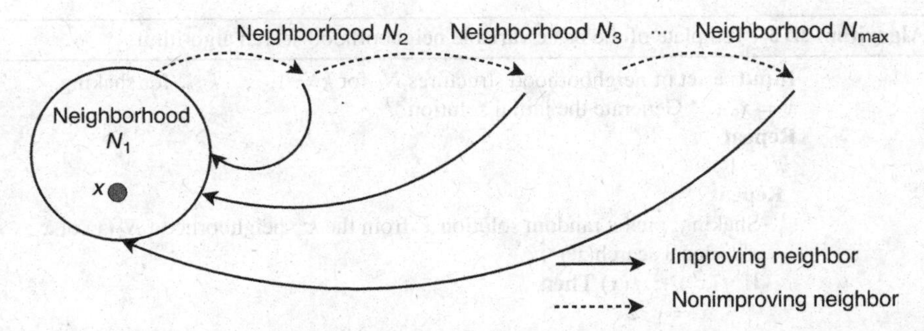

FIGURE 2.31 The principle of the variable neighborhood descent algorithm.

Algorithm 2.11 Template of the variable neighborhood descent algorithm.

Input: a set of neighborhood structures N_l for $l = 1, \ldots, l_{max}$.
$x = x_0$; /* Generate the initial solution */
$l = 1$;
While $l \leq l_{max}$ **Do**
  Find the best neighbor x' of x in $N_l(x)$;
  If $f(x') < f(x)$ **Then** $x = x'$; $l = 1$;
  Otherwise $l = l + 1$;
Output: Best found solution.

The design of the VND algorithm is mainly related to the selection of neighborhoods and the order of their application. The complexity of the neighborhoods in terms of their exploration and evaluation must be taken into account (see Section 2.1.1). The larger are the neighborhoods, the more time consuming is the VND algorithm. Concerning the application order, the most popular strategy is to rank the neighborhoods following the increasing order of their complexity (e.g., the size of the neighborhoods $|N_l(x)|$).

2.7.2 General Variable Neighborhood Search

VNS is a stochastic algorithm in which, first, a set of neighborhood structures N_k ($k = 1, \ldots, n$) are defined. Then, each iteration of the algorithm is composed of three steps: shaking, local search, and move. At each iteration, an initial solution is shaked from the current neighborhood N_k. For instance, a solution x' is generated randomly in the current neighborhood $N_k(x)$. A local search procedure is applied to the solution x' to generate the solution x''. The current solution is replaced by the new local optima x'' if and only if a better solution has been found (i.e., $f(x'') < f(x)$). The same search procedure is thus restarted from the solution x'' in the first neighborhood N_1. If no better solution is found (i.e., $f(x'') \geq f(x)$), the algorithm moves to the next neighborhood N_{k+1}, randomly generates a new solution in this neighborhood, and attempts to improve it. Let us notice that cycling is possible (i.e., $x'' = x$). Algorithm 2.12 presents the template of the basic VNS algorithm.

Algorithm 2.12 Template of the basic variable neighborhood search algorithm.

Input: a set of neighborhood structures N_k for $k = 1, \ldots, k_{max}$ for shaking.
$x = x_0$; /* Generate the initial solution */
Repeat
  $k = 1$;
  Repeat
    Shaking: pick a random solution x' from the kth neighborhood $N_k(x)$ of x ;
    x'' =local search(x') ;
    If $f(x'') < f(x)$ **Then**
      $x = x''$;
      Continue to search with N_1 ; $k = 1$;
    Otherwise k=k+1 ;
  Until $k = k_{max}$
Until Stopping criteria
Output: Best found solution.

A more general VNS algorithm where the simple local search procedure is replaced by the VND algorithm can be found in Algorithm 2.13.

Algorithm 2.13 Template of the general variable neighborhood search algorithm.

Input: a set of neighborhood structures N_k for $k = 1, \ldots, k_{max}$ for shaking.
  a set of neighborhood structures N_l for $k = 1, \ldots, l_{max}$ for local search.
$x = x_0$; /* Generate the initial solution */
Repeat
  For k=1 **To** k_{max} **Do**
  Shaking: pick a random solution x' from the kth neighborhood $N_k(x)$ of x ;
  Local search by VND ;
  For l=1 **To** l_{max} **Do**
    Find the best neighbor x'' of x' in $N_l(x')$;
    If $f(x'') < f(x')$ **Then** $x' = x''$; l=1 ;
    Otherwise l=l+1 ;
    Move or not:
    If local optimum is better than x **Then**
      $x = x''$;
      Continue to search with N_1 $(k = 1)$;
    Otherwise k=k+1 ;
Until Stopping criteria
Output: Best found solution.

In addition to the design of a simple local search (see Section 2.3) or a VND algorithm, the design of the VNS algorithm is mainly related to the selection of neighborhoods for the shaking phase. Usually, nested neighborhoods are used, where each neighborhood $N_k(x)$ contains the previous one $N_{k-1}(x)$:

$$N_1(x) \subset N_2(x) \subset \cdots \subset N_k(x), \forall x \in S$$

A compromise must be found between intensification of the search and its diversification through the distribution of work between the local search phase and the shaking phase. An increased work in the local search phase will generate better local optima (more intensification), whereas an increased work in the shaking phase will lead to potentially better regions of the search space (more diversification).

Example 2.34 Nested neighborhoods for the shaking phase. For many combinatorial optimization problems, there is a natural definition of nested neighborhoods. For instance, for routing problems such as the traveling salesman problem and the vehicle routing problem, the k-opt operator can be used for different values of k ($k = 2, 3, \ldots$).

As in local search, VNS requires a small number of parameters. For the shaking phase, the single parameter is the number of neighborhood structures k_{max}. If large values of k_{max} are used (i.e., very large neighborhoods are considered), VNS will be similar to a multistart local search. For small values of k_{max}, VNS will degenerate to a simple local search algorithm.

Example 2.35 Many neighborhoods in a real-life application. This example illustrates the use of many neighborhoods ($k = 9$) to solve a scheduling problem [26]. Many oil wells in onshore fields rely on artificial lift methods. Maintenance services such as cleaning, stimulation, and others are essential to these wells. They are performed by workover rigs. Workover rigs are available in a limited number with respect to the number of wells demanding service. The decision which workover rig should be sent to perform some maintenance services is based on factors such as the well production, the current location of the workover rig in relation to the demanding well, and the type of service to be performed. The problem of scheduling workover rigs consists in finding the best schedule S^* for the available m workover rigs, so as to minimize the production loss associated with the wells awaiting service. A schedule is represented by an ordered set of wells serviced by workover rigs. A variable neighborhood search metaheuristic has been proposed for this problem using the following neighborhoods in the shaking procedure:

1. Swapping of routes (SS) where the wells associated with two workover rigs are exchanged.
2. Swapping of wells from the same workover rig (SWSW) where two wells serviced by the same workover rig are exchanged.
3. Swapping of wells from different workover rigs (SWDW) where two wells affected by two different workover rigs are exchanged.
4. Add/drop (AD) where a well affected by a workover rig is reassigned to any position of the schedule of another workover rig.
5. Two applications of the SWSW transformation.
6. Two applications of the SWDW transformation.
7. Three applications of the SWDW transformation.

8. Successive application of two AD transformations.
9. Successive application of three AD transformations.

Many extensions of the GVNS algorithm have been proposed such as VNDS and SVNS [366]. These extensions are not related to the main concept of the VNS algorithm, which is the neighborhood change. In VNDS, the optimization problem is decomposed into subproblems, whereas in SVNS the algorithm addresses how to get out of large valleys (basin of attraction).

2.8 GUIDED LOCAL SEARCH

Guided local search is a deterministic S-metaheuristic that has been mainly applied to combinatorial optimization problems. Its adaptation to continuous optimization problems is straightforward given that GLS sits on top of a local search algorithm [805]. The basic principle of GLS is the dynamic changing of the objective function according to the already generated local optima [808]. The features of the obtained local optima are used to transform the objective function (Fig. 2.32). It allows the modification of the landscape structure to be explored by an S-metaheuristic to escape from the obtained local optima.

In GLS, a set of m features ft_i $(i = 1, \ldots, m)$ of a solution are defined. A solution feature defines a given characteristic of a solution regarding the optimization problem to solve. A cost c_i is associated to each feature. When trapped by a local optima, the algorithm will penalize solutions according to some selected features. To each feature i is associated a penalty p_i that represents the importance of the

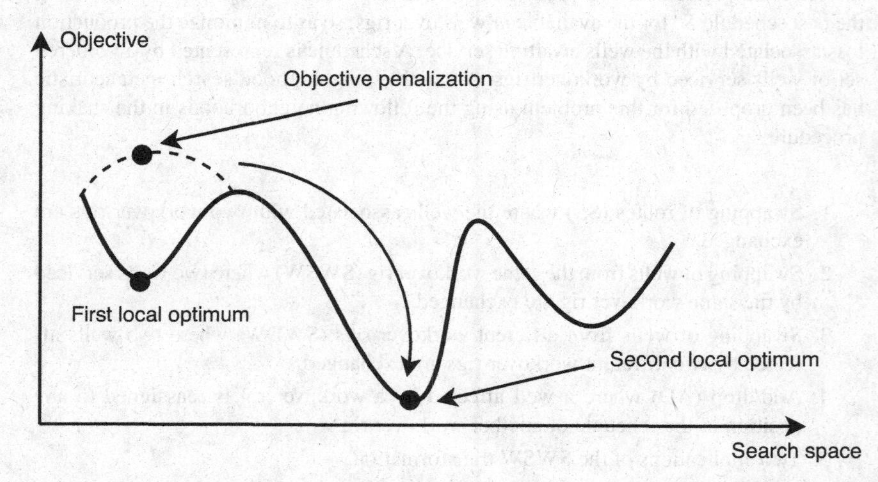

FIGURE 2.32 Guided local search penalizing the solutions found to escape from the local optimum. The objective function is increased according to the features of the obtained solutions.

feature. The objective function f associated with a solution s is then penalized as follows:

$$f'(s) = f(s) + \lambda \sum_{i=1}^{m} p_i I_i(s)$$

where λ represents the weights associated with different penalties and, $I_i(s)$ an indicator function that determines whether the feature ft_i is present in the solution s:

$$I_i(s) = \begin{cases} 1 & \text{if the feature } ft_i \in s \\ 0 & \text{otherwise} \end{cases}$$

All penalties p_i are initialized to 0.

Example 2.36 Identification of suitable features. The application of guided local search to a given optimization problem requires the identification of suitable features of the solutions. The choice of features depends mainly on the model associated with the optimization problem:

- **Routing problems:** In routing problems such as the traveling salesman problem and the vehicle routing problem, a feature may be associated with the presence of an edge (a, b) in the solution. The cost corresponds to the distance (or travel time) associated with the edge.
- **Assignment problems:** In assignment problems, such as the generalized assignment problem and location facility problems, a solution represents an assignment of a given number of objects to a set of locations. A feature may be represented by the pair (i, k), where i represents an object and k represents a specific location.

$$I_{ik}(s) = \begin{cases} 1 & \text{if } s(i) = k \\ 0 & \text{otherwise} \end{cases}$$

The cost will be handled by the cost c_{ik} in assigning the object i to the location k.

- **Satisfiability problems:** In satisfiability problems, such as the MAX-SAT, the objective is generally related to the number of violated constraints. A feature may be associated with each constraint. The cost of a feature will be related to the constraint violation.

The main question that arises is the way the features are selected and penalized. The goal is to penalize the features that are present in the obtained local optimum or unfavorable features. Given a local optima s^*, a utility u_i is then associated with each feature i as follows:

$$u_i(s^*) = I_i(s^*) \frac{c_i}{1 + p_i}$$

where c_i represents the cost of the feature i. For instance, if a given feature i is not present in the local optimum s^*, the utility of penalizing feature i is 0. Otherwise, the utility will be proportional to the cost c_i and inversely proportional to the penalty p_i. Then, the feature associated with the highest utility will be penalized. Its penalty is incremented by 1, and the scaling of the penalty is normalized by λ.

On one hand, GLS will intensify the search of promising regions defined by lower costs of the features. On the other hand, the GLS algorithm will diversify the search by penalizing the features of the generated local optima to avoid them. The common use of GLS approach is within a S-metaheuristic (local search) framework. However, an extension to P-metaheuristics can be easily envisaged [839]. In addition to penalizing the objective function, one may take into account the penalties to bias the recombination operators of P-metaheuristics (crossover, mutation, etc.). For instance, the encoded features that contribute more to the penalties will be more likely to be changed in the reproduction operators. For efficiency issues, the incremental evaluation of the objective function in local search (see Section 2.1.4) may be extended easily for the augmented objective functions in GLS. Algorithm 2.14 describes the template of the GLS algorithm.

Algorithm 2.14 Template of the guided local search algorithm.

Input: S-metaheuristic LS, λ, Features I, Costs c.
$s = s_0$ /* Generation of the initial solution */
$p_i = 0$ /* Penalties initialization */
Repeat
  Apply a S-metaheuristic LS ; /* Let s^* the final solution obtained */
  For each feature i of s^* **Do**
    $u_i = \frac{c_i}{1+p_i}$; /* Compute its utility */
  $u_j = max_{i=1,..m}(u_i)$; /* Compute the maximum utilities */
  $p_j = p_j + 1$; /* Change the objective function by penalizing the feature j */
Until Stopping criteria /* e.g. max number of iterations or time limit */
Output: Best solution found.

The input design parameters of the GLS algorithm are represented by the choice of the features (indicator function), their costs, and the λ parameter. The features and the costs are related to the optimization problem at hand. The literature suggests that the performance of the algorithm is not very sensitive to the value of λ [556]. Large values of λ will encourage the diversification, while small values of λ will intensify the search around the local optima. A common strategy to initialize λ consists in dividing the value of the objective function of the local optimum by the average number of features present in the local optimum or near the average change of the objective function in the neighborhood. The more the S-metaheuristic used is effective, the less is the value of the λ parameter. The penalty needed to escape from local optima must decrease with the increase of the effectiveness of the S-metaheuristic used within GLS.

Example 2.37 Guided local search for the symmetric TSP. A solution of the TSP is encoded by a permutation s. The original objective function consists in minimizing the total distance:

$$f(s) = \sum_{i=1}^{n} d_{i,s(i)}$$

where n represents the number of cities. As mentioned above, the features of the TSP may be represented by the edges composing a tour. Then, the indication of the presence of a feature may be represented as follows:

$$I_{(i,j)}(s) = \begin{cases} 1 & \text{if edge } (i, j) \in s \\ 0 & \text{otherwise} \end{cases}$$

The cost associated with an edge (i, j) is the distance d_{ij}. Penalties are represented by a matrix $P_{n,n}$, where p_{ij} represents the penalty of the edge (i, j). All the elements of the matrix P are initialized to 0. The augmented objective function of the problem is given by

$$f'(s) = \sum_{i=1}^{n} d_{i,s(i)} + \lambda p_{i,s(i)}$$

The utility function is defined as follows:

$$u(s^*, (i, j)) = I_{(i,j)}(s) \frac{d_{ij}}{1 + p_{ij}}$$

2.9 OTHER SINGLE-SOLUTION BASED METAHEURISTICS

Some existing S-metaheuristics use other strategies to escape from local optima. Search space smoothing and noisy methods are based on the transformation of the landscape of the problem by changing the input data associated with the problem altering the objective function.

2.9.1 Smoothing Methods

Search space smoothing consists in modifying the landscape of the target optimization problem [326,343]. The smoothing of the landscape associated with the problem

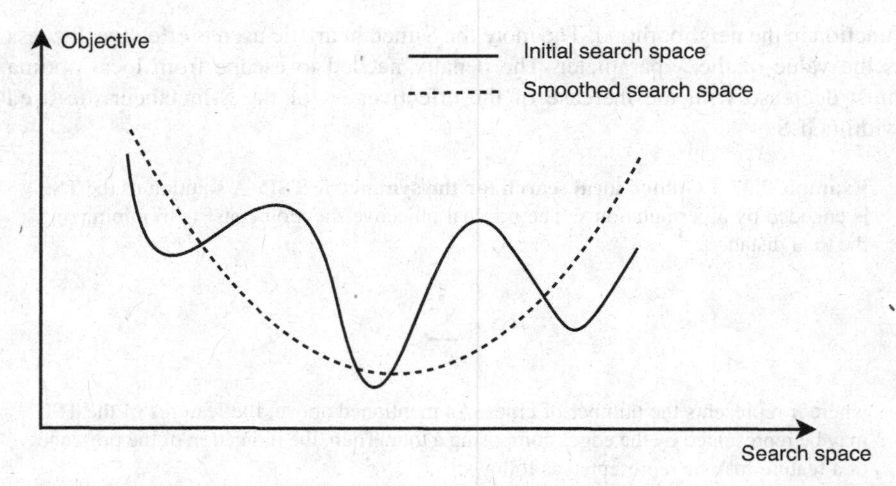

FIGURE 2.33 Search space smoothing that results in an easiest problem to solve. The smoothed landscape has less local optima than the original one.

reduces the number of local optima and the depth of the basins of attraction without changing the location region of the global optimum of the original optimization problem (Fig. 2.33). The search space associated with the landscape remains unchanged, and only the objective function is modified. Once the landscape is smoothed by "hiding" some local optima, any S-metaheuristic (or even a P-metaheuristic) can be used in conjunction with the smoothing technique.

The main idea of the smoothing approach is the following: given a problem instance in a parameter space, the approach will transform the problem into a sequence of successive problem instances with different associated landscapes. Initially, the most simplified smoothed instance of the problem is solved. A local search is then applied. The probability to be trapped by a local optima is minimized. In the ideal case, there is only one local optimum that corresponds to the global optimum (Fig. 2.34). The less the number of local optima, the more efficient a S-metaheuristic. Then, a more complicated problem instance with a rougher landscape is generated. It takes the solution of the previously solved problem as an initial solution and further improves that solution. The solutions of smoothed landscapes are used to guide the search in more rugged landscapes. Any S-metaheuristic can be used in conjunction with the smoothing operation. The last step of the approach consists in solving the original problem.

If the global minimum in the smoothed landscape is used as the initial solution in the original space (see Fig. 2.34), the probability to find the global optimum in the original space may increase considerably.

The main design question concerns the smoothing operation. There are many strategies to smooth a landscape. The smoothing factor α is used to characterize the strength of a smoothing operation. Using different levels of strength will generate various degrees of smoothness. When $\alpha = 1$, there is no smoothing operation, and the landscape is the same as the original one. A smoothing operation is carried out if $\alpha > 1$. The larger the smoothing factor ($\alpha >> 1$), the stronger a smoothing operation and more

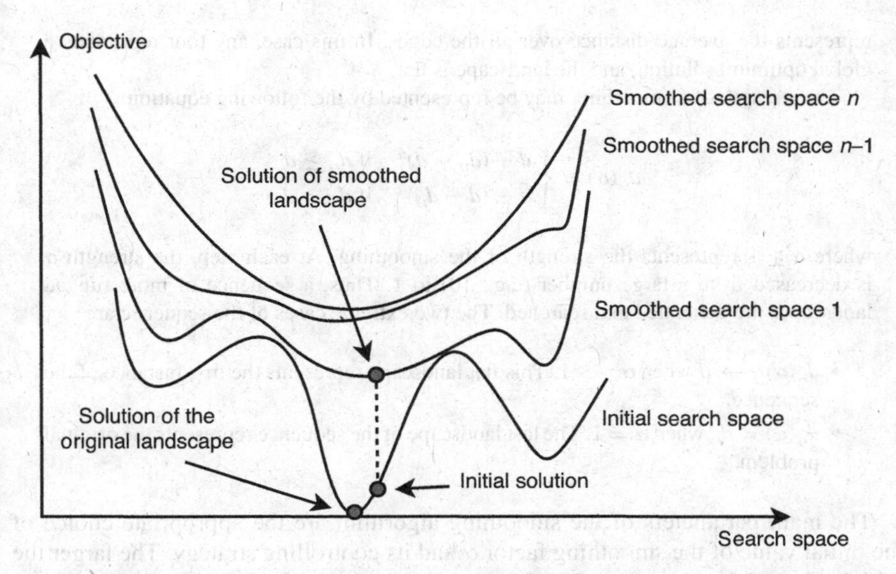

FIGURE 2.34 Successive smoothing of the landscape. The solution found at the step i will guide the search at the iteration $i+1$ in a more rugged landscape.

flat a landscape. Algorithm 2.15 illustrates the principles of the smoothing algorithm. The original idea of the algorithm relies on the reduced complexity of solving smoothing instances of the original problem and the effectiveness of using intermediate local optima solutions to guide the search toward increasingly complex instances.

Algorithm 2.15 Template of the smoothing algorithm.

Input: S-metaheuristic LS, α_0, Instance I.
$s = s_0$; /* Generation of the initial solution */
$\alpha = \alpha_0$; /* Initialization of the smoothing factor */
Repeat
  $I = I(\alpha)$; /* Smoothing operation of the instance I */
  $s = LS(s, I)$; /* Search using the instance I and the initial solution s */
  $\alpha = g(\alpha)$; /* Reduce the smoothing factor, e.g. $\alpha = \alpha - 1$ */
Until $\alpha < 1$ /* Original problem */
Output: Best solution found.

Example 2.38 Smoothing operation for the TSP. The smoothing strategy has been applied successfully to many discrete optimization problems [326]. In the case of the TSP, the smoothing operation is based on the fact that a trivial case for the TSP is the one where all the distances between cities are equal: $d_{ij} = \bar{d}, \forall i, j$, where

$$\bar{d} = \frac{1}{n(n-1)} \sum_{i \neq j} d_{ij}$$

represents the average distance over all the edges. In this case, any tour represents a global optimum solution, and the landscape is flat.

The strength of a smoothing may be represented by the following equation:

$$d_{ij}(\alpha) = \begin{cases} \bar{d} + (d_{ij} - \bar{d})^{\alpha} & \text{if } d_{ij} \geq \bar{d} \\ \bar{d} - (\bar{d} - d_{ij})^{\alpha} & \text{if } d_{ij} < \bar{d} \end{cases}$$

where $\alpha \geq 1$ represents the strength of the smoothing. At each step, the strength α is decreased from a large number (e.g., 10) to 1. Thus, a sequence of more rugged landscapes are generated and searched. The two extreme cases of the sequence are

- $d_{ij}(\alpha) \longrightarrow \bar{d}$ when $\alpha >> 1$. This flat landscape represents the first instance of the sequence.
- $d_{ij}(\alpha) = d_{ij}$ when $\alpha = 1$. The last landscape of the sequence represents the original problem.

The main parameters of the smoothing algorithm are the appropriate choice of the initial value of the smoothing factor α and its controlling strategy. The larger the initial value of the smoothing factor α_0, the more time consuming the algorithm.

Some meta-modeling strategies (see Section 1.4.2.5) may also be used to approximate and smooth the objective function such as Gaussian kernels [833] and global polynomial models [505].

2.9.2 Noisy Method

The noisy method is another S-metaheuristic algorithm that is based on the landscape perturbation of the problem to solve [124]. Instead of taking the original data into account directly, the NM considers that they are the outcomes of a series of fluctuating data converging toward the original ones. Some random noise is added to the objective function f. At each iteration of the search, the noise is reduced. For instance, the noise is initially randomly chosen into an interval $[-r, +r]$. The range of the interval r decreases during the search process until a value of 0. Different ways may be used to decrease the noise rate r.

The noising method can be considered as a succession of local searches applied to perturbed data. The data parameters are replaced by "noised" data. For instance, if the input data are completely represented by a graph $G = (V, E)$ and the considered parameters are the weights w_{ij} of the edges (i, j), the noising method will replace those values as follows:

$$w_{ij}^{\text{noised}} = w_{ij} + \rho_{ij}$$

where ρ_{ij} is a noise. Then, a local search procedure is applied to the noised graph. Once a local optimum is obtained, the noise rate r is decreased by decreasing the standard deviation or the absolute value of the mean. The search terminates when the noise is low enough. The extreme stopping creterion is when the mean and the standard deviation of the noise are equal to 0. Contrary to traditional S-metaheuristics, an improving move may be rejected in the noising algorithm. As in simulated annealing, for instance, a nonimproving move may be accepted.

A more general noising method considers the original data, but the noise is considered in computing the incremental evaluation of the neighbor s' obtained by a transformation carried on the current solution s. Instead of considering the original variation $\Delta(s, s')$, a noised variation $\Delta_{\text{noised}}(s, s')$ is considered by adding a noise to $\Delta(s, s')$: $\Delta_{\text{noised}}(s, s') = \Delta(s, s') + \rho_k$, where ρ_k is a noise changing at each iteration k and depending on the noise rate. This second noising method is a more general one in the sense that the first one may be reduced to this method by summing up the impact of the noises added to the data. The main difference between the two strategies is that randomness does not occur in the same way. In the first noising method, after fixing the noises affecting the original data, the local search process can be deterministic, while in the second noising method, randomness takes place at each iteration of the local search. Algorithm 2.16 shows the general template of the noising algorithm. Noise is added to the data or the variations of the objective function in an absolute or relative way.

Algorithm 2.16 Template of the noising method.

Input: r.
$s = s_0$; /* Generation of the initial solution */
$r = r_{max}$; /* Initialization of the noising factor */
Repeat
  $\Delta_{noised}(s, s') = \Delta(s, s') + r$; /* Noising operation of f */
  $s = LS(s, r)$; /* Search using the noising factor r */
  $r = g(r)$; /* Reduce the noising factor */
Until $r = r_{min}$ /* Original problem */
Output: Best solution found.

The are different ways to add noise to data. The choice of the noising method scheme may have a great impact on the performance of the noising algorithm. A noise is a value taken by a certain random variable following a given probability distribution (e.g., a uniform law or a Gaussian one). The mean and the standard deviation of this probability distribution converge toward 0, and the standard deviation decreases during the search process. The added noise is progressively reduced and becomes nonexistent. The noise rate r introduced characterizes the "strength" of the noise for a chosen probability distribution. Then the decreasing of the noise is obtained by decreasing the noise rate r.

For other S-metaheuristics, some parameters must be tuned for the noising method:

- **Noise rate:** The extremal values of the noise rate r_{max} and r_{min} depend on the data. It is always possible to choose $r_{\text{min}} = 0$.
- **Decreasing noise rate:** The geometrical decreasing function is usually used ($r = r\alpha$ with $\alpha \in]0, 1[$). More advanced noising methods may be applied [125] (Fig. 2.35).

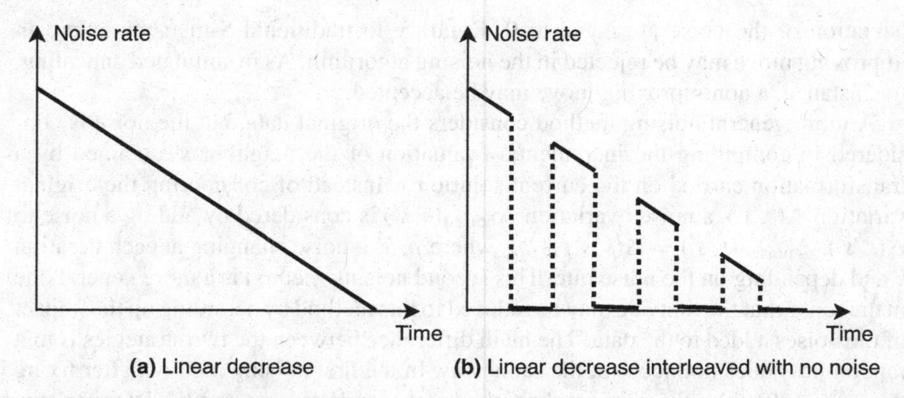

FIGURE 2.35 Different noising methods. (a) The noise rate is decreased linearly down to 0. (b) The noise decreases linearly, but "unperturbed" local searches are applied from time to time.

- **Probability distribution:** In adding the noise, it is possible to apply different probability distributions. In most of the cases, uniform distribution is applied. The noise added could be nonuniform and even close to a Gaussian distribution. The efficiency of a given probability distribution depends on the problem to solve. There is no absolute best probability distribution for all problems.

Example 2.39 Noising algorithm for graph partitioning. Given a complete nonoriented graph $G = (V, E)$ weighted by positive or negative integers, find a partition of V into subsets of which the number is not fixed. The objective is to minimize the sum of the weights of edges with their two extremities in the same subset. A noising method where the noise is randomly added to the weights of the edges, with a uniform distribution into $[-r, +r]$ and a arithmetical decrease of the noise rate r, may be applied [124]. Noised local searches are alternated with unnoised ones. There is a periodical restart of the current solution. The edges have weights in the range $[-w_{\max}, w_{\max}]$. The neighborhood consists in transferring a vertex from the subset to which it currently belongs to another one, which can be empty if we want to create a new subset (if a solution is coded by associating with each vertex the number of the subset to which it belongs, then this neighborhood is a substitution). The examination of the neighborhood for the local search (the noised ones as well as the unnoised ones) is systematic. The best tuning of the parameters depends on the studied graphs: the maximum rate noise $r_{\max}$ is chosen between $0.8w_{\max}$ and $0.95w_{\max}$ and the minimum rate noise $r_{\min}$ is chosen between $0.15w_{\max}$ and $0.5w_{\max}$. For instance, using $0.8w_{\max}$ for $r_{\max}$ and $0.4w_{\max}$ for $r_{\min}$, good results have been obtained. Of course, the total number of iterations depends on the search time that the user wishes to spend to solve the problem. For the frequency of the restart, if α denotes the number of pairs (noised local search, unnoised local search) applied between two restarts and β the number of restarts (so the total number of noised local searches and unnoised ones is equal to $\alpha\beta$), then a good tuning of α and β was to choose α between β and 2β.

Example 2.40 Different noising methods for a clique partitioning problem. Let us consider the clique partitioning problem of Example 2.22. Different noising methods may be applied to the weights of the input graph or on incremental evaluation of the objective function [125]:

- **Uniform noise:** For a node i and for each current class C, $W_{\text{noised}}(i, C)$ is given by the sum of $W(i, C)$ and a noise $\rho \times$ rate where ρ is randomly picked in the interval $[-1, 1]$ with a uniform law.

$$W_{\text{noised}}(i, C) = W(i, C) + \rho \times \text{rate}$$

- **Logarithmic noise:** For a node i and for each current class C, the added noise will be

$$W_{\text{noised}}(i, C) = W(i, C) + \log(\rho) \times \text{rate}$$

  where ρ is picked with a uniform random law in the interval $]0, 1]$.

- **Relative uniform noise:** Here, the noise is added to the weights of the input graph. Then, for a vertex i and for each current class C, we have

$$W_{\text{noised}}(i, C) = \sum_{j \in C, i \neq j} w(i, j) \times (1 + \rho_j \times \text{rate})$$

  where ρ_j is chosen with a uniform random law in the interval $[-1, 1]$.

- **Forgotten vertices noise:** In this unusual noising method, some selected nodes of the graph will not participate in the cyclic exploration of the neighborhood of a solution s. At each neighborhood exploration, a given percentage (rate) of vertices of the input graph G are removed from the exploration. The best perturbed class for a forgotten node is not searched. For a nonforgotten node, the following value is minimized to find the best class for a nonforgotten node:

$$W_{\text{noised}}(i, C) = \sum_{j \in C, i \neq j, j \textbf{ nonforgotten}} w(i, j)$$

- **Forgotten edge noise:** Instead of deleting nodes, this noised method forgets some edges of the graph. The rate ρ denotes the probability that the edge (i, j) is forgotten (random uniform law). For each node i and for each current class C of the current solution,

$$W_{\text{noised}}(i, C) = \sum_{j \in C, i \neq j, (i,j) \textbf{ nonforgotten}} w(i, j)$$

2.9.3 GRASP

The GRASP metaheuristic is an iterative greedy heuristic to solve combinatorial optimization problems. It was introduced in 1989 [255]. Each iteration of the GRASP algorithm contains two steps: construction and local search [256]. In the construction step, a feasible solution is built using a randomized greedy algorithm, while in the next step a local search heuristic is applied from the constructed solution. A similar idea, known as the *semigreedy heuristic*, was presented in 1987, where a multistart greedy approach is proposed but without the use of local search [367]. The greedy algorithm must be randomized to be able to generate various solutions. Otherwise, the local search procedure can be applied only once. This schema is repeated until a given number of iterations and the best found solution are kept as the final result. We notice that the iterations are completely independent, and so there is no search memory. This approach is efficient if the constructive heuristic samples different promising regions of the search space that makes the different local searches generating different local optima of "good" quality. Algorithm 2.17 resumes the template for the GRASP algorithm. The *seed* is used as the initial seed for the pseudorandom number generator.

Algorithm 2.17 Template of the greedy randomized adaptive search procedure.

```
Input: Number of iterations.
Repeat
    s = Random-Greedy(seed) ; /* apply a randomized greedy heuristic */
    s' = Local - Search(s) ; /* apply a local search algorithm to the solution */
Until Stopping criteria /* e.g. a given number of iterations */
Output: Best solution found.
```

The main design questions for GRASP are the greedy construction and the local search procedures:

- **Greedy construction:** In the constructive heuristic, as mentioned in Section 1.3.4, at each iteration the elements that can be included in the partial solution are ordered in the list (decreasing values) using the local heuristic. From this list, a subset is generated that represents the *restricted candidate list*. The RCL list is the key component of the GRASP metaheuristic. It represents the probabilistic aspect of the metaheuristic.

  The restriction criteria may depend on

  - **Cardinality-based criteria:** In this case, the RCL list is made of the p best elements in terms of the incremental cost, where the parameter p represents the maximum number of elements in the list.
  - **Value-based criteria:** It is the most commonly used strategy [649]. It consists in selecting the solutions that are better than a given threshold value. Let $c^{\max}$ (resp. $c^{\min}$) be the maximum (resp. the minimum) values for the set of elements

using the local heuristic. The list RCL may be constructed as follows:

$$\{e_i/c_i \leq c^{\min} + \alpha(c^{\max} - c^{\min})\}$$

where α is a user-defined parameter.

At each iteration, a random element is picked from the list RCL. Once an element is incorporated in the partial solution, the RCL list is updated. To update the RCL list, the incremental costs $c'(e)$ of the elements e composing the RCL list must be reevaluated. Algorithm 2.18 shows the template of the randomized part of the GRASP metaheuristic.

Algorithm 2.18 Template of the greedy randomized algorithm.

$s = \{\}$; /* Initial solution (null) */
Evaluate the incremental costs of all candidate elements ;
Repeat
  Build the restricted candidate list RCL ;
  /* select a random element from the list RCL */
  e_i = Random-Selection(RCL) ;
  If $s \cup e_i \in F$ **Then** /* Test the feasibility of the solution */
  $s = s \cup e_i$;
  Reevaluate the incremental costs of candidate elements ;
Until Complete solution found.

- **Local search:** Since the solutions found by the construction procedure are not guaranteed to be local optima, it is beneficial to carry out a local search step in which the constructed solution is improved. Traditionally, a simple local search algorithm is applied. Nevertheless, any S-metaheuristic can be used: tabu search, simulated annealing, noisy method, and so on.

Example 2.41 GRASP for the capacitated minimum spanning tree problem. The capacitated minimum spanning tree problem is a key problem in network design such as in telecommunication and transportation applications. It consists in connecting a set of customer nodes to a root node through a minimum cost connected network subjected to a capacity constraint on all connections. Given a connected undirected graph $G = (V, E)$, where $V = \{v_1, \ldots, v_n\}$ represents the set of vertices and E is the set of edges. Each node (resp. edge) is weighted by nonnegative integers b_i (resp. c_{ij}). The weight c_{ij} represents the cost of the edge, whereas b_i represents the flow of the node. Given an integer Q denoting the capacity that must not be exceeded by any edge and a node $r \in V$ defining the sink node (concentrator or central node) to which all the flows go. The CMST consists of finding a minimum spanning tree T of G that minimizes the total cost of edges and satisfies the following constraint: the sum of the weights of vertices in each connected component of the graph induced in T by $V - \{r\}$ is less than or equal to Q; that is, for each subtree originated from the root r, the total flow does not exceed the link capacity C.

The greedy heuristic is based on the well-known saving heuristic EW of Esau and Williams [246]. This greedy heuristic is popular and widely used into metaheuristics to solve constrained spanning tree problems. Initially, every node is connected directly to the sink node. Hence, there are as many subtrees as the number of nodes. The iteration step consists of selecting the two nodes i and j belonging to two different subtrees and providing the largest saving and satisfying the capacity constraint. The saving is defined as

$$s_{ij} = (G_i + G_j) - (G_i + c_{ij}) = G_j - c_{ij}$$

where G_i and G_j are the costs of the links connecting the subtrees associated with vertices i and j to the sink node. Since the nodes of V_j have an edge (r, i) as a new link with connection cost G_i, the savings can be computed as follows:

$$s_{kl} = \begin{cases} s_{kl} - G_j + G_i & \text{for } k \in V \backslash (V_i \cup V_j \cup r) \text{ and } l \in V_j \\ 0 & \text{for } k, l \in V_j \text{ and } k \neq l \\ s_{kl} & \text{otherwise} \end{cases}$$

The algorithm stops when there is no more pair of nodes with positive saving or not exceeding the capacity constraint. The time complexity of the algorithm is $O(n^2 \log(n))$, where n is the number of nodes of the graph G $(n = |V|)$. Figure 2.36 illustrates the application of the saving heuristic EW to a given graph.

Let C be the set of all candidate edges, that is, edges satisfying the capacity constraint and belonging to two different subtrees. The saving associated with candidate edges is used to randomize the heuristic. The RCL list associated with the randomized greedy

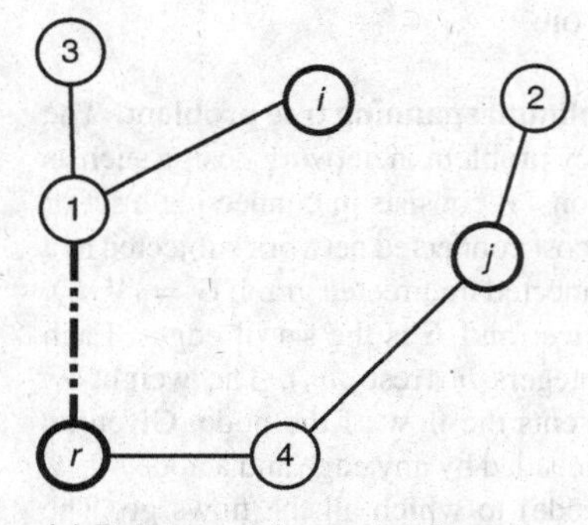

(a) Before merging nodes i and j

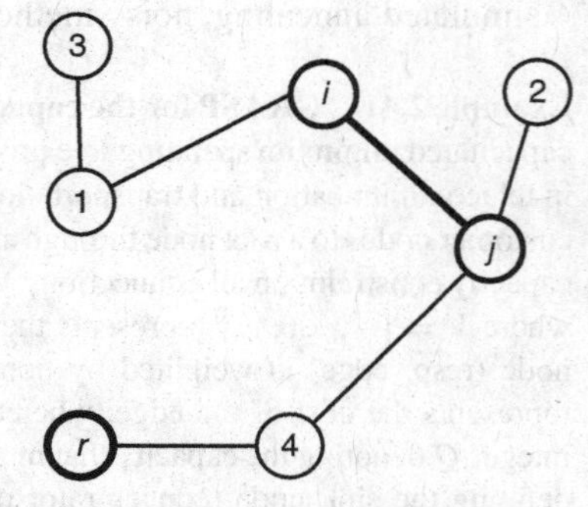

(b) After merging nodes i and j

FIGURE 2.36 An iteration of the saving heuristic EW. (a) We have two subtrees of vertices $\{1, i, 3\}$ and $\{2, j, 4\}$. We suppose that s_{ij} is the largest saving so that the total flow of vertices $\{1, 2, 3, 4, i, j\}$ does not exceed the capacity Q. (b) Represents the new solution after merging the nodes i and j.

heuristic is defined as follows [190]:

$$\mathrm{RCL} = \{(i, j) \in C / s_{ij} > s^{\min} + \alpha \cdot (s^{\max} - s^{\min})\}$$

where $s^{\min}$ (resp. $s^{\max}$) represents the minimum (resp. maximum) saving of the candidate edges (i, j) ($(i, j) \in C$). Then, any local search algorithm may be applied to the constructed solution.

The main parameter for GRASP is α parameter ($\alpha \in [0, 1]$). It defines the compromise between search exploitation (intensification using more greediness) and search exploration (diversification using more randomness). In fact, small values for α allow larger values for the average quality of the RCL list elements and then encourage exploitation. When $\alpha = 1$, the algorithm is a deterministic greedy algorithm. When $\alpha = 0$, the algorithm is a random greedy algorithm. Smaller values for α generate more elements in the list RCL and then encourage diversification. Many experimental results show a Gaussian normal distribution for the obtained solutions. Figure 2.37 shows the distribution of the constructed solutions as a function of α parameter [649]. The smaller is the α parameter, the larger is the variance between the solutions of the construction phase and worst is the average quality of solutions.

The performance of the GRASP metaheuristic is very sensitive to α parameter. Since this parameter is critical, many strategies may be applied for its initialization:

- **Static:** In the static strategy, the value of α is initialized to a constant value before the search. The commonly used range is naturally closer to the greedy choice: [0.7, 0.9].

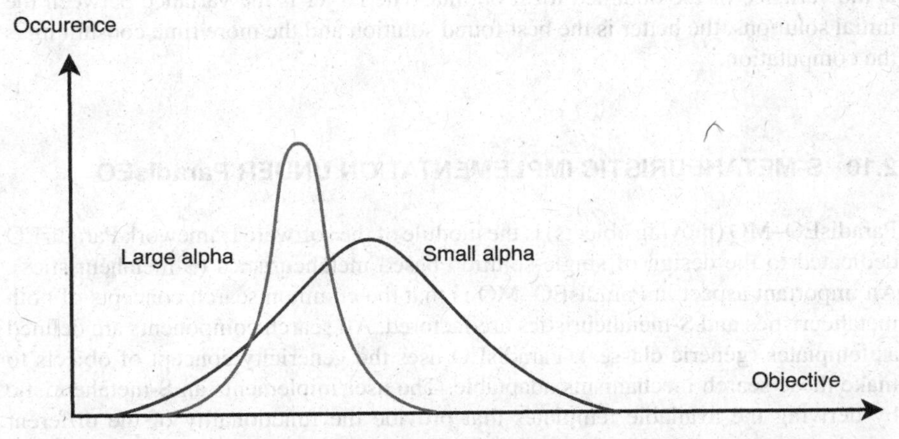

FIGURE 2.37 The distribution of the obtained local optima as a function of α parameter. We suppose a minimization problem in which small values of α tend to a purely random greedy search.

- **Dynamic:** The dynamic strategy often initializes the α value to a random value at each iteration of the GRASP metaheuristic. For instance, a uniform distribution may be used in the range $[0.5, 0.9]$, or a decreasing nonuniform distribution.
- **Adaptive:** In this strategy, the value of α is self-tuned. The value is updated automatically during the search function of the memory of the search.

Example 2.42 Self-tuning in reactive GRASP. In reactive GRASP, the value of the parameter α is periodically updated according to the quality of the obtained solutions [623]. At each iteration, the parameter value is selected from a discrete set of possible values $\Psi = \{\alpha_1, \ldots, \alpha_m\}$. The probability associated with each α_i is initialized to a same value $p_i = 1/m, i \in [1, \ldots, m]$. The adaptive initialization in the reactive GRASP consists in updating these probabilities according to the quality of solutions obtained for each α_i. Let z^* be the incumbent solution and A_i the average value of all solutions found using $\alpha = \alpha_i$. Then, the probability p_i for each value of α is updated as follows:

$$p_i = \frac{q_i}{\sum_{j=1}^{m} q_j}, \quad i \in [1, \ldots, m]$$

where $q_j = z^*/A_i$. Hence, larger values of p_i correspond to more suitable values for the parameter α_i.

In addition to the parameters associated with the randomized greedy heuristic, the GRASP metaheuristic will inherit the parameters of the embedded S-metaheuristic. The larger is the variance between the solutions of the construction phase, the larger is the variance of the obtained local optima. The larger is the variance between the initial solutions, the better is the best found solution and the more time consuming is the computation.

2.10 S-METAHEURISTIC IMPLEMENTATION UNDER ParadisEO

ParadisEO–MO (moving objects) is the module of the software framework ParadisEO dedicated to the design of single-solution based metaheuristics (S-metaheuristics). An important aspect in ParadisEO–MO is that the common search concepts of both metaheuristics and S-metaheuristics are factored. All search components are defined as templates (generic classes). ParadisEO uses the genericity concept of objects to make those search mechanisms adaptable. The user implements an S-metaheuristic by deriving the available templates that provide the functionality of the different search components: problem-specific templates (e.g., objective function, representation) and problem-independent templates (e.g., neighbor selection, cooling schedule, and stopping criteria).

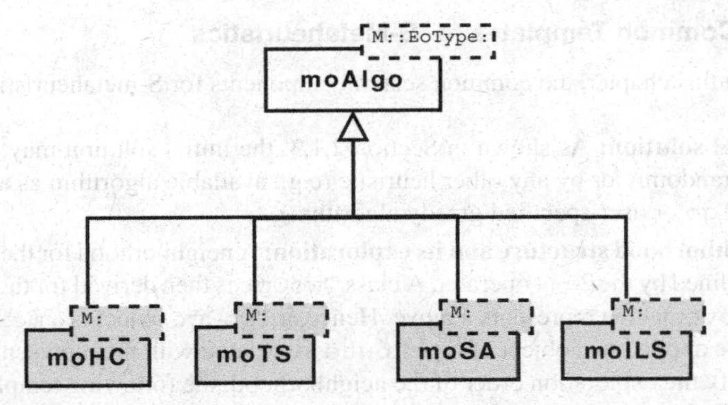

FIGURE 2.38 UML diagram of the `moAlgo` template representing an S-metaheuristic such as hill climbing, tabu search, simulated annealing, iterated local search.

In ParadisEO–MO, the `moAlgo` template represents an S-metaheuristic such as local search (hill climbing), tabu search, simulated annealing, and iterated local search (Fig. 2.38).

Figure 2.43 shows the common concepts and relationships in single-solution based metaheuristics. Hence, most of the search components will be reused by different S-metaheuristics. The aim of this section is to show not only the easy way to design an S-metaheuristic but also the high flexibility to transform an S-metaheuristic to another one reusing most of the design and implementation work. The different implementations are illustrated using the symmetric TSP problem.

2.10.1 Common Templates for Metaheuristics

As seen in Chapter 1, the common search components that have to be designed for any metaheuristic are

- **Objective function:** The objective function is associated with the template `eoEvalFunc`, which is a problem-specific template. For the TSP problem, it corresponds to the total distance. It is straightforward to implement.
- **Representation of solutions:** The encoding used for the TSP is based on permutations. Hence, an object `Route` is designed to deal with this structure. It corresponds to a permutation vector and its associated fitness. This is also a problem-specific template. However, one can reuse some popular representations. In fact, in ParadisEO, the template associated with the encoding of solutions defines, for instance, the binary, discrete vector, real vectors, and trees. Those encodings may be reused to solve an optimization problem.
- **Stopping criteria:** The stopping criteria for hill climbing are implicit, that is, the algorithm stops when a local optimal solution is found. Then there is nothing to specify.

2.10.2 Common Templates for S-Metaheuristics

As seen in this chapter, the common search components for S-metaheuristics are

- **Initial solution:** As shown in Section 2.1.3, the initial solution may be generated randomly or by any other heuristic (e.g., available algorithm as a template `moAlgo` or user-specified greedy algorithm).
- **Neighborhood structure and its exploration:** A neighborhood for the TSP may be defined by the 2-opt operator. A class `TwoOpt` is then derived for the template `moMove`, which represents a move. Hence, a `TwoOpt` object is a `moMove` that can be applied to a object of type `Route` associated with the representation. To specify the exploration order of the neighborhood, the following templates have to defined:
  - **First move:** The template `moMoveInit` defines the initial move to apply. The corresponding class in our example is

```
class TwoOptInit : public moMoveInit <TwoOpt>
```

  - **Next move:** The template `moNextMove` defines the next move to apply. This template has also to check the end of the exploration.
- **Incremental evaluation function:** The incremental objective function is associated with the template `moIncrEval`. The user must derive this template to implement the function. According to a solution and a move, this template is able to compute the fitness of the corresponding neighbor with a higher efficiency.

2.10.3 Local Search Template

Figure 2.39 shows the architecture of the hill-climbing template `moHC`. Once the common templates for all metaheuristics and S-metaheuristics are defined, `only one` search component is left, the neighbor selection strategy. The template associated with the selection strategy of the next neighbor is `moMoveselect`. The usual standard strategies are available in the template (see Section 2.3.1). The user has to choose one of them:[17]

- **Best improvement** which corresponds to `moBestImprSelect` template.
- **First improvement** which corresponds to `moFirstImprSelect` template.
- **Random improvement** which corresponds to `moRandImprSelect` template.

From those defined templates, building a hill-climbing algorithm is completely done. The detailed description of the program associated with a hill-climbing algorithm using the defined search components and their associated templates is as follows:

[17] As the framework is a white box, the user can also design other selection strategies.

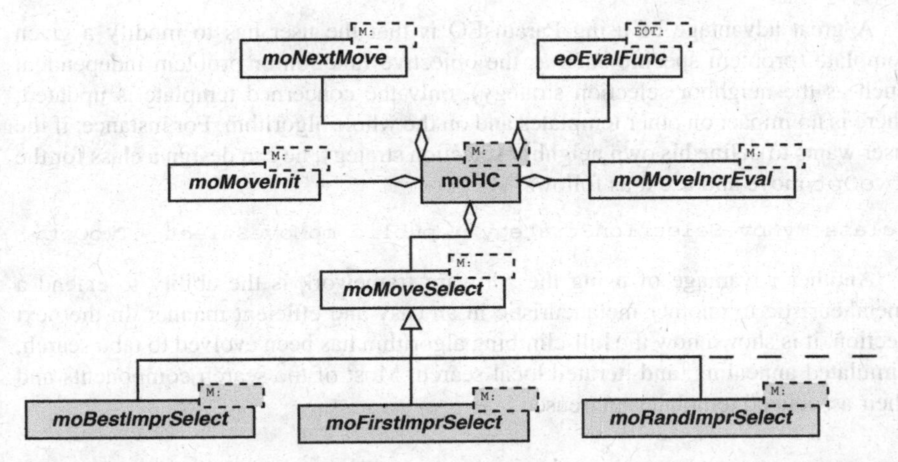

FIGURE 2.39 UML diagram of the hill-climbing template moHC. The templates moEvalFunc, moNextMove, moMoveIncrEval, and moMoveInit are problem specific and need to be completed by the user. The template moMoveSelect is problem independent, that is, "plug and play" that can be completely reused.

```
...
//An initial solution.
Route route;
//An eoInit object (see ParadisEO-EO).
RouteInit route_init;
//Initialization.
route_init(route);
//The eoEvalFunc.
RouteEvaluation full_eval;
//Solution evaluation.
full_eval (route);
//The moMoveInit object.
TwoOptInit two_opt_init;
//The moNextMove object.
TwoOptNext two_opt_next;
//The moIncrEval object.
TwoOptIncrEval two_opt_incr_eval;
//The moMoveSelect.
moFirstImprSelect <TwoOpt> two_opt_select;
//or moBestImprSelect <TwoOpt> two_opt_select;
//or moRandImprSelect <TwoOpt> two_opt_select;
//or MyMoveSelect <TwoOpt> two_opt_select;
//The moHC object.
moHC <TwoOpt> hill_climbing (two_opt_init, two_opt_next,
    two_opt_incr_eval, two_opt_select,full_eval);
//The HC is launched on the initial solution.
hill_climbing (route) ;
```

A great advantage of using ParadisEO is that the user has to modify a given template (problem specific such as the objective function or problem independent such as the neighbor selection strategy), only the concerned template is updated; there is no impact on other templates and on the whole algorithm. For instance, if the user wants to define his own neighbor selection strategy, he can design a class for the `TwoOpt` move and use it as follows:

```
class MyMoveSelectionStrategy : public moMoveSelect <TwoOpt>
```

Another advantage of using the software framework is the ability to extend a metaheuristic to another metaheuristic in an easy and efficient manner. In the next section, it is shown how the hill-climbing algorithm has been evolved to tabu search, simulated annealing, and iterated local search. Most of the search components and their associated templates are reused.

2.10.4 Simulated Annealing Template

Figure 2.40 shows the architecture of the simulated annealing template `moSA`. If a comparison between Figs 2.39 and 2.40 is done, one can notice that most of the templates (search components) are the same.

The following search components and their associated templates are reused from the hill-climbing S-metaheuristic (moHC):

- Objective function that corresponds to the template `eoEvalFunc`.
- Incremental evaluation function that corresponds to `moMoveIncrEval`.

In addition to the search components associated with local search, the following components have to be defined for simulated annealing algorithm in the template `moSA`:

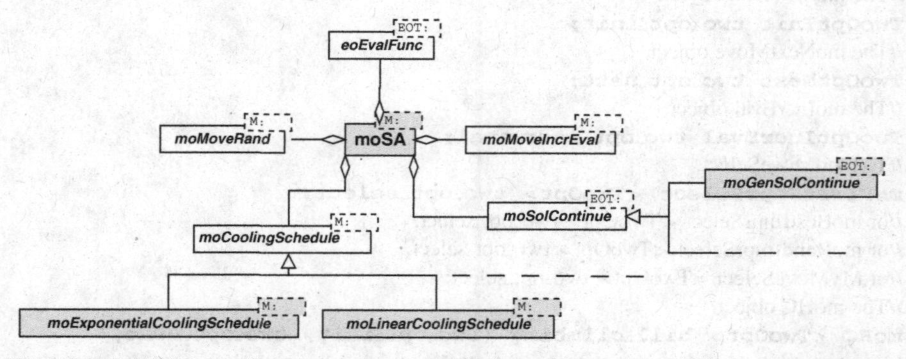

FIGURE 2.40 UML diagram of the simulated annealing template `moSA`. The template `moMoveRand` is specific to the problem; that is, the user has to define it, and the templates `moCoolingSchedule` and `moSolContinue` are problem independent and ready to use.

- **Cooling schedule:** The cooling schedule of simulated annealing is specified in the template `moCoolingSchedule`. Some cooling functions are available, such as the linear function `moLinearCoolingSchedule` and the geometric one `moExponentialCoolingSchedule`.
- **Stopping criteria** For any S-metaheuristic (e.g., tabu search), many defined stopping criteria in the template `moSolContinue` may be used.
- **Random neighbor generation:** The template `moMoveRand` defines how a random neighbor is generated.

In the following simulated annealing program, the lines different from the hill-climbing program are represented in bold. It is easy to extract the characteristics of the implemented SA: a maximum number of iterations as stopping criteria, the Boltzmann distribution acceptance probability, and so on.

```
...
// An initial solution.
Route route;
// An eoInit object (see ParadisEO-EO).
RouteInit route_init;
// Initialization.
route_init(route);
// The eoEvalFunc.
RouteEvaluation full_eval;
// Solution evaluation.
full_eval (route);
// The moRandMove object.
TwoOptRand two_opt_rand;
// The moIncrEval object.
TwoOptIncrEval two_opt_incr_eval;
// The chosen cooling schedule object.
moExponentialCoolingSchedule cool_sched (T_min, ratio);
// or moLinearCoolingSchedule cool_sched (T_min, quantity);
// or MyCoolingSchedule cool_sched;
// The moSolContinue.
moGenSolContinue <Route> cont (max_step);
// The moSA object.
moSA <TwoOpt> simulated_annealing (two_opt_rand, two_opt_incr_eval,
                                   cont, T_init, cool_sched, full_eval);
// The simulated_annealing is launched on the initial solution.
simulated_annealing (route) ;
```

2.10.5 Tabu Search Template

Figure 2.41 shows the architecture of the tabu search template `moTS`. If a comparison between Figs 2.39 and 2.41 is done, one can notice that most of the templates (search components) are the same.

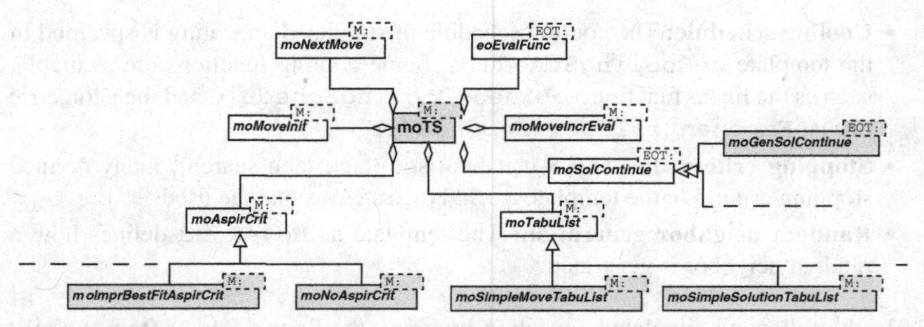

FIGURE 2.41 UML diagram of the tabu search template (moTS object). The templates `moAspirCrit`, `moTabuList`, and `moSolContinue` are problem-independent and ready-to-use templates.

The following search components and their associated templates are reused from the hill-climbing S-metaheuristic (moHC):

- Objective function that corresponds to the template `eoEvalFunc`.
- Incremental evaluation function that corresponds to `moMoveIncrEval`.
- Neighborhood structure and its exploration that corresponds to the templates `moMoveInit`, `moNextMove`.

To design a tabu search algorithm, only the following search components have to be defined in the template `moTS`:

- **Aspiration criteria** that corresponds to the template `moAspirCrit`. Two aspiration criteria are provided: the `moNoAspirCrit` that always rejects a move and the `moImpBestFitAspirCrit` that accepts a move if the fitness of the neighbor is better than the best found solution.
- **Tabu list (short-term memory)** that corresponds to the template `moTabuList`. Two basic tabu lists already exist: the ready-to-use template `moSimpleMoveTabuList` that contains the moves and the template `moSimpleSolutionTabuList` that contains the solutions.
- **Stopping criteria** that corresponds to the template `moSolContinue`. This template allows to select different stopping criteria for tabu search such as
  - `moGenSolContinue`, where the S-metaheuristic stops after a given maximum number of iteration.
  - `moFitSolContinue`, where the algorithm continues its execution until a target fitness (quality) is reached.
  - `moNoFitImprSolContinue`, where the algorithm stops when the best found solution has not be improved since a given number of iterations.
  - `moSteadyFitSolContinue`, a combination of the first and the third criteria: the algorithm performs a given number of iterations and then it stops if the best found solution is not improved for a given number of iterations.

In the following tabu search program, the lines different from the hill-climbing program are represented in bold. It is easy to extract the characteristics of this tabu search: a maximum number of iterations as stopping criterion.

```
...
// An initial solution.
Route route;
// An eoInit object (see ParadisEO-EO).
RouteInit route_init;
// Initialization.
route_init(route);
// The eoEvalFunc.
RouteEvaluation full_eval;
// Solution evaluation.
full_eval (route);
// The moMoveInit object.
TwoOptInit two_opt_init;
// The moNextMove object.
TwoOptNext two_opt_next;
// The moIncrEval object.
TwoOptIncrEval two_opt_incr_eval;
// The moTabuList.
moSimpleSolutionTabuList<TwoOpt> tabu_list(10);
// or moSimpleMoveTabuList<TwoOpt> tabu_list(10);
// or MyTabuList<TwoOpt> tabu_list;
// The moAspirCrit.
moNoAspirCrit <TwoOpt> aspir_crit;
// or moImprBestFitAspirCrit<TwoOpt> aspir_crit;
// or MyAspirCrit<TwoOpt> aspir_crit;
//The moSolContinue.
moGenSolContinue <Route> cont (10000);
// or MySolContinue<TwoOpt> cont;
// The moTS object.
moTS <TwoOpt> tabu_search (two_opt_init, two_opt_next, two_opt_incr_eval,
                           tabu_list, aspir_crit, cont, full_eval);
// The TS is launched on the initial solution.
tabu_search (route) ;
```

2.10.6 Iterated Local Search Template

Figure 2.42 shows the architecture of the iterated local search template moILS. Once a given S-metaheuristic designed, it is very easy to construct an iterated local search algorithm.

The following search components have to be defined for the ILS algorithm in the template moILS:

- **Local search algorithm:** The local search algorithm to be used must be specified in the moAlgo template. Any developed S-metaheuristic may be used,

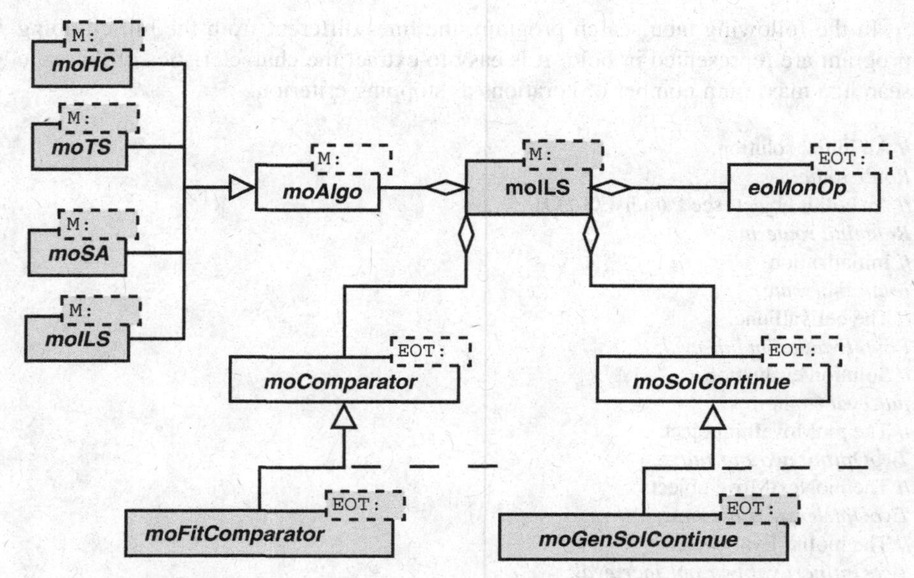

FIGURE 2.42 UML diagram of the iterated local search template `moILS`.

such as hill climbing (`moHC` template), tabu search (`moTS` template), simulated annealing (`moSA` template), any other user-defined S-metaheuristic, or why not another ILS `moILS`.

- **Perturbation method:** The perturbation method is defined in the template `eoMonOp`.
- **Acceptance criteria:** The search component dealing with the acceptance of the generated solution is defined in the template `moComparator`. Some usual acceptance functions are available such as `moFitComparator` that selects the new solution if it is better than the best found. Nevertheless, any specific acceptance method can be implemented; that is, a new class must be defined:

```
class MyComparisonStrategy : public moComparator <Route>
```

- **Stopping criteria:** For any S-metaheuristic (e.g., simulated annealing, tabu search), many defined stopping criteria in the template `moSolContinue` may be used.

Starting from any S-metaheuristic program, the user can easily design an ILS for the symmetric TSP problem. In the following program, the additional lines to a S-metaheuristic program are represented in bold:

...
// An initial solution.
Route route;
// An object to initialise this solution.
RouteInit route_init;

```
// Initialization.
route_init(route);
// A full evaluation method <=> eoEvalFunc.
RouteEvaluation full_eval;
// Solution evaluation.
full_eval (route);
// The moMoveInit object.
TwoOptInit two_opt_init;
// The moNextMove object.
TwoOptNext two_opt_next;
// The moIncrEval object.
TwoOptIncrEval two_opt_incr_eval;
// moMoveSelect.
moFirstImprSelect <TwoOpt> two_opt_select;
// or moBestImprSelect <TwoOpt> two_opt_select;
// or moRandImprSelect <TwoOpt> two_opt_select;
// or MyMoveSelect <TwoOpt> two_opt_select;
// The moHC object.
moHC <TwoOpt> hill_climbing (two_opt_init, two_opt_next,
                              two_opt_incr_eval, two_opt_select, full_eval);

  // The moSolContinue object.
moGenSolContinue <Route> cont (1000);
// The moComparator object.
moFitComparator <Route> comparator;
// The eoMonOp, in this example the well known CitySwap.
CitySwap perturbation;
// The moILS object.
moILS<TwoOpt> iterated_local_search(hill_climbing, comparator,
                                     perturbation, full_eval);
//The iterated local search is launched on the initial solution.
iterated_local_search (route) ;
```

2.11 CONCLUSIONS

In addition to the representation, the objective function and constraint handling that are common search concepts to all metaheuristics, the common concepts for single-solution based metaheuristics are as follows (Fig. 2.43):

- **Initial solution:** An initial solution may be specified randomly or by a given heuristic.
- **Neighborhood:** The main concept of S-metaheuristics is the definition of the neighborhood. The neighborhood has an important impact on the performances of this class of metaheuristics. The interdependency between representation and neighborhood must not be neglected. The main design question in S-metaheuristics is the trade-off between the efficiency of the representation/neighborhood and its effectiveness (e.g., small versus large neighborhoods).

- **Incremental evaluation of the neighborhood:** This is an important issue for the efficiency aspect of an S-metaheuristic.
- **Stopping criteria.**

Hence, most of the search components will be reused by different single-solution based metaheuristics (Fig. 2.43). Moreover, an incremental design and implementation of different S-metaheuristics can be carried out. In addition to the common search concepts of S-metaheuristics, the following main search components have to be defined for designing the following S-metaheuristics:

- **Local search:** Neighbor selection strategy.
- **Simulated annealing, demon algorithms, threshold accepting, great deluge and record-to-record travel:** Annealing schedule.
- **Tabu search:** Tabu list, aspiration criteria, medium- and long-term memories.
- **Iterated local search:** Perturbation method, acceptance criteria.
- **Variable neighborhood search:** Neighborhoods for shaking and neighborhoods for local search.

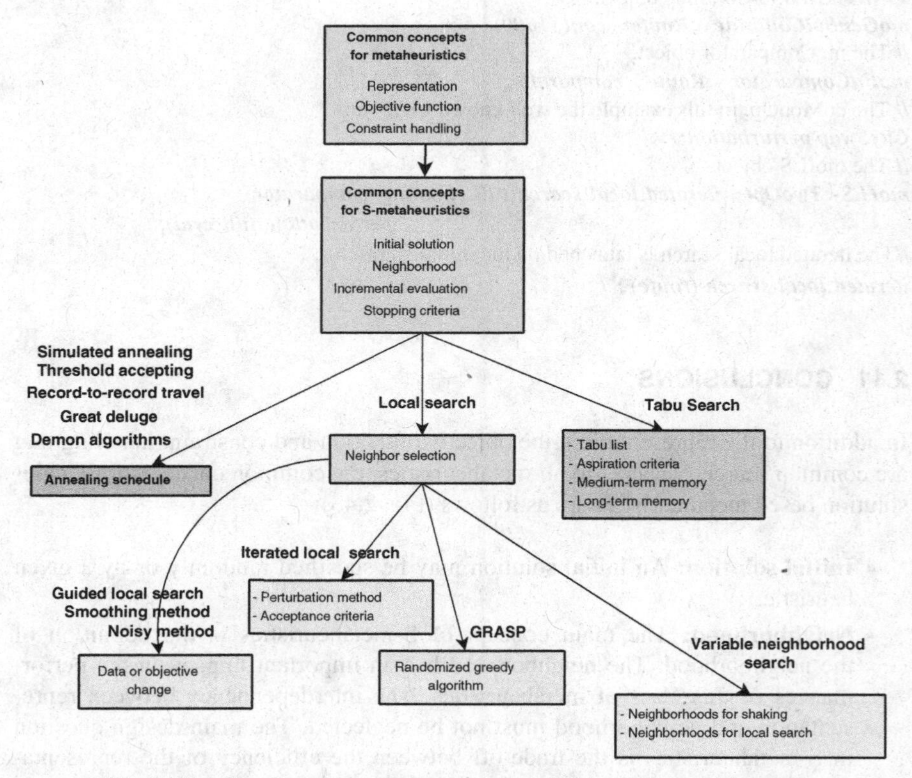

FIGURE 2.43 Common concepts and relationships in S-metaheuristics.

- **Guided local search, smoothing method, noisy method:** Function changing the input data or the objective.
- **GRASP:** Randomized greedy heuristic.

Moreover, there is a high flexibility to transform a S-metaheuristic into another one reusing most of the design and implementation work.

The analysis of landscapes of optimization problems is an important aspect in designing a metaheuristic (Fig. 2.44). It will be one of the most challenging problems in the theory of heuristic search algorithms. Indeed, the properties of the landscape has an important impact on the performance of metaheuristics. They have a major role in describing, explaining, and predicting the behavior of metaheuristics. One of the main lessons to learn is to analyze and exploit the structural properties of the landscape associated with a problem. One can also modify the landscape by changing the representation/neighborhood structure or the guiding function so that it becomes more "easy" to solve (e.g., deep valley landscape).

Once the S-metaheuristic is designed, the ParadisEO–MO software framework allows to implement it easily. The architecture modularity reduces the time and the complexity of designing S-metaheuristics. An expert user can without difficulty extend the already available boxes to suit to his problem and obtain more effective methods. Nevertheless, ParadisEO–MO can be used by newbies with a minimum

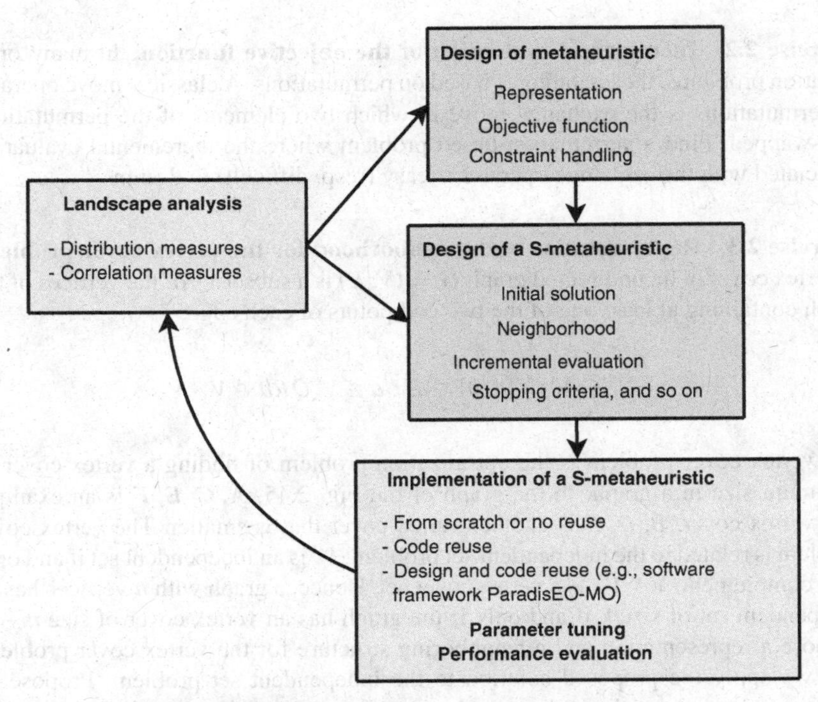

FIGURE 2.44 Development process of a S-metaheuristic.

of code to produce to implement diverse search strategies. A natural perspective is to evolve the open-source software by integrating more search components, heuristics (e.g., variable neighborhood search), and problem-solving environments (e.g., routing, scheduling, and assignment).

Each S-metaheuristic has some parameters to tune. The performance of the different metaheuristics is more or less sensitive to those parameters. However, the optimal tuning of the parameters will never overcome the bad design of search components (e.g., representation, neighborhood, and objective functions). The actual theory in S-metaheuristics, such as simulated annealing, focuses on the asymptotic convergence of the algorithms. It would be interesting to study and analyze more deeply the finite-time behavior of single-solution based metaheuristics. This will help the practical use of theoretical results, for instance, in the parameter tuning of a S-metaheuristics.

2.12 EXERCISES

Exercise 2.1 Initial solution for highly constrained problems. Let us consider the graph coloring problem. We would like to design a S-metaheuristic to solve the problem. Is it easy to generate a feasible random initial solution? Propose a greedy strategy to find a feasible initial solution.

Exercise 2.2 Incremental evaluation of the objective function. In many optimization problems, the encoding is based on permutations. A classical move operator in permutations is the exchange move in which two elements of the permutations are swapped. Find a permutation-based problem where the incremental evaluation associated with the exchange operator is easy (resp. difficult) to design.

Exercise 2.3 Representation and neighborhood for the vertex cover problem. A vertex cover of an undirected graph $G = (V, E)$ is a subset V' of the vertices of the graph containing at least one of the two end points of each edge:

$$V' \subseteq V : \forall \{a, b\} \in E : a \in V' \, OR b \in V'$$

The vertex cover problem is the optimization problem of finding a vertex cover of minimum size in a graph. In the graph of the Fig. 2.45, A, C, E, F is an example of a vertex cover. B, D, E is another vertex cover that is smaller. The vertex cover problem is related to the independent set problem: V' is an independent set if and only if its complement, $V \setminus V'$, is a vertex cover set. Hence, a graph with n vertices has an independent set of size k if and only if the graph has an vertex cover of size $n - k$. Propose a representation and a neighboring structure for the vertex cover problem. Can we apply the proposed solution to the independent set problem. Propose an incremental way to evaluate the neighbors.

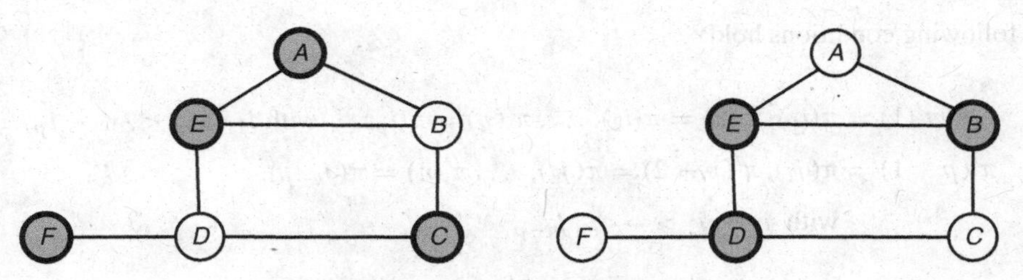

FIGURE 2.45 The vertex cover problem.

Exercise 2.4 Large neighborhood for the capacitated spanning tree problem. Let us consider the capacitated spanning tree problem presented in Example 2.41. The two-exchange neighborhood structure is based on exchanging a single node or a set of nodes between two subtrees. Generalize this neighborhood structure into a very large neighborhood structure based on the cyclic exchange neighborhood.

Exercise 2.5 Large neighborhood for the graph partitioning problem. The graph partitioning problem consists in finding a partitioning of a graph $G = (V, E)$ into two subsets of vertices V_1 and V_2 with $|V_1| = |V_2|$ such that the number of edges connecting vertices from V_1 and V_2 is minimized. Propose a representation and a neighborhood structure for the GPP problem.

The variable-depth search method implements a way to search an exponentially large neighborhood in polynomial time. This is made possible by some intelligent pruning of the search and heuristic rules. Devise a variable-depth search algorithm for the GPP problem. *Hint*: find the best pair $x_1 \in V_1$ and $y_1 \in V_2$ to swap. Swap these vertices and fix their position, that is, they cannot be swapped again in the step. In the kth iteration, $1 \leq k \leq n$, find the best pair x_k, y_k among the remaining $(n - k)^2$ pairs, swap this pair, and fix the position of x_k, y_k. These may not be swapped again. If k reaches n, then the roles of V_1 and V_2 are simply interchanged. It is important then to stop when $k < n$ swaps have been found such that the improvement in the quality of the partition is maximized. How can this be done efficiently?

Exercise 2.6 Neighborhood for different encodings of the JSP. Let us consider the job-shop scheduling problem and the various direct and indirect encodings proposed in Example 1.33. For each encoding, propose a neighborhood and compute its associated size.

Exercise 2.7 Large neighborhood based on cyclical shift. Let us consider the TSP problem. A tour is *pyramidal* if it starts in city 1, then visits cities in increasing order until it reaches city n, and finally returns through the remaining cities in decreasing order. Let $\pi(i)$ represent the city in the ith position of the tour π. A tour π' is a pyramidal neighbor of a tour π if there exists an integer p $(0 \leq p \leq n)$ such that the following conditions hold:

$$\pi'(1) = \pi(i_1), \pi'(2) = \pi(i_2), \ldots, \pi'(p) = \pi(i_p), \quad \text{with } i_1 < i_2 < \cdots < i_p$$

$$\pi'(p+1) = \pi(j_1), \pi'(p+2) = \pi(j_2), \ldots, \pi'(n) = \pi(j_{n-p}),$$

$$\text{with } j_1 > j_2 > \cdots > j_{n-p}$$

For instance, if $\pi = (1, 2, 3, 4, 5, 1)$, then a pyramidal neighbor may be $\pi' = (1, 2, 5, 4, 3, 1), (1, 3, 5, 4, 2, 1)$, and so on. What is the size of this pyramidal neighborhood? Design an efficient algorithm to explore it knowing that its complexity may be reduced to $O(n^3)$. The algorithm can be based on the shortest path algorithm in the improvement graph. The drawback of this pyramidal neighborhood is that the edge $(1, 2)$ is always contained in the tours. Find an alternative to solve this issue. Show that if a solution is a local optimum for the pyramidal neighborhood, then it is a local optimum for the 2-opt neighborhood.

Exercise 2.8 Size versus time to explore a large neighborhood. The critical issue in selecting a large neighborhood is the trade-off between the size of the neighborhood and the time to explore it. Let us consider the TSP problem. Compute the size and the time complexities for the following neighborhoods: city swap, 2-opt, k-opt, pyramidal, cyclical shift, compound swaps, and Halin graphs. What is the diameter of the above neighborhoods?

Exercise 2.9 Incremental objective function evaluation for the QAP. The incremental evaluation of the objective function in single-solution based algorithms is a very important issue to reduce the complexity of the evaluation of the neighborhood. In this exercise, we will tackle this question for a well-known assignment problem the quadratic assignment problem. The QAP arises in many applications such as facility location, data analysis, VLSI design, image synthesis, and so on. The problem can be defined as follows. Given a set of n objects $O = \{O_1, O_2, \ldots, O_n\}$, a set of n locations $L = \{L_1, L_2, \ldots, L_n\}$, a flow matrix C, where each element c_{ij} denotes a flow cost between the objects O_i and O_j, a distance matrix D, where each element d_{kl} denotes a distance between location L_k and L_l, find an object–location mapping $m : O \rightarrow L$ that minimizes the objective function f:

$$f = \sum_{i=1}^{n} \sum_{j=1}^{n} c_{ij} \cdot d_{M(i)M(j)}$$

Define an incremental function for the following encoding and move operator. The encoding of a solution is based on a permutation of n integers $s = (l_1, l_2, \ldots, L_n)$ where l_i denotes the location of the object O_i. The move operator is based on the exchange operator where two elements of the permutation are exchanged.

Exercise 2.10 Efficient evaluation of the neighborhood. Let us consider the maximum independent set problem defined in Example 2.27. The neighborhood is defined by the exchange of a vertex $v \in X$ with a vertex $w \in E - X$. The size of the neighborhood is $k(n-k) = O(nk)$ where n represents the number of vertices. Let us denote $\Gamma_X(v)$ the set of vertices $w \in X$ that are connected to $v \in V$ by an edge. The vertices v in X are sorted according to nonincreasing values of $\Gamma_X(v)$, and the vertices $w \in V - X$ are sorted according to nondecreasing values of $\Gamma_X(w)$. Show that the best neighbor may be found in $O(n)$ instead of $O(kn)$.

Exercise 2.11 Difficult incremental objective function evaluation. Identify some optimization problems and local search operators in which it is difficult to compute the incremental objective function.

Exercise 2.12 Distance in permutation space. Find an algorithm with time complexity $O(n)$ that computes the distance between any two permutations. The problem may be reduced to the shortest path between two solutions of the search space.

Exercise 2.13 Distance using 2-opt operator. Let us consider the traveling salesman problem. An S-metaheuristic using the 2-opt neighborhood has been designed to solve the problem. We need a definition of a distance to perform a landscape analysis of the problem. The distance $\Delta_{2-\text{opt}}(t_1, t_2)$ denotes the minimum number of applications of the 2-opt move to obtain t_2 from t_1. Is there any polynomial algorithm to compute such as distance? If not, propose an approximation of such a distance that can be computed efficiently.

Exercise 2.14 Hard unimodal problem for local search. The goal of this exercise is to construct a difficult problem for local search-based algorithms. The well-known types of difficulties for local search are multimodality, full deception, and isolation (needle in a haystack).

Construct an optimization problem in which the landscape is unimodal (any local optimum is a global optimum) and where a simple hill climber finds the global optimal solution in exponential time. Thus, unimodality is not a sufficient indicator to analyze the landscape difficulty of problems for local search-based algorithms.

Exercise 2.15 Greedy algorithms and epistasis. Starting from scratch, a greedy algorithm selects at each iteration a decision variable or component of a solution to be assigned until a complete solution is generated. Show that greedy algorithms are suitable for optimization problems with low epistasis. The response may be based on the following design questions of a greedy algorithm: selection of the order of the components and the value assignment to the components.

Exercise 2.16 Fractal landscape. Show that the NK-model landscape, TSP with the 2-opt operator, and the GBP are fractal landscapes ($h = \frac{1}{2}$).

Exercise 2.17 NFL theorem. Following the NFL theorem, one can state that all optimization algorithms are equivalent. Is it correct?

Exercise 2.18 Fitness distance correlation. The main drawback of the FDC analysis is that it requires the knowledge of the global optimal solution of the target optimization problem. Give some responses to this limitation when

- There are many known global optimal solutions.
- No global optimal solution is known for the problem.

Exercise 2.19 Tabu list representation. Suppose we have to solve the vehicle routing problem that has been defined in Example 1.11. The transformation operator used consists in moving a customer c_k from route R_i to route R_j. The tabu list is represented by the moves attributes. Propose three representations that are increasing in terms of their severity.

Exercise 2.20 Tabu list with random size. The commonly used representation for fixed size tabu lists are circular lists. Indeed, at each iteration, the last move is added to the list, whereas the oldest move is removed from the list. Determine the representation for tabu lists where the size is randomly updated during the search.

Exercise 2.21 Multiple tabu list. In scheduling problems such as the permutation flow-shop scheduling problem, various move operators may be used in parallel during the search. Propose multiple tabu list for the permutation flow-shop scheduling problem.

Exercise 2.22 Strategic oscillation, GRASP, and noisy method. The strategic oscillation approach introduced in tabu search is characterized by alternation between diversification in the search space and intensification of the search into a promising region. We would like to introduce strategic oscillation into the constructive procedure of the GRASP metaheuristic. How can we use the noisy method as a strategic oscillation strategy? Illustrate using a constrained spanning tree problem where the noisy method consists in perturbing the weights w_e of the graph edges e by $w_e \cdot r_i(e)$, where $r_i(e)$ is the perturbation coefficient applied to iteration i. We use the following search memory t, where $t_{i-1}(e)$ represents the number of locally optimal solutions in which the edge e appeared ($0 \leq t_{i-1}(e) \leq i$). The search memory can be viewed as a medium-term memory in tabu search.

Exercise 2.23 Black box for local search. Suppose that we have a black-box solver available to solve a given problem. This black-box solver is based on a local search procedure that has as an input an initial solution and as an output the local optima obtained. Which single-solution based metaheuristic can we use to solve the problem?

Exercise 2.24 Guided local search for the QAP. The quadratic assignment problem has been defined in Exercise 2.9. The goal of this exercise is to design a guided local search algorithm for the QAP. Suppose we have already at hand a local search (or any S-metaheuristic) procedure for the QAP. Then, it is required to define the augmented objective function. Hence, the following concepts have to be formulated: the features of a solution and the cost associated with a feature.

Exercise 2.25 Smoothing algorithms for graph problems. The landscape smoothing strategy has been widely used for the TSP problem. The smoothing operation consists in changing the weights (distances) of the input graph. Propose a smoothing operation for the graph partitioning problems and weighted clique problems.

Exercise 2.26 Smoothing constraints for covering and matching problems. Traditional smoothing techniques focus on the objective function. For some constrained problems, such as covering and matching problems, it would be interesting to smooth the constraints to generate a problem with an idealized landscape structure. Propose such a smoothing operation for constraints.

Exercise 2.27 Smoothing algorithm using P-metaheuristics. Traditionally, the smoothing algorithm has been used in conjunction with local search algorithms (S-metaheuristics). The smoothing algorithm can be extended to be used in conjunction with a population-based metaheuristic. Propose such an extension.

Exercise 2.28 Smoothing factor controlling. There are different ways of controlling the smoothing factor α that represents the strength of the landscape smoothing operation. Which properties must have such a controlling scheme?

Exercise 2.29 Links of the noising method with simulated annealing and threshold accepting. In the way the noising method operates, it may be similar to simulated annealing and threshold accepting algorithms. For which noise distributions may the noising algorithm be reduced to simulated annealing? The same question holds for threshold accepting. One consequence of these generalizations is that they also provide results on the convergence of some noising schemes. These convergence results for simulated annealing [3] and threshold accepting [28] show that there exist noising schemes for which the noising methods converge toward an optimal solution when the number of iterations is infinite. In Ref. [732], the authors present the convergence of the first kind of a noising method by giving sufficient conditions for convergence toward an optimal solution.

Similarly, we may consider that the noising method is a generalization of the threshold accepting algorithm. In this method, the neighborhood is systematically explored and the current solution s is replaced with one of its neighbors s' if s' is better than s or if the increase (for a minimization problem) does not overpass a given threshold; this threshold depends on the iteration and decreases during the process to 0. So, with respect to simulated annealing, the two main differences rely on the neighborhood exploration and on the fact that the acceptance criterion is no longer the exponential and nondeterministic Metropolis criterion but the following one: at the kth trial, s' is accepted instead of s if $f(s') - f(s) < T_k$, where T_k is the threshold of the kth trial, with $T_k \geq 0$ and $T_{k+1} < T_k$ and $T_K = 0$ if K is the total number of trials. It is quite easy to see that these thresholds can be seen as noises added to the variation of f (i.e., according to the second way of adding a noise described above).

Exercise 2.30 Automatic setting of parameters for the noising method. The objective here is to design an automatic tuning of the parameters of the noising methods. Our goal is to have a noising framework independent of the problem to solve and of the probability distribution of the noises, and with only one parameter: the search time fixed by the user. Propose such an automatic tuning. It would be preferable to spend more time on less noised objective function.

Exercise 2.31 Elite set in an iterative S-metaheuristic. In the design of an iterative S-metaheuristic such as iterated local search or GRASP, our goal is to maintain an elite set of solutions E_s. An iterative S-metaheuristic generates a single solution at each iteration of the algorithm. The elite set has a given maximum size k_{max} in terms of the number of solutions that is updated during the search. In the first k_{max} iterations of the iterative S-metaheuristic, the obtained solution is systematically integrated into the elite set. Which integration policies can we apply to the future iterations taking into account the quality of solutions and the diversity of the elite set E_s.

Exercise 2.32 Toward a dependency of iterations in GRASP. In most of the GRASP metaheuristic implementations, the independence between iterations is assumed. The iterations are memoryless; that is, there is no use of a search memory between successive iterations. For instance, the search does not learn from the history of solutions found. Hence, the same results are obtained independent of the order of the iterations. Which kind of search memory can be introduced into GRASP to

- Improve the quality of solutions.
- Avoid redundant work.
- Speed up the search.

Propose such a strategy that makes the iterations of the GRASP dependent on each other.

Exercise 2.33 From the capacitated vehicle routing problem to the capacitated spanning tree problem. The objective of this exercise is to show how problem-solving results can be reused thanks to a problem reduction. Let us consider the well-known capacitated vehicle routing problem where many metaheuristics have been designed. Our objective is to solve the capacitated minimum spanning tree problem presented in Example 2.41. The concept of clustering of nodes satisfying the capacity constraint is present in both problems. Show that the CMST problem is a relaxation of the CVRP problem. Then, in solving the CVRP, we obtain an upper bound for the

CMST. Once we have a cluster of nodes, finding a minimum spanning tree problem is a polynomial problem where well-known greedy heuristics may be used, such as the Prim or Kruskal ones. Combine these two ideas to design a S-metaheuristic (e.g., GRASP algorithm) for the CMST problem. The same exercise may be applied for a P-metaheuristic (e.g., ant colony optimization) presented in Chapter 3.

Exercise 2.34 GRASP construction method and the noisy method. In the design of a GRASP metaheuristic to solve an optimization problem, there is a need of a randomized greedy heuristic. For some problems, no such randomized greedy heuristic is available. How can we use the noisy method to replace the construction phase of the GRASP metaheuristic. Illustrate the answers using the clique partitioning problem of Example 2.22.

Exercise 2.35 Perturbation in ILS versus shaking in VNS. In the design of an ILS metaheuristic, a perturbation method must be defined. In the VNS metaheuristic, shaking is used to generate an initial solution for local search or the VND method. What are the similarities between these two procedures: perturbation in ILS and shaking in VNS.

Exercise 2.36 Bias functions in the construction procedure of GRASP. In the construction procedure of the GRASP metaheuristic, the next element to introduce in the partial solution from the RCL list is chosen randomly. Indeed, the elements belonging to RCL are assigned an equal probability. Let $r(\sigma)$ denote the rank of element σ and $\text{bias}(r(\sigma))$ a bias function. The probability $\pi(\sigma)$ of selecting an element from the set RCL is

$$\pi(\sigma) = \frac{\text{bias}(r(\sigma))}{\sum_{\sigma' \in \text{RCL}} \text{bias}(r(\sigma'))}$$

The random bias function commonly used in GRASP is $\text{bias}(r) = 1$ for $r \in$ RCL. Propose other probability distributions that may be used to bias the selection of elements from the set RCL.

Exercise 2.37 Robust optimization using S-metaheuristics. Suppose that we have used a S-metaheuristic to solve a given optimization problem. How can we estimate the robustness of the obtained solution in terms of the disturbance of the decision variables.

Exercise 2.38 Local search for the N-Queens problem. The N-Queens puzzle is the problem of putting N chess queens on an $N \times N$ chessboard such that none of them is able to capture any other using the standard chess queen's moves. Any queen is assumed to be able to attack any other. Suppose that the objective function f is to reduce the number of conflicts. The neighborhood is defined as a move of a queen toward its eight neighbor positions on the chess (Fig. 2.46). Design and implement a basic local search algorithm to solve the problem under the ParadisEO framework.

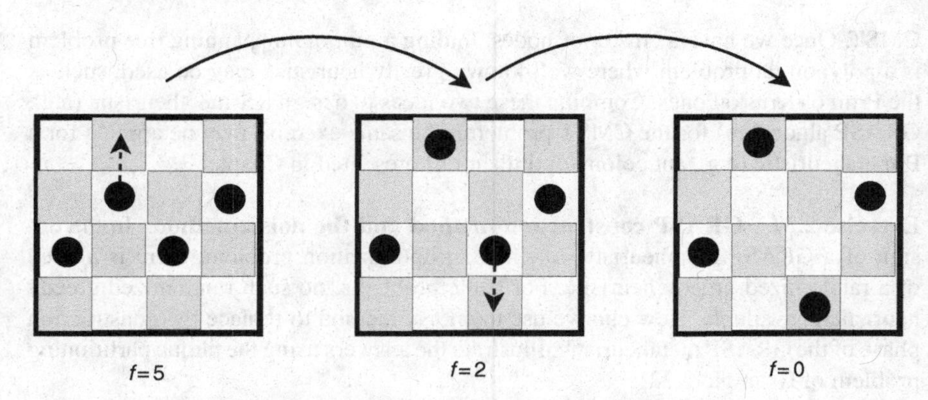

FIGURE 2.46 A local search procedure for the N-Queens problem.

Propose an improvement of the local search procedure for a more effective search algorithm.

Exercise 2.39 Flexibility of the local search template. Given a local search template developed under ParadisEO-MO to solve an optimization problem P (see Section 2.10.3 or many examples on the Web site of the framework), what the user has to perform if he wants to

- Change the neighbor selection strategy.
- Modify the guiding objective function to solve the same problem P.
- Transform the neighborhood but keep the same representation.
- Extend the local search to tabu search, simulated annealing, and iterated local search.
- Solve another optimization problem Q that uses the same representation and neighborhood.

Exercise 2.40 Local search under ParadisEO. Evaluate the performance (quality of solutions) of the developed local search algorithm on different benchmarks. Experiment different neighbor selection strategies (first improvement, best improvement) in terms of solution quality and computational time. Test if the algorithm is sensitive to the initial solution by running the algorithm for different random initial solutions. Compare the performances of the local search approach with

- Random walk, which generates randomly successive neighbor solutions. The best found solution is always updated.
- Random sampling, which is a variation of random walk, where a neighbor-generated solution is accepted if it is better than the current solution.

Exercise 2.41 Flexibility of the tabu search template. Given a tabu search developed under ParadisEO–MO to solve an optimization problem *P* (see Section 2.10.5 or the examples on the Web site of the framework), what the user has to perform if he wants to

- Modify the tabu list definition.
- Change the aspiration function.
- Experiment another stopping criteria (e.g., stops when a given fitness (quality) is attained)
- Include medium-term or long-term memories.

Exercise 2.42 Flexibility of the simulated annealing template. Given a simulated annealing template developed under ParadisEO-MO to solve an optimization problem *P* (see Section 2.10.4 or the examples on the Web site of the framework), what the user has to perform if he wants to

- Modify the cooling schedule.
- Include a more efficient incremental objective function. Can is this new function be used by any S-metaheuristic?
- Implement the other SA-inspired algorithms such as threshold accepting, demon algorithms, great deluge, and record-to-record algorithms to solve the problem *P*. Afterward, these algorithms will be available to be used by other users.

Exercise 2.43 Threshold accepting template. The threshold accepting algorithm belongs to the family of simulated annealing algorithms. Show how the simulated annealing template of ParadisEO-MO can be easily modified to implement a threshold accepting template.

Exercise 2.44 Flexibility of the iterated local search template. Given an iterated local search template developed under ParadisEO-MO to solve an optimization problem *P* (see Section 2.10.6 or the examples on the Web site of the framework), what the user has to perform if he wants to

- Replace the S-metaheuristic algorithm (e.g., from local search to tabu search or simulated annealing).
- Experiment another perturbation method and/or acceptance criteria.

CHAPTER 3

Population-Based Metaheuristics

Population-based metaheuristics (P-metaheuristics) share many common concepts. They could be viewed as an iterative improvement in a population of solutions. First, the population is initialized. Then, a new population of solutions is generated. Finally, this new population is integrated into the current one using some selection procedures. The search process is stopped when a given condition is satisfied (stopping criterion). Algorithms such as evolutionary algorithms (EAs), scatter search (SS), estimation of distribution algorithms (EDAs), particle swarm optimization (PSO), bee colony (BC), and artificial immune systems (AISs) belong to this class of metaheuristics.

This chapter is organized as follows. After the high-level template of P-metaheuristics is presented, Section 3.1 details the common search components for P-metaheuristics, namely, the determination of the initial population and the stopping criteria. In Section 3.2, the focus is on evolutionary algorithms such as genetic algorithms, evolution strategies (ESs), evolutionary programming, and genetic programming. The common search components of this family of P-metaheuristics (e.g., selection, variation operators, and replacement) are outlined in Section 3.3. Section 3.4 presents other evolutionary algorithms such as estimation of distribution algorithms, differential evolution, coevolutionary algorithms, and cultural algorithms. Section 3.5 presents the scatter search and path relinking, and Section 3.6 deals with swarm intelligence algorithms (e.g., ant colonies (ACs), particle swarm optimization). Other nature-inspired P-metaheuristics such as bee colonies (e.g., food foraging, queen bee marriage) and artificial immune systems (e.g., clonal selection, immune network) are presented in Section 3.7. Finally, Section 3.8 presents the ParadisEO–EO (evolving objects) module of the ParadisEO software framework that is dedicated to the implementation of P-metaheuristics. Some design and implementation issues of P-metaheuristics such as evolutionary algorithms, particle swarm optimization, and estimation of distribution algorithms are illustrated.

Metaheuristics: From Design to Implementation, by El-Ghazali Talbi

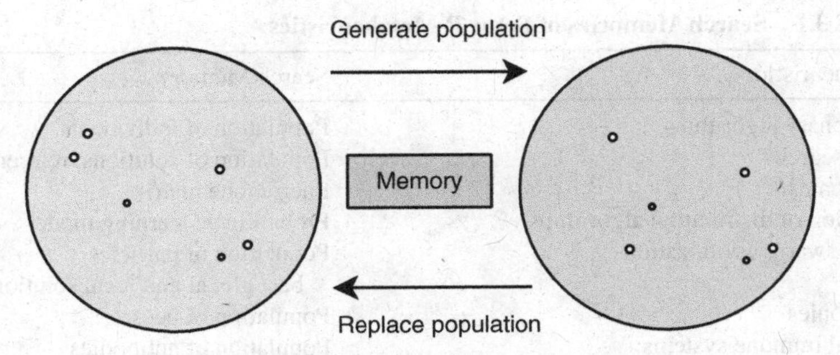

FIGURE 3.1 Main principles of P-metaheuristics.

3.1 COMMON CONCEPTS FOR POPULATION-BASED METAHEURISTICS

Population-based metaheuristics start from an initial population of solutions.[1] Then, they iteratively apply the generation of a new population and the replacement of the current population (Fig. 3.1). In the generation phase, a new population of solutions is created. In the replacement phase, a selection is carried out from the current and the new populations. This process iterates until a given stopping criteria. The generation and the replacement phases may be *memoryless*. In this case, the two procedures are based only on the current population. Otherwise, some history of the search stored in a memory can be used in the generation of the new population and the replacement of the old population. Most of the P-metaheuristics are nature-inspired algorithms. Popular examples of P-metaheuristics are evolutionary algorithms, ant colony optimization, scatter search, particle swarm optimization, bee colony, and artificial immune systems. Algorithm 3.1 illustrates the high-level template of P-metaheuristics.

Algorithm 3.1 High-level template of P-metaheuristics.

$P = P_0$; /* Generation of the initial population */
$t = 0$;
Repeat
  Generate(P'_t); /* Generation a new population */
  P_{t+1} = Select-Population($P_t \cup P'_t$); /* Select new population */
  $t = t + 1$;
Until Stopping criteria satisfied
Output: Best solution(s) found.

P-metaheuristics differ in the way they perform the generation and the selection procedures and the search memory they are using during the search.

[1]Some P-metaheuristics such as ant colony optimization start from partial or empty solutions.

TABLE 3.1 Search Memories of Some P-Metaheuristics

P-metaheuristic	Search Memory
Evolutionary algorithms	Population of individuals
Scatter search	Population of solutions, reference set
Ant colonies	Pheromone matrix
Estimation of distribution algorithms	Probabilistic learning model
Particle swarm optimization	Population of particles, best global and local solutions
Bee colonies	Population of bees
Artificial immune systems: clonal selection	Population of antibodies

- **Search memory:** The memory of a P-metaheuristic represents the set of information extracted and memorized during the search. The content of this memory varies from a P-metaheuristic to another one (Table 3.1). In most of the P-metaheuristics such as evolutionary algorithms and scatter search, the search memory is limited to the population of solutions. In ant colonies, the pheromone matrix is the main component of the search memory, whereas in estimation distribution algorithms, it is a probabilistic learning model that composes the search memory.
- **Generation:** In this step, a new population of solutions is generated. According to the generation strategy, P-metaheuristics may be classified into two main categories (Fig. 3.2):
  - **Evolution based:** In this category of P-metaheuristics, the solutions composing the population are selected and reproduced using variation operators (e.g., mutation, recombination[2]) acting *directly* on their representations. A new solution is constructed from the different attributes of solutions belongingto the current population. Evolutionary algorithms and scatter search represent

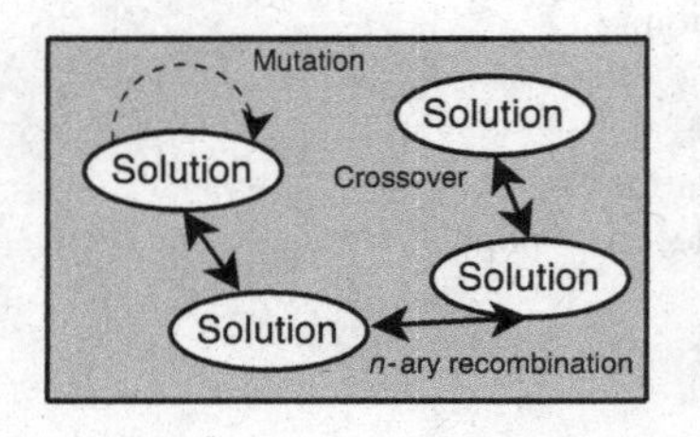

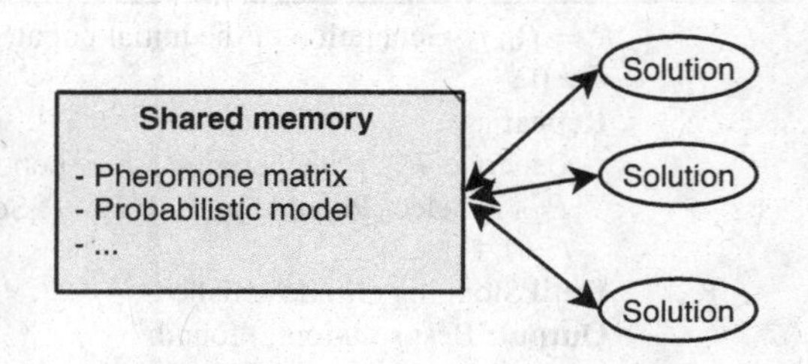

(a) Evolutionary-based P-metaheuristics: evolutionary algorithms, scatter search, ... (b) Blackboard-based P-metaheuristics: ant colonies, estimation distribution algorithms, ...

FIGURE 3.2 Evolution based versus blackboard based strategies in P-metaheuristics.

[2] Also called crossover and merge.

well-known examples of this class of P-metaheuristics. In EAs, the recombination operator is generally a binary operator (crossover), while in SS, the recombination operator may be an n-ary operator ($n > 2$).

- **Blackboard based**[3]**:** Here, the solutions of the population participate in the construction of a shared memory. This shared memory will be the main input in generating the new population of solutions. The recombination in this class of algorithm between solutions is indirect through this shared memory. Ant colonies and estimation distribution algorithms belong to this class of P-metaheuristics. In the former strategy, the shared memory is represented by the pheromone matrix, while in the latter strategy, it is represented by a probabilistic learning model. For instance, in ant colonies, the generated solutions by past ants will affect the generation of solutions by future ants via the pheromone. Indeed, the previously generated solutions participate in updating the pheromone.

- **Selection:** The last step in P-metaheuristics consists in selecting the new solutions from the union of the current population and the generated population. The traditional strategy consists in selecting the generated population as the new population. Other strategies use some *elitism* in the selection phase where they provide the best solutions from the two sets. In blackboard-based P-metaheuristics, there is no explicit selection. The new population of solutions will update the shared search memory (e.g., pheromone matrix for ant colonies, probabilistic learning model for estimation of distribution algorithms), which will affect the generation of the new population.

As for S-metaheuristics, the search components that allow to define and differentiate P-metaheuristics have been identified. The common search concepts for P-metaheuristics are the determination of the initial population and the definition of the stopping criteria.

3.1.1 Initial Population

Due to the large diversity of initial populations, P-metaheuristics are naturally more exploration search algorithms whereas S-metaheuristics are more exploitation search algorithms. The determination of the initial population is often disregarded in the design of a P-metaheuristic. Nonetheless, this step plays a crucial role in the effectiveness of the algorithm and its efficiency. Hence, one should pay more attention to this step [522].

In the generation of the initial population, the main criterion to deal with is diversification. If the initial population is not well diversified, a premature convergence can occur for any P-metaheuristic. For instance, this may happen if the initial population is generated using a greedy heuristic or a S-metaheuristic (e.g., local search, tabu search) for each solution of the population.

[3] A blackboard system is an artificial intelligence application based on the blackboard architectural model, where a shared knowledge base, the "blackboard," is iteratively updated by a diverse group of agents [245].

TABLE 3.2 Analysis of the Different Initialization Strategies

Strategy	Diversity	Computational Cost	Quality of Initial Solutions
Pseudo-random	++	+++	+
Quasi-random	+++	+++	+
Sequential diversification	++++	++	+
Parallel diversification	++++	+++	+
Heuristic	+	+	+++

The evaluation is better with more plus (+) sign. Sequential and parallel diversification strategies provide in general the best diversity followed by the quasi-random strategy. The heuristic initialization provides in general better solutions in terms of quality but with the expense of a higher computational cost and a reduced diversity. This will depend on the fitness landscape of the tackled optimization problem. For some landscapes (e.g., flat rugged), the diversity may remain important.

In some P-metaheuristics such as scatter search, the diversification criterion is explicitly taken into account in the generation of the initial population. Some diversification criteria are optimized in the generation of the initial population such as maximizing the minimum distance between any two solutions of the initial population:

$$\text{Max}_{i=1,n}(\text{Min}_{j=1,i-1}\{d_{ij}\})$$

where d_{ij} represents the distance in the decision space between two solutions i and j and n is the size of the population.

Strategies dealing with the initialization of the population may be classified into four categories: random generation, sequential diversification, parallel diversification, and heuristic initialization. They may be analyzed according to the following criteria: diversity, computational cost, and quality of the solutions (Table 3.2).

3.1.1.1 Random Generation Usually, the initial population is generated randomly. For instance, in continuous optimization, the initial real value of each variable may be generated randomly in its possible range.

Example 3.1 Uniform random population in global optimization. In continuous optimization, each decision variable x_j is defined to be in a given range $[l_j, u_j]$. Let us generate a randomly distributed initial population P_0 of size n. Each solution x_i of the population is a k-dimensional real vector x_{ij}, $j \in [1, k]$. Each element of the vector x_{ij} is generated randomly in the range $[l_j, u_j]$, representing the lower and the upper bounds for each variable:

$$x_{ij} = l_j + \text{rand}_j[0, 1] \cdot (u_j - l_j), i \in [1, n], j \in [1, k]$$

where rand_j is a uniformly distributed random variable in the range [0, 1]. If the limits (lower and upper bounds) are not well defined, the bounds should be initialized large enough to encompass the search space delimited by optimal solutions.

The random generation may be performed according to *pseudo-random* numbers or a *quasi-random* sequence of numbers. The most popular random generation of the population is the pseudo-random one[4] (Fig. 3.4). Indeed, as it is impossible in practice to generate algorithmically truly independent random numbers (genuine random), pseudo-random numbers are generated using various classical generators (e.g., congruential quadratic, recursive lagged Fibonacci) [313]. Care should be taken to use pseudo-random generators that provide good properties (e.g., sensibility to seeds and coefficients).

In a quasi-random sequence, the goal of the generator is related not only to the independence between the successive numbers but also to their dispersion. Many quasi-random generators that try to cover the search space exist in the literature (e.g., Niederreiter) [313]. In a quasi-random sequence, the diversity of the population is generally better than in a pseudo-random generation (Table 3.2).

In discrete optimization, the same uniform random initialization may be applied to binary vectors, discrete vectors, and permutations.

3.1.1.2 Sequential Diversification

The initial population can also be uniformly sampled in the decision space. Some initialization procedures do not require any evaluation of the objective function or constraints associated with the optimization problem. In a sequential diversification, the solutions are generated in sequence in such a way that the diversity is optimized.

Example 3.2 Simple sequential inhibition process. A well-known sequential diversification strategy in statistics is the simple sequential inhibition (SSI) process [210]. Given Q the current subpopulation, which initially is composed of only one randomly picked solution. Any new selected solution must be at a minimum distance Δ to all other solutions of the current subpopulation Q. Hence, a pseudo-random solution is generated until it verifies this property. This process is repeated until the population is filled with the specified number of solutions. The drawback of this strategy is its relatively high computation cost. The number of iterations performed cannot be known *a priori*. However, it ensures a good distribution of the population, that is, the minimum distance between any two solutions of the initial population is greater than Δ. Let us notice that the distance threshold $\Delta > 0$ is a parameter of the strategy.

3.1.1.3 Parallel Diversification

In a parallel diversification strategy, the solutions of a population are generated in a parallel independent way.

Example 3.3 Uniform sampling using Latin hypercube sampling. Let n be the size of the population and k be the number of variables. The variable range of each variable i is divided into n equal segments of size $(u_i - l_i)/k$, where l_i and u_i represent successively the lower and upper bounds for each variable i. A Latin hypercube sample

[4] A sequence of infinite size is random if the amount of information it contains is also infinite. It is impossible to test the randomness of a finite sequence [471]. In this book, the term random refers to pseudo-random.

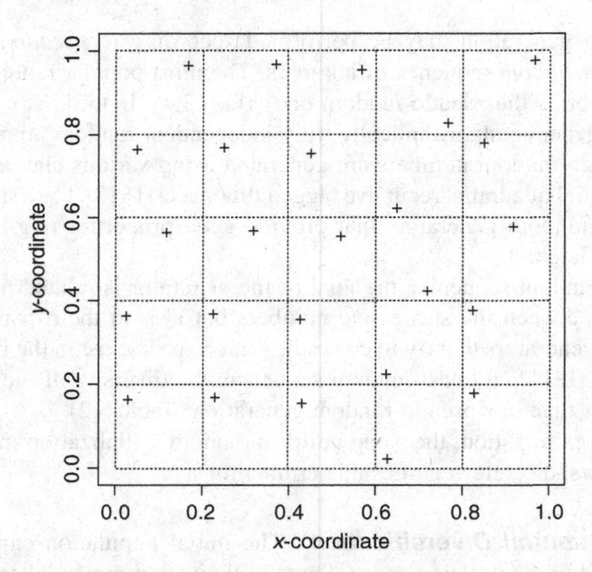

FIGURE 3.3 In the Latin hypercube strategy, the search space is decomposed into 25 blocks and a solution is generated pseudo-randomly in each block.

is generated by sampling a random real number that is generated in each segment [536]. This strategy is similar to nonaligned systematic sampling, a well-known sampling design procedure in statistics [658]. Figures 3.3 and 3.4 illustrate the difference between pseudo-random generation and uniform sampling. It is clearly shown that using Latin hypercube sampling, the coverage is much better with uniform sampling than using pseudo-random generation.

To generalize this procedure to a population of vector solutions, an unbiased Knuth shuffling strategy may be used. A random permutation of n elements (from 1 to n) is generated. The solution with index j is assigned the value located at the position $\pi(j)$th of the permutation. This procedure is iterated for all variables. This strategy gives a good overall random unbiased distribution of the population in the decision space and does not require any evaluation of the objective function or constraints [513].

Example 3.4 Diversified initial population of permutations. Let us consider a permutation problem, the quadratic assignment problem (QAP), which is defined in Exercise 2.9. A solution is represented by a permutation π of m integers $\{1, 2, \ldots, m\}$, where m is the size of the problem (number of locations and objects). A diversification criterion may be selected such as for each object i and for each location j, there is a solution of the initial population in which the object i is mapped on the location j [167]. The maximum distance between any two solutions will be equal to $\sqrt{2n}$. First, a random initial solution X_1 is generated. The second solution X_2 is constructed by initializing $\pi(k_i^1)$ to site i, where k_i^1 represents the object on the location i in X_1. Then, the third solution X_3 is constructed by initializing $\pi(k_i^2)$ to site i, where k_i^2 represents the object on the location i in X_2. The same process is iterated $n - 1$ times to

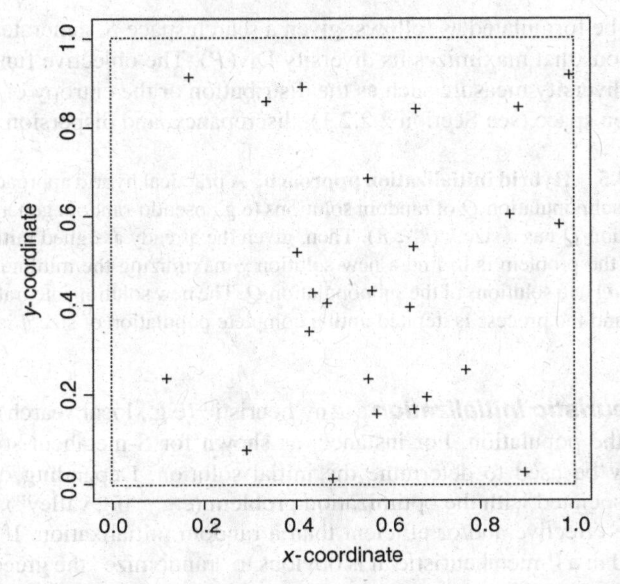

FIGURE 3.4 In the pseudo-random generation, 25 solutions are generated independently in the search space.

generate a population of size n. Figure 3.5 illustrates such a diversified initial population of permutations.

More generally, the generation of the initial population in a way to optimize a given diversification criterion can be defined as an optimization problem. This problem may be as (or more) difficult as the original problem to solve. This is why in most of the cases, heuristic or metaheuristic algorithms (e.g., greedy algorithms) are used to solve the optimization problem dealing with generation of a diversified population. The

X_1	5	3	2	1	6	4
X_2	6	2	3	5	4	1
X_3	4	5	6	2	1	3
X_4	3	1	4	6	5	2
X_5	2	6	1	4	3	5
X_6	1	4	5	3	2	6

FIGURE 3.5 Deterministic diversification of the initial population of permutations in an assignment problem.

problem can be formulated as follows: given a search space S, generate a population P of n solutions that maximizes its diversity Div(P). The objective function Div(P) may be any diversity measure such as the distribution or the entropy of the solutions in the decision space (see Section 2.2.2.1), discrepancy, and dispersion [581].

Example 3.5 Hybrid initialization approach. A practical hybrid approach may first generate a subpopulation Q of random solutions (e.g., pseudo-random generation). The subpopulation Q has a size k ($k < n$). Then, given the already assigned initial subpopulation Q, the problem is to find a new solution s maximizing the minimum distance min(dist(s, Q)) to solutions of the subpopulation Q. The new solution integrates the population Q and the process is iterated until a complete population of size n is initialized (Fig. 3.6).

3.1.1.4 Heuristic Initialization Any heuristic (e.g., local search) can be used to initialize the population. For instance, as shown for S-metaheuristics, a greedy heuristic may be used to determine the initial solution. Depending on the fitness landscape associated with the optimization problem (e.g., "big valley"), this strategy may be more effective and/or efficient than a random initialization. If this strategy has to be used in a P-metaheuristic, it is obvious to "randomize" the greedy procedure to obtain different solutions from the greedy procedure. The main drawback of this approach is that the initial population may lose its diversity, which will generate a premature convergence and stagnation of the population (Table 3.2).

3.1.2 Stopping Criteria

Many stopping criteria based on the evolution of a population may be used. Some of them are similar to those designed for S-metaheuristics.

- **Static procedure:** In a static procedure, the end of the search may be known *a priori*. For instance, one can use a fixed number of iterations (generations), a limit on CPU resources, or a maximum number of objective function evaluations.
- **Adaptive procedure:** In an adaptive procedure, the end of the search cannot be known *a priori*. One can use a fixed number of iterations (generations) without improvement, when an optimum or a satisfactory solution is reached (e.g., a

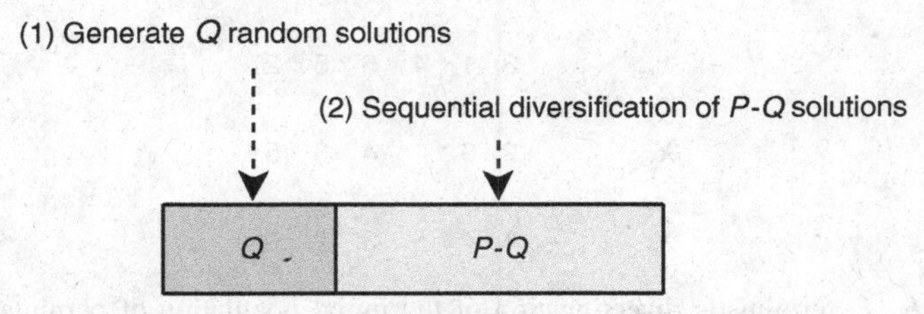

FIGURE 3.6 Hybrid initialization of the population.

given error to the optimum or an approximation to it when a lower bound is known beforehand).

Some stopping criteria are specific to P-metaheuristics. They are generally based on some statistics on the current population or the evolution of the population. Mostly, they are related to the diversity of the population. It consists in stopping the algorithm when the diversity measure falls below a given threshold. This stopping criteria deal with the stagnation of the population. When the population stagnates, keeping the execution of a P-metaheuristic is useless.

3.2 EVOLUTIONARY ALGORITHMS

In the nineteenth century, J. Mendel was the first to state the baselines of heredity from parents to offsprings. Then in 1859, C. Darwin presented the theory of evolution in his famous book *On the Origin of Species* [176]. In the 1980s, these theories of creation of new species and their evolution have inspired computer scientists in designing evolutionary algorithms. Different main schools of evolutionary algorithms have evolved independently during the past 40 years: *genetic algorithms* (GA), mainly developed in Michigan, USA, by J. H. Holland [383,384]; *evolution strategies*, developed in Berlin, Germany, by I. Rechenberg [642,643] and H-P. Schwefel [685,687]; and *evolutionary programming* by L. Fogel in San Diego, USA [272,273]. Later, in the end of 1980s, *genetic programming* has been proposed by J. Koza [480]. Each of these constitutes a different approach; however, they are inspired by the same principles of natural evolution [43]. A good introductory survey can be found in Ref. [45].

Evolutionary algorithms are stochastic P-metaheuristics that have been successfully applied to many real and complex problems (epistatic, multimodal, multiobjective, and highly constrained problems). They are the most studied population-based algorithms. Their success in solving difficult optimization problems in various domains (continuous or combinatorial optimization, system modeling and identification, planning and control, engineering design, data mining and machine learning, artificial life) has promoted the field known as *evolutionary computation* (EC) [45].

EAs are based on the notion of *competition*. They represent a class of iterative optimization algorithms that simulate the evolution of species (Fig. 3.7). They are based

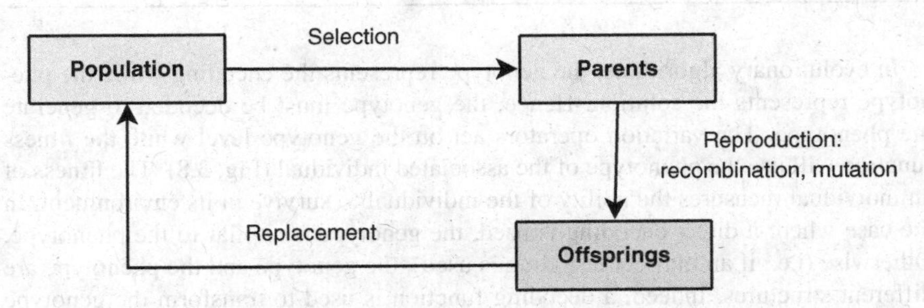

FIGURE 3.7 A generation in evolutionary algorithms.

TABLE 3.3 Evolution Process Versus Solving an Optimization Problem

Metaphor	Optimization
Evolution	Problem solving
Individual	Solution
Fitness	Objective function
Environment	Optimization problem
Locus	Element of the solution
Allele	Value of the element (locus)

on the evolution of a population of individuals. Initially, this population is usually generated randomly. Every individual in the population is the encoded version of a tentative solution. An objective function associates a fitness value with every individual indicating its suitability to the problem. At each step, individuals are selected to form the parents, following the selection paradigm in which individuals with better fitness are selected with a higher probability. Then, selected individuals are reproduced using variation operators (e.g., crossover, mutation) to generate new offsprings. Finally, a replacement scheme is applied to determine which individuals of the population will survive from the offsprings and the parents. This iteration represents a generation (Fig. 3.7). This process is iterated until a stopping criteria hold. Table 3.3 makes the parallel between the metaphor of the evolution process and solving an optimization problem. Algorithm 3.2 illustrates the template of an evolutionary algorithm.

Algorithm 3.2 Template of an evolutionary algorithm.

Generate($P(0)$) ; /* Initial population */
$t = 0$;
While not Termination_Criterion($P(t)$) **Do**
  Evaluate($P(t)$) ;
  $P'(t) = $ Selection($P(t)$) ;
  $P'(t) = $ Reproduction($P'(t)$); Evaluate($P'(t)$) ;
  $P(t+1) = $ Replace($P(t)$, $P'(t)$) ;
  $t = t + 1$;
End While
Output Best individual or best population found.

In evolutionary algorithms, the genotype represents the encoding while the phenotype represents the solution. Hence, the genotype must be decoded to generate the phenotype. The variation operators act on the genotype level while the fitness function will use the phenotype of the associated individual (Fig. 3.8). The fitness of an individual measures the ability of the individual to survive in its environment. In the case where a direct encoding is used, the genotype is similar to the phenotype. Otherwise (i.e., if an indirect encoding is used), the genotype and the phenotype are different structures. Indeed, a decoding function is used to transform the genotype into a phenotype (see Section 4.8.2.1).

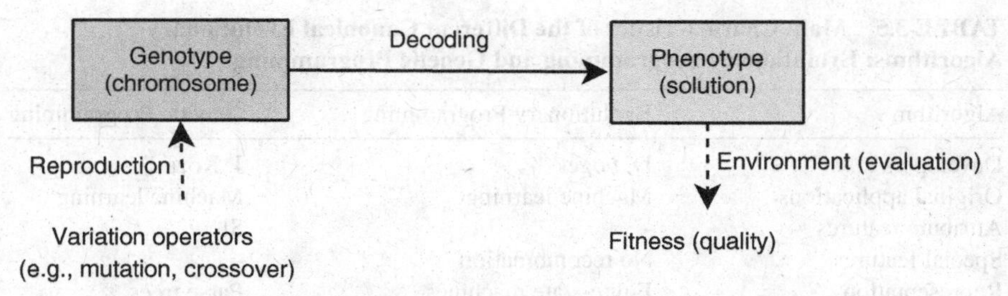

FIGURE 3.8 Genotype versus phenotype in evolutionary algorithms.

In terms of theoretical asymptotic convergence, many studies show the convergence properties of evolutionary algorithms in which the algorithms are generally limited to mutation operators and elitist replacement [669].

In the following sections, the main difference between the various families of evolutionary algorithms is outlined. Then, focus is made on their common search components.

3.2.1 Genetic Algorithms

Genetic algorithms have been developed by J. Holland in the 1970s (University of Michigan, USA) to understand the adaptive processes of natural systems [384]. Then, they have been applied to optimization and machine learning in the 1980s [328,431].

GAs are a very popular class of EAs. Traditionally, GAs are associated with the use of a binary representation but nowadays one can find GAs that use other types of representations. A GA usually applies a crossover operator to two solutions that plays a major role, plus a mutation operator that randomly modifies the individual contents to promote diversity (Tables 3.4 and 3.5). GAs use a probabilistic selection

TABLE 3.4 Main Characteristics of the Different Canonical Evolutionary Algorithms: Genetic Algorithms and Evolution Strategies

Algorithm	Genetic Algorithms	Evolution Strategies
Developers	J. Holland	I. Rechenberg, H.-P. Schwefel
Original applications	Discrete optimization	Continuous optimization
Attribute features	Not too fast	Continuous optimization
Special features	Crossover, many variants	Fast, much theory
Representation	Binary strings	Real-valued vectors
Recombination	*n*-point or uniform	Discrete or intermediary
Mutation	Bit flipping with fixed probability	Gaussian perturbation
Selection (parent selection)	Fitness proportional	Uniform random
Replacement (survivor selection)	All children replace parents	(λ, μ) $(\lambda + \mu)$
Specialty	Emphasis on crossover	Self-adaptation of mutation step size

TABLE 3.5 Main Characteristics of the Different Canonical Evolutionary Algorithms: Evolutionary Programming and Genetic Programming

Algorithm	Evolutionary Programming	Genetic Programming
Developers	D. Fogel	J. Koza
Original applications	Machine learning	Machine learning
Attribute features	–	Slow
Special features	No recombination	–
Representation	Finite-state machines	Parse trees
Recombination	No	Exchange of subtrees
Mutation	Gaussian perturbation	Random change in trees
Selection	Deterministic	Fitness proportional
Replacement (survivor selection)	Probabilistic $(\mu + \mu)$	Generational replacement
Specialty	Self-adaptation	Need huge populations

that is originally the proportional selection. The replacement (survivor selection) is generational, that is, the parents are replaced systematically by the offsprings. The crossover operator is based on the n-point or uniform crossover while the mutation is bit flipping. A fixed probability p_m (resp. p_c) is applied to the mutation (resp. crossover) operator.

3.2.2 Evolution Strategies

Evolution strategies are another subclasses of EAs such as GAs or GPs. They were originally developed by Rechenberg and Schewefel in 1964 at the Technical University of Berlin [642,643]. ESs are mostly applied to continuous optimization where representations are based on real-valued vectors. Early applications include real-valued parameter shape optimization [466]. They usually use an elitist replacement and a specific normally (Gaussian) distributed mutation. Crossover is rarely used. In an ES, there is a distinction between the population of parents of size μ and the population of the offsprings of size $\lambda \geq \mu$. An individual is composed of the float decision variables plus some other parameters guiding the search. Thus, an ES facilitates a kind of *self-adaptation* by evolving the solution as well as the strategy parameters (e.g., mutation step size) at the same time (see Example 3.10). The selection operator is deterministic and is based on the fitness ranking. Hence, the parameterization of an ES is highly customizable. The recombination is discrete (similar to uniform crossover of GAs) or intermediary (arithmetic crossover). Their main advantage is their efficiency in terms of time complexity. Much more theory on convergence exists for evolution strategies [73].

Example 3.6 From basic to contemporary versions of ES. The basic version of ES, the $(1 + 1)$-ES, has a population composed of two individuals: the current point (parent) and the result of its mutation (offspring). The parent is replaced by its offspring if it is better; otherwise the offspring is disregarded. More generally, in the $(1 + \lambda)$-ES strategy, λ offsprings can be generated and compete with the parent. In a $(1, \lambda)$-ES the best individual of the λ offsprings becomes the parent of the next population while the current parent is always deleted. Most of the recent derivatives of ES use a population of μ parents and also recombination of ρ offsprings as an additional operator, which defines the $(\mu/\rho + \lambda)$-ES strategy (resp. $(\mu/\rho, \lambda)$-ES strategy) where the new population is selected from the parents μ and the offsprings λ (resp. the offsprings λ).

Algorithm 3.3 illustrates the evolution strategy template.

Algorithm 3.3 Template of evolution strategies.

Initialize a population of μ individuals ;
Evaluate the μ individuals ;
Repeat
  Generate λ offsprings from μ parents ;
  Evaluate the λ offsprings ;
  Replace the population with μ individuals from parents and offsprings ;
Until Stopping criteria
Output Best individual or population found.

3.2.3 Evolutionary Programming

Evolutionary programming emphasizes on mutation and does not use recombination. Traditional EPs have been developed to evolve finite state machines to solve time series prediction problems and more generally to evolve learning machines [273]. Contemporary EPs have been later applied to solving continuous optimization problems using real-valued representations. They use normally distributed mutations and self-adaptation principle of the parameters as in ESs. The parent selection mechanism is deterministic. The survivor selection process (replacement) is probabilistic and is based on a stochastic tournament $(\mu + \mu)$ selection [240]. The framework of EP is less used than the other families of EAs due to its similarity with ES.

3.2.4 Genetic Programming

Genetic programming is a more recent evolutionary approach, which extends the generic model of learning to the space of programs [480]. Its major variation, with respect to other evolutionary families, is that the evolving individuals are themselves programs (nonlinear representation based on trees) instead of fixed length strings from a limited alphabet of symbols (linear representation). GP is a form of *program induction* that allows to automatically generate programs that solve a given task. In general, the parent selection is a fitness proportional and the survivor selection is a generational replacement. The crossover operator is based on subtrees exchange and the mutation is based on random change in the tree. One of the main problems in GP is the uncontrolled growth of trees; this phenomenon is called *bloat*.

Originally, J. Koza used Lisp expressions to encode programs. More generally, representations of solutions (programs) are S-expressions (or parse trees) where the leaves are terminals and the internal nodes are operators (functions). The definition of the leaves and the operators depend on the target application. They need a huge population (e.g., thousands of individuals) and then they are very computationally intensive. Theory of GP is less developed than in evolution strategies and genetic algorithms [493]. Contemporary GPs are widely used in machine learning and data mining tasks such as prediction and classification.

Example 3.7 Symbolic regression problem. The objective of the symbolic regression problem is to find a program that matches a given mathematical equation. It is a well-known problem in statistics. The terminals of the tree represent significant variables and constants for the problem while the internal nodes of the tree represent arithmetic operators $F = \{*, +, -, /\}$ (Fig. 3.9). The objective function to minimize may be formulated as the sum of the square errors for each test data point.

Example 3.8 Artificial ant on the Santa Fe trail. This is another classical example in the GP community. An artificial ant is placed on a cell of a $32 \cdot 32$ toroidal grid (Fig. 3.10). Food pellets are mapped on some cells of the grid. The objective of this problem is to find a path planning strategy to maximize the food intake of the ant. The objective function will be the number of food pellets lying in the path minus the amount of food the ant eats during the move. For the representation, leaves may represent move operators in several directions (turn left, turn right, move forward) and the internal nodes represent conditional if statements that are sensing functions.

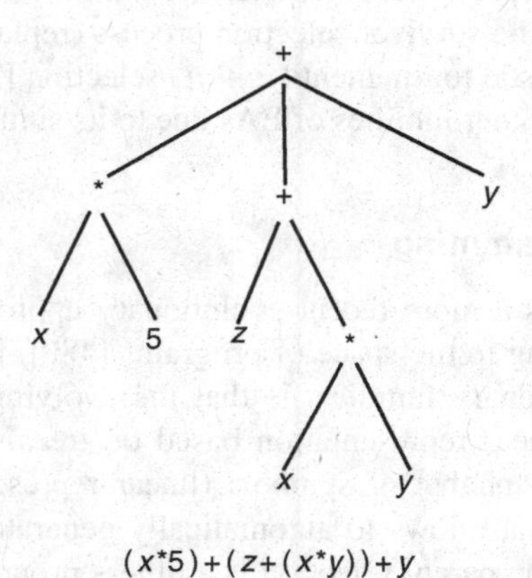

FIGURE 3.9 Tree-like representation in genetic programming. For the regression problem, a function is represented by a tree structure.

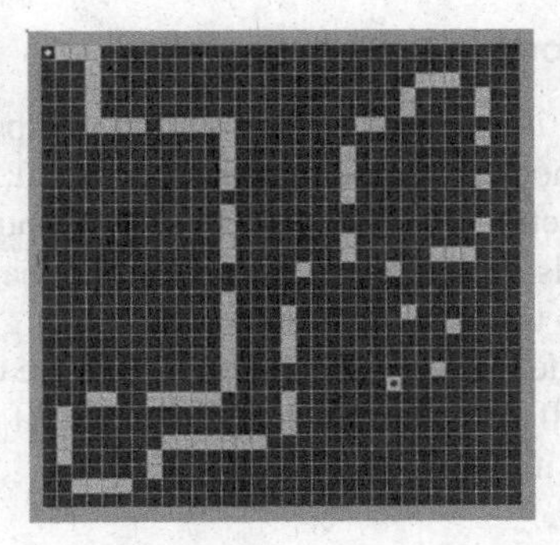

FIGURE 3.10 Artificial ant on the Santa Fe trail. A program is represented by a tree. The IF statements are sensing functions that detect if there is a food around. Leaves represent move operators in several directions (left, right, forward).

3.3 COMMON CONCEPTS FOR EVOLUTIONARY ALGORITHMS

The main search components for designing an evolutionary algorithm are as follows:

1. **Representation:** This is a common search component for all metaheuristics (see Section 4.8.2.1). In the EA (specially GA) community, the encoded solution is referred as *chromosome* while the decision variables within a solution (chromosome) are genes. The possible values of variables (genes) are the *alleles* and the position of an element (gene) within a chromosome is named *locus*.
2. **Population initialization:** This is a common search component for all P-metaheuristics (see Section 3.1.1).
3. **Objective Function:** This is a common search component for all metaheuristics. In the EA community, the term fitness refers to the objective function (see Section 1.4.2).
4. **Selection strategy:** The selection strategy addresses the following question: "Which parents for the next generation are chosen with a bias toward better fitness?"
5. **Reproduction strategy:** The reproduction strategy consists in designing suitable mutation and crossover operator(s) to generate new individuals (offsprings).
6. **Replacement strategy:** The new offsprings compete with old individuals for their place in the next generation (survival of the fittest).
7. **Stopping criteria:** This is a common search component for all metaheuristics. Some stopping criteria are specific to P-metaheuristics (see Section 3.1.2).

The following sections deal with the specific search components for evolutionary algorithms: selection, reproduction, and replacement.

3.3.1 Selection Methods

The selection mechanism is one of the main search components in EAs. The main principle of selection methods is "the better is an individual, the higher is its chance of being parent." Such a selection pressure will drive the population to better solutions. However, worst individuals should not be discarded and they have some chance to be selected. This may lead to useful genetic material.

The selection strategy determines which individuals are chosen for mating (reproduction) and how many offspring each selected individual produces. In EAs, fitness assignment to individuals may take two different ways:

- *Proportional fitness assignment* in which the absolute fitnesses are associated with individuals.
- *Rank-based fitness assignment* in which relative fitnesses are associated with individuals. For instance, a rank in the population is associated with each individual according to its rank in a decreasing sorting of individuals.[5]

Then, the parents are selected according to their fitness by means of one of the following strategies: roulette wheel selection, stochastic universal sampling (SUS), tournament selection, and rank-based selection.

3.3.1.1 Roulette Wheel Selection It is the most common selection strategy. It will assign to each individual a selection probability that is proportional to its relative fitness. Let f_i be the fitness of the individual p_i in the population P. Its probability to be selected is $p_i = f_i \Big/ \left(\sum_{j=1}^{n} f_j\right)$. Suppose a pie graph where each individual is assigned a space on the graph that is proportional to its fitness (Fig. 3.11). An outer roulette wheel is placed around the pie. The selection of μ individuals is performed by μ independent spins of the roulette wheel. Each spin will select a single individual. Better individuals have more space, and then more chance to be chosen.

In the roulette wheel selection, outstanding individuals will introduce a bias in the beginning of the search that may cause a premature convergence and a loss of diversity. Moreover, when all individuals are equally fit, this selection strategy does not introduce a sufficient pressure to select the best individuals.

3.3.1.2 Stochastic Universal Sampling To reduce the bias of the roulette selection strategy, the stochastic universal sampling may be used. An outer roulette wheel is placed around the pie with μ equally spaced pointers. In the SUS strategy, a *single* spin of the roulette wheel will simultaneously select all the μ individuals for reproduction. Figure 3.11 illustrates the principles of the roulette wheel and the SUS selection strategies.

[5]In this section, a maximization optimization problem is considered.

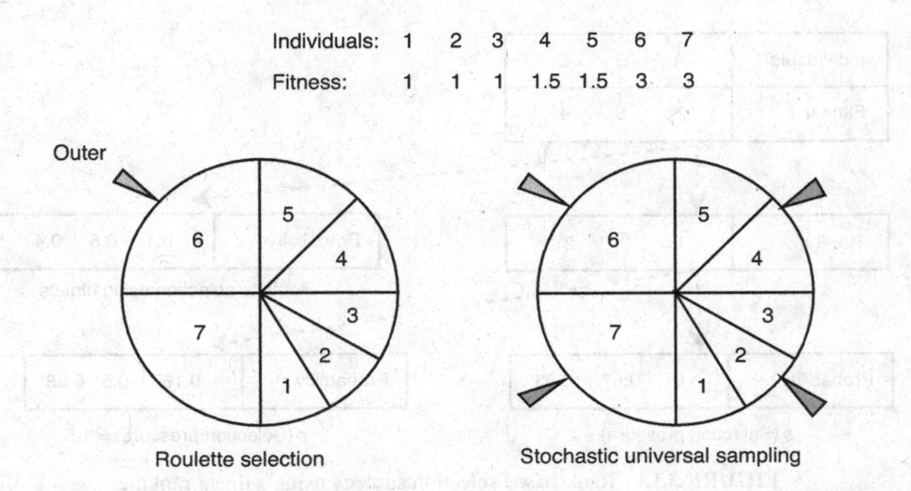

FIGURE 3.11 Roulette selection strategies. In the standard roulette selection, each spin selects a single individual. In SUS, a spin will select as individuals as outers (e.g., four individuals in the example).

3.3.1.3 Tournament Selection Tournament selection consists in randomly selecting k individuals; the parameter k is called the size of the tournament group. A tournament is then applied to the k members of the group to select the best one (Fig. 3.12). To select μ individuals, the tournament procedure is then carried out μ times.

3.3.1.4 Rank-Based Selection Instead of using the fitness value of an individual, the rank of individuals is used. The function is biased toward individuals with a high rank (i.e., good fitness). The rank may be scaled linearly using

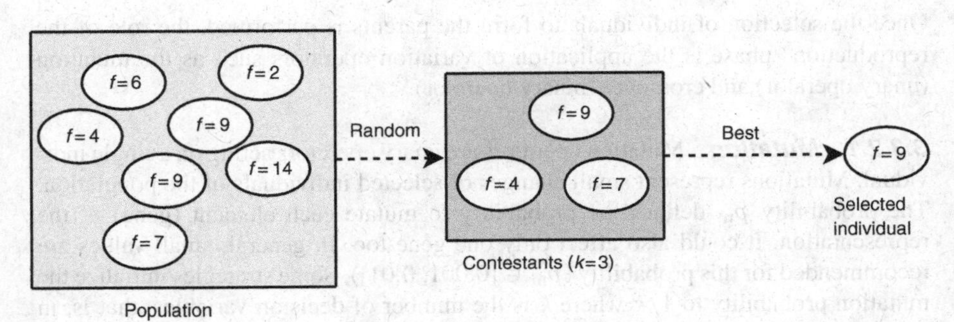

FIGURE 3.12 Tournament selection strategy. For instance, a tournament of size 3 is performed. Three solutions are picked randomly from the population. The best solution from the picked individuals is then selected.

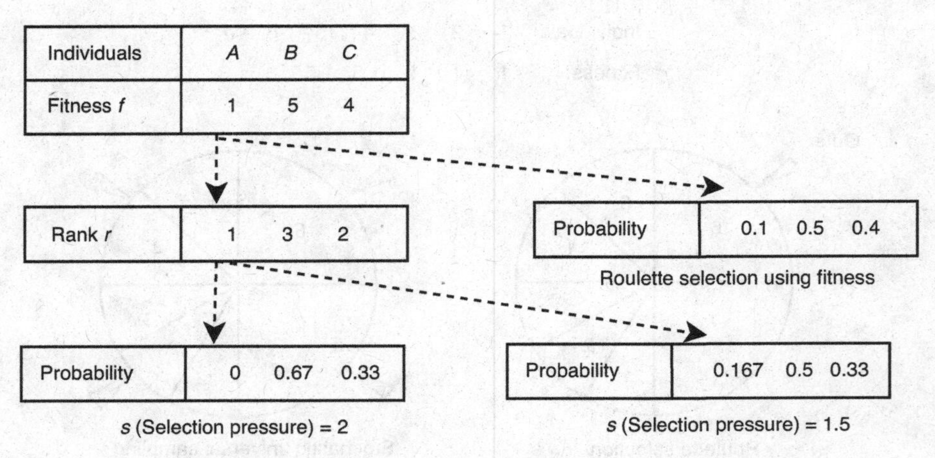

FIGURE 3.13 Rank-based selection strategy using a linear ranking.

the following formula:

$$P(i) = \frac{2-s}{\mu} + \frac{2 \cdot r(i)(s-1)}{\mu(\mu-1)}$$

where s is the selection pressure ($1.0 < s \leq 2.0$), μ is the size of the population, and $r(i)$ is the rank associated with the individual i. Greater is the selection pressure s, more importance to better individuals is given (Fig. 3.13).

In addition to the above selection mechanisms, other selection methods can be applied such as Boltzmann selection based on simulated annealing, soft brood selection used in GP, disruptive selection, nonlinear ranking selection, competitive selection, and variable life span [44].

3.3.2 Reproduction

Once the selection of individuals to form the parents is performed, the role of the reproduction[6] phase is the application of variation operators such as the mutation (unary operator) and crossover (binary operator).

3.3.2.1 Mutation Mutation operators are unary operators acting on a single individual. Mutations represent small changes of selected individuals of the population. The probability p_m defines the probability to mutate each element (gene) of the representation. It could also affect only one gene too. In general, small values are recommended for this probability ($p_m \in [0.001, 0.01]$). Some strategies initialize the mutation probability to $1/k$ where k is the number of decision variables, that is, in average only one variable is mutated.

[6] Also referred as variation phase.

Some important points that must be taken into account in the design or use of a mutation operator are as follows:

- **Ergodicity:** The mutation operator should allow every solution of the search space to be reached.
- **Validity:** The mutation operator should produce valid solutions. This is not always possible for constrained optimization problems.
- **Locality:** The mutation should produce a minimal change. The size of mutation is important and should be controllable. As for the neighborhood definition in S-metaheuristics, the main property that must characterize a mutation operator is *locality*. Locality is the effect on the solution (phenotype) when performing the move (perturbation) in the representation (genotype). When small changes are made in the genotype, the phenotype must reveal small changes. In this case, the mutation is said to have a strong locality. Hence, an evolutionary algorithm will carry out a meaningful search in the landscape of the problem. Weak locality is characterized by a large effect on the phenotype when a small change is made in the genotype. In the extreme case, the search will converge toward a random search in the landscape.

Example 3.9 Highly disruptive mutation. In grouping problems, a classical encoding consists in a linear discrete representation that associates each element with its assigned group (see Example 1.32). Let us consider a mutation that modifies the value of a given element. For instance, let us suppose a high-quality individual $AAACCC$ that contains two groups. A mutation may produce the individual $AAABCC$, which contains a group with only one element. This mutation operator is highly disruptive as it may generate very low-quality individuals from good solutions.

The mutation in evolutionary algorithms is related to neighborhood operators of S-metaheuristics (see Section 2.1.1). Hence, the neighborhood structure definitions for traditional representations (e.g., linear discrete) may be reused as mutation operators.

- **Mutation in binary representation:** The commonly used mutation is defined as the flip operator.
- **Mutation in discrete representation:** It consists generally in changing the value associated with an element by another value of the alphabet.
- **Mutation in permutations:** Mutation in order-based representations are generally based on the *swapping*, *inversion*, or the *insertion* operators.

In GP where parse trees are used as representations, some distinct forms of mutations may be defined as follows:

- **Grow:** A terminal node is selected randomly and replaced by a randomly generated subtree (Fig. 3.14).

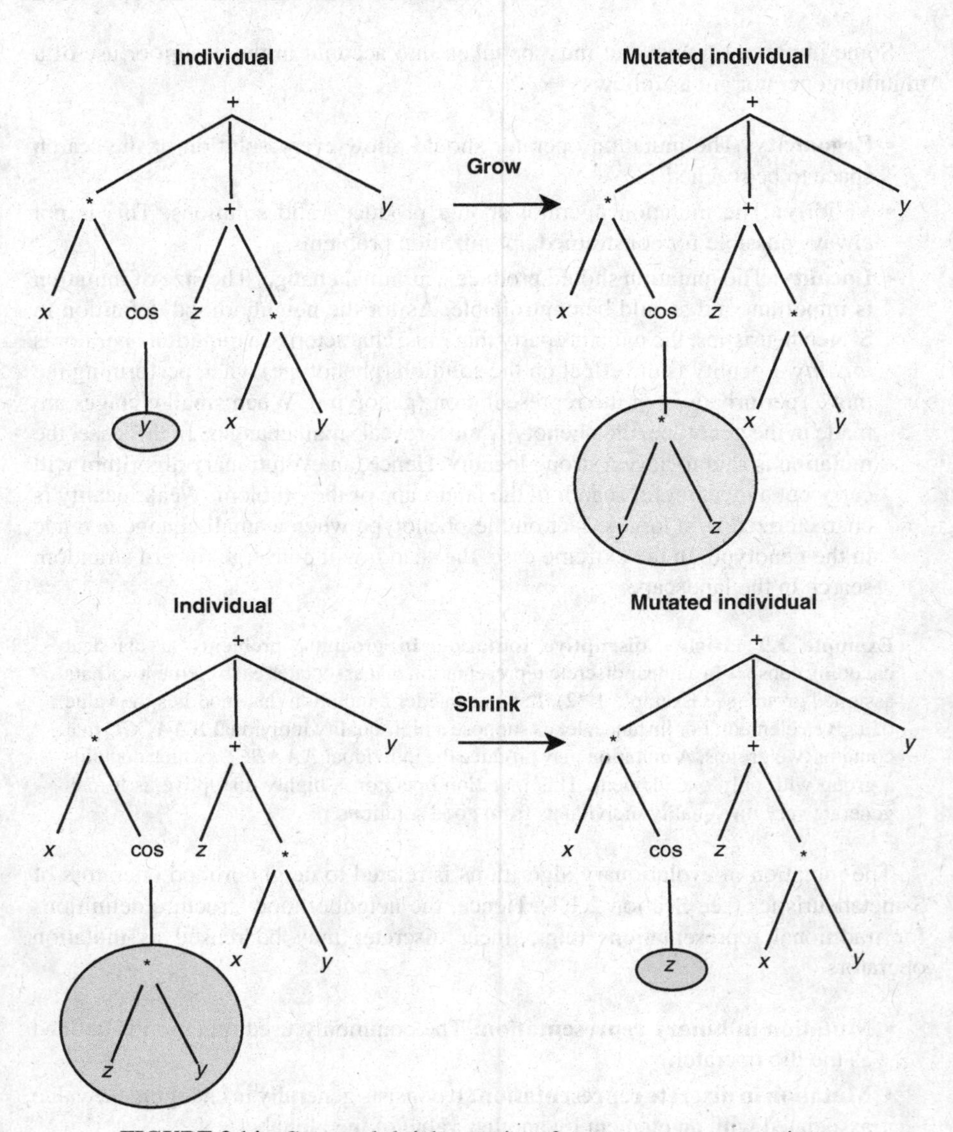

FIGURE 3.14 Grow and shrink mutations for parse tree representations.

- **Shrink:** An internal node is selected randomly and replaced by a randomly generated terminal (Fig. 3.14).
- **Switch:** An internal node is selected randomly, two of its subtrees are selected randomly and their positions in the tree are switched (Fig. 3.15).
- **Cycle:** A single node (internal or terminal) is selected randomly and replaced by a randomly node with the same number of arguments (Fig. 3.15).

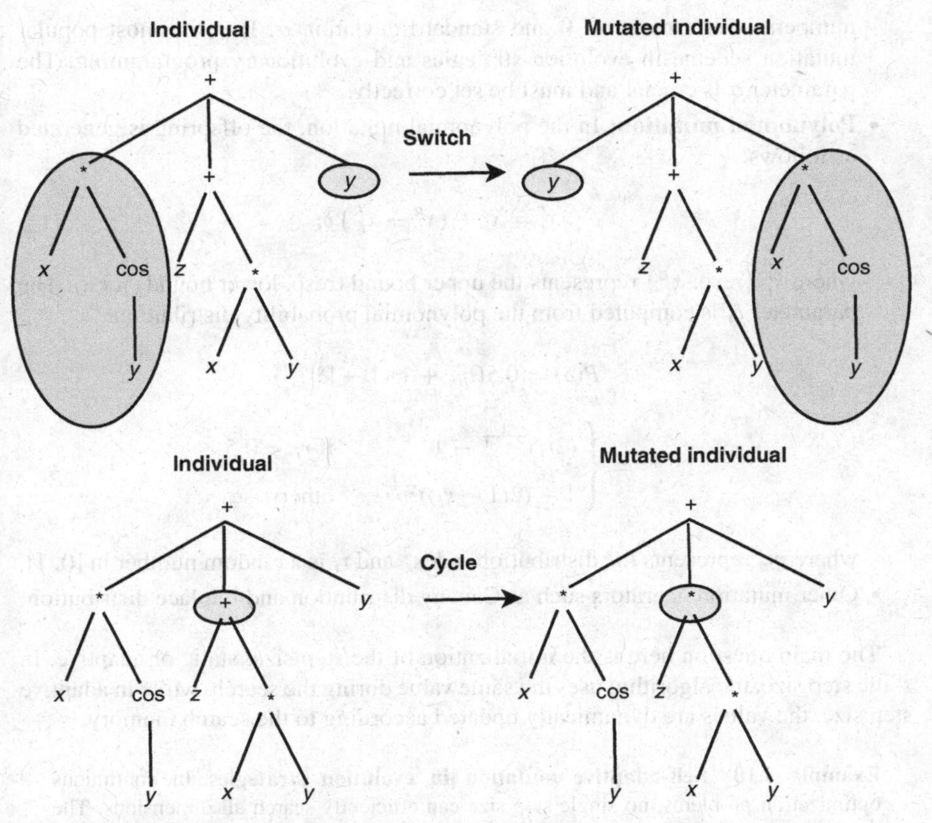

FIGURE 3.15 Switch and cycle mutations for parse tree representations.

For real-valued vectors, there are many distinct mutation operators. The most used class of mutation operators has the form:

$$x' = x + M$$

where M is a random variable. The value of M can take the following different forms:

- **Uniform random mutation:** A uniform random variable in the interval $[a, b]$ is generated. The parameter a is in general equal to $-b$. The offspring is generated within the hyperbox $x + U(-b, b)^n$ where b represents a user-defined constant.
- **Normally distributed mutation:** A Gaussian (or normal) distribution $M = N(0, \sigma)$ is used, where $N(0, \sigma)$ is a vector of independent random Gaussian

numbers with a mean of 0 and standard deviation σ. It is the most popular mutation scheme in evolution strategies and evolutionary programming. The parameter σ is crucial and must be set correctly.

- **Polynomial mutation:** In the polynomial mutation, the offspring is generated as follows:

$$x_i' = x_i + \left(x_i^u - x_i^L\right)\delta_i$$

where x_i^u (resp. x_i^L) represents the upper bound (resp. lower bound) for x_i. The parameter δ_i is computed from the polynomial probability distribution:

$$P(\delta) = 0.5(\eta_m + 1)(1 - |\delta|^{\eta m})$$

$$\delta_i = \begin{cases} (2r_i)^{\frac{1}{\eta m+1}} - 1 & \text{if } r_i < 0.5 \\ 1 - (2(1 - r_i))^{\frac{1}{\eta m+1}} & \text{otherwise} \end{cases}$$

where η_m represents the distribution index[7] and r_i is a random number in [0, 1].

- Other mutation operators such as Cauchy distribution and Laplace distribution.

The main question here is the initialization of the step size: static or adaptive. In static step size, the algorithm uses the same value during the search, while in adaptive step size, the values are dynamically updated according to the search memory.

Example 3.10 Self-adaptive mutation in evolution strategies. In continuous optimization problems, no single step size can efficiently search all dimensions. The mutation scheme for continuous optimization should dynamically scale the mutation strength (step width) to suit each variable. In evolution strategies, the answer provided is the use of "self-adaptation" to scale and orient the mutation vectors. Each solution vector $x_i(t)$ is paired with a strategy vector $\sigma_i(t)$ that is used to scale the variation operation. As already mentioned in this chapter, the decision variables evolve in parallel with their associated strategy vector. The strategy vectors are adjusted with log-normal noise according to the following rule:

$$\sigma_{ij}(t+1) = \sigma_{ij}(t) \cdot \exp(\tau' \cdot N(0,1) + \tau \cdot N_j(0,1))$$

where $\tau = \left(\sqrt{2\sqrt{D}}\right)^{-1}$ and $\tau' = \left(\sqrt{2D}\right)^{-1}$. The vectors are mutated as follows:

$$x_{ij}(t+1) = x_{ij}(t) + \sigma_{ij}(t+1) \cdot N_j(0,1)$$

[7] $\eta_m \approx 20$ is generally used.

where $N(0, 1)$ represents a normally Gaussian distributed variable with a zero mean and a standard deviation of 1. A new random value $N_j(0, 1)$ is generated for each variable.

Example 3.11 The CMA evolution strategy. CMA-ES is one of the most successful optimization algorithms to solve continuous optimization problems. In the CMA[8] evolution strategy, individual step sizes for each coordinate or correlations between coordinates are governed by CMA [362]. CMA-ES adapts the covariance matrix of the multivariate normal mutation distribution. The mutation distribution conducts the generation of new candidate solutions. CMA-ES is a second-order optimization approach, that is, it captures dependencies between variables. The covariance matrix defines the pairwise dependencies between the variables in the distribution. Adaptation of the covariance matrix is based on learning a second-order model of the target objective function, which is reduced to the approximation of the inverse Hessian matrix in the quasi-Newton method, a traditional method in continuous optimization.

The CMA-ES is based on two adaptation principles, which make it an efficient procedure for multimodal continuous problems [361]:

- **Maximum likelihood:** The idea behind this principle is to increase the probability of a successful mutation step. For this purpose, the algorithm updates the covariance matrix of the distribution such that the likelihood of already applied successful steps is increased. Then, the CMA-ES algorithm uses an iterated PCA (principal components analysis) of successful mutation steps while retaining all principal axes.
- **Evolution path:** The other adaptation principle is based on memorizing the time evolution path of the distribution mean. This path will contain important information of the correlation between successive steps. During the search, the evolution path is used for the covariance matrix adaptation procedure in place of single successful mutation steps. Moreover, the evolution path is used to apply an additional step-size control. The goal of this step-size control is to make successive moves of the distribution mean orthogonal in expectation.

3.3.2.2 Recombination or Crossover

Unlike unary operators such as mutation, the crossover operator is binary and sometimes n-ary. The role of crossover operators is to inherit some characteristics of the two parents to generate the offsprings. As for the mutation operator, the design of crossover operators mainly depends on the representation used. Unlike S-metaheuristics, where the search operators are always unary, this part has been independently developed in the evolutionary computation community.

Some important points must be taken into account in the design or use of a crossover operator:

- **Heritability:** The main characteristic of the crossover operator is *heritability*. The crossover operator should inherit a genetic material from both parents. An

[8]CMA stands for covariance matrix adaptation.

operator is a pure recombination operator (strong heritability) if two identical individuals generate identical offsprings. Hence, the mutation and crossover operators are complementary. In this case, mutation introduces some diversification in the individuals by introducing some missing values in the current individuals of a population.

A crossover operator Ox is *respectful* if the common decisions in both parents are preserved, and is *assorting* if the distance between the parents (p_1, p_2) and the offspring o is lower or equal to the distance between the parents [629]:

$$d(p_1, o) \leq d(p_1, p_2) \text{ and } d(p_2, o) \leq d(p_1, p_2), \quad \forall o \in O(p_1, p_2, Ox)$$

where $O(p_1, p_2, Ox)$ is the set of all possible offsprings generated by the crossover operator Ox.

- **Validity:** The crossover operator should produce valid solutions. This is not always possible for constrained optimization problems.

The crossover rate p_c ($p_c \in [0, 1]$) represents the proportion of parents on which a crossover operator will act. The best parameter value for p_c is related to other parameters among them such as the population size, the mutation probability, and the selection procedure. The most commonly used rates are in the interval [0.45, 0.95]. Adaptive techniques for the crossover rate may also be useful.

For linear representations excluding permutations, the well-known crossover operators are the 1-point crossover, its generalized form the n-point crossover, and the uniform crossover.

The basic crossover operator is the 1-point crossover and its generalization the n-point crossover. These operators have been initially proposed for binary representations. In the 1-point crossover, a crossover site k is randomly selected, and two offsprings are created by interchanging the segments of the parents (Fig. 3.16). In general, a uniform random distribution is used to select the crossover point k. An effect of *disruption* can be generated by the 1-point crossover. Suppose that the elements A and E are coadapted in the sense that their presence is beneficial in the individual (e.g., `ABCDE`). In most of the offsprings, this coadaptation will be lost, given that the crossover point is always between the two elements. Indeed, the elements in the beginning and in the end of the individual are disrupted with a higher probability.

To eliminate the effect of disruption, all positions have to be treated equally. In the n-point crossover, n crossover sites are randomly selected (Fig. 3.16). For instance, the 2-point crossover uses two crossing sites. The individuals `A|BCD|E` and `a|bcd|e` generate the offsprings `A|bcd|E` and `a|BCD|e`.

Using the uniform crossover, two individuals can be recombined without regard to the size of segments. Each element of the offspring is selected randomly from either parent (Fig. 3.17). Each parent will contribute equally to generate the offsprings.

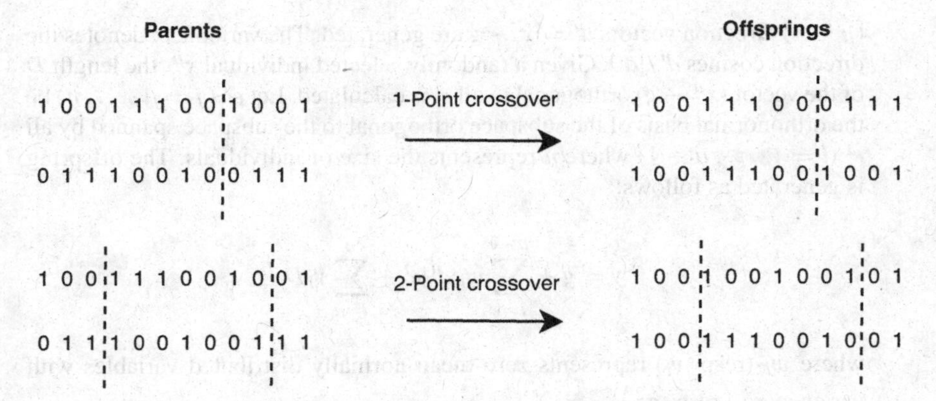

FIGURE 3.16 1-point and *n*-point crossover operators.

For real-valued representations, in addition to the 1-point, *n*-point, and the uniform crossover operators, the following two types of crossover operators are commonly used: mean-centric recombination and parent-centric recombination.

In mean-centric recombination, the offsprings are generated closer to the centroid of their parents. One may use the following crossover operators:

- **Intermediate crossover:** The intermediate crossover operators attempt to average the elements of the parents. Given two parents p_1 and p_2, the *arithmetic crossover* creates an offspring o using the weighted average:

$$o_i = \alpha x_{1i} + (1 - \alpha) x_{2i}$$

- **Geometrical crossover:** The geometrical crossover generates an offspring in the following form [548]:

$$o_i = ((x_{11}x_{21})^{0.5}, \ldots, (x_{1n}x_{2n})^{0.5})$$

- **Unimodal normal distribution crossover (UNDX):** In this mean-centric crossover operator, $(\mu - 1)$ parents x^i are randomly selected from the population [594]. The mean value g of the selected individuals is computed. Then,

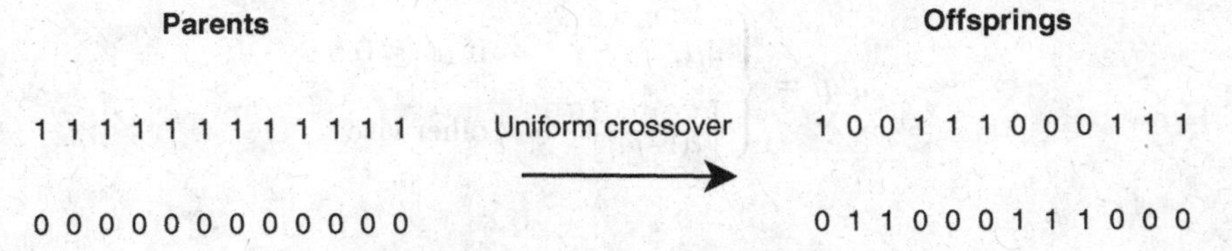

FIGURE 3.17 The uniform crossover operator.

$(\mu - 1)$ direction vectors $d^i = x^i - g$ are generated. The variable e^i denotes the direction cosines $d^i/|d^i|$. Given a randomly selected individual x^μ, the length D of the vector $(x^\mu - g)$ orthogonal to all e^i is calculated. Let e^j $(j = \mu, \ldots, n)$ be the orthonormal basis of the subspace orthogonal to the subspace spanned by all e^i $(i = 1, \ldots, \mu - 1)$ where n represents the size of individuals. The offspring is generated as follows:

$$y = g + \sum_{i=1}^{\mu-1} w_i |d^i| e^i + \sum_{i=\mu}^{n} v_i D e^i$$

where w_i (resp. v_i) represents zero-mean normally distributed variables with variance σ_ξ^2 $\left(\text{resp. } \sigma_\eta^2\right)$.

- **Simplex crossover (SPX):** The SPX crossover generates the offsprings around the mean [779]. The operator restricts the offsprings in a predefined region: a simplex similar but $\lambda = \sqrt{\mu + 1}$ bigger than the parent simplex. Unlike the UNDX operator, the SPX operator uses a uniform distribution probability in the generation of the offsprings.

In parent-centric recombination, the offsprings are generated closer to their parents. Each parent is assigned an equal probability of creating an offspring in its neighborhood. One may use the following crossover operators:

- **Simulated binary crossover (SBX):** A random number μ_i is first generated between 0 and 1 [196]. Given a probability distribution function:

$$P(\beta) = \begin{cases} 0.5(\eta + 1)\beta_i^\eta & \text{if } \beta_i \leq 1 \\ 0.5(\eta + 1)\beta_i^{\frac{1}{\eta+2}} & \text{otherwise} \end{cases}$$

The distribution index η[9] gives a higher probability for generating offsprings that are near their parents. The ordinate βq_i is found so that the area under the probability curve from 0 to βq_i is equal to the generated random number μ_i:

$$\beta q_i = \begin{cases} 2\mu_i^{\frac{1}{\eta+1}} & \text{if } \mu_i \leq 0.5 \\ \left[\frac{1}{2(1-\mu_i)}\right]^{\frac{1}{\eta+1}} & \text{otherwise} \end{cases}$$

[9]For monoobjective EAs, the value of 2 is generally used for η whereas for multiobjective optimization the interval value [5, 10] is commonly used.

The two offsprings y^1 and y^2 are then computed as follows:

$$y_i^1 = 0.5 \left[(1 + \beta q_i) x_i^1 + (1 - \beta q_i) x_i^2 \right]$$

$$y_i^2 = 0.5 \left[(1 - \beta q_i) x_i^1 + (1 + \beta q_i) x_i^2 \right]$$

where x^1 and x^2 represent the parents.

- **Parent-centric crossover (PCX):** First the mean vector g is calculated [199]. One parent x^p is selected in equal probability for each offspring. Then, the direction vector $d^p = x^p - g$ is computed. From each of the other $(\mu - 1)$ parents, perpendicular distances D_i to the line d^p are computed and their average $\bar{D}$ is found. The offspring is generated as follows:

$$y = x^p + \omega_\xi |d^p| + \sum_{i=1, i \neq p}^{\mu} \omega_\eta \bar{D} e^i$$

where e^i represents the $(\mu - 1)$ orthonormal bases spanning the subspace perpendicular to d^p, and ω_ξ (resp. ω_η) represents a zero-mean normally distributed variable with variance σ_ξ^2 (resp. σ_η^2).

Figure 3.18 shows the distribution of the offsprings using the three crossover operators UNDX, SPX, and PCX.

Example 3.12 Highly disruptive and nonheritable crossover. Let us use the straightforward encoding for grouping problems which associates to each element its group member (see example 1.32). As pointed out, a classical crossover for linear representations is the 1-point crossover. Applying the 1-point crossover leads to nonefficient search. Given the two parents $AA|BBCC$ and $BB|AACC$,

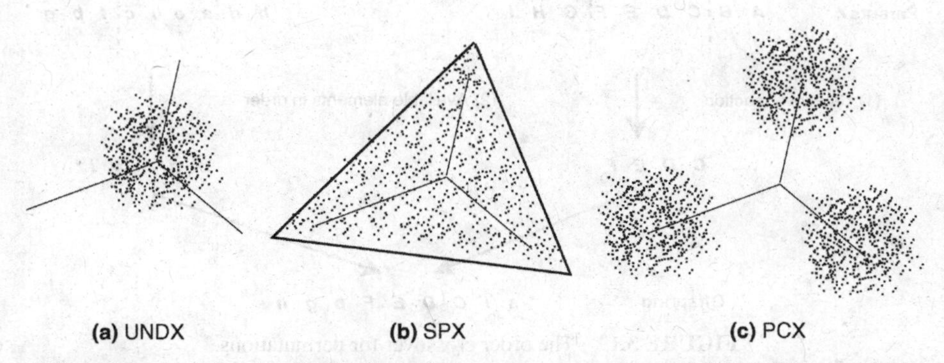

FIGURE 3.18 Offspring distribution using the crossover operators UNDX, SPX, and PCX.

the 1-point crossover may produce the individual $AAAACC$ that contains only two groups. This crossover operator is highly disruptive and does not satisfy the heritability property as it generates solutions that will not share the good schemata of the parents and may produce very low-quality individuals from high-quality solutions.

Moreover, if the parents are identical (e.g., $A|BC|ADD$ and $C|AD|CBB$), one of the offsprings may be $CBCCBB$. This offspring is completely different from its parent and then this crossover operator is highly disruptive. The strong heritability property is not satisfied.

Applying classical crossover operators to permutations will generate solutions that are not permutations (i.e., nonfeasible solutions). Hence, many permutation crossover operators have been designed as follows:

- **Order crossover (OX):** First, two crossover points are randomly selected. From parent 1, one will copy in the offspring, at the same absolute positions, the part between the two points. From parent 2, one will start at the second crossover point and pick the elements that are not already selected from parent 1 to fill them in the offspring from the second crossover point (Fig. 3.19). The OX crossover operator is a pure recombination operator. If one starts filling or picking at the first crossover point, the operator will not be pure. From parent 1, the relative order, the adjacency, and the absolute positions are preserved. From parent 2, only the relative order is preserved [181].
- **Partially mapped crossover (PMX):** As in the order crossover, two crossover points are selected randomly. From parent 1, one will copy in the offspring, at the same absolute positions, the part between the two points (Fig. 3.20) [330].
- **Two-point crossover:** In this operator, two points are randomly selected. The elements outside the selected two points are inherited from one parent of the

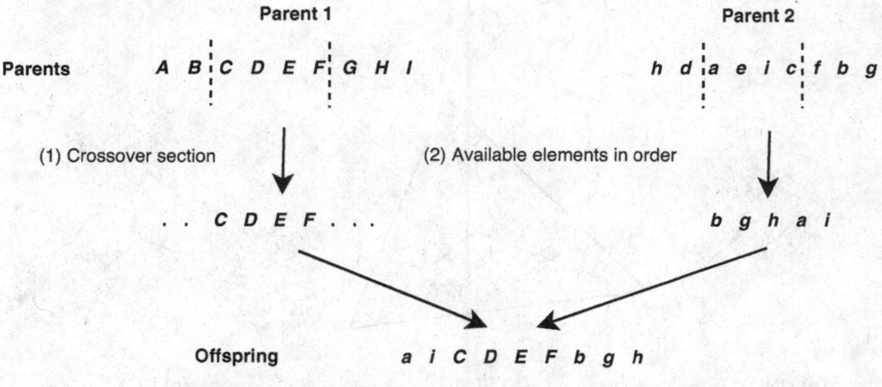

FIGURE 3.19 The order crossover for permutations.

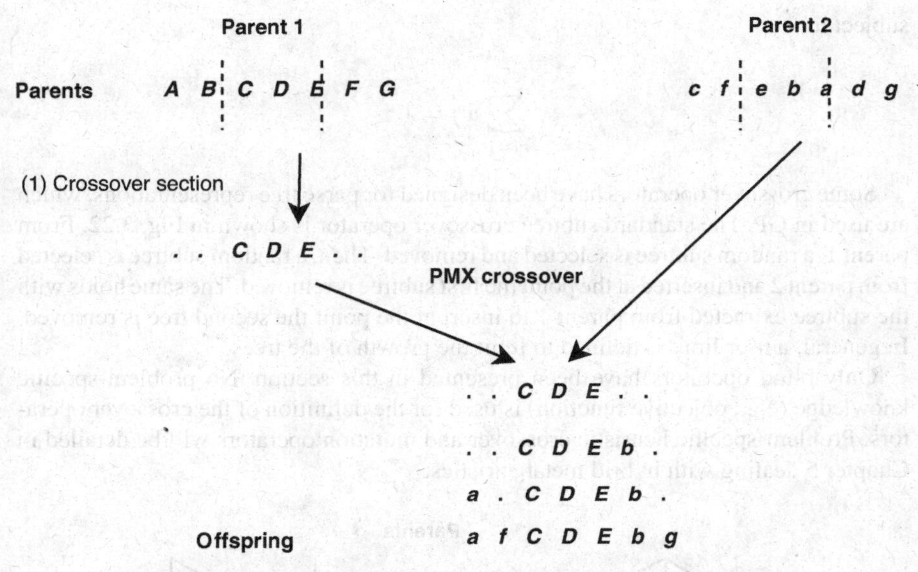

FIGURE 3.20 The partially mapped crossover for permutations.

child, and the other elements are placed in the order of their appearance in the other parent as shown in Fig. 3.21.

- Other crossover operators may be used such as the maximum preservative crossover [569], cycle crossover (CX) that preserves the absolute positions of the elements [592], merge crossover [78], and position-based crossover (POS) [735].

Most of the crossover operators may be extended to more than two parents. For instance, the arithmetic crossover may be extended using the following formula:

$$o_i = w_1 x_{1i} + w_2 x_{2i} + \cdots + w_k x_{ki}$$

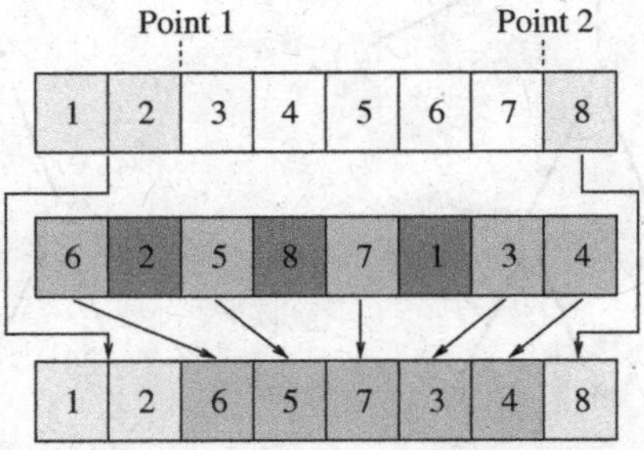

Point 1 Point 2

1	2	3	4	5	6	7	8

6	2	5	8	7	1	3	4

1	2	6	5	7	3	4	8

FIGURE 3.21 Two-Point crossover operator for permutations.

subject to

$$\sum_{j=1}^{k} w_j = 1$$

Some crossover operators have been designed for parse tree representations, which are used in GP. The standard subtree crossover operator is shown in Fig. 3.22. From parent 1, a random subtree is selected and removed. Then, a random subtree is selected from parent 2 and inserted at the point the first subtree is removed. The same holds with the subtree extracted from parent 1 to insert at the point the second tree is removed. In general, a user limit is defined to limit the growth of the trees.

Only blind operators have been presented in this section. No problem-specific knowledge (e.g., objective function) is used for the definition of the crossover operators. Problem-specific heuristic crossover and mutation operators will be detailed in Chapter 5 dealing with hybrid metaheuristics.

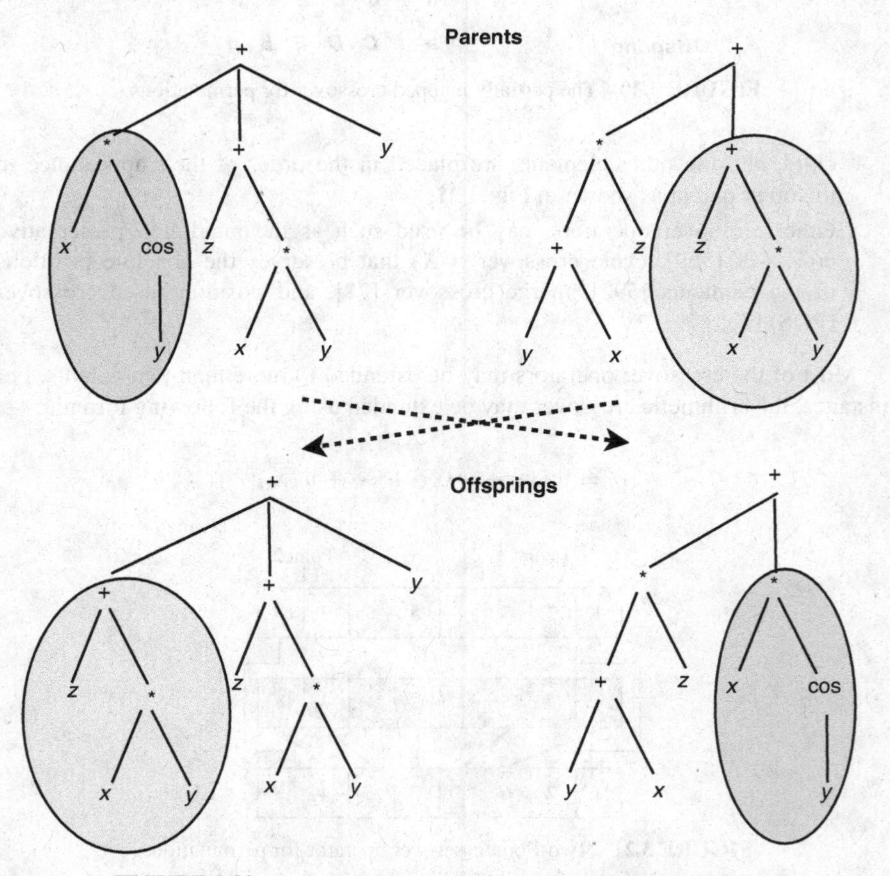

FIGURE 3.22 A crossover operator for parse tree representations.

3.3.3 Replacement Strategies

The replacement phase concerns the survivor selection of both the parent and the offspring populations. As the size of the population is constant, it allows to withdraw individuals according to a given selection strategy. First, let us present the extreme replacement strategies:

- **Generational replacement:** The replacement will concern the whole population of size μ. The offspring population will replace systematically the parent population. This strategy is applied in the canonical GA as proposed by J. Holland.
- **Steady-state replacement:** At each generation of an EA, only one offspring is generated. For instance, it replaces the worst individual of the parent population.

Between those two extreme replacement strategies, many distinct schemes that consist in replacing a given number of λ individuals of the population may be applied $(1 < \lambda < \mu)$. Elitism always consists in selecting the best individuals from the parents and the offsprings. This approach leads to a faster convergence and a premature convergence could occur. Sometimes, selecting bad individuals is necessary to avoid the sampling error problem. Those replacement strategies may be stochastic or deterministic.

Let us summarize the common parameters of EAs:

- **Mutation probability p_m:** A large mutation probability will disrupt a given individual and the search is more likely random. Generally, small values are recommended for the mutation probability ($p_m \in [0.001, 0.01]$). Usually, the mutation probability is initialized to $1/k$ where k is the number of decision variables. Hence, on average, only one variable is mutated.
- **Crossover probability p_c:** The crossover probability is generally set from medium to large values (e.g., [0.3, 0.9]).
- **Population size:** The larger is the size of the population, the better is the convergence toward "good" solutions. Sampling errors are more important in smaller populations. However, the time complexity of EAs grows linearly with the size of the population. A compromise must be found between the quality of the obtained solutions and the search time of the algorithms. In practice, the population size is usually between 20 and 100. Some theoretical results indicate that the size of the population should grow exponentially with the size of individuals, which lead to very large populations to be practical.

3.4 OTHER EVOLUTIONARY ALGORITHMS

In the past 15 years, other models of evolutionary algorithms have been developed. Among them, one can find estimation of distribution algorithms, differential evolution, coevolutionary algorithms, and cultural algorithms.

3.4.1 Estimation of Distribution Algorithms

Estimation of distribution algorithms are a recent class of optimization techniques based on the concept of using probability distribution of the population in reproducing new offsprings [519,609]. EDAs are an outgrowth of genetic algorithms in which statistical information is extracted from the population to construct a probability distribution and then are created new individuals by sampling this probability distribution. This class of algorithms is classified as non-Darwinian evolutionary algorithms as they replace Darwinian operators with probability distributions. The first algorithms belonging to this class have been proposed in Refs. [48,568].

Example 3.13 Estimation of distribution algorithms versus genetic algorithms. Let us consider an optimization problem with a bit vector representation of size 6. In a GA, the population of k individuals is represented explicitly by an array of k vectors. New solutions are created using recombination and mutation variation operators (Fig. 3.23). In an EDA, the population is represented by the probability distribution that is used to reproduce new individuals. For instance, the probability distribution will be represented by a single vector of six probability elements $P = (p_1, p_2, \ldots, p_6)$. Each element of the vector p_i represents the probability that the value associated with the bit vector i is 1 (i.e., a value equal to 0 with a probability $1 - p_i$) (Fig. 3.24). It is possible to create any solution of the search space using the probability distribution P.

The principal idea in EDA is then to transform the optimization problem into a search over probability distributions. They maintain a population of individuals. A probabilistic model for promising individuals is constructed. For instance, EDA

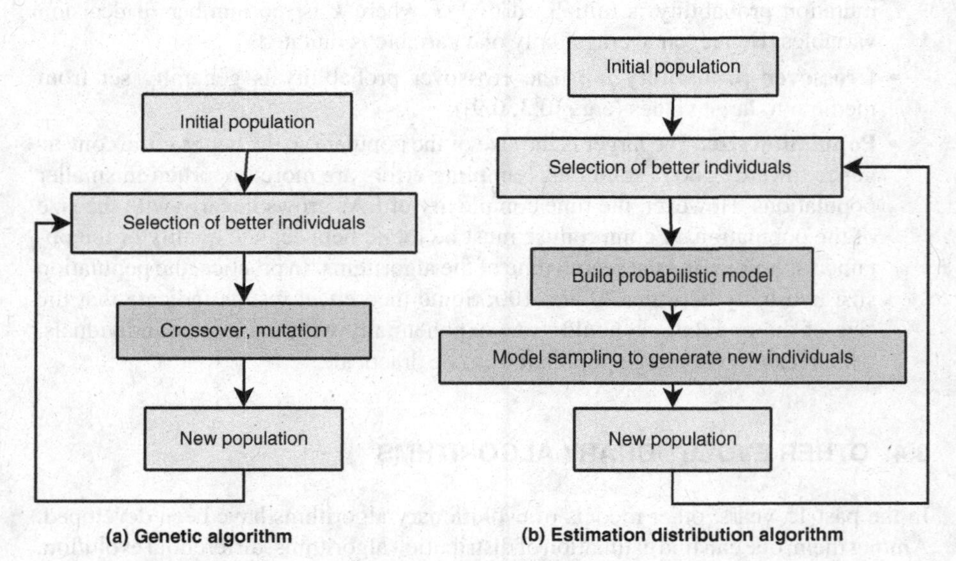

FIGURE 3.23 Estimation of distribution algorithms versus genetic algorithms.

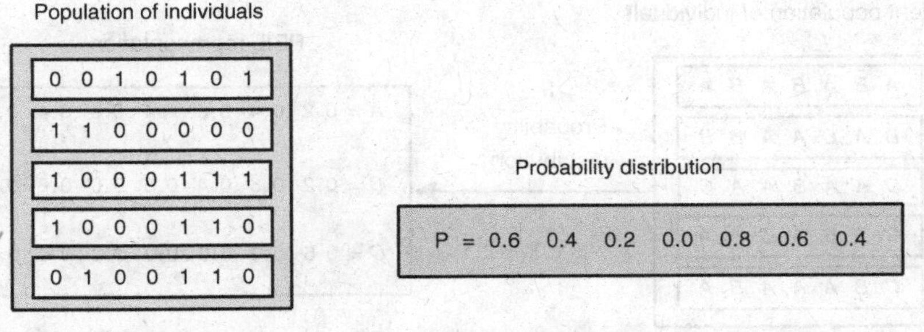

FIGURE 3.24 EDA and GA in solving a bit vector optimization problem.

estimates the probability distribution of each decision variable of the optimization problem. The probabilistic model represents an explicit model of promising regions of the search space. The induced probabilistic model will be used to generate new solutions. The generated individuals will replace the old population in a full or a partial manner. This process iterates until a given stopping criteria. The general EDA can be sketched as follows (Algorithm 3.4):

Algorithm 3.4 Template of the EDA algorithm.

$t = 1$;
Generate randomly a population of n individuals ;
Initialize a probability model $Q(x)$;
While Termination criteria are not met **Do**
  Create a population of n individuals by sampling from $Q(x)$;
  Evaluate the objective function for each individual ;
  Select m individuals according to a selection method ;
  Update the probabilistic model $Q(x)$ using selected population and $f()$ values ;
  $t = t + 1$;
End While
Output: Best found solution or set of solutions.

The main step in this algorithm is to estimate the probability model $Q(x)$ to generate new points according to this distribution. This process represents a clear difference with respect to other evolutionary algorithms that use recombination and/or mutation operators to compute a new population of tentative solutions.

EDAs can be classified according to the level of variable interaction that their probabilistic model takes into account [607]:

- **Univariate:** In this class of EDA, no interaction between the problem variables is taken into account in the construction of the probabilistic model.
- **Bivariate:** In bivariate EDAs, the interactions between two variables will define the probabilistic model.

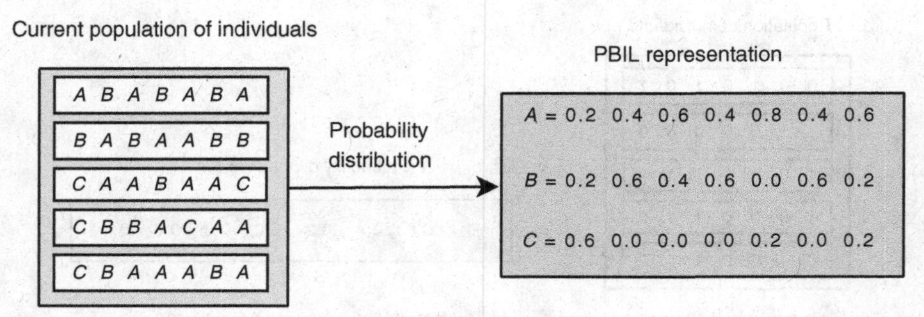

FIGURE 3.25 Probability distribution in the PBIL algorithm.

- **Multivariate:** In this general class of EDAs, the probabilistic distribution models the interactions between more than two variables. For optimization problems having no significant interaction between variables, univariate and bivariate models provide better results, whereas in problems where higher order interaction occurs, multivariate models must be used to improve the results.

EDAs are mainly based on the use of (unsupervised) density estimators/generative statistical models. The different EDA algorithms differ by the probabilistic models used and their construction. The most known EDAs include the PBIL (population-based incremental learning), UMDA (univariate marginal distribution algorithm), BOA (Bayesian optimization algorithm), and EMNA (estimation of multivariate normal algorithm).

In 1994, the PBIL algorithm was the first EDA strategy applied to solve optimization problems. The algorithm creates a probability vector characterizing high fitness solutions (see Fig. 3.25). A marginal probability is associated with each variable of the problem. Then, each element of the vector is represented as a real value in the range [0, 1], indicating the probability that the associated value appears in that element. This probability vector is then used to create new solutions. Algorithm 3.5 illustrates the PBIL algorithm for a binary optimization problem. The initial distribution is $D = (0.5, \ldots, 0.5)$. A new population is generated using the distribution D. The fitness of each member is evaluated and ranked. Then, the probability distribution D is updated according to the new fitness evaluation. This process is repeated until a given population-based stopping criterion.

Algorithm 3.5 Template of the PBIL algorithm.

Initial distribution $D = (0.5, \ldots, 0.5)$;
Repeat
  Generation of the population ;
  If $r < D_i$ (r uniform in [0, 1]) **Then** $X_i = 1$
  Else $X_i = 0$;
  Evaluate and sort the population ;
  Update the distribution $D = (1 - \alpha)D + \alpha X_{best}$;
Until Stopping criteria

The UMDA approach introduced in Ref. [568] estimates the probability density functions for binary encodings of solutions by the product of the individual probability density. Other probabilistic models may be used:

- Gaussian networks for continuous optimization.
- Bayesian networks for discrete optimization.
- Mutual information maximization for input clustering (MIMIC) regards pairwise dependencies.

The BOA for multivariate dependencies extend the above ideas by using Bayesian networks to model the individuals of superior fitness (see Algorithm 3.6) [608].

Algorithm 3.6 Template of the BOA algorithm.

```
Initialize the population P(0) randomly ; Evaluate (P(0)) ;
Repeat
  Select a set of promising solutions S(t) from P(t) ;
  Construct the network B using a given metric and constraints ;
  Generate new solutions O(t) according to the joint distribution encoded by B ;
  Create population P(t + 1) by replacing some solutions from P(t) with O(t) ;
  Evaluate P(t) ; t = t + 1 ;
Until Stopping criteria
```

The results obtained from the EDA family of algorithms are not yet competitive compared to more traditional metaheuristics.

3.4.2 Differential Evolution

Differential evolution (DE) is one of the most successful approaches for continuous optimization [627]. DE grew out of K. Price's attempts to solve the Chebycheff polynomial fitting problem that had been posed to him by R. Storn [724,725]. The main idea of DE is using vector differences for perturbing the vector population. This idea has been integrated in a novel recombination operator of two or more solutions and a self-referential mutation operator to direct the search toward "good" solutions. The DE community is relatively new and has been growing since 1995.

Like any evolutionary algorithm, DE generates a randomly distributed initial population P_0 of size k ($k \geq 4$). Each individual is a D-dimensional real vector x_{ij}. Each individual is encoded as a vector of floating-point numbers. Each element of the vector x_{ij} is generated randomly in the range $[x_j^{lo}, x_j^{hi}]$ representing the lower and the upper bounds for each variable:

$$x_{ij} = x_j^{lo} + \text{rand}_j[0, 1] \cdot (x_j^{hi} - x_j^{lo}), i \in [1, k], j \in [1, D]$$

where rand_j is a uniformly distributed random variable in the range [0, 1].

Instead of using the classical crossover operators of EAs where parts of the parents are recombined, the DE recombination operator is based on a linear combination in which the distance concept plays an important role. Algorithm 3.7 shows the algorithm associated with the crossover operator. Given a parent i and three randomly selected individuals of the population r_1, r_2, and r_3. The parameter F represents a scaling factor ($F \in [0, 1]$) while the parameter CR represents a probability (CR $\in [0, 1]$). When $\text{rand}_j[0, 1] < \text{CR}$ or $j = j_{\text{rand}}$, the offspring-associated variable will be a linear combination of three randomly chosen solutions. Otherwise, the offspring variable will inherit the value of its parent. The condition $j = j_{\text{rand}}$ is included to ensure that at least one variable of the offspring will be different from its parent (for instance, for CR= 0). The scaling factor F controls the amplification of the difference between the individuals r_1 and r_2 and is used to avoid stagnation of the search process.

Algorithm 3.7 Recombination operator in DE.

Input: Parent i, three randomly selected individuals $r_1, r_2, r_3, i \neq r_1 \neq r_2 \neq r_3$.
$j_{rand} = int(rand_i[0, 1].D) + 1$;
For $(j = 1, j \leq D, j++)$ **Do**
  If $(rand_j[0, 1]) < CR)$ or $(j = j_{rand})$ **Then**
    $u_{ij} = v_{ij} = x_{r_3 j} + F.(x_{r_1 j} - x_{r_2 j})$;
  Else
    $u_{ij} = x_{ij}$;
Output: Offspring u_i.

As no single step size can efficiently search all dimensions, the mutation scheme for continuous optimization should dynamically scale the distribution to suit each variable. Moreover, the mutation operator should use a zero-mean distribution in generating mutation vectors, and correlate mutations to ensure rotational invariance. In evolution strategies, the answer to this crucial question is the use of "self-adaptation" (see Example 3.10).

The notation `DE/x/y/z` is generally used to define a DE strategy, where x specifies the vector to be mutated, which currently can be rand (a randomly chosen population vector) or best (the vector of lowest cost from the current population), y is the number of difference vectors used, and z denotes the crossover scheme. The standard variant is the bin crossover due to independent binomial experiments. Algorithm 3.8 shows the template for the basic DE algorithm (i.e., `DE/rand/1/bin algorithm`), where `bin` represents the binary crossover variant. An elitist replacement is considered, that is, the offspring will replace its parent if its objective value is better or equal to the parent one:

$$x_i(t+1) = \begin{cases} u_i(t+1) & \text{if } f(u_i(t+1)) \leq f(x_i(t)) \\ x_i(t) & \text{otherwise} \end{cases}$$

During the evolution process, each individual (i) is iteratively refined. The modification process has two steps:

- **Mutation/crossover:** This step consists in creating a variant solution using randomly selected members of the population. Then, a trial solution is created by recombining the variant solution with the individual i (crossover step).
- **Replacement:** This step performs a selection procedure to determine whether the trial solution replaces the individual i in the population.

Algorithm 3.8 Template of the DE/rand/1/bin algorithm.

Input: Parameters: F (scaling factor), CR (crossover constant).
Initialize the population (uniform random distribution) ;
Repeat
  For $(i = 1, i \leq k, i++)$ **Do** /* Each individual */
    Mutate and Recombine:
      $j_{rand} = int(\text{rand}_i[0, 1] \cdot D) + 1$;
      For $(j = 1, j \leq D, j++)$ **Do**
        If $(\text{rand}_j[0, 1]) < CR$) or $(j = j_{rand})$ **Then**
          $u_{ij} = v_{ij} = x_{r_3 j} + F \cdot (x_{r_1 j} - x_{r_2 j})$
        Else
          $u_{ij} = x_{ij}$
    Replace:

$$x_i(t+1) = \begin{cases} u_i(t+1) & \textbf{If} f(u_i(t+1)) \leq f(x_i(t)) \\ x_i(t) & \textbf{Otherwise} \end{cases}$$

  End For
Until Stopping criteria /* ex: a given number of generations */
Output: Best population or solution found.

DE has shown its efficiency in solving many continuous optimization problems: nonlinear constraint optimization, flat landscapes, noisy and epistatic functions, and so on. Moreover, it is a simple method and effective (algorithmic complexity of $O(n)$). Let us summarize some important search concepts in DE:

- **Initial population:** The diversity of the initial population in DE is very important since the search is guided by the difference between vector elements.
- **Repair strategy:** Using the variation operators (recombination, mutation) if the value of a variable exceeds its range, many strategies can be applied to reset the value as follows:
  - **Extreme strategies:** The first extreme strategy is to set the value to the limit it exceeds. The drawback of this method is that it decreases the diversity of the population. The second strategy is to reinitialize the value to a random value. This strategy is extreme in terms of diversity maintenance.
  - **Intermediate:** Some intermediate strategies may be applied. An example of intermediate strategy consists in initializing the offending value to a

point, which is the midway between its old value (before variation) and the bound being violated:

$$u_{ij}(t+1) = \begin{cases} \frac{x_{ij}(t)+x_j^{lo}}{2} & \text{if } u_{ij}(t+1) < x_j^{lo} \\ \frac{x_{ij}(t)+x_j^{hi}}{2} & \text{if } u_{ij}(t+1) > x_j^{hi} \\ u_{ij}(t+1) & \text{otherwise} \end{cases}$$

The bounds will be approached asymptotically and the amount of disruption is minimized.

DE is very easy to tune. There is no probability distribution to specify for the mutation operator. A guideline in designing a DE algorithm may be to choose a given method (e.g., `DE/rand/1/exp`[10]), set the number of parents NP to 10 times the number of decision variables of the target optimization problem, and initialize the weighting factor to $F = 0.8$ and the crossover constant to $CR = 0.9$. If this tuning does not converge, one has to increase the number of parents NP, but often one has only to adjust the scaling factor F to be a little lower or higher than 0.8. There is always a trade-off between the convergence speed and robustness. If the value of NP is increased and the value of F is decreased a little bit, convergence is more likely to happen but it generally takes longer time (i.e., DE is more robust).

DE is much more sensitive to the value of F than it is to the value of CR. CR is more like a fine-tuning element. High values of CR (e.g., CR = 1) give quicker convergence if convergence occurs. Sometimes, however, one has to go down as much as CR = 0 to make DE robust enough for a specific problem. If a binomial crossover is selected (e.g., `DE/rand/1/bin`), CR is usually higher than the exponential crossover variant (i.e., `DE/rand/1/exp`). The range of both the values F and CR are generally in [0.5, 1] for most encountered problems. Different problems usually require different settings for NP, F, and CR. If the algorithm does not converge, one has to try a different DE method. The mostly used DE methods are `DE/rand/1/` or `DE/best/2/`. The crossover method is not so important although it is known that binomial is generally better than exponential.

3.4.3 Coevolutionary Algorithms

Coevolution may be defined as complementary evolution of closely associated species [231]. Many observations from nature show the coevolving of various species represented by a collection of similar individuals in terms of their phenotype. Such an example of cooperative interaction from nature is the interlocking adaptation of many flowering plants and their pollination insects. An example of competitive interaction is the predator–prey relationships where an evolutionary advance in the predator launches an evolutionary response in the prey. This phenomena lead to highly complex adaptations of populations.

[10] `exp` stands for exponential crossover variant.

Unlike traditional EAs where a population is composed of a single species, a coevolutionary algorithm may be viewed as a cooperative–competitive strategy involving different populations in which each population represents a given species. The traditional coevolutionary algorithm involves interacting populations in which the different populations are optimizing coupled objectives, that is, the fitness of an individual of a given population will depend on the fitness of individuals of the other populations [375,397].

There are two different models of coevolution: *competitive* coevolutionary models in which the different populations compete in solving the global problem (e.g., access to limited resources) and *cooperative* coevolutionary models in which the various populations cooperate to solve the problem (e.g., access to hard-attained resource).

In a competitive coevolutionary algorithm, the individual fitness is related to competition ("arm races") with individuals of other populations, which evolve independently in their own species [662]. This inverse fitness interaction will increase the capabilities of each population until the global optimal solution is attained. Populations in competitive coevolutionary algorithms use game-theoretic mechanism of competition. Each population minimizes a local cost specified by a local objective function. The competition between populations leads to an equilibrium in which the local objectives cannot be improved and hopefully the global objective is achieved. The global solution is not directly evaluated.

A well-known example of competitive coevolutionary algorithms is the predator–prey model, where the selection process on the solutions in one population will depend on the quality of the solutions in the other population [584,600]. The predator–prey model is inspired by animals grouped in flocks. When chased, animals will have some difficulty to stay around their most preferable places (e.g., water source, better pasture) and have to find other locations that are free of predators and of good quality. The success of a given population will be a failure for another population, which must respond to survive (i.e., fitness inverse interaction). This interaction using inverse objectives is the main driving force of the evolution of various populations (Fig. 3.26).

Example 3.14 Predator–prey coevolutionary model for constraint satisfaction. Let us consider a constrained optimization problem. In this coevolutionary model, there are two populations evolving in parallel [599]. The main population is composed

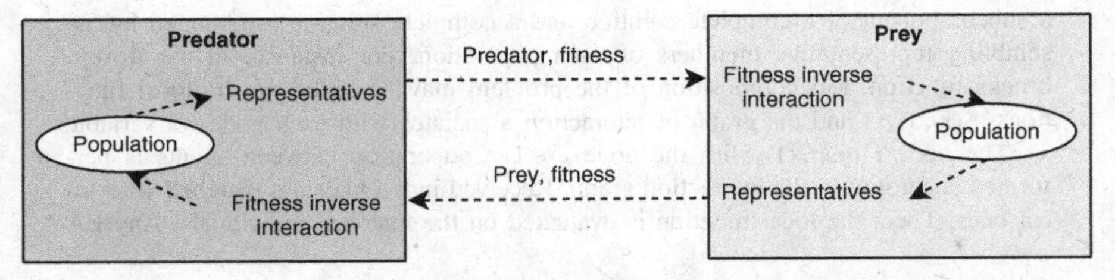

FIGURE 3.26 Competitive coevolutionary algorithms based on the predator–prey model.

of potential solutions to the problem. The secondary population contains the handled constraints. A solution with high quality in the main population represents a solution that satisfies a large number of constraints, whereas a solution with high quality in the secondary population represents a constraint that is violated by many solutions.

Constraints and solutions have encounters in which solutions belonging to both populations are evaluated. The quality of a solution is evaluated according to its encounters. The principle of this coevolutionary approach is to increase the quality of those constraints that are harder to satisfy so that the search methods concentrate on them. The more a constraint is satisfied in the main population, the lower is the fitness of the constraint in the secondary population. Hence, the search will focus on difficult constraints.

In cooperative[11] coevolutionary algorithms, the populations associated with different species cooperate to improve their survival. This scheme may be found in different organisms: eukaryotes that result from the interaction between prokaryotes and infected cells, birds obtain food by cleaning the skin of animals, and so on. Each population (i.e., species) evolves a subcomponent of the solution. Then, a global solution (complex structure) emerges from the assembling of species subcomponents according to a cooperative interaction between the different populations. The fitness of an individual of a given species will depend on its ability to cooperate with individuals from other populations.

Example 3.15 Competitive versus cooperative coevolutionary models for function optimization. Let us consider a continuous function f of n variables x_i ($i = 1, n$) to optimize, for instance, the RosenbrockÂ's function:

$$f(x) = \sum_{i=1}^{n} (100(x_i^2 - x_{i+1})^2 + (1 - x_i)^2),\ x \in \mathbb{R}$$

The coevolutionary approach may be viewed as a multiagent in which each agent optimizes a local objective function. The problem must be analyzed in terms of its possible decomposition into subcomponents. The relations between subcomponents will define a communication graph G_{com} called interaction graph. The function f is then decomposed into n local functions f_i. Thus, the coevolutionary algorithm will contain n populations evolving in parallel. For each population P_i, a local function f_i is associated. A local individual s_{ij} in the population P_i represents a single variable j of the problem. Hence, each population (species) defines a subcomponent of a complete solution and a complete solution is obtained by assembling representative members of each population. For instance, in the Rosenbrocks function, a decomposition of the problem may be based on the local functions $f_i(x_i; x_{i+1})$ and the graph of interaction associates with each node i a variable x_i. The node i interacts with the node $i+1$. Cooperation between agents is performed according to the interaction graph. Received individuals are matched with local ones. Then, the local function is evaluated on the matched individuals. Any EA

[11] Also named symbiotic and mutualistic.

algorithm can be applied to the local population. These coevolving populations compete to minimize their local function. The global system can achieve some equilibrium equivalent to Nash point equilibrium in noncooperative models of game theory. The performance of the whole system is evaluated using a global objective function (e.g., sum of the local function values). The global objective is unknown for the subpopulations that optimize their local objective function. Many real-life problems (e.g., economics) are intrinsically decomposable in terms of the global objective function. In the most unfavorable case, the interaction graph is a fully connected graph, where the global objective function represents the local function for each population. Competitive models can be viewed as noncooperative models of game theory.

In a cooperative coevolutionary model, the interaction graph is fully connected [620]. First, individuals of a given population are randomly matched with individuals from all other populations to construct a global solution. Then, the fitness of each generated individual is computed and the best individual I_i^{best} is found. Then, at each generation the evolving of the populations is performed in two phases. In the first phase, there is only one active population and the others are frozen. The individuals composing the active population are matched with the best individuals of the other frozen populations (Fig. 3.27). Then, the new best solution of the active population is found. This process is iterated for each population. In the second phase, the best individual of each population is matched with a randomly selected individual from each population. The best of the two generated solutions is considered as the winner and constitutes the new individual. At the end of the evolution process, the best complete solution of the problem is constructed from the best individuals (subcomponents) of each population.

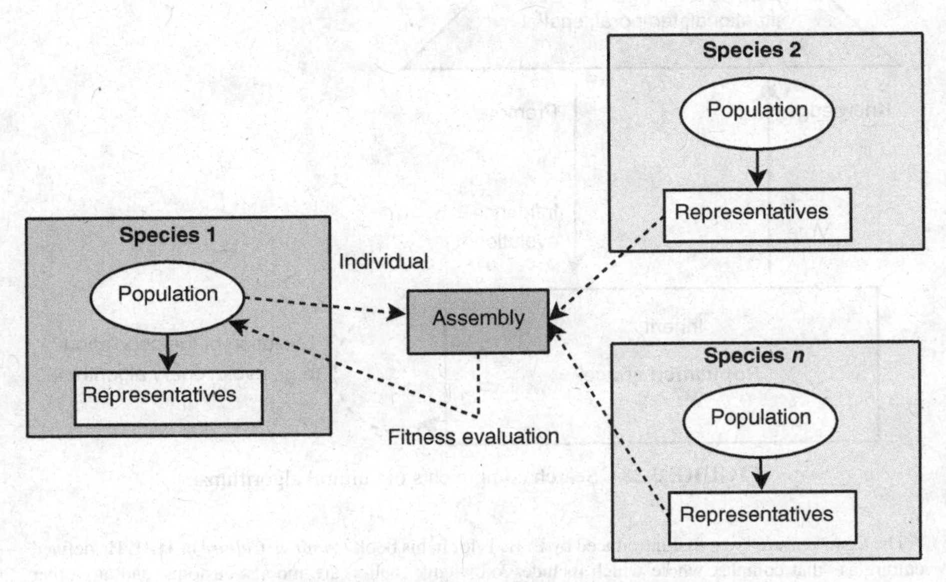

FIGURE 3.27 A cooperative coevolutionary algorithm.

3.4.4 Cultural Algorithms

Cultural algorithms (CAs)[12] are special variants of evolutionary algorithms. CAs have been introduced by R. G. Reynolds in 1994 [652]. They are computational models of cultural evolution based upon principles of human social evolution. They employ a model of cultural change within an optimization problem, where culture might be symbolically represented and transmitted between successive populations [231]. The main principle behind this process is to preserve beliefs that are socially accepted and discard unacceptable beliefs.

Cultural algorithms contain two main elements, a *population space* at the microevolutionary level and a *belief space* at the macroevolutionary level (Fig. 3.28). The two elements interact by means of a vote–inherit–promote or VIP protocol. This enables the individuals to alter the belief space and allows the belief space to influence the ways in which individuals evolve. The population space at the microevolutionary level may be carried out by EAs. At each generation, the knowledge acquired by the search of the population (e.g., best solutions of the population) can be memorized in the belief space in many forms such as logic- and rule-based models, schemata, graphical models, semantic networks, and version spaces [559] among others to model the macroevolutionary process of a cultural algorithm. The belief space is divided into

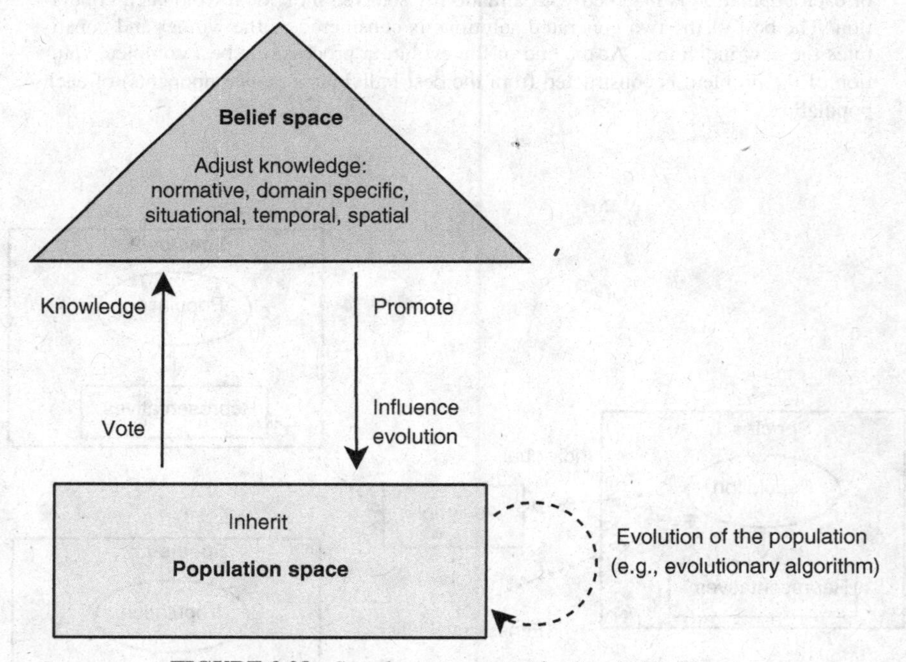

FIGURE 3.28 Search components of cultural algorithms.

[12]The term "culture" was first introduced by E. B. Tylor in his book *Primitive Culture* in 1881. He defined culture as "that complex whole which includes knowledge, belief, art, morals, customs, and any other capabilities and habits acquired by man as a member of society."

distinct categories that represent different domains of knowledge that the population has acquired on the search space: normative knowledge (i.e., a collection of desirable value ranges for some decision variables of the individuals in the population), domain-specific knowledge (i.e., information about the domain of the problem CA is applied to), situational knowledge, temporal knowledge (i.e., information of important events about the search), and spatial knowledge (i.e., information about the landscape of the tackled optimization problem). Algorithm 3.9 illustrates the template of a cultural algorithm.

Algorithm 3.9 Template of the cultural algorithm.

Initialize the population *Pop*(0) ;
Initialize the Belief $BLF(0)$;
$t = 0$;
Repeat
  Evaluate population *Pop*(t) ;
  Adjust(BLF(t), Accept(POP(t))) ;
  Evolve(Pop(t+1), Influence(BLF(t))) ;
  $t = t + 1$;
Until Stopping criteria
Output: Best found solution or set of solutions.

As such, cultural algorithms represent a P-metaheuristic based on hybrid evolutionary systems that integrate evolutionary search and symbolic reasoning. They are particularly useful for problems whose solutions require extensive domain knowledge (e.g., constrained optimization problems) and dynamic environments (e.g., dynamic optimization problems).

3.5 SCATTER SEARCH

Scatter search has its origin in the paper of F. Glover [320]. SS is a deterministic strategy that has been applied successfully to some combinatorial and continuous optimization problems. Even if the principles of the method have been defined since 1977, the application of SS is in its beginning.

SS is a evolutionary and population metaheuristic that recombines solutions selected from a reference set to build others [491]. The method starts by generating an initial population Pop satisfying the criteria of diversity and quality. The reference set (RefSet) of moderate size[13] is then constructed by selecting good representative solutions from the population. The selected solutions are combined to provide starting solutions to an improvement procedure based on a S-metaheuristic. According to the result of such procedure, the reference set and even the population of solutions are updated to incorporate both high-quality and diversified solutions. The process is iterated until a stopping criterion is satisfied.

[13]Typically, the reference set is composed of more or less 10 solutions.

The SS approach involves different procedures allowing to generate the initial population, to build and update the reference set, to combine the solutions of such set, to improve the constructed solutions, and so on. SS uses explicitly strategies for both search intensification and search diversification. It integrates search components from P-metaheuristics and S-metaheuristics. The algorithm starts with a set of diverse solutions, which represents the reference set (initial population) (see Algorithm 3.10). This set of solutions is evolved by means of recombination of solutions as well as by the application of local search (or another S-metaheuristic).

Algorithm 3.10 Template of the scatter search algorithm.

```
/* Initial phase */
Initialize the population Pop using a diversification generation method ;
Apply the improvement method to the population ;
Reference set Update Method ;
/* Scatter search iteration */
Repeat
  Subset generation method ;
  Repeat
     Solution Combination Method ;
     Improvement Method ;
  Until Stopping criteria 1
Reference Set Update Method ;
Until Stopping criteria
Output: Best found solution or set of solutions.
```

The design of a scatter search algorithm is generally based on the following five methods (Fig. 3.29) :

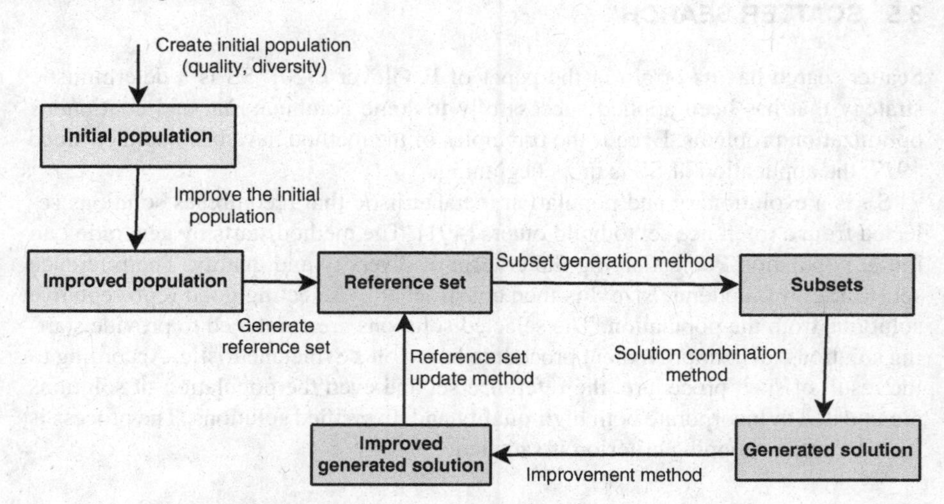

FIGURE 3.29 Search components of scatter search algorithms.

- **Diversification generation method:** This method generates a set of diverse initial solutions. In general, greedy procedures are applied to diversify the search while selecting high-quality solutions.
- **Improvement method:** This method transforms a trial solution into one or more enhanced trial solutions using any S-metaheuristic. In general, a local search algorithm is applied and then a local optimum is generated.
- **Reference set update method:** In this search component, a reference set is constructed and maintained. The objective is to ensure diversity while keeping high-quality solutions. For instance, one can select RefSet1 solutions with the best objective function and then adding RefSet2 solutions with the best diversity (RefSet = RefSet1 + RefSet2).
- **Subset generation method:** This method operates on the reference set RefSet, to produce a subset of solutions as a basis for creating combined solutions. This method usually selects all the subsets of fixed size r (in general, $r = 2$). This procedure is similar to the selection mechanism in EAs. However, in SS, it is a deterministic operator, whereas in EAs, it is generally a stochastic operator. Moreover, the size of the reference set in SS is much smaller than the size of the population in EAs. This is why more enumerative selection mechanisms can be applied.
- **Solution combination method:** A given subset of solutions produced by the subset generation method are recombined. In general, weighted structured combinations are used via linear combinations and generalized rounding to discrete variables. This operator may be viewed as a generalization of the crossover operator in EAs where more than two individuals are recombined.

The three search components (diversification generation method, improvement method, and combination method) are problem specific whereas the two other search components (reference set update method, subset generation method) are generic. Those methods are combined, as shown in Fig. 3.29 and Algorithm 3.10.

Example 3.16 Scatter search algorithm for the p-median problem. The p-median problem is a p-facility location–allocation problem with a wide class of logistic and clustering applications such as location of warehouses and public facilities [297]. Given a set $L = \{v_1, v_2, \ldots, v_m\}$ of m potential locations for p facilities. Given a set $U = \{u_1, u_2, \ldots, u_n\}$ of n customers. Given an $n \times m$ matrix, $D = (d_{ij})_{n \times m}$ that represents the distance (or a given cost) to satisfy the demand of the customer located at u_i from the facility located at v_j. The p-median problem consists in locating the p facilities at locations L and allocating every customer u_i to a facility to minimize the objective function, which represents the total distance between the customers and their associated closest facilities.

$$f(X) = \min \sum_{u_i \in U} \min_{v_j \in S} d_{u_i v_j}$$

where S represents the set of facilities ($S \subseteq L$ and $|S| = p$). Let us design a SS to solve this problem. Let us suppose that without loss of generality, $L = U$ and $m = n$. The problem will consist in selecting a set S of p locations from U to locate the facilities. In the rest of this section, some solutions for the different design issues of a scatter search algorithm are presented.

Encoding: A solution of the p-median problem may be encoded as a discrete vector $v = \{v_1, v_2, \ldots, v_n\}$ of size n, which represents the arrangement of all customers U. The variable v_i defines a facility in S for $i \leq p$ and it is a nonfacility point for $i > p$.

Neighborhood: A move operator may be the interchange operator. The neighborhood of a solution is defined by the set of interchanges $I = \{(i, j) : 1 \leq i \leq p, p < j \leq n\}$. For an interchange $(i, j) \in I$, the neighbor of a solution x is $x - \{v_i\} + \{v_j\}$.

Initial population: The set L of points is partitioned into disjoint subsets. A greedy heuristic is applied to each subset L_i as follows: an initial point u of L_i is selected arbitrary, and $p - 1$ iterations of selecting the farthest point to the already selected points are performed. This greedy procedure is applied from different initial points to obtain different solutions for each subset L_i. For each obtained solution, an improvement method is performed. To optimize the diversity, one needs to define a distance between two solutions. The distance may be defined as follows:

$$\text{dist}(X, Y) = f_Y(X) + f_X(Y)$$

where $f_Y(X) = \sum_{v \in Y} \min_{u \in X} d_{uv}$. Given that the size of the population Pop is Popsize, the parameter α specifies the proportion of solutions selected using the objective function. For the $(1 - \alpha)$Popsize remaining solutions, they are selected using the diversification scoring function h:

$$h(X) = f(X) - \beta \text{dist}(X, \text{Pop})$$

where $\text{dist}(x, \text{Pop}) = \min_{Y \in \text{Pop}} \text{dist}(X, Y)$ and β is a constant parameter.

Generation of the reference set: RefSet1 solutions are selected in terms of the quality of the objective function. RefSet2 solutions are selected using the diversity criteria (RefSet = RefSet1+ RefSet2). Once the best RefSet1 solutions have been included in the reference set RefSet, the farthest solution from the solutions already in the reference set is iteratively included. This procedure of diversification is repeated RefSet2 times.

Subset generation method: All subsets of size $r = 2$ are selected. Repetitions can be avoided by storing information on the already selected combinations.

Solution combination method: A recombination crossover operator involving two solutions may be applied. First, the common points X to both solutions are selected. The construction of the set

$$L(u) = \{v \in L : d_{un} \leq \beta d_{\max}\}$$

is performed, where $u \in L \backslash X$ and $d_{\max} = \max_{u,v \in L} d_{uv}$. Then, the point $u^* \in L$ such that $d_{xu^*} = \max_{u \in L} d_{Xu}$ and a random point $v \in L(u^*)$ that is included in X are selected. This procedure is applied until $|X| = p$.

Improvement method: A straightforward local search is applied using the encoding and the neighborhood defined above. The improvement method can be extended to any S-metaheuristic such as tabu search and simulated annealing. The output of this procedure is the set ImpSolSet of improved solutions.

Reference set update method: The "generate reference set" procedure is applied to the set composed of the union between RefSet and the set of improved solutions ImpSolSet.

3.5.1 Path Relinking

Path relinking (PR) was proposed by Glover within the framework of scatter search [325]. It allows to explore paths connecting elite solutions found by scatter search. However, this strategy may be generalized and applied to any metaheuristic generating a pool of "good" solutions such as evolutionary algorithms, greedy adaptive search procedure (GRASP), ant colonies, and iterative local search.

The main idea of path relinking is to generate and to explore the trajectory in the search space connecting a starting solution s and a target solution t. The idea is to reinterpret the linear combinations of points in the Euclidean space as paths between and beyond solutions in a neighborhood space. The path between two solutions in the search space (neighborhood space) will generally yield solutions that share common attributes with the input solutions. A sequence of neighboring solutions in the decision space are generated from the starting solution to the target solution. The best found solution in the sequence is returned. Algorithm 3.11 shows the template for a basic PR algorithm. At each iteration, the best move in terms of the objective function and decreasing the distance d between the two solutions is selected. This is repeated until the distance is equal to 0. The best solution found in the trajectory is returned by the algorithm.

Algorithm 3.11 Template of the basic PR algorithm.

Input: Starting solution s and target solution t.
$x = s$;
While $dist(x, t) \neq 0$ **Do**
  Find the best move m which decreases $dist(x \oplus m, t)$;
  $x = x \oplus m$; /* Apply the move m to the solution x */ ;
Output: Best solution found in trajectory between s and t.

The main design issues in path relinking are as follows:

- **Path selection:** The issue here is what should be considered in the generation of the path. A guiding heuristic to generate the path has to be used to minimize the distance toward the guiding solution. Hence, a distance d must be defined in the search space associated with the problem (see Section 2.2.1). The computational complexity of this procedure must be taken into account. While it is polynomial for some problems, it may be more complex for other optimization problems. Moreover, many paths may also be considered in parallel.

Let s and t be respectively the starting and the guiding solutions. A sequence $(s, x_1, x_2, \ldots, t)$ has to be generated. For instance, the candidate set $S(x_i)$ for x_{i+1} may be generated from x_i by selecting in the neighborhood of the solution x_i those of minimum distance to the guiding solution x':

$$S(x_i) = x_{i+1}/x_{1+1} \in N(x_i) \text{ and } \mathrm{Min}(d(x_{i+1}, t))$$

The cardinality of this set may be greater than one. Hence, an additional selection criteria have to be used to select a solution from the candidate set $S(x_i)$. The selection mechanism may be based on different criteria:

- **Quality:** Choosing the solution based on the objective function of the problem. Choosing the best or the worst solutions will have a different impact on the search (intensification, diversification).
- **History of the search:** The memory of the search may be used in the selection phase. For instance, the use of the recency memory in tabu search may discard some solutions (see Section 2.5).

If the choice rules do not forbid cycles in the generation of the path, then a tabu list may be maintained. The path selection may also be guided by the set $\Delta(s, t)$ that represents the set of different components (e.g., edges in routing problems) in the starting solution s and the target solution t.

- **Intermediate operations:** This design question deals with the operations to apply at each step of the path construction. Some selected solutions on the path may be considered. For instance, one may apply a S-metaheuristic at each intermediate solution. Figure 3.30 illustrates such a case where a local search procedure is applied on an intermediate solution to improve the quality of the search.

Moreover, for each pair of solutions s and t, various alternatives exist to select the starting and the target solutions (Fig. 3.31):

- **Forward:** The worst solution among s and t is used as the starting solution.
- **Backward:** The role of each solution is interchanged. The better solution among s and t is used as the starting solution. As the neighborhood of the starting solution is more explored than of the target solution, the backward strategy is in general better than the forward one.
- **Back and forward relinking:** Two paths are constructed in parallel, using alternatively s as the starting and the target solutions. This strategy adds an overhead in the computation time that is not surely balanced by the quality of the obtained solutions.
- **Mixed relinking:** As in the back and forward relinking strategy, two paths are constructed in parallel from s and t but the guiding solution is an intermediate

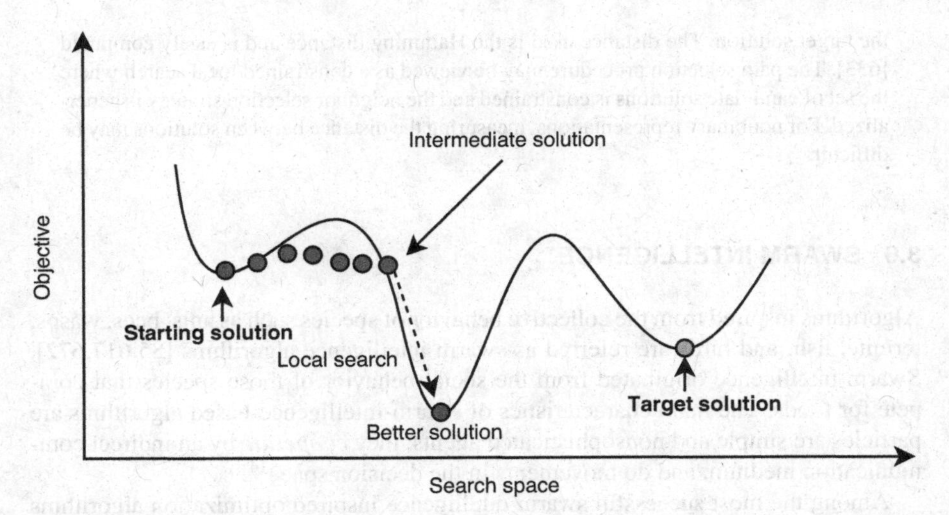

FIGURE 3.30 Application of a local search procedure to an intermediate solution in path relinking. In a "big valley" landscape structure, an intermediate solution between two local optima may be reasonably guided to a third basin of attraction. This third basin of attraction may contain a better local optima.

solution m at the same distance from s and t. This parallel strategy may reduce the computational time.

Example 3.17 Optima linking in a binary search space. In the context of binary representation of optimization problems, a path may be found by finding at each step the best move (flip operator) that would guide the current solution one step nearer to

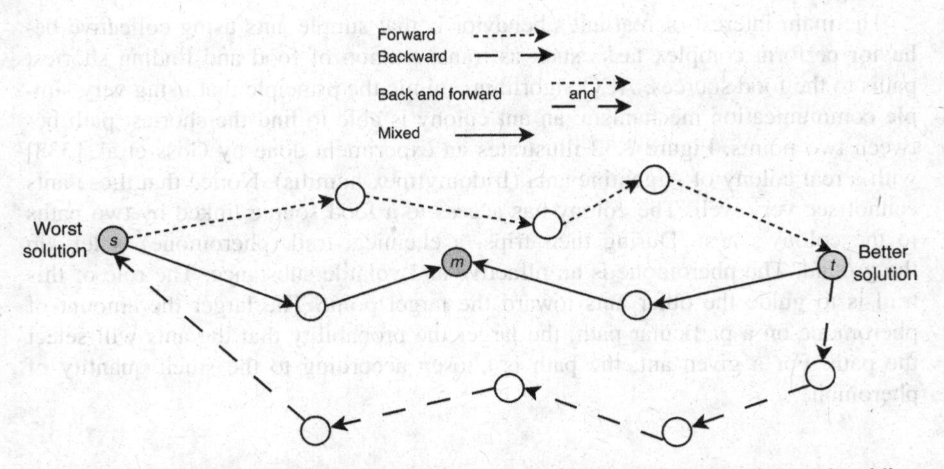

FIGURE 3.31 Different path relinking strategies in terms of the starting and guiding solutions.

the target solution. The distance used is the Hamming distance and is easily computed [633]. The path selection procedure may be viewed as a constrained local search where the set of candidate solutions is constrained and the neighbor selection strategy is generalized. For nonbinary representations, measuring the distance between solutions may be difficult.

3.6 SWARM INTELLIGENCE

Algorithms inspired from the collective behavior of species such as ants, bees, wasps, termite, fish, and birds are referred as swarm intelligence algorithms [85,617,672]. Swarm intelligence originated from the social behavior of those species that compete for foods. The main characteristics of swarm-intelligence-based algorithms are particles are simple and nonsophisticated agents, they *cooperate* by an indirect communication medium, and do movements in the decision space[14].

Among the most successful swarm intelligence inspired optimization algorithms are ant colony and particle swarm optimization.

3.6.1 Ant Colony Optimization Algorithms

The basic idea in ant colony optimization algorithms (ACO) is to imitate the cooperative behavior of real ants to solve optimization problems. ACO metaheuristics have been proposed by M. Dorigo [215]. They can be seen as multiagent systems in which each single agent is inspired by the behavior of a real ant. Traditionally, ACO have been applied to combinatorial optimization problems and they have achieved widespread success in solving different problems (e.g., scheduling, routing, assignment) [219].

The main interest of real ant's behavior is that simple ants using collective behavior perform complex tasks such as transportation of food and finding shortest paths to the food sources. ACO algorithms mimic the principle that using very simple communication mechanism, an ant colony is able to find the shortest path between two points. Figure 3.32 illustrates an experiment done by Goss et al. [338] with a real colony of Argentine ants (Iridomyrmex humilis). Notice that those ants cannot see very well. The colony has access to a food source linked by two paths to the colony's nest. During their trips, a chemical trail (pheromone) is left on the ground. The pheromone is an olfactive and volatile substance. The role of this trail is to guide the other ants toward the target point. The larger the amount of pheromone on a particular path, the larger the probability that the ants will select the path. For a given ant, the path is chosen according to the smelt quantity of pheromone.

[14]Self-organization using indirect cooperation is an important issue in biological systems [105].

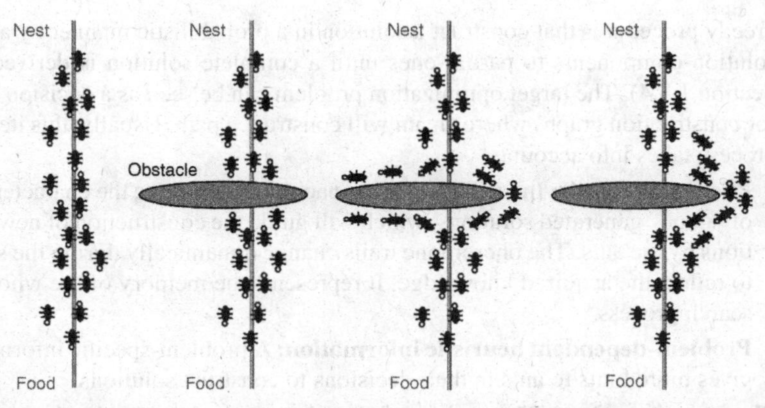

FIGURE 3.32 Inspiration from an ant colony searching an optimal path between the food and the nest.

Furthermore, this chemical substance has a decreasing action over time (evaporation process) and the quantity left by one ant depends on the amount of food (reinforcement process). As shown in Fig. 3.32, when facing an obstacle, there is an equal probability for every ant to choose the left or right path. As the left trail is shorter than the right one and so requires less travel time, the ant will end up leaving a higher level of pheromone. The more the ants take the left path, the higher the pheromone trail. Hence, there is an emergence of the shortest path. This fact will be increased by the evaporation stage. This indirect form of cooperation is known as *stigmergy*.

Algorithm 3.12 presents the template algorithm for ACO. First, the pheromone information is initialized. The algorithm is mainly composed of two iterated steps: solution construction and pheromone update.

Algorithm 3.12 Template of the ACO.

Initialize the pheromone trails ;
Repeat
  For each ant **Do**
    Solution construction using the pheromone trail ;
    Update the pheromone trails:
      Evaporation ;
      Reinforcement ;
Until Stopping criteria
Output: Best solution found or a set of solutions.

- **Solution construction:** The construction of solutions is done according to a probabilistic state transition rule. Artificial ants can be considered as stochastic greedy procedures that construct a solution in a probabilistic manner by adding solution components to partial ones until a complete solution is derived (see Section 1.3.4). The target optimization problem can be seen as a decision graph (or construction graph) where an ant will construct a path. Usually, this iterative process takes into account

– **Pheromone trails:** Indeed, the pheromone trails memorize the characteristics of "good" generated solutions, which will guide the construction of new solutions by the ants. The pheromone trails change dynamically during the search to reflect the acquired knowledge. It represents the memory of the whole ant search process.
– **Problem-dependent heuristic information:** A problem-specific information gives more hints to ants in their decisions to construct solutions.

- **Pheromone update:** The update of the pheromone is carried out using the generated solutions. A global pheromone updating rule is applied in two phases:

– An *evaporation phase* where the pheromone trail decreases automatically. Each pheromone value is reduced by a fixed proportion:

$$\tau_{ij} = (1 - \rho)\tau_{ij}, \quad \forall i, j \in [1, n]$$

where $\rho \in]0, 1]$ represents the reduction rate of the pheromone. The goal of the evaporation is to avoid for all ants a premature convergence toward "good" solutions and then to encourage the diversification in the search space (exploration).

– A *reinforcement phase* where the pheromone trail is updated according to the generated solutions. Three different strategies may be applied [155]:

  ◦ **Online step-by-step pheromone update:** The pheromone trail τ_{ij} is updated by an ant at each step of the solution construction [217].
  ◦ **Online delayed pheromone update:** The pheromone update of τ is applied once an ant generates a complete solution [527]. For instance, in the ACS, each ant will update the pheromone information with a value that is proportional to the quality of the solution found. The better the solution found, the more accumulated the pheromone.
  ◦ **Off-line pheromone update:** The pheromone train update is applied once *all* ants generate a complete solution. This is the most popular approach where different strategies can be used [541]:
    ▪ **Quality-based pheromone update:** This strategy updates the pheromone value associated with the best found solution among all ants (or the best k solutions where the number k is smaller than the number of ants) [218]. The added values depend on the quality of the selected solutions. For instance, for each component belonging to the best solution π^*, a positive

value Δ is added:

$$\tau_{i\pi^*(i)} = \tau_{i\pi^*(i)} + \Delta, \quad \forall i \in [1, n]$$

- **Rank-based pheromone update:** The best k ant solutions are allowed to update the pheromone with an amount depending on the ranking of the solutions [95].
- **Worst pheromone update:** The ant generating the worst solution will decrease the pheromone trails related to the components of the solution [154].
- **Elitist pheromone update:** The best solution found so far will update the pheromone to enforce an intensification of the search [728]. A minimum (resp. maximum) value for the pheromone is defined such as each choice has a minimum (resp. maximum) probability to be selected.

Theoretical convergence analysis of ACO algorithms may be found in Ref. [348]. The first convergence results were presented in Ref. [727]. The author proves convergence with probability $1 - \epsilon$ to an optimal solution of a particular ACO algorithm, the graph-based ant system (GBAS). In Ref. [727], a convergence result has been obtained for a more general class of ACO algorithms among the most efficient in practice, the class of algorithms that uses a lower bound $\tau_{\min}$ to all pheromone values. Indeed, the lower bound allows the probability to generate any solution to be different from zero. For a comprehensive survey of theoretical results for ant colony optimization, the reader may refer to Ref. [216].

In addition to classical and common search components in metaheuristics (e.g., representation), the main issue in designing an ACO is the determination of the following:

- **Pheromone information:** The pheromone model represents the central component of ACO algorithms. It consists in defining a vector of model parameters τ called *pheromone trail parameters*. The pheromone values $\tau_i \in \tau$ should reflect the relevant information in the construction of the solution for a given problem. They are usually associated with the components of a solution.
- **Solution construction:** In the solution construction, the main question is concerned with the definition of the local heuristic to be used in guiding the search in addition to the pheromone. The ACO metaphor is easy to adapt in solving problems where relatively efficient greedy algorithms already exist.
- **Pheromone update:** Mainly the reinforcement learning strategy for the pheromone information has to be defined.

Example 3.18 ACO for the TSP problem. Let us consider the application of ACO algorithms to the TSP problem. The ant system (AS) was the first application of ACO in the domain of combinatorial optimization [215]. Let $G = (V, E)$ be the input graph. Designing an ACO algorithm for the TSP needs the definition of the pheromone trails and the solution construction procedure (Algorithm 3.13).

Algorithm 3.13 Ant colony algorithm for the TSP problem (ACO–TSP).

```
Initialize the pheromone information ;
Repeat
  For each ant Do
    Solution construction using the pheromone trails:
      S = {1, 2, ..., n} /* Set of potentially selected cities */
      Random selection of the initial city i ;
      Repeat
        Select new city j with probability p_ij = (τ_ij^α × η_ij^β) / (Σ_{k∈S} τ_ik^α × η_ik^β) ;
        S = S − {j} ; i = j ;
      Until S = ∅
  End For
  Update the pheromone trail:
    For i, j ∈ [1, n] Do
      τ_ij = (1 − ρ)τ_ij /* Evaporation */ ;
    For i ∈ [1, n] Do
      τ_iπ(i) = τ_iπ(i) + Δ /* π: best found solution */ ;
Until Stopping criteria
Output: Best solution found or a set of solutions.
```

- **Pheromone trails:** A pheromone τ_{ij} will be associated with each edge (i, j) of the graph G. The pheromone information can be represented by an $n \times n$ matrix τ where each element τ_{ij} of the matrix expresses the desirability to have the edge (i, j) in the tour. The pheromone matrix is generally initialized by the same values[15]. During the search, the pheromone will be updated to estimate the utility of any edge of the graph.
- **Solution construction:** Each ant will construct a tour in a stochastic way. Given an initial arbitrary city i, an ant will select the next city j with the probability

$$p_{ij} = \frac{\tau_{ij}}{\sum_{k \in S} \tau_{ik}}, \quad \forall j \in S$$

where the set S represents the not yet visited solutions of the graph G. The ants may use a randomly selected initial city in the construction phase.

The additional problem-dependent heuristic is defined by considering the values η_{ij} equal to $1/d_{ij}$ where d_{ij} represents the distance between the cities i and j. The higher the heuristic value η_{ij}, the shorter the distance d_{ij} between cities i and j. Computing the decision transition probabilities, p_{ij} is performed as follows:

$$p_{ij} = \frac{\tau_{ij}^{\alpha} \times \eta_{ij}^{\beta}}{\sum_{k \in S} \tau_{ik}^{\alpha} \times \eta_{ik}^{\beta}}, \quad \forall j \in S$$

[15]The values of $\tau_{ii}, i \in [1, n]$ are useless.

where α and β are parameters representing the relative influence of the pheromone values and the problem-dependent heuristic values. If $\alpha = 0$, the ACO algorithm will be similar to a stochastic greedy algorithm in which the closest cities are more likely selected. If $\beta = 0$, only the pheromone trails will guide the search. In this case, a rapid emergence of *stagnation* may occur where all ants will construct the same suboptimal tour. Hence, a good trade-off must be found in using those two kinds of information.

Then, the pheromone update procedure has to be specified. For instance, each ant will increment the pheromone associated with the selected edges in a manner that is proportional to the quality of the obtained tour π:

$$\tau_{i\pi(i)} = \tau_{i\pi(i)} + \Delta, \quad \forall i \in [1, n]$$

where $\Delta = 1/f(\pi)$. Then, good tours will emerge as the result of the cooperation between ants through the pheromone trails.

The classical evaporation procedure is applied for the pheromone trails. For each edge, its pheromone τ_{ij} will evaporate as follows:

$$\tau_{ij} = (1 - \rho)\tau_{ij}, \quad \forall i, j \in [1, n]$$

where $\rho \in]0, 1]$ represents the reduction rate of the pheromone.

Compared to other metaheuristics, an important aspect in ACO is the differential path length (DPL) effect of ants. The decentralized and asynchronous nature of ants is crucial in solving distributed problems where there is no global view of the objective function. Decisions must be taken under a local view of the problem.

Example 3.19 Solving distributed and dynamic problems with ACO. This example illustrates the efficient way ACO can solve distributed network problems. For instance, in network routing, the problem deals with building and using routing tables to route the data traffic so that a given measure of network performance (e.g., throughput) is maximized. The network can be modeled by a weighted graph $G = (V, E)$ where the vertices of the set V represent the network nodes (processing/queuing/forwarding capabilities) and the edges of the graph represent the links of the network (directional transmission system). The weight associated with the edges is defined by the physical properties of the link (static measure) and the crossing traffic flow (dynamic measure). Given a network application with data flow from any source to any destination, the problem consists in constructing the routing tables R_i for each node of the network. The routing table $R_i = r_{ijd}$ at the node i and for message destined to d will forward the message to the neighbor node j.

Pheromone trail will be associated with each link of the network. A pheromone trail associated with a given edge (i, j) is a vector composed of $N - 1$ trails $\tau_{ijd} \in [0, 1]$ where N is the number of nodes of the network and d the destination node. Indeed, the pheromone trail of an edge will also depend on the final destination node. To each ant of the colony is assigned a pair (routing task) (f, d), which is defined by the starting node

f and the destination node d. Unlike classical optimization problems such as the TSP, two properties characterize this problem:

- **Distribution:** Each ant will solve a partial problem. The global problem is to build all paths defined by (f, d) whereas an ant will find a single path of the whole problem.
- **Dynamicity:** The weights associated with the edges are not static and can change dynamically according to the traffic.

ACO algorithms can be designed for this problem as follows [108]: ants are launched from each node of the network taking into account the traffic patterns. Each ant will search for the minimum cost path from its assigned starting node f to its assigned destination node d. When an ant k is in the node i, it will select the next neighbor j according to a probabilistic transition rule that depends on the pheromone trails associated with the edges and a heuristic value. A heuristic value η_{ij}, which depends on the destination node d, is associated with each edge (i, j) as given below.

$$\eta_{ij} = 1 - \frac{q_{ij}}{\sum_{l \in N_i} q_{il}}$$

where q_{ij} is the length of the message queue in the link connecting node i with its neighbor j.

The solution construction is based on the routing table $A_i = [a_{ijd}(t)]$ at each node i. This routing table is a composition of the pheromone trails τ_{ijd} and the heuristic values η_{ij}:

$$a_{ijd}(t) = \frac{w\tau_{ijd}(t) + (1-w)\eta_{ij}}{w + \frac{1-w}{|N_i|-1}}$$

where $j \in N_i$, d is the destination node, $w \in [0, 1]$ a weighting factor, and the denominator is a normalization factor. Then, the ant k located in the node i for the destination d will choose a not yet visited node j with the probability

$$p_{ijd}^{k}(t) = \begin{cases} a_{ijd}(t) & \text{if } j \notin M^k \\ 0 & \text{if } j \in M^k \end{cases}$$

where M^k is the set of already visited nodes. If all nodes are already visited by the ant, a neighbor node $j \in N_i$ is chosen randomly.

The reinforcement procedure of the pheromone trails works as follows: once an ant k completes a path, it updates the pheromone trails by an amount $\Delta\tau^k(t)$ that is proportional to the quality of the builded path. So the ant moves back to the source node by using the same reverse path. For each link l_{ij}, the ant increases the pheromone trail intensity by $\Delta\tau^k(t)$.

$$\tau_{ijd}(t) = \tau_{ijd}(t) + \Delta\tau^k(t)$$

Then, the pheromone values of all the output connections of the same node i evaporate.

$$\tau_{ijd}(t) = \frac{\tau_{ijd}(t)}{(1 + \Delta\tau^k(t))}, \quad \forall j \in N_i$$

where N_i is the set of neighbors of the node i.

3.6.1.1 *ACO for Continuous Optimization Problems* ACO algorithms have been extended to deal with continuous optimization problems. The main issue in adapting the ACO metaheuristic is to model a continuous nest neighborhood by a discrete structure or change the pheromone model by a continuous one. Indeed, in ACO for combinatorial problems, the pheromone trails are associated with a finite set of values related to the decisions that the ants make. This is not possible in the continuous case. ACO was first adapted for continuous optimization in Ref. [75]. Further attempts to adapt ACO for continuous optimization were reported in many works [224,708,778]. Most of these approaches do not follow the original ACO framework [709]. The fundamental idea is the shift from using a discrete probability distribution to using a continuous one (e.g., probability density function [709]).

Initializing the numerous parameters of ACO algorithms is critical. Table 3.6 summarizes the main parameters of a basic ACO algorithm. Some sensitive parameters such as α and β can be adjusted in a dynamic or an adaptive manner to deal with the classical trade-off between intensification and diversification during the search [635]. The optimal values for the parameters α and β are very sensitive to the target problem. The number of ants is not a critical parameter. Its value will mainly depend on the computational capacity of the experiments.

3.6.2 Particle Swarm Optimization

Particle swarm optimization is another stochastic population-based metaheuristic inspired from swarm intelligence [459]. It mimics the social behavior of natural organisms such as bird flocking and fish schooling to find a place with enough food. Indeed, in those swarms, a coordinated behavior using local movements emerges without any central control. Originally, PSO has been successfully designed for continuous optimization problems. Its first application to optimization problems has been proposed in Ref. [457].

TABLE 3.6 Parameters of the ACO Algorithm

Parameter	Role	Practical Values
α	Pheromone influence	–
β	Heuristic influence	–
ρ	Evaporation rate	[0.01, 0.2]
k	Number of ants	[10, 50]

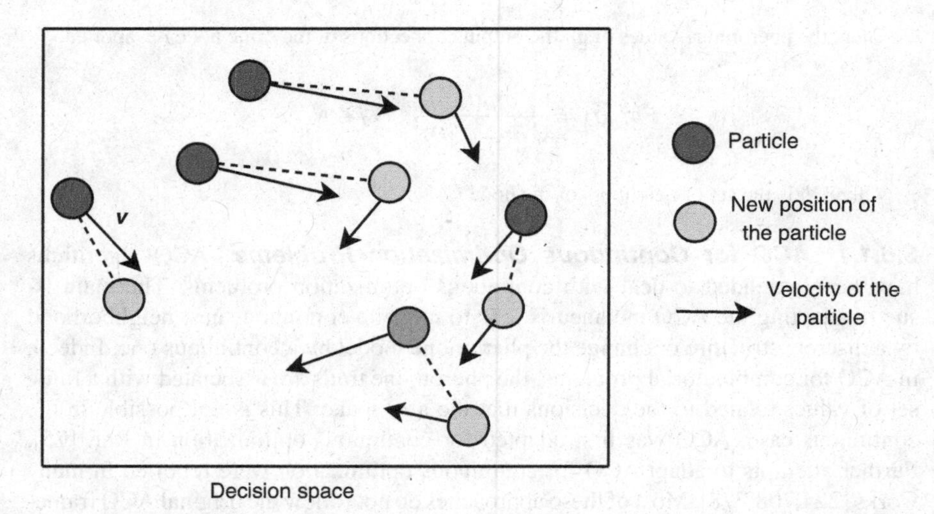

FIGURE 3.33 Particle swarm with their associated positions and velocities. At each iteration, a particle moves from one position to another in the decision space. PSO uses no gradient information during the search.

In the basic model, a swarm consists of N particles flying around in a D-dimensional search space. Each particle i is a candidate solution to the problem, and is represented by the vector x_i in the decision space. A particle has its own position and velocity, which means the flying direction and step of the particle (Fig. 3.33). Optimization takes advantage of the cooperation between the particles. The success of some particles will influence the behavior of their peers. Each particle successively adjusts its position x_i toward the global optimum according to the following two factors: the best position visited by itself (pbest_i) denoted as $p_i = (p_{i1}, p_{i2}, \ldots, p_{iD})$ and the best position visited by the whole swarm (gbest) (or lbest, the best position for a given subset of the swarm) denoted as $p_g = (p_{g1}, p_{g2}, \ldots, p_{gD})$. The vector $(p_g - x_i)$ represents the difference between the current position of the particle i and the best position of its neighborhood.

3.6.2.1 Particles Neighborhood A neighborhood must be defined for each particle. This neighborhood denotes the social influence between the particles. There are many possibilities to define such a neighborhood. Traditionally, two methods are used:

- **gbest Method:** In the global best method, the neighborhood is defined as the whole population of particles (Fig. 3.34).
- **lbest Method:** In the local best method, a given topology is associated with the swarm. Hence, the neighborhood of a particle is the set of directly connected particles. The neighborhood may be empty in which the articles are isolated (i.e., $C_2 = 0$) [244]. Figure 3.34 shows three different topologies: complete

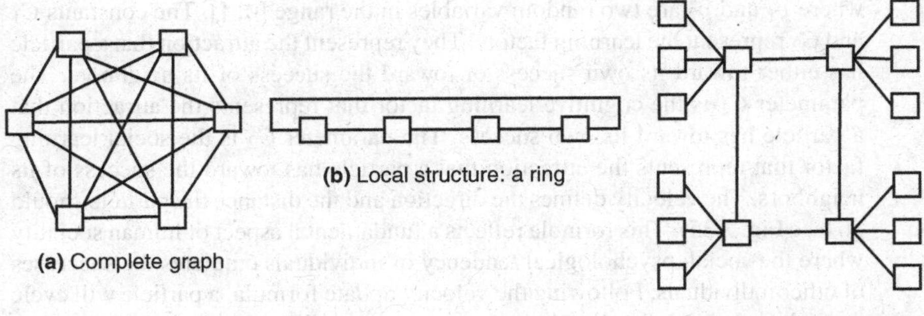

FIGURE 3.34 Neighborhood associated with particles. (a) gbest Method in which the neighborhood is the whole population (complete graph). (b) lbest Method where a noncomplete graph is used to define the neighborhood structure (e.g., a ring in which each particle has two neighbors). (c) Intermediate topology using a small world graph.

graph, ring world graph, and small world graph. This model is similar to social science models based on population members' mutual imitation, where a stabilized configuration will be composed of homogeneous subpopulations. Each subpopulation will define a sociometric region where will emerge a like-minded "culture." Individuals into the same sociometric region tend to become similar and individuals belonging to different regions tend to be different [40,585].

According to the neighborhood used, a *leader* (i.e., lbest or gbest) represents the particle that is used to guide the search of a particle toward better regions of the decision space.

A particle is composed of three vectors:

- The x-vector records the current position (location) of the particle in the search space.
- The p-vector records the location of the best solution found so far by the particle.
- The v-vector contains a gradient (direction) for which particle will travel in if undisturbed.
- Two fitness values: The x-fitness records the fitness of the x-vector, and the p-fitness records the fitness of the p-vector.

A particle swarm may be viewed as a *cellular automata* where individual cell (particles in PSO) updates are done in parallel; each new cell value depends only on the old value of the cell and its neighborhood, and all cells are updated using the same rules. At each iteration, each particle will apply the following operations:

- **Update the velocity:** The velocity that defines the amount of change that will be applied to the particle is defined as

$$v_i(t) = v_i(t-1) + \rho_1 C_1 \times (p_i - x_i(t-1)) + \rho_2 C_2 \times (p_g - x_i(t-1))$$

where ρ_1 and ρ_2 are two random variables in the range [0, 1]. The constants C_1 and C_2 represent the learning factors. They represent the attraction that a particle has either toward its own success or toward the success of its neighbors. The parameter C_1 is the cognitive learning factor that represents the attraction that a particle has toward its own success. The parameter C_2 is the social learning factor that represents the attraction that a particle has toward the success of its neighbors. The velocity defines the direction and the distance the particle should go (see Fig. 3.35). This formula reflects a fundamental aspect of human sociality where the social–psychological tendency of individuals emulates the successes of other individuals. Following the velocity update formula, a particle will cycle around the point defined as the weighted average of p_i and p_g:

$$\frac{\rho_1 p_i + \rho_2 p_g}{\rho_1 + \rho_2}$$

The elements of v_i are limited to a maximal value $[-V_{\max}, +V_{\max}]$ such as the system will not explode due to the randomness of the system. If the velocity v_i exceeds $V_{\max}$ (resp. $-V_{\max}$), it will be reset to $V_{\max}$ (resp. $-V_{\max}$).

In the velocity update procedure, an inertia weight w is generally added to the previous velocity [699]:

$$v_i(t) = w \times v_i(t-1) + \rho_1 \times (p_i - x_i(t-1)) + \rho_2 \times (p_g - x_i(t-1))$$

The inertia weight w will control the impact of the previous velocity on the current one. For large values of the inertia weight, the impact of the previous velocities will be much higher. Thus, the inertia weight represents a trade-off between global exploration and local exploitation. A large inertia weight encourages global exploration (i.e., diversify the search in the whole search space) while a smaller inertia weight encourages local exploitation (i.e., intensify the search in the current region).

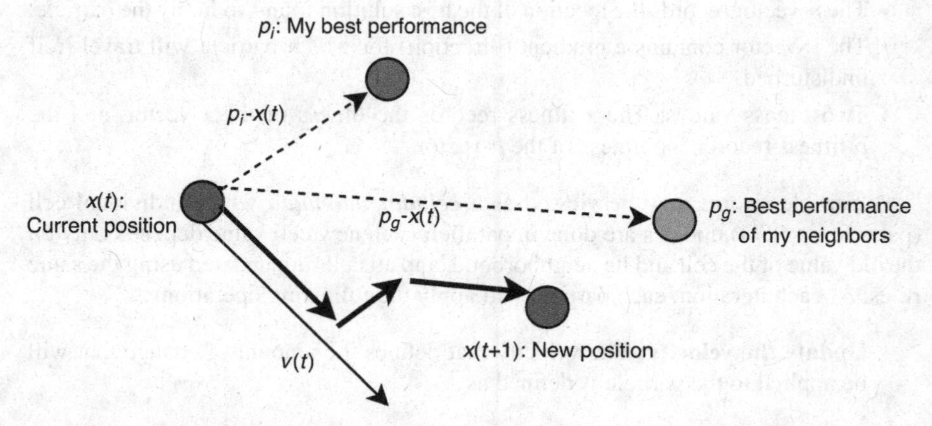

FIGURE 3.35 Movement of a particle and the velocity update.

- **Update the position:** Each particle will update its coordinates in the decision space.

$$x_i(t) = x_i(t-1) + v_i(t)$$

Then it moves to the new position.

- **Update the best found particles:** Each particle will update (potentially) the best local solution:

$$\text{If } f(x_i) < \text{pbest}_i, \text{ then } p_i = x_i$$

Moreover, the best global solution of the swarm is updated:

$$\text{If } f(x_i) < \text{gbest, then } g_i = x_i$$

Hence, at each iteration, each particle will change its position according to its own experience and that of neighboring particles.

As for any swarm intelligence concept, agents (particles for PSO) are exchanging information to share experiences about the search carried out. The behavior of the whole system emerges from the interaction of those simple agents. In PSO, the shared information is composed of the best global solution gbest.

Algorithm 3.14 shows the template for the PSO algorithm.

Algorithm 3.14 Template of the particle swarm optimization algorithm.

Random initialization of the whole swarm ;
Repeat
  Evaluate $f(x_i)$;
  For all particles i
    Update velocities:
      $v_i(t) = v_i(t-1) + \rho_1 \times (p_i - x_i(t-1)) + \rho_2 \times (p_g - x_i(t-1))$;
    Move to the new position: $x_i(t) = x_i(t-1) + v_i(t)$;
    If $f(x_i) < f(pbest_i)$ **Then** $pbest_i = x_i$;
    If $f(x_i) < f(gbest)$ **Then** $gbest = x_i$;
    Update(x_i, v_i) ;
  EndFor
Until Stopping criteria

Example 3.20 PSO for continuous function optimization. Let us illustrate how the general PSO algorithm solves a continuous 2D function f. Let us notice the lower bound (resp. upper bound) for each dimension i by l_i (resp. u_i). The position of a particle i is represented by its coordinates (x_{i1}, x_{i2}). First, the initial position $(x_{i1}(0), x_{i2}(0)$ of a particle i will be generated by a random uniform law in the range of the domain for x_1 and x_2. Each particle will evaluate its position in the two-dimensional space according to the objective function f. Let us suppose a neighborhood based on the whole population. Then, the best particle gbest of the population is defined. Each particle i updates its velocities (v_{i1}, v_{i2}) according to the current velocity, and the best local and global solutions as follows: $v_i(t) = v_i(t-1) + \rho_1 \times (p_i - x_i(t-1)) + \rho_2 \times (p_g - x_i(t-1))$. For a particle i, if there is a maximum range for the location of the variables x_{i1} or x_{i2} (i.e., $x_{ij} \in [l_i, u_i]$), the particle is reflected. Each particle will move to its next position $X(t+1)$. Each particle will compute the next local and global best solutions and the same process is iterated until a given stopping criteria.

3.6.2.2 PSO for Discrete Problems

Unlike ACO algorithms, PSO algorithms are applied traditionally to continuous optimization problems. Some adaptations must be made for discrete optimization problems. They differ from continuous models in

- **Mapping between particle positions and discrete solutions:** Many discrete representations such as binary encodings [458] and permutations can be used for a particle position. For instance, in the binary mapping, a particle is associated with an n-dimensional binary vector.
- **Velocity models:** The velocity models may be real valued, stochastic, or based on a list of moves. In stochastic velocity models for binary encodings, the velocity is associated with the probability for each binary dimension to take value 1. In the binary PSO algorithm [458], a sigmoid function

$$S(v_{id}) = \frac{1}{1 + \exp(-v_{id})}$$

transforms the velocities values v_i into the [0, 1] interval. Then, a random number is generated in the same range. If the generated number is less than $S(v_{id})$, then the decision variable x_{id} will be initialized to 1, otherwise the value 0 is assigned to x_{id}. The velocity tends to increase when the $(p - x)$ term is positive (p_{id} or $p_{gd} = 1$) and decreases when p_{id} or $p_{gd} = 0$. Then, when v_{id} increases, the probability that $x_{id} = 1$ also increases.

Velocity models for discrete optimization problems have been generally inspired from mutation and crossover operators of EAs.

Example 3.21 Geometric PSO. Geometric PSO (GPSO) is an innovative discretization of PSO, which is based on the geometric framework of recombination operators [563]. The location of each particle i is represented by a binary vector $x_i = (x_{i1}, x_{i2}, \ldots, x_{iN})$ where each element x_{ij} (with j in $\{1, N\}$) takes a binary value 0 or 1. The key issue of the GPSO is the concept of particle movement. In this approach, instead of using the notion of velocity, a three-parent mask-based crossover (3PMBCX) operator is applied to each particle to "move" it. According to the definition of the 3PMBCX operator, given three parents a, b, and c in $\{0, 1\}^n$, it generates randomly a crossover mask of length n with symbols from the alphabet a, b, and c. Then, the offspring is constructed by filling each element with the value from the parent appearing in the crossover mask at the corresponding position. For a given

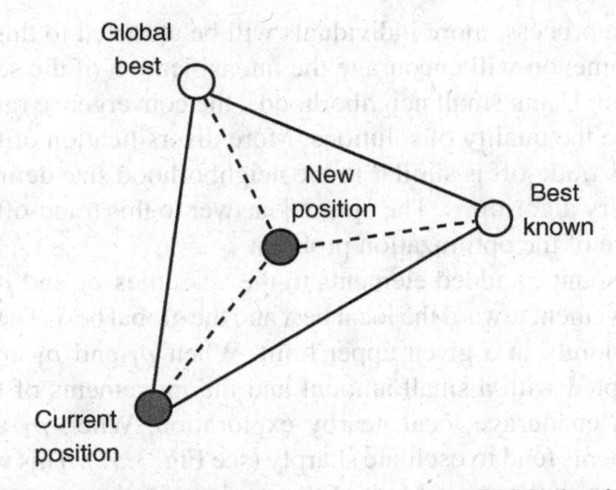

FIGURE 3.36 Geometric crossover in the GPSO algorithm.

particle i, three parents take part in the 3PMBCX operator: the current position x_i, the social best position g_i, and the historical best position found h_i of this particle (Fig. 3.36). The weight values w_1, w_2, and w_3 indicate for each element in the crossover mask the probability of having values from the parents x_i, g_i, or h_i, respectively. These weight values associated with each parent represent the inertia value of the current position (w_1), the social influence of the global/local best position (w_2), and the individual influence of the historical best position found (w_3). A constriction of the geometric crossover forces w_1, w_2, and w_3 to be nonnegative and add up to 1.

Table 3.7 summarizes the main parameters of a basic PSO algorithm. The number of particles n has an inverse relationship with the number of required iterations of the algorithm. Increasing the population size will improve the results but is more time consuming. There is a trade-off between the quality of results and the search time as in any P-metaheuristic. Most of the PSO implementations use an interval of [20,60] for the population size.

The two extremes for the neighborhood size k are the use of the global population of individuals ($k = n(n-1)/2$, where n is the population size) and a local neighborhood structure based on the ring topology ($k = 2$). Many intermediate neighborhood structures may be used (e.g., torus, hypercubes). Using large neighborhoods, the convergence will be faster but the probability to obtain a premature convergence will be more significant. There is a great impact of the best solution on the whole population

TABLE 3.7 Parameters of the PSO Algorithm

Parameter	Role	Practical Values
n	Number of particles	[20, 60]
τ_1, τ_2	Acceleration coefficients	≤ 2.0
k	Neighborhood size	$\left[2, n \cdot \frac{n-1}{2}\right]$
w	Inertia weight	[0.4, 0.9]

in the convergence process, more individuals will be attracted to this best global solution. This phenomenon will encourage the intensification of the search toward the best global solution. Using small neighborhoods, the convergence rate will be slower but it may improve the quality of solutions. More diversification of the search space is carried out. This trade-off is similar to the neighborhood size definition in parallel cellular evolutionary algorithms. The optimal answer to this trade-off depends on the landscape structure of the optimization problem.

The relative amount of added elements to the velocities ρ_1 and ρ_2 represents the strength of the movement toward the local best and the global best. The two parameters are generated randomly in a given upper limit. When ρ_1 and ρ_1 are near zero, the velocities are adapted with a small amount and the movements of the particles are smooth. This will encourage local nearby exploration. When ρ_1 and ρ_1 are high values, the movements tend to oscillate sharply (see Fig. 3.37). This will tend to more global wide-ranging exploration. Most of the implementations use a value of 2.0 for both parameters [455].

The upper limit $V_{\max}$ is recommended to be dependent on the range of the problem. This parameter may be discarded if the following formula is used to update the velocities [139]:

$$v_i(t) = \chi \times (v_i(t-1) + \rho_1 \times (p_i - x_i(t-1)) + \rho_2 \times (p_g - x_i(t-1)))$$

where χ represents the constriction coefficient:

$$\chi = \frac{\kappa}{\text{abs}\left(\frac{1-\frac{\rho}{2}-\sqrt{\text{abs}(\rho^2-4\rho)}}{2}\right)}$$

where $\kappa \in [0, 1]$ (a value of 1.0 has been used), $\rho = \rho_1 + \rho_2$ (should be greater than 4, e.g., limit each ρ_i to 2.05). Using the constriction coefficient will decrease the amplitude of the particle's oscillation.

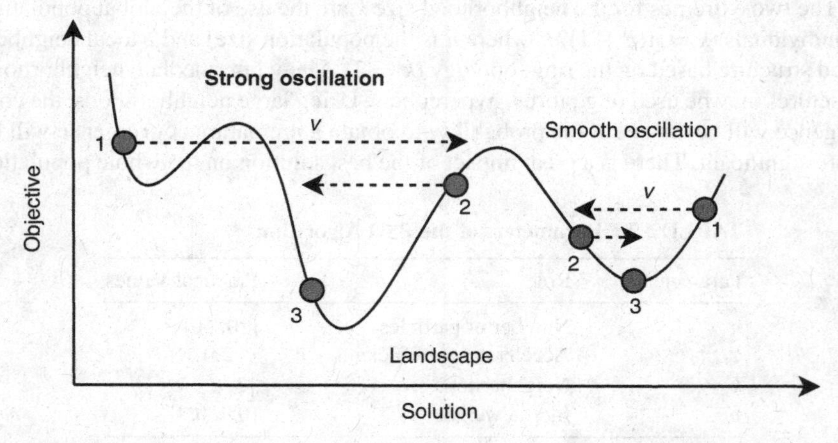

FIGURE 3.37 Strong oscillations versus smooth oscillations in a particle swarm.

These various parameters may also be initialized in a dynamic or adaptive way to deal with the trade-off between intensification and diversification during the search. Typically, the value of the inertia weight w is initialized to 0.9 to decrease to 0.4. The number of particles can vary during the search. For instance, a particle can be removed when its performance is the worst one [138].

3.7 OTHER POPULATION-BASED METHODS

Other nature-inspired P-metaheuristics such as bee colony and artificial immune systems may be used for complex optimization problem solving.

3.7.1 Bee Colony

The bee colony optimization-based algorithm is a stochastic P-metaheuristic that belongs to the class of swarm intelligence algorithms. In the last decade, many studies based on various bee colony behaviors have been developed to solve complex combinatorial or continuous optimization problems [77]. Bee colony optimization-based algorithms are inspired by the behavior of a honeybee colony that exhibits many features that can be used as models for intelligent and collective behavior. These features include nectar exploration, mating during flight, food foraging, waggle dance, and division of labor.

Bee colony-based optimization algorithms are mainly based on three different models: food foraging, nest site search, and marriage in the bee colony. Each model defines a given behavior for a specific task.

3.7.1.1 Bees in Nature Bee is social and flying insect native to Europe, the Middle East, and the whole of Africa and has been introduced by beekeepers to the rest of the world [689,707]. There are more than 20,000 known species that inhabit the flowering regions and live in a social colony after choosing their nest called a *hive*. There are between 60,000 and 80,000 living elements in a hive. The bee is characterized by the production of a complex substance, the honey, and the construction of its nest using the wax. Bees feed on the nectar as energy source in their life and use the pollen as protein source in the rearing of their broods. The nectar is collected in pollen baskets situated in their legs.

Generally, a bee colony contains one reproductive female called *queen*, a few thousand males known as *drones*, and many thousand sterile females that are called the *workers*. After mating with several drones, the queen breeds many young bees called *broods*. Let us present the structural and functional differences between these four honeybee elements:

- **Queen:** In a bee colony, there is a unique queen that is the breeding female with life expectancy between 3 and 5 years. It is developed from special and very young larvae and eggs selected by workers, from which the colony produce a new queen to become sexually mature, after killing the old unfertilized one. It is an exclusive development that will be raised in special queen cells with rich-protein secretion. The main role of the queen is the reproduction by the egg laying [492]. It mates with 7–20 drones in a reproductive operation called *mating flight*. It stores the sperms in her spermatheca and then lays up to 2000 eggs per day. The fertilized eggs become female (worker) and the unfertilized eggs become male (drones).

- **Drones:** Drones represent the males varying between 300 and 3000 in the hive. Drones are developed when the queen lays unfertilized eggs and they play the role of fertilizing with a receptive queen generally in the summer and exceptionally in the autumn. The drone has a life expectancy of 90 days. It dies after a successful mating.
- **Workers:** Workers are female bees but are not reproductive. They live from 4 to 9 months in the cold season and their number reaches up to 30,000. However, in summer, they live approximately for 6 weeks when their number attains up to 80,000. The worker is responsible for the beehive defense using its barbed stinger. Consequently, it dies after stinging. One can enumerate the worker activities by the day criterion as follows: cell cleaning (day 1–2), nurse bee (day 3–11), wax production (day 12–17), guard honeybees (day 18–21), and foraging honeybees (day 22–42). The worker ensures the habitual activities of the bee colony such as honey sealing, pollen packing, fanning honeybees, water carrying, egg moving, queen attending, drone feeding, mortuary honeybees, and honeycomb building.
- **Broods:** The young bees are named broods. They born following the laying of eggs by the queen in special honeycomb cells called: the brood frames. Thereafter, the workers add royal jelly on the brood heads. Few female larvae are selected to be future queens. In this case, they are flooded by royal jelly. The unfertilized eggs give birth to the broods. The young larvae are spinning by cocoon, capping the cell by the older sisters; it is the pupa stage. Then, they reach the development stage in which they receive nectar and pollen from foragers until leaving the beehive and spending its life as forager.

The foraging behavior (nest site selection, food foraging) and the marriage behavior in a bee colony are the main activities in the life of a bee colony that attract researchers to design optimization algorithms.

3.7.1.2 Nest Site Selection In late spring or early summer, bees belonging to a colony are divided into two sets: the queen and half of the workers and the daughter queen and the rest half of the workers. The former aims to establish a new colony and the latter perpetuate the old colony. For selecting a new nest site, few hundreds of scout bees among several thousands explore some nest sites. The other bees remain quiescent, probably to conserve the swarms energy supply, until decision making and then migrate to the selected nest site. The foraging bees indicate various nest sites by several dances having eight patterns called *waggle dances*[16] (Fig. 3.38). The

[16] The waggle dance of the honeybee was elucidated by Karl von Frisch, an Austrian ethologist. For this work, he received the Nobel Prize in Physiology or Medicine in 1973.

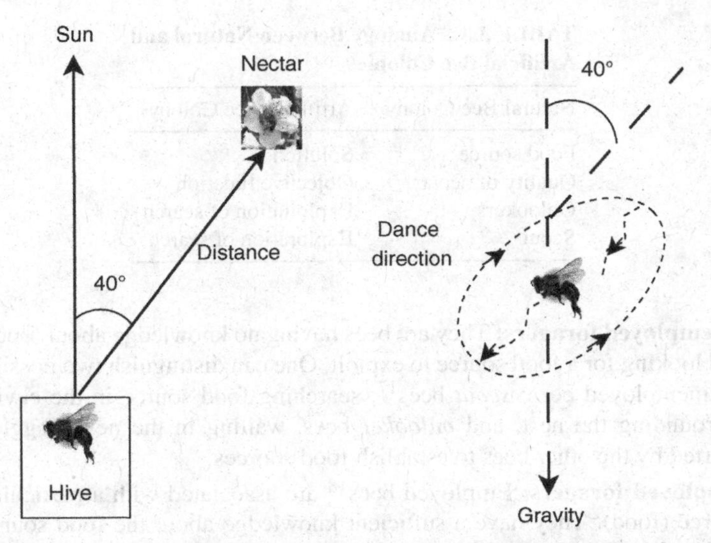

FIGURE 3.38 The waggle dance. The direction is indicated by the angle from the sun; the distance is defined by the duration of the waggle part of the dance. A waggle run oriented 40° to the right indicates a food source 40° to the right of the direction of the sun outside the hive. The bee runs through a figure-eight pattern on a vertical comb. It passes through the central, and performs the waggle run with vibrating her body laterally. The waggle run duration is related to the food source distance with a rate of increase of about 75 ms [691].

speed and the orientation of the dance are related with the nest sites quality. Various attributes are used to characterize a nest site (e.g., entrance area, entrance direction, entrance height, cavity volume). Within time, the advertising sites decline until the bee's dance focus on one site. In other words, scouts vote by dancing for their favorite site and then they make a group decision via a quorum sensing and not via consensus sensing. Thereafter, scouts inform their nest mates by waggle dances. Finally, the entire bee cluster migrates toward the new nest site [690,691].

The waggle dance is used to inform other bees about nest site location or even food sources. The quality of the nest site is related to cavity volume and entrance hole, perched several meters off the ground, facing south, and located at the cavity floor.

Searching for a nest site is more or less similar to searching food source. Indeed, this behavior starts with the environment exploration. The food source is discovered via waggle dance and then the exploitation of the nectar is performed. The quality (profitability) of a food source depends on many indicators such as the richness of the energy, the distance to the nest, and the difficulty of extracting the energy.

3.7.1.3 Food Foraging

The role of a bee colony in foraging is to find rich food sources to obtain maximum quantity of nectar. According to their role, there are different types of bee foragers:

TABLE 3.8 Analogy Between Natural and Artificial Bee Colonies

Natural Bee Colony	Artificial Bee Colony
Food source	Solution
Quality of nectar	Objective function
Onlookers	Exploitation of search
Scout	Exploration of search

- **Unemployed foragers:** They are bees having no knowledge about food sources and looking for a food source to exploit. One can distinguish two possible types of unemployed bees: *scout* bees[17], searching food source in the environment surrounding the nest, and *onlooker* bees, waiting in the nest waggle dances exerted by the other bees to establish food sources.
- **Employed foragers:** Employed bees[18] are associated with a particular nectar source (food). They have a sufficient knowledge about the food source. They find and exploit food source, memorize its location, load a portion of nectar to the beehive, and unload it to the food area in the hive. One can mention three possible states related to the amount of nectar; if it is in low level or exhausted, the recruit honeybees abandon food source and become unemployed honeybees. If the amount of nectar is still sufficient, they forage and do not share food source with the nest mates. Finally, if an important amount of nectar is found, they exert a waggle dance for recruiting the other bees of the nest.

Searching a food source is based on two strategies (see Table 3.8 that illustrates the analogy between natural and artificial bee colonies):

- **Exploration of food sources:** A scout bee explores the neighboring area to find a food source. In the positive case, it returns to the dancing floor of the hive and informs the nest mates by a waggle dance. The onlookers become recruit bees and then they become employed foragers.
- **Exploitation of a food source:** An employed forager calculates the amount of food sources and takes a decision according to the quality of nectar. Either it continues the exploitation by the memorization of the best food found so far or it abandons. In that case, the employed bee becomes an unemployed one, either a scout or an onlooker bee using a probabilistic dividing.

A colony of bees can extend itself over long distances (up to 14 km) and in multiple directions in parallel to exploit a large number of food sources. A colony prospers by deploying its foragers to food sources of good quality. In principle, flower patches with plentiful amounts of nectar or pollen that can be collected with less effort should be visited by more bees, whereas patches with less nectar or pollen should receive

[17]The mean number of scout bees in a colony is 10% and varies from 5 to 30% [689].
[18]As they must recruit, they are also called recruit bees.

fewer bees. The foraging process begins in a colony by scout bees being sent to search for promising flower patches. Scout bees move randomly from one patch to another. During the harvesting season, a colony continues its exploration, keeping a percentage of the population as scout bees. When they return to the hive, those scout bees that found a patch that is rated above a certain quality threshold (measured as a combination of some constituents, such as sugar content) deposit their nectar or pollen and go to the "dance floor" to perform a waggle dance (Fig. 3.39). This dance is primordial for communication between bees and contains three types of information regarding a flower patch: the direction in which it will be found, its distance from the hive, and its fitness (i.e., quality). This information guides the colony to send its bees to flower patches precisely. Each beeÂ's knowledge of the neighboring environment

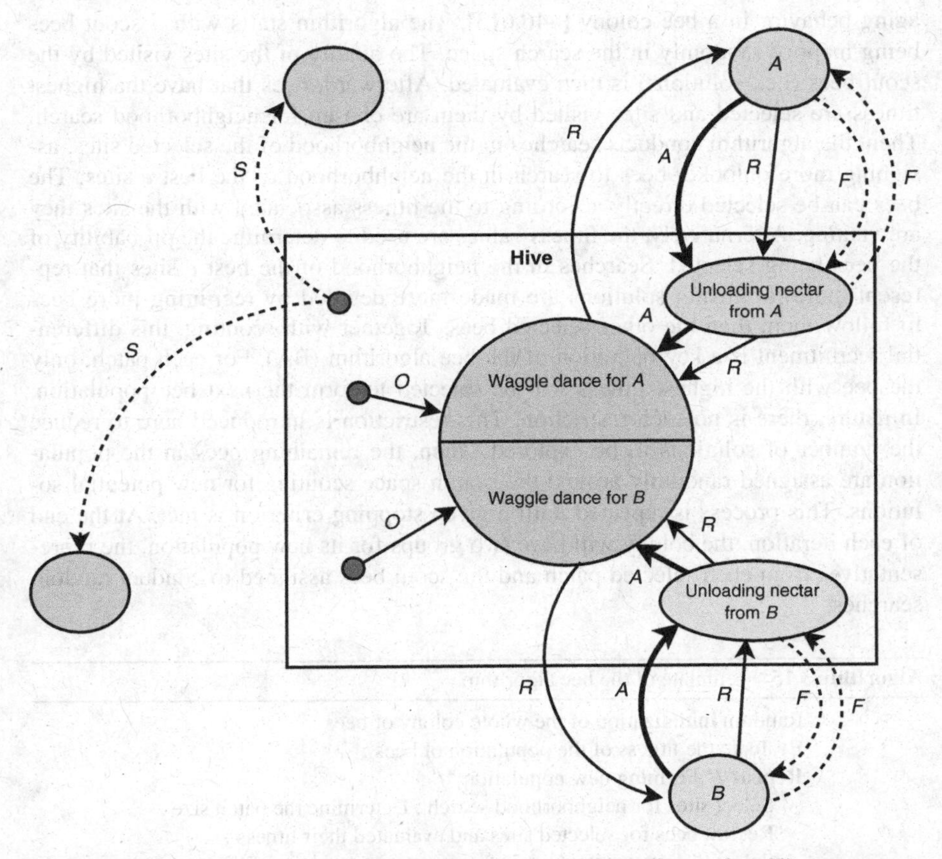

FIGURE 3.39 Bee colony behavior for food source (nectar) discovering. We assume two discovered food sources A and B [445]. An unemployed bee has no knowledge about food source. It can be a scout bee S, starting to explore the neighborhood of the nest, or an onlooker bee O, watching for the waggle dances. After the localization of a food source, the bee becomes an employed bee. After unloading the nectar, the employed bee has three alternatives: abandoning the food source (A), recruit other bees from the nest (R), and foraging without recruiting other bees (F).

is extracted solely from the waggle dance. This dance enables the colony to evaluate the relative merit of different patches according to both the quality of the food they provide and the amount of energy needed to harvest it. After waggle dancing on the dance floor, the dancer (i.e., the scout bee) goes back to the flower patch with follower bees that were waiting inside the hive. More follower bees are sent to more promising patches. This allows the colony to gather food quickly and efficiently. While harvesting from a patch, the bees monitor its food level. This is necessary to decide upon the next waggle dance when they return to the hive. If the patch is still good enough as a food source, then it will be advertised in the waggle dance and more bees will be recruited to that source (Fig. 3.39). The recruitment is proportional to the profitability of the food source.

Algorithm 3.15 shows the template of the bee algorithm inspired by the food foraging behavior in a bee colony [446,613]. The algorithm starts with n scout bees being mapped randomly in the search space. The quality of the sites visited by the scout bees (i.e., solutions) is then evaluated. Afterward, bees that have the highest fitness are selected and sites visited by them are chosen for neighborhood search. Then, the algorithm conducts searches in the neighborhood of the selected sites, assigning more onlooker bees to search in the neighborhood of the best e sites. The bees can be selected directly according to the fitness associated with the sites they are visiting. Alternatively, the fitness values are used to determine the probability of the bees being selected. Searches in the neighborhood of the best e sites that represent more promising solutions are made more detailed by recruiting more bees to follow them than the other selected bees. Together with scouting, this differential recruitment is a key operation of the bee algorithm (BA). For each patch, only the bee with the highest fitness will be selected to form the next bee population. In nature, there is no such restriction. This restriction is introduced here to reduce the number of solutions to be explored. Then, the remaining bees in the population are assigned randomly around the search space scouting for new potential solutions. This process is repeated until a given stopping criterion is met. At the end of each iteration, the colony will have two groups for its new population, the representatives from each selected patch and the scout bees assigned to conduct random searches.

Algorithm 3.15 Template of the bee algorithm.

```
Random initialization of the whole colony of bees ;
Evaluate the fitness of the population of bees ;
Repeat /* Forming new population */
   Select sites for neighborhood search ; Determine the patch size ;
   Recruit bees for selected sites and evaluated their fitness ;
   Select the representative bee from each patch ;
   Assign remaining bees to search randomly and evaluate their fitness ;
Until Stopping criteria
```

The algorithm requires a number of parameters to be initialized: the number of scout bees (n), the number of sites selected out of n visited sites (m) for neighborhood search, the number of best sites out of m selected sites (e), the number of bees recruited for best e sites (nep), the number of bees recruited for the other ($m - e$) selected sites (nsp), and the initial size of patches (ngh), which includes site and its neighborhood and a stopping criterion.

Example 3.22 Bee colony optimization for the job-shop scheduling problem. Let us consider the application of the bee foraging model to solve the job-shop scheduling problem (JSP) (see Example 1.33 for the definition of the problem). A feasible solution in a JSP is a complete schedule of operations specified in the problem. One can think of each solution as a path from the hive to the food source.

The makespan of the solution is analogous to the profitability of the food source in terms of distance and sweetness of the nectar. Hence, the shorter the makespan, the higher the profitability of the solution path. One can thus maintain a colony of bees, where each bee will traverse a potential solution path (i.e., disjunctive graph). The foragers move along branches from one node to another node in the disjunctive graph (Fig. 3.40). A forager must visit every node once, starting from the source node

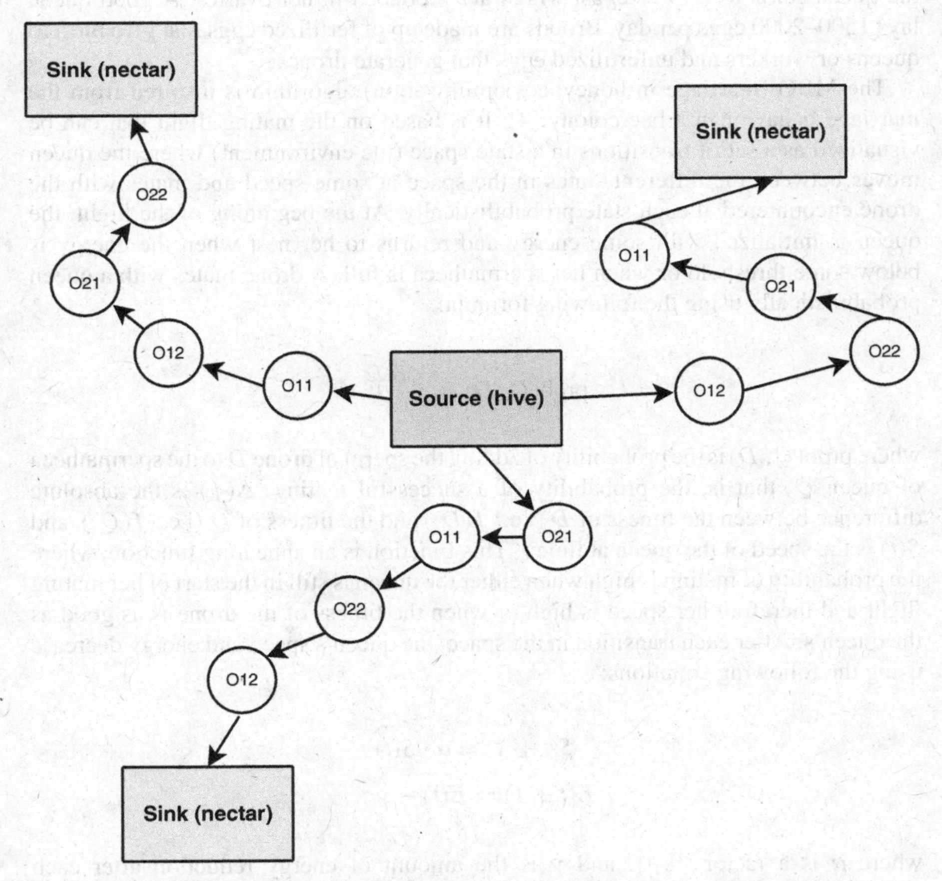

FIGURE 3.40 Bee colony optimization for the job-shop scheduling problem.

(e.g., hive) and finishing at the sink node (e.g., nectar). Once a feasible solution is found, each bee will return to the hive to perform a waggle dance. The waggle dance will be represented by a list of elite solutions, from which other bees can choose to follow another bee's path [132]. Bees with a better objective function will have a higher probability of adding its path to the list of elite solutions, promoting a convergence to a "good" solution.

3.7.1.4 Marriage Process

The reproduction phenomenon in a bee colony is guaranteed by the queen that mates with 7–20 drones [10]. This phenomenon is called the mating flight [657]. It carries out far from the nest in the air. First, the queen initializes with some energy and then performs a special dance. Drones follow and mate with the queen. They put their sperms in the queen spermatheca. It forms the genetic pool of the colony. Next, the queen returns to the nest either when the energy is below a given threshold or when her spermatheca is full (retrieving at random a mixture sperms about 5,000,000 spermatozoa). Three days after her last mating flight, the queen starts to lay her eggs, which are produced in her ovaries. A good queen lays 1500–2000 eggs per day. Broods are made up of fertilized eggs that give birth to queens or workers and unfertilized eggs that generate drones.

The MBO (marriage in honeybees optimization) algorithm is inspired from the marriage behavior in a bee colony [4]. It is based on the mating flight that can be visualized as a set of transitions in a state space (the environment) where the queen moves between the different states in the space at some speed and mates with the drone encountered at each state probabilistically. At the beginning of the flight, the queen is initialized with some energy and returns to her nest when the energy is below some threshold or when her spermatheca is full. A drone mates with a queen probabilistically using the following formula:

$$\text{prob}(Q, D) = e^{\frac{-\Delta(f)}{S(t)}}$$

where $\text{prob}(Q, D)$ is the probability of adding the sperm of drone D to the spermatheca of queen Q, that is, the probability of a successful mating, $\Delta(f)$ is the absolute difference between the fitness of D (i.e., $f(D)$) and the fitness of Q (i.e., $f(Q)$), and $S(t)$ is the speed of the queen at time t. This function is an annealing function, where the probability of mating is high when either the queen is still in the start of her mating flight and therefore her speed is high or when the fitness of the drone is as good as the queen's. After each transition in the space, the queen's speed and energy decrease using the following equations:

$$S(t+1) = \alpha \cdot S(t)$$

$$E(t+1) = E(t) - \gamma$$

where α is a factor $]0, 1[$, and γ is the amount of energy reduction after each transition.

Algorithm 3.16 shows the template for the MBO algorithm [4]. The algorithm starts with initializing the queen's genotype at random. After that, workers (i.e., S-metaheuristics) are used to improve the queen's genotype, thereby preserving the assumption that a queen is usually a good bee. Afterward, a set of mating flights are performed. In each mating flight, the queen's energy and speed are initialized randomly. The queen then moves between different states (i.e., solutions) in the space according to her speed and mates with the drone she encounters at each state using the previously presented function. The transition made by the queen in the space is based on her speed. Therefore, at the beginning of the process, the speed is usually high and the queen makes very large steps in the space. If a drone is successfully mated with the queen, his sperm is added to the queen's spermatheca (i.e., a set of partial solutions). Then, the speed and the energy of the queen are reduced. Once the queen finishes her mating flight, she returns to the nest and starts breeding by selecting a sperm from her spermatheca at random followed by crossover with the queen's genome that complements the chosen sperm. This crossover operation results in a brood. This is the haploid crossover [4]. The mutation operator then acts on the brood. Therefore, if the same sperm is used once more to generate a brood, the resultant brood will be different because of mutation. This process is followed by applying the worker to improve the broods. The fitness of each worker is then updated based on the amount of improvement performed by the worker to the drone. Afterward, the queen is replaced with the fittest brood if the brood is better than the queen. The remaining broods are then killed and a new mating flight is launched [4].

Algorithm 3.16 Template of the MBO algorithm.

```
Random initialization of the queen's ;
Improve the queen with workers (S-metaheuristic) ;
For predefined maximum number of mating-flights Do
   Initialize energy and speed ;
   While queen's energy > 0 Do
      The queen moves between states and probabilistically chooses drones ;
      If a drone is selected Then
         Add its sperm to the queen's spermatheca ;
      Update the queen's internal energy and speed ;
   Endwhile
   Generate broods by haploid-crossover and mutation ;
   Use the workers (S-metaheuristic) to improve the broods ;
   Update workers' fitness ;
   If The best brood is fitter than the queen Then
      Replace the queen's chromosome with the best brood's chromosome ;
   Kill all broods ;
Endfor
```

The user-defined parameters are the number of queens, the queen's spermatheca size representing the maximum number of matings per queen in a single mating flight, the number and type of workers, and the number of broods that will be created by all queens.

3.7.2 Artificial Immune Systems

Recently, attention has been drawn to mimic biological immune systems for the development of novel optimization algorithms. Indeed, the immune system is highly robust, adaptive, inherently parallel, and self-organized. It has powerful learning and memory capabilities and presents an evolutionary type of response to infectious foreign elements [70,253]. This rapidly growing field that applies immune system principles to optimization and machine learning problems is known as artificial immune systems. An AIS may be seen as an adaptive system that is inspired by theoretical immunology and observed immune processes. They have been mainly applied to data mining problems [395,770]. In the last years, their application to optimization problems is increasing [119,170].

The biological processes that are simulated to design AIS algorithms include pattern recognition, clonal selection for B cells, negative selection of T cells, affinity maturation, danger theory, and immune network theory. In designing an AIS algorithm, three main questions occur [185]:

- **Representation:** This question addresses the representation of the components (e.g., antigens, antibodies, cells, molecules) of the system. Some traditional representation may be used (see Section 4.8.2.1).
- **Affinity:** This question is concerned with the evaluation of the interaction of the system's components (i.e., each other and with their environment). The affinity measure may be represented by a similarity (or dissimilarity) distance. The distance will depend on the representation used (e.g. Hamming distance for binary representation, Euclidean or Manhattan distance for real-value representation).
- **Adaptation:** This question is related to the procedures that govern the dynamics of the whole system.

AIS algorithms may be classified into two classes [184]:

- **Population based:** Population-based AIS algorithms do not take into account the immune network. For instance, they are inspired by the *clonal selection* theory and the *negative selection* theory.
- **Network based:** Network-based AIS algorithms are inspired by the network theory of the immune system such as the *immune network theory* and the *danger theory*.

3.7.2.1 Natural Immune System

The main purpose of the immune system[19] is to keep the organism free from *pathogens* that are unfriendly foreign microorganisms, cells, or molecules. The immune system is a complex set of cells, molecules, and organs that represents an identification mechanism capable of perceiving and combating a dysfunction from our own cells (infectious self), such as tumors and cancerous cells, and the action of exogenous microorganisms (infectious nonself) [178].

[19]The word *immunity* from Latin *immunitas* means "freedom from."

In the surface of *pathogens* like viruses, fungi, bacteria, and parasites, there are *antigens* (Ag) that simulate the immune responses. Antigens represent substances such as toxins or enzymes in the microorganisms that the immune system considers foreign. There exist two types of immunities: the innate immune system and the adaptive immune system.

- **Innate immune system:** The innate immune system plays a crucial role in the initiation and regulation of immune responses. The innate system is so called because the body is born with the ability to recognize a microbe and destroy it immediately. It protects our body from nonspecific pathogens.
- **Adaptive immune system:** The adaptive or acquired immune system completes the innate one and removes the specific pathogens that persist to it. The adaptive immunity is made essentially by *lymphocytes*, a certain type of white blood cells that has two types of cells: the B cells[20] and the T cells[21]. These cells are responsible of recognizing and destroying any antigen.

3.7.2.2 Clonal Selection Theory

Clonal selection is a widely accepted theory for modeling the immune system responses to infection. The theory of clonal selection was proposed by M. Burnet in 1959 [100]. It is based on the concept of cloning and *affinity maturation*. B and T lymphocytes are selected to destruct specific antigens invading the body. When the body is exposed to an exogenous antigen, those B cells that best bind the antigen proliferate by cloning. The B cells are programmed to clone a specific type of antibodies `Ab` that will bind to a specific antigen `Ag`. The binding between an antigen `Ag` and an antibody `Ab` is governed by how well a paratope on the `Ab` matches an epitope of the `Ag` (Fig. 3.41). The closer is this match, the stronger is the bind. This property is called *affinity*. Some of the cloned cells are differentiated into *plasma cells* that are antibody secretors. The other cloned cells become *memory cells*. A high-rate *somatic mutation* (hypermutation) is applied to the cloned cells that promote a genetic diversity. Moreover, a selection pressure is performed, which implies a survival of the cells with higher affinity. Let us notice that clonal selection is a kind of an evolutionary process. Clonal selection immune algorithms may be viewed as a class of evolutionary algorithms that are inspired by the immune system.

One of the main algorithms based on clonal selection theory is the `CLONALG` algorithm [186]. The main design questions for this algorithm are maintenance of a specific memory set, selection and cloning of the most stimulated antibodies, death of nonstimulated antibodies, affinity maturation and selection of the clones proportionally to their antigenic affinity, and generation and maintenance of diversity [188]. An antibody `Ab` represents a solution and an antigen `Ag` represents the value of the objective function to optimize. Antibody and antigen representations are commonly implemented by traditional encodings (e.g., strings of attributes). The attributes may

[20]B because they mature within bone marrow.
[21]T because they mature within the thymus.

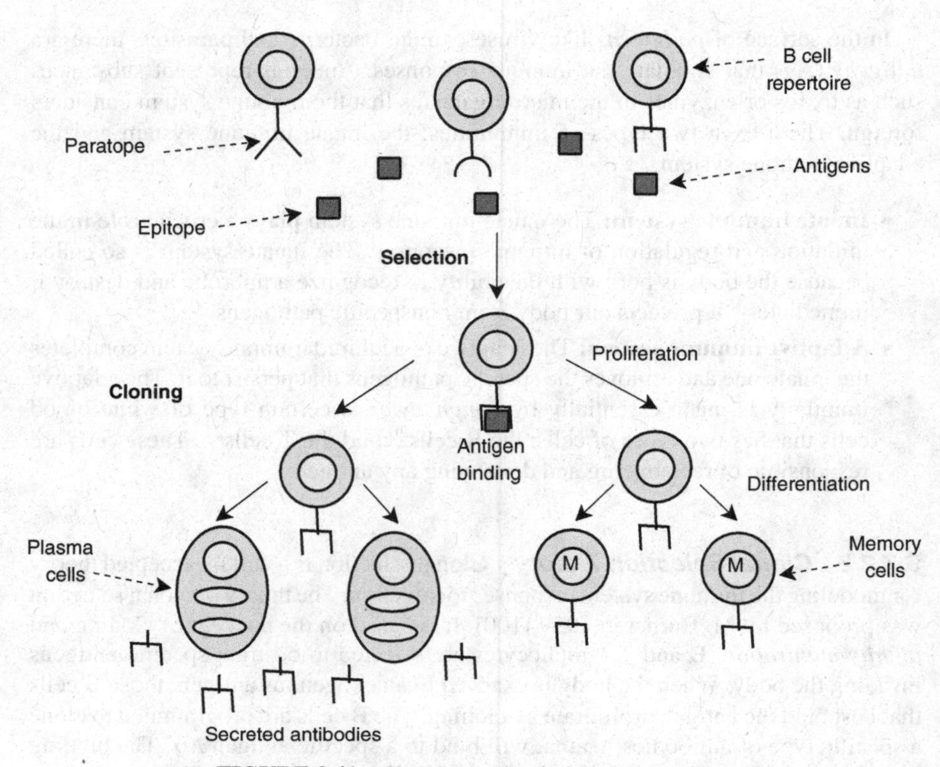

FIGURE 3.41 Clonal selection in immune systems.

be binary, integer, or real valued. Matching is performed according to a distance metric (e.g., Euclidean distance, Manhattan distance or Hamming distance). The Ag−Ab affinity is then related to the distance. The Ag−Ab representation will partially determine which type of distance measure shall be used to compute degree of interaction between an antibody and an antigen.

Algorithm 3.17 illustrates the general scheme of the CLONALG algorithm. First, a population of N antibodies is generated randomly. Each antibody represents a solution for the target optimization problem. Then, n antibodies are selected according to a selection scheme. The selected antibodies are cloned and mutated to construct new candidate population of antibodies. The n antibodies generate N_c clones proportionally to their affinities[22]. The higher the affinity, the larger the clone size. The number of cloned antibodies N_c can be computed as follows:

$$N_c = \sum_{i=1}^{n} \text{round} \frac{\beta \cdot N}{i}$$

[22]The affinity in CLONALG for optimization tasks is defined as the objective function rather than the similarity (e.g., machine learning tasks).

where β is a multiplying factor. Each term of this sum corresponds to the clone size of each selected antibody. For instance, for $N = 100$ and $\beta = 1$, the highest affinity antibody ($i = 1$) produces 100 clones while the second highest affinity antibody produces 50 clones. Afterward, the clones undergo a *hypermutation* and *receptor editing*. The receptor editing offers the ability to escape from a local region on an affinity landscape and the possibility to obtain the global optimum (i.e., diversification). The mutation rate of clones is inversely proportional to their antigenic affinity. The higher is the affinity, the smaller is the mutation rate. The new population is evaluated and some of its members are selected to be added to the original population. Finally, a given percentage of the worst members of the previous population of antibodies are replaced with new randomly generated solutions. This step will introduce some diversity in the population.

Algorithm 3.17 Template of the CLONALG.

Input: Initial population P_0.
$P = P_0$; /* Generation of the initial population of random antibodies */
Repeat
  Evaluate all existing antibodies and compute their affinities ;
  Select $N\%$ of antibodies with highest affinities ;
  Clone the selected antibodies ;
  Maturate the cloned antibodies ;
  Evaluate all cloned antibodies ;
  Add $R\%$ of best cloned antibodies to the pool of antibodies ;
  Remove worst members of the antibodies pool ;
  Add new random antibodies into the population ;
Until Stopping criteria satisfied
Output: Best population found.

Other AIS algorithms based on clonal selection have been proposed in the literature such as the CLIGA algorithm [171], the B cell algorithm [454], and the Forrest's algorithm [279]. According to the clonal selection theory, Table 3.9 shows the analogy between natural immune systems and optimization problem solving.

TABLE 3.9 Analogy Between the Natural Immune System and the Optimization Problem According to the Clonal Selection Theory

Natural Immune System	Optimization Problem
Antibody	Solution
Affinity	Objective function
Antigen	Optimization problem
Cloning	Reproduction of solutions
Somatic mutation (hypermutation)	Multiple mutation of a solution
Affinity maturation	Mutation and selection of best solutions
Receptor editing	Diversification

3.7.2.3 Negative Selection Principle The immune system may present a dysfunction, where it confuses the nonself cells with the cells that belong to our body (i.e., self cells or antigens). To avoid this dysfunction, our body eliminates the lymphocytes T cells that react to our self cells from the repertoire through a process called "negative selection." Hence, only the lymphocytes that do not respond to the self cells will survive. Those lymphocytes are called tolerant. Negative selection can be viewed as the process of eliminating cells, which recognize self cells and molecules.

Negative selection algorithm (NSA) is based on the principles of the maturation of the T cells and self/nonself discrimination in the biological immune systems. The immature T cells are a sort of anomaly detectors. NSA has been developed by Forrest et al. in 1994 to solve computer security problems [280]. As NSAs are used to generate a set of anomaly detectors, they are usually applied to computer security, network intrusion detection problems [381], and classification problems [336]. Recently, many algorithms inspired by negative selection have been proposed to solve optimization problems [106,296].

3.7.2.4 Immune Network Theory The theoretical development of the immune network theory was initiated by Jerne in 1974 [412]. The immune network is defined as a dynamic and autoregulated system formed by immune cells that have the capability to communicate and recognize not only the antigens but also the other immune cells. Those immune cells simulate, activate, and suppress each other even in the absence of antigens.

Let us recall that according to the clonal selection theory, the immune system is composed of discrete cells and molecules that are stimulated only by nonself antigens; whereas in the immune network theory, the immune system is composed of cells and molecules that communicate with each other. In the immune network theory, no antigen foreign stimulation is necessary. There are two levels of interaction an immune network: the interaction with the environment (external environment such as foreign antigens) and the interaction with other components of the network (i.e., internal environment).

One of the most known AIS algorithms based on immune network theory is the aiNET algorithm (artificial immune network) [187].

Algorithm 3.18 illustrates the general scheme of the aiNET algorithm. First, a population S of antigens to be recognized is assumed, and a population P of antibodies (i.e., B cell) in the network is randomly generated. A vector of real values is used to represent antigens and antibodies. The affinity between antigens and antibodies is defined by the Euclidean distance. Then, a given number of antibodies are selected and cloned. The selection is based on their affinity with the antigens. The higher is the affinity of an antibody, the more significant is the probability of its selection and the higher is the number of its clones. The generated cloned undergo a somatic mutation. The somatic mutation is inversely proportional to their antigenic affinity. The higher is the affinity with the antigens, the lower is the mutation rate. Afterward, a given number of affinity clones is selected to be the member of the immune network (i.e., clonal memory). Moreover, antibodies with an affinity with other antibodies lower than a given threshold are eliminated from the immune network (i.e., clonal suppression). Antibodies with an affinity with antigens lower than a given threshold are eliminated from the immune network (i.e., natural death rate). Finally, a given number of new randomly generated antibodies are incorporated into the immune network and evaluated according to their affinity with existing antibodies (i.e., metadynamics). Antibodies whose affinities are lower than a given threshold are eliminated.

Algorithm 3.18 The aiNET algorithm.

Input: Initial random population P of antibodies. Initial population S of antigens.
Repeat
Antigenic presentation:
For each antigenic pattern s **Do**
Clonal selection and expansion:
For each antibody determine its affinity with antigen ;
Select a number n_1 of antibodies ; Clone the selected antibodies ;
Affinity maturation:
Mutate each clone ; Re-select a number n_2 of clones ;
Place the selected clones in the clone memory set ;
Metadynamics:
Eliminate all memory clones whose affinities with antigen is less than ϵ ;
Clonal interactions:
Determine the network interactions (affinity) between all antibodies of the clone memory set ;
Clonal suppression:
Eliminate memory clones whose affinities is less than σ_s ;
Network construction:
Incorporate remaining clones if the clonal memory set into the network ;
EndFor
Network interactions:
Determine the similarity between each pair of network antibodies ;
Network suppression:
Eliminate all antibodies whose affinity with each other is less than σ_s ;
Diversity:
Introduce a number n_3 of new randomly generated antibodies into the network ;
Until Stopping criteria
Output: Population P of memory antibodies (solutions).

3.7.2.5 Danger Theory Danger theory was proposed by P. Matzinger in 1994 [533]. Traditional immune system theories are based on the self/nonself distinction. The danger theory suggests that there exists a concept that is more important than self/nonself distinction. It proposes that the immune system may not be stimulated by nonself foreign cells. For instance, there is no immune reaction to foreign bacteria. It also suggests that the immmune system may react to self cells. For instance, it recognizes self molecules expressed by stressed or damaged cells [534].

In danger theory, foreign dangerous antigens stimulate the production of danger signals by stimulating cellular stress or cell death. Those signals are recognized by antigen-presenting cells (APCs). Then, the immune system manipulates these danger signals to recognize the *danger zone* and then evaluates the danger. Let us notice that there is currently a hot debate among immunologists on the danger theory. This theory is far to be widely accepted and still controversial. AIS algorithms based on danger theory have been recently used to solve computer security and machine learning problems [17,616].

3.8 P-METAHEURISTICS IMPLEMENTATION UNDER ParadisEO

This section will illustrate the implementation of evolutionary algorithms, particle swarm optimization, and estimation of distribution algorithms under the ParadisEO–EO framework. The EO library has been developed initially for evolutionary algorithms (genetic algorithms, evolution strategies, evolutionary programming, genetic programming, estimation distribution algorithms, and differential evolution) [453]. It has been extended to population-based metaheuristics such as particle swarm optimization and ant colony[23] optimization.

3.8.1 Common Components and Programming Hints

Besides the classes dedicated to the implementation of a specific population-based metaheuristic, ParadisEO–EO contains a huge set of tools that can be used independent of the metaheuristic involved. Most of them are written using templates. This allows to write generic code, that is, involving a class that does not have to be known when writing the code but only when compiling it. Although the advantages are obvious (writing generic reusable code instead of rewriting the same pieces of code for different types), there are some drawbacks, namely, it makes some of the compiler error messages hard to understand. It also forbids the compilation of most parts of ParadisEO–EO into an object library file as the actual types are not known in advance.

3.8.1.1 Main Core Templates—ParadisEO–EO's Functors A functor *function object* is a computer programming construct allowing an object to be invoked or called as if it were an ordinary function with the same syntax. In C++, a functor may be used instead of an ordinary function by defining a class that overloads the function call operator by defining an *operator()* member function. The term *class type functor* is commonly used to identify this kind of construct. The C++ functors have three main advantages:

- Functors introduce a high level of generalization (*horizontal generalization* here).
- Unlike a function pointer, a function object can be in-lined.
- They can maintain states between calls.

[23]The model implemented is inspired from the self-organization of *Pachycondyla apicalis* ant species.

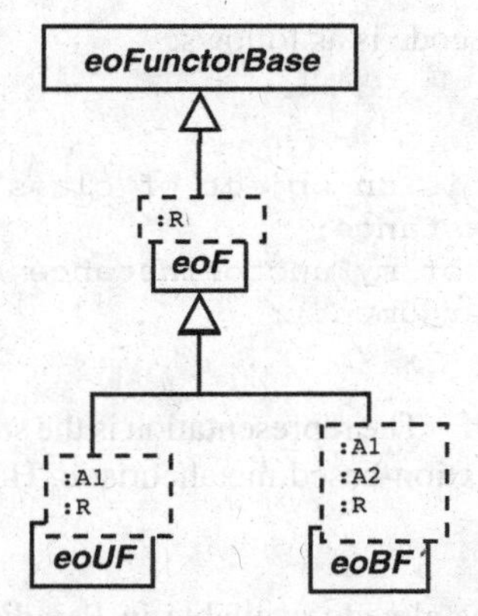

FIGURE 3.42 eoFunctors: the base classes and templates of ParadisEO–EO.

ParadisEO–EO mainly contains functors, which have a method called *operator()*. The functors of ParadisEO–EO are the base classes and templates at the top level of the inheritance tree. By having all functors derived from the same base class `eoFunctorBase`, one can also easily manage the memory.

Notice that these functors are template based. The UML diagram defined in Fig. 3.42 implies that

- Any object extending `eoF` must have an overloaded operator `operator()` that returns the templatized type `R`. `eoF` is for arity-zero functors, that is, `operator()` method does not require any argument. It has a single template parameter, the return type of the `operator()` method.
- `eoUF` tends for *eo unary functors*. Any object extending `eoUF` must have an overloaded operator `operator(A1)` that takes an object of type `A1` and returns an object of type `R`.
- `eoBF` is for *eo binary functors*. Their `operator()` method requires two arguments. It has three template parameters, the types of the arguments and the return type of the `operator()` method.

All the operators, initializers, stopping criteria, and evaluation functions available within ParadisEO–EO inherit these functors. The following is a short basic example of how to program and use a functor object:

```
class MyFunctor
{...
    void operator()(ArgType arg)
    {
            // what you have to do
    }
}; // end of class declaration
```

The way it is used in the code is as follows:

```
ArgType myArgument;
// myFunctorInstance is an object of class MyFUnctor.
MyFunctor myFunctorInstance;
 // calls operator() of myFunctorInstance acting on myArgument.
myFunctorInstance(myArgument);
```

3.8.1.2 Representation The representation is the starting point for anyone who plans to implement a population-based metaheuristic. However, there are two ways to define a *solution*:

- Use the representations already available in ParadisEO–EO. That is the most frequent case. The only thing to code is the mono-objective fitness computation function.
- Design and implement a specific one and the representation-dependent parts of the algorithm.

The `EO` template is the base class for evolvable objects, that is, the representation of a solution. EOs have only got a fitness whose type is given by the template argument. It confers to the solution it represents a sense in the objective space. For evolutionary algorithms, an `EO` defines the individual and its phenotype. Extensions are made for particles or individuals that need several fitnesses (multiobjective optimization). An `EO` inherits from `eoPersistent`: it must know how to write and read itself. At this point, the representation in the search space is not exposed yet. Bit strings, real-valued vectors or parse trees extends all `EO` to complete the representation (Fig. 3.43):

- `eoVector` templatized with the fitness type and the genotype, that is, the type of the coded representation will suit for almost all the cases. For example, `eoReal` contains a fitness of type `F` and a vector of double. Of course, it extends the standard vector of the Standard Template Library (STL).
- `eoParseTree` implements a parse tree for genetic programming.
- `eoString` is just an adaptor that turns an STL `std::string` into an EO.
- `eoExternalEO` allows an external `struct` (in C++ sense) to be inserted in EO.

In case these representations do not suit for a given problem, a specific one can be easily coded by extending the *evolving object* `EO` template or by plugging it into an `eoExternalEO`. Hence, the user may have to define representation–dependent parts of the algorithm. Similarly, for particle swarm optimization (particles must keep their best fitness as a memory) and multiobjective optimization (many objectives means many fitness functions), it is clear that the basic `EO` is not sufficient. That is why several extensions are provided (see Section 4.8.1). Notice that for most of the generic components that will be described in the following sections, the type of the

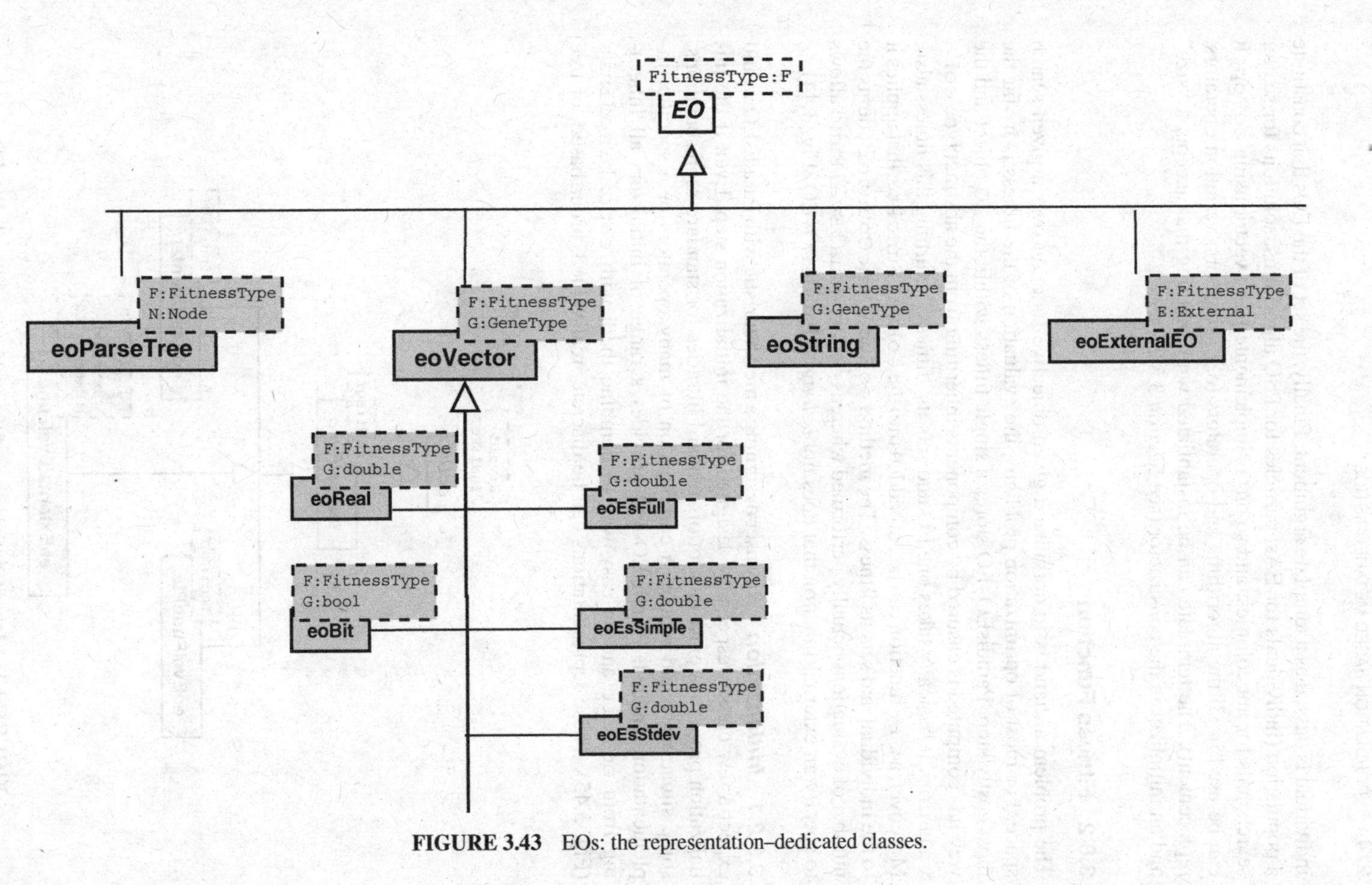

FIGURE 3.43 EOs: the representation–dedicated classes.

individual is passed as a template argument. Finally, the set of the EOs that constitute a population (individuals for EAs, particles for PSO algorithms, solutions for scatter search, ants for ant colonies, and so on) is implemented as a vector using `eoPop`. It can be used in all the algorithms and operators (e.g., selectors, variation operators, replacement). The template can be instantiated with anything that accepts a "size" and an initializer in the constructor (see Section 3.8.2.1).

3.8.2 Fitness Function

The problem at hand is to optimize a given objective function over a given search space. For most of optimization problems, the evaluation of the fitness is by far the most costly step. ParadisEO–EO stores a single fitness within the `EO` object and the way it is computed is ensured by components inheriting from the abstract type `eoEvalFunc`. It basically takes one EO and sets its "fitness" returning this fitness also. Moreover, a C++ function can be embedded into the `eoEvalFuncPtr` that applies it to the individual and sets its fitness. The method `eoEvalFuncCounter` counts the number of evaluations actually performed whereas `eoExternalEvalFunc` allows to specify an external function that does not *belong* to ParadisEO–EO (Fig. 3.44).

3.8.2.1 Initialization Any user designing a metaheuristic with ParadisEO would expect a few classes especially designed for the initialization step. Even if the initialization properties exist in a lot of standard libraries for standard representations, some situations could require a combination of many operators or a specific implementation. Indeed, ParadisEO–EO provides a range of initializers all inheriting from `eoInit` and an easy way to combine them with `eoCombinedInit` (Fig. 3.45). These representations can be discrete, real valued, order based, or tree

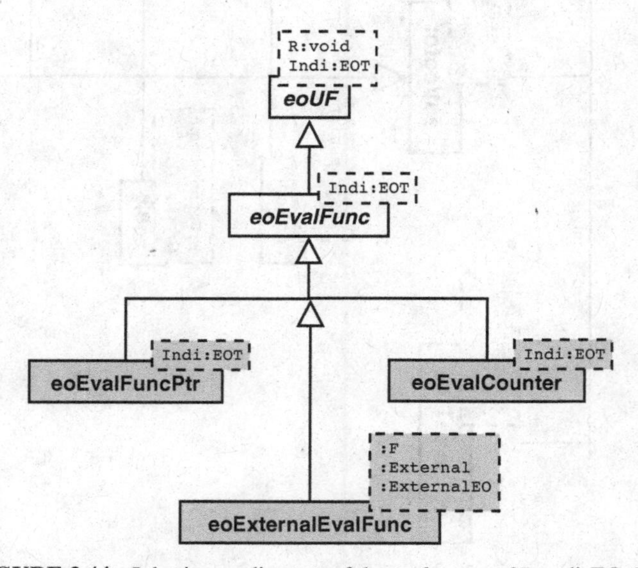

FIGURE 3.44 Inheritance diagram of the evaluators of ParadisEO–EO.

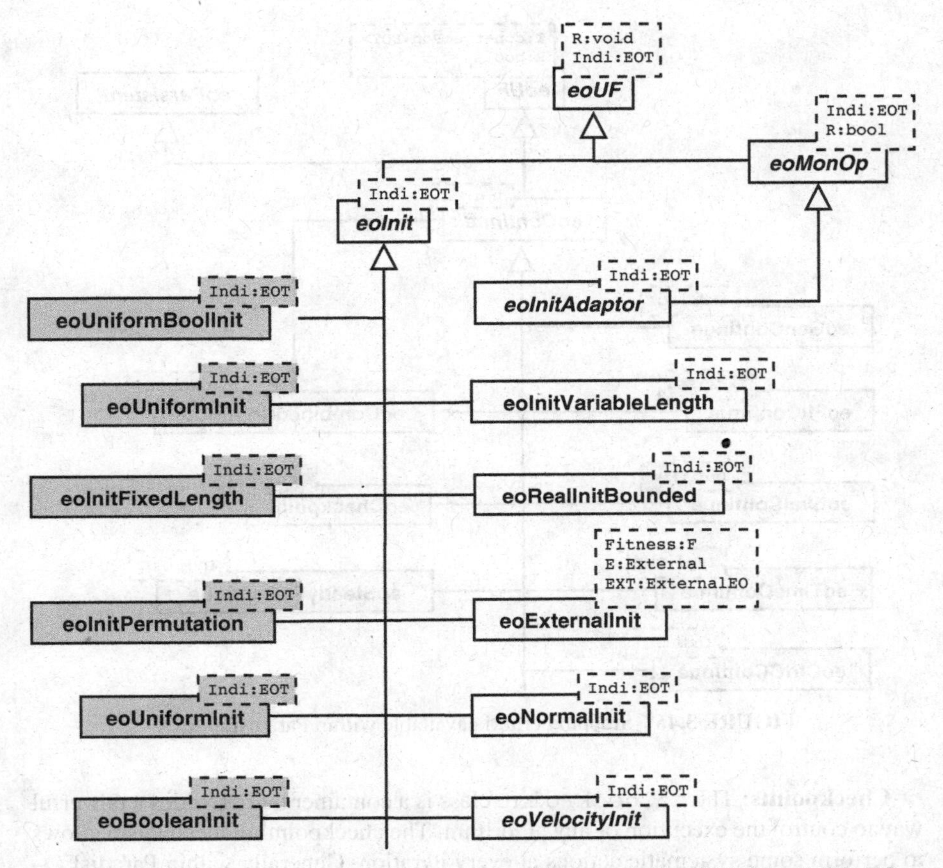

FIGURE 3.45 A summary of initialization procedures available within ParadisEO–EO.

based. Nevertheless, one could still consider that it is not enough for some kind of problems. That is why any mutation operator inheriting from `eoMonOp` can be wrapped by the `eoInitAdaptor` and used as an initializer. Other components also exist to initialize particles (see Section 3.8.4). Moreover, one can use S-metaheuristics within ParadisEO–MO that can generate promising solutions for the initial population.

3.8.2.2 Stopping Criteria, Checkpoints, and Statistics

Stopping criteria: Since an iterative method computes successive approximations, a practical test is needed to determine when to stop an iteration. In addition, other procedures may be called for at each step or loop of the main algorithm. Many stopping criteria extending `eoContinue` are offered (Fig. 3.46), including

- `eoGenContinue` that performs a fixed number of iterations.
- `eoTimeContinue` that continues until a duration is reached.
- `eoEvalContinue` that continues until the maximum fitness level is reached.

The stopping criteria can be combined with `eoCombinedContinue`.

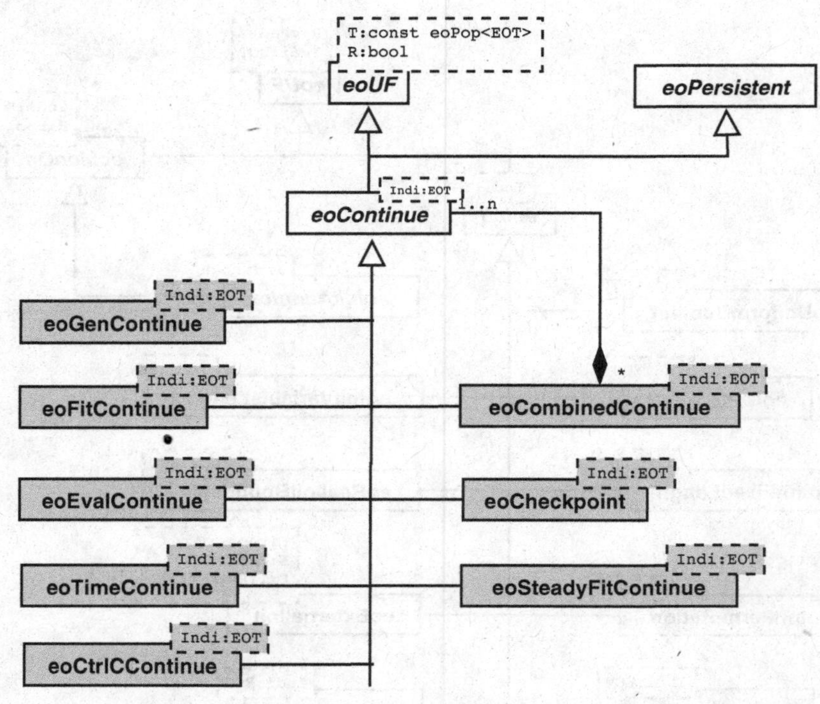

FIGURE 3.46 Stopping criteria available within ParadisEO–EO.

Checkpoints: The `eoCheckPoint` class is a container that provides a powerful way to control the execution of any algorithm. The checkpointing mechanism allows to perform some systematic actions at every iteration. Generally within ParadisEO–EO, checkpoints are called for at each iteration in a transparent manner. These methods expect an `eoCheckPoint` to be instantiated and their implemented structures do not depend on the control one might want to impose. The `eoCheckPoint` just returns if the algorithm should go on according to the states of the components it contains.

- `eoContinue`: The checkpoint examines if the algorithm should continue by evaluating the combination of the stopping criteria.
- `eoStat`: Refer to the next paragraph.
- `eoMonitor`: Derived classes will stream or pipe the current values of the parameters to wherever the user wants it to get streamed or piped. For example, the `eoStdoutMonitor` allows to print out the states of a population (e.g., representation, fitnesses, deviations) on the standard output.
- `eoUpdater`: It encapsulates anything a user wish to do that does not fit into one of the above categories.

Statistics: The `eoStatBase` is the abstract top-level class for all the statistics. It is extended so that there is nothing to do in order to use any statistic anybody could

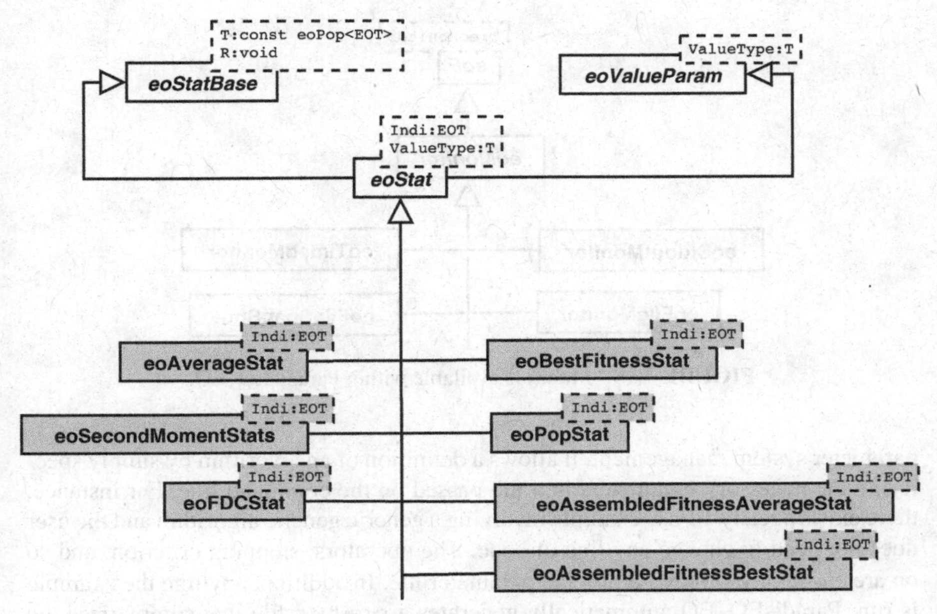

FIGURE 3.47 Statistics available within ParadisEO–EO.

think of. The user needs to declare the corresponding `eoStat` objects and add them to the `eoCheckpoint` used in the algorithm. But it makes no sense if those statistics are not monitored (i.e., either displaying on the screen or storing them into a file). A few monitors are implemented (Fig. 3.48):

- `eoStdoutMonitor` displays its parameters in text format on the screen by evaluating the combination of the stopping criteria.
- `eoFileMonitor` writes its parameters in text format in a file. A file name is necessary in the constructor, and an optional separator character can be added.
- `eoGnuplot1DMonitor` displays its parameters in graphical format on the screen by calling the Gnuplot program[24].

These monitors compute the statistics as shown in Fig. 3.47.

3.8.2.3 Dynamic Parameter Management and State Loader/Register

Dynamic parameter management: When a metaheuristic is implemented to tackle an optimization problem, there is often a wide set of parameters to choose. If those parameters are hard coded, the user will have to compile the program each time one of them has changed. To avoid this waste of time, ParadisEO–EO proposes an advanced

[24]It only works on the Unix platforms (e.g., Linux, MacOs).

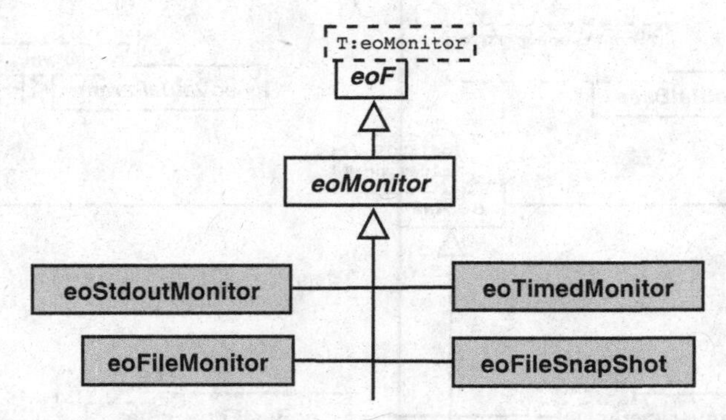

FIGURE 3.48 Monitors available within ParadisEO–EO.

parameter system management. It allows a definition of an algorithm by simply specifying the necessary parameters in a file passed on the command line. For instance, there exists a ready-to-use example involving a generic genetic algorithm and the user does not need to change any line of code. The operators, stopping criterion, and so on are chosen by simply editing the parameter file. In addition, anytime the example is run, ParadisEO–EO automatically generates a `status` file that summarizes the parameters used.

State loader/register: Generally, it is very useful to register the state of a running algorithm (e.g., parameters, population at each iteration). It can give of lot of information about the algorithm's behavior and allow an easy restart in case of run-time error. ParadisEO–EO proposes, for example, to start an algorithm using an existing population. This population could have been registered previously by another algorithm run in a different context. The `eoState` can be used to register objects inheriting from `eoPersistent`. It implements the persistence framework through members load and save. The `eoState` can merely be embedded into an `eoUpdater`.

3.8.3 Evolutionary Algorithms Under ParadisEO

Once the common components have been designed and implemented, it becomes quite easy to present the way evolutionary algorithms are designed within ParadisEO–EO. The problem is always to optimize a given objective function in a given search space by making a population of individuals undergo some Darwinian evolution. This evolution is made of steps. These steps define the architecture of the components involved to implement it. So the current section aims to answer this question: What do I need to implement my EA and how does ParadisEO help me to do it?

3.8.3.1 Representation The individual is represented as a genotype and it must be relevant regarding the tackled problem. When choosing a representation, one has to bear in mind how the genotypes will be evaluated and how the variation operators will be used. The components dedicated to the representation have been described in Section 4.8.2.1.

3.8.3.2 *Initialization* The initialization of the population is fundamental in an EA event if it has no natural counterpart in the biological models of evolution. Initializers are common objects within ParadisEO–EO that can be combined and extended. The reader may refer to Section 3.8.2.1.

3.8.3.3 *Evaluation* For EAs, the evaluation consists in the computation of the fitnesses of the newborn offspring. The fitness measure is directly associated with its objective function value. Evaluators are common components within the framework, they are presented in Section 3.8.2.

3.8.3.4 *Variation Operators* Variation operators modify the genotype of individuals, or, equivalently, move them in the search space. In EAs, variation operators are almost stochastic. Depending on the number of arguments they use and/or modify, they are classified as follows:

- **Binary and quadratic operators:** Variation operators involving two individuals are called crossover operators. They can either modify one of the parents according to the material of the other parent or modify both parents. In ParadisEO–EO, the former are called binary operators and the latter are called quadratic operators.
- **Unary operators:** Variation operators involving one single individual are called mutation operators.
- **Combined operators:** Straightforward extensions of these simple operators allow to combine them. In proportional combinations, one operator is chosen from a given set of operators of same arity according to some weights.

In ParadisEO–EO, one can also define and use variation operators that generate any number of offsprings from any number of parents[25] as in scatter search metaheuristics. These operators are called general operators. However, the interface of such operators was designed for their use inside general combinations: proportional combination can be used, in which one operator is chosen from a given set of operators of same arity according to some weights, as for simple operators except that operators of different arities can be mixed.

Basically, variation operators operate on genotypes only. Hence, there should be generally no reference to anything related to the fitness within a variation operator. However, whenever the genotype of an individual has been modified, it will be necessary to recompute its fitness before any selection process. This is why all the variation operators return a `bool` that indicates whether the genotype argument has been modified or not. Four abstract classes derive from `eoOp`, namely, `eoMonOp` (for mutations), `eoBinOp` and `eoQuadOp` (for crossovers), and `eoGenOp` for all other operators. Variation operators can be combined using `eoProportionalCombinedMonOp`, `eoProportionalCombinedBinOp`,

[25] Sometimes termed orgy operators.

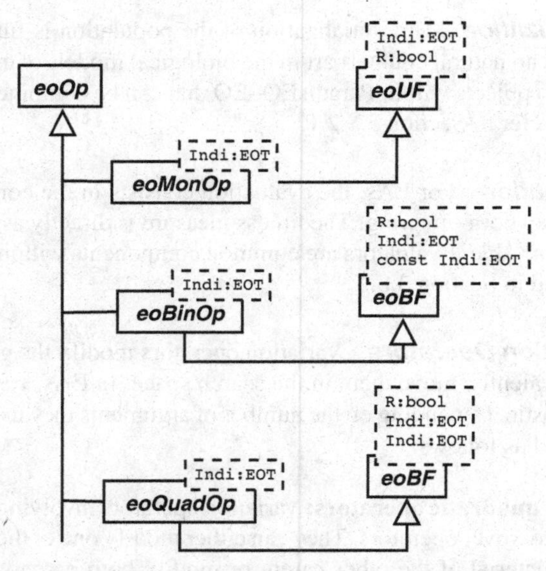

FIGURE 3.49 Mutators are unary operators (`MonOp`) within ParadisEO–EO.

and `eoProportionalCombinedQuadOp`. The operators `eoGenOp` can be combined into an abstract class `eoOpContainer` with two implementations: `eoProportionalOp` and `eoSequentialOp`.

Mutation operators: The fact that mutation operators or *mutators* are usually defined from the search space E to E is directly translated to the architecture. The `eoMonOp` template defines an unary genetic operator that takes and modify only one individual (Fig. 3.49). The general approach in ParadisEO–EO about simple variation operators is to perform in-place modifications. It consists in modifying the arguments rather than generating new (modified) individuals. This results in the following interface for the functor objects `eoMonOp`:

```
bool operator()(EOT & )
```

Here is a brief list of the available mutations extending `eoMonOp` (Fig. 3.50):

- `eoBitMutation`, `eoBitInversion`, and many others for the binary representation.
- `eoSwapMutation`, `eoNormalMutation`, and `eoUniformMutation` for permutations, real-valued and integer representations.
- `eoBranchMutation` and `eoCollapseSubtreeMutation` for tree-based representations.
- `eoPropCombinedMutation` that allows to combine several mutations and choose one of them using a given rate and a roulette-wheel selection.

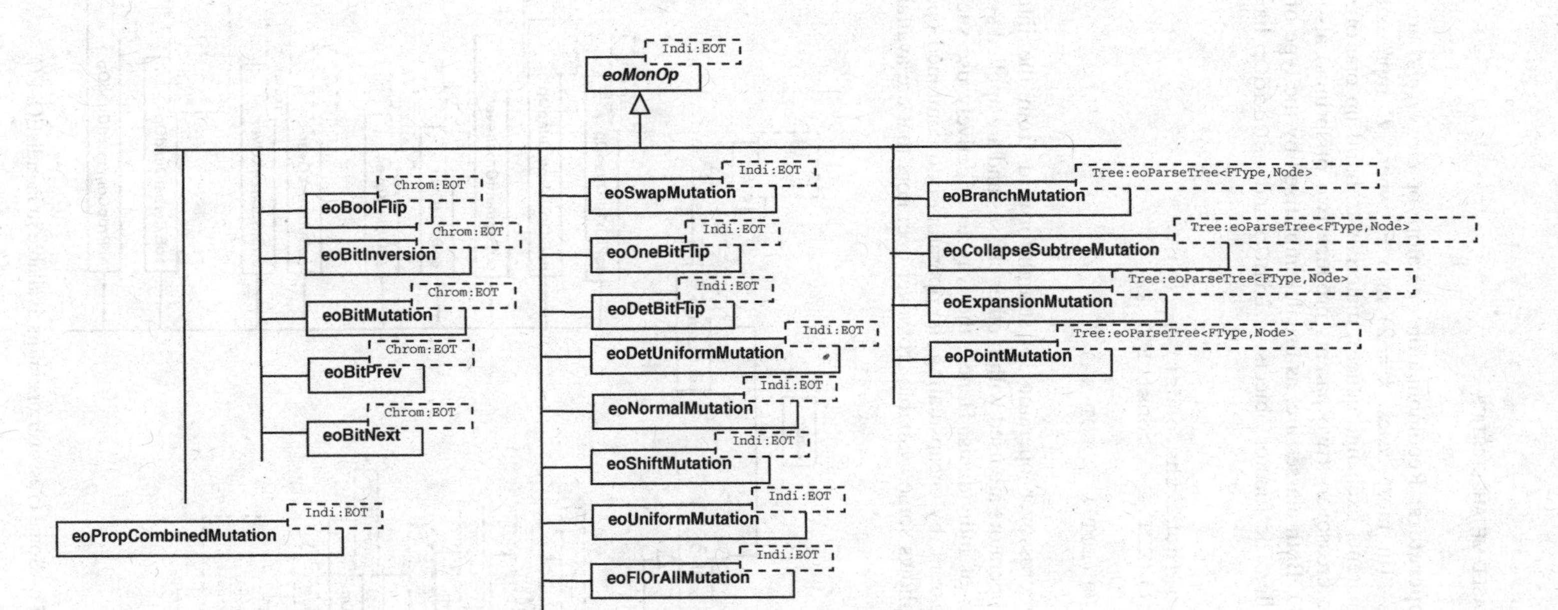

FIGURE 3.50 Some mutation operators: inheritance UML diagram.

Recombination operators: Recombination operators or *crossovers*, are operators acting from E^k (in most cases, $k = 2$) into E, where E represents the search space. Some parents exchange genetic materials to build up one offspring `eoBinOp`. Quadratic crossovers (two parents produce two offsprings) also exist within ParadisEO–EO. Both classes are, as usual, templatized by the type of individual they can handle. The functor objects `eoBinOp` and `eoQuadOp` have the following interfaces:

```
// For eoBinOp (note the const)
bool operator()(EOT & , const EOT &)
//  For eoQuadOp
bool operator()(EOT & , EOT & )
```

Directly applying crossover operators is straightforward from the interface above. Nevertheless, operators are used within other classes and are applied systematically to whole sets of individuals. Hence, the way to effectively use such operators will be transparent, by encapsulating the operators into combined operator objects. Figure 3.51 shows some available crossover operators that are available in ParadisEO–EO.

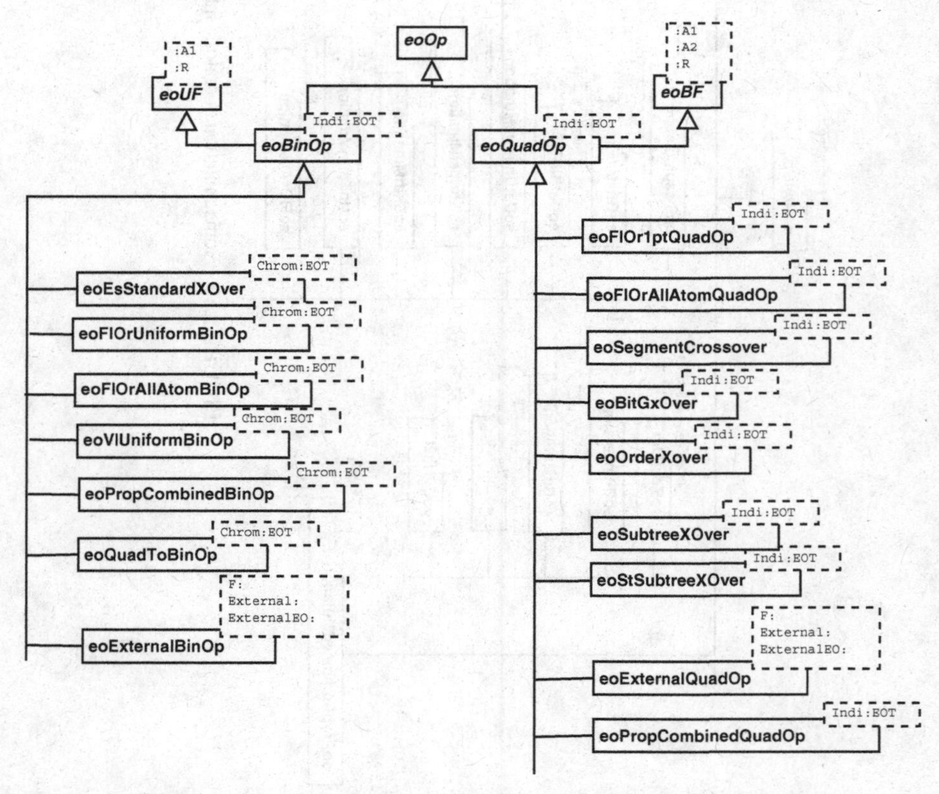

FIGURE 3.51 Some crossover operators available in ParadisEO–EO.

3.8.3.5 *Evolution Engine* The term evolution engine denotes the different parts of an evolutionary algorithm that simulate the Darwinism. Darwinism considers that the fittest individuals have more chance to reproduce and survive. This idea takes place in two different phases of an EA:

- The selection is the Darwinistic choice of parents that will perform the reproduction.
- The replacement is performed after the reproduction. It represents the Darwinistic choice of the individuals that will survive. The survivors become the parents of the next generation.

Both selection and replacement will be discussed in turn. Additional classes used within selection and replacement procedures are also presented.

Selection: Conceptually, there are two distinct ways to choose the individuals from the population that will become the parents:

- One by one from the same population. The same individual could be chosen every time.
- As a whole in some sort of a batch procedure.

Consequently, ParadisEO–EO provides two basic abstract classes for the selection: `eoSelectOne` and `eoSelect`. `eoSelectOne` derives from class `eoUF`. It takes one population and return an unchanged individual. Any class extending `eoSelectOne` must implement the following operator (inheritance from `eoUF`):

```
const EOT & operator()(const eoPop<EOT>& _parents)
```

That is the case for several selection procedures:

- `eoDetTournamentSelect` uses the (deterministic) tournament selection to choose one individual.
- `eoStochTournamentSelect` uses the binary stochastic tournament selection to choose one individual.
- `eoProportionalSelect` is the original roulette-wheel selection. Each parent is selected with a probability proportional to its fitness and so on.

On the other hand, `eoSelect` derives from `eoBF` and takes two populations. It fills the second one with individuals from the first one without modifying it. Indeed, the user should give the number of individuals to select and the way the selection of one individual is repeated. For example, `eoDetSelect` selects individuals deterministically, that is, it starts from the best ones down to the worse ones. Its constructor needs a number of individuals to select or a percentage of the source population size.

There is also an easy way to repeat the selection of one individual by using `eoSelectMany`, which is derived from `eoSelect` and encapsulates an `eoSelectOne`. The number of individuals it should select is expected in the constructor, according to the `eoHowMany` paradigm.

Replacement: The replacement occurs after the creation of all offsprings through variation operators. The new population will be built upon the old parents and the newborn offspring. In all EAs implemented within ParadisEO–EO, the population size is supposed to be constant from one generation to the next one. Of course, it is quite easy to overload the algorithms to skip this constraint.

The `eoReplacement` class is the abstract class for replacement procedures. It inherits from `eoBF<eoPop<EOT>&, eoPop<EOT>&, void>`. This means that it takes two populations (the parents and the offspring) and is free to modify both. The resulting population is the first argument. Anyone could think of a broad range of specific replacements for an EA and it would be quite easy to extend `eoReplacement` to implement them. The Paradiseo–EO framework proposed many well-known replacement procedures (Fig. 3.52):

- `eoGenerationalReplacement`: This is the most straightforward replacement procedure. All offsprings replace systematically all parents. This generational replacement is used in traditional genetic algorithms.

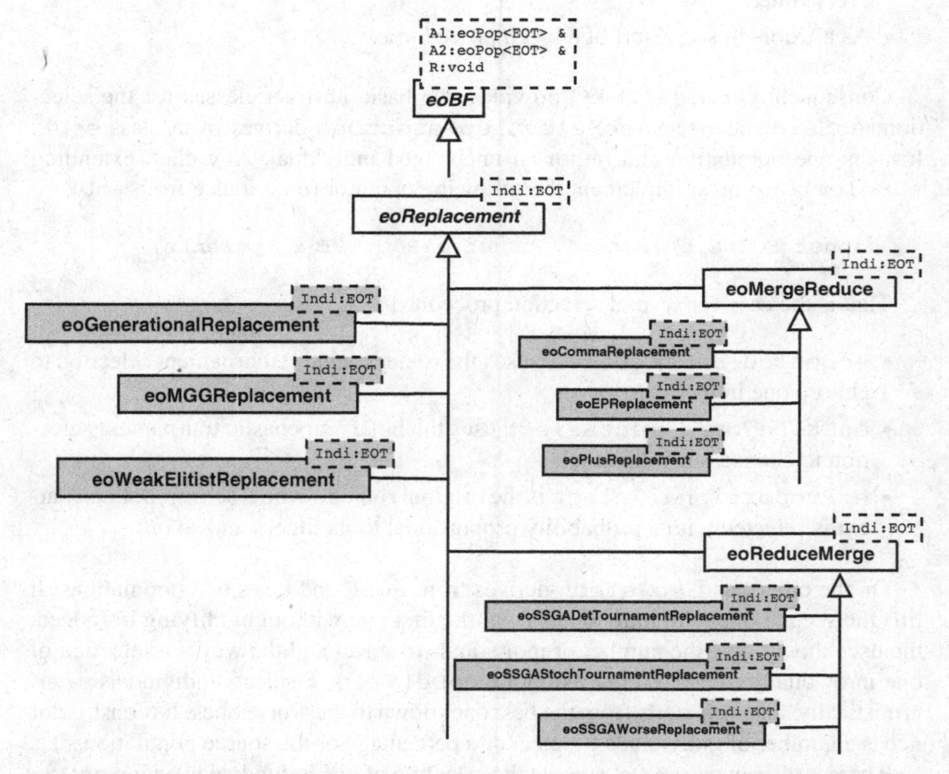

FIGURE 3.52 Inheritance UML diagram of the main replacement–dedicated classes. The basic abstract class is `eoReplacement`. The reduce–merge strategies are represented for the classes on the right side.

- eoMergeReduce: It has two major steps, namely, merging both populations of parents and offsprings and reducing this large population to the right size. It contains two objects of respective types eoMerge and eoReduce. There are many merge and reduce classes that are implemented in the framework (e.g., eoLinearTruncate, eoElitism).
- eoSurviveAndDie: This procedure takes one population, kills the worse, and moves the best to a safe place. The corresponding replacement applies an eoSurviveAndDie to the parents, another one to the offspring, and finally merges the remaining parents and offspring before reducing the resulting population to the right size. For instance, the template eoDeterministic-SaDReplacement uses a deterministic merge–reduce operation.

3.8.3.6 *Evolutionary Algorithms*

The generic EA: When all the algorithmic elements that compose an evolutionary algorithm have been chosen, the last thing to do is the instantiation of the algorithm itself. The eoEasyEA class should suit for all the cases as its structure is really generic. Its derives from eoAlgo, the interface of all the algorithms, and launches the generation loop using the *operator()* that receives a population (eoPop). The following steps are performed in Algorithm 3.19.

Algorithm 3.19 Template of the eoEasyEA evolutionary algorithm.

```
Perform a first evaluation of the given population
Repeat
  Select parents ;
  Make them reproduce ;
  Evaluate the offspring ;
  Replace the parent by the offspring ;
Until Stopping criteria
```

Many constructors exist for the eoEasyEA and each one needs a set of classes (given as parameters) that define completely the algorithm. The variety of the constructors ensures that all the combination of the strategies can be easily made. Any chromosome, any selection transformation, and any merging and evaluation algorithms can be chosen. At the end, designing and implementing an EA is as easy as choosing its components (Fig. 3.53).

Simple genetic algorithm (SGA): The simple genetic algorithm is also implemented. It needs a selector (class eoSelectOne), a crossover (eoQuad, i.e., a $2->2$ operator), and a mutation with their respective rates, of course an evaluation function (eoEvalFunc) and a continuator (eoContinue) that defines the stopping criterion. It performs the full generational replacement. As it only has one constructor, the eoSGA is the easiest way to implement a genetic algorithm. Here is the code corresponding to that constructor; the type of the individuals is passed in template argument (EOT):

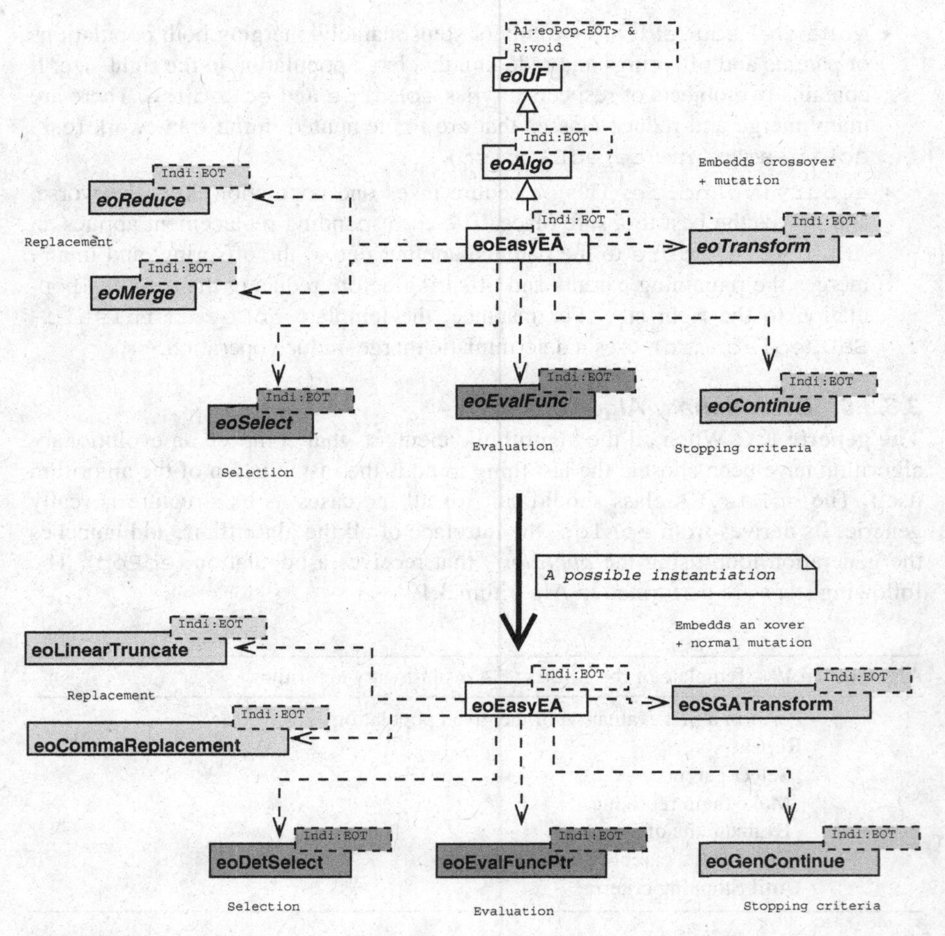

FIGURE 3.53 A possible design for `eoEasyEA`: the upper part describes one of the constructors with the abstract classes expected. Then, a possible instantiation is proposed.

```
// SGA constructor
eoSGA(
  eoSelectOne<EOT>& _select,                // selection
  eoQuadOp<EOT>& _cross, float _crate,      // crossover
  eoMonOp<EOT>& _mutate, float _mrate,      // mutation
  eoEvalFunc<EOT>& _eval)                   // evaluation function
```

3.8.4 Particle Swarm Optimization Under ParadisEO

This section show how to implement a particle swarm optimization algorithm using ParadisEO–EO. Some definitions, design concepts, and code examples are detailed for PSO algorithms.

The implementation of PSO algorithms under ParadisEO is quite easy as the framework is object oriented and provides fine-grained components. An abstract class is always defined for PSO search components. Thus, the whole framework is extensible and can be adapted to best suit any new scheme or strategy according to a given algorithm. Particularly for the PSO, any new feature a user could think of could be quickly integrated as the classes and templates have a high flexibility degree. In this section, a description of the PSO-dedicated common components are detailed. Furthermore, it will be shown that any of these components can be extended to design a specific PSO algorithm. The design components required to implement a PSO algorithm are the following:

- **Representation of a particle:** A particle of any optimization problem needs to be represented both in the decision space and in the objective space. The ParadisEO's template `EO` is the base class for evolvable objects. To each individual, only a fitness is associated. Thus, an additional template PO inheriting from EO is proposed to store the best fitness of the particle; that is the only element a particle needs to have regarding the representation in the objective space. Consequently, several other templates are designed to take the decision variables into account. The `eoVector` template is mainly used to encode a genetic individual, so the `eoVectorParticle` template is also proposed. The `eoVectorParticle` owns all the information a particle must encode: current position, best position associated with the best fitness value reached, and velocities. These elements are stored as vectors inheriting from the standard vector of the C++ library.

  ParadisEO also provides templates inheriting from `eoVectorParticle`: `eoRealParticle`, a full real-coded particle and `eoBitParticle` whose velocities are real but the positions are encoded by a binary vector.

- **Particle swarm initialization (positions, velocities):** As soon as a representation is designed, the next important step consists in finding a way to initialize the particles. This must be done according to the problem specifications (e.g., discrete/continuous optimization problem, problem-specific constraints). ParadisEO provides a wide range of components dedicated to the initialization, but allows the user to define his own class by using inheritance. The templates extending `eoInit` initialize the positions, some examples are presented in Fig. 3.54.

  The `eoVelocityInit` is the basic template for the initialization of the velocities (Fig. 3.55).

  The particle's initial best positions and fitness also need to be initialized. The abstract template `eoParticleBestInit` is extended by `eoFirstIsBestInit` that initializes the best positions and the best fitness. Indeed, an important constraint is underlined: an evaluation must be performed before initializing the best positions and the best fitness. Let us assume that anyone would set the initial best positions and fitness of a particle, respectively, as the initial positions and fitness, the `eoFirstIsBestInit` inheriting from the abstract `eoParticleBestInit` is proposed. But the template `eoParticleBestInit` can be easily extended.

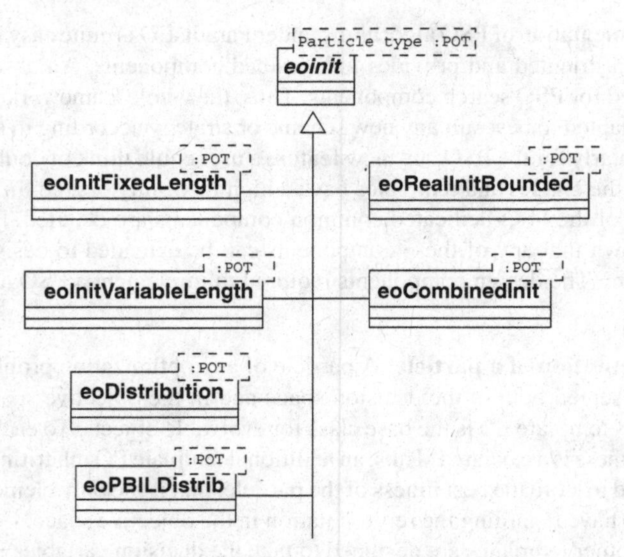

FIGURE 3.54 Core classes for the initialization of a particle.

Finally, an additional template called `eoParticleFullInitializer` performs a complete initialization using the components given as parameters. It allows the user to implement with a minimum of code (Fig. 3.56).

- **Evaluation of the particles:** The evaluation is by far the most costly step for real applications. Depending on the problem, it can be a subroutine, a black box, or an external process. Taking these constraints into account, ParadisEO provides generic templatized components especially dedicated to the evaluation. The base class is `eoEvalFunc` ; it sets the individual's fitness. It has been extended by `eoEvalFuncPtr`, which takes an existing function pointer and converts it into a evaluation function class, and `eoEvalFuncCounter` that counts the number of evaluations actually performed. Any other component inheriting from `eoEvalFunc` could be the interface with a linked procedure, an external process; in fact, any procedure that can be plugged using the C++ calls.

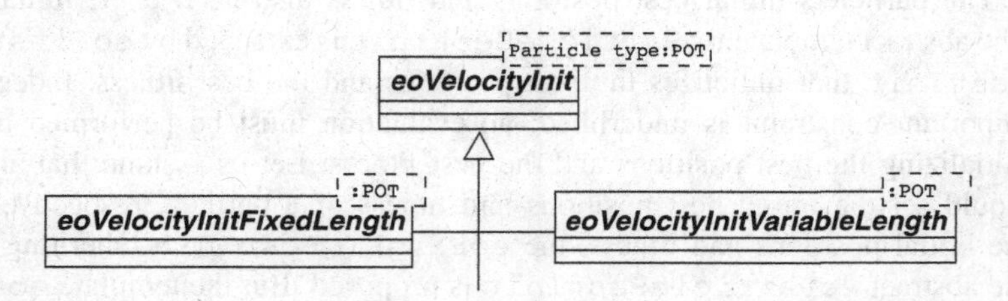

FIGURE 3.55 Core classes for the initialization of the velocities.

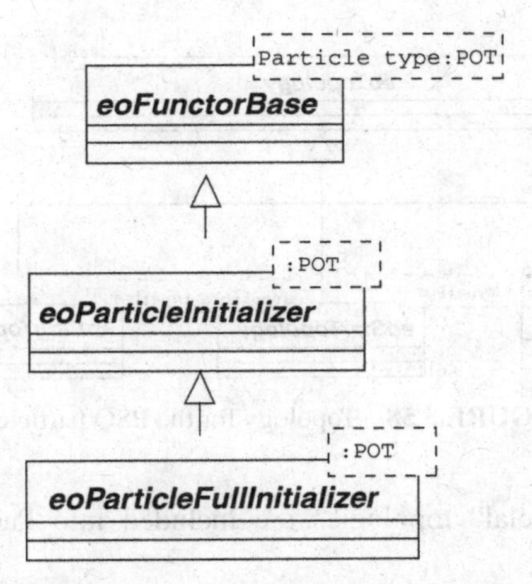

FIGURE 3.56 A complete initializer for the PSO particles.

- **Neighborhood:** The important point that must be underlined here is the necessity of defining a topology. It is directly associated with the neighborhood structure as it allows a particle to define the "best" particle in its neighborhood. So the topology is expected to be defined before the velocity update. The same remark can be done for the neighborhood as the social and physical ones can be distinguished.

  The physical neighborhood is based on the distance contrary to the social neighborhood that considers relationships between the particles. Knowing these aspects, ParadisEO provides an `eoSocialNeighborhood` and an `eoPhysicalNeighborhood` inheriting from the abstract template `eoNeighborhood` (Fig. 3.57). Then a few convenient methods exist to retrieve a particle in the neighborhood or to know if the particle is contained in one of them.

  The next step consists in choosing a topology, which means determining the way the neighborhoods will be built using the swarm's members. This choice is problem dependent and highly important in terms of convergence and any velocity needs its topology. This constraint is inserted into ParadisEO–EO: all the components extending `eoVelocity` must be constructed with an `eoTopology` (Fig. 3.58).

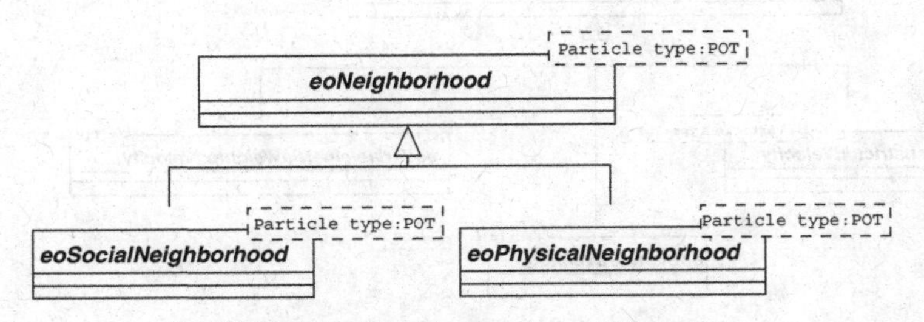

FIGURE 3.57 Neighborhoods for PSO particles.

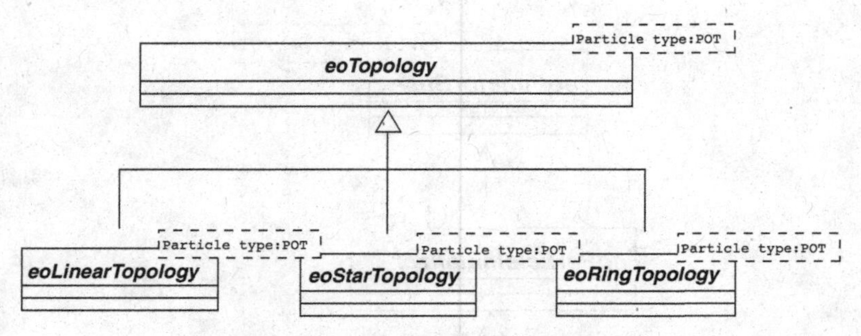

FIGURE 3.58 Topology for the PSO particles.

The basic "social" topologies are included into ParadisEO–EO such as (Fig. 3.58):

– The star topology defined by the template `eoStarTopology`.
– The grid topology defined by the template `eoLinearTopology`.
– The ring topology defined by the template `eoRingTopology`.

- **Velocity update:** ParadisEO proposes an abstract class `eoVelocity` and a set of ready-to-use velocities inheriting from it (Fig. 3.59):
  – **Standard velocity:** The template `eoStandardVelocity` performs the most common calculation of a velocity i:

$$v(t+1) = \omega \cdot v(t) + c_1 \cdot \rho_1 \cdot (bx(t) - x(t)) + c_2 \cdot \rho_2 \cdot (T_b(i)[j] - x(t))$$

  – **Constricted velocity:** The template `eoConstrictedVelocity` updates the current velocities as follows:

$$v(t+1) = K \cdot [\omega \cdot v(t) + c_1 \cdot \rho_1 \cdot (bx(t) - x(t)) + c_2 \cdot \rho_2 \cdot (T_b(i)[j] - x(t))]$$

  where the parameter K is fixed for all the particles and all the generations. The `eoConstrictedVariableWeightVelocity` template is more flexible as it introduces a constriction factor for the previous velocity.

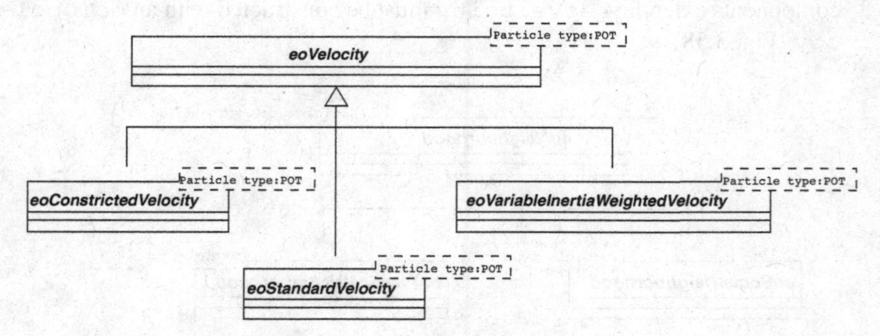

FIGURE 3.59 Velocity for the PSO particles.

At step t+1: $v(t+1) = K \cdot (\omega \cdot v(t) + c_1 \cdot \rho_1 \cdot (bx(t) - x(t)) + c_2 \cdot \rho_2 \cdot (g(t) - x(t)))$. K is fixed for all the time steps contrary to ω, updated at each iteration using an `eoWeightUpdater`. The abstract class `eoWeightUpdater` is extended by `eoLinearDecreasingWeightUp` that updates a weight according to $\omega(t) = (\omega(0) - \omega(N_t)) \cdot (N_t - t)/N_t + \omega(N_t)$ where t is the current generation/event, N_t is the total number of generations/event, $\omega(0)$ is the initial weight, and $\omega(N_t)$ is the last inertia weight.

– **Variable inertia weight velocity:** The provided ready-to-use template `eoVariableInertiaWeightedVelocity` suggests another kind of velocity update:

$$v(t+1) = \omega \cdot v(t) + c_1 \cdot \rho_1 \cdot (bx(t) - x(t)) + c_2 \cdot \rho_2 \cdot (\text{topology.best}(i) - x(t))$$

where ω is updated each time the velocity performer is called for, using the `eoWeightUpdater` given in the constructor. Furthermore, for most of these operators, vectorial bound constraints can be applied to restrict the displacement of the particles. These bounds can also be updated at each time step.

- **Flight:** The flight operators allow the calculation of the particle next positions. The most natural way to apply it is to add the previously evaluated velocities to the current positions (Fig. 3.60):

$$x(t+1) = x(t) + v(t+1)$$

That is the basic task of the `eoStandardFlight`-templatized component inheriting from `eoFlight`. The flight can be constrained between real bounds even if it can be applied to any other data structure supporting the operator +. Moreover, `eoBinaryFlight` is the abstract base template for binary particle swarm optimization. Using `eoSigBinaryFlight`, the velocities are expected to be real and considering P_i to be the ith position of a particle P and V_i to be

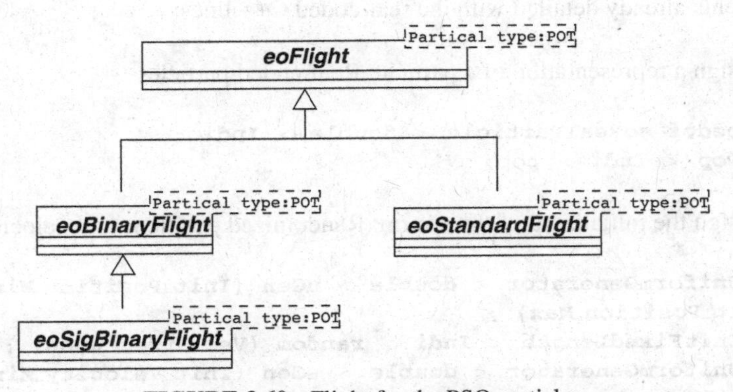

FIGURE 3.60 Flight for the PSO particles.

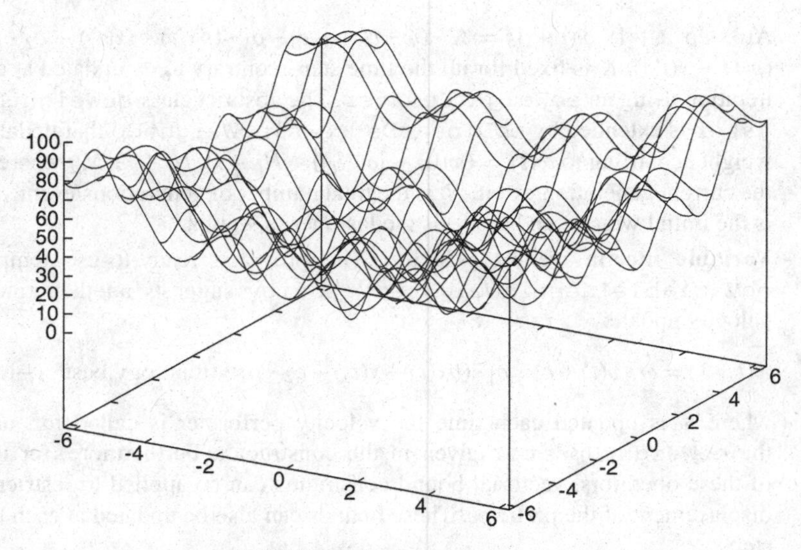

FIGURE 3.61 Eggcrate function.

the ith velocity of the same particle, the flight expression is

$$P_i = \begin{cases} 1 & \text{random } [0, 1] < \text{sig}(V_i) \\ 0 & \text{otherwise} \end{cases}$$

- **Stopping criteria:** Any stopping criteria defined in the ParadisEO–EO module for P-metaheuristics may be used.

3.8.4.1 Illustrative Example Let us design a PSO algorithm to solve the continuous two-dimensional function `Eggcrate` that is a nonconvex function (Fig. 3.61).

The implementation of a PSO algorithm using ParadisEO consists in choosing the main components and adjust a few parameters. The next paragraph presents the main components already detailed with the real-coded C++ lines:

▷ Design a representation of a particle: Real-coded particles.

```
typedef eoRealParticle < double > Indi ;
eoPop < Indi > pop;
```

▷ Design the initializing of the swarm: Randomized positions and velocities.

```
eoUniformGenerator < double > uGen (Init_Position_Min,
Init_Position_Max) ;
eoInitFixedLength < Indi > random (Vec_Size, uGen) ;
eoUniformGenerator < double > sGen (Init_Velocity_Min,
Init_Velocity_Max) ;
```

```
eoVelocityInitFixedLength < Indi > veloRandom (Vec_Size,
sGen) ;
```

▷ Design a way of evaluating the particles: The eggcrate function.

```
eoEvalFuncPtr<Indi, double, const Indi& >
plainEval(eggcrate) ;
eoEvalFuncCounter< Indi > eval(plainEval) ;
```

▷ Design a topology and the velocity: The linear topology for the standard velocity with a static inertia.

```
eoLinearTopology<Indi> topology(Neighborhood_Size);
eoStandardVelocity < Indi > velocity (topology,inertia,
C1,C2);
```

▷ Design the flight: The standard flight.

```
eoStandardFlight < Indi > flight() ;
```

▷ Design the way the "best" particles are updated: The first fitness is the first best fitness.

```
eoFirstIsBestInit < Indi > localInit;
```

▷ Design a stopping criteria: A fixed number of iterations.

```
eoGenContinue < Indi > genContPara (Max_Gen);
```

▷ The algorithm itself is coded using

```
eoEasyPSO <Indi> psa(init,checkpoint,eval,velocity,
flight);
```

3.8.5 Estimation of Distribution Algorithm Under ParadisEO

The abstract class for algorithms that evolve a probability distribution on the spaces of populations rather than a population is `eoEDA.h` (Fig. 3.62). It is an unary functor applied to an `eoDistribution.h` and effectively extended by the `eoSimpleEDA.h` template. This simple estimation of distribution algorithm (`eoSimpleEDA.h`) repeats the following steps:

- Generates a population from the current distribution.
- Evaluates that population.
- Updates the probability distribution.

The update of the probability distribution is ensured by a class inheriting from `eoDistribUpdater` passed through the constructor. The `eoPBILAdditive`

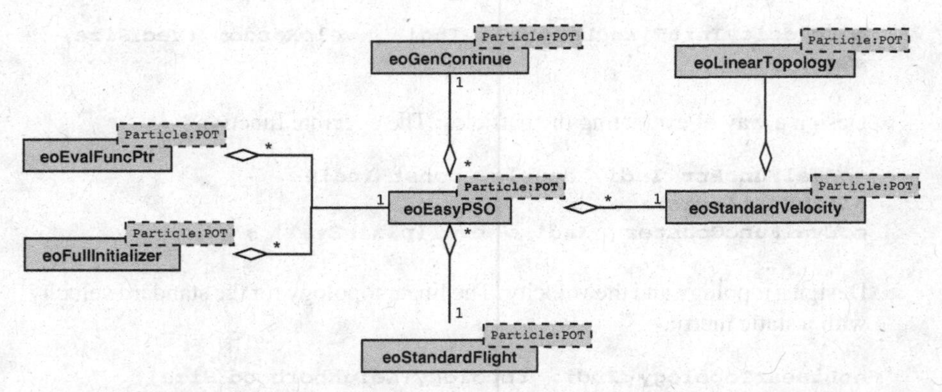

FIGURE 3.62 UML diagram of a particle swarm optimization algorithm.

and `eoPBILOrg` classes can be used within the PBIL (population-based incremental learning) algorithm:

- `eoPBILAdditive` where the probability distribution is updated according to the following rule: $p^s(i)(t+1) = (1 - LR) \cdot p(i)(t) + LR \cdot best(i)$.
- `eoPBILOrg` where the probability distribution is updated according to the following rule: $p^s(i)(t+1) = (1 - LR) \cdot p(i)(t) + LR \cdot best(i)$.

Obviously, all the abstract classes can be freely extended to go forward the existing implementations.

3.9 CONCLUSIONS

In addition to the representation, the objective function, and constraint handling that are common search concepts to all metaheuristics, following are the common concepts for population-based metaheuristics:

- **Initial population**[26]**:** An initial population may be specified randomly (e.g., pseudo-random, quasi-random) or by a given procedure(e.g., sequential diversification, parallel diversification, and heuristic).
- **Stopping criteria:** In addition to the traditional stopping criteria of S-metaheuristics, the stopping criteria in P-metaheuristics may be based on some statistics of the current population (e.g., population diversity) or the evolution of a population.

In addition to the common search concepts of P-metaheuristics, the following main search components have to be defined for designing the P-metaheuristics (Fig. 3.63):

[26]The initial population is not to be defined for P-metaheuristics based on greedy procedures such as ant colonies.

- **Evolution based:** In evolutionary P-metaheuristics such as evolutionary algorithms, differential evolution, scatter search, bee colony (marriage process of bees), and artificial immune systems (clonal selection), the selection and variation operators (e.g., recombination) constitute the main search components.
- **Blackboard based:** In blackboard-based P-metaheuristics such as ant colonies, estimation of distribution algorithms, particle swarm optimization, and bee food foraging, the construction of the shared memory (e.g., probabilistic model, pheromone trails, global best, waggle dance) and the generation of operator that create a solution according to the global shared memory are the main search components.

Most of the search components will be reused by different population-based metaheuristics (Fig. 3.63). Hence, an incremental design and implementation of different P-metaheuristics can be carried out. Moreover, there is a high flexibility to transform a P-metaheuristic to another one reusing most of the design and implementation work.

Once the P-metaheuristic is designed, the ParadisEO–EO software framework allows to implement it easily. The architecture modularity reduces the time and the

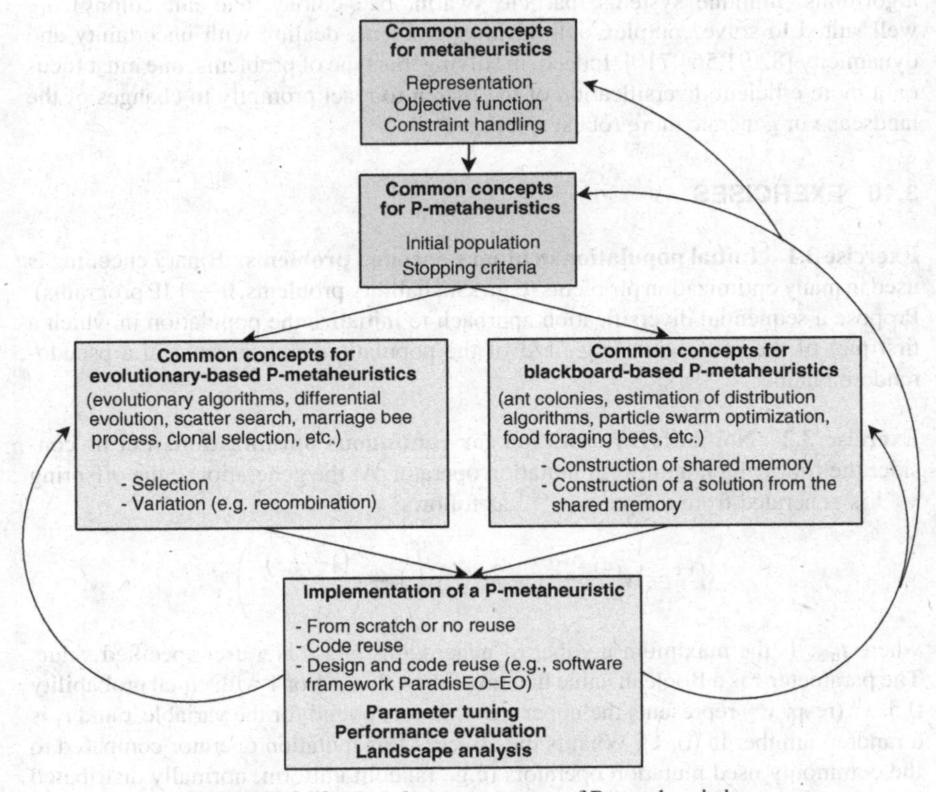

FIGURE 3.63 Development process of P-metaheuristics.

complexity of designing P-metaheuristics. An expert user can extend the already available boxes to more suit to his problem without difficulty and obtain more effective methods. Nevertheless, ParadisEO–EO can be used by newbies with a minimum of code to produce to implement diverse search strategies (e.g., evolutionary algorithm, estimation of distribution algorithm, particle swarm optimization, and differential evolution). A natural perspective is to evolve the open-source software by integrating more search components, heuristics (e.g., bee colony, artificial immune systems), and problem-solving environments (e.g., routing, scheduling, assignment).

Each P-metaheuristic has some parameters to tune. The performance of the different metaheuristics is more or less sensitive to these parameters. However, the optimal tuning of the parameters will never overcome the bad design of search components (e.g., representation, recombination, and global shared memory). In terms of theoretical convergence, there are some global convergence properties for all algorithms. The results refer to the question if the algorithm converges toward the global optimal solution when unlimited search time is available (asymptotic convergence). As for S-metaheuristics, it would be interesting to study and analyze more deeply the finite-time behavior of P-metaheuristics.

P-metaheuristics and especially nature-inspired algorithms (e.g., evolutionary algorithms, immune systems, particle swarm, bee colony, and ant colony) are well suited to solve complex optimization problems dealing with uncertainty and dynamicity [82,91,564,710]. Indeed, in solving this type of problems, one must focus on a more efficient diversification of the search to react promptly to changes of the landscape or generate more robust solutions.

3.10 EXERCISES

Exercise 3.1 Initial population in binary encoded problems. Binary encoding is used in many optimization problems (e.g., satisfiability problems, $0-1$ IP programs). Propose a sequential diversification approach to initialize the population in which a first part of the population (e.g., $1/3$ of the population) is generated in a pseudo-random manner.

Exercise 3.2 Nonuniform mutation for continuous optimization. Let us consider the following nonuniform mutation operator. At the generation t, the offspring y^{t+1} is generated from the parent x^{t+1} as follows:

$$y_i^{t+1} = x_i^{t+1} + \tau(x_i^u - x_i^L)\left(1 - r_i^{\left(1-\frac{t}{t_{\max}}\right)^b}\right)$$

where $t_{\max}$ is the maximum number of generations and b is a user-specified value. The parameter τ is a Boolean value that takes the value -1 or 1 with equal probability 0.5. x^{u} (resp. x^{L}) represents the upper (resp. lower) bound for the variable x and r_i is a random number in [0, 1]. What is the effect of this mutation operator compared to the commonly used mutation operators (e.g., random uniform, normally distributed mutations).

Exercise 3.3 Yet another crossover property. The crossover operator inherits some characteristics of the two parents to generate an offspring. Suppose a distance d measures the similarity between any two individuals. In the design of a crossover operator, to force an offspring to share genetic material from both parents, the following property has to be satisfied:

$$\text{Max}\{d(p_1, o), d(p_2, o)\} \leq d(p_1, p_2), \quad \forall o \in O(p_1, p_2, Ox)$$

where p_1 and p_2 are the parents, o is the generated offspring, and $O(p_1, p_2)$ is the set of all possible offsprings generated by the crossover operator Ox.

Let us consider a problem with a binary encoding in which the Hamming distance is used. Which crossover operators among the 1-point crossover and the uniform crossover verify the property?

Exercise 3.4 Elite set out of a P-metaheuristic. In the design of a P-metaheuristic, our goal is to maintain (in parallel) an elite set of solutions E_s found during the search. This elite set E_s contains a limited number of solutions $k_{\max}$. At each iteration, the P-metaheuristic generates a new population P of n solutions (individuals, particles, ants, etc.). Which replacement strategies can be applied to update the elite set E_s by the union of the elite set and the new population P ($E_s = E_s \cup P$)? Those replacement strategies must take into account the quality of solutions and their diversity.

Exercise 3.5 Genetic algorithms for the "casse tête" problem. Let us consider a 2D grid of size $4 \cdot 4$ covered by 16 tokens (Fig. 3.64). The aim of the problem is to delete six tokens from the grid such as for each row and each column of the grid there will be a pair number of tokens. Our goal is to design a genetic algorithm to solve this problem. Propose a representation of individuals of the population. Propose an objective function for the problem. Which crossover and mutation operators will you apply using the selected representation?

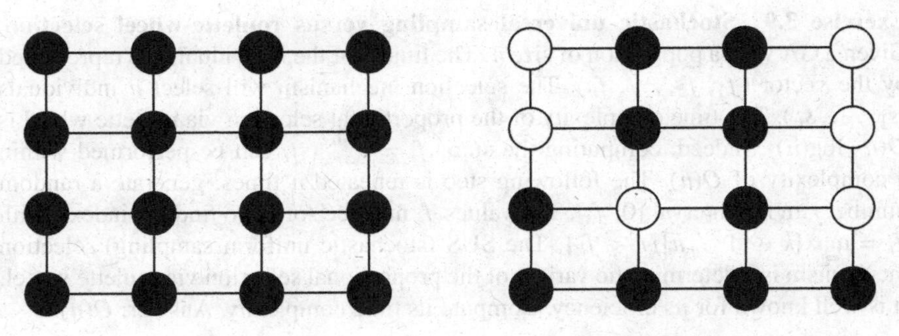

FIGURE 3.64 The "casse tête" problem.

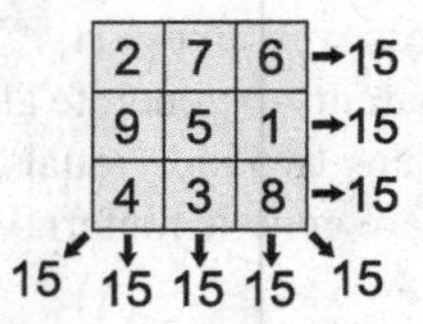

FIGURE 3.65 The magic square for $n = 3$.

Exercise 3.6 Reproduction operators for the magic square problem. Given distinct n^2 integers (from 1 to n^2) over a matrix $n \cdot n$, a magic square of order n is an arrangement such that the n numbers in all rows, all columns, and both diagonals sum to the same constant (Fig. 3.65). To the best of our knowledge, no polynomial-time algorithm exists for this problem. A magic square exists for all $n > 2$. Figure 3.65 shows a magic square for $n = 3$. The constant sum in every row, column, and diagonal is called the magic sum M. The magic sum has the value $M(n) = (n^3 + n)/2$. For normal magic squares of order $n = 3, 4, 5, \ldots$, the magic constants are 15, 34, 65, 111, 175, 260, and so on. Propose a representation for this problem and the objective function to optimize. Which genetic operators (mutation and crossover) can be used for the proposed representation?

Exercise 3.7 Encoding for network design. Consider the network design problem defined is Example 6.13. Propose an encoding for this problem. Our goal is to design a genetic algorithm to solve the problem. Propose some specific crossover and a mutation operator for the problem.

Exercise 3.8 Efficiency of selection mechanisms. Given a population P of λ individuals associated with their fitness values $(f_1, f_2, \ldots, f_\lambda)$. A selection mechanism allows to select μ individuals $(s_1, \ldots, s_\mu)$ from the population P. Compute the complexity of the k-ary tournament selection, (μ, λ) selection, $\mu + \lambda$ selection, and the q-fold binary tournament selection used in EP. Answer: $O(q \cdot \mu)$, $O(\mu + (\lambda - \mu)\log\mu)$, $O(\lambda + \mu)$, $O((\lambda + \mu)q)$.

Exercise 3.9 Stochastic universal sampling versus roulette-wheel selection. Given a GA with a population of size n. The fitness of the individuals are represented by the vector $(f_1, f_2, \ldots, f_n)$. The selection mechanism will select n individuals $(s_1, \ldots, s_n)$. The time complexity of the proportional selection via roulette wheel is $O(n \cdot \log(n))$. Indeed, computing the sum, $f_s = \sum_{i=1}^{n} f_i$ can be performed within a complexity of $O(n)$. The following step is repeated n times: generate a random number r in the interval $[0, f_s]$. The values f_i must be sorted to find the index i with $f_i = \max\{k \in [1 \ldots n]/r < f_k\}$. The SUS (stochastic uniform sampling) selection mechanism is a deterministic variant of the proportional selection via roulette wheel. It is well known for its efficiency. Compute its time complexity. Answer: $O(n)$.

Exercise 3.10 Redundant evaluation. The most computational part of an EA is the evaluation of the objective function. One of the solutions consists in avoiding a redundant evaluation of the same individuals. Propose an implementation of this solution. Answer: (i) When creating an offspring clone from a parent, copy the parent's objective function value into the offspring. Mark the offspring as evaluated. (ii) After the application of a genetic operator, such as the mutation or crossover, to an individual, check to see whether the resulting individual is different from the original one. If so, mark the individual as unevaluated. (iii) Evaluate only individuals that are marked unevaluated.

Exercise 3.11 Mutation complexity. Given an individual of n elements (n-tuple). In GAs, the mutation is applied with a probability p_{m} to each element of the individual. So, for each element of the n-tuple, a random number generation is performed and a Bernoulli trial is applied using the probability p_{m}. In general, the probability p_{m} has small values ($p_{\mathrm{m}} << 1$). Find a geometric distribution that models the interarrival time of a sequence of Bernoulli trials of probability p_{m}.

Exercise 3.12 Crossover connectivity. The question in this exercise is to see if the crossover operators can generate solutions having all possible combinations of elements of their parents. For simplification reasons, let us suppose a binary representation and the following crossovers: 1-point crossover, n-point crossover, uniform crossover, shuffle crossover, and random respectful recombination. *Hint*: Consider the strings 0 and 1 for the parents. What is about discrete (nonbinary) strings. Answer 1 yes for uniform, shuffle, and random respectful recombination. Answer 2 yes for random respectful recombination.

Exercise 3.13 Distance preservation crossover. Design a crossover operator for permutation-based representations that ensure the same distance between the offspring and the two parents as

$$d(p_1, o) = d(p_2, o) = d(p_1, p_2), \quad \forall o \in O(p_1, p_2, Oy)$$

where p_1 and p_2 are the parents, o is the generated offspring, and $O(p_1, p_2)$ is the set of all possible offsprings generated by the crossover operator Oy.

Exercise 3.14 Complexity of crossover. Given a subpopulation of p individuals. Each individual is represented by a vector of size n. The recombination operator takes as input the subpopulation to generate a single individual. Compute the time complexity of the recombination operator in the case of application of the following operators: 1-point crossover, k-point crossover, intermediate recombination, gene pool recombination, and the uniform crossover.

Exercise 3.15 Landscape analysis for crossover operators. In Section 2.2, the presented indicators to analyze fitness landscapes are more adapted to mutation in evolutionary algorithms and neighborhood in S-metaheuristics. Indeed, in the correlation analysis, mutation and neighborhoods are well suited to generate random walks in the landscape. These operators generate a time series of fitness values. How can those indicators (for instance, the FDC (fitness distance correlation) and the autocorrelation function) be extended to crossover operators? The main difficulty is that crossover operator works on a pair of solutions (parents) and produces a pair of solutions (offsprings). The presented question may be reduced to how a time series of fitness values can be generated from the crossover operator.

Exercise 3.16 GA for the minimum label spanning tree (MLST) and the colorful traveling salesman (CTSP) problems. Given a connected undirected graph $G = (V, E)$ where each edge is denoted by a unique color, the MLST problem consists in constructing a spanning tree that minimizes the number of colors. This NP-hard problem has many applications such as in communication network design. Unlike the minimum spanning tree problem, where the focus is on the edges, for the MLST problem it makes sense to focus on colors. Propose a GA to solve the problem.

The colorful TSP (CTSP) problem consists in finding a tour that minimizes the number of colors. This is also a NP-hard problem [829]. Are any search components used to solve the MLST that can be reused for the CTSP (representation, mutation, crossover, etc.)?

Exercise 3.17 Even-parity-4 problem using GP. In its general formulation, the Boolean even-parity k function of k Boolean arguments returns $true$ if an even number of its Boolean arguments evaluates $true$, otherwise it returns *false*. For the special case where $k = 4$, 16 fitness cases must be checked to evaluate the fitness of an individual. Formulate the objective function for this problem. Our goal is to design a genetic programming approach to solve the problem. Propose a tree-like representation for this problem. For this purpose, the operators and the terminal set of the tree have to be defined.

Exercise 3.18 Distance measure for GP trees. Genetic programming use parse trees to encode solutions. Defining a distance between trees is not a trivial task. Propose such a distance to deal with tree-based representations. As shown in the previous chapter, the distance measure may be important in the landscape analysis of the problem and the design of diversification or intensification search mechanisms. Is the distant proposed coherent with the mutation operators?

Exercise 3.19 Decision tree generation using GP. Decision trees represent a classical model in data mining for classification tasks. The problem consists in the induction using GP of the "optimal" decision tree from a training set (or learning set) of data. Each record from the training set is composed of several attributes and one goal attribute that is the class attribute. The decision tree will be used to predict the class of new records with an unknown class (label).

A decision tree is a tree where the terminal nodes are defined by classes c_i, $i = 1, n$, and the nonterminal nodes represent the different attributes a_j, $j = 1, m$. Each edge of the tree is defined by a test on the attribute values $a_j = v_j$ where v_j represents the possible values of the attribute a_j.

Design a GP algorithm for this problem.

Exercise 3.20 Recombination and mutation operator for different encodings of the JSP. Let us consider the job-shop scheduling problem and the various direct and indirect encodings proposed in Example 1.33. For each encoding, propose a recombination and mutation operators.

Exercise 3.21 Scatter search for unconstrained quadratic binary programs. Unconstrained quadratic programming represents a well-known framework for modeling and solving various academic optimization problems (e.g., many satisfiability problems, graph problems, and scheduling problems) and real-life problems (e.g. financial analysis, network design, molecular conformation, and traffic management). An unconstrained quadratic binary programs (UQP) may be defined as follows:

$$QP: \min xQx$$

where Q is an $n \times n$ matrix of constants and x is a binary vector. The representation of solutions is straightforward; it is based on the binary encoding. Design a scatter search strategy to solve such a class of problems. Rounding approaches may be considered for the subset generation procedure. For instance, one can round the fractional variables in an iterative manner. At each iteration, the variable that produces the best rounding for the objective function is selected.

Exercise 3.22 Scatter search for the linear ordering problem. The linear ordering problem (LOP) is a NP-hard combinatorial optimization problem with many applications (e.g., matrix triangulation, individual preferences ranking in group decision making) [118]. Given the set S of all permutations $(1, 2, \ldots, m)$ and a matrix $E_{m,m} = (e_{i,j})$, find the permutation p of the columns (and rows) that maximizes the sum of the weights in the upper triangle of the matrix E:

$$C_E(p) = \sum_{i=1}^{m-1} \sum_{j=i+1}^{m} e_{p_i p_j}$$

The LOP problem has a symmetry property, that is, maximizing the permutation $(p_1, p_2, \ldots, p_m)$ is equivalent to minimizing the permutation $(p_m, p_{m-1}, \ldots, p_1)$. In graph theory, the problem is equivalent to search in a complete weighted graph for an acyclic tournament with a maximal sum of arcs weights [342]. Design a scatter search algorithm to solve the LOP problem. The diversification generator may be based on frequencies, the number of times an element i appears in the position j. In the improvement procedure, the neighborhood based on an insertion or swapping operators may be considered.

Exercise 3.23 Evolutionary algorithms versus scatter search. What is the difference between the selection mechanism (resp. crossover operator) in evolutionary algorithms and the subset generation method (resp. solution combination method) in scatter search?

Exercise 3.24 Identical solutions in a population. In the design of P-metaheuristics for monoobjective and multiobjective optimizations (see Chapter 4), it would be desirable to eliminate duplicate copies of the same solution in a population (current or elite). What is the complexity of the algorithm removing all identical solutions in a population of size n.

Exercise 3.25 Diversity and dynamic optimization. When a dynamic change of the problem is detected by an evolutionary algorithm, some strategies are based on generating more diversity in the population to increase the probability in tracking the new optimum. Which operations may be carried out to increase the diversity in the population at the time a change is detected.

Exercise 3.26 Selection of starting and guiding solutions in path relinking. Let us suppose the application of a P-metaheuristic (or even a S-metaheuristic such as iterative local search or GRASP) to generate a population of k "good" solutions in solving a given optimization problem. The application of the path relinking strategy to this final population would be interesting. The number of pairs of solutions that have to be considered is $k \cdot (k-1)$, if the path (x, x') may be different from the path (x', x). As the computational complexity of such a procedure is very important, propose some selection mechanisms among this set of pairs. Justify the considered selection procedures.

Exercise 3.27 Path relinking in constrained spanning tree problems. In constrained spanning tree problems such as the CMST (capacitated spanning tree problem) defined in Example 2.41, the set of $\Delta(s, t)$ different edges between two feasible spanning trees s and t may be used to generate the path. Each move may be characterized by a pair of edges, one to be inserted and the other to be deleted from an intermediate solution. Propose such a path relinking strategy for the CMST problem. Will your strategy always find a path? If not, propose such a strategy that ensures a path from any two solutions s and t. Note that the objective for path relinking is to hopefully find better solutions.

Exercise 3.28 ACO design for a permutation scheduling problem. The single machine total weighted tardiness problem (SMTWTP) is a well-known NP-hard scheduling problem. Given n jobs to be scheduled on a single machine. Each job i is characterized by its weight w_i, a processing time p_i, and a due date d_i. For a given schedule, let C_i define the completion time of the job i. The objective of the SMTWTP problem is to minimize the total weighted tardiness:

$$\sum_{i=1}^{n} w_i \times T_i$$

where $T_i = \max(0, C_i - d_j)$ represents the tardiness for the job i.

The main problem-dependent elements in designing an ACO algorithm are the pheromone information and the solution construction. Propose a pheromone information that is suitable to the problem. How this pheromone information will be used in the solution construction? Notice that the relative position of the job is much more important than its direct predecessor or successor in the schedule such as in the traveling salesman problem. In addition to the pheromone, a heuristic to guide the ants toward good solutions must be proposed. Which priority greedy heuristic may be used to decide the next job to schedule?

Exercise 3.29 ACO for the set covering problem. The set covering problem (SCP) represents an important class of NP-hard combinatorial optimization problems with many applications in different domains: transportation network, integer coefficients linear programming, assignment problems, simplification of Boolean expressions, and so on. The SCP problem is generally defined by its Boolean covering matrix: $(a_{ij})_{m \cdot n}$ where $i \in I = 1, \ldots, m$ and $j \in J = 1, \ldots, n$. An element of the matrix $a_{ij} = 1$ if the row i is covered by the column j, and $a_{ij} = 0$ otherwise. Each column j of the matrix is characterized by a positive cost c_j and a cardinality (card_j), which is the number of rows covered by the column j. The SCP problem consists in choosing a subset of columns at a minimal cost in a way to cover all the rows (at least a 1 on each line). The SCP can be stated as minimizing

$$\sum_{j=1}^{n} c_j x_j$$

such as:

$$x_j = \begin{cases} 1 & \text{if the column } j \text{ belong to the solution} \\ 0 & \text{otherwise} \end{cases}$$

$$\sum_{j=1}^{n} a_{ij} x_j \geq 1, i = 1, \ldots, m$$

$$x_j \in \{0, 1\}, j = 1, \ldots, n$$

The constraint maintains the integrity of the system, that is, each row is covered at least by one column. The parameter α_i is defined as the set of columns that cover the line i and β_j and as the set of lines covered by the column j:

$$\alpha_i = \{j \in J / a_{ij} = 1\}$$

$$\beta_j = \{i \in I | a_{ij} = 1\}$$

Propose a greedy algorithm to solve the SCP problem. Based on this greedy algorithm, design a solution construction strategy for the ACO algorithm. Once a covering has been established by an ant, an iterative function that eliminates the redundant columns is performed, that is, those that are useless (superfluous) since their elements are covered by other columns of the covering. This function iterates on the columns, beginning from the last one whose cost is more significant, to optimize the cost.

Exercise 3.30 ACO for the shortest common supersequence (SCS) problem. String problems are one of the most important and well-studied problems in computer science. Such an example of string problems is the SCS problem. Given an alphabet $\sum$ and a set L of strings over this alphabet, the SCS problem consists in finding a minimal length of supersequence of each string of L. A string S is a supersequence of a string A if S can be obtained from A by inserting in A zero or more characters. For instance, if the set L is $\{bbbaaa, bbaaab, cbaab, cbaaa\}$, the optimal supersequence, the one minimizing its length, will be *cbbbaaab*. The SCS problem has many applications in various domains [552]:

- **Phylogenetics in bioinformatics:** The strings represent DNA from different species. One of the main questions concerning the evolution of those species is what will be their ancestor. For simplicity, let us assume that only mutations based on deletion of nucleotides can occur during the evolution process. Then, most probably the ancestor is the shortest supersequence of the input DNA strings.
- **Conveyer belt design:** Given a set of workpieces $\{W_1, W_2, \ldots, W_n\}$ to be designed. To each workpiece W_i is associated a sequence of operations for designing it, $W_i = s_1 s_2 \ldots s_k$. The problem is to produce a conveyer belt on which the n workpieces can be designed. Such a conveyer belt can be defined as a supersequence. The cost of producing the conveyer belt is mainly related to the size of the string representing its sequence. For instance, let us have three workpieces $\{W_1, W_2, W_3\}$ and their associated sequences to produce them: $W_1 =$ `bcbacb`, `caac`, `bbacac`. A conveyer belt on which the three workpieces are designed can be `bbacbaacb`. Figure 3.66 presents an example of a supersequence for the conveyer belt.

Ant can construct solutions by iteratively removing characters from the front of the input strings of L, and appending them to the supersequence. Then, each ant

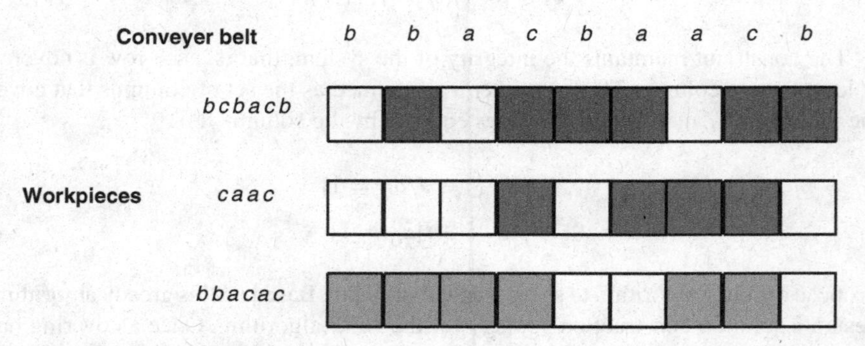

FIGURE 3.66 Design of a conveyer belt to produce workpieces. A feasible nonoptimal solution is shown. The optimal solution has a size of 8: *bcbacacb*.

must maintain a set of pointers to the current front of the strings that represent the selectable components of the constructed solution. The transitions are defined by the rules that select the next character of the supersequence. Only feasible supersequences are generated. Design an ACO algorithm for this problem.

Exercise 3.31 Diversification in particle swarm optimization. To prevent the swarm from a premature convergence toward a small region of the search space, some diversification strategies must be introduced. Given a swarm S of n particles with their associated position $x_i = x_{i1}, x_{i2}, \ldots, x_{iD}$ where D represents the dimension of the continuous problem to optimize. Propose a diversity measure. The PSO algorithm can have two different phases, a repulsion phase and an attraction phase. When the diversity is below a given threshold d_{low}, the repulsion phase is launched. When the diversity measure is greater than another given threshold d_{high} ($d_{\text{high}} > d_{\text{low}}$), the attraction phase is launched. Propose velocity update strategies to be applied in the repulsion and attraction phases.

Exercise 3.32 Mutation versus velocity update. What is the difference between the concept of mutation in evolutionary algorithms and the velocity update in particle swarm optimization?

Exercise 3.33 Inertia weight update in PSO. In particle swarm optimization, the inertia weight w constitutes a trade-off between global and local explorations. A large inertia weight tends to global exploration (i.e., more diversification) while a smaller inertia weight tends to local exploration in the current search region (i.e., more intensification). Is it interesting to vary the inertia weight during the search from a relatively large value to a small value. If yes, propose such a decreasing scheme of the inertia weight (dynamic or adaptive).

Exercise 3.34 Adaptive application of variation operators. In a given metaheuristic, the efficiency of a variation operator (mutation, recombination, etc.) may change during the algorithm: an operator may be more efficient during the beginning of the search while another operator is more efficient at the end of the search. Moreover, the success of an operator may also depend on the instance of the problem to solve. This motivates the use of an adaptive operator probability to automate the dynamic selection of efficient operators [57]. Let us consider k operators O_i ($i = [1, k]$) belonging to the class O. For instance, if O represents the mutation operator in an evolutionary algorithm, the operators O_i may be k different mutation operators. For this case, the purpose is to use simultaneously the different mutations O_i during the GA search, and to change automatically the selection probability of each operator according to its efficiency. So, the algorithm after uses the best operators than the worst ones.

The initial selection probabilities for the different operators may be equal: $P(O_i) = p_o/k$ where p_o is the probability of the application of the operator O (i.e., in GA, it will be the probability of the mutation application p_{m}).

For each operator O_i, a progress value $G(O_i)$ is associated. Each time the operator O_i is applied, its progress $G(O_i)$ is computed. This progress value depends on the criteria one wishes to optimize: quality of solution, diversity, and so on.

At the end of an iteration of the metaheuristic, the average progress $\bar{G}(O_i)$ is updated for each operator:

$$\bar{G}(O_i) = \frac{\sum_{j=1}^{m_i} G(O_i)}{m_i}$$

where m_i represents the number of applications of the operator O_i. Then, the new selection probabilities are updated as follows:

$$P_{O_i} = \frac{\bar{G}(O_i)}{\sum_{j=1}^{k} \bar{G}(O_j)} \times (1 - k \times \delta) + \delta$$

where δ is the minimal selection probability value of the operators.

Define the progress function $G(O_i)$ that encourages the operators generating better solutions in terms of quality.

Exercise 3.35 Positive feedback in swarm intelligence. Positive feedback is a basic property on which self-organization relies. It promotes the creation of "good" solutions. Give some examples of positive feedback found in ant colonies and particle swarm optimization-based algorithms.

Exercise 3.36 Bee marriage versus evolutionary algorithms. What are the major differences between the MBO algorithm and traditional evolutionary algorithms?

Exercise 3.37 Self-organization in swarms. The main properties on which self-organization relies are positive feedback, negative feedback, fluctuations, and multiple interactions. Illustrate these properties for bee colony-based algorithms.

Exercise 3.38 Clonal selection versus evolutionary algorithms. What are the major differences between the CLONALG algorithm and traditional evolutionary algorithms?

Exercise 3.39 PSO for continuous optimization. A PSO algorithm has been implemented under ParadisEO–EO to solve the eggcrate continuous function (*eoEasyPSO* template available). Perform 20 runs of the program with the following values of parameters:

- Size of each particle: $VEC\_SIZE = 2$
- Swarm's size: $POP\_SIZE = 30$
- Neighborhood size: $NEIGHBORHOOD\_SIZE = 6$

- Static inertia factor: $INERTIA = 0.5$
- Learning factor: $C_1 = 1.5$ and $C_2 = 1.5$
- Number of iterations: $MAX\_GEN = 20$ (first run) $MAX\_GEN = 50$ (second run)

Analyze the obtained results in terms of the quality of solutions (minimum, average, and standard deviation).

Exercise 3.40 Intensification versus diversification. For the following P-metaheuristics, identify the search components dealing with the diversification of the search or the intensification of the search: evolutionary algorithms, particle swarm optimization, scatter search, ant colonies, bee colonies, artificial immune systems, and estimation of distribution algorithms.

CHAPTER 4

Metaheuristics for Multiobjective Optimization

Many industrial domains are concerned about large and complex optimization problems involving many criteria. Indeed, optimization problems encountered in practice are seldom monoobjective. In general, there are many conflicting objectives[1] to handle. For instance, in designing a given product, one must have to minimize its cost, maximize its quality (e.g., in terms of physic, mechanic, or service), and minimize its environmental impact. In fact, many diverse areas (e.g., engineering design, bioinformatics, logistics, transportation, telecommunication, environment, aeronautics, finance) are concerned about multiobjective optimization problems (MOPs)[2].

Multiobjective optimization[3] has its roots in the nineteenth century, in the work of Edgeworth and Pareto in economics [236,600]. It has been used in economics and management science for several decades [472,485], and then gradually in engineering sciences [720]. Nowadays, multiobjective optimization is an important area in science and engineering. The complexity of MOPs becomes more and more significant in terms of the size of the problem to be solved (e.g., number of objectives, size of the search space). Moreover, the search time for solving these problems has to be reasonable for most of the MOPs encountered in practice. Hence, the development of advanced multiobjective metaheuristics has been widely investigated since the end of the 1980s. This is an important issue in solving complex and large MOPs.

The optimal solution for MOPs is not a single solution as for monoobjective optimization problems, but a set of solutions defined as Pareto optimal solutions. A solution is Pareto optimal if it is not possible to improve a given objective without deteriorating at least another objective. This set of solutions represents the compromise solutions between the different conflicting objectives. The main goal of the resolution of a multiobjective problem is to obtain the Pareto optimal set and, consequently, the Pareto front. Notwithstanding this, when metaheuristics are applied, the goal becomes to obtain an approximation of the Pareto optimal set having two

[1]The terms criteria, attribute, and objective are used indifferently.
[2]Note that the terms multiobjective and multicriteria are used interchangeably throughout this chapter.
[3]Sometimes referred to as vector optimization.

properties: convergence to the Pareto optimal front and uniform diversity. The first property ensures the generation of near-optimal Pareto solutions, while the second property indicates a good distribution of the obtained solutions around the Pareto optimal front, so that no valuable information is lost.

Compared to monoobjective optimization, the difficulty in solving MOPs lies in the following general facts:

- There are no commonly used definitions on the global optimality of a solution as in monoobjective optimization. The order relation between solutions of a MOP problem is partial, and the final choice depends on the decision maker.
- The number of Pareto optimal solutions increases according to the size of the problem and mainly with the number of objectives being considered. Indeed, at least all Pareto solutions of an n-objective problem are necessary Pareto solutions of the same problem with an additional objective function. For instance, the number of Pareto optimal solutions may be exponential with respect to the problem size (e.g., some NP-hard combinatorial multiobjective optimization problems) [238].
- The structure of the Pareto front (e.g., continuity, convexity, multimodality) depends on the studied MOP. For instance, the Pareto optimal solutions may be localized on the frontier and inside the convex hull of feasible solutions. Moreover, most of the MOPs are NP-hard problems.

This chapter presents the main issues related to the design and implementation of multiobjective metaheuristics. In recent years, the application of metaheuristic techniques to solve MOPs has become a very active research and development area. Solving this class of problems implies obtaining a set of Pareto optimal solutions in such a way that the corresponding set fulfills the requirements of convergence to the true Pareto front and uniform diversity. Most of studies about metaheuristics for multiobjective optimization are focused on P-metaheuristics, such as evolutionary algorithms that are more suited to solve MOPs [144,195]. Our main interest is the development of metaheuristics that allow the approximation of the Pareto front in solving MOP problems. A unifying view for designing and analyzing multiobjective metaheuristics (S-metaheuristics and P-metaheuristics) is provided. The focus is made on the search components that must be adapted to transform metaheuristics to solve MOPs. The aspect of decision making, for the choice of a final solution among the Pareto solutions, is not addressed [555].

The chapter is organized as follows. After introducing the main concepts of multiobjective optimization in Section 4.1, Section 4.2 illustrates some examples of multiobjective optimization problems. It also shows the various possible interactions between the problem solver and the decision maker. Section 4.3 extracts the main search components of a multiobjective metaheuristic: fitness assignment, diversity preservation, and elitism. Sections 4.4–4.6 discuss how these three search components can be defined independently to design a multiobjective metaheuristic. Some examples dealing with popular metaheuristics are also illustrated. Section 4.7 is devoted to the performance evaluation of multiobjective metaheuristics and the characterization of the Pareto front landscape. Finally, the implementation issues of multiobjective metaheuristics under the ParadisEO framework will be outlined in Section 4.8.

4.1 MULTIOBJECTIVE OPTIMIZATION CONCEPTS

This section covers the main concepts of multiobjective optimization, such as dominance, Pareto optimality, Pareto optimal set, and Pareto front. In these definitions, the minimization of all the objectives is assumed, without loss of generality.

Definition 4.1 Multiobjective optimization problem. *A multiobjective optimization problem may be defined as*

$$\text{MOP} = \begin{cases} \min F(x) = (f_1(x), f_2(x), \ldots, f_n(x)) \\ \text{s.c. } x \in S \end{cases} \tag{4.1}$$

where n ($n \geq 2$) is the number of objectives, $x = (x_1, \ldots, x_k)$ is the vector representing the decision variables, and S represents the set of feasible solutions associated with equality and inequality constraints and explicit bounds. $F(x) = (f_1(x), f_2(x), \ldots, f_n(x))$ is the vector of objectives to be optimized.

The search space S represents the *decision space* or parameter space of the MOP. The space in which the objective vector belongs to is called the *objective space*. The vector F can be defined as a cost function from the decision space in the objective space that evaluates the quality of each solution $(x_1, \ldots, x_k)$ by assigning an objective vector $(y_1, \ldots, y_n)$, which represents the quality of the solution (or *fitness*) (Fig. 4.1). In the field of multiobjective optimization, the decision maker uses it to work in terms of evaluation of a solution on each criterion, and is naturally placed in the objective space. The set $Y = F(S)$ represents the feasible points in the objective space, and $y = F(x) = (y_1, y_2, \ldots, y_n)$, where $y_i = f_i(x)$, is a point of the objective space.

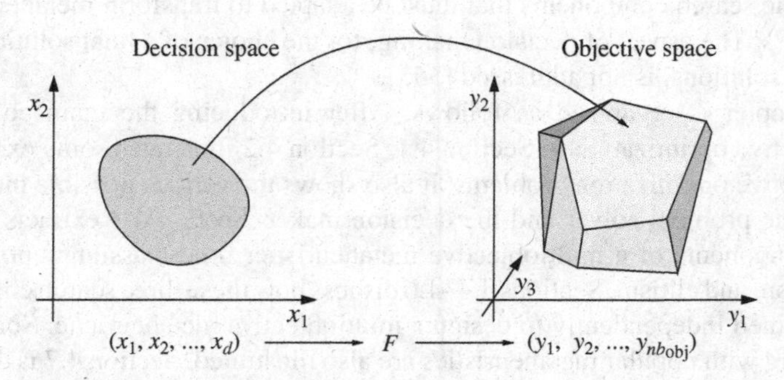

FIGURE 4.1 Decision space and objective space in a MOP.

It is not usual to have a solution x^*, associated with a decision variable vector, where x^* is optimal for all the objectives:

$$\forall x \in S, \; f_i(x^*) \leq f_i(x), \quad i = 1, 2, \ldots, n \tag{4.2}$$

Given that this situation is not usual in real-life MOPs where the criteria are in conflict, other concepts were established to consider optimality. A partial order relation could be defined, known as dominance relation.

Definition 4.2 Pareto dominance. *An objective vector $u = (u_1, \ldots, u_n)$ is said to dominate $v = (v_1, \ldots, v_n)$ (denoted by $u \prec v$) if and only if no component of v is smaller than the corresponding component of u and at least one component of u is strictly smaller, that is,*

$$\forall i \in \{1, \ldots, n\} : u_i \leq v_i \; \wedge \; \exists i \in \{1, \ldots, n\} : u_i < v_i$$

The generally used concept is *Pareto optimality.* Pareto optimality definition comes directly from the dominance concept. The concept was proposed initially by F.Y. Edgeworth in 1881 [236] and extended by W. Pareto in 1896 [600]. A Pareto optimal solution denotes that it is impossible to find a solution that improves the performances on a criterion without decreasing the quality of at least another criterion.

Definition 4.3 Pareto optimality. *A solution $x^* \in S$ is Pareto optimal*[4] *if for every $x \in S$, $F(x)$ does not dominate $F(x^*)$, that is, $F(x) \nprec F(x^*)$.*

Graphically, a solution x^* is Pareto optimal if there is no other solution x such that the point $F(x)$ is in the dominance cone of $F(x^*)$ that is the box defined by $F(x)$, with its projections on the axes and the origin (Fig. 4.2). In general, searching in a monoobjective problem leads to find a unique global optimal solution. A MOP may have a set of solutions known as the *Pareto optimal set.* The image of this set in the objective space is denoted as the *Pareto front.*

Definition 4.4 Pareto optimal set. *For a given MOP (F, S), the Pareto optimal set is defined as $\mathcal{P}^* = \{x \in S / \nexists x' \in S, F(x') \prec F(x)\}$.*

Definition 4.5 Pareto front. *For a given MOP (F, S) and its Pareto optimal set $\mathcal{P}^*$, the Pareto front is defined as $\mathcal{PF}^* = \{F(x), x \in \mathcal{P}^*\}$.*

The Pareto front is the image of the Pareto optimal set in the objective space. Obtaining the Pareto front[5] of a MOP is the main goal of multiobjective optimization. However, given that a Pareto front can contain a large number of points, a good approximation of the Pareto front may contain a limited number of Pareto solutions,

[4] The Pareto optimal solutions are also known as *acceptable solutions, efficient, nondominated, noninferior.*
[5] For some applications, it is also important to obtain the complete Pareto set.

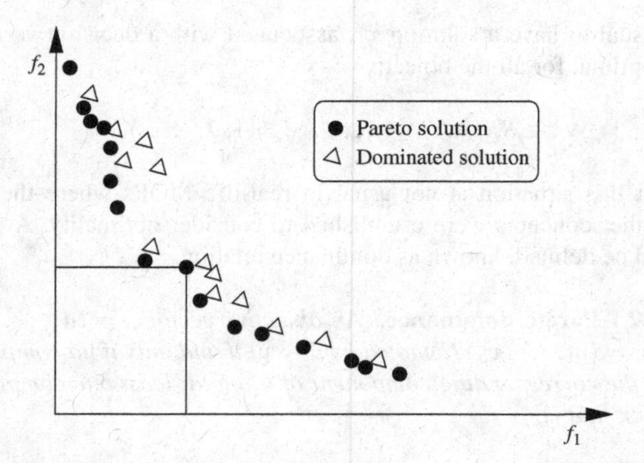

FIGURE 4.2 Nondominated solutions in the objective space.

which should be as close as possible to the exact Pareto front, as well as they should be uniformly spread over the Pareto front. Otherwise, the obtained approximation of the Pareto front would not be very useful to the decision maker who should have a complete information on the Pareto front. Let us examine the three fronts shown in Fig. 4.3 that represents several approximations. The first plot (left) shows a front having a very good spread of solutions, but the points are far from the true Pareto front; this front is not attractive because it does not provide Pareto optimal solutions. The second example (center) contains a set of solutions that are very close to the true Pareto front; thus, some regions of the true Pareto front are not covered, so the decision maker could lose important information on the Pareto front. Finally, the last front (right) has the two desirable properties of good convergence and diversity.

Let us notice that depending on the considered space (decision space or objective space), the number of Pareto solutions may be different. In the objective space, two solutions having the same objective vector will be considered as a single point,

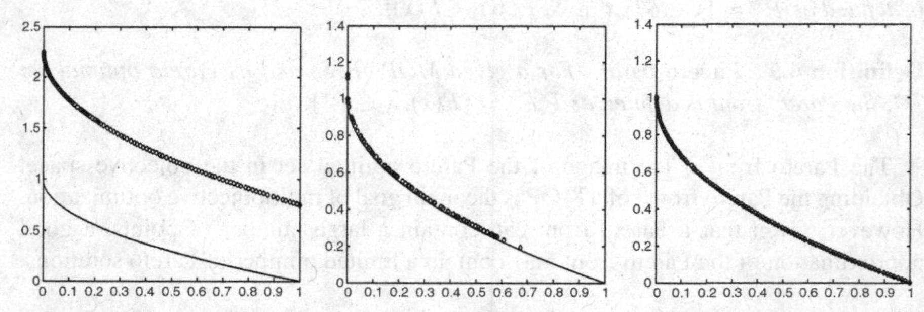

FIGURE 4.3 Examples of Pareto fronts: bad convergence and good diversity (left), good convergence and bad diversity (center), good convergence and diversity (right).

whereas they represent two different solutions in the decision space. The Pareto optimal set in the objective space is called the *minimal complete Pareto set*, whereas it is the *maximal complete Pareto set* in the decision space.

It is worth to point out that ideally one would like to obtain a solution minimizing all the objectives. Let us suppose that the optimum for each objective function is known, the objective functions being separately optimized.

Definition 4.6 Ideal vector. *A point* $y^* = (y_1^*, y_2^*, \ldots, y_n^*)$ *is an ideal vector if it minimizes each objective function* f_i *in* $F(x)$*, that is,* $y_i^* = \min(f_i(x)), x \in S, i \in [1, n]$.

The ideal vector is generally an utopian solution in the sense that it is not a feasible solution in the decision space. In certain cases, the decision maker defines a *reference vector*, expressing the goal to reach for each objective. This generalizes the concept of ideal vector. The decision maker may specify some aspiration levels $\overline{z}_i, i \in [1, n]$ to attain for each objective function f_i. Aspiration levels represent acceptable or desirable levels in the objective space. A Pareto optimal solution satisfying all aspiration levels is called a *satisficing solution* [680].

Definition 4.7 Reference point. *A reference point* $z^* = [\overline{z}_1, \overline{z}_2, \ldots, \overline{z}_n]$ *is a vector that defines the aspiration level (or goal)* $\overline{z}_i$ *to reach for each objective* f_i.

Definition 4.8 Nadir point. *A point* $y^* = (y_1^*, y_2^*, \ldots, y_n^*)$ *is the nadir point if it maximizes each objective function* f_i *of* F *over the Pareto set, that is,* $y_i^* = \max(f_i(x)), \quad x \in \mathcal{P}^*, i \in [1, n]$.

The ideal and nadir points give some information on the ranges of the Pareto optimal front (Fig. 4.4).

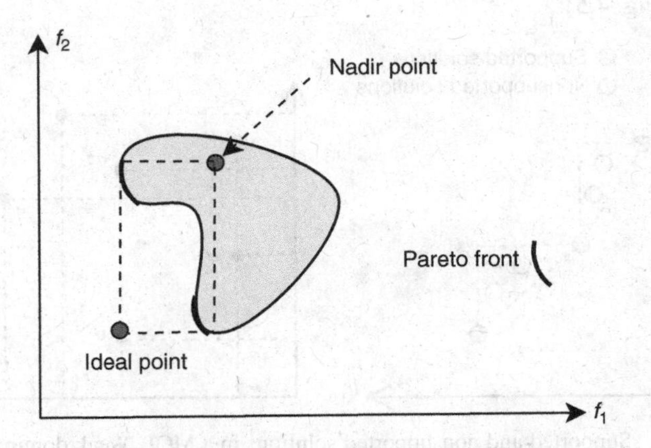

FIGURE 4.4 Nadir and ideal points in a MOP.

Definition 4.9 Utility function. *A utility (or value) function v, which represents the preferences of the decision maker, maps the objective vector to a scalar-valued function: $v : \mathcal{R}^n \longrightarrow \mathcal{R}$.*

The utility function has to be minimized to suit the preferences of the decision maker.

In multiobjective optimization, the concept of local minima can be generalized to the *locally Pareto optimal solution*. This notion is related to the concept of *neighborhood*, usually applied to S-metaheuristics (see Section 2.1.1).

Definition 4.10 Locally Pareto optimal solution. *A solution x is locally Pareto optimal if and only if $\forall w \in N(x)$, $F(w)$ does not dominate $F(x)$, and $N(x)$ represents the neighborhood of the solution x.*

Some Pareto optimal solutions may be obtained by the resolution of the following mathematical program:

$$(\text{MOP}_\lambda) \begin{cases} \min F(x) = \sum_{i=1}^{n} \lambda_i f_i(x) \\ \text{s.c. } x \in S \end{cases} \tag{4.3}$$

with $\lambda_i \geq 0$ for $i = 1, \ldots, n$, and $\sum_{i=1}^{n} \lambda_i = 1$.

Such solutions are known as *supported solutions* [314]. Supported solutions are generated by the resolution of (MOP_λ) for various values of the weight vector λ. The complexity of (MOP_λ) is equivalent to the subjacent monoobjective optimization problems. If the subjacent optimization problems are polynomial, it will be relatively easy to generate the supported solutions. Nevertheless, there exists other Pareto optimal solutions that cannot be obtained by the resolution of a (MOP_λ) mathematical program. Indeed, these solutions, known as *nonsupported solutions*, are dominated by convex combinations of supported solutions, that is, points of the convex hull of $Y = F(S)$ (Fig. 4.5).

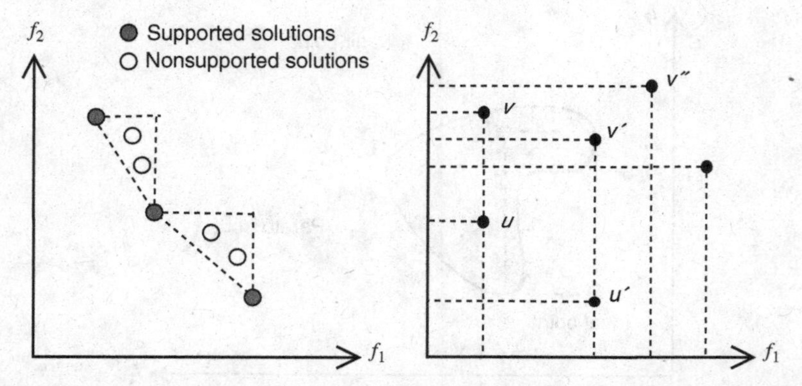

FIGURE 4.5 Supported and nonsupported solutions in a MOP. Weak dominance and strict dominance concepts. Solution u weakly dominate solution v; solution u' weakly dominates solution v'; solution u strictly dominates solutions v' and v''.

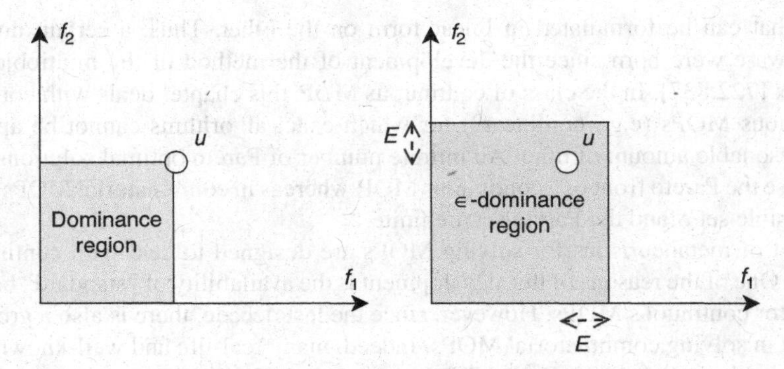

FIGURE 4.6 ϵ-Dominance concept.

Other types of domination definitions exist, such as the concept of weak dominance, strict dominance, and ϵ-dominance [370].

Definition 4.11 Weak dominance. *An objective vector* $u = (u_1, \ldots, u_n)$ *is said to weakly dominate* $v = (v_1, \ldots, v_n)$ *(denoted by* $u \preccurlyeq v$*) if all components of u are smaller than or equal to the corresponding components of v, that is,* $\forall i \in \{1, \ldots, n\}$, $u_i \leq v_i$ *(Fig. 4.5).*

Definition 4.12 Strict dominance. *An objective vector* $u = (u_1, \ldots, u_n)$ *is said to strictly dominate* $v = (v_1, \ldots, v_n)$ *(denoted by* $u \prec\prec v$*) if all components of u are smaller than the corresponding components of v, that is,* $\forall i \in \{1, \ldots, n\}$, $u_i < v_i$ *(Fig. 4.5).*

Definition 4.13 ϵ-Dominance. *An objective vector* $u = (u_1, \ldots, u_n)$ *is said to* ϵ*-dominate* $v = (v_1, \ldots, v_n)$ *(denoted by* $u \prec_\epsilon v$*) if and only if no component of v is smaller than the corresponding component of* $u - \epsilon$ *and at least one component of* $u - \epsilon$ *is strictly better, that is,* $\forall i \in \{1, \ldots, n\} : u_i - \epsilon_i \leq v_i \ \wedge \ \exists i \in \{1, \ldots, n\} : u_i - \epsilon_i < v_i$ *(Fig. 4.6).*

4.2 MULTIOBJECTIVE OPTIMIZATION PROBLEMS

As in monoobjective optimization, MOPs can be divided into two categories: those whose solutions are encoded with *real-valued* variables, also known as *continuous MOPs*, and those where the solutions are encoded using *discrete* variables such as *combinatorial MOPs*.

In the past 40 years, the majority of the works concerned the multiobjective continuous linear programming. The principal reasons of this interest are the development of the monoobjective linear programming in operations research and the relative facility to deal with such problems, on the one hand, and the abundance of the practical cases that can be formulated in linear form on the other. Thus, a certain number of software were born since the development of the method of the multiobjective simplex [722,837]. In the class of continuous MOP, this chapter deals with complex continuous MOPs (e.g., nonlinear[6]) for which exact algorithms cannot be applied in a reasonable amount of time. An infinite number of Pareto optimal solutions may compose the Pareto front of a continuous MOP, whereas in combinatorial MOPs, both the feasible set S and the Pareto set are finite.

Most of metaheuristics for solving MOPs are designed to deal with continuous MOPs. One of the reasons of this development is the availability of "standard" benchmarks for continuous MOPs. However, since the last decade, there is also a growing interest in solving combinatorial MOPs. Indeed, many real-life and well-known academic problems (e.g., TSP, QAP, VRP, knapsack, scheduling) have been modeled as combinatorial MOPs. In the following sections, some academic examples of MOPs as well as real-life ones are presented.

4.2.1 Academic Applications

The majority of the benchmarks used in the comparison of multiobjective metaheuristics were carried out on academic problems. Let us point out that, in many cases, continuous functions are used to perform the first experimentations of a new multiobjective metaheuristic.

4.2.1.1 Multiobjective Continuous Problems A continuous MOP can be mathematically formulated as follows:

$$\min F(x) = (f_1(x), f_2(x), \ldots, f_n(x))$$

subject to

$$g_i(x) \leq 0, \quad i = 1, \ldots, m$$

$$h_i(x) = 0, \ i = 1, \ldots, p$$

with $x = (x_1, \ldots, x_k)$, $F : \mathbb{R}^k \longrightarrow \mathbb{R}^n$ the objective vector, m inequality constraints g_i, and p equality constraints h_i.

In the recent years, some continuous test functions have been proposed to easily carry out experimentations of multiobjective metaheuristics [277,488,841,799]. Test problems allow a more fair evaluation of the efficiency and the effectiveness of MOP algorithms. Some well-known test problems are used in the literature for continuous MOPs, such as the ZDT and DTLZ benchmarks [794]. For some test problems, the exact Pareto front is known *a priori* that makes easier the performance assessment of multiobjective metaheuristics. Indeed, in the ZDT class of instances, a simple procedure has been designed to construct biobjective optimization problems

[6]The problem formulation contains at least one nonlinear function.

in which different characteristics of the Pareto front landscape and difficulties are introduced [194]. However, the ZDT class of instances is relatively simple and inadequate to represent real-life MOPs. Hence, more complex test MOPs have been introduced [201,393,591]. For instance, in the DTLZ class, nine benchmarks have been proposed with a scalable number of decision variables and objectives [202]. For the DTLZ class of test problems, except DTLZ1, the Pareto optimal solutions satisfy the equation $\sum_{m=1}^{M} (f_m^*)^2 = 1$, that is, the radius of any solution of the Pareto front is equal to 1.

Example 4.1 Test instances for constrained multiobjective continuous optimization problems. A number of constrained test problems with nonlinear objective functions and constraints exist in the literature such as the CTP problems [195]. Different tunable degrees of difficulties are introduced in the benchmarks, among them are:

- Feasible islands in the objective space
- Long narrow tunnel to optimality
- Piecewise activeness of different constraints on the optimal Pareto front.

4.2.1.2 Multiobjective Combinatorial Problems

For combinatorial MOPs, there is a lack of "standard" benchmarks even if recently there is an interest in providing test instances for classical combinatorial MOPs that can be classified into two complexity classes:

- **Polynomial problems:** Many multiobjective models of polynomially solvable optimization problems have been tackled: shortest path problems [811,814], spanning tree problems [840], assignment problems [786], and so on.
- **NP-hard problems:** Most of the multiobjective models concern NP-hard optimization problems: scheduling problems [56,572,681], routing problems [601], quadratic assignment problems, and so on.

An increasing number of combinatorial multiobjective test functions are available in the literature[7]. However, in most of the cases, they are biobjective optimization problems. Globally, there is also a lack of test functions for real-life combinatorial MOPs, especially problems that are subject to many objectives [405], uncertainty [506], and dynamicity [252].

Example 4.2 Multiobjective scheduling problems. The permutation flow-shop scheduling problem (FSP) is one of the most well-known scheduling problems [771]. The problem can be presented as a set of n jobs $J_1, J_2, \ldots, J_n$ to be scheduled on m machines. Machines are critical resources: one machine cannot be assigned to two jobs

[7] For instance, see http://www.lifl.fr/OPAC for static and stochastic biobjective flow-shop scheduling and vehicle routing problems.

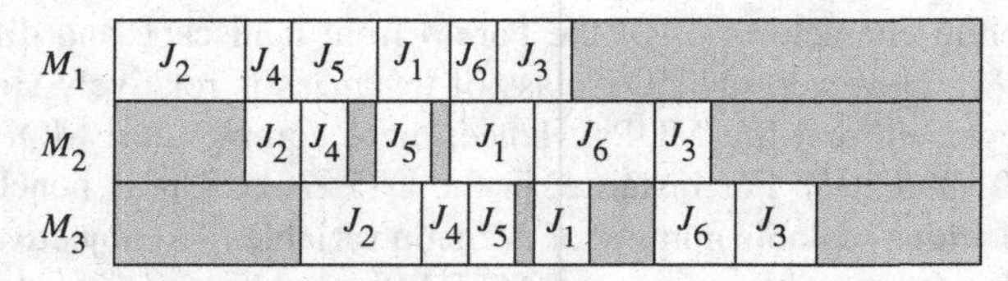

FIGURE 4.7 A permutation flow-shop scheduling problem.

simultaneously. Each job J_i is composed of m consecutive tasks $t_{i1}, \ldots, t_{im}$, where t_{ij} represents the jth task of the job J_i requiring the machine M_j. To each task t_{ij} is associated a processing time p_{ij}, and to each job J_i a release time r_i and a due date d_i (deadline of the job) are given. In permutation flow-shop problems, the jobs must be scheduled in the same order on all the machines (Fig. 4.7). A comprehensive survey of multiobjective scheduling problems may be found in Ref. [771].

Many objectives may be used in scheduling tasks on different machines. These objectives vary according to the particularities of the treated problem:

$C_{\max}$	Makespan (total completion time): $\max\{C_i \mid i \in [1 \ldots n]\}$
$\bar{C}$:	Mean value of jobs completion time
$T_{\max}$:	Maximum tardiness: $\max\{[\max(0, C_i - d_i)] \mid i \in [1 \ldots n]\}$
T:	Total tardiness: $\sum_{i=1}^{n} [\max(0, C_i - d_i)]$
U:	Number of jobs delayed with regard to their due date d_i
$F_{\max}$:	Maximum job flow-time: $\max\{C_i - r_i \mid i \in [1 \ldots n]\}$
$\bar{F}$:	Mean job flow-time

where s_{ij} represents the time at which the task t_{ij} is scheduled and $C_i = s_{im} + p_{im}$ represents the completion time of job J_i. The size of the Pareto front is not very important as the correlation of the two objectives is positively important that restricts the number of Pareto solutions (see Fig. 4.5).

4.2.2 Real-Life Applications

A huge number of works dealing with MOPs are dedicated to real-life applications [794]. Two key aspects are responsible for this interest: many real-life applications involve various conflicting objectives, and efficient multiobjective metaheuristics have been developed (e.g., evolutionary multiobjective algorithms). Indeed, multiobjective metaheuristics have been applied to real-life applications since 1960. Moreover, several domains were dealt with various multiobjective applications:

- **Engineering design:** In the past 20 years, the design of systems in engineering sciences (e.g., mechanics, aeronautics, chemistry) has boosted the research and development of multiobjective metaheuristics. Indeed, many design problems have been formulated as MOPs (e.g., plane wings [588], car engines [289]). Multiobjective formulation of design problems has gained a large success in the engineering domain.

- **Environment and energetics:** In the literature, one of the first papers deals with multiobjective modeling of optimization problems concerned with the environment and energetic domains [472] (e.g., management of water distribution [355], management of the air quality [515]). This domain will be more critical in years to come due to the deterioration of our environment and the lack of energetic resources (e.g., water [702] and nonrenewable resources such as petrol).
- **Telecommunications:** In the last decade, the telecommunication area has been one of the most exciting domains in which multiobjective metaheuristics have been applied (e.g., design of antennas [796], design of cellular networks [544], design of constellation of satellites [242], frequency assignment [172]). This domain will remain to be exciting due to the continuing evolution of network technologies (e.g., sensor networks, ad hoc networks, cognitive networks).
- **Control:** The classical applications around optimal design of controllers are very active in terms of multiobjective modeling and solving of optimization problems (see Ref. [268] for a survey).
- **Computational biology and bioinformatics:** Numerous key problems in computational biology and bioinformatics can be formulated as MOPs. Multiobjective optimization is in its starting phase in this application domain. A lot of potential works are still to be done in this challenging area (e.g., classification, feature selection, clustering, association rules [460], inverse problems such as gene regulatory network modeling and phylogenetic inference, sequence and structure alignment, structure prediction and design such as protein identification, protein structure prediction [766], and molecular docking). A comprehensive review of multiobjective optimization in bioinformatics and computational biology may be found in Ref. [357].
- **Transportation and logistics:** Nowadays, this domain generates a large number of MOP applications (e.g., containers management [772], design of grid systems [286], traced motorway [144]).

Example 4.3 Multiobjective routing problems. Routing problems such as the traveling salesman and the vehicle routing problems are widely studied because of their numerous real-life applications (e.g., logistics, transportation). The most common objectives include minimizing the total distance traveled, the total time required, the total tour cost, and/or the fleet size, and maximizing the quality of the service and/or the collected profit. Numerous other aspects such as balancing of workloads (e.g., time, distance) can be taken into account.

Multiobjective routing problems are mainly used in three ways: to extend classical academic problems to improve their practical application (while never losing sight of the initial objective), to generalize classic problems, and to study real-life cases in which the objectives have been clearly identified by the decision maker and are dedicated to a specific real-life application:

- **Extending classic academic problems:** Multiobjective optimization is one possible way to study objectives other than the one initially defined, which is often related to solution cost. In this context, the problem definition remains unchanged, and new objectives are added. The purpose of such extensions is often to enhance the practical applications of the model by recognizing that logistics problems are not only cost driven. Some of the different extensions found in the literature are driver workload [497], customer satisfaction [696], commercial distribution [655], and multiobjective traveling salesman problem and variants [359,409,503].

- **Generalizing classic problems:** Another way to use multiobjective optimization is to generalize a problem by adding objectives instead of one or several constraints and/or parameters. In the literature, this strategy has notably been applied to the vehicle routing problem with time window constraints, where the time windows are replaced by one or several objectives [302,385,593,763].
- **Real-life cases:** Multiobjective routing problems are also studied for a specific real-life situation, in which decision makers define several clear objectives that they would like to get optimized. Several examples of these real-life problems may be found: transport delivery routing [241], urban school bus route planning [87], rural school bus routing [153], urban trash collection [490], merchandise transport routing [762], hazardous product distribution [315], and tour planning for mobile health care facilities [206].

A more comprehensive survey of multiobjective routing problems can be found in Ref. [439].

4.2.3 Multicriteria Decision Making

The aim of solving MOPs is to help a decision maker to find a Pareto solution that copes with his preferences. One of the fundamental questions in MOPs resolution is related to the interaction between the problem solver (e.g., metaheuristic) and the decision maker. Indeed, the Pareto optimal solutions cannot be ranked globally. The role of the decision maker[8] is to specify some extra information to select his favorite solution. This interaction[9] can take one of the three following forms [400,555]:

- ***A priori:*** In this approach, the decision maker provides his preferences before the optimization process. Different forms may be used to formulate the preferences. In many cases, the suggested approaches consist in combining the different objective functions according to some *utility function* (or value function) v, to obtain only one objective function to be optimized (aggregation method). The reduced problem to solve will be

$$\text{Min } v(f(x)), x \in S$$

[8] Group decision making may also be considered [399].
[9] The whole procedure is called solution process.

The value function will provide a complete order between the Pareto optimal solutions. For instance, if the value function is a linear one, the decision maker is supposed to evaluate *a priori* the weight of each objective to define the utility function. However, in most of the cases, it is difficult to define the utility function before the optimization process. For some problems, it has been demonstrated that it is impossible to represent the decision maker utility function in a reliable manner [207].

Moreover, the various objectives are not comparable[10]. The search space defined by the aggregation does not represent the initial problem. If the decision maker is not able to indicate *a priori* the type of wished compromise between criteria, it is not relevant to seek one and only one effective solution carrying out an aggregation between these criteria. In using this approach, the decision maker must have a minimum knowledge on his problem in terms of possibilities and limitations. In terms of problem solving, in general, it results in the transformation of the MOP into a monoobjective problem, which can be solved by any traditional metaheuristic (S-metaheuristic or P-metaheuristic).

- ***A posteriori:*** In the *a posteriori* approach, the search process determines a set of Pareto solutions. This set helps the decision maker to have a complete knowledge of the Pareto front. In some sense, the Pareto front constitutes an acquired knowledge on the problem. Then, the decision maker chooses one solution from the set of solutions provided by the solver. This approach is practical when the number of objectives is small and the cardinality of the set is reduced [681]. Otherwise, to help the decision maker to make a choice, it is advisable to enable him to explore the whole Pareto set (or an approximation) according to its preferences, so that he can better apprehend the arbitration to be operated between the criteria. In terms of problem solving, this approach is more complex in a sense that a set of good Pareto solutions must be found.
- ***Interactive:*** In this case, there is a progressive interaction between the decision maker and the solver (Fig. 4.8). From the knowledge extracted during the problem resolution, the decision maker defines his preferences in an understandable way. Many preference information have been used in the literature (e.g., reference point [817], reference direction [475], marginal rate of return [555]).

  These preferences are taken into account by the solver in the problem resolution. This process is iterated during several steps. As the interaction occurs during the search, the solver must not require too much time. At the end of the guided exploration of the Pareto front, the decision maker has a thorough knowledge to select a solution from the Pareto front, representing an acceptable compromise that will convince the decision maker. If the decision maker is rational and the problem is well formulated, the final solution is always Pareto optimal.

Each approach has its weaknesses and strengths. The choice of a method depends on the problem properties and the abilities of the decision maker. In this chapter, our

[10]Several objective are not comparable if their values are expressed in different ways. For example, if one objective seeks to maximize the profit and another one try to minimize the ecological impact.

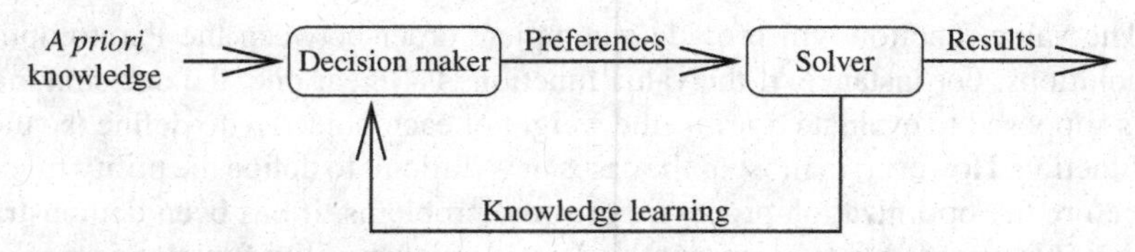

FIGURE 4.8 Interactive approach: progressive cooperation between the solver and the decision maker.

focus is on noninteractive multiobjective metaheuristics, where the decision maker is involved before the search process (*a priori* interaction) or after the search process is finished (*a posteriori* interaction). The background presented can be easily adapted to design interactive multiobjective metaheuristics.

4.3 MAIN DESIGN ISSUES OF MULTIOBJECTIVE METAHEURISTICS

As in monoobjective optimization, the optimization algorithms that can be used to solve MOPs can be classified into *exact* and *approximate* algorithms. In the literature, more attention has been devoted to bicriteria optimization problems by using *exact methods* such as *branch and bound* algorithms [499,681,694,787,800], branch and cut [438], *A* algorithm* [526,723], and *dynamic programming* [109,814]. Exact search methods are effective for problems of small sizes. Moreover, for problems with more than two criteria, there are no many effective exact procedures, given the simultaneous difficulties of NP-hardness complexity of problems and the multicriterion framework of the problems. However, there exists some new advances in this area, with several exact approaches proposed in the literature for biobjective [495,498,500] and multiobjective problems [498].

Heuristic methods are necessary to solve large-scale or many criteria problems. They do not guarantee to find in an exact way the Pareto set but an approximation of this set. Approximate methods can be divided into two classes: on one hand, algorithms that are specific to a given problem using some knowledge on the problem and, on the other hand, the metaheuristics that are general-purpose algorithms, applicable to a large variety of MOPs. In the last two decades, the application of metaheuristics to solve MOPs has become an active research and development area. For instance, in the EMO[11] community, a surge of research activity on using evolutionary algorithms has been observed. Solving this class of problems implies obtaining an approximation set of Pareto optimal solutions in such a way that the corresponding set fulfills the requirements of convergence to the Pareto front and uniform diversity. A unifying view for analyzing, designing, and implementing multiobjective metaheuristics (S-metaheuristics and P-metaheuristics) is provided in this chapter.

[11]Evolutionary multicriterion optimization.

In addition to the common concepts of monoobjective metaheuristics (see previous chapters), a multiobjective metaheuristic contains three main search components:

- **Fitness assignment:** The main role of this procedure is to guide the search algorithm toward Pareto optimal solutions for a better convergence. It assigns a scalar-valued fitness to a vector objective function.
- **Diversity preserving:** The emphasis here is to generate a diverse set of Pareto solutions in the objective and/or the decision space.
- **Elitism:** The preservation and use of elite solutions (e.g., Pareto optimal solutions) allows a robust, fast, and a monotonically improving performance of a metaheuristic.

A unified view of multiobjective metaheuristics is presented in an attempt to provide a common terminology and classification mechanisms. The goal of the general classification is to provide a mechanism that allows a common description and comparison of multiobjective metaheuristics in a qualitative way. It also allows the design of new multiobjective metaheuristics, borrowing ideas from current ones. The following sections discuss how these three search components can be defined independently to design a multiobjective metaheuristic. Some examples dealing with popular multiobjective metaheuristics are also illustrated.

4.4 FITNESS ASSIGNMENT STRATEGIES

For a given solution, a fitness assignment procedure maps a fitness vector to a single value. The fitness scalar value measures the quality of the solution. According to the fitness assignment strategy, multiobjective metaheuristics can be classified into four main categories (Fig. 4.9):

- **Scalar approaches:** They are based on the MOP problem transformation into a monoobjective problem. This class of approaches includes, for example, the methods based on aggregation that combine the various objectives f_i into a single objective function F. These approaches require for the decision maker to have a good knowledge of his problem.
- **Criterion-based approaches:** In criterion-based approaches, the search is performed by treating the various noncommensurable objectives separately.
- **Dominance-based approaches:** The dominance-based approaches[12] use the concept of dominance and Pareto optimality to guide the search process. The objective vectors of solutions are scalarized using the dominance relation.
- **Indicator-based approaches:** In indicator-based approaches, the metaheuristics use performance quality indicators to drive the search toward the Pareto front.

In the following sections, the different approaches are detailed.

[12] Also named Pareto approaches.

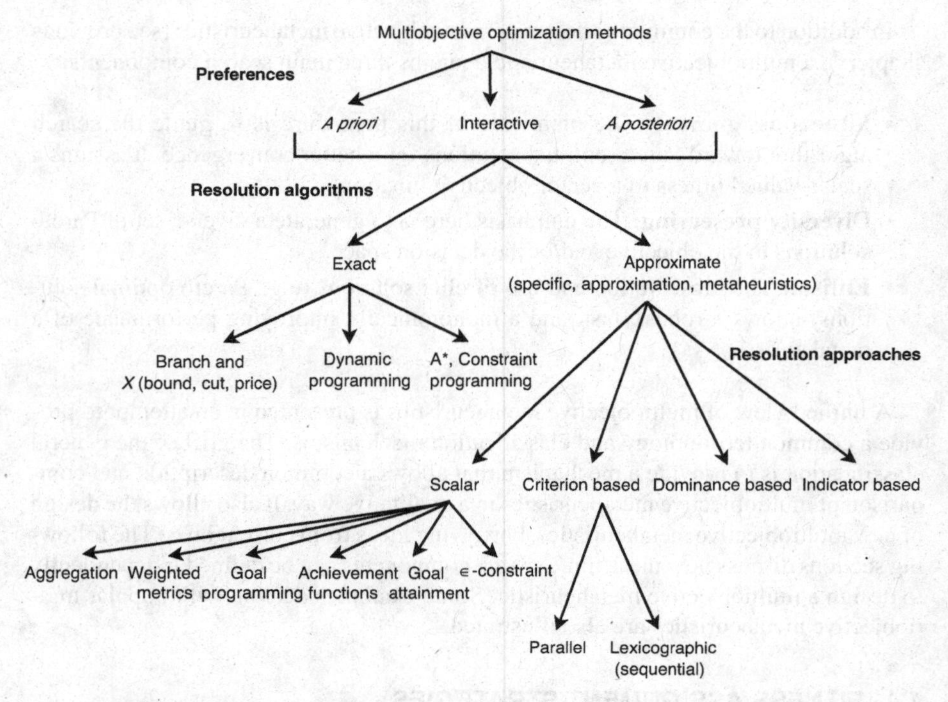

FIGURE 4.9 Classification of multiobjective optimization algorithms.

4.4.1 Scalar Approaches

This class of multiobjective metaheuristics contains the approaches that transform a MOP problem into a monoobjective one or a set of such problems. Many proposed algorithms in the literature are scalar approaches. Among these methods one can find the aggregation methods, the weighted metrics, the goal programming methods, the achievement functions, the goal attainment methods, and the ϵ-constraint methods. The use of scalarization approaches is justified when they generate Pareto optimal solutions.

4.4.1.1 Aggregation Method The aggregation (or weighted) method is one of the first and most used methods for the generation of Pareto optimal solutions. It consists in using an aggregation function to transform a MOP into a monoobjective problem (MOP_λ) by combining the various objective functions f_i into a single objective function f generally in a linear way [400,715]:

$$f(x) = \sum_{i=1}^{n} \lambda_i f_i(x), \qquad x \in S \tag{4.4}$$

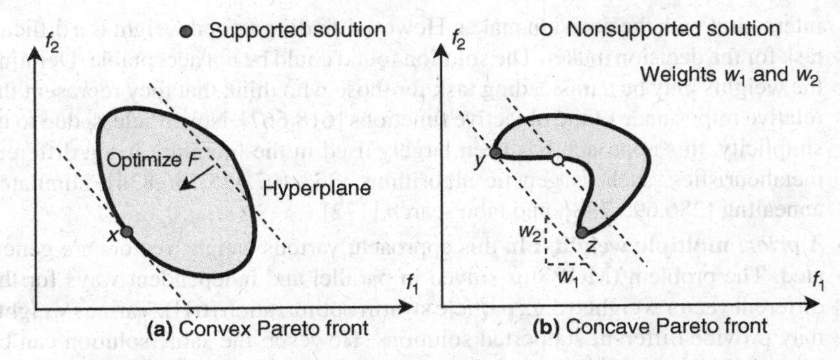

FIGURE 4.10 The aggregation method generates only supported solutions.

where the weights $\lambda_i \in [0 \ldots 1]$ and $\sum_{i=1}^{n} \lambda_i = 1$. The solution of the weighted problem is weakly Pareto optimal. The final solution is Pareto optimal if $\lambda_i > 0$, for all $i \in [1, n]$ or the solution is unique [555]. Figure 4.10 illustrates the linear aggregation method for a biobjective problem. A weight vector is defined by a hyperplane in the objective space (a line for a bicriteria problem). Generating of the Pareto optimal solution is reduced to find the point where the hyperplane has a common tangent with the feasible space (point x in the figure minimizing the objective functions). A Pareto optimal solution is always on the border of the feasible objective space. The main drawback of this method is that it generates only supported solutions. In Fig. 4.10b, characterized by a nonconvex Pareto border, only the solutions y and z can be generated. No matter how the weights are initialized, all other Pareto optimal solutions between the points y and z cannot be found. Then, for MOPs with a concave Pareto front, the decision maker will have a misleading information of the Pareto front.

If the various objectives are not in the same scale, a normalization of the objectives must be realized. For instance, one can transform the previous equation in the form

$$F(x) = \sum_{i=1}^{n} \lambda_i \frac{f_i(x) - f_i^{\min}}{f_i^{\max} - f_i^{\min}} \tag{4.5}$$

where $f_i^{\max}$ and $f_i^{\min}$ represent the upper and lower bounds of the different objectives f_i.

Once a weighted function is defined, the problem is reduced to a classical monoobjective problem. Hence, any metaheuristic (S-metaheuristic or P-metaheuristic) described in the previous chapters can be designed to solve the problem (e.g., ant colonies [403], tabu search [64]) [273,661]. The obtained results in the resolution of the problem (MOP$_\lambda$) depend strongly on the parameters chosen for the weight vector λ. Different strategies may be applied:

- ***A priori* single weight:** This strategy consists in defining the weights λ_i to be selected according to the preferences of a decision maker. This is possible when the decision maker has a utility function that is linear. The advantage of this approach is the generation of only one solution and thus do not require any interaction with the decision maker. However, finding a good weight is a difficult task for the decision maker. The solution found could be not acceptable. Defining the weights may be a misleading task for those who think that they represent the relative importance of the objective functions [618,667]. Nevertheless, due to its simplicity, this approach has been largely used in the literature using different metaheuristics, such as genetic algorithms [353,407,425,736,834], simulated annealing [286,695,788], and tabu search [172].

- ***A priori* multiple weights:** In this approach, various weight vectors are generated. The problem (MOP_λ) is solved in parallel and independent ways for the different vector weights (e.g., particle swarm optimization [61]). Various weights may provide different supported solutions. However, the same solution can be generated by using different weights. An automatic way to generate the weights to obtain different Pareto solutions may be found in Refs [121,722]. A uniformly distributed set of weights does not produce necessarily a uniform distribution of Pareto optimal solutions in the objective space [177]. Moreover, for some problems, a small change in the weights can generate completely different solutions in the objective space.
- **Dynamic multiple weights:** In this approach, the weights are varied during the search to approximate the Pareto front. The search memory is not used to update the weights. For instance, the weights can be updated randomly during the search (e.g., in evolutionary algorithms [404]).
- **Adaptive multiple weights:** In this approach, the weights are varied according to the search memory of a metaheuristic (e.g., particle swarm optimization [605]).

Example 4.4 Self-adaptive weights. In evolutionary algorithms, the representation of the solution may include the weights of each objective in addition to the solution of the problem [353]. Hence, the weights evolve during the search. The advantage of this approach is that it encourages the diversity of the weights used in the population through self-adaptation. The goal of this approach is to generate, in a parallel way, a set of Pareto optimal solutions corresponding to various selected weights.

Example 4.5 Scalarized S-metaheuristics. S-metaheuristics are mainly used in scalar approaches to solve MOPs:

- **Simulated annealing:** One of the first attempts to use simulated annealing to solve MOPs was presented in Ref. [695]. At present, there are many proposals in the literature [130,447]. Weighted metrics are used to aggregate the objectives into a single score to be used in the acceptance function. Most of these algorithms do not have a population, but they use an archive to store the nondominated solutions discovered during the search process. Another precursor-scalarized simulated annealing is the MOSA (multiobjective simulated annealing) algorithm [785].
- **Tabu search:** The MOTS (Multiobjective Tabu Search) algorithm is one of the first scalar approaches adapted to tabu search [358]. The algorithm works with a set of solutions that, through manipulation of weights, are optimized toward the nondominated frontier, while at the same time it tries to disperse them over the

Pareto front. Several other scalarized tabu search strategies have been proposed in the literature [64,373].

4.4.1.2 Weighted Metrics In this approach[13], the decision maker must define the reference point z to attain. Then, a distance metric between the referenced point and the feasible region of the objective space is minimized. The aspiration levels of the reference point are introduced into the formulation of the problem, transforming it into a monoobjective problem. For instance, the objective function can be defined as a weighted norm that minimizes the deviation from the reference point. Using the L_p-metric, the problem can be formulated in the following way:

$$(\text{MOP}(\lambda, z)) \begin{cases} \min \left(\sum_{j=1}^{n} \lambda_j |f_j(x) - z_j|^p \right)^{\frac{1}{p}} \\ \text{s.c. } x \in S \end{cases} \tag{4.6}$$

where $1 \leq p \leq \infty$ and z is the reference point.

The obtained solutions depend on the used metric. Generally, p is equal to 2, which corresponds to the Euclidean metric. Problem 4.6 generates a Pareto optimal solution if the solution is unique or all the weights are strictly positive. As for the weighted method, the convexity property is needed to guarantee that every Pareto optimal solution can be generated. If $p = \infty$, the equation becomes a min–max function (weighted Tchebycheff problem):

$$(\text{MOP}(\lambda, z)) \begin{cases} \min \max_{j \in [1,n]} [\lambda_j (f_j(x) - z_j)] \\ \text{s.c. } x \in S \end{cases} \tag{4.7}$$

If the reference point z represents the ideal vector, the absolute values may be ignored. Problem 4.7 generates a weak Pareto optimal solution for all positive weights and has at least one Pareto optimal solution [555]. By changing the weights and using the ideal point as a reference point, any Pareto optimal solution can be generated. An arbitrary selection of the reference point cannot be carried out, since a bad choice of the reference point can lead to a solution that is not Pareto optimal. To avoid the weakly Pareto optimal solution in solving the problem 4.7, an *augmented Tchebycheff problem* may be used to give a slight slope to the contours of the feasible objective space [722]:

$$(\text{MOP}(\lambda, z)) \begin{cases} \min \max_{j \in [1,n]} [\lambda_j (f_j(x) - z_j)] + \rho \sum_{j=1}^{n} (f_j(x) - z_j) \\ \text{s.c. } x \in S \end{cases} \tag{4.8}$$

where ρ is a small positive value.

[13] Also called compromise programming

Example 4.6 Compromise programming using metaheuristics. As the problem is transformed to a monoobjective optimization problem, any metaheuristic (S-metaheuristic or P-metaheuristic) can be used to solve this class of problems. For instance, one can use

- **Genetic algorithms:** Evolutionary algorithms have been largely used to solve the weighted metrics formulation of MOPs [678,816]. A min–max function comparing the relative deviations according to attainable minima (ideal vector) may be used [141,143]. Let us consider the function objective f_i, where the deviation can be calculated in the following way:

$$z'_i(x) = \frac{|f_i(x) - f_i^0|}{|f_i^0|} \tag{4.9}$$

where

$$z''_i(x) = \frac{|f_i(x) - f_i^0|}{|f_i(x)|} \tag{4.10}$$

Suppose that $\forall X,\ f_i(x) \neq 0$. The function to be optimized is

$$F(x) = \sum_{i=1}^{n} \lambda_i \left| \frac{f_i(x) - f_i^0}{\alpha_i} \right| \tag{4.11}$$

where $\alpha_i = f_i^0$ or $f_i(x)$, n represents the number of objectives, and λ_i represents the weights associated with the aggregation function. The user provides several sets of weight λ_L. A weighted GA is executed in which each GA solves the optimization problem with the associated aggregation. A selection procedure, based on the paradigm of the *fuzzy logic*, may also be used [640,641]. The calculation of a utility function F is based on fuzzy rules:

$$F = \frac{1}{n} \sum_{i=1}^{n} f'(f_i) \tag{4.12}$$

where f' represents the set of fuzzy rules. It can be defined as follows:

$$\begin{cases} \text{If } f_i \leq (O_i - E_i), \text{ then } f'(f_i) = \left(\frac{S_{\min}}{f_i\min - (O_i - E_i)} \right) (f_i - (O_i - E_i)) \\ \text{If } (O_i - E_i), \leq f_i \leq (O_i + E_i), \text{ then } f'(f_i) = 0 \\ \text{If } f_i \geq (O_i + E_i), \text{ then } f'(f_i) = \left(\frac{-S_{\max}}{(O_i + E_i) - f_i\max} \right) (f_i - (O_i + E_i)) \end{cases} \tag{4.13}$$

where O_i is the goal associated with each objective, E_i is the acceptable error for O_i, $S_{\min(\max)}$ is the scale factor for the values lower (or higher) than the accepted value, $f_{\min(\max)}$ is the lower (or upper) bound for each objective. Figure 4.11 illustrates

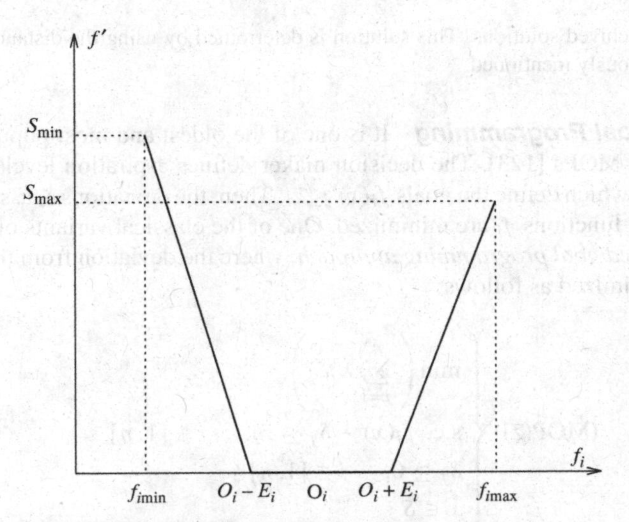

FIGURE 4.11 Fuzzy rule applied to objective functions.

these rules. This approach allows the uncertain calculation of each objective with a tolerance threshold level equal to O_i.

- **Simulated annealing:** For instance, simulated annealing was used to solve a biobjective traveling salesman problem with the following acceptance function [695]:

$$P_{xy}(T) = \min\left(1, e^{\frac{\max_i(\lambda_i(f_i(x)-z_i))-\max_i(\lambda_i(f_i(y)-z_i))}{T}}\right) \tag{4.14}$$

  where x is the current solution, y is the solution generated from x neighborhood, the norm used is the Tchebycheff norm L_∞, and z_i is the reference value. The weights λ_1 and λ_2 are initialized to 1, and for each iteration, a random number, generated in the interval $[-0.05, +0.05]$, update the two weights. This allows a small variation of the weights during the search, and thus the determination of several Pareto optimal solutions.

- **Tabu search:** A traditional tabu search may be used to solve the weighted metrics formulation of a MOP, except for the determination of the best neighbor [294]. The selected solution is represented by the best compromise among all the solutions of the neighborhood that are not in the tabu list. To determine this solution, a distance measure is introduced so that the neighbor accepted "satisfies" all the objective functions. The cost function used to select the best neighbor is a balanced standard (Tchebycheff L_p standard) compared to the ideal vector. Throughout this process, M solutions are archived. Every solution, accepted during the tabu search process, is compared with the M archived solutions. If one or more solutions are dominated, they are eliminated from this set and replaced by new ones (that are not dominated). Finally, a solution is proposed, which represents the best compromise among the

M archived solutions. This solution is determined by using the distance concept previously mentioned.

4.4.1.3 Goal Programming It is one of the oldest and most popular methods dealing with MOPs [123]. The decision maker defines aspiration levels $\overline{z}_i$ for each objective f_i, which define the goals $f_i(x) \leq \overline{z}_i$. Then, the deviations δ_i associated with the objective functions f_i are minimized. One of the classical variants of the method is the *weighted goal programming approach*, where the deviation from the aspiration levels is minimized as follows:

$$(\text{MOP}(\overline{z}))\begin{cases} \min\left(\sum_{j=1}^{n} \lambda_j \delta_j\right) \\ \text{s.c. } f_j(x) - \delta_j \leq \overline{z}_j, \quad j \in [1, n] \\ \delta_j \geq 0, \quad j \in [1, n] \\ x \in S \end{cases} \tag{4.15}$$

where δ_j represents the deviation variables ($\delta_j = \max[0, f_j(x) - \overline{z}_j]$).

The solution found is Pareto optimal if the aspiration levels form a Pareto optimal reference point or all the deviation variables δ_j are strictly positive. For instance, if the aspiration levels form a feasible solution, then the obtained solution is equal to the reference point. The popularity of goal programming is due to the fact that the goals are easy to define by the decision maker.

4.4.1.4 Achievement Functions Achievement functions have been introduced by Wierzbicki [817]. Unlike the previous methods where the reference point must be chosen carefully (e.g., ideal point), an arbitrary reference point $\overline{z}$ can be selected in the objective space (feasible or nonfeasible). Then, the following scalarization function is optimized:

$$(\text{MOP}(\lambda, z))\begin{cases} \min \max_{j\in[1,n]}[w_j(f_j(x) - \overline{z}_j)] + \rho \sum_{j=1}^{n} (f_j(x) - \overline{z}_j) \\ \text{s.c. } x \in S \end{cases} \tag{4.16}$$

where w_j are normalizing factors. For instance, they can be initialized as $w_j = 1/(z_i^{nadir} - z_i^{ideal})$.

A Pareto optimal solution is produced for each location of the reference point. Different Pareto optimal solutions may be generated by using various reference points. Without using the augmentation factor, weakly Pareto optimal solutions are generated.

4.4.1.5 Goal Attainment The goal attainment method constitutes another approach that is based on the preference specification of the intermediary of a goal to reach. In this approach, a weight vector $(\lambda_1, \lambda_2, \ldots, \lambda_n)$ and the goals $z_1^*, z_2^*, \ldots, z_n^*$ for

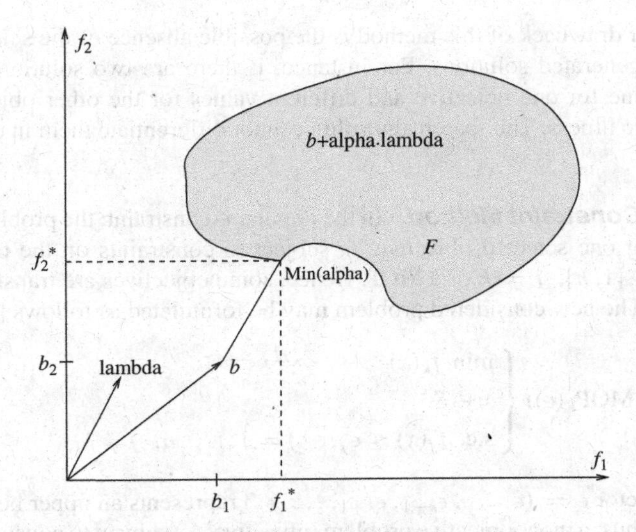

FIGURE 4.12 The goal attainment method.

all the objectives have to be chosen by the decision maker. To find the best compromise solution x^*, the following problem is solved:

$$\begin{cases} \min \alpha \\ \text{s.c. } x \in S \\ f_i(x) \leq z_i^* + \alpha\lambda_i, \quad i = 1, \ldots, n \\ \sum_{i=1}^{n} \lambda_i = 1 \end{cases} \tag{4.17}$$

where α is a scalar variable. If a weight λ_i is null, the maximum limit of the objective $f_i(x)$ is z_i^*. The advantage of this model compared to the weighted metrics method is that the function is differentiable[14] and can be solved using gradient-based algorithms.

The set of Pareto optimal solutions can be generated by varying the weights λ_i, either for convex and nonconvex MOPs [129]. The approach is illustrated in Fig. 4.12. The vector b represents the goal determined by the decision maker, who also chooses the direction vector λ. The direction of the vector $b + \alpha\lambda$ can be determined, and the problem consists in finding a feasible solution in the objective space, as closed as possible to the origin and in the direction of the vector $b + \alpha\lambda$. If this solution exists, it is necessarily Pareto optimal.

The optimal value of α indicates if the goals are attainable. A negative α value implies that the goals are attainable. If not ($\alpha > 0$), the goal is not attainable. The formulated problem can be solved by using any metaheuristic (e.g., genetic algorithms [820]).

[14]If all the original objective functions were also differentiable.

The major drawback of this method is the possible absence of the selection pressure of the generated solutions. For instance, if there are two solutions that have the same value for one objective and different values for the other objective, they have the same fitness. The search algorithm cannot differentiate them in the problem resolution.

4.4.1.6 ϵ-Constraint Method In the popular ϵ-constraint, the problem consists in optimizing one selected objective f_k subject to constraints on the other objectives f_j, $j \in [1, n]$, $j \neq k$ of a MOP. Hence, some objectives are transformed into constraints. The new considered problem may be formulated as follows [351]:

$$(\text{MOP}_k(\epsilon)) \begin{cases} \min f_k(x) \\ x \in S \\ \text{s.c. } f_j(x) \leq \epsilon_j, \quad j = 1, \ldots, n, \ j \neq k \end{cases} \tag{4.18}$$

where the vector $\epsilon = (\epsilon_1 \ldots, \epsilon_{k-1}, \epsilon_{k+1}, \ldots, \epsilon_n)$ represents an upper bound for the objectives. Thus, a monoobjective problem (objective f_k) subject to constraints on the other objectives is solved. Figure 4.13 illustrates the ϵ-constraint method for a biobjective problem, by minimizing the function f_2 and adding the constraint $f_1(x) \leq e_i$.

The solution of the problem is always weakly Pareto optimal. An optimal solution x^* of the problem is Pareto optimal if it is unique or it solves the problem for every $k \in [1, n]$ where $\epsilon_j = f_j(x^*)$ for $j \in [1, n]$, $j \neq k$ [555]. Unlike the weighted method, this method works for nonconvex MOPs; it can generate the nonsupported solutions (i.e., solutions in a concave region of the objective space).

Various values of ϵ_i can be used to be able to generate various Pareto optimal solutions. The *a priori* knowledge of the suitable intervals for the ϵ_i values is necessary for all the objectives and may constitute a difficult task. Obtaining information on the range of the different objective functions may be useful in the generation of the

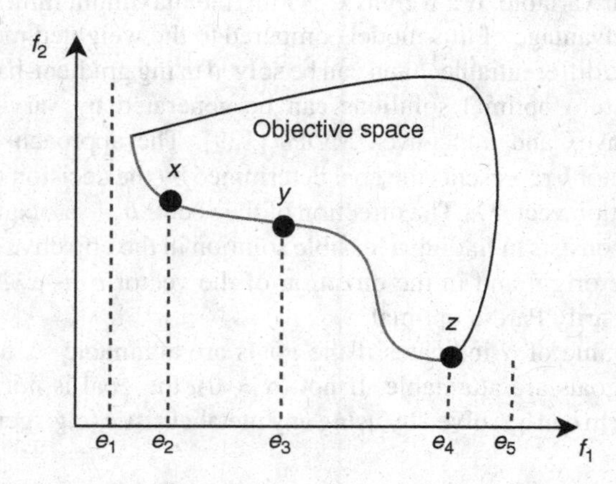

FIGURE 4.13 ϵ-Constraint method. According to the constraints associated with $f_1 \leq e_1, \ldots, f_1 \leq e_5$, the Pareto solutions x, y, and z are obtained.

upper bounds ϵ_i associated with the constraints. For instance, the ideal vector may be computed to determine the lower limits, to be able to define the adequate values for ϵ_i (nonempty feasible region). Thus, one will have

$$\epsilon_i \geq f_i(x^*), \quad i = 1, 2, k-1, k+1, n \tag{4.19}$$

An automatic way to generate a set of constraints may be found in Ref. [121]. If an *a priori* method is used, it would be easier for the decision maker to specify the upper bounds than the weights for the aggregation method.

Example 4.7 ϵ-Constraint metaheuristics. As for any scalar method, the ϵ-constraint model has been solved with different metaheuristics (e.g., tabu search [438]). For instance, several evolutionary algorithms have been designed to solve ϵ-constraint MOP [796]. For instance, an evolutionary algorithm can be carried out several times with various values of the vector ϵ, to generate various Pareto optimal solutions [659].

An EA in which the ϵ-vector values are generated in a different manner into the individuals may also be used [514,515]. Let us consider a biobjective problem, the associated thresholds of the individuals 1 and k will be initialized respectively to the minimal threshold $\epsilon_{\min}$ and the maximum threshold $\epsilon_{\max}$. The threshold associated with the individual i of the population will take the following form:

$$\epsilon_i = \epsilon_{\min} + \frac{(i-1) \cdot (\epsilon_{\max} - \epsilon_{\min})}{(k-1)} \tag{4.20}$$

where k represents the population size.

The generation of several solutions requires multiple executions of the algorithm with various constraints, which is an expensive exercise in terms of computation time. There exists a relation between the model based on aggregation and the model based on the ϵ-constraint method.

Theorem 4.1 *Suppose that S and f are convex. If, for some k, x^* is solution of $MOP_k(\epsilon)$, then there exists λ such as x^* is solution of MOP_λ, and inversely [121].*

Several hybridization of scalar methods may be used. An example of such hybrid models is the combination of the aggregation model MOP_λ and the ϵ-constraint model $\text{MOP}_k(\epsilon)$:

$$(\text{MOP}(\lambda, \epsilon)) \begin{cases} \min F(x) = \sum_{i=1}^{n} \lambda_i f_i(x) \\ \text{s.c. } x \in S \\ f_j(x) \leq \epsilon_j, \quad j = 1, \ldots, n \end{cases} \tag{4.21}$$

Analysis of scalar methods: The transformation of a multiobjective problem into a single-objective problem requires *a priori* knowledge on the considered problem that is not always available. This type of approach proved highly successful in practice due to its simplicity and its relatively low computational cost. The optimization of a monoobjective problem can guarantee Pareto optimality of the obtained solutions, but naturally finds only one solution. Hence, there is a loss of diversity of the obtained solutions. In practical situations, the decision makers generally need several alternatives. Indeed, if the objectives are disturbed or if data are uncertain, these methods are not effective. They are also sensitive to the landscape of the Pareto front (e.g., convexity, discontinuity). The other drawback of these methods is their sensitivity to the selected weights, the constraints, and the reference points. The obtained solutions depend strongly on these parameters. For several situations, various parameters are used; then the problem must be solved several times to find several Pareto optimal solutions. Thus, the computational cost associated will be more significant. Indeed, it requires several independent runs for each considered parameter values. Moreover, repetitive runs do not guarantee to find distinct Pareto optimal solutions. The following sections provide how to overcome the difficulties presented previously.

4.4.2 Criterion-Based Methods

In this class that is mainly based on P-metaheuristics, the search is carried out by treating the various noncommensurable objectives separately. Few studies belonging to this class exist in the literature. Among them one can find the parallel selection in evolutionary algorithms, parallel pheromone update in ant colony optimization, and lexicographic optimization.

4.4.2.1 Parallel Approach In this approach, the objectives are handled in parallel. P-metaheuristics may be transformed easily to parallel criterion-based multiobjective optimization algorithms. Indeed, the generation of new solutions will be carried out independently according to the objectives.

Example 4.8 Parallel selection in evolutionary algorithms. The first historical work consisting in using nonscalar EAs to solve MOPs has been proposed by Schaffer [682]. The developed algorithm, named VEGA (vector evaluated genetic algorithm), selects the individuals from the current population according to each objective, independently from the other ones. At each generation, the population is divided into a number of subpopulations that is equal to the number of objectives to optimize. Each subpopulation i is selected according to the objective f_i. The VEGA algorithm composes the entire population, and applies the classical steps of an EA (mutation, crossover, replacement) (Fig. 4.14).

As this algorithm randomly assigns the individuals to the subpopulations for each generation, an individual can be evaluated differently according to the selected objective, from one generation to another. The analysis of VEGA algorithm indicates that its behavior is more or less similar to an algorithm carrying out a linear aggregation; the results correspond to a weighted combination of the objectives with variable weights, according to the distribution of the individuals of the current population [656]. In spite

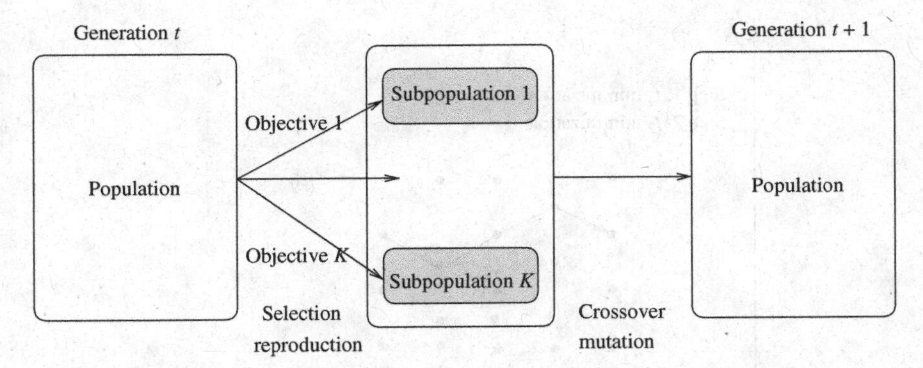

FIGURE 4.14 Parallel selection in the VEGA evolutionary algorithm.

of this effect, the VEGA algorithm provides good results in the search of Pareto optimal solutions in solving continuous MOP. However, there is a certain tendency to be unaware of the "compromised" solutions, and the nonsupported solutions cannot be generated. Indeed, there is a bias toward the best individuals regarding the objectives (i.e., extreme solutions).

Example 4.9 Parallel criterion-based P-metaheuristics. In population-based metaheuristics such as particle swarm optimization, ant colonies, evolutionary algorithms, and scatter search, the parallel approach involves several subpopulations solving single-objective problems. Then, the subpopulations exchange some information (e.g., solutions) to produce trade-offs among the different solutions previously generated for the objectives that were separately optimized. For instance, this approach has been used for particle swarm optimization in which the information exchanged is the global best particles of the subswarms [133,604].

In criterion-based parallel ant colony optimization, one ant colony is tackling each objective (e.g., ANT-Q algorithm [529], P-ACO [213]). Hence, a pheromone matrix will be associated with a given objective of the MOP [49,131]. Cooperation between colonies may be performed by exchanging information through pheromone updating [292].

4.4.2.2 *Sequential or Lexicographic Approach*

In this traditional approach, the search is carried out according to a given preference order of the objective defined by the decision maker. This order defines the significance level of the objectives [264]. Let us suppose that the objective indices of the functions also indicate their priority; the function f_1 has the greatest priority. Then, a set of monoobjective problems are solved in a sequential manner. The first solved problem will be formulated in the following way:

$$\text{Min } f_1(x), \text{ s.t. } X \in S \tag{4.22}$$

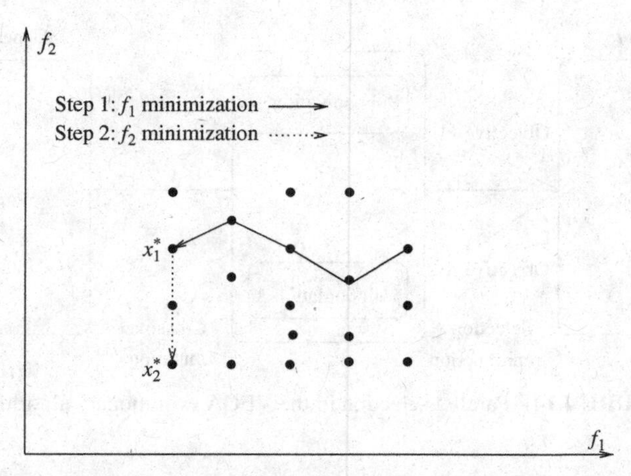

FIGURE 4.15 Biobjective lexicographic ordering.

If the problem associated with the most significant objective function has a unique solution, the search provides the optimal solution found x_1^* and stops. Otherwise, the problem associated with the second most significant objective function is solved, including the constraint that the most significant objective function preserves its optimal value (i.e., an equality constraint is associated with the already optimized functions). The second problem treated would be

$$\text{Min } f_2(x), \text{ s.t. } X \in S, \quad \text{with} f_1(x) = f_1(x_1^*) \tag{4.23}$$

The same stopping criteria and process are iterated until the treatment of the function f_n. Figure 4.15 illustrates the course of this procedure in the case of a biobjective problem.

The solution obtained with lexicographic ordering of the objective is Pareto optimal. A relaxation may be applied to the constraint regarding the previous objective functions. For instance, a small decrease in the performance of the most significant objective functions may be allowed to obtain trade-off solutions.

Example 4.10 Lexicographic metaheuristics. As for any scalar method, the lexicographic approach has been experimented with different metaheuristics [159,169]:

- **P-metaheuristics:** For instance, several genetic algorithms [142] and particle swarm optimizers [391] were used to solve MOPs in a lexicographic manner. In genetic algorithms, a lexicographical selection is performed. The lexicographical selection is carried out by comparing pairs of individuals; each pair of individuals is compared according to the objective with the highest priority level [282]. If the result is the same for the first priority objective, then the objective with the second priority level is used, and so on. The same approach based on a lexicographical selection may be used in any evolutionary algorithm (e.g., evolution strategies [488]). Instead of a deterministic ordering, a predetermined probability distribution may be used for the objectives. The individuals are compared according to an objective, which is selected in a random way, following the predetermined probability.

- **S-metaheuristics:** S-metaheuristics are also naturally adapted to solve lexicographic models of MOPs. For instance, tabu search may be used to solve a succession of monoobjective subproblems under several constraints [373]. In each subproblem, one objective is considered, following the relative importance of the objective (lexicographic order). In fact, the tabu search seeks for a good solution for the most significant function. Then, the second function, in the relative order of importance, is optimized, while having an additional constraint to deteriorate as less as possible the value obtained for the first objective function (application of a threshold). This process is reiterated for each function. This approach was tested for biobjective problems. The problem (MOP_q) solved with the stage $q = 1, \ldots, n$ is

$$(\text{MOP}_q) \begin{cases} f_q^* = \min f_q(x) \\ \text{s.c. } f_r(x) \leq f_r' \quad r = 1, \ldots, q-1 \\ x \in S \end{cases} \tag{4.24}$$

where f_r' is the threshold applied to the ideal value f_r, calculated from the optimum f_r^* of the MOP_r problem, plus one maximum value of deterioration, accepted for the objective f_r. The relative importance of each objective can be checked by changing the threshold value.

4.4.3 Dominance-Based Approaches

The dominance-based approaches use the concept of dominance in the fitness assignment, contrary to the other approaches that use a scalarization function or treat the various objectives separately. This idea was introduced initially into GAs by Goldberg [328]. The main advantage of dominance-based approaches is that they do not need the transformation of the MOP into a monoobjective one. In a single run, they are able to generate a diverse set of Pareto optimal solutions and Pareto solutions in the concave portions of the convex hull of feasible objective space.

Since the beginning of the nineties, interest concerning MOPs area with Pareto approaches always grow. Most of Pareto approaches use EMO algorithms. One can mention the commonly used ones: NSGA-II (nondominated sorting genetic algorithm), and SPEA2 (strength Pareto evolutionary algorithm). Many other competent EMOs have been developed, such as multiobjective messy GA, MOMGA [795], and neighborhood constraint GA [515]. P-metaheuristics seem particularly suitable to solve MOPs, because they deal simultaneously with a set of solutions that allow to find several members of the Pareto optimal set in a single run of the algorithm. Moreover, Pareto P-metaheuristics are less sensitive to the shape of the Pareto front (continuity, convexity).

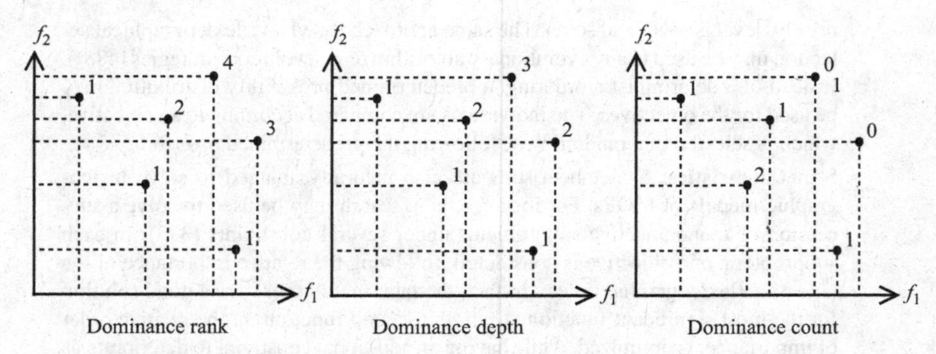

FIGURE 4.16 Fitness assignment: some dominance-based ranking methods.

Our concern here is to design a fitness assignment procedure to guide the search toward the Pareto border. *Ranking methods* are usually applied to establish an order between the solutions. This order depends on the concept of dominance and thus directly on Pareto optimality. Most of these fitness assignment procedures have been proposed in the EMO community. The most popular dominance-based ranking procedures are as follows (see Fig. 4.16) [843]:

- **Dominance rank:** In this strategy, the rank associated with a solution is related to the number of solutions in the population that dominates the considered solution [276]. This strategy was first employed in the MOGA algorithm (multiobjective genetic algorithm) [276]. In the MOEA algorithm, the fitness of a solution is equal to the number of solutions of the population that dominate the considered solution, plus one.
- **Dominance depth:** The population of solutions is decomposed into several fronts. The nondominated solutions of the population receive rank 1 and form the first front E_1. The solutions that are not dominated except by solutions of E_1 receive rank 2; they form the second front E_2. In a general way, a solution receives the row k if it is only dominated by individuals of the population belonging to the unit $E_1 \cup E_2 \cup \cdots \cup E_{k-1}$. Then, the depth of a solution corresponds to the depth of the front to which it belongs. For instance, this strategy is applied to the NSGA-II algorithm [197].
- **Dominance count:** The dominance count of a solution is related to the number of solutions dominated by the solution. This measure can be used in conjunction with the other ones. For instance, in the SPEA algorithm family, the dominance count is used in combination with the dominance rank [845,848].

Since a single value fitness (rank) is assigned to every solution in the population, any search component of a monoobjective metaheuristic can be reused to solve MOPs. For instance, the selection mechanism in EAs can be derived from the selection mechanisms used in monoobjective optimization. The interest of Pareto-based fitness assignment, compared to scalar methods, is that they evaluate the quality of

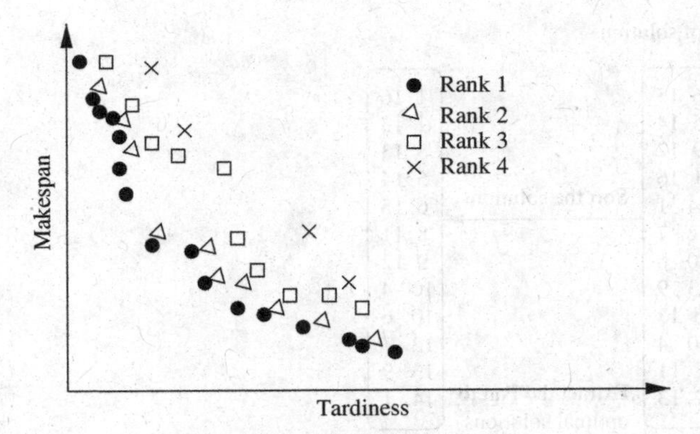

FIGURE 4.17 NSGA ranking.

a solution in relation to the whole population. No absolute values are assigned to solutions.

Example 4.11 An efficient algorithm for biobjective NSGA ranking. The computation of the dominance depth is time consuming (Fig. 4.17). The intuitive algorithm has a $O(N^3)$ complexity, with N the number of solutions. An algorithm in $O(N^2 \times \log(N))$ has been designed [200]. Sorting the solutions according to one objective allows the design of an efficient algorithm for the biobjective case [57] (see Algorithm 4.1). Figure 4.18 illustrates the effectiveness of the algorithm for biobjective NSGA ranking. The algorithm is divided into two parts. The first part consists in sorting the solutions with an algorithm such as quick sort. The complexity of this sorting algorithm is in $O(N \times \log(N))$. In the second part of the algorithm, the population is explored to extract nondominated solutions. Then this exploration

---

Algorithm 4.1 A biobjective NSGA ranking algorithm.

Sorting: Sort the solutions according to the first objective f_1 ;
If two solutions are equal regarding f_1 sort them according to f_2 ;
Initialization of the rank: $r_k = 1$;
While all the solutions are not treated **Do**
  Let s_c be the first non-treated solution ;
  $R_k s_c = r_k$;
   For all non-treated solution s_n **Do**
   If s_n and s_c have the same fitness **Then** $R_k s_n = r_k$
   Else if $f_2(s_n) < f_2(s_c)$ **Then** $R_k s_n = r_k$
   End if
   $s_c = s_n$;
  End For
  $r_k = r_k + 1$;
End While

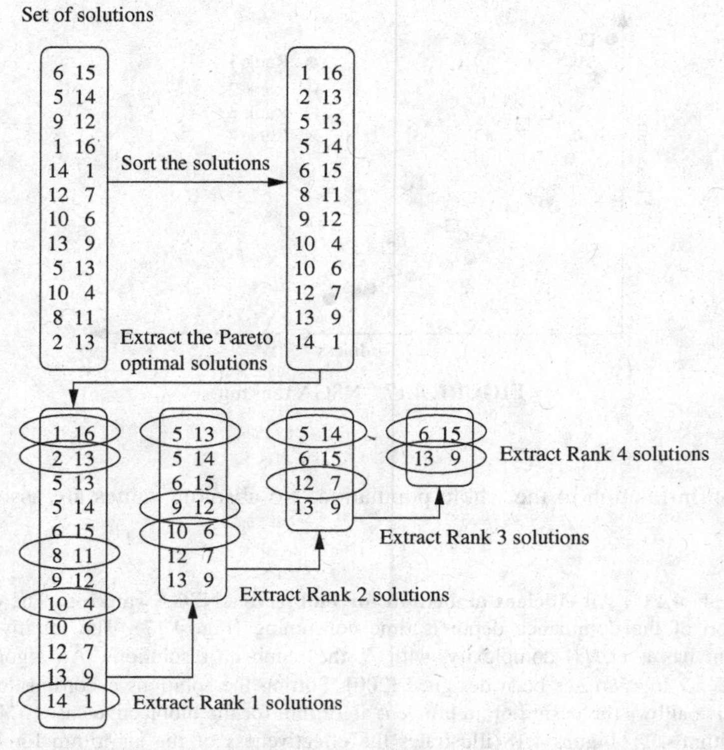

FIGURE 4.18 Efficient NSGA ranking for biobjective MOPs.

is restarted with the remaining solutions. So, the maximum applied comparisons is in $O(N \times \mathrm{Rk}_m)$ with Rk_m the maximum rank given to a solution. In the worst case, Rk_m is equal to N. So the worst complexity of this part of algorithm is $O(N^2)$. However, in general, Rk_m is small in comparison with the number of solutions and experiments show that the ratio between Rk_m and N becomes small when N becomes great. So, the complexity of the algorithm is less than $O(N^2)$ and its average complexity is $O(N \times \log(N) + N \times \mathrm{Rk}_m)$.

Other dominance concepts may be used in the fitness assignment procedure such as the ϵ-dominance concept. For instance, one can also use the following:

- **Guided dominance:** First, a weighted function of the objectives is defined [182]:

$$\Omega_i(f(x)) = f_i(x) + \sum_{j=1, j \neq i}^{n} a_{ij} f_j(x), \quad i = 1, 2, \ldots, n$$

A solution x dominates another solution y, if $\Omega_i(f(x)) \leq \Omega_i(f(y))$ for all $i = 1, 2, \ldots, n$, and the strict inequality occurs at least for one objective

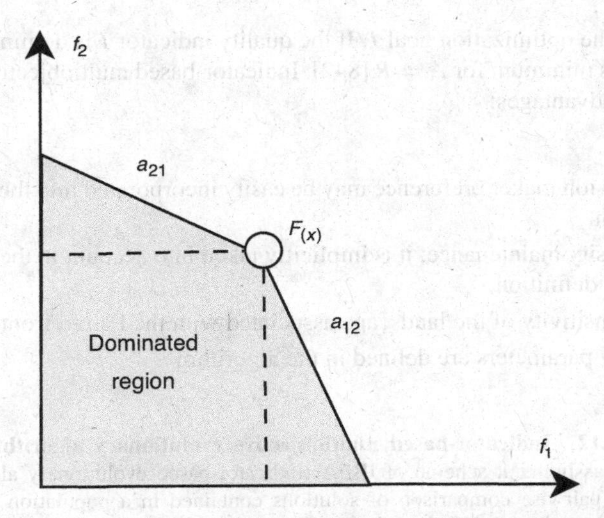

FIGURE 4.19 An example of another domination concept that can be used in dominance-based multiobjective metaheuristics: guided domination.

(Fig. 4.19). Guided domination allows a larger region to become dominated by a single solution than the classical domination.

- **Fuzzy dominance:** The fuzzy dominance concept is based on a fuzzy logic pairwise comparison [247]. The probability of nondominance is related to the margins between the objectives values. The larger the margins, the more significant the probability of nondominance. Hence, the obtained Pareto front is defined with a fuzzy boundary.
- Other domination concepts such as cone dominance concept.

4.4.4 Indicator-Based Approaches

In indicator-based approaches, the search is guided by a performance quality indicator [842]. The optimization goal is given in terms of a binary quality indicator I that can be viewed as an extension of the Pareto dominance relation. A value $I(A, B)$ quantifies the difference in quality between two approximated efficient sets A and B. So, if R denotes a reference set (which can be the Pareto optimal set X_E), the overall optimization goal can be formulated as

$$\arg\min_{A\in\Omega} I(A, R)$$

where Ω represents the space of all efficient set approximations.

The reference set R does not have to be known, it is just required for the formalization of the optimization goal. Since R is fixed, the indicator I actually represents a unary function that assigns a fitness reflecting the quality of each approximation set according to the optimization goal I. If the quality indicator I is dominance preserving, $I(A, R)$ is minimum for $A = R$ [842]. Indicator-based multiobjective algorithms have several advantages:

- The decision maker preference may be easily incorporated into the optimization algorithm.
- No diversity maintenance; it is implicitly taken into account in the performance indicator definition.
- Small sensitivity of the landscape associated with the Pareto front.
- Only few parameters are defined in the algorithm.

Example 4.12 Indicator-based multiobjective evolutionary algorithm (IBEA). The fitness assignment scheme of IBEA (indicator-based evolutionary algorithm) is based on a pairwise comparison of solutions contained in a population by using a binary quality indicator [842]. Indeed, several quality indicators can be used within IBEA (see Section 4.7.1). The binary additive ϵ-indicator, inspired by the concept of ϵ-dominance, is particularly well adapted to indicator-based search and seems to be efficient on different kinds of problems [54,842]. It is capable of obtaining both a well-converged and a well-diversified Pareto set approximation. This indicator computes the minimum value by which a solution $x_1 \in X$ can be translated in the objective space to weakly dominate another solution $x_2 \in X$. For a minimization problem, it is defined as follows:

$$I_{\epsilon+}(x_1, x_2) = \max_{i\in\{1,\ldots,n\}}(f_i(x_1) - f_i(x_2))$$

Furthermore, to evaluate the quality of a solution according to a whole population P and a binary quality indicator I, different approaches exist. For instance, an additive technique that amplifies the influence of solutions mapping to dominating points over solutions mapping to dominated ones that can be outlined as follows [842]:

$$I(P\backslash\{x\}, x) = \sum_{x^* \in P\backslash\{x\}} -e^{\frac{-I(x^*, x)}{\kappa}}$$

where $\kappa > 0$ is a scaling factor.

Algorithm 4.2 illustrates the template of the IBEA algorithm. The selection scheme in IBEA is a binary tournament between randomly chosen individuals. The replacement strategy is an environmental one that consists in deleting, one-by-one, the worst individuals and in updating the fitness values of the remaining solutions each time there is a deletion; this step is iterated until the required population size is reached. Moreover, an archive stores solutions mapping to potentially nondominated solutions, to prevent their loss during the stochastic search process.

Algorithm 4.2 Template of the IBEA algorithm.

Input: α (pop. size), N (max. nb. of generations), κ (fitness scaling factor).
Initialization:
Generate an initial population P of size α ; set the generation counter m to 0 ;
Fitness assignment:
Calculate fitness values of individuals in P, i.e. for all $x^1 \in P$ set:

$$F(x^1) = \sum_{x^2 \in P \backslash x^1} -e^{-I(x^2, x^1)/\kappa}$$

Environmental selection:
Iterate the following 3 steps until the population size P does not exceed α:
Choose an individual $x^* \in P$ with the smallest fitness value, i.e.

$$F(x^*) \leq F(x), \forall x \in P$$

Remove x^* from the population;
Update the fitness values of the remaining individuals, i.e.

$$F(x) = F(x) + e^{-I(x^*, x)/\kappa}, \forall x \in P$$

Termination test:
If $m \geq N$ or another stopping criterion is satisfied **Then**
Set A to the set of non-dominated individuals in P ; Stop.
Mating selection:
Perform binary tournament selection with replacement from P to P' ;
Variation:
Apply recombination and mutation operators to the mating pool P' ;
Add the resulting offspring to P;
Increment the generation counter (m = m + 1) ; Goto fitness assignment step ;
Output: A (Pareto set approximation).

4.5 DIVERSITY PRESERVATION

P-metaheuristics are reputed to be very sensitive to the choice of the initial population and the biased sampling during the search. Diversity loss is then observable in many P-metaheuristics[15]. To face this drawback related to the stagnation of a population, diversity must be maintained in the population. The fitness assignment methods presented previously tend to favor the convergence toward the Pareto optimal front. However, these methods are not able to guarantee that the approximation obtained will be of good quality in terms of diversity, either in the decision or objective space.

[15]This phenomenon is called genetic drift in evolutionary algorithms.

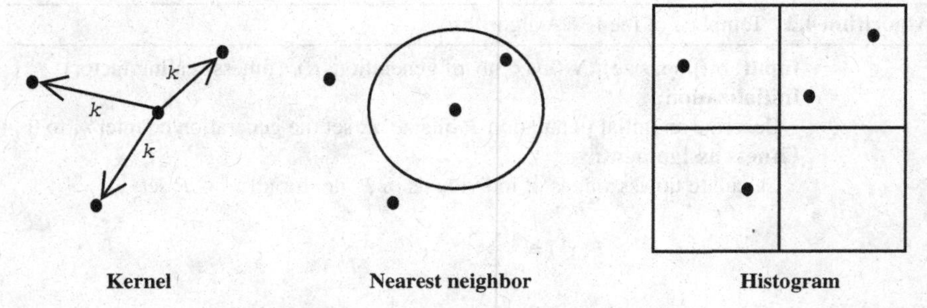

FIGURE 4.20 Diversity maintaining strategies.

Thus, diversity preservation strategies must be incorporated into multiobjective metaheuristics. In general, diversification methods deteriorate solutions that have a high density in their neighborhoods. As suggested in Ref. [843], the diversity preservation methods may be classified into the same categories used in statistical density estimation [704] (see Fig. 4.20).

4.5.1 Kernel Methods

Kernel methods define the neighborhood of a solution i according to a Kernel function K, which takes the distance between solutions as the argument. For a solution i, the distances d_{ij} between i and all other solutions of the population j are computed. The Kernel function $K(d_i)$ is applied to all distances. Then, the density estimate of the solution i is represented by the sum of the Kernel functions $K(d_i)$.

Example 4.13 Fitness sharing. Fitness sharing is the most popular diversification strategy in the evolutionary computation community [331]. It is a kernel method that has been widely used in multiobjective metaheuristics such as MOGA [276], NSGA [715], and NPGA [388].

Fitness sharing consists in degrading the fitness of individuals belonging to search regions with a high density of solutions. The degradation of the fitness of an individual is realized, thanks to a function sh called sharing function [331]. The new fitness $f'(x)$ of an individual x is equal to the original fitness $f(x)$ divided by the sharing counter $m(x)$ (niche count) of the individual:

$$f'(x) = \frac{f(x)}{m(x)}$$

with $m(x) = \sum_{y \in pop} sh(d(x, y))$ where $d(x, y)$ represents the distance between x and y. The sharing function sh is defined as follows:

$$\text{sh}(d(x, y)) = \begin{cases} 1 - \frac{d(x,y)}{\sigma} & \text{if } d(x, y) < \sigma \\ 0 & \text{otherwise} \end{cases}$$

The constant σ represents the nonsimilarity threshold (niche size), that is, the distances from which two individuals x and y are not considered as belonging to the same niche.

Three variants of sharing were developed, depending on how the sharing function is computed: distance in the decision space or the objective space. In general, fitness sharing is performed in the objective space. Indeed, the diversity in MOPs is mainly needed in the objective space. Hence, metaheuristics will have some difficulties in finding multiple Pareto solutions in MOPs where different Pareto optimal solutions in the decision space correspond to the same point in the objective space.

To overcome this problem, a combined sharing approach may be used. In combined sharing, the new fitness $f'(x)$ of an individual x is

$$f'(x) = \frac{f(x)}{m(x)}$$

with

$$m(x) = \sum_{y \in pop} \mathrm{sh}(d_d(x, y), d_o(x, y))$$

where $d_d(x, y)$ represents the distance between x and y in the decision space (the minimal number of mutations that must be applied to x to obtain y) and $d_o(x, y)$ represents the distance between x and y in the objective space (the difference between the fitness of the two solutions on each objective). The sharing function sh is defined as follows:

$$\mathrm{sh} = \begin{cases} 1 - \dfrac{d_d(x, y)}{\sigma_d} & \text{if } d_d(x, y) < \sigma_d \text{ and } d_o(x, y) \geq \sigma_o \\ 1 - \dfrac{d_o(x, y)}{\sigma_o} & \text{if } d_d(x, y) \geq \sigma_d \text{ and } d_o(x, y) < \sigma_o \\ 1 - \dfrac{d_d(x, y) d_o(x, y)}{\sigma_d \sigma_o} & \text{if } d_d(x, y) < \sigma_d \text{ and } d_o(x, y) < \sigma_o \\ 0 & \text{otherwise} \end{cases}$$

The σ_d and σ_o parameters are respectively the niche sizes in the decision space and in the objective space. The effectiveness of the sharing principle depends mainly on these two parameters that must be set carefully. Indeed, diversification becomes inefficient with a low value of σ, but the convergence speed of the front becomes too small when this value is too high.

4.5.2 Nearest-Neighbor Methods

In the nearest-neighbor approach, the distance between a given solution i and its kth nearest neighbors is taken into account to estimate the density of the solution. For instance, this approach is used in the SPEA2 algorithm [845], where the estimator is a function of the inverse of this distance.

Example 4.14 Nondominated sorting genetic algorithm (NSGA-II). One of the most popular evolutionary multiobjective algorithms is the NSGA-II algorithm. Individuals are ranked according to two criteria. First, the solutions are ranked using the nondominance concept; all nondominated solutions of the population are assigned to rank 1, then they are removed from the population. Iteratively, nondominated solutions are determined and assigned the rank 2. This process is iterated until the population is empty. Fig. 4.21a illustrates the results of this ranking procedure. Within a given rank, solutions are ranked again according to the crowding distance. The crowding distance is defined as the circumference of the rectangle defined by its left and right neighbors, and infinity if there is no neighbor. Figure 4.21b illustrates the concept of crowding. Solutions with high crowding distance are considered better solutions, as they introduce more diversity in the population. In Fig. 4.21b, the solutions a and d belonging to the rank 1 in terms of nondominance have the best score in terms of crowding. Then, follows the solutions b and c. The rectangle associated with c is the smallest one.

At each iteration of the algorithm, p offsprings are generated, where p is the population size. The replacement phase of the population works as follows: the old and offspring population are combined and ranked according to the two criteria: nondominance and crowding as shown above. The better half of the union of the two populations form the new population. A binary tournament selection is used, where two solutions are picked randomly from the population. First, the nondominance ranking is used to select the best individuals. If their rankings in terms of nondominance are equal, the crowding criteria are used to select the individual that give the largest crowding distance.

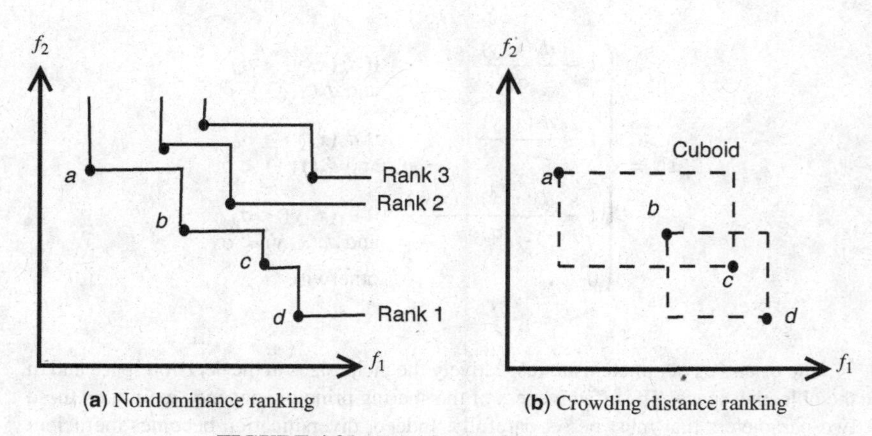

FIGURE 4.21 Ranking method in NSGA-II.

4.5.3 Histograms

The histograms approach consists in partitioning the search space into several hypergrids defining the neighborhoods. The density around a solution is estimated by the number of solutions in the same box of the grid. For instance, this approach is used in the PAES (Pareto archived evolution strategy) algorithm [156]. The hypergrid can be fixed *a priori* (statically) or adaptively during the search with regard to the current population.

One of the most important issues in the diversity preservation approaches is the distance measure. Many metrics can be used. Moreover, the distance may be computed in the decision and/or objective space of the problem. In general, in MOPs, the diversity is preserved in the objective space. However, for some problems, a diversity in the decision space may be important in terms of decision making, and may also improve the search.

4.6 ELITISM

In general terms, elitism consists in archiving the "best" solutions generated during the search (e.g., Pareto optimal solutions). A secondary population, named *archive*, is used to store these high-quality solutions. First, elitism has been used to prevent the loss of the obtained Pareto optimal solutions. In this passive elitism strategy, the archive is considered as a separate secondary population that has no impact on the search process (Fig. 4.22a). Elitism will only guarantee that an algorithm has a monotonically nondegrading performance in terms of the approximated Pareto front. Then, elitism has been used in the search process of multiobjective metaheuristics (active elitism), that is, the archived solutions are used to generate new solutions (Fig. 4.22b). Active elitism allows to achieve faster and robust convergence toward the Pareto front for a better approximation of the Pareto front [545,588,846]. However, a care should be taken to be trapped by a premature convergence if a high-elitist pressure is applied to the generation of new solutions.

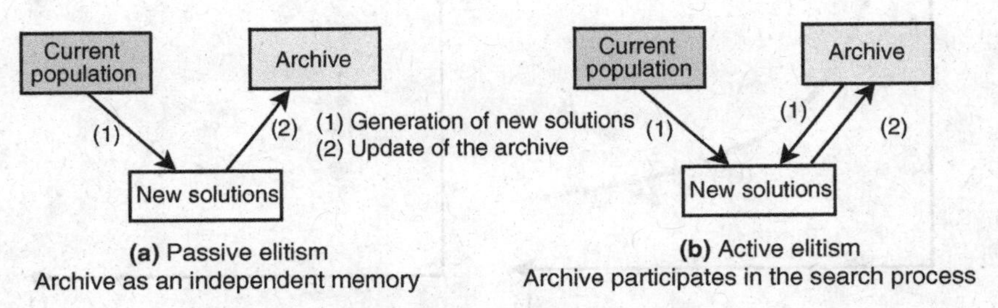

FIGURE 4.22 Elitism in multiobjective metaheuristics.

The archive maintains a set of "good" solutions encountered during the search. The strategy used in updating the archive (elite population) relies on size, convergence, and diversity criteria.

- **Size criteria:** A simple updating strategy consists in storing all Pareto solutions generated during the search (unbounded archive). For some MOP problems, the size of the Pareto set may be very large (infinite number of solutions in continuous MOPs) and then a maximum allowed size for the archive may be fixed. In that case, the convergence and the diversity criteria are used to update the archive.
- **Convergence criteria:** Any fitness assignment procedure may be used to update the archive (e.g., scalar function, dominance based, indicator based). The dominance-based approach is the most used approach, that is, only Pareto optimal solutions compose the archive. However, if the number of Pareto solutions is greater than the size of the archive, another criterion must be used, such as diversity criteria. Otherwise, relaxed forms of dominance may be used. For instance, the ϵ-dominance concept can be used to update the archive [494]. It allows the reduction of both the archive size (i.e., bounded archive) and the computational time to update the archive. It consists in partitioning the objective space into a set of boxes of appropriate size ϵ. For each box, only one nondominated solution is retained (Fig. 4.23). Usually, the number of boxes is logarithmic with respect to the number of objectives. This concept can be destructive for problems where the number of feasible solutions is small.
- **Diversity criteria:** Any diversity preservation approach may be used to update the archive.

Other criteria may be used such as the age of solutions that represents the number of iterations the solution is present in the archive [670]. In general, a combination of both criteria (convergence and diversity) is carried out to update the archive.

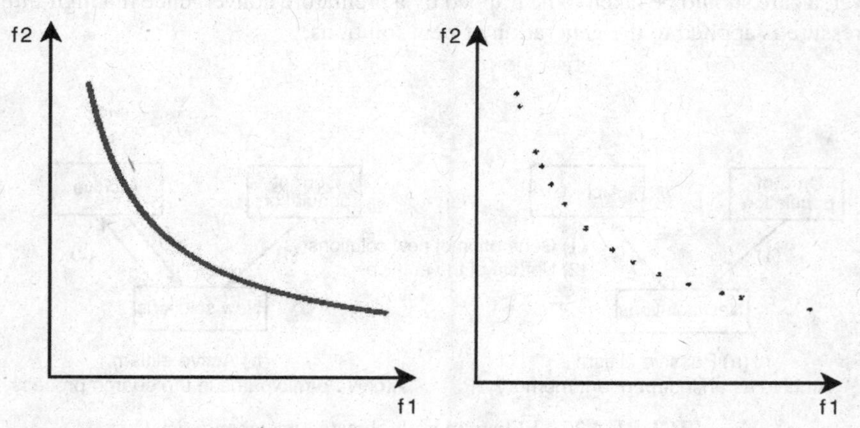

FIGURE 4.23 ϵ-Dominance concept used in updating the archive. In the left figure, the classical dominance is used whereas in the right figure the ϵ-dominance concept is used.

Example 4.15 Elitism in multiobjective evolutionary algorithms. In evolutionary algorithms, the elitism consists in maintaining a secondary population of individuals, different from the current population, which allows to memorize all (or a subset of) the Pareto optimal individuals found during all generations. The elitism is widely used in the selection process. For instance, it consists in carrying out the selection of the individuals as well from the current population as from the archive [545,602]. Then, the archive takes part in the application of the genetic operators (e.g., mutation, crossover).

In SPEA2, the archive is exclusively used to generate new solutions. The algorithm maintains a fixed number of Pareto solutions in a separate archive [846]. This elite archive participates exclusively in the generation of the solutions and is used in the fitness assignment procedure. A clustering algorithm is used to control the cardinality of the archive by maintaining the diversity among the Pareto solutions of the archive. The algorithm uses a density information and nearest-neighbor methods to guide the search.

In the original SPEA algorithm, the fitness is assigned as follows. For each member of the archive, a strength value proportional to the number of solutions this member dominates is computed. Then, the fitness of a solution is obtained according to the strength values of the archive's individuals that dominate it (Fig. 4.24). Moreover, a clustering algorithm is used to keep diversity. The three main aspects in which SPEA2 differ from SPEA are that it incorporates (i) a fine-grained fitness assignment strategy that takes into account the number of individuals that a solution dominates and is dominated by; (ii) a density estimation technique that leads the search process more precisely; and (iii) an enhanced archive truncation method that ensures the preservation of boundary solutions.

Example 4.16 Pareto-based elitist multiobjective particle swarm optimizers. Unlike in monoobjective optimization where a particle has a single leader (i.e., global best

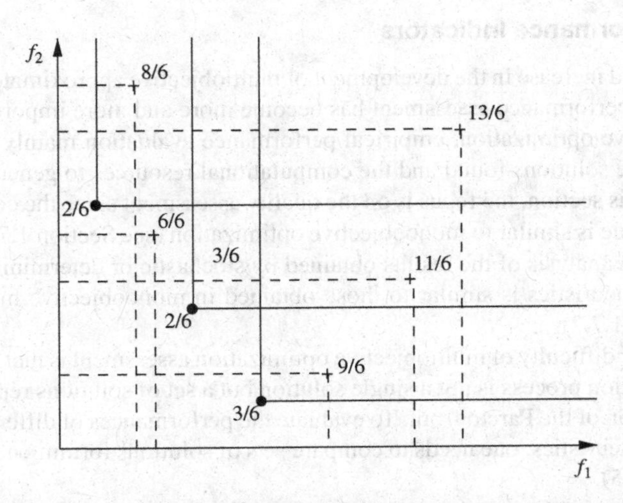

FIGURE 4.24 Fitness assignment in the SPEA algorithm on a biobjective optimization problem. The external population members are shown by circles and the EA population members are shown by crosses.

or local best); in the case of MOPs, each particle may have a set of different leaders from which just one can be selected to update its position [651]. The main issues in designing a multiobjective PSO are the selection and the update of the archive (i.e., leaders). In Pareto-based PSO, the fitness assignment of the leaders is based on the dominance concept. Using elitism, these leaders are stored in an external archive. Moreover, to encourage diversity in the decision and/or the objective space, the fitness assignment of the leaders may be based on density measure strategies that have been used in evolutionary algorithms:

- Nearest-neighbor density estimator [639]. The SPEA2 (resp. NSGA-II) fitness assignment strategy has been used in PSO [379] (resp. [504].
- Kernel density estimator [636,716].
- Histograms [103]. The ϵ-dominance fitness assignment strategy has been used in PSO [567,703].

Then, any stochastic or deterministic selection mechanism (e.g., roulette wheel selection, tournament selection) can be used to select the leaders according to their fitness.

4.7 PERFORMANCE EVALUATION AND PARETO FRONT STRUCTURE

In this section, the performance evaluation of multiobjective metaheuristics and the characterization of the Pareto front structure are outlined.

4.7.1 Performance Indicators

With the rapid increase in the development of multiobjective approximate algorithms, the issue of performance assessment has become more and more important. As with monoobjective optimization, empirical performance evaluation mainly involves the quality of the solutions found and the computational resources to generate these solutions. In this section, the focus is on the quality assessment since the computational resources issue is similar to monoobjective optimization (see Section 1.7). Moreover, the statistical analysis of the results obtained by stochastic or deterministic multiobjective metaheuristics is similar to those obtained in monoobjective metaheuristics (see Section 1.7.2).

The major difficulty of multiobjective optimization assessment is that the output of the optimization process is not a single solution but a set of solutions representing an approximation of the Pareto front. To evaluate the performances of different multiobjective metaheuristics, one needs to compare sets of solutions forming nondominated sets (Fig. 4.25).

Various metrics for nondominated sets have been suggested, but there exists no generally accepted standard for performance evaluation. Quality indicators may be classified using different properties.

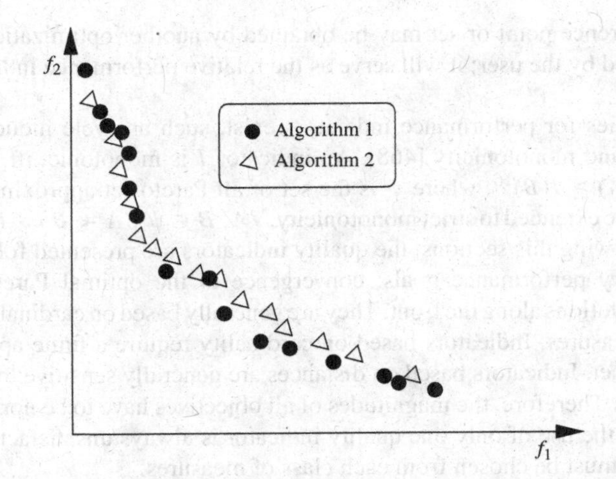

FIGURE 4.25 Comparing two Pareto fronts in a biobjective case. The situation where a set A completely dominates a set B is uncommon. Some solutions of the set A dominates solutions of the set B (and vice versa). Moreover, some solutions of the two sets are incomparable.

- **Unary indicators/binary indicators:** Unary indicators assign to each approximated Pareto front a scalar value: $I : \Omega \longrightarrow \mathbb{R}$ (e.g., generational distance measure, hypervolume I_H) that represents its quality. Some combinations of unary measures can also be used (e.g., average distance to the exact Pareto front, diversity of the obtained Pareto front, and the number of solutions in the approximation [795]). Such combinations may lose important quality information. Unary indicators (or their combination) have some theoretical limitations [233]. There exists no unary indicator that is able to indicate whether an approximation A is better than an approximation B. A single unary performance measure cannot adequately determine the best approximation, as both aspects of convergence and diversity cannot be measured by a single performance metric [233]. In binary indicators, a measure is related to two approximations A and B (e.g., ϵ-quality measure): $I : \Omega \times \Omega \longrightarrow \mathbb{R}$ [360]. Binary performance metrics are better measures for comparing two approximations. Most of the unary indicators may be generalized to binary ones (e.g., hypervolume $I_H(A, B)$, ϵ-indicator).
- **Known Pareto optimal set/unknown Pareto optimal set:** If the exact Pareto set is known, some specific quality indicators may be used [785]. Indeed, the availability of the exact Pareto set allows the definition of good indicators in terms of convergence and diversity. However, in most real-life problems, the exact Pareto set cannot be known.
- **Parameter less/additional parameters:** Some quality indicators need the definition of some parameters (e.g., ideal point, nadir point, reference set, reference front). For instance, some approaches need a reference point (e.g., hypervolume) or a reference set (e.g., ϵ-indicator) to evaluate an approximation front.

The reference point or set may be obtained by another optimization algorithm or defined by the user; it will serve as the relative performance indicator.

Other properties for performance indicators exist, such as cycle inducing, scaling dependence, and monotonicity [468]. An indicator I is monotonic, iff $\forall A, B \in \psi : A \preceq B \Rightarrow I(A) \geq I(B)$[16], where ψ is the set of all Pareto set approximations. This property can be extended to strict monotonicity: $\forall A, B \in \psi : A \prec B \Rightarrow I(A) > I(B)$.

In the following this sections, the quality indicators are presented following their complementary performance goals: convergence to the optimal Pareto front and diversity of solutions along the front. They are generally based on cardinality, distance, or volume measures. Indicators based on cardinality require a finite approximation of the Pareto set. Indicators based on distances are generally sensitive to the scale of the objectives. Therefore, the magnitudes of all objectives have to be normalized. Let us notice that the use of only one quality indicator is always unsatisfactory. At least one indicator must be chosen from each class of measures.

4.7.1.1 Convergence-Based Indicators Convergence metrics evaluate the effectiveness of the solutions in terms of the closeness to the optimal Pareto front. Many convergence-based quality indicators have been proposed in the literature (e.g., contribution, error ratio, distance from reference).

Contribution: The contribution is a cardinality-based binary measure [545,746]. The contribution of an approximation PO_1 relatively to another approximation PO_2 is the ratio of nondominated solutions produced by PO_1 in PO^*, which is the set of Pareto solutions of $PO_1 \cup PO_2$. Let PO be the set of solutions in $PO_1 \cap PO_2$. Let W_1 (resp. W_2) be the set of solutions in PO_1 (resp. PO_2) that dominate some solutions of PO_2 (resp. PO_1). Let L_1 (resp. L_2) be the set of solutions in PO_1 (resp. PO_2) that are dominated by some solutions of PO_2 (resp. PO_1). Let N_1 (resp. N_2) be the noncomparable solutions of PO_1 (resp. PO_2): $N_i = PO_i/(PO \cup W_i \cup L_i)$.

$$\text{Cont}(PO_1/PO_2) = \frac{\frac{\|PO\|}{2} + \|W_1\| + \|N_1\|}{\|PO^*\|}$$

Let us remark that $\|PO^*\| = \|PO\| + \|W_1\| + \|N_1\| + \|W_2\| + \|N_2\|$ and $\text{Cont}(PO_1/PO_2) + \text{Cont}(PO_2/PO_1) = 1$. Figure 4.26 illustrates the calculation of the contribution indicator, comparing two sets of solutions PO_1 and PO_2. Solutions of PO_1 (resp. PO_2) are represented by circles (resp. crosses). The obtained results are $\text{Cont}(PO_1, PO_2) = 0.7$ and $\text{Cont}(PO_2, PO_1) = 0.3$. The contribution metric measures the proportion of Pareto solutions given by each front. Using this metric, the results are easily interpreted. For instance, $\text{Contribution}(A, B) = 0.8$ indicate that 80% of the solutions of the nondominated set of $A \cup B$ are provided by A, and then 20% provided by B. So, this value has to be greater than 0.5 to indicate that A is better than B in terms of convergence to the Pareto front.

[16] The indicator is supposed to be maximized.

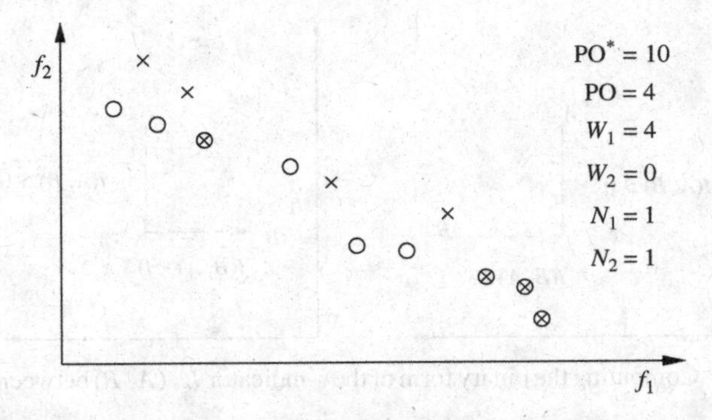

FIGURE 4.26 Computing the contribution between two Pareto fronts PO_1 and PO_2. $\text{Cont}(PO_1, PO_2) = 0.7$ and $\text{Cont}(PO_2, PO_1) = 0.3$.

Generational distance: the generational distance I_{GD} computes the average distance between the approximated set A and a reference set R [795]. The reference set is generally represented by the exact Pareto front PF*. At a given iteration t, the distance between the two sets is averaged over the pairwise minimum distances:

$$I_{GD}^{t}(A, R) = \frac{\left(\sum_{u \in A} (\min_{v \in R} \| F(u) - F(v) \|^2)\right)^{1/2}}{|R|}$$

where the distance represents the Euclidean distance in the objective space. If the approximated front A is included in the reference set A, the generational distance will be equal to 0.

The relative improvement in the search may be approximated by the generational convergence velocity I_{GCV}^{t} as follows [795]:

$$I_{GCV}^{t}(A, R) = \ln \frac{I_{GD}^{1}(A, R)}{I_{GD}^{t}(A, R)^{1/2}}$$

ϵ-Indicator: The unary additive *ϵ-indicator* $I_{\epsilon+}^{1}$, which is a distance-based indicator, gives the minimum factor by which an approximation A has to be translated in the objective space to weakly dominate the reference set Z_N^* [233]. $I_{\epsilon+}^{1}$ can be defined as follows (Fig. 4.27):

$$I_{\epsilon+}^{1}(A) = I_{\epsilon+}(A, Z_N^*)$$

where

$$I_{\epsilon+}(A, B) = \min_{\epsilon \in \mathbb{R}} \{\forall z \in B, \exists z' \in A : z'_i - \epsilon \leq z_i, \forall 1 \leq i \leq n\}$$

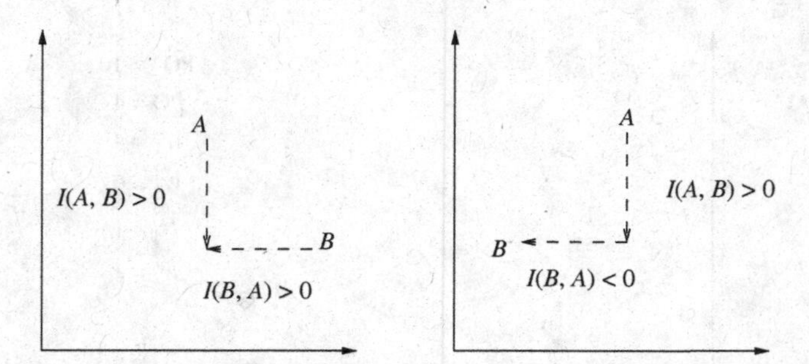

FIGURE 4.27 Computing the binary form of the ϵ-indicator $I_{\epsilon+}(A, B)$ between two solutions.

A negative value for the indicator implies that the approximated set A weakly dominates the reference set Z_N^*. The indicator is monotonic. The complexity of its calculation is relatively reduced, that is, $O(n.|A|.|Z_N^*|)$ where n is the number of objectives.

If the optimal Pareto set PO is known, one may use the following [785]:

- **Cardinality measure:** For instance, the proportion of solutions in the approximation set A that belong to the optimal Pareto set PO:

$$I_{\mathrm{p}}(A, \mathrm{PO}) = \frac{|A \cap \mathrm{PO}|}{|\mathrm{PO}|}$$

- **Distance measure:** Such a measure may be the average Euclidean distance of the approximation A to the optimal Pareto set PO:

$$I_{\mathrm{ad}}(A, \mathrm{PO}) = \frac{\sum_{u \in A} \min_{v \in \mathrm{PO}}(\| F(u) - F(v) \|)}{|\mathrm{PO}|}$$

4.7.1.2 Diversity-Based Indicators Diversity indicators measure the uniformity of distribution of the obtained solutions in terms of dispersion and extension. In general, the diversity is researched in the objective space. Diversity measures are generally nonmonotonic and they involve a higher computational cost compared to convergence indicators; at least a quadratic complexity function of the size of the approximated set is obtained (Table 4.1). In these class of metrics, one can find spread, spacing, and the entropy.

Spread: The spread indicator I_{S} combines the distribution and cardinality to measure the dispersion of the approximated set A [841]:

$$I_{\mathrm{S}} = \frac{\sum_{u \in A} |\{u' \in A : \| F(u) - F(u') \| > \sigma\}|}{|A| - 1}$$

where $\sigma > 0$ is a neighborhood parameter. The closer is the measure to 1, the better is the spread of the approximated set A.

Extent: a metric taking into account the extent of the Pareto approximation A may be defined as follows:

$$I_{\text{ex}}(A) = \left(\sum_{i=1}^{n} (\max_{u,u' \in A} \parallel f_i(u) - f_i(u') \parallel) \right)^{1/2}$$

where $\|.\|$ is a metric distance (e.g., Euclidean distance).

Entropy: The entropy measure, originally used in information theory, is a natural indicator of diversity in a population [545,746]. The objective space is partitioned into μ^n equal-sized hypergrids (i.e., niches, clusters), each objective is divided into μ intervals. Each grid is a hypercube of dimension n; it is defined as the indifferent region, that is, the region where any two solutions are considered as equivalent. Then, the entropy indicator measures the dispersion of the solutions around these hypergrids. Let PO_1 and PO_2 be two sets of solutions, PO^* be the set of Pareto solutions of $\text{PO}_1 \cup \text{PO}_2$, N_i be the cardinality of solutions of $\text{PO}_1 \cup \text{PO}^*$ that are in the niche of the ith solution of $\text{PO}_1 \cup \text{PO}^*$. Let n_i be the cardinality of solutions of PO_1 that are in the niche of the ith solution of $\text{PO}_1 \cup \text{PO}^*$, Cd be the cardinality of $\text{PO}_1 \cup \text{PO}^*$. Let $\gamma = \sum_{i=1}^{\text{Cd}} (1/N_i)$ be the sum of the coefficients of each solution. The more concentrated is a region of the solution space, the lower is the coefficients of its solutions. Then, the following formula is applied to evaluate the entropy E of PO_1, relatively to the space occupied by PO^*:

$$E(\text{PO}_1, \text{PO}_2) = \frac{-1}{\log(\gamma)} \sum_{i=1}^{\text{Cd}} \left(\frac{1}{N_i} \frac{n_i}{\text{Cd}} \log \frac{n_i}{\text{Cd}} \right)$$

This indicator may be generalized to a unary one. An approximation A has a good diversity if every solution of A belongs to a different hypergrid (i.e., maximal entropy equal to 1).

4.7.1.3 Hybrid Indicators

Some quality indicators combine convergence and diversity measures (e.g., hypervolume, R-metrics).

Hypervolume: in its unary form, the *hypervolume* indicator I_H associated with an approximation A is given by the volume of the objective space portion that is weakly dominated by the set A [847]. This intuitive quality indicator needs the specification of a reference point Z_{ref} that denotes an upper bound over all the objectives (Fig. 4.28). In its binary form, computing the hypervolume metric needs a reference set Z_N^*. It represents the hypervolume dominated by Z_N^* and not by A (Fig. 4.28). The more this binary measure is close to 0, the better is the approximation S. In general, the reference set Z_N^* may be the optimal Pareto front or extracted from the union of all obtained fronts. The choice of the reference point affects the ordering of nondominated sets. The reference point Z_{ref} may be fixed as $(1.05 \times Z_1^{\max}, \ldots, 1.05 \times Z_n^{\max})$ where $Z_i^{\max}$ represents the upper bound of the objective i obtained from the reference set. The unary hypervolume indicator is strictly monotonic but needs a

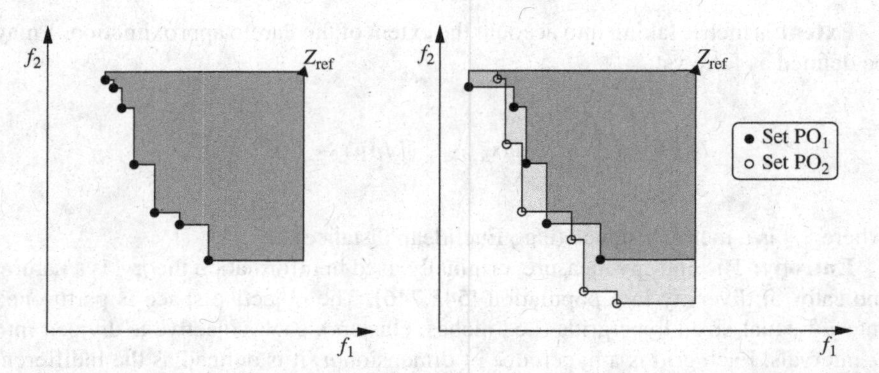

FIGURE 4.28 Unary versus binary hypervolume indicator for a nondominated approximation set of solutions. The binary hypervolume indicator is computed for two Pareto sets of solutions PO_1 and PO_2.

high computational cost, that is, it has an exponential complexity in the number of objectives.

R-metrics: Computing of R-metrics is based on a set of utility functions u [360]. Suppose that the preferences of the decision maker are given in terms of a parameterized utility function u_λ and the corresponding set of parameters Λ. As an example, the utility function u_λ may be defined by a weighted sum of the objectives, where $\lambda = (\lambda_1, \lambda_2, \ldots, \lambda_n) \in \Lambda$. The set Λ contains a sufficiently large number of uniformly dispersed normalized weight combinations λ where $\lambda_i \geq 0$ and $\sum_{i=1}^{n} \lambda_i = 1$. Then, there exist several ways to transform the utility functions to a performance indicator. For instance, the R_2 and R_3 indicators can be defined as follows:

$$I_{R_2}(A, B) = \frac{\sum_{\lambda \in \Lambda} u^*(\lambda, A) - u^*(\lambda, B)}{|\Lambda|}$$

$$I_{R_3}(A, B) = \frac{\sum_{\lambda \in \Lambda} [u^*(\lambda, B) - u^*(\lambda, A)]/u^*(\lambda, B)}{|\Lambda|}$$

where u^* represents the maximum value of the utility function u_λ using the weight vector λ and the Pareto approximation A:

$$u^*(\lambda, A) = \max_{x \in A}\{u_\lambda(f(x))\}$$

The R-metrics can be transformed into a unary form by replacing one set by a reference set R: $I^1_{R_2}(A) = I_{R_2}(A, R)$ and $I^1_{R_3}(A) = I_{R_3}(A, R)$. Many utility functions may be used [360]:

- **Weighted linear function:**

$$u_\lambda(z) = -\sum_{i=1}^{n} \lambda_i |z_i^* - z_i|$$

where z^* represents the ideal point or any point that weakly dominates all points of the corresponding Pareto front approximation. Using the weighted linear function, the points that are not in the convex hull of the approximated front will not be rewarded. Nonlinear functions such as Tchebycheff function can be used to avoid this situation.

- **Weighted Tchebycheff function:**

$$u_\lambda(z) = -\max_{i\in[1,n]}\{\lambda_i |z_i^* - z_i|\}$$

Using the weighted Tchebycheff function, the utility of a point and one that weakly dominates it will be the same. Augmented Tchebycheff functions are used to avoid this situation.

- **Augmented Tchebycheff function:**

$$u_\lambda(z) = -(\max_{i\in[1,n]}\{\lambda_i |z_i^* - z_i|\} + \varphi \sum_{i=1}^{n} \lambda_i |z_i^* - z_i|)$$

where φ is a small positive real number.

Table 4.1 summarizes the characteristics of the presented performance indicators: goal achieved by the indicator (convergence or diversity), monotonicity property,

TABLE 4.1 Main Characteristics of Performance Indicators in Multiobjective Optimization

Indicator	Goal	Monotone	Complexity	Parameter	[], Min–Max
Contribution	Conv.	Mon.	$O(\|A\|.\|R\|)$	Ref. set	[0, 1], Max
Gen. Dist.	Conv.	No	$O(\|A\|.\|R\|)$	Ref. set	$[0, \infty)$, Min
ϵ-indicator	Conv.	Mon.	$O(n.\|A\|.\|R\|)$	Ref. set	$[0, \infty)$, Min
I_p	Conv.	Mon.	$O(\|A\|.\|PO\|)$	Opt. set	[0, 1], Max
I_{ad}	Conv.	No	$O(\|A\|.\|PO\|)$	Opt. set	$[0, \infty)$, Min
Spread	Div.	No	$O(\|A\|^2)$	—	[0, 1], Min
Extent	Div.	No	$O(\|A\|^2)$	—	$[0, \infty)$, Max
B. Entropy	Div.	No	$O((\|R\| + \|A\|).\mu^n)$	Ref. set,μ	[0, 1], Max
U. Entropy	Div.	No	$O((\|A\|.\mu^n)$	μ	[0, 1], Max
Hypervolume	Hybrid	Strict	$O(\|A\|^n)$	Ref. point	$[0, \infty)$, Max
R-metrics	Hybrid	Mon.	$O(n.\|\Lambda\|.\|A\|.\|R\|)$	Ref. set ideal point	$[0, \infty)$, Min

complexity of its computation, information required for its calculation, the range of its values, and the objective that consists in minimizing or maximizing the indicator.

4.7.2 Landscape Analysis of Pareto Structures

The structure of the landscape of a Pareto front can provide useful information to the decision maker. It also defines the difficulty of a MOP relatively to a given class of optimization algorithms. Then, it can guide the user for a better design of a multiobjective metaheuristic. The Pareto front (or Pareto set) structure can be characterized in different ways:

- **Convex versus concave structure:** The metaheuristic performances differ according to whether the structure of the Pareto front is convex or concave. A MOP is defined to be convex if the feasible objective space is convex, or the feasible decision space is convex and the objective functions are quasi-convex with at least one strictly quasi-convex function [555]. In convex MOPs, any local Pareto optimal solution is a global Pareto optimal solution. For instance, the use of a weighted aggregation method is more effective when the structure of the Pareto front is convex than if the structure is concave (existence of nonsupported Pareto optimal solutions).

  Moreover, the fitness assignment procedures based on dominance may have an important effect on the results, according to whether the structure of the Pareto front is convex or concave [193]. In some population-based metaheuristics, the fitness of a solution is proportional to the number of solutions it dominates [846]. This ranking procedure supports the compromised Pareto solutions, if the Pareto border is convex. The algorithm tends to find more compromised solutions than solutions at the extremities of the Pareto front. This tendency does not arise if the Pareto border is concave.

  To measure the Pareto front convexity, one can make a distinction between the supported solutions and the nonsupported solutions. Let PO be the set of supported solutions. In a biobjective optimization problem, the nonsupported solutions belong to the triangles built by two close supported solutions (Fig. 4.5). These triangles are thus regions of existence of nonsupported solutions. The indicator Conv, which characterizes the convexity of the Pareto set, represents the proportion of supported solution of the Pareto front: $\text{Conv} = \frac{|SPO|}{|PO|}$. Computing the proportion of supported solutions is not sufficient. One has to also measure their diversity over the Pareto front using, for instance, the entropy indicator. Figure 4.29 illustrates the importance of analyzing the distribution of nonsupported solutions. For the first instance, there are only two supported solutions that are represented by the extreme solutions.

- **Continuous versus discontinuous structure:** The discontinuity of the Pareto set may be a hard task to tackle with S-metaheuristics that are based on the concept of neighborhoods. Let us introduce the concept of *efficient graph*, where the

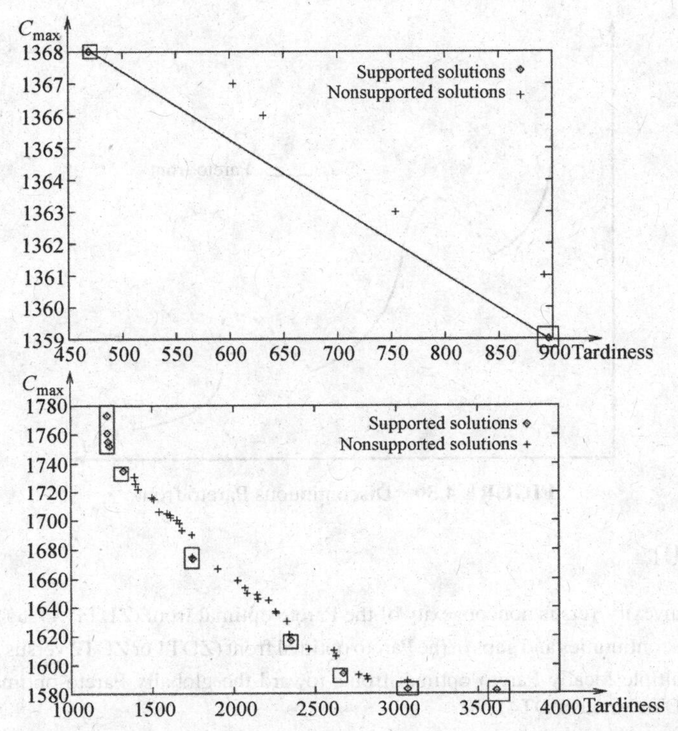

FIGURE 4.29 Distribution of supported solution on an optimal Pareto front. Instance of a biobjective permutation flow-shop where the makespan C_{max} and total tardiness T have to be minimized with (20 jobs, 5 machines) and (20 jobs, 10 machines) [499].

nodes represent the Pareto solutions and the arcs represent their neighborhood structure. The efficiency of S-metaheuristics depends on the connexity of the efficient graph [239].

The performance of diversity preservation strategies is also sensitive to the discontinuity and nonuniformity of the Pareto front (Fig. 4.30). In this case, even if some Pareto solutions can be found in each Pareto region, the competition between the solutions does not encourage the exploration of the whole solutions. Adaptive diversification parameters must be considered.

- **Multimodal and deceptive structures:** The multimodal structure of the Pareto front rises from the existence of locally Pareto optimal solutions. The multi-modality raises difficulties for the convergence through the optimal Pareto set PO. Some S-metaheuristics escaping from local optima have to be used (e.g., tabu search, simulated annealing, VNS) (see Chapter 2).

Example 4.17 ZDT benchmarks. ZDT test instances for continuous optimization MOPs have been constructed following different landscape structures of the Pareto

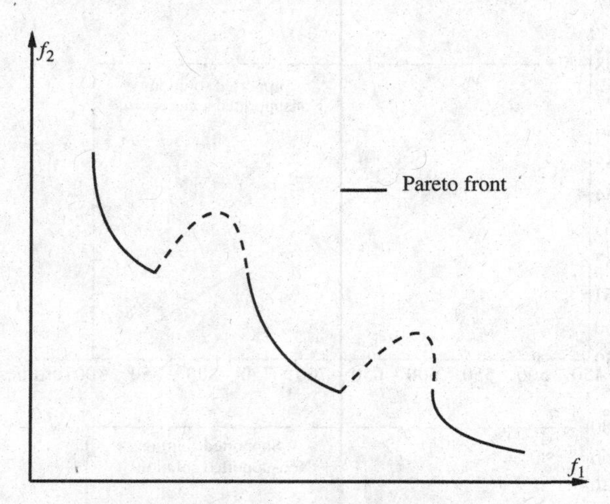

FIGURE 4.30 Discontinuous Pareto front.

front [841]:

- Convexity versus nonconvexity of the Pareto optimal front (ZDT1 versus ZDT2).
- Discontinuities and gaps in the Pareto optimal front (ZDT1 or ZDT2 versus ZDT3).
- Multiple locally Pareto optimal fronts toward the globally Pareto optimal front (ZDT1 versus ZDT4).
- Isolation and deception of the globally Pareto optimal front (ZDT1 versus ZDT5).
- Nonuniform density of solutions across the Pareto optimal front (ZDT2 versus ZDT6).

Example 4.18 Multiobjectivization. Multiobjectivization may be viewed as a way to improve the search of a monoobjective optimization problem by extending its formulation to a multiobjective one. For instance, if the landscape associated with a monoobjective optimization problem is characterized by a high multimodality (ruggedness) or flat networks (plateaus), its transformation into a multiobjective problem may improve the search by reducing the complexity of the original problem. Indeed, the multiobjectivization will transform the landscape of the problem into a smoother one in which the application of metaheuristics will be more efficient. Two main strategies are applied:

- **Objective function decomposition:** This strategy consists in partitioning the original objective function into several subobjectives. The subobjectives may be defined over a subset of the decision variables. This decomposition process will separate the potentially conflicting goals of the monoobjective function and will then reduce the number of local optima associated with the problem [470,766].
- **Helper objectives:** This strategy consists in adding new objectives. The added objectives are generally correlated with the primary objective function [411,580]. These new secondary objectives may be viewed as helper objectives whose introduction will reduce the difficulty of the original monoobjective problem. For

instance, in a landscape characterized by neutral networks (i.e., plateaus), adding helper objectives may break those plateaus into smooth networks in which the search is more easy for any metaheuristic. For instance, the reduction of a well-known difficulty in genetic programming, called the "bloating," by minimizing the size of programs as an additional objective may help to find better solutions with more compact program (i.e., reduce the effect caused by bloating) [80,189]. The proposed approach considers the program size as a second independent objective besides the program functionality.

Multiobjectivization has to satisfy the following property [470]:

$$\forall x^* \in S, \exists x_E \in \mathrm{PO} : x_E = x^*$$

where x^* is the global optimal solution of the monoobjective problem, PO is the Pareto optimal set of the associated multiobjective problem, and S is the feasible set of solutions. It means that a Pareto optimal solution x_E has to be the global optimal solution according to the original monoobjective problem.

4.8 MULTIOBJECTIVE METAHEURISTICS UNDER ParadisEO

A software framework for multiobjective metaheuristics is usually intended to be generic and could then be useful only if some important criteria are fulfilled. Hence, in addition to the identified goals of a software framework for monoobjective metaheuristics (see Section 1.8.2), a software framework for multiobjective metaheuristics must satisfy the following criteria:

- **Utility:** The framework must cover a wide range of features related to multiobjective metaheuristics (e.g., scalarization methods, Pareto-based approaches, indicator-based approaches).
- **Code and design reuse:** In terms of design, the framework must provide a whole unified architecture of the different approaches (e.g., fitness assignment, diversity preserving, elitism). This goal also requires a clear and maximal conceptual distinction between the algorithm design and the problem definitions. The designer must, therefore, write only the minimal problem-specific code and the development process of the algorithm should be done in an incremental way. In terms of code, the framework must allow the programmer to rewrite code as little as possible. Everything that is already coded might be reusable. Then, it must be a commonplace to extend a problem from the monoobjective (e.g., MO and EO frameworks) to the multiobjective case (e.g., MOEO framework), and from the sequential and pure metaheuristics to hybrid and parallel metaheuristics (e.g., PEO, see Chapters 5 and 6) without reimplementing the whole algorithm. For instance, it should not be necessary to recode the neighborhoods, variation operators, solution, population initialization, and so on.

- **Extensibility, adaptability, and flexibility:** New features for some search components must be easily added or modified without involving other search components. Furthermore, existing search components must be adaptable, in practice, to the existing as well as evolving problems. Hence, the framework must be white box; users must have access to source code and must use inheritance or specialization concepts of object-oriented programming to derive new components from base or abstract classes.

4.8.1 Software Frameworks for Multiobjective Metaheuristics

Many software frameworks dedicated to multiobjective metaheuristics have been developed. However, very few reached all the goals stated above. Table 4.2 shows a nonexhaustive comparison study between some existing software frameworks or libraries for multiobjective metaheuristics: TEA [243], PISA [81], Open BEAGLE [290], MOMHLib++, MOEA-Matlab [764], and MALLBA [22]. The frameworks are described according to the following criteria: available metaheuristics, framework type (black box or white box), availability of hybridization features, availability of parallel features, and programming language. All the frameworks are open source except MOEA, which is based on Matlab that is not an open source. Moreover, a large part of these frameworks are white box frameworks. Even so, only a few includes all the most popular S-metaheuristics, P-metaheuristics, and performance indicators. Parallel and hybrid features for S-metaheuristics and P-metaheuristics are provided only by ParadisEO and MALLBA. Furthermore, even if these two frameworks are portable on distributed-memory and shared-memory parallel machines, ParadisEO offers more flexibility and is the only one portable on grid computing platforms (see Chapter 6). Many indicators are available under the ParadisEO, PISA,

TABLE 4.2 Main Characteristics of some Software Frameworks for Multiobjective Metaheuristics

Framework/ Library	Meta	Type	Metrics	Hybrid	Parallel	Language
ParadisEO	S-meta P-meta	White	Many	Yes	Yes	C++
TEA	EA	White	No	No	Yes	C++
PISA	EA	Black	Many	No	No	Any
O. BEAGLE	EA	White	No	Yes	Yes	C++
MOMHLib++	EA,LS,SA	White	Many	Yes	No	C++
MOEA–Matlab	EA	Black	No	No	Yes	Matlab
MALLBA	S-meta P-meta	White	No	Yes	Yes	C++

S-meta: S-metaheuristics; P-meta: P-metaheuristics; White: white box software; Black: black box software; LS: local search; SA: simulated annealing; EA: evolutionary algorithms.

and MOMHLib++ frameworks (e.g., coverage, R-metrics, ϵ-indicator, hypervolume, contribution, entropy, generational distance).

ParadisEO–MOEO provides a flexible and modular framework to design multiobjective metaheuristics. The implementation of ParadisEO–MOEO is conceptually divided into fine-grained components. On each level of its architecture, a set of abstract classes is proposed and a wide range of concrete classes are already provided. But, as the framework aims to be extensible, flexible, and easily adaptable, all its components are generic to provide a modular architecture allowing to quickly and conveniently develop any new scheme with a minimum code writing. The goal is to follow new strategies coming from the literature and, if need be, to provide any additional components required for their implementation. Also, ParadisEO–MOEO constantly evolves and new features might be added to the framework regularly to provide a wide range of efficient and modern concepts and to reflect the most recent academic advances in the MOP field.

This section gives a detailed description of the MOP-dependent components provided within the MOEO module of ParadisEO to design a whole efficient multiobjective metaheuristic. The flexibility of the framework and its modular architecture around the three main search components (fitness assignment, diversity preservation, elitism) allow the design of multiobjective metaheuristics in solving various MOPs. For instance, some popular EMO algorithms (e.g., NSGA-II, IBEA, SPEA2) have been designed in an easy way by simply transforming the three search components.

4.8.2 Common Components

4.8.2.1 Representation A solution of a MOP problem needs to be represented both in the decision space and in the objective space. In the monoobjective case, a single value is usually used for the representation in the unidimensional objective space. For MOPs, where the criterion space is multidimensional, a tuple of n values (called *objective vector*) might be used for such a representation.

Using ParadisEO–MOEO, the first thing is to set the number of objectives for the problem under consideration and for each one to indicate if it has to be minimized or maximized. This can be done using the static class `moeoObjectiveVectorTraits`. Then, a class templatized with the last one and inheriting of `moeoObjectiveVector` have to be created for the formulation of an objective vector, as illustrated in Fig. 4.31. Besides, as a majority of MOPs deal with real-coded objective values, a class modeling real-coded objective vectors is already proposed within ParadisEO–MOEO.

As already noticed, an important issue about the design of metaheuristics for MOP is the concept of convergence and diversity. To every solution is assigned a *fitness*[17] value representing its quality in terms of convergence and a *diversity* value

[17] In the multiobjective case, the word "fitness" is not employed in the same sense than it is in the monoobjective case (and in ParadisEO–EO), where it usually denotes the (single) objective value of a solution.

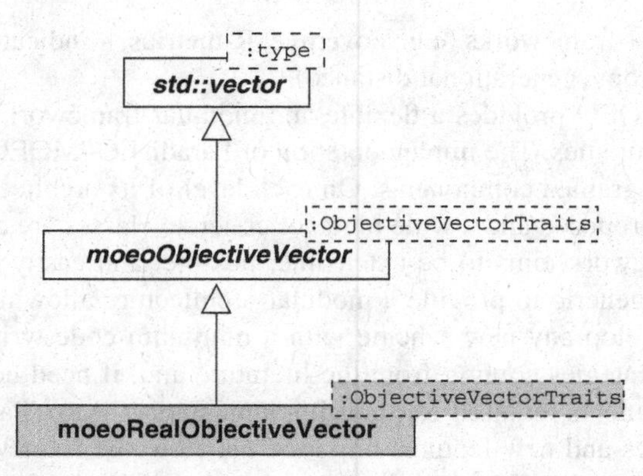

FIGURE 4.31 Core classes for the representation of a solution in the objective space.

representing its quality in terms of diversity (in the decision space and/or in the objective space).

The class used to represent a whole solution within ParadisEO–MOEO is then templatized within an objective vector type, a fitness type, and a diversity type, and it must define its representation in the decision space, which fully depends on the tackled problem. At the implementation level, the way to do so is to extend the `MOEO` class to be used for a specific problem. This modeling tends to be applicable for every kind of problems with the aim of being as general as possible. But ParadisEO–MOEO also provides easy-to-use classes for standard vector-based representations and, in particular, implementations for vectors composed of bits or of real-coded values that can thus directly be used in a ParadisEO–MOEO-designed application. These classes are summarized in Fig. 4.32 using the UML notation. Some standard variation mechanisms are provided within the ParadisEO–EO module and can thus directly be used for such representations.

4.8.2.2 Fitness Assignment Schemes There exists a huge number of different ways to assign fitness values to a set of solutions. Following the taxonomy introduced in this chapter, the fitness assignment schemes are classified into four main categories within ParadisEO–MOEO, as illustrated in Fig. 4.33:

- **Scalar**: `moeoScalarFitnessAssignment`.
- **Criterion based**: `moeoCriterionBasedFitnessAssignment`.
- **Pareto based**: `moeoParetoBasedFitnessAssignment`.
- **Indicator based**: `moeoIndicatorBasedFitnessAssignment`.

The details of the concrete features of ParadisEO–MOEO for fitness assignment schemes are listed below. The most common fitness assignment strategies are implemented: scalarization approaches (e.g., achievement functions), criterion-based approaches, Pareto-based approaches (e.g., MOGA, NSGA, SPEA), and indicator-

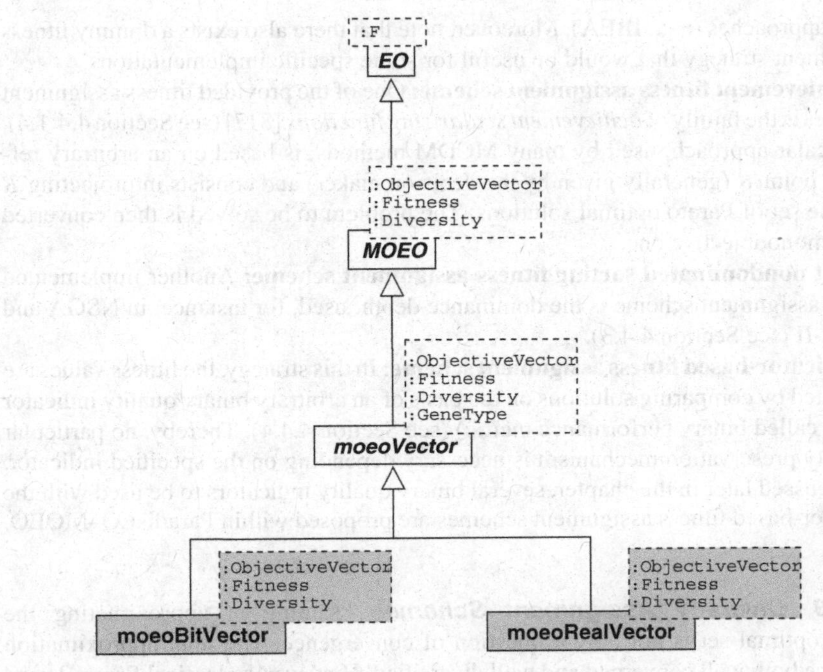

FIGURE 4.32 Core classes for the representation of a solution.

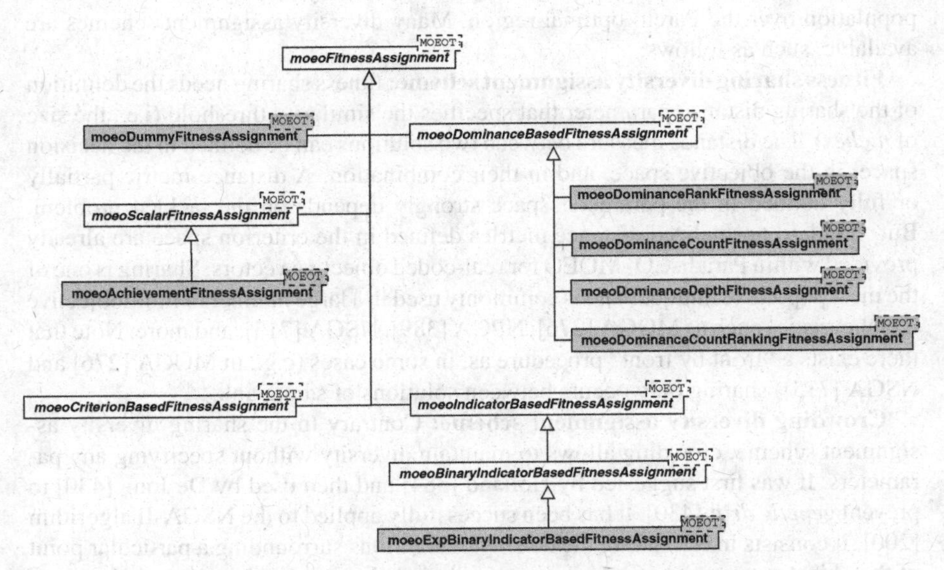

FIGURE 4.33 Core classes for fitness assignment schemes.

based approaches (e.g., IBEA). Moreover, note that there also exists a dummy fitness assignment strategy that would be useful for some specific implementations.

Achievement fitness assignment scheme: One of the provided fitness assignment schemes is the family of *achievement scalarizing functions* [817] (see Section 4.4.1.4). This scalar approach, used by many MCDM methods, is based on an arbitrary reference point R (generally given by the decision maker) and consists in projecting R onto the set of Pareto optimal solutions. The problem to be solved is then converted into a monoobjective one.

Fast nondominated sorting fitness assignment scheme: Another implemented fitness assignment scheme is the dominance depth, used, for instance, in NSGA and NSGA-II (see Section 4.4.3).

Indicator-based fitness assignment scheme: In this strategy, the fitness values are computed by comparing solutions on the basis of an arbitrary binary quality indicator I (also called binary performance metric) (see Section 4.4.4). Thereby, no particular diversity preservation mechanism is necessary depending on the specified indicator. As discussed later in the chapter, several binary quality indicators to be used with the indicator-based fitness assignment schemes are proposed within ParadisEO–MOEO.

4.8.2.3 Diversity Assignment Schemes Aiming at approximating the Pareto optimal set is not only a question of convergence. The final approximation has to be both well converged and well diversified. However, a classical Pareto-based fitness assignment scheme often tends to produce premature convergence by favoring nondominated solutions, what does not guarantee a uniformly sampled output set. To prevent that, a diversity-maintaining mechanism is usually employed to distribute the population over the Pareto optimal region. Many diversity assignment schemes are available, such as follows:

Fitness sharing diversity assignment scheme: fitness sharing needs the definition of the sharing distance parameter that specifies the similarity threshold (i.e., the size of *niches*). The distance measure between two solutions can be defined in the decision space, in the objective space, and in their combination. A distance metric partially or fully defined in the parameter space strongly depends on the tackled problem. But, standard normalized distance metrics defined in the criterion space are already provided within ParadisEO–MOEO for real-coded objective vectors. Sharing is one of the most popular techniques and is commonly used in a large number of multiobjective metaheuristics such as MOGA [276], NPGA [389], NSGA [715], and more. Note that there exists a "front by front" procedure as, in some cases (e.g., in MOGA [276] and NSGA [715]) sharing only occurs between solutions of same rank.

Crowding diversity assignment scheme: Contrary to the sharing diversity assignment scheme, crowding allows to maintain diversity without specifying any parameters. It was first suggested by Holland [384] and then used by De Jong [430] to prevent *genetic drift* [430]. It has been successfully applied to the NSGA-II algorithm [200]. It consists in estimating the density of solutions surrounding a particular point of the objective space. As previously, a similar mechanism working on subclasses of solutions is also provided within ParadisEO–MOEO (Fig. 4.34).

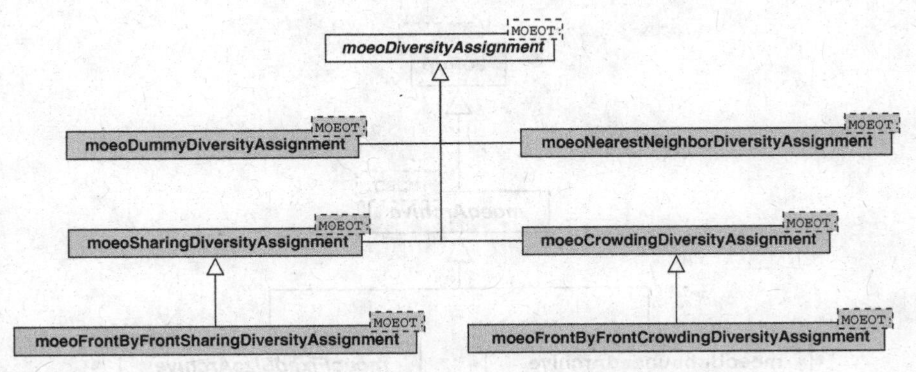

FIGURE 4.34 Core classes for diversity assignment schemes.

4.8.2.4 Elitism Another essential point about Pareto-based resolution is the concept of *elitism*. The concept is very popular since the end of the nineties and is used in a majority of recent MOMHs [467,844]. It consists in maintaining an external set, the so-called *archive*, that allows to store all the non-dominated or the most preferred solutions found during the search. This archive mainly aims at preventing these solutions from being lost during the (often stochastic) optimization process. As shown in Fig. 4.35, in terms of implementation, an archive is an unbounded population using a particular dominance relation to update its contents. The Pareto dominance criterion is the most commonly employed and is used as default, but ParadisEO–MOEO also gives the opportunity to use any other dominance relation (as shown in Fig. 4.36). The archive is basically used as an external storage. The next section will show that its members can also be included during the selection phase of an EMO algorithm.

4.8.2.5 Statistical Tools Some useful statistical tools are also provided within ParadisEO–MOEO. It is, for instance, possible to save the contents of the archive at each iteration, so that the evolution of the nondominated set can be observed or studied using graphical tools such as GUIMOO[18]. Furthermore, an important issue in MOO is the performance analysis, commonly done by using performance metrics. As shown in Fig. 4.37, a couple of metrics are featured within ParadisEO–MOEO. Some are used to quantify the quality of a Pareto set (or a solution), while others are used for pairwise comparisons (between two Pareto sets or two solutions). The *entropy* [56] and the *contribution* [545] metrics are both already implemented and can thus be used to compare two sets of solutions. Moreover, it is possible to compare the current archive with the archive of the previous iteration using a binary metric, and to print the progression of this measure iteration after iteration. Besides, some metrics for pairwise comparison of solutions (that are then usable with the binary indicator-based fitness assignment schemes) are proposed, such as the additive

[18]GUIMOO is a graphical user interface for multiobjective optimization available at `http://guimoo.gforge.inria.fr/`.

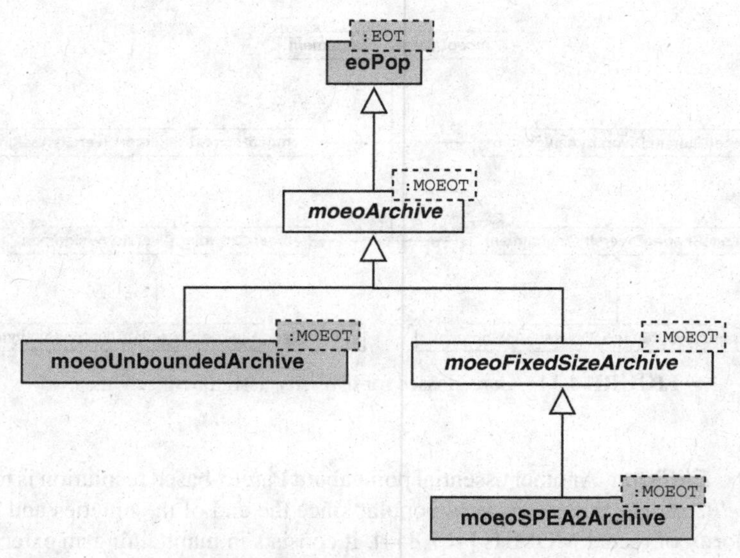

FIGURE 4.35 Core classes for archiving.

ϵ-indicator and the *hypervolume* indicator. Of course, other metrics can easily be implemented.

4.8.3 Multiobjective EAs-Related Components

As a multiobjective P-metaheuristic differs from a monoobjective one only in a few aspects, many of the ParadisEO–EO components are reusable within ParadisEO–MOEO. The reader is referred to Section 3.8 for more details about the multiobjective independent components of ParadisEO. Using these two modules (namely, ParadisEO–EO and ParadisEO–MOEO), it is possible to build a complete and efficient multiobjective optimization solver. Generally speaking, the two main differences between a multiobjective and a monoobjective P-metaheuristic appear during the fitness assignment and diversity preserving phases of the algorithms. For instance, as the representation in the objective space does not correspond to a scalar value in the multiobjective case, ParadisEO–EO's selection and replacement schemes of evolutionary

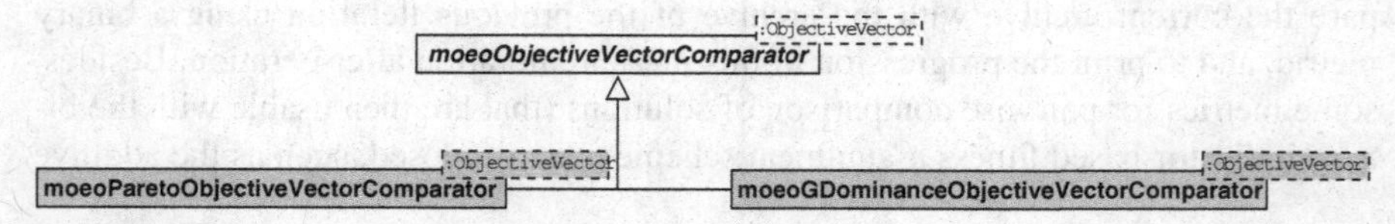

FIGURE 4.36 Core classes for dominance relations (used for a pairwise objective vector comparison).

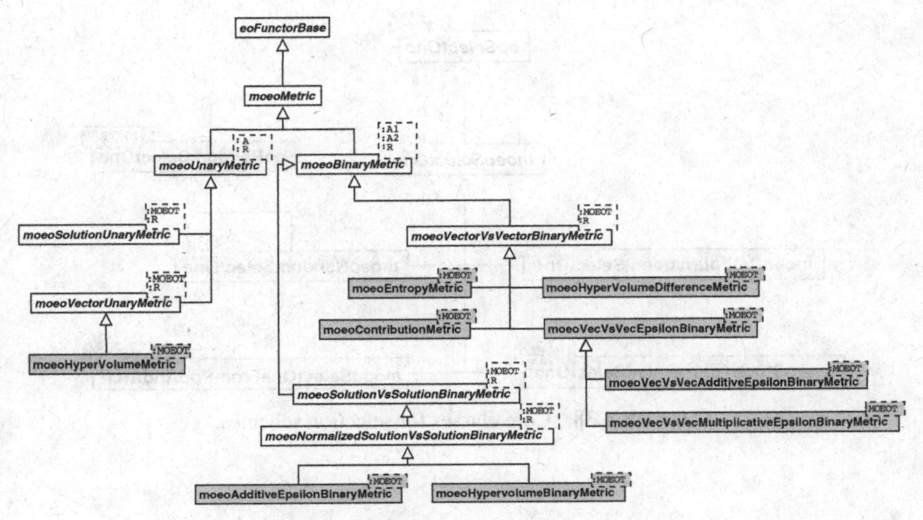

FIGURE 4.37 Core classes for metrics.

algorithms cannot be used in a multiobjective EA. Therefore, the major contributions of this framework refer to

- Fitness assignment, diversity preservation, and elitism (as suggested by the multiobjective metaheuristics design issues introduced in Section 4.3).
- The selection and replacement schemes that need to be defined for the specific case of MOO, where the fitness and diversity values are used instead of a single scalar objective value (as it is generally the case in monoobjective optimization). Of course, the representation of a solution as well as the way to build a P-metaheuristic also need to be redefined for the multiobjective case.

4.8.3.1 Selection Schemes As noticed earlier, two main differences between a monoobjective EA and a multiobjective EA appear on the selection and the replacement steps of the algorithm, during which the fitness and/or the diversity values are usually used. The selection step consists in choosing some solutions that will be used to generate the offspring population. There exist a large number of selection strategies in the case of MOP, some of them are already provided within ParadisEO–MOEO (see Fig 4.38):

- **Random selection scheme:** It consists in randomly selecting a parent from the population members, without taking into account the fitness values or the diversity values.
- **Deterministic tournament selection scheme:** It consists in performing a tournament between n randomly chosen population members and in selecting the best one.

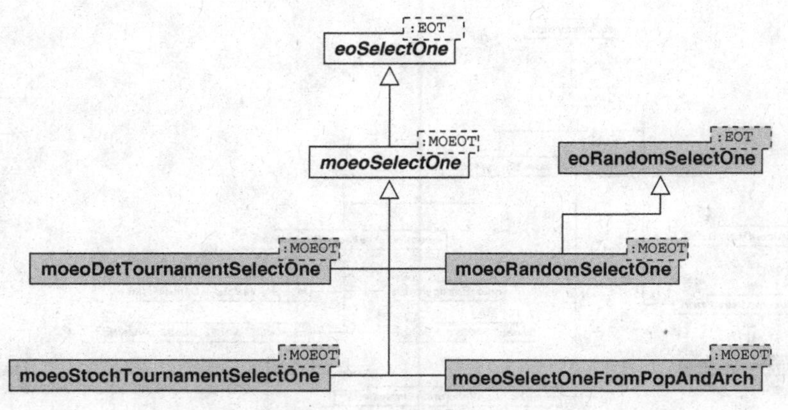

FIGURE 4.38 Core classes for selection schemes.

- **Stochastic tournament selection scheme:** It consists in performing a binary tournament between randomly chosen population members and in selecting the best one with a probability p or the worst one with a probability $(1 - p)$.
- **Selection scheme from the population and the archive:** It consists in selecting a population member using a particular selection scheme with a probability p or in selecting an archive member using another particular selection scheme with a probability $(1 - p)$. So, nondominated or most-preferred solutions also contribute to the evolution engine as they are used to create the offspring. This scheme has been successfully applied to various elitist MOEAs with efficient performances as it is the case, for instance, in SPEA [846] or SPEA2 [844] among others.

Everything is done to easily implement a new selection scheme with a minimum programming effort.

4.8.3.2 Replacement Schemes The replacement step of an EA consists in choosing which solutions will be part of the next generation by using both the offspring and the parent populations. The majority of the replacement strategies depend on the fitness and/or the diversity values and are then MOP specific. Three replacement schemes are already provided within ParadisEO–MOEO (see Fig. 4.39), but this is not exhaustive as new ones can easily be implemented due to the genericity of the framework:

- **Generational replacement scheme**: It consists in keeping the offspring population only, while all parents are deleted.
- **Elitist replacement scheme**: It consists in choosing the N best solutions (where N is the population size).

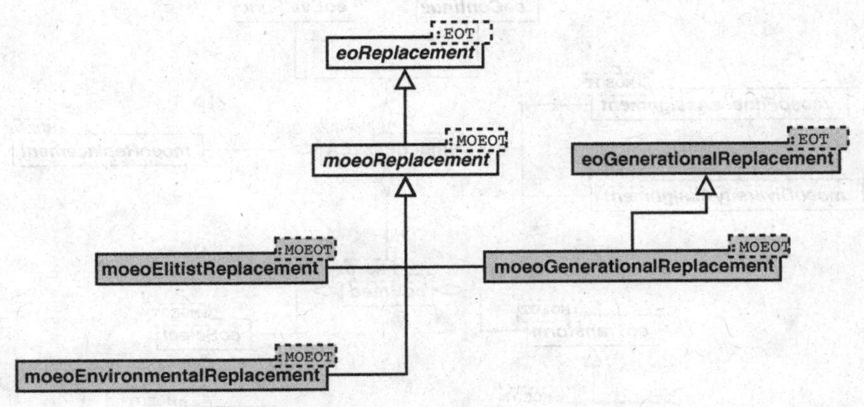

FIGURE 4.39 Core classes for replacement schemes.

- **Environmental replacement scheme**: It consists in deleting one-by-one the worst individuals, and in updating the fitness and the diversity values of the remaining solutions each time there is a deletion. The process ends when the desired population size is reached.

4.8.3.3 Multiobjective Evolutionary Algorithms Now that all the MOP-specific components are defined, a multiobjective EA can easily be developed using the fine-grained classes of both ParadisEO–EO and ParadisEO–MOEO. As the implementation is conceptually divided into components, different operators can be experimented without engendering significant modifications in terms of code writing. As seen before, a wide range of components are already provided. But this list is not exhaustive as the framework perpetually evolves and offers all that are necessary to develop new ones with a minimum effort, as ParadisEO is a white box framework that tends to be flexible while being as user-friendly as possible.

Figure 4.40 illustrates the use of the `moeoEasyEA` class that allows to define a multiobjective EA in a common fashion by specifying all the particular components required for its implementation. As often within ParadisEO, all the classes use a template parameter *MOEOT* that defines the type of a solution for the problem under consideration. This type might be represented by inheriting of the `MOEO` class that is described in Section 4.8.2.1.

To satisfy both the common and the more experimented users, ParadisEO–MOEO also provides even more ready-to-use multiobjective metaheuristics (see Fig. 4.41). These classes propose an implementation of standard multiobjective EAs such as NSGA, NSGA-II, or IBEA by using the fine-grained components of ParadisEO while requiring a minimum number of problem- or algorithm-specific parameters. These easy-to-use algorithms also tend to be used as state-of-the-art references for a fair performance comparison in the academic world, even if they are also well suited for a straight use on a real-world problem.

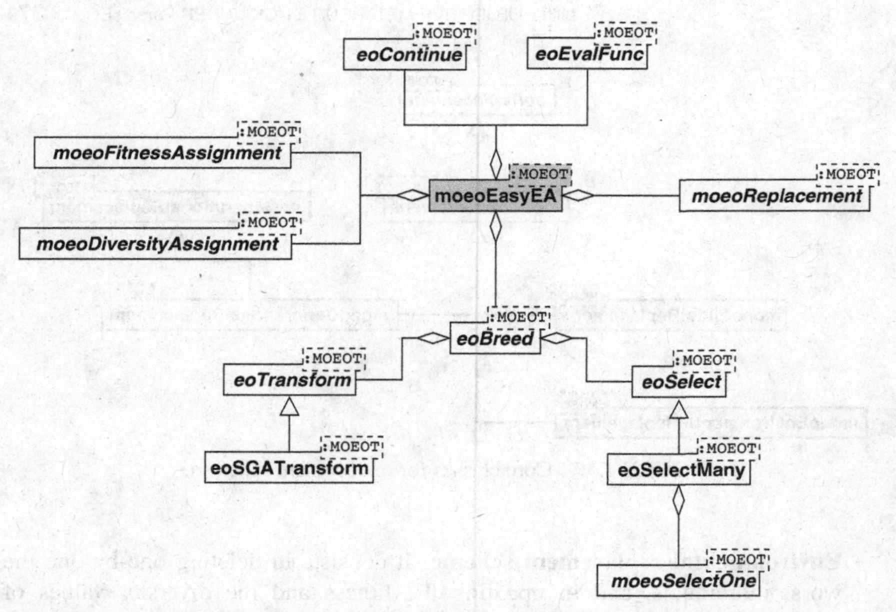

FIGURE 4.40 Core classes required by *moeoEasyEA* to design a MOEA.

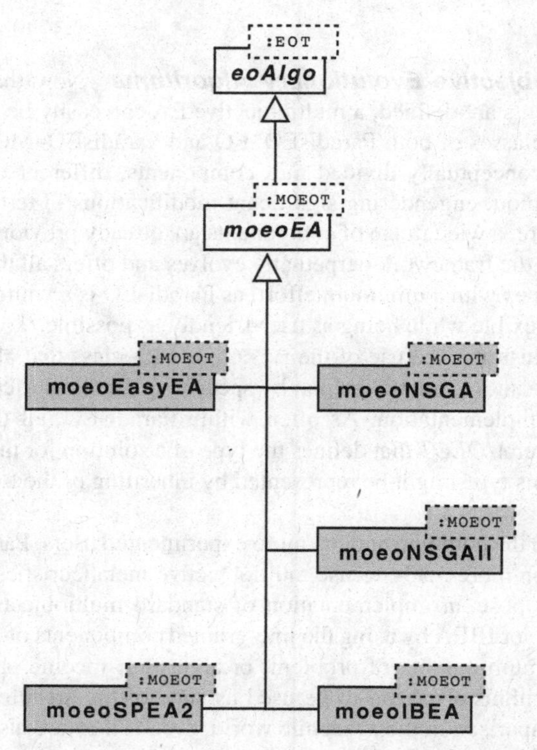

FIGURE 4.41 Core classes for easy-to-use evolutionary algorithms.

4.9 CONCLUSIONS AND PERSPECTIVES

Multiobjective optimization is certainly a crucial area in engineering and science. Indeed, uncountable real-life optimization problems are characterized by multiple objectives. The most popular approach nowadays to tackle complex multiobjective problems is the use of metaheuristics. P-metaheuristics are good candidates for solving MOPs, where the output is generally a set of Pareto optimal solutions rather than a single solution as in monoobjective optimization. Indeed, in the last decade, the EMO community has been very active [142,278,195]. Recently, some alternative P-metaheuristics to evolutionary algorithms have been investigated, such as ant colonies [298], particle swarm optimization [651], scatter search and path relinking [65], bee colony [612], differential evolutions [830], and artificial immune systems [140].

In addition to classical search components of monoobjective metaheuristics (e.g., representation, constraint handling, search operators), multiobjective metaheuristics must handle the following three search components: fitness assignment, diversity preservation, and elitism (Fig. 4.42).

In this chapter, the need of a software framework dedicated to the reusable design and implementation of multiobjective metaheuristics has been outlined. The framework ParadisEO–MOEO provides the most common search components and metaheuristic algorithms for multiobjective optimization. A high level of flexibility and adaptability is also provided. The user can modify or add new search components or solve new problems. Some popular multiobjective metaheuristics (e.g., NSGA-II,

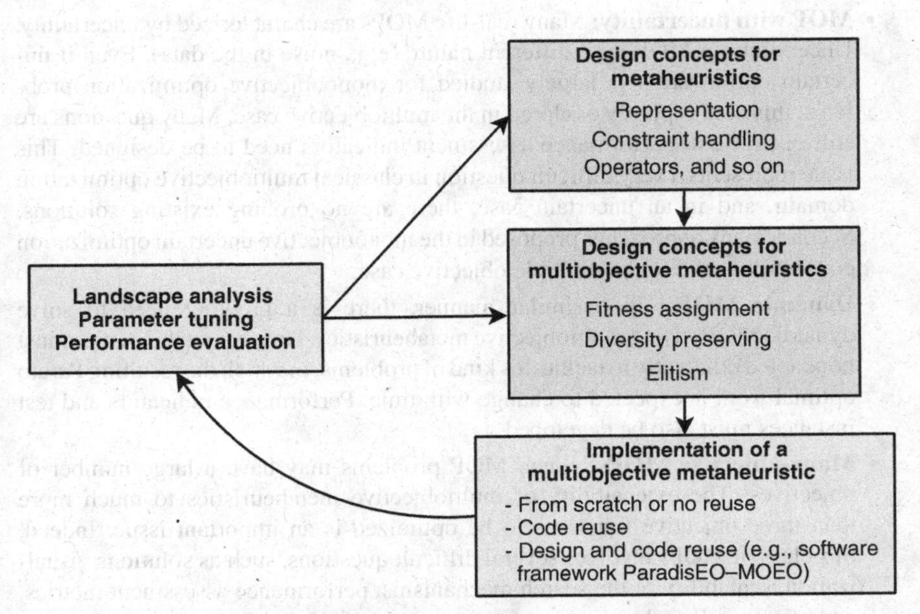

FIGURE 4.42 Development process of a multiobjective metaheuristic.

IBEA, SPEA2) are available in the ParadisEO framework. Their whole design and invariant code could be reused. Moreover, using the ParadisEO framework in designing an algorithm, several concepts and their implementation can be reused.

- Monoobjective metaheuristics such as the representation, neighborhoods, stopping criteria, variation operators (mutation, crossover), selection, and replacement mechanisms.
- Multiobjective metaheuristics such as fitness assignment procedures, diversity preservation approaches, and elitism.
- Hybrid and parallel metaheuristics. Indeed, parallel and hybrid multiobjective metaheuristics can be implemented in an incremental manner. In Chapter 5 (resp. Chapter 6), specific sections are dedicated to hybrid (resp. parallel) multiobjective metaheuristics. A growing interest is actually focused on hybrid and parallel metaheuristics for solving complex MOPs.

Assessing the performance of multiobjective metaheuristics is a multiobjective optimization problem! Indeed, no single measure is sufficient to assess the quality of an approximation. Some representative indicators must be used for each class of measure: convergence class and diversity class (extension and dispersion). These quality indicators can also be used to design indicator-based multiobjective metaheuristics or stopping criteria.

In terms of perspectives, some concerns related to multiobjective metaheuristics are as follows:

- **MOP with uncertainty:** Many real-life MOPs are characterized by uncertainty. Uncertainty in MOP is of different nature (e.g., noise in the data). Even if uncertain optimization is largely studied for monoobjective optimization problems, this area is poorly explored in the multiobjective case. Many questions are still open. First, performance assessment indicators need to be designed. This issue represents a very difficult question in classical multiobjective optimization domain, and in an uncertain case, there are no probing existing solutions. Second, many approaches proposed in the monoobjective uncertain optimization could be adapted to the multiple objective case.
- **Dynamic MOPs:** In a similar manner, there is a growing need to solve dynamic MOPs using multiobjective metaheuristics. Hence, metaheuristics must be adapted efficiently to tackle this kind of problems, in which the resulting Pareto optimal front is expected to change with time. Performance indicators and test instances must also be developed.
- **Many-objective MOPs:** Some MOP problems may have a large number of objectives. The extensibility of multiobjective metaheuristics to much more than three objective functions to be optimized is an important issue. Indeed, this class of MOPs involves several difficult questions, such as solutions visualization, scalability of the search mechanisms, performance assessment metrics, and benchmark problems.

- **Interactive optimization:** The aim of solving MOPs is to help a decision maker find the solution that copes with his preferences. Hence, finding the Pareto optimal set is not enough in solving multicriteria decision-making problems. In interactive multiobjective metaheuristics, the decision maker specifies the preference information progressively during the search. One of the crucial questions is which kind of information is exchanged between the decision maker and the multiobjective metaheuristic.

4.10 EXERCISES

Exercise 4.1 Multiobjective combinatorial problems. Many academic combinatorial optimization problems have been generalized to multiobjective models by taking into account multiple input data for the problem. For instance, let us consider the multiobjective knapsack problem that can be formulated in the following way [6]:

$$\begin{cases} \text{Max}(f_i(x)) = \sum_{j=1}^{m} c^i_j x_j, \quad (i = 1, \ldots, n) \\ \sum_{j=1}^{m} w_j x_j \leq w \\ x_j \in \{0, 1\}, \quad j = \{1, \ldots, m\} \end{cases} \tag{4.25}$$

where

$$x_j = \begin{cases} 1 & \text{if } j \text{ is in the knapsack} \\ 0 & \text{otherwise} \end{cases} \tag{4.26}$$

w_j is the weight (volume) of the element j, and c^i_j is the utility of the element j according to the criterion i. Hence, different values c^i_j are associated with the utility input of the problem instead of a single utility value for the classical monoobjective form of knapsack problems. Apply the same principle to the well-known traveling salesman problem and the quadratic assignment problem.

Exercise 4.2 No preference methods. In some MCDM approaches, the decision maker does not take part in the solution process. Such no preference methods are used to find a compromise solution, typically in the middle of the Pareto front. These methods, also known as methods of neutral preferences, can be used when there is no decision maker available. The obtained compromise solution may also be used as an initial solution for interactive approaches. Which formulation of a MOP can be used to find such solutions?

Exercise 4.3 Weak Pareto optimal solution. Some scalarization methods generate weakly Pareto optimal solutions. Our objective is to check if the generated solution

$x^* \in S$ is a Pareto optimal one. Let us consider the following problem to solve:

$$\text{Maximize} \sum_{i=1}^{n} \epsilon_i$$

Subject to

$$f_i(x) + \epsilon_i = f_i(x^*), \forall i \in [1, n]$$

$$\epsilon_i \geq 0, \forall i \in [1, n]$$

$$x \in S$$

where $x \in \mathbb{R}^n$ and $\epsilon \in \mathbb{R}^n_+$ are variables. What will be the result of this problem if the solution x^* is a Pareto optimal solution? What will be the property of the obtained solution x' in the resolution of the problem if it corresponds to a finite and nonzero optimal objective function? One can consider that the equality constraints can be replaced by inequalities $f_i(x) + \epsilon_i \leq f_i(x^*)$.

Exercise 4.4 Multiobjective modeling of portfolio selection. In financial engineering, the problem of portfolio selection is a popular standard problem. The problem has received a lot of attention in its multiobjective formulation. A portfolio is a set of assets held by a banking company. The objective is to distribute a given budget on a set of available assets. The optimal return depends on the risk aversion of the client. What represent the two families of objectives generally used in portfolio selection? For each family of objectives, formulate some related objective functions.

Exercise 4.5 Tournament selection in constrained MOPs. Let us consider an evolutionary algorithm solving a constrained multiobjective optimization problem. The algorithm uses the binary tournament selection procedure. Adapt the binary tournament selection procedure to handle such problems. One has to define a "constrained-domination" concept between two solutions using the domination concept and feasibility of solutions (constraint violation).

Exercise 4.6 Multiobjective model for robust optimization. In general, the robustness issue in optimization is tackled by defining an expected objective function such as the Monte Carlo integration or the averaging function into the neighborhood of the final solution. In some cases, this strategy is not sufficient. For instance, positive and negative deviations of the objective values will cancel each other. An alternative could be the use of multiobjective model where the robustness criterion is handled separately. Propose such a MOP (biobjective or triobjective) to solve a monoobjective function f.

Exercise 4.7 Niche size in sharing-based diversification. The effectiveness of the sharing principle mainly depends on the niche size σ_0. In this exercise, our interest is the automatic computation of the niche size in the objective space σ_o. The parameter σ_o must be computed to spread solutions over all the Pareto front, with the hypothesis that the solutions are ideally distributed on the front. The size niche σ_o must be fixed at some known minimal separation between desired optima. Let $\text{Area}_{\text{Pareto}}$ be the surface of the Pareto front and N the number of desired solutions. How can be approximated the niche size σ_o?

In a k-dimensional space volume, a niche is a hypersphere of dimension k and the Pareto front is a space of dimension $k - 1$. Their intersection is a space of dimension $k - 1$ that can be approximated by $(\sigma_o)^{k-1}$. Let us suppose that the considered distance is based on the Euclidean distance, $\max_j$ and $\min_j$ are respectively the maximum and the minimum value for the objective j (Fig. 4.43). Compute a lower and an upper bound for the Pareto area for a bicriteria MOP. Give an approximation of the niche size.

When $\dim \geq 3$, the lower bound approximation is more difficult. So, when $\dim \geq 3$, only the upper bound of $\text{Area}_{\text{Pareto}}$ is used to approximate σ_o. Compute an upper bound for the Pareto area.

In the general case, the distance is computed by Euclidean metric, but the Holder metric p can also be used:

$$\text{dist}(x, y) = \left(\sum_{i=1}^{\dim} |x_i - y_i|^p \right)^{\frac{1}{p}}$$

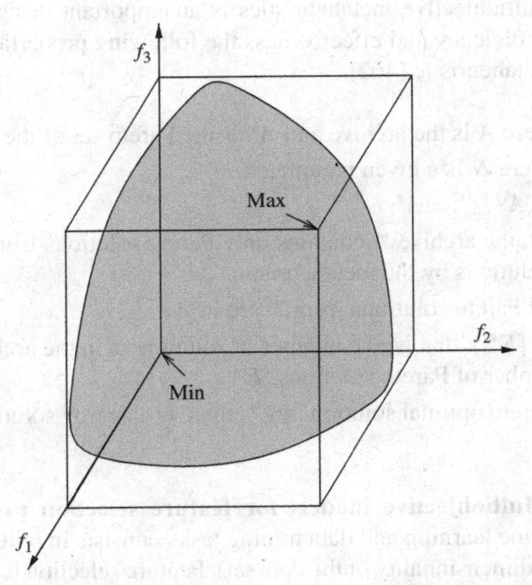

FIGURE 4.43 Space occupied by the front approximated by a hypercube: Example with three objectives.

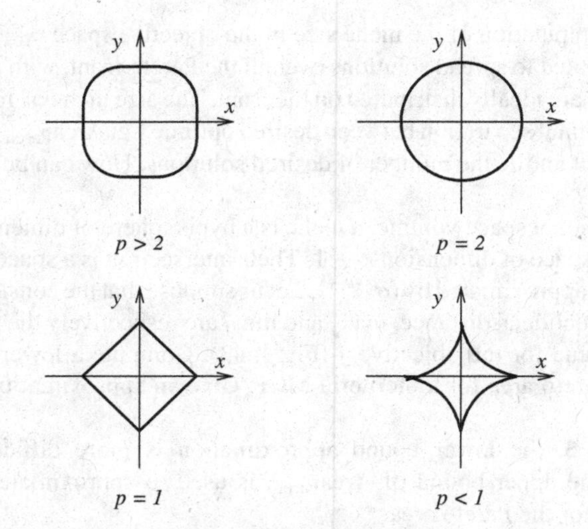

FIGURE 4.44 Niche shapes in two dimensions, as the degree p of the Holder metric varies.

The shape of the niche is changed according to p value of the defined distance (Fig. 4.44).

Why the Manhattan distance ($p = 1$) is encouraged?

Exercise 4.8 Elitism using archiving. Maintaining archives of potential Pareto solutions into multiobjective metaheuristics is an important design concept. Analyze in terms of efficiency and effectiveness the following properties for the archive produced by a metaheuristic [469]:

- $A = A^*$ where A is the archive and A^* is the Pareto set of the archive.
- $|A| \leq N$ where N is a given parameter.
- $\exists t, \forall u > 0 : A^{(t+u)} = A^t$.
- $A \subseteq F^*$, i.e., the archive A contains only Pareto solutions from the set F of all generated solutions by the metaheuristic.
- All extremal Pareto solutions from F are in A.
- $S \simeq \min(N, |F^*|)$, that is, the number of solutions S in the archive A is close to N or the number of Pareto solutions $|F^*|$.
- For every Pareto optimal solution in F^*, there is a nearby solution in the archive A.

Exercise 4.9 Multiobjective models for feature selection problems. Feature selection in machine learning and data mining tasks consists in reducing the number of attributes (i.e., dimensionality of the data set). Feature selection is often considered as a necessary preprocessing step in analyzing data characterized by a large number of attributes. The monoobjective formulation of feature selection can be defined as follows: Given a set of n features $F = \{f_1, f_2, \ldots, f_i, \ldots, f_n\}$, find a subset $F' \subseteq F$ that maximizes a scoring function $\Theta : \Gamma \longrightarrow G$ such that

$$F' = \arg\max_{G \in \Gamma}\{\Theta(G)\}$$

where Γ is the space of all possible feature subsets of F, G is a subset of Γ, and Θ the objective function that measures the accuracy of the classification phase.

Feature selection allows to improve the accuracy of the extracted models. The wrapper method for feature selection, which carries out the feature subset selection and the classification (e.g., k-NN, support vector machines) in the same process, engages a classification algorithm to measure the accuracy (Fig. 4.45). The encoding of a solution is based on a binary vector of size n, where each element denotes the presence or absence of the feature. Propose a multiobjective model for feature selection that uses an additional objective rather than the accuracy of the classification. One may use a P-metaheuristic to solve the problem. Propose a strategy for the initialization of the population.

Exercise 4.10 Crowding in many-objective problems. The diversity preservation strategy in NSGA-II algorithm is based on crowding. Show that the crowding distance operator does not work well for more than two objectives. Indeed, many MOPs comprise a relatively large number of objectives (e.g., engineering design problems). Such problems pose new challenges for algorithm design and implementation.

Exercise 4.11 Adaptive application of variation operators. In Exercise 3.34, the question of adapting dynamically the selection probability of different search operators in a given metaheuristic has been addressed. Generalize the adaptive procedure for multiobjective optimization. The difficulty in MOP lies in the partial order of solutions defined by the Pareto optimality concept.

Exercise 4.12 NSGA-II and archiving. The NSGA-II algorithm does not use any archiving strategy in which the algorithm stores all generated nondominated solutions as they are found. Is this archiving strategy useful to include in the NSGA-II algorithm?

Exercise 4.13 Archive update complexity. In elitist multiobjective metaheuristics, a nonbounded archive contains all encountered nondominated solutions. The

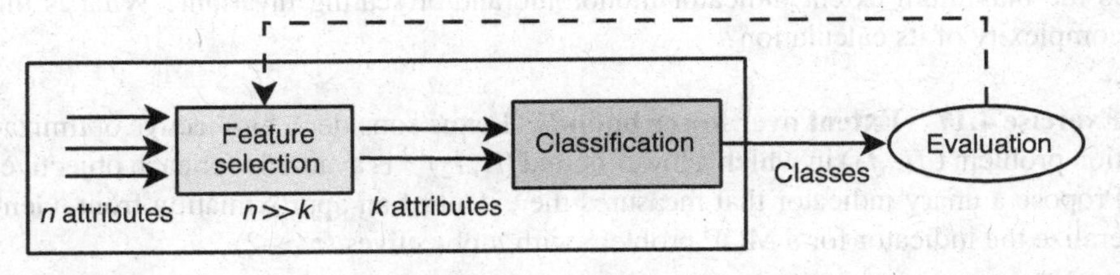

FIGURE 4.45 A wrapper method for feature selection within a classification task (supervised classification).

update of the archive may become expensive if the size of the archive grows too much. Given N the size of the population of a P-metaheuristic, M the size of the archive, and k the number of objectives of the MOP, at each iteration N solutions are generated. What is the computational complexity of the update procedure for each iteration of the algorithm? Propose some solutions to reduce this computational cost.

Exercise 4.14 Deterioration of the archive. Hybrid strategies combining Pareto-based fitness assignment and density-based diversity preservation to update the archive are widely used in practice. Indeed, the Pareto-based criteria encourage the convergence of the archive toward the optimal Pareto front, while the density-based information encourages the diversity of the limited size population of the archive. Show that a combined strategy may deteriorate the archive, that is, solutions belonging to the archive at iteration t may be dominated by old members of the archive at iteration s ($s < t$). Propose an approach that avoids this deterioration problem.

Exercise 4.15 Scaling invariance of performance indicators. Let us consider a strictly monotonic transformation of the objectives associated with a MOP: $s : \mathbb{R}^n \to \mathbb{R}^n$. For instance, usually the following normalization of the objectives is used in practice:

$$s(f(x)) = \frac{f(x) - f_l}{f_u - f_l}$$

where f_l (resp. f_u) represents the lower (resp. upper) bound for the objective f. It transforms the objective values of f in the interval $[0, 1]$.

A performance indicator I is scaling invariant iff it is not affected by any strictly monotonic scaling of the objective functions of the target MOP, that is, the values of the performance indicator I do not change. Are the following performance indicators scaling invariant: hypervolume, ϵ-indicator, and the R-metrics?

Exercise 4.16 Maximum extent. The maximum extent unary performance indicator I_{ME} of an approximation A may be defined as follows:

$$I_{\mathrm{ME}}(A) = \max_{1 \leq i \leq n}(\max_{x \in A} f_i(x) - \min_{x \in A} f_i(x))$$

Is the maximum extent indicator monotonic and/or scaling invariant? What is the complexity of its calculation?

Exercise 4.17 Extent over lower bounds. Let us consider a biobjective optimization problem (f_1, f_2) in which a lower bound (l_1, l_2)[19] is available for each objective. Propose a unary indicator that measures the extent of an approximation front. Generalize the indicator for a MOP problem with n objectives ($n > 2$).

[19] A minimization problem is supposed.

Exercise 4.18 Monotonicity of performance indicators. A nonmonotonic performance indicator may be considered as unreliable, that is, the indicator can yield a preference for an approximation set A over another approximation set B, when $B \preceq A$. Are the following performance indicators monotonic: generational distance, spacing, and maximum extent indicators?

Show that the unary additive ϵ-indicator $I^1_{\epsilon+}$ is not strictly monotonic.

Exercise 4.19 Performance relative to the exact Pareto front. When the exact Pareto front P^* is known, some performance indicators may be designed to measure the convergence property of an approximated front A. The number of Pareto solutions is supposed finite (i.e., combinatorial MOP). Propose such indicators for each class of measures: a cardinality measure and a distance measure. Analyze their properties in terms of monotonicity, scaling invariance, and computational complexity.

Exercise 4.20 Ideal performance indicator. An ideal performance indicator must have a reduced computational complexity, does not need any specific parameter, strictly monotonic, and objective scaling invariant. Does such an ideal performance indicator exist?

Exercise 4.21 Deceptive MOPs. There are some optimization problems that are easy for a given search algorithm and difficult for other algorithms. For instance, below is a deceptive biobjective problem for local search that is easy for genetic algorithms. The first objective is

$$f_1(x \neq 1111\ldots) = |2 \cdot x_1 - x_2| \tag{4.27}$$

$$f_1(1111\ldots) = x_1 \cdot x_2 \tag{4.28}$$

where x is a string of bits, x_1 represents the number of bits equal to 1 in the first half of the chain, and x_2 the number of bits equal to 1 in the second half of the chain. The second objective is formulated as follows:

$$f_2(x \neq 1111\ldots) = |2 \cdot x_2 - x_1| \tag{4.29}$$

$$f_2(1111\ldots) = x_1 \cdot x_2 \tag{4.30}$$

Show that using a genetic algorithm (especially the crossover operator) one can produce the global optimum, if the population contains representative solutions of the two local optima whereas the local search is trapped by the two local optima associated with the bit-flip neighborhood.

Exercise 4.22 From NSGA-II to IBEA under ParadisEO. Let us consider a NSGA-II program to solve any MOP (e.g., bicriteria flow-shop scheduling problem) that is available under the ParadisEO–MOEO framework. What has to be modified in the program to solve the same problem using the IBEA algorithm?

Exercise 4.23 Solving various formulations of MOPs within ParadisEO. The architecture of a multiobjective metaheuristic under ParadisEO is based on the three search components: fitness assignment, diversity preservation, and elitism. The modification of these three components allows to solve various formulations of multiobjective problems. Let us consider the NSGA-II algorithm. Propose modifications of the search components associated with the NSGA-II algorithm to

- generate a partial Pareto front in the objective space,
- find knee points (i.e., points in which a small improvement according to one objective requires a large deterioration in at least another objective.),
- estimate the nadir point,
- generate a robust Pareto front using neighborhood average function values in the decision space,
- generate a diverse Pareto front using the ϵ-dominance concept,
- generate a diverse Pareto front using the K-mean clustering algorithm, and
- generate solutions around a set of reference points.

Exercise 4.24 Handling many-objective problem. A simple domination concept may be used to handle a MOP with a large number of objectives. A solution x dominates a solution y, if the solution x has a larger number of better objective values than y (i.e., if $(f_i(x) < f_i(y))$ is satisfied for more objectives than $(f_i(y) < f_i(x))$). This dominance concept identifies intermediate solutions in the Pareto optimal front. Moreover, a preference information (e.g., priority, hierarchy, weight) may be assigned to the objectives [486]. Based on this dominance concept, a fast and effective dominance-based multiobjective metaheuristic may be designed to prune nondominated solutions in many-objective problems. What has to be modified in a multiobjective dominance-based metaheuristic (e.g., NSGA-II) to integrate this concept of dominance? What is the impact on the implementation under ParadisEO?

Exercise 4.25 Welded beam design problem. The welded beam design problem is one of the classical benchmarks for testing multiobjective metaheuristics [647]. The problem can be defined as follows [700]: Given a uniform beam, made of steel, of rectangular cross section need to be welded to a base to be able to carry a load of F lbf (Fig. 4.46), the objective of the design is to minimize the cost of the production and beam deflection while satisfying the constraints of weld thickness h, weld length l, beam thickness t, and beam width b. The cost function f_1 includes the setup cost, welding labor cost, and material cost:

$$\min f_1 = (1 + c_1)h^2 l + c_2 tb(L + l)$$

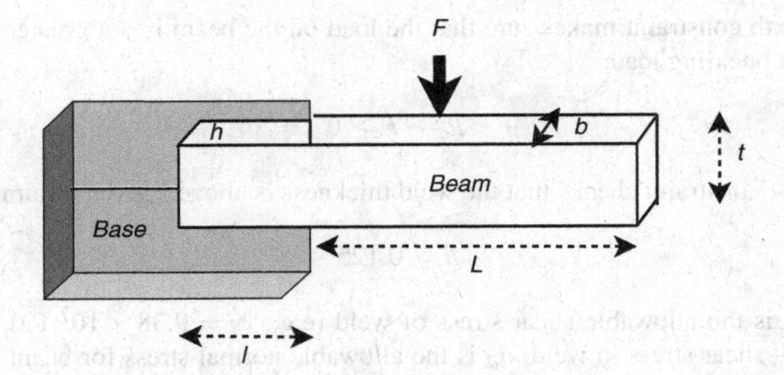

FIGURE 4.46 A welded beam.

where c_1[20] represents the unit volume of weld material cost, c_2[21] is the unit volume of bar stock cost, and L is the fixed distance from load to support ($L = 356$ mm).

The beam end deflection f_2 can be formulated as follows:

$$\min f_2 = \delta$$

where δ is the beam end deflection.

Some constraints must be considered that are related to the mechanical properties of the weld and bar, shear and normal stresses, physical constraints, and maximum deflection. The first constraint

$$\tau_d - \tau \geq 0$$

ensures that the maximum developed shear stress is less than the allowable shear stress of the weld material. The second constraint checks that the maximum developed normal stress is lower than the allowable normal stress in the beam.

$$\sigma_d - \sigma \geq 0$$

The third constraint ensures that the beam thickness exceeds that of the weld:

$$b - h \geq 0$$

The following fourth and fifth constraints are practical checks to prevent negative lengths or thicknesses.

$$l \geq 0$$

$$t \geq 0$$

[20]($c_1 = 6.3898 \times 10^{-6}$ \$/mm^3).
[21]($c_2 = 2.9359 \times 10^{-6}$ \$/mm^3).

The sixth constraint makes sure that the load on the beam is not greater than the allowable buckling load:

$$P_c - F \geq 0$$

The last constraint checks that the weld thickness is above a given minimum:

$$h \geq 0.125$$

where τ_d is the allowable shear stress of weld (e.g., $\tau_d = 9.38 \times 10^7$ Pa), τ is the maximum shear stress in weld, σ_d is the allowable normal stress for beam material (e.g., $\sigma_d = 2.07 \times 10^8$Pa), σ is the maximum normal stress in beam, P_c is the bar buckling load, and F is the load (e.g., $L = 6000 lbf$).

Solve this problem using the classical algorithms: NSGA-II, IBEA, and SPEA-II that are implemented in the ParadisEO framework. Compare the obtained results.

CHAPTER 5

Hybrid Metaheuristics

Over the last years, interest in hybrid metaheuristics has risen considerably in the field of optimization. The best results found for many real-life or classical optimization problems are obtained by hybrid algorithms [747]. Combinations of algorithms such as P-metaheuristics, S-metaheuristics, mathematical programming, constraint programming (CP), and machine learning techniques have provided very powerful search algorithms. Four different types of combinations are considered in this chapter:

- Combining metaheuristics with (complementary) metaheuristics.
- Combining metaheuristics with exact methods from mathematical programming approaches that are mostly used in operations research.
- Combining metaheuristics with constraint programming approaches deveoped in the artificial intelligence community.
- Combining metaheuristics with machine learning and data mining techniques.

This chapter deals with the design of hybrid metaheuristics and their implementation. A taxonomy of hybrid algorithms is presented in an attempt to provide a common terminology and classification mechanisms. The goal of the general taxonomy given here is to provide a mechanism to allow comparison of hybrid algorithms in a qualitative way. In addition, it is hoped that the categories and their relationships to each other have been chosen carefully enough to indicate areas in need of future work as well as to help classify future work. Among existing classifications in other domains, one can find examples of flat and hierarchical classifications schemes [295]. The taxonomy proposed here is a combination of these two schemes—hierarchical as long as possible to reduce the total number of classes and flat when the descriptors of the algorithms may be chosen in an arbitrary order. The same classification is used for all types of combinations. For each type of hybrids, the main ideas in combining algorithms are detailed. Each class of hybrids is illustrated with some examples. A critical analysis is also carried out.

Metaheuristics: From Design to Implementation, by El-Ghazali Talbi

In fact, the taxonomy could be usefully employed to classify any hybrid optimization algorithm (specific heuristics, exact algorithms). The basic classification is extended by defining the space of hybrid metaheuristics as a grammar, where each sentence is a method that describes a combination of metaheuristics, mathematical programming, and constraint programming. In this chapter, a "high-level" description of hybrid metaheuristics is proposed. The internal working and the algorithmic aspects of a given metaheuristic are not considered. Indeed, as Shown in Chapter 3, a term like evolutionary algorithms(EAs) may cover many quite different algorithms nowadays.

The chapter is organized as follows. Section 5.1 is concerned with hybrid algorithms combining metaheuristics. The design and implementation issues of hybrid metaheuristics are detailed. A taxonomy is presented to encompass all published work to date in the field and to provide a unifying view of it. A grammar that generalizes the basic hybridization schemes is proposed. In Section 5.2, the combination of metaheuristics with mathematical programming approaches is considered. Section 5.3 deals with the combination of metaheuristics with constraint programming techniques. In Section 5.4, the combination of metaheuristics with machine learning and data mining algorithms is addressed. Hybrid metaheuristics for multiobjective optimization are addressed in Section 5.5. Finally, Section 5.6 illustrates some implementations of hybrid metaheuristics under the ParadisEO software framework.

5.1 HYBRID METAHEURISTICS

Hybridization of metaheuristics involves a few major issues that may be classified as design and implementation. The former category is concerned with the hybrid algorithm itself, involving issues such as functionality and architecture of the algorithm. The implementation consideration includes the hardware platform, programming, model, and environment on which the algorithm is to be run. In this chapter, a difference is made between the design issues used to introduce hybridization and implementation issues that depend on the execution model of the algorithms.

5.1.1 Design Issues

The taxonomy will be kept as small as possible by proceeding in a hierarchical way as long as possible, but some choices of characteristics may be made independent of previous design choices, and thus will be specified as a set of descriptors from which a subset may be chosen.

5.1.1.1 Hierarchical Classification The structure of the hierarchical portion of the taxonomy is shown in Fig. 5.1. A discussion about the hierarchical portion then follows. At the first level, one may distinguish between low-level and high-level hybridizations. The low-level hybridization addresses the functional composition of a single-optimization method. In this hybrid class, a given function of a metaheuristic

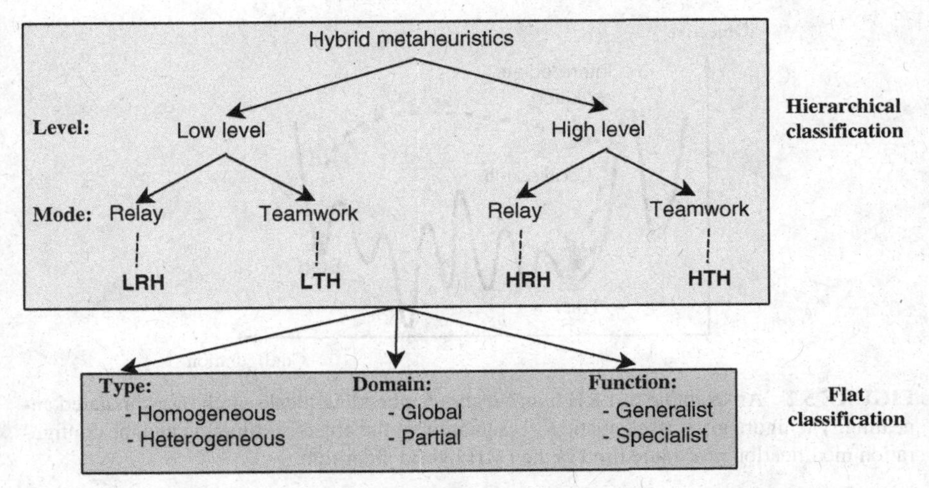

FIGURE 5.1 Classification of hybrid metaheuristics in terms of design issues.

is replaced by another metaheuristic. In high-level hybrid algorithms, the different metaheuristics are self-contained. There is no direct relationship to the internal workings of a metaheuristic.

In relay hybridization, a set of metaheuristics is applied one after another, each using the output of the previous as its input, acting in a pipeline fashion. Teamwork hybridization represents cooperative optimization models in which many cooperating agents evolve in parallel; each agent carries out a search in a solution space.

Four classes are derived from this hierarchical taxonomy:

- **LRH (low-level relay hybrid):** This class of hybrids represents algorithms in which a given metaheuristic is embedded into a S-metaheuristic. Few examples of hybrid metaheuristics belong to this class.

    Example 5.1 Embedding local search into simulated annealing. The main idea is to incorporate deterministic local search (LS) techniques into simulated annealing so that the Markov chain associated with simulated annealing explores only local optima [532]. The algorithm proceeds as follows: suppose the configuration is currently locally optimal. This is labeled `Start` in Fig. 5.2. A perturbation or a "kick" is applied to this configuration, which significantly changes the current solution `Start`. After the kick, the configuration labeled `Intermediate` in the figure is reached. It is much better to first improve `Intermediate` by a local search and then only apply the accept/reject test of simulated annealing. The local search takes us from `Intermediate` to the configuration labeled `Trial`, and then the accept/reject test is applied. If `Trial` is accepted, one has to find an interesting large change to `Start`. If `Trial` is rejected, return to `Start`. Many of the barriers (the "ridges") of the fitness landscape are jumped over in one step by the hybrid metaheuristic.

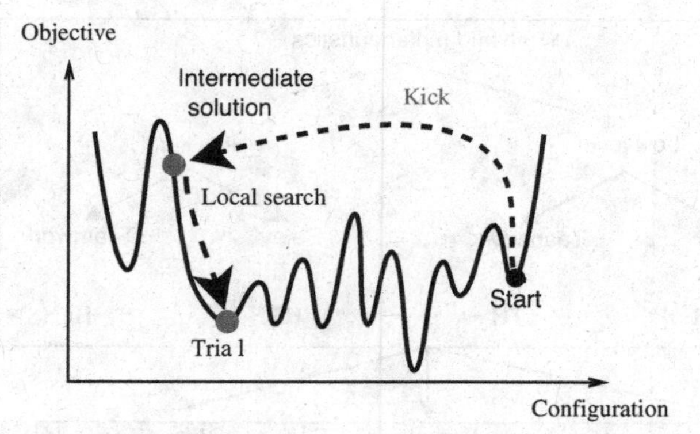

FIGURE 5.2 An example of LRH hybridization embedding local search into simulated annealing. The figure gives a schematic representation of the objective function and the configuration modification procedure used in the LRH hybrid algorithm.

To implement the above hybridization, the choice for an appropriate "kick" should be adapted to both the optimization problem and the local search method used. For the traveling salesman problem, if the local search algorithm used is the 2-opt local search heuristic, the "kick" move must apply a k-change with $k > 2$ to prevent cycles. The "kick" operator must attain solutions that are always outside the neighborhood associated with the local search algorithm.

- **LTH (low-level teamwork hybrid):** As mentioned in Chapter 1, two competing goals govern the design of a metaheuristic: exploration and exploitation. Exploration is needed to ensure that every part of the space is searched enough to provide a reliable estimate of the global optimum. Exploitation is important since the refinement of the current solution will often produce a better solution. P-metaheuristics (e.g., evolutionary algorithms, scatter search, particle swarm, ant colonies (AC)) are powerful in the exploration of the search space and weak in the exploitation of the solutions found.

  Therefore, most efficient P-metaheuristics have been coupled with S-metaheuristics such as local search, simulated annealing, and tabu search, which are powerful optimization methods in terms of exploitation. The two classes of algorithms have complementary strengths and weaknesses. The S-metaheuristics will try to optimize locally, while the P-metaheuristics will try to optimize globally. In LTH hybrid, a metaheuristic is embedded into a P-metaheuristic[1] (Fig. 5.3). This class of hybrid algorithms is very popular and has been applied successfully to many optimization problems. Most of the state-of-the-art P-metaheuristics integrate into S-metaheuristics.

[1]This class of hybrid metaheuristics includes *memetic algorithms*.

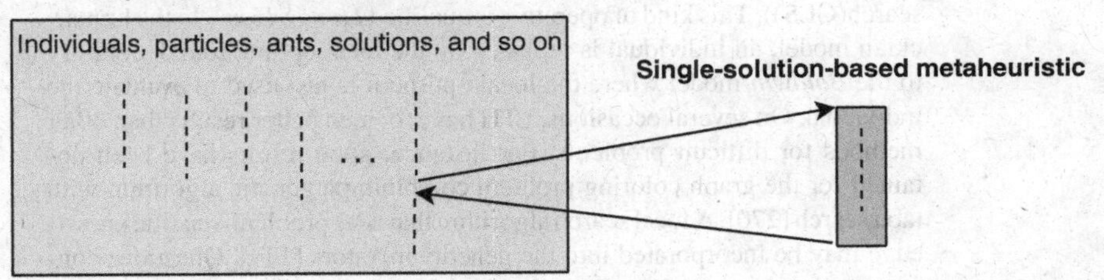

FIGURE 5.3 Low-level teamwork hybrid. S-metaheuristics are embedded into P-metaheuristics.

Example 5.2 Embedding S-metaheuristics into evolutionary algorithms. When an evolutionary algorithm is used as a global optimizer, its standard operators may be augmented with the ability to perform local search. Instead of using a blind operator acting regardless of the fitness of the original individual and the operated one, a heuristic operator that considers an individual as the origin of its search applies itself, and finally replaces the original individual by the enhanced one (see Fig. 5.4). The use of local search with evolutionary algorithms is also inspired by biological models of learning and evolution. EAs take many cues from mechanisms observed in natural evolution. Similarly, models of learning are often equated with techniques for local optimization [671]. Research on the interaction between evolution and learning had naturally led computer scientists to consider interactions between evolutionary algorithms and local optimization [67].

The genetic operators replaced or extended are generally mutation[2] and crossover.

- **Mutation:** The local search algorithm may be a simple local search [417,731,784], tabu search [269,462,768], simulated annealing algorithm

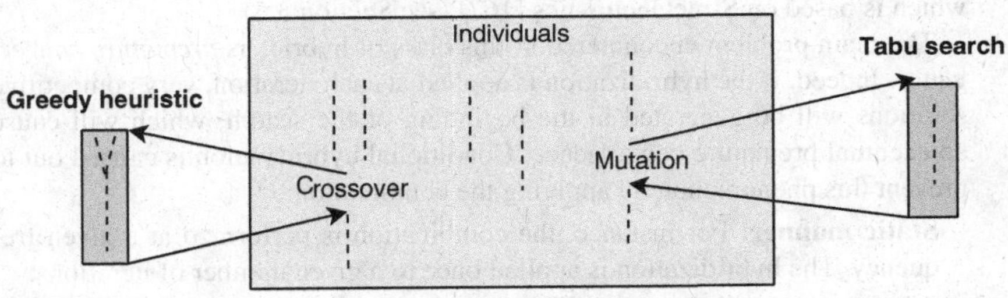

FIGURE 5.4 Illustration of a LTH hybrid. For instance, a tabu search is used as a mutation operator and a greedy heuristic as a crossover operator into a genetic algorithm.

[2]Also known as evolutionary local search algorithms.

[128,810], or any S-metaheuristic (e.g., threshold accepting, guided local search(GLS)). This kind of operators is qualified *Lamarckian*[3]. In the Lamarckian model, an individual is replaced by the local optima found, contrary to the *Baldwin* model where the local optimum is just used to evaluate the individual. On several occasions, LTH has provided better results than other methods for difficult problems. For instance, good results have been obtained for the graph coloring problem combining a genetic algorithm with tabu search [270]. A local search algorithm that uses problem-specific knowledge may be incorporated into the genetic operators [134]. Questions concerning the best use of local search with a genetic algorithm (GA) have been addressed in Ref. [368].

– **Crossover:** Classical crossover operators do not use any heuristic information about a specific application domain. They are blind operators. One can introduce heuristic crossover to account for problem-specific information [340]. For instance, greedy heuristics for the crossover operator have shown to improve EAs results when applied to job-shop scheduling, set covering, and traveling salesman problems [181].

  Many crossover operators including heuristic information have been proposed for continuous optimization:

  ∘ Heuristic crossover where the offspring has the following form: $x' = u(x_2 - x_1) + x_2$, where u is a uniform random value in [0, 1] and x_1 and x_2 are the two parents with the condition that x_2 is better than x_1 [826]. This heuristic crossover uses the objective function in determining the direction of the search.

  ∘ Simplex crossover where more than two parents are selected, the worst (resp. the best) individuals x_2 (resp. x_1) are determined. The centroid of the group c is then computed without taking into account the solution x_2. The offspring has the following form: $x' = c + (c - x_2)$ [648].

This hybrid model can be used to improve any P-metaheuristic: ant colonies [729,743], genetic programming [595], particle swarm optimization, and so on. The S-metaheuristic has been introduced to intensify the search. Let us notice that the scatter search metaheuristic already includes an improvement procedure, which is based on S-metaheuristics [167] (see Section 3.5).

The main problem encountered in this class of hybrids is *premature convergence*. Indeed, if the hybridization is applied at each iteration, very competitive solutions will be generated in the beginning of the search, which will cause an eventual premature convergence. Conditional hybridization is carried out to prevent this phenomenon by applying the combination.

– **Static manner:** For instance, the combination is performed at a given frequency. The hybridization is applied once to a given number of iterations.

– **Adaptive manner:** When a given event occurs during the search, the hybridization is performed. For instance, if there is no improvement of the search for a given number of iterations.

[3]The name is an allusion to Jean Batiste de Lamarck's contention that phenotype characteristics acquired during lifetime can become heritable traits.

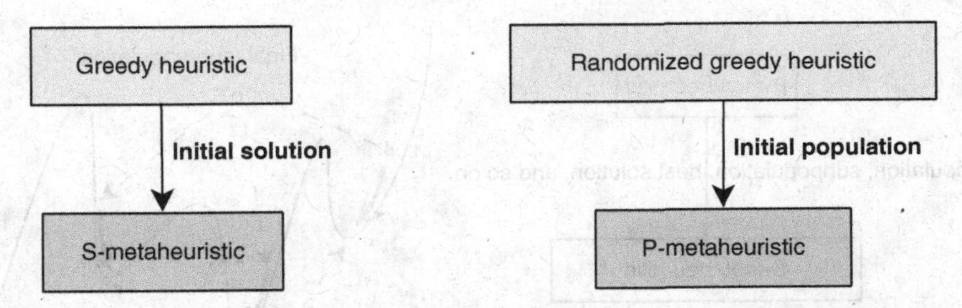

FIGURE 5.5 High-level relay hybridization. (Left) Generation of the initial solution of a S-metaheuristic by a greedy algorithm. (Right) Generation of the initial population of a P-metaheuristic by a randomized greedy heuristic.

- **HRH (high-level relay hybrid):** In HRH hybrids, the self-contained metaheuristics are executed in a sequence. For example, the initial solution of a given S-metaheuristic may be generated by another optimization algorithm. Indeed, the initial solution in S-metaheuristics has a great impact on their performances. A well-known combination scheme is to generate the initial solution by greedy heuristics, which are in general of less computing complexity than iterative heuristics (Fig. 5.5).

  This scheme may also be applied to P-metaheuristics, but a randomized greedy heuristic must be applied to generate a diverse population (Fig. 5.5). Greedy heuristics are in general deterministic algorithms and then they generate always the same solution. On the other hand, the diversity of the initial population has a great impact on the performance of P-metaheuristics. This hybrid scheme is carried out explicitly in the scatter search metaheuristic (see Section 3.5).

  Combining P-metaheuristics with S-metaheuristic in the HRH scheme is also largely applied. It is well known that P-metaheuristics are not well suited for fine-tuning structures, which are very close to optimal solutions. Indeed, the strength of P-metaheuristics is in quickly locating the high-performance regions of vast and complex search spaces. Once those regions are located, it may be useful to apply S-metaheuristics to the high-performance structures evolved by the P-metaheuristic.

  A fundamental practical remark is that after a certain amount of time, the population is quite uniform and the fitness of the population is no longer decreasing. The odds to produce fitter individuals are very low. That is, the process has fallen into a basin of attraction from which it has a low probability to escape.

  The exploitation of the already found basin of attraction to find as efficiently as possible the optimal point in the basin is recommended. It is experimentally clear that the exploitation of the basin of attraction that has been found may be more efficiently performed by another algorithm than by a P-metaheuristic. Hence, it is much more efficient to use a S-metaheuristic such as a hill-climbing or tabu search (see Fig. 5.6). The HRH hybridization may use a greedy heuristic

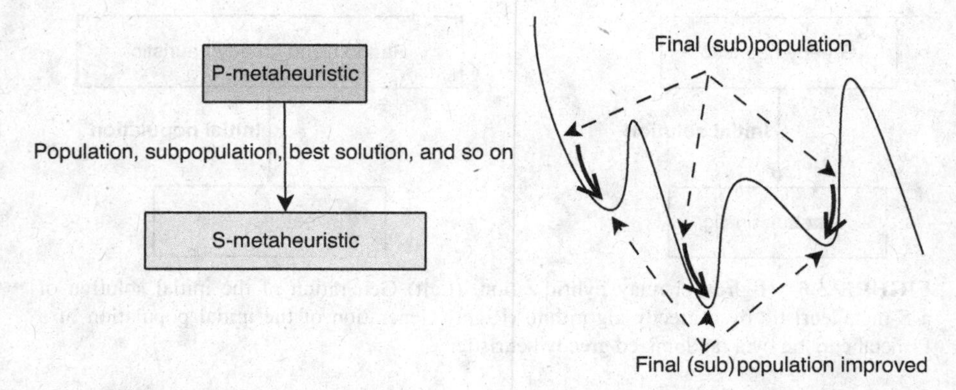

FIGURE 5.6 High-level relay hybridization. There may be more than two algorithms to be pipelined.

to generate a good initial population for the P-metaheuristic (see Fig. 5.6). At the end of a simulated annealing search, it makes sense to apply local search on the best found solution to ensure that it is a local optimum.

In this hybrid scheme, the S-metaheuristics may be applied to the following:

- **The whole population:** This will lead to the best final solutions but with a more significant computational cost of the search.
- **A subpopulation:** The selection of the subpopulation may be based to the diversity of the solutions. This is a good compromise between the complexity of the search and the quality of the final results.
- **The best solution of the population:** The S-metaheuristic is applied once to the best solution of the obtained population. This procedure will reduce the search time but does not ensure to find the best solution.

A path relinking strategy may be applied to a population or a set of elite solutions found by a metaheuristic [18]. Path relinking may be seen as an intensification task over a given population of solutions.

Example 5.3 HRH hybrid evolutionary algorithms. Many research works of the literature have used the idea of HRH hybridization for EAs. In Refs [524,754], the considered hybrid scheme introduces, respectively, simulated annealing and tabu search to improve the population obtained by a GA. In Ref. [582], the author introduces hill-climbing to improve the results obtained by an evolution strategy (ES). In Ref. [507], the algorithm proposed starts from simulated annealing and uses GAs to enrich the solutions found. Experiments performed on the graph partitioning problem using the tabu search algorithm exploiting the result found by a GA give better results than a search performed either by the GA or the tabu search alone [754].

- **HTH (high-level teamwork hybrid):** The HTH[4] scheme involves several self-contained algorithms performing a search in parallel and cooperating to find an optimum. Intuitively, HTH will ultimately perform at least one algorithm alone, more often perform better, and each algorithm provides information to the others to help them.

Example 5.4 Island model for genetic algorithms. The first HTH hybrid model has been proposed for genetic algorithms. This is the well-known island model[5]. The population in this model is partitioned into small subpopulations by geographic isolation. A GA evolves each subpopulation and individuals can migrate between subpopulations (Fig. 5.7). This model is controlled by several parameters: the topology that defines the connections between subpopulations, the migration rate that controls the number of migrant individuals, the replacement strategy used, and a migration interval that affects how often migration occurs. In some island models, the individuals really migrate and therefore leave empty space in the original population. In general, the migrated individuals remain in the original population (i.e., pollination model [714]).

Let us present some pioneering island models for GAs. Tanese proposed a GA -based HTH scheme that used a 4D hypercube topology to communicate individuals from one subpopulation to another [765]. Migration is performed at uniform periods of time between neighbor subpopulations along one dimension of the hypercube. The migrants are chosen probabilistically from the best individuals of the subpopulation and they replace the worst individuals in the receiving subpopulation.

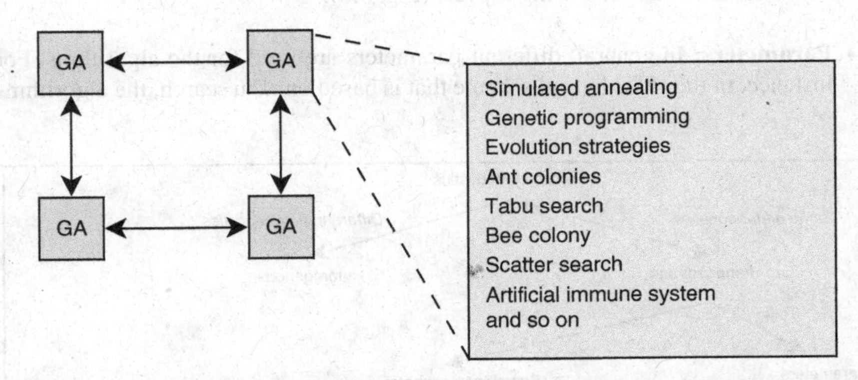

FIGURE 5.7 The island model of genetic algorithms as an example of high-level teamwork hybrid. The same model has been used with different topologies for simulated annealing, genetic programming, evolution strategy, ant colony, tabu search, bee colony, artificial immune system, and so on.

[4]HTH hybrids is referred as *multiple interacting walks* [798], *multiagent algorithms* [83], and *cooperative search algorithms* [136,137,382,394,776].

[5]Also known as migration model, diffusion model, and coarse-grain model.

Cohoon, Hedge, Martin, and Richards proposed a HTH based on the theory of "punctuated equilibria" [147]. A linear placement problem was used as a benchmark and experimented using a mesh topology. They found that the algorithm with migration outperforms the algorithm without migration and the standard GA. This work was later extended using a VLSI design problem (graph partitioning) on a 4D hypercube topology [148,149].

Belding [66] attempted to extend the Tanese's work using the Royal Road continuous functions. Migrant individuals are sent to a selected subpopulation randomly, rather than using a hypercube topology. The global optimum was found more often when migration (i.e., cooperating GAs) occurred than in completely isolated cases (i.e., noncooperating GAs).

The HTH hybrid model has been generalized to other P-metaheuristics and S-metaheuristics. Indeed, the HTH hybrid model has also been applied to simulated annealing [249], genetic programming [479], evolution strategies [801], ant colonies [528], scatter search [168], tabu search [250], and so on.

The conceptual and implementation details of this model will be detailed in Chapter 6.

5.1.1.2 Flat Classification

Homogeneous/Heterogeneous: In homogeneous hybrids, all the combined algorithms use the same metaheuristic. Hybrid algorithms such as the island model for GAs belong to this class of hybrids. The homogeneous metaheuristics may differ in the initialization of their following aspects (Fig. 5.8):

- **Parameters:** In general, different parameters are used for the algorithms. For instance, in the HTH hybrid scheme that is based on tabu search, the algorithms

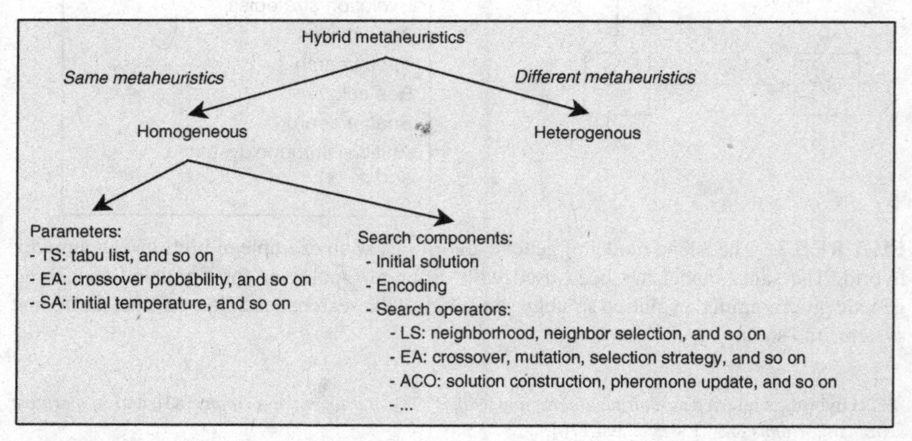

FIGURE 5.8 Homogeneous versus heterogeneous hybrid metaheuristics. Some illustrative examples of parameters and search components are illustrated.

may be initialized with different tabu list sizes [802]; different crossover and mutation probabilities may be used in evolutionary algorithms and so on.

- **Search components:** Given a metaheuristic, one can use different strategies for any search component of the metaheuristic, such as the representation of solutions, objective function approximations [234,692], initial solutions, search operators (neighborhood, mutation, crossover, etc.), termination criteria, and so on.

Using different parameters or search components in a given metaheuristic will increase the robustness of the hybrid algorithm.

Example 5.5 Heterogeneous hybrids. In heterogeneous algorithms, different metaheuristics are used (Fig. 5.9). A heterogeneous HTH algorithm based on genetic algorithms and tabu search has been proposed in Ref.[160] to solve a network design problem. The population of the GA is asynchronously updated by multiple tabu search algorithms. The best solutions found by tabu search algorithms build an elite population for the GA.

The GRASP method (greedy randomized adaptive search procedure) may be seen as an iterated heterogeneous HRH hybrid in which local search is repeated from a number of initial solutions generated by a randomized greedy heuristic [257,258]. The method is called adaptive because the greedy heuristic takes into account the decisions of the precedent iterations [256].

Global/Partial: From another point of view, one can also distinguish two kinds of cooperation: global and partial. In global hybrids, all the algorithms explore the same whole search space. The goal is here to explore the space more thoroughly. All the

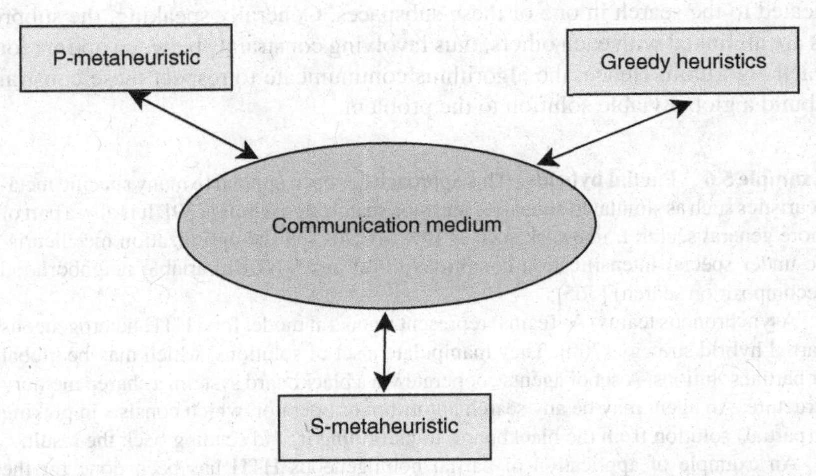

FIGURE 5.9 High-level teamwork hybridization (heterogeneous, global, general). Several search algorithms cooperate, coadapt, and coevolve a solution.

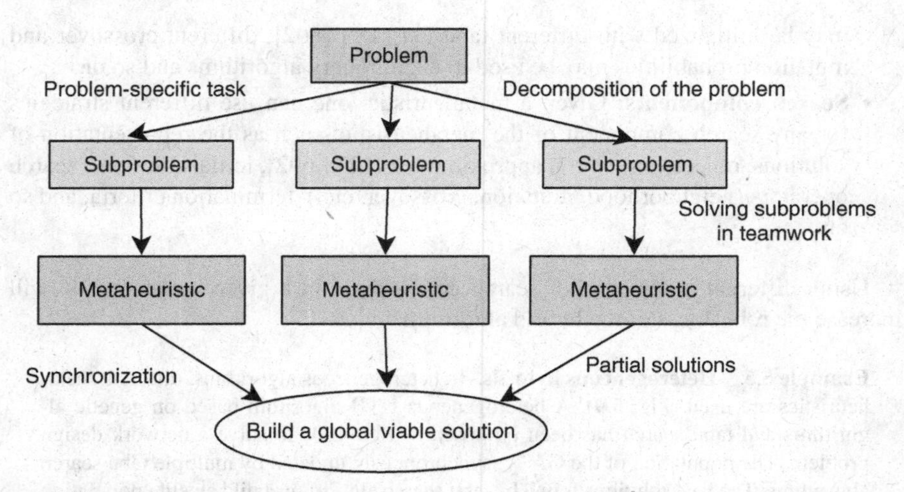

FIGURE 5.10 Partial hybrid schemes. Several search algorithms cooperate in solving subproblems. A synchronization is performed to build a global solution from the partial solutions found.

above-mentioned hybrids are *global* hybrids in the sense that all the algorithms solve the whole optimization problem. A global HTH algorithm based on tabu search has been proposed in Ref. [161], where each tabu search task performs a given number of iterations and then broadcasts the best solution. The best of all solutions becomes the initial solution for the next phase.

In partial hybrids, the problem to be solved is decomposed *a priori* into subproblems, each one having its own search space (Fig. 5.10). Then, each algorithm is dedicated to the search in one of these subspaces. Generally speaking, the subproblems are all linked with each others, thus involving constraints between optima found by each algorithm. Hence, the algorithms communicate to respect these constraints and build a global viable solution to the problem.

Example 5.6 Partial hybrids. This approach has been applied to many specific metaheuristics such as simulated annealing and tabu search algorithms [739]. It is also a part of more general search framework such as POPMUSIC (partial optimization metaheuristic under special intensification conditions [742] and VNDS (variable neighborhood decomposition search) [365].

Asynchronous teams (A-Teams) represent a general model for a HTH heterogeneous partial hybrid strategy [760]. They manipulate a set of solutions, which may be global or partial solutions. A set of agents cooperate via a blackboard system, a shared memory structure. An agent may be any search algorithm or operator, which consists in picking a (partial) solution from the blackboard, transforming it, and sending back the result.

An example of application of partial homogeneous HTH has been done for the job-shop scheduling problem [398]. The search algorithm is a GA. Each GA evolves individuals of a species that represent the process plan for one job. Hence, there are as many cooperating GAs as there are jobs. The communication medium collects fitted individuals from each GA and evaluates the resulting schedule as a whole, rewarding the best process plans.

Decomposition techniques based on partitioning time have been used to solve many problems such as the production lot sizing (partitioning of time) [254]. Decomposition techniques based on partitioning a geographical region have been largely applied to optimization problems associated with Euclidean distances such as the TSP [450], the VRP, and the P-median problem [741].

Example 5.7 Partitioning a continuous objective function. A function f is separable if

$$(\text{argmin}_{x_1} f(x_1, \ldots), \ldots, \text{argmin}_{x_n} f(\ldots, x_n)) = \text{argmin}(f(x_1, x_2, \ldots, x_n))$$

It follows that the function f can be optimized in a parallel way using n independent algorithms. Each algorithm will solve a 1D optimization problem.

Generalist/Specialist: All the above-mentioned hybrids are *general hybrids*, in the sense that all the algorithms solve the same target optimization problem. *Specialist hybrids* combine algorithms that solve different problems. The COSEARCH generic model belongs to this class of hybrids (Fig. 5.11). COSEARCH manages the cooperation of a search agent (a local search), a diversifying agent, and an intensifying agent. The three agents exchange information via a passive coordinator called the adaptive memory[6]. A main key point of the COSEARCH approach is the design of this memory, which focuses on high-quality regions of the search and avoids attractive but deceptive areas. The adaptive memory contains a history of the search; it stores

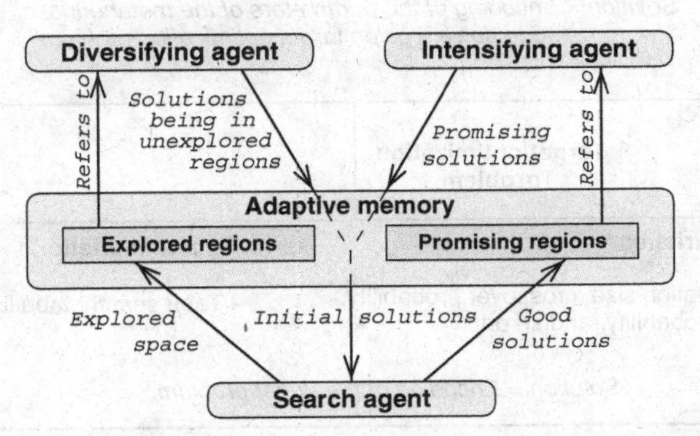

FIGURE 5.11 The COSEARCH HTH specialist hybrid model for metaheuristics. Several search algorithms solve different problems.

[6]The concept of adaptive memory has been proposed in the domain of combinatorial optimization [744]. It is similar to the concept of blackboard in the field of artificial intelligence [245].

information about the already visited areas of the search space and about the intrinsic nature of the good solutions already found. When diversifying, the local search agent receives starting solutions in unexplored regions; when intensifying, the search agent receives an initial solution in a promising region. The diversifying agent refers to the adaptive memory (information about the explored areas) to yield a solution from an unexplored region. The intensifying agent refers to the adaptive memory (information about promising regions) to produce a promising starting solution.

Example 5.8 COSEARCH for the quadratic assignment problem. An example of the application of the COSEARCH approach has been developed in Ref. [749] to solve the quadratic assignment problem (QAP). A parallel tabu search is used to solve the QAP, while a genetic algorithm makes a diversification task that is formulated as another optimization problem. The frequency memory stores information relative to all the solutions visited during the tabu search. The genetic algorithm refers to the frequency memory to generate solutions being in unexplored regions.

Another approach of specialist hybrid HRH heuristics is to use a heuristic to optimize another heuristic, that is, find the optimal values of the parameters of the heuristic (Fig. 5.12). This approach is known as *meta-optimization* (see Section 1.6.1). For instance, it has been used to optimize simulated annealing and noisy methods (NM) by GA [484], ant colonies by GA [5], simulated annealing-based algorithms by a GA [333], and a GA by a GA [697][7]. In Ref. [697], the three parameters optimized are the crossover rate, inversion rate, and mutation rate. The individuals of the population

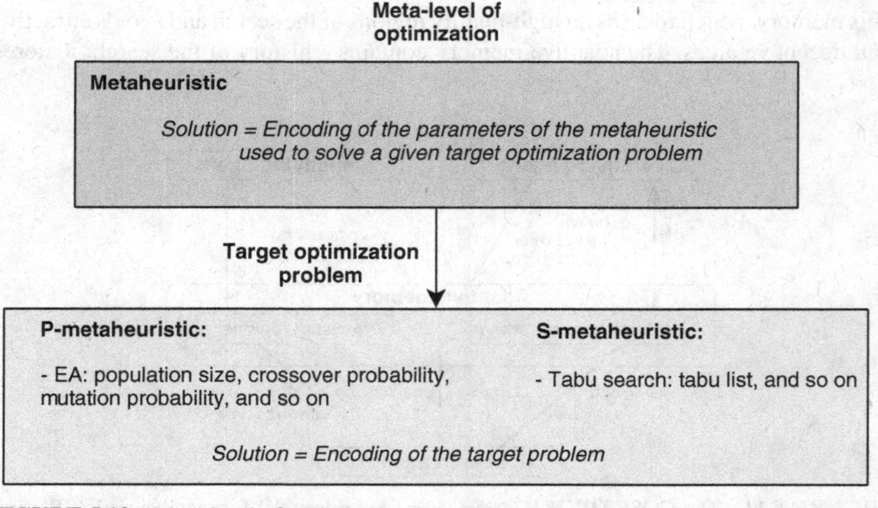

FIGURE 5.12 Meta-level of optimization in metaheuristics. Metaheuristics are used to optimize the parameters of another metaheuristic.

[7]This procedure is also called meta-evolution.

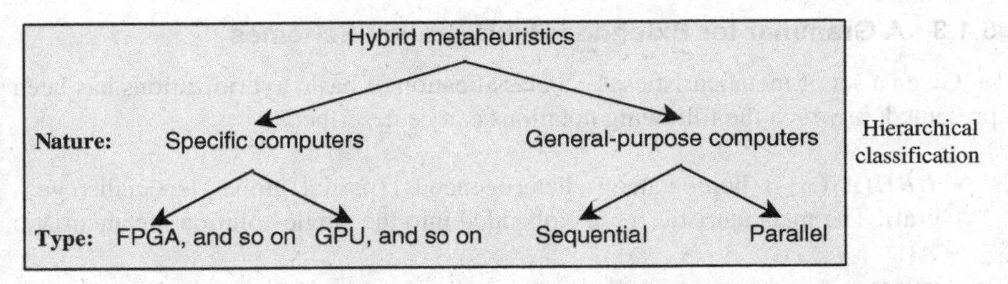

FIGURE 5.13 Classification of hybrid metaheuristics (implementation issues).

associated with the optimizer consist of three integers representing the mutation rate, inversion rate, and crossover rate. The fitness of an individual is taken to be the fitness of the best solution that the GA can find in the entire run, using these parameters.

5.1.2 Implementation Issues

The structure of the taxonomy concerning the implementation issues is shown in Fig. 5.13. This taxonomy has been discussed in the following sections.

5.1.2.1 Dedicated Versus General-Purpose Computers Application of specific computers differ from general purpose ones in that they usually solve only a small range of problems, but often at much higher rates and lower cost. Their internal structure is tailored for a particular problem, and thus can achieve much higher efficiency and hardware utilization than a processor that must handle a wide range of tasks.

In the last years, the advent of programmable logic devices has made easier to build specific computers for metaheuristics such as simulated annealing [8] and genetic algorithms [676]. A general architecture acting as a template for designing a number of specific machines for different metaheuristics (SA, TS, etc.) may be constructed [7]. The processor is built with XILINX FPGAs and APTIX interconnection chips. Experiments evaluating a simulated annealing algorithm to solve the traveling salesman problem achieved a speedup of about 37 times over an IBM RS6000 workstation. To our knowledge, this approach has not yet been proposed for hybrid metaheuristics.

Nowadays, the use of GPU (graphical processing unit) devices is more and more popular in many application domains. Indeed, those devices are integrated into many workstations to deal with visualization tasks. The idea is to exploit those available resources to improve the effectiveness of hybrid metaheuristics.

5.1.2.2 Sequential Versus Parallel Most of the proposed hybrid metaheuristics are sequential programs. According to the size of problems, parallel implementations of hybrid algorithms have been considered. The easiness to use a parallel and distributed architecture has been acknowledged for the HTH hybrid model. Parallel hybrids are detailed in the next chapter.

5.1.3 A Grammar for Extended Hybridization Schemes

Given a set of metaheuristics A_i, a classification of basic hybridizations has been presented, in which the following notations can be described:

- $LRH(A_1(A_2))$ (homogeneous, heterogeneous) (partial, global) (specialist, general): The metaheuristic A_2 is embedded into the single-solution metaheuristic A_1.
- $HRH(A_1 + A_2)$ (homogeneous, heterogeneous) (partial, global) (specialist, general): The self-contained metaheuristics A_1 and A_2 are executed in sequence.
- $LTH(A_1(A_2))$ (homogeneous, heterogeneous) (partial, global) (specialist, general): The metaheuristic A_2 is embedded into the population-based metaheuristic A_1.
- $HTH(A_1, A_2)$ (homogeneous, heterogeneous) (partial, global) (specialist, general): The self-contained metaheuristics A_1 and A_2 are executed in parallel and they cooperate.

These hybridizations should be regarded as primitives that can be combined in different ways. The grammar given in Fig. 5.14 generalizes the basic hybridization schemes. One of the practical importances of the grammar is to specify the hybrid heuristic to use, if a metaheuristic problem-solving tool is used.

Example 5.9 Extended hybridization schemes. Let us present some examples of extended hybridization schemes (Fig. 5.15). Boese et al. [84] suggested an adaptive multistart (AMS) approach, which may be seen as a HRH(LS + LTH(GA(LS))) scheme.

<hybrid-metaheuristic> ⟶ <design-issues> <implementation-issue>
<design-issues> ⟶ <hierarchical> <flat>
<hierarchical> ⟶ <LRH> | <LTH> | <HRH> | <HTH>
<LRH> ⟶ LRH(<S-metaheuristic> (<metaheuristic>))
<LTH> ⟶ LTH(<P-metaheuristic> (<metaheuristic>))
<HRH> ⟶ HRH(<metaheuristic> + <metaheuristic>)
<HTH> ⟶ HTH(<metaheuristic>)
<HTH> ⟶ HTH(<metaheuristic> , <metaheuristic>)
<flat> ⟶ (<type> , <domain> , <function>)
<type> ⟶ homogeneous | heterogeneous
<domain> ⟶ global | partial
<function> ⟶ general | specialist
<implementation-issue> ⟶ *<specificcomputers>* | *<general-purpose computers>*
<specific computers> ⟶ FPGA | GPU | ...
<general-purpose computers> ⟶ sequential | parallel
<metaheuristic> ⟶ *<S-metaheuristic>* | *<P-metaheuristic>*
<S-metaheuristic> ⟶ LS | TS | SA | TA | NM | GDA | ILS | GRASP | ...
<P-metaheuristic> ⟶ EA | SS | ACO | PSO | AIS | BC | EDA | CA | CEA | ...
<metaheuristic> ⟶ <hybrid-metaheuristic>

FIGURE 5.14 A grammar for extended hybridization schemes.

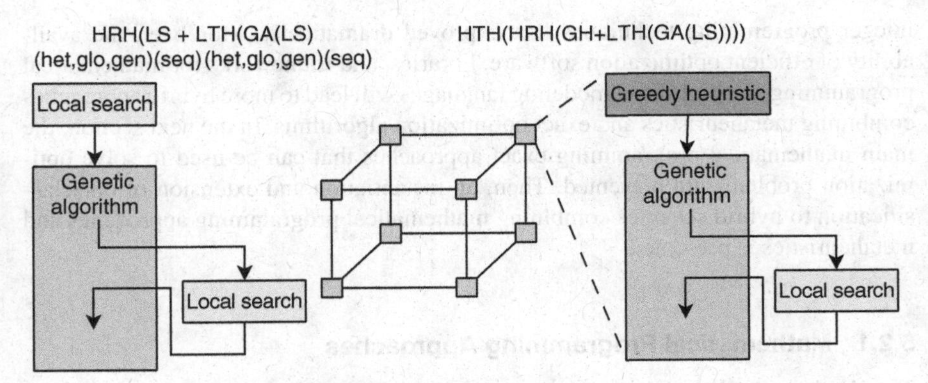

FIGURE 5.15 Extended hybridization schemes.

First, AMS generates a set of random starting solutions and runs an LS algorithm for each solution to find corresponding local optima. Then, AMS generates new starting solutions by combining features of the T best local optima seen so far, with T being a parameter of the approach. This mechanism bears some resemblance to GAs, but differs in that many solutions (instead of just two) are used to generate the new starting solutions. New local optima are obtained by running the LS algorithm from these new starting solutions, and the process iterates until some stop criterion is met.

D. Levine has used a HTH(HRH(GH+LTH(GA(LS)))) hierarchical scheme in his PhD to solve set partitioning problems. Efficient results have been obtained with a parallel static implementation in solving big-sized problems in real-world applications (airline crew scheduling) [502]. At the first level, a HTH hybrid based on the island model of parallel genetic algorithms is used. The initial population of each GA was generated by a greedy heuristic (the Chvatal heuristic [135]), and a local search algorithm was used to improve the solutions at each generation of the GA. The same hybrid scheme with a sequential implementation has been used in Ref. [92] to solve the traveling salesman problem. The local search algorithms used are the well-known 2-opt and or-opt heuristics. The author reported some interesting results for the 442-and 666-city problems. He found the optimum of the 442-city problem, and a solution within 0.04% of the optimum for the 666-city problem.

The objective of this chapter is far from providing an exhaustive list of research works using hybrid metaheuristics. Following this grammar, more than 125 annotated hybrid metaheuristics may be found in Ref. [747]. This shows the usefulness of the taxonomy.

5.2 COMBINING METAHEURISTICS WITH MATHEMATICAL PROGRAMMING

Metaheuristics and exact algorithms are complementary optimization strategies in terms of the quality of solutions and the search time used to find them. In the last few years, solving exactly the important optimization problems using, for example, integer programming techniques has improved dramatically. Moreover, the availability of efficient optimization software, libraries, and frameworks for mathematical programming and high-level modeling languages will lead to more hybrid approaches combining metaheuristics and exact optimization algorithms. In the next section, the main mathematical programming exact approaches that can be used to solve optimization problems are presented. Then, an instantiation and extension of our classification to hybrid schemes combining mathematical programming approaches and metaheuristics is presented.

5.2.1 Mathematical Programming Approaches

The main mathematical programming approaches may be classified as follows:

- **Enumerative algorithms:** This class of algorithms contains tree search algorithms, such as branch and bound, and dynamic programming. They are based on a divide and conquer strategy to partition the solution space into subproblems and then optimizing individually each subproblem.
- **Relaxation and decomposition methods:** This class of methods is based on relaxation techniques, such as the Lagrangian relaxation [265], and decomposition methods such as the Bender's decomposition and the continuous semidefinite programming.
- **Cutting plane and pricing algorithms:** This class of algorithms is based on polyhedral combinatorics in which the search space is pruned.

5.2.1.1 Enumerative Algorithms Enumerative methods include branch and bound algorithm, dynamic programming, $A*$, and other tree search algorithms. The search is carried out over the whole search space, and the problem is solved by subdividing it into simpler subproblems.

Branch and bound algorithm is one of the most popular methods to solve optimization problems in an exact manner. The algorithm is based on an implicit enumeration of all solutions of the considered optimization problem. The search space is explored by dynamically building a tree whose root node represents the problem being solved and its whole associated search space. The leaf nodes are the potential solutions and the internal nodes are subproblems of the total solution space. The size of the subproblems is increasingly reduced as one approaches the leaves.

The construction of such a tree and its exploration are performed using two main operators: *branching* and *pruning* (Fig. 5.16). The algorithm proceeds in several iterations during which the best found solution is progressively improved. The generated nodes and not yet treated are kept in a list whose initial content is limited only to the root node. The two operators intervene at each iteration of the algorithm. The branching strategy determines the order in which the branches are explored. Many branching strategies may be applied such as the *depth-first*, the *breadth-first*, and the *best-first* strategies. The *pruning* strategy eliminates the partial solutions that do not lead to optimal solutions. This is done by computing the lower bound associated with

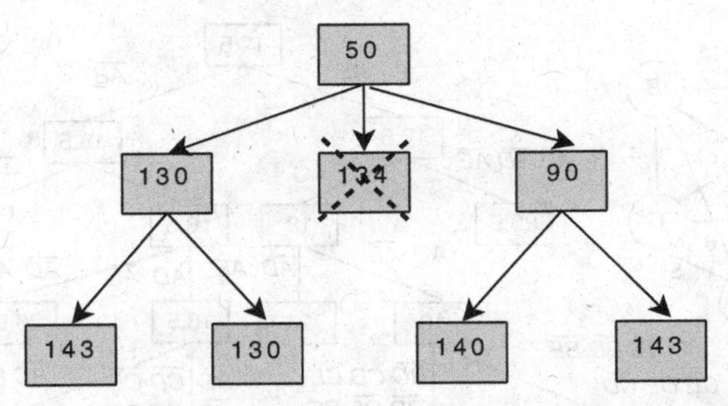

FIGURE 5.16 The branch and bound algorithm. This figure shows the nodes actually explored in the example problem, assuming a depth-first and left-to-right search strategy. The subtree rooted at the second node on level 2 is pruned because the cost of this node (134) is greater than that of the cheapest solution already found (130).

a partial solution. If the lower bound of a node (partial solution) is greater than the best solution found so far or a known upper bound of the problem, the exploration of the node is not needed. The algorithm terminates if there are no more nodes to branch or all nodes are eliminated. Hence, the most important concepts in designing an efficient branch and bound algorithm are the quality of the bounds and the branching strategy.

Example 5.10 Branch and bound algorithm on the TSP. Let us consider the TSP problem. A straightforward method for computing a lower bound on the cost of any solution may be the following:

$$\frac{1}{2}\sum_{v \in V} \text{sum of the costs of the two least cost edges adjacent to } v$$

For the example shown in Fig. 5.17, the lower bound is associated with the edges $(A, D), (A, B), (B, A), (B, E), (C, B), (C, A), (D, A), (D, C), (E, B), (E, D)$ and is equal to 17.5. In the search tree (Fig. 5.17), each node represents a partial solution. Each partial solution is represented by the set of associated edges (i.e., edges that must be in the tour) and the nonassociated edges (i.e., set of edges that must not be on the tour). The branching consists in generating two children nodes. A set of additional excluding and including edges is associated with each child. Two rules may be applied. An edge (a, b) must be included if its exclusion makes it impossible for a or b to have two adjacent edges in the tour. An edge (a, b) must be excluded if its inclusion causes for a or b to have more than two adjacent edges in the tour or would complete a nontour with edges already included. The pruning consists first in computing the lower bounds for each child. For instance, if the edge (A, E) is included and the edge (B, C) is excluded, the lower bound will be associated with the following selected edges $(A, D), (A, E), (B, A), (B, E), (C, D), (C, A), (D, A), (D, C), (E, B), (E, A)$ and is equal to 20.5. If the lower bound associated with a node is larger than the known upper

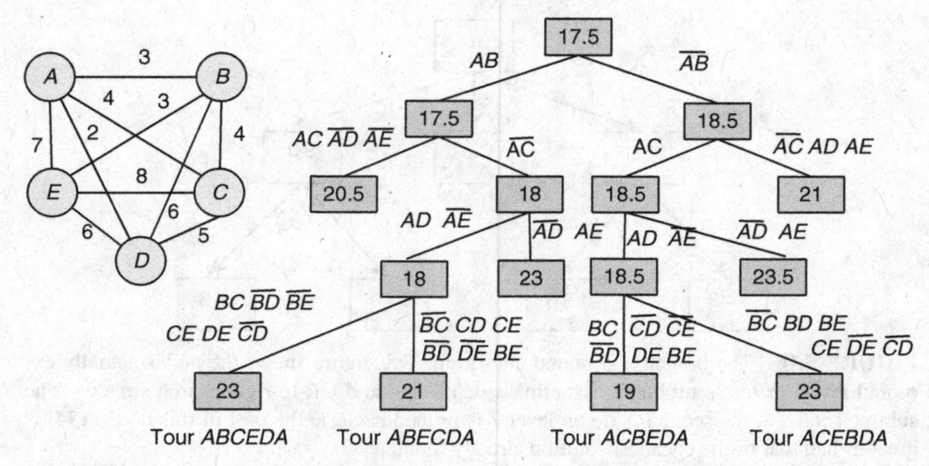

FIGURE 5.17 Illustration of the branch and bound algorithm on the traveling salesman problem.

bound, the node is proved to be unable to generate an optimal solution and then is not explored. A best-first search heuristic is considered in which the child with the smaller lower bound is explored first. The upper bound is updated each time a new complete solution is found with a better cost.

The *dynamic programming* (DP) approach is based on the recursive division of a problem into simpler subproblems. This procedure is based on the *Bellman's principle* that says,"the subpolicy of an optimal policy is itself optimal with regard to the start and end states" [68].

Designing a dynamic programming procedure for a given problem needs the definition of the following components [71]:

- Define the *stages* and the *states*. A problem can be divided into a number of stages N. A number of states are associated with each stage.
- Define the cost of the initial stage and states. There is an initial state of the system x_0.
- Define the recursive relation for a state at stage k in terms of states of previous stages. The system takes the state x_k at the stage k. At the k stage, the state of the system changes from x_k to x_{k+1} using the following equation

$$x_{k+1} = f_k(x_k, u_k)$$

where u_k is a control that takes values from a given finite set, which may depend on the stage k. The transition from the state k to $k+1$ involves a cost $g_k(x_k, u_k)$. The final transition from $N-1$ to N involves the terminal cost $G(x_N)$. The functions f_k, g_k, and G must be determined.

TABLE 5.1 An Instance for the Knapsack problem with a Capacity of 5

Item (i)	Weight (w_i)	Utility (u_i)
1	2	65
2	3	80
3	1	30

Given a control sequence $(u_1, u_2, \ldots, u_{N-1})$, the corresponding state sequence will be $(x_0, \ldots, x_N)$, which is determined from the initial state x_0 using the following equation. In dynamic programming, the objective is to find the optimal control sequence minimizing the total cost:

$$G(x_N) + \sum_{k=0}^{N-1} g_k(x_k, u_k)$$

DP have been successfully applied to knapsack, planning, and routing-type problems, in which it is easy to define efficient recursive relationships between stages.

Example 5.11 Dynamic programming for the {0,1} knapsack problem. Let us consider the following instance for the knapsack problem with a total capacity equal to 5 (see Table 5.1).

The stages are represented by the items. The number of stages are then equal to the number of items (3). The state y_i at stage i represents the total weight of items i and all following items in the knapsack. The decision at stage i corresponds to how many items i to place in the knapsack. Let us call this value k_j. This leads to the following recursive formulas: let $f_j(y_j)$ be the value of using y_j units of capacity for items j and following. Let $\lfloor a \rfloor$ represent the largest integer less than or equal to a.

$$f_3(y_i) = 30 \cdot y_i$$

$$f_j(y_i) = \max_{k_i \leq \lfloor \frac{y_i}{w_i} \rfloor} \{u_i k_i + f_{i+1}(y_i - w_i k_i)\}$$

5.2.1.2 *Relaxation and Decomposition Methods*

Relaxation methods consist in relaxing a strict requirement in the target optimization problem. In general, a given strict requirement is simply dropped completely or substituted by another one that is more easily satisfied. The most used relaxation techniques are the linear programming relaxation (LP-relaxation) and the Lagrangian relaxation. In addition to their use in solving optimization problems, relaxation methods are also used to generate bounds.

Linear programming relaxation: Linear programming relaxation is a straightforward approach that consists in ignoring the integrity constraints of an integer program (IP). Once the integrity constraints are dropped, the problem can be solved using LP solvers. This gives a lower bound for the problem. If the solution found satisfies the integer constraints (generally not true), it will be considered as the optimal solution for the IP program. If the relaxed problem is infeasible, then so is the IP program. LP-relaxation is widely used in branch and bound algorithm to solve IP problems in which the branching is performed over the fractional variables.

Lagrangian relaxation: Lagrangian relaxations are widely used to generate tight lower bounds for optimization problems. The main idea is to remove some constraints and incorporate them in the objective function. For each constraint, a penalty function is associated. The choice of which constraints are handled in the objective function is important. More complicated constraints to satisfy are preferable as they generate an easiest problem to solve. Given the following LP problem:

$$\text{Max } \; c^T x$$

$$\text{s.t. } \; Ax \leq b$$

with $x \in \mathbb{R}^n$ and $A \in \mathbb{R}^{m,n}$

The set of constraints A is split into two sets: $A_1 \in \mathbb{R}^{m_1,n}$ and $A_2 \in \mathbb{R}^{m_2,n}$, where $m_1 + m_2 = m$. Then, the subset of constraints A_2 is integrated into the objective function, which gives the following Lagrangian relaxation of the original problem:

$$\text{Max } \; c^T x + \lambda^T (b_2 - A_2 x)$$

$$\text{s.t. } \; A_1 x \leq b_1$$

with $x \in \mathbb{R}^n$, $A_1 \in \mathbb{R}^{m_1,n}$, and $A_2 \in \mathbb{R}^{m_2,n}$
where $\lambda = (\lambda_1, \ldots, \lambda_{m_2})$ are nonnegative weights ,which penalize the violated constraints A_2. The efficiency of Lagrangian relaxation depends on the structure of the problem; there is no general theory applicable to all problems. Lagrangian relaxation may find bounds that are tighter than the LP-relaxation. The problem is solved iteratively until optimal values for the multipliers are found. One of the main issues in the Lagrangian relaxation is the generation of the optimal multipliers. This difficult problem can be solved by metaheuristics.

In practice, decomposition methods are used to solve large IP problems. Among the numerous decomposition approaches, one can refer to Bender's decomposition and Dantzig–Wolfe decomposition.

Bender's decomposition: The Bender's decomposition algorithm is based on the notion of complicated variables. It consists in fixing the values of complicated variables and solves the resulting reduced problem iteratively [69]. Given a MIP problem:

$$\text{Max } \; c^T x + h^T y$$

$$\text{s.t. } \; Ax + Gy \leq b$$

with $x \in \mathbb{Z}_+^n$ and $y \in \mathbb{R}_+^p$

If the set of variables x is fixed, the following linear program (LP) is obtained

$$z_{\text{LP}}(x) = \max\{hy/Gy \leq b - Ax\}$$

and its dual

$$\min\{u(b - Ax)/uG \geq h, u \in \mathbb{R}^m_+\}$$

If the dual polyhedron is assumed to be not empty and bounded, the MIP model can be formulated as follows:

$$z = \max_{x \in \mathbb{Z}^n_+}(cx + \min_{i \in 1,\ldots,T}(u^i(b - Ax)))$$

This model can be reformulated as

$$z = \max\{\eta/\eta \leq u^i(b - Ax), \quad i \in 1,\ ldots, T, x \in \mathbb{Z}^n_+\}$$

Then, the algorithm finds cutting planes based on the dual problem. The cutting planes are added to the problem and the problem is resolved.

5.2.1.3 Branch and Cut and Price Algorithms

The objective of the following popular techniques is to generate tighter IP relaxations.

Cutting plane: Cutting plane approaches have been proposed in 1958 by Gomory [335]. The use of cuts can greatly improve branch and bound algorithms. In general, cutting plane algorithms consist in iteratively adding some specific constraints to the LP-relaxation of the problem. Those constraints represent restrictions to the problem so that the linear programming polytope closely approximates the polyhedron represented by the convex hull of all feasible solutions of the original IP problem. A good survey of branch and cut algorithms and their use for different families of optimization problems may be found in Refs [440,579].

Column generation: Column generation has been first applied by Gilmore and Gomory [317]. Column generation (i.e., Dantzig–Wolfe decomposition) generates a decomposition of the problem into a master and subproblems (Fig. 5.18). A good survey may be found in Ref. [50].

5.2.2 Classical Hybrid Approaches

Exact MP algorithms are known to be time and/or memory consuming. In general, they cannot be applied to large instances of difficult optimization problems. On one hand, their combination with metaheuristics may improve the effectiveness of heuristic search methods (i.e., getting better solutions). On the other hand, this type of combination allows the design of more efficient exact methods (i.e., finding optimal solutions in shorter time). The following sections illustrate, for each class of hybrids

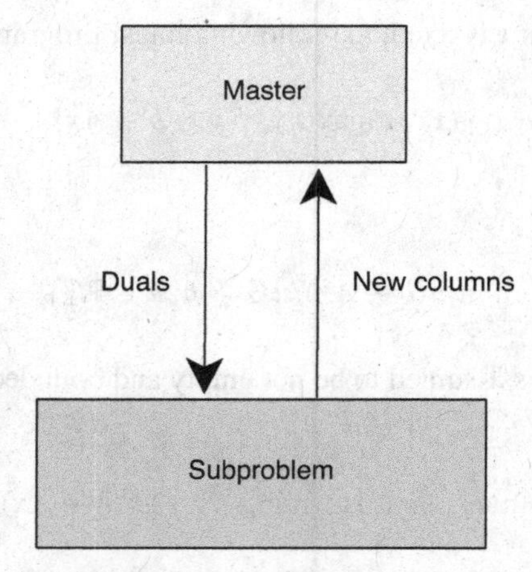

FIGURE 5.18 Branch and price approach.

belonging to the presented taxonomy, some hybridization schemes combining exact MP algorithms and metaheuristics.

5.2.2.1 *Low-Level Relay Hybrid* This class of algorithms represents hybrid schemes in which a metaheuristic approach (resp. exact approach) is embedded into an exact approach (resp. S-metaheuristic approach) to improve the search strategy. In this usual combination, a given metaheuristic or exact algorithm solves a problem of a different nature of the considered optimization problem.

Embedding S-metaheuristics into exact algorithms: Indeed, metaheuristics may solve many search problems involved in the design of an exact method such as the node selection strategy, upper bound generation, and column generation (Fig. 5.19):

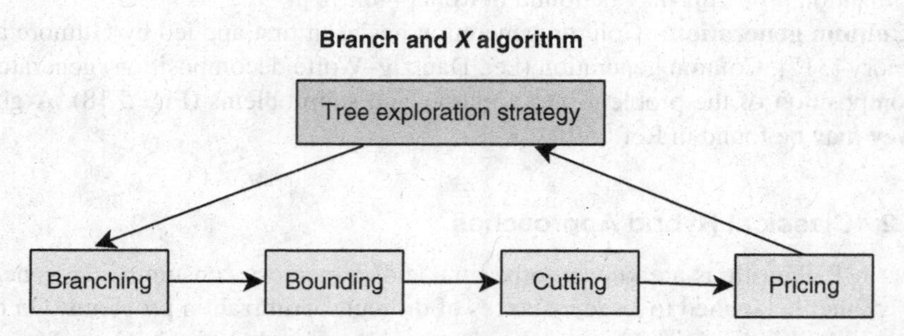

FIGURE 5.19 LRH cooperation in which a metaheuristic can be used in the design of some search components of branch and X family of algorithms (e.g., branch and bound, branch and cut, branch and price): selection of the node to explore, generation of an upper bound, cutting plane generation, column generation selection, and so on.

- **Bounding:** Providing an upper bound associated with a node of the branch and bound algorithm can be designed using a metaheuristic. Indeed, the partial solution is completed by a given metaheuristic and then a local upper bound is provided.
- **Cutting:** In the branch and cut algorithm, the cutting plane generation problem is a crucial part of the algorithm: the part that looks for valid inequalities that cut off the current nonfeasible linear program solution. Metaheuristics may be used in this *separation procedure*. For instance, this approach has been proposed for the CVRP (capacitated vehicle routing problem) [39]. Some metaheuristics (e.g., tabu search, greedy heuristics) have been designed to extract a set of violated capacity constraints of the relaxed problem.
- **Pricing:** In the branch and price algorithm, the pricing of columns may be carried out by a metaheuristic [261].

Some metaheuristic ingredients may also be used in tree search algorithms such as the concepts of tabu lists and aspiration criteria [625].

Embedding exact algorithms into S-metaheuristics: Many combinations may be designed in which exact algorithms are embedded into search components of S-metaheuristics.

Very large neighborhoods: As seen in Section 2.1.2, S-metaheuristics may be improved using very large neighborhoods. The concept of large neighborhoods is also used in the ILS (perturbation operator [517]) and the variable neighborhood search (VNS) metaheuristics. Mathematical programming approaches may be used to efficiently search these large neighborhoods to find the best or an improving solution in the neighborhood (Fig. 5.20). Algorithms such as branch and bound, dynamic programming [621], network flow algorithms [221], and matching algorithms [346] have been used to explore large neighborhoods defined for different important optimization problems. Some hybrid schemes explore the *whole* neighborhood while other neighborhood search algorithms explore a *subset* of the neighborhood. If no

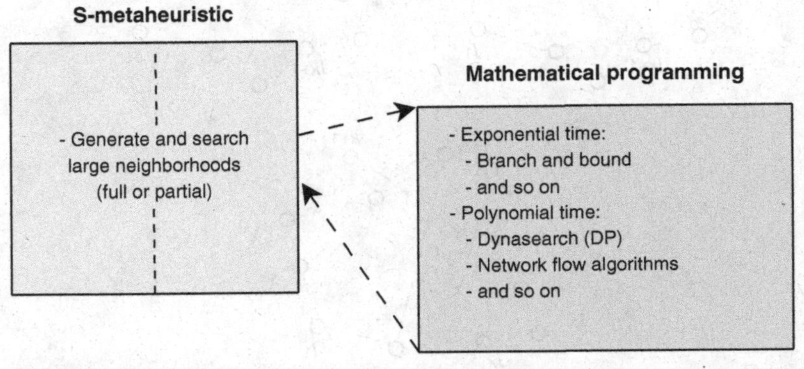

FIGURE 5.20 LRH cooperation where a mathematical programming approach can be used for the efficient search of a very large neighborhood in S-metaheuristics.

polynomial-time algorithm exists to search the whole neighborhood, a partial search is generally performed.

Example 5.12 Hyperopt. The hyperopt S-metaheuristic explores only a subset of a very large neighborhood [97]. The hybrid algorithm has been used to solve the asymmetric traveling salesman problem. The move operator is based on hyperedges that represent subpaths of the tour. A hyperedge $H(i, j)$ is represented by its start node i, end node j, and length k. A k-hyperopt move consists in deleting two hyperedges $H(i_1, i_{k+1})$ and $H(j_1, j_{k+1})$ of length k. It is supposed that $H(i_1, i_{k+1}) \cap H(j_1, j_{k+1}) = \phi$, that is, the hyperedges share no common edges. Then, the move operator adds edges to the hyperedges $H(i_{k+1}, j_1)$ and $H(j_{k+1}, i_1)$ to construct a feasible tour (Fig. 5.21). The size of the hyperedge neighborhood grows exponentially with k. The neighborhood search algorithm is reduced to a smaller TSP problem. The algorithms used are based on enumeration for small k and a dynamic programming algorithm for medium values of k.

Some search concepts of exact algorithms may be used in S-metaheuristics. Efficient mathematical programming approaches that generate "good" lower bounds exist for many optimization problems. Information related to lower bounds, obtained, for example, by Lagrangian relaxation, can be exploited into a metaheuristic to intensify the search in promising regions of the search space. For instance, information based on Lagrangian multipliers are exploited to guide the metaheuristic in solving the set covering problem [63]. Lower bounds have been used in S-metaheuristics such as tabu search to improve the search [221,376].

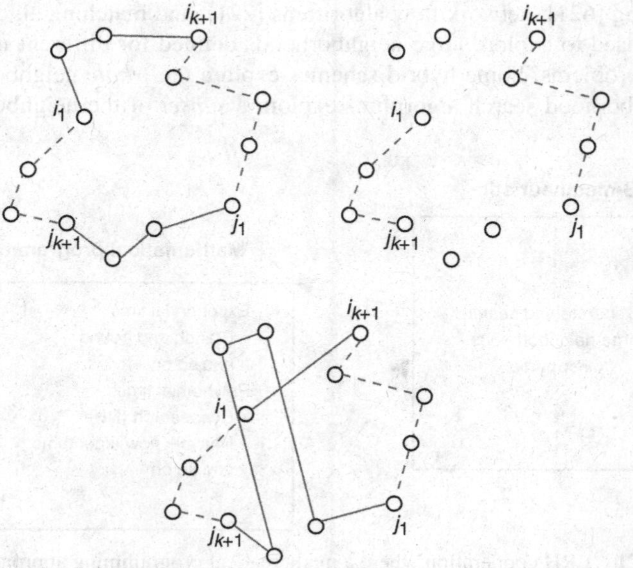

FIGURE 5.21 Large neighborhood based on hyperedge for the asymmetric traveling salesmen problem.

5.2.2.2 Low-Level Teamwork Hybrids Recall that in this class of hybrid algorithms, a search component of a P-metaheuristic is replaced by another optimization algorithm. Concerning the combination of P-metaheuristics and MP algorithms, two main hybrid approaches may be considered: exact search hybrid algorithms in which a P-metaheuristic is embedded into an exact algorithm and heuristic search algorithms in which an exact algorithm is embedded into a P-metaheuristic.

Embedding a P-metaheuristic into an exact algorithm: As mentioned previously in this chapter, the following questions arise in designing a branch and bound algorithm:

- **Branch ordering:** How the problem to solve (node of the tree) is decomposed into subproblems? On which variable the next branching is applied? Indeed, near-optimal solutions obtained by metaheuristics may guide the branch and bound to apply an efficient branch ordering by giving preference to branches that share common values with near-optimal solutions.

  The node selection problem in tree search based on branch and bound may be solved by metaheuristics. For instance, genetic programming approaches have been used to deal with the node selection problem [477].
- **Variable selection:** In which subproblem (child node) the search will be performed in the next step? What value should first be assigned to the branching variable? Information obtained from branch and bound tree can be used by heuristic algorithms to determine a better strategy for variable selection [477].

An exact algorithm constructs partial solutions that are used to define a search space for a metaheuristic. Then, the obtained results are exploited to refine the bounds or generate the columns into a branch and cut algorithm.

Example 5.13 Local branching. The *local branching* exact approach has been proposed in Ref. [263]. It uses the principle of local search heuristics. The search space is partitioned by introducing branching conditions expressed through (invalid) linear inequalities called local branching cuts. Let us consider a MIP problem with {0, 1} variables. The k-opt neighborhood is considered. The main principle of the local branching method is to iteratively solve a subproblem corresponding to the neighborhood k-opt of a partial solution s. Two partitions are then considered: $p_1 = \{x \in \{0, 1\}^n / \Delta(x, s) \leq k\}$ and $p_2 = \{x \in \{0, 1\}^n / \Delta(x, s) \geq k + 1\}$, where Δ represents the Hamming distance and n the size of the problem. The problem associated with p_1 is solved. A new subproblem is generated if an improved solution is found. Otherwise, the other problem is solved using the standard procedure.

Embedding an exact algorithm into P-metaheuristic: In this hybrid scheme, some search components of a P-metaheuristic induce optimization problems that are solved by exact algorithms (Fig. 5.23).

Example 5.14 Exact algorithms into recombination operators. Exact algorithms may be integrated into recombination operators of P-metaheuristics such as evolutionary algorithms to find the best offspring from a large set of possibilities. The induced problem `Recombination` (S_1, S_2) is defined to generate the best offsprings

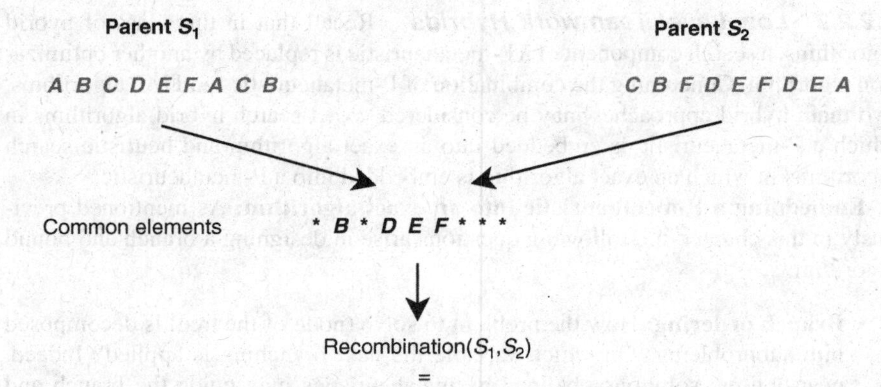

FIGURE 5.22 Using exact algorithms in recombination operators (e.g., crossover) of P-metaheuristics.

from the parents S_1 and S_2. A common idea is to keep the common elements of the parents and explore all the other possibilities to generate better offsprings (Fig. 5.22). For instance, a branch and bound algorithm (resp. dynamic programming) has been used into the crossover operator of a genetic algorithm in solving permutation problems [163] (resp. [831]). For some specific problems, polynomial exact algorithms may also be used such as minimum spanning tree algorithms [406], matching algorithms in a bipartite graph [11,46] for optimized crossover operators.

Large neighborhood search algorithms integrated into P-metaheuristics belong typically to the LTH class of hybrids. For instance, the mutation operator in EAs can also be substituted by MP algorithms, which explore large neighborhoods (Fig. 5.23).

Exact decoding: Exact algorithms can also be used as decoders of incomplete solutions carried out by metaheuristics. This hybrid strategy is applied in the case where metaheuristics use an incomplete encoding for the problem. Once a good

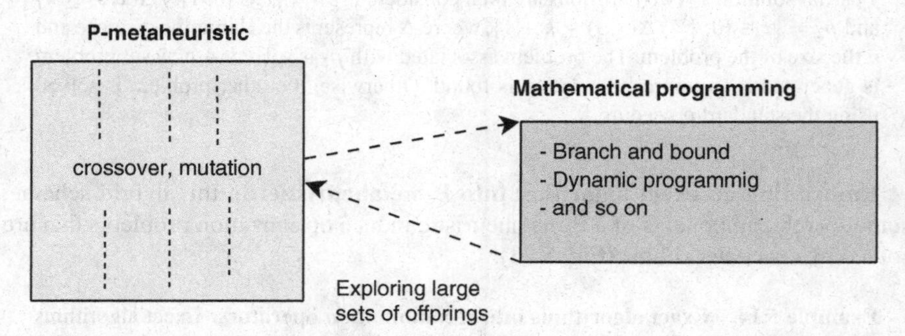

FIGURE 5.23 LTH heuristic cooperation: exact algorithms are used as search components of a P-metaheuristic (e.g., recombination, mutation).

incomplete solution is found, exact algorithms complete optimally the missing part of the encoding.

Exact search ingredients: Some search ingredients of exact algorithms can also be used in P-metaheuristics:

- **Lower bounds:** The use of lower bounds in a P-metaheuristic can improve the search. Lower bounds have been used in the construction phase of the ant colonies P-metaheuristic to solve the quadratic assignment problem [527]. The well-known Gilmore–Lawler lower bound and the values of the dual variables are used to order the locations during the construction phase. The impact of the location on a given QAP instance depends on the value of its associated dual variable. The concept of bounds has been used into evolutionary algorithms for the mutation and the crossover operators [222,761]. Indeed, partial solutions that exceed a given bound are deleted. The bounds are computed using the linear and Lagrangian relaxation and tree search methods.
- **Partial solutions:** The evaluated partial solutions (subproblems) maintained by the branch and bound family of algorithms may provide interesting initial solutions to improve. The evaluation of these partial solutions will guide the metaheuristics to more promising regions of the search space [527]. The partial solution with the least cost lower bound suggests a promising region by giving additional information.

5.2.2.3 *High-Level Relay Hybrids*

This class of cooperation, where self-contained algorithms are used in sequence, is the most popular in practice. This may be seen as a preprocessing or a postprocessing step. Some information is provided in the sequence between the two families of algorithms (metaheuristics and MP algorithms) (Fig. 5.24).

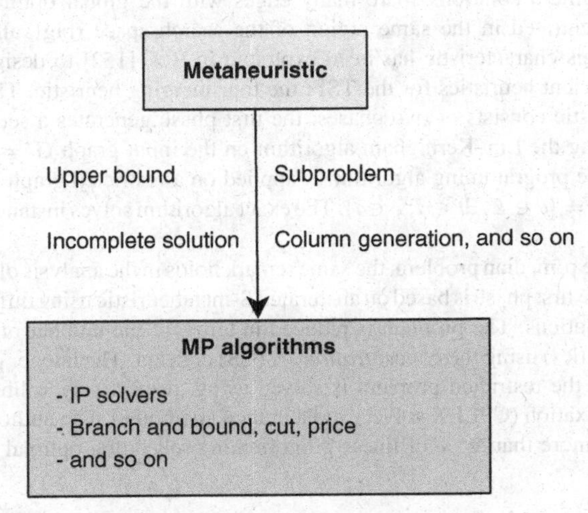

FIGURE 5.24 HRH cooperation: information provided by metaheuristics to MP algorithms.

Information provided by metaheuristics: In the case where the information is provided by the metaheuristics, the most natural and trivial hybrid approach is to start with a metaheuristic to find a "good" *upper bound* that will be used by a MP algorithm in the bounding phase (Fig. 5.24). Indeed, the efficiency of the search (pruning phase) largely depend on the quality of the upper bound.

Using the characteristics of generated high-quality solutions, metaheuristics can be used to reduce the size of the original problem. Then, the exact method can be applied to solve the reduced problem. This approach is interesting for optimization problems where "good solutions" share many components [33]. This allows to reduce the problem into a much smaller problem that can be solved exactly by state-of-the-art mathematical programming algorithms. The reduction phase may be concerned with the following:

- **Partitioning of decision variables:** In this strategy, the decision variables are partitioned into two sets X and Y. The metaheuristic will fix the variables of the set X and the exact method will optimize the problem over the set Y. Hence, the generated subproblems are subject to free variables in the set Y and freezed variables in the set X. Those subproblems are solved exactly.

  A set of high-quality solutions may be obtained by a P-metaheuristic or an iterated S-metaheuristic. The characteristics of this set can be exploited to define smaller problems by fixing some variables and solve the resulting subproblems by exact algorithms. An example of such strategy is the Mimausa method for the quadratic assignment problem [535]. The method builds at each iteration a subproblem by fixing k decision variables and solves it by a branch and bound algorithm.

  Example 5.15 Reducing problems by metaheuristics to be solved by MP algorithms. Analyzing the landscape for the TSP problem, one can observe that local optimum solutions share many edges with the global optimum and they are concentrated in the same region of the search space (big valley structure) [750]. This characteristic has been exploited in Ref. [152] to design one of the most efficient heuristics for the TSP: the tour merging heuristic. The tour merging heuristic consists of two phases: the first phase generates a set T of "good" tours using the Lin–Kernigham algorithm on the input graph $G = (V, E)$. Then, a dynamic programming algorithm is applied on a restricted graph $G' = (V, E')$, where $E' = \{e \in E / \exists t \in T, e \in t\}$. The exact algorithm solves instances up to 5000 cities.

  For the p-median problem, the same remark holds in the analysis of its landscape [663]. The first phase is based on an iterated S-metaheuristic using different random initial solutions. The problem is reduced in terms of the number of nodes (location facilities) using the *concentration set* (CS) concept. The integer programming model of the restricted problem is solved using, respectively, a linear programming relaxation (CPLEX solver) and a branch and bound. The authors exploit the fact that more than 95% of linear programming relaxation optimal solutions are integers.

For continuous optimization, HRH hybrid schemes are very popular. For instance, a hybrid method combining tabu search and the simplex algorithm provides interesting results in solving complex continuous functions [127].

- **Domain reduction:** This strategy consists in reducing the domain of values that the decision variables can take. The metaheuristic will perform a domain reduction for the decision variables and then an exact method is used over the reduced domains. For instance, a GA may be used to find promising ranges for decision variables and then tree search algorithms are considered to find the optimal solution within those ranges [572].

Information provided by exact algorithms: In the case where the information is provided by an exact algorithm, many hybrid approaches may be designed:

- **Partial solutions:** Partial solutions are first provided by an exact algorithm which are then completed by a metaheuristic (Fig.5.25).
- **Problem reduction:** In this strategy, a problem reduction is carried out by an exact algorithm. For instance, a tree search algorithm has been used to reduce the size of a nurse scheduling problem [223]. Then, a tabu search strategy is applied to solve the problem within a simplified objective function [223].
- **Relaxed optimal solutions and their duals:** The optimal solutions for relaxed formulation (e.g., LP-relaxation, Lagrangian relaxation) of the problem and its duals may be exploited by metaheuristics.

Example 5.16 LP-relaxations as an input for metaheuristics. Information gathered from solutions obtained by LP-relaxations of MIP problems may be used as an input for a metaheuristic. A straightforward approach is the "dive and fix" strategy, where

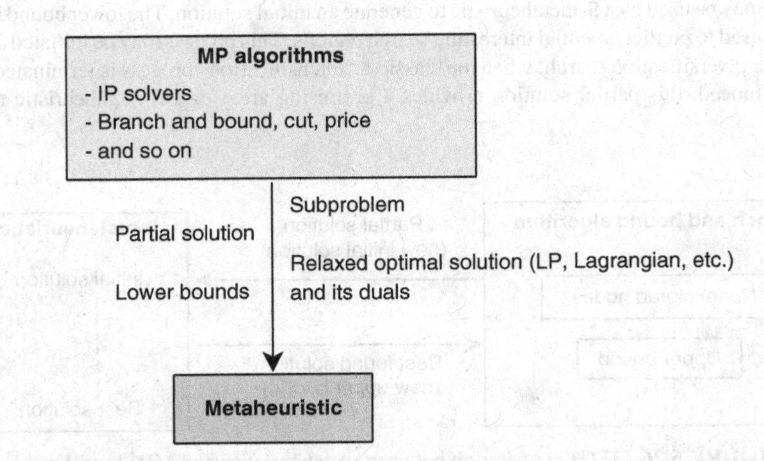

FIGURE 5.25 HRH cooperation: information provided by MP algorithms to metaheuristics.

the value of a subset of the integer variables are fixed and the resulting LP problem is solved. This strategy iterates until the LP finds an integer solution. This will restrict the search space of metaheuristics in promising regions. This idea has been used to design an efficient hybrid approach for the 0–1 multidimensional knapsack problem [792]. Many linear relaxations of the MIP formulation of the problem, including different constraints on the number of elements of the knapsack, are solved exactly. The obtained solutions are exploited to generate initial solutions for multiple tabu search metaheuristics.

5.2.2.4 High-Level Teamwork Hybrids Few strategies belong to this class of hybrid that combine metaheuristics and MP algorithms in a parallel cooperative way. However, this is a promising class of hybrids. A set of agents representing metaheuristics and MP algorithms are solving global, partial, or specialist optimization problems and exchanging useful informations. The majority of proposed approaches fall in the class of partial and specialist hybrids. Indeed, the search space is generally too large to be solved by an exact approach. One of the main issues in the HTH hybrid is the information exchanged between metaheuristics and MP algorithms. The different complementary algorithms solving different problems may exchange any information gathered during the search to improve the efficiency and the effectiveness of the hybrid approach: solution(s), subproblems, relaxed optimal solutions and its duals, upper bounds, lower bounds, optimal solutions for subproblems, partial solutions, and so on.

Example 5.17 Parallel cooperation between a branch and bound algorithm and a S-metaheuristic. In a parallel cooperation between branch and bound algorithm and a S-metaheuristic, the following information may be exchanged (Fig. 5.26):

- **From a branch and bound algorithm to a S-metaheuristic:** A subproblem of the branch and bound (node of the tree, partial solution) with least-cost lower bound may be used by a S-metaheuristic to generate an initial solution. The lower bound is used to predict potential interesting search regions. This process may be initiated as a diversification search, when the classical "intensification" process is terminated. Indeed, this partial solution provides a promising area for a S-metaheuristic to

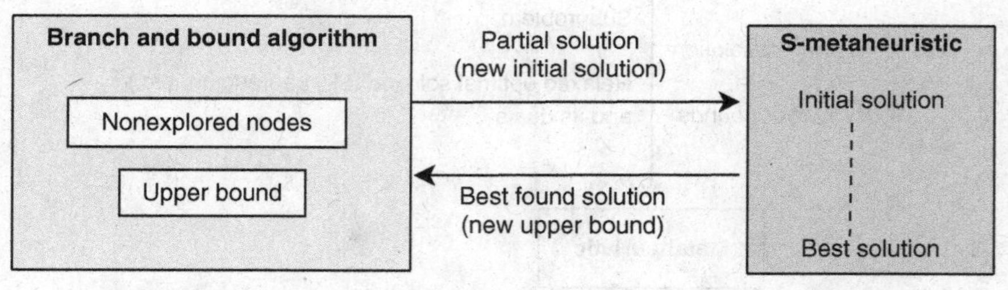

FIGURE 5.26 HTH cooperation between metaheuristics and MP algorithms.

explore. The nonexplored node list maintained by a branch and bound provides a metaheuristic with new initial solutions.

- **From a S-metaheuristic to a branch and bound algorithm:** The best solution identified so far by a metaheuristic may be used in branch and bound algorithms for a better pruning of the search tree. Indeed, the better is the upper bound, the more efficient is the pruning of the search tree. This information is exchanged each time the best solution found is improved.

In generalist and global hybrids, where all the algorithms are solving the same target problem, the space of design is reduced. For instance, a parallel HTH hybrid that consists in combining a branch and bound algorithm with simulated annealing has been designed [587]. The SA algorithm sends improved upper bounds to the exact algorithm. Any integer bound obtained by the B&B execution is passed to SA and used as an alternative reheated solution.

In specialist hybrids, where the algorithms are solving different problems, many strategies may be proposed (Fig. 5.27). For instance, a parallel cooperation between a local search metaheuristic and a column generation (branch and price) algorithm to solve the VRP problem has been proposed [116]. The local search algorithm is used to generate new columns for a branch and cut algorithm.

Extending the grammar, presented in Section 5.1.3, with hybrid schemes combining metaheuristics with exact optimization algorithms has been presented in Ref. [433]. More than 60 annotated hybrid approaches are detailed in the paper. Other examples of combining metaheuristics with exact algorithms may be found in the survey papers [212,433,628].

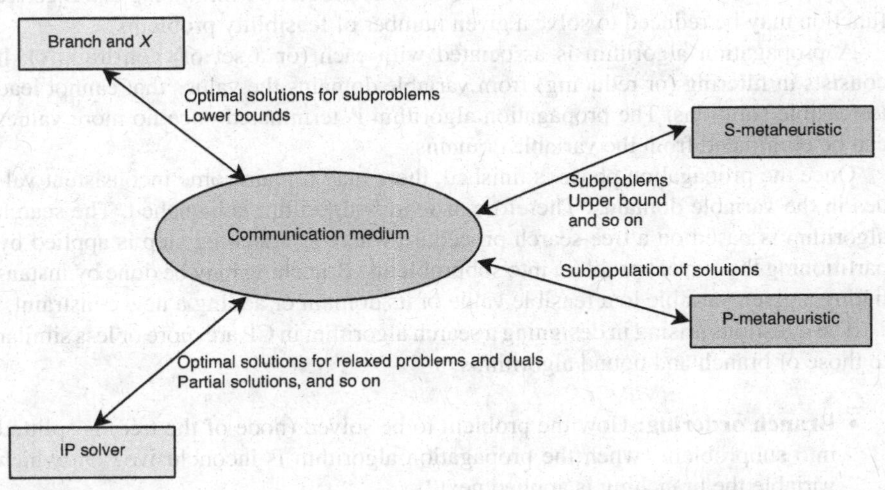

FIGURE 5.27 Specialist HTH cooperation between S-metaheuristics and MP algorithms.

5.3 COMBINING METAHEURISTICS WITH CONSTRAINT PROGRAMMING

Constraint programming is a modeling and an exact[8] search paradigm based on constraint satisfaction techniques, which are largely used in the artificial intelligence community [34]. CP has been applied successfully to many combinatorial optimization problems with tightly constrained search problems, while metaheuristics perform well for underconstrained optimization problems.

Nowadays, more and more hybrid approaches combining metaheuristics and constraint programming are used to solve optimization problems. Indeed, metaheuristics and constraint programming are complementary search and modeling approaches, which may be combined naturally to solve optimization problems in a more efficient manner [271]. One of the main advantages of using constraint programming is its flexibility. Models are based on a declarative programming paradigm. Hence, the addition/deletion of new constraints in the model is straightforward.

5.3.1 Constraint Programming

Optimization problems in constraint programming are modeled by means of a set of variables linked by a set of constraints. The variables take their values on a finite domain of integers. The constraints may have mathematical or symbolic forms. *Global constraints* refer to a set of variables of the problem. An example of such global constraints is `all_different`$(x_1, x_2, ..., x_n)$, which specifies that all the variables $x_1, x_2, ..., x_n$ must be different.

Solving a feasibility problem in CP is based on interleaving the *propagation* and the *search* processes to find a feasible solution for the problem. Minimizing an objective function may be reduced to solve a given number of feasibility problems.

A propagation algorithm is associated with each (or a set of) constraint(s). It consists in filtering (or reducing) from variable domains the values that cannot lead to feasible solutions. The propagation algorithm is terminated once no more values can be eliminated from the variable domains.

Once the propagation phase is finished, there may remain some inconsistent values in the variable domains. Therefore, a *search* algorithm is launched. The search algorithm is based on a tree search procedure where a branching step is applied by partitioning the current problem into subproblems. Branching may be done by instantiating a given variable to a feasible value of its domain or adding a new constraint.

The questions arising in designing a search algorithm in CP are more or less similar to those of branch and bound algorithms:

- **Branch ordering:** How the problem to be solved (node of the tree) is splitted into subproblems when the propagation algorithm is inconclusive? On which variable the branching is applied next?

[8] The term complete is always used in the CP community.

- **Variable selection:** In which subproblem (child node) the search continue next? What value should be first assigned to the branching variable?

Example 5.18 A CP model for Sudoku. Nowadays, the Sudoku logic game is very popular. The principle of the game is to fill a 9×9 grid so that each row and each column contains the numbers from 1 to 9. Moreover, each of the nine 3×3 boxes contains the numbers from 1 to 9. A partially completed grid is provided as an input for each game setting. A CP model using the Gecode solver may be the following:

Algorithm 5.1 CP model for Sudoku.

```
class Sudoku < Gecode::Model
  def initialize(predefined_values)
  # Create the squares representing the integer variables.
  @squares = int_var_matrix(9, 9, 1..9)
   # Distinctness constraint.
   9.times do |i|
   # All rows must contain distinct numbers.
   @squares.row(i).must_be.distinct
   # All columns must contain distinct numbers.
   @squares.column(i).must_be.distinct
   # All 3x3 boxes must contain distinct numbers.
   @squares.minor((i % 3) * 3, 3, (i / 3) * 3, 3).must_be.distinct
   end
  # Place the constraints from the predefined squares on them.
   predefined_values.row_size.times do |i|
    predefined_values.column_size.times do |j|
     unless predefined_values[i,j].zero?
      @squares[i,j].must == predefined_values[i,j]
     end
    end
   end
    end
  end
```

The `must_be.distinct` constraint has been used to model the three constraints of the problem (row, column, 3×3 boxes). The rest of the model represents the input setting of the game. It assigns the predefined values to squares of the grid (otherwise by default it is 0). Figure 5.28 illustrates a solution for a given game input.

5.3.2 Classical Hybrid Approaches

Many combination schemes show that the hybridization of metaheuristics and CP is fruitful for some optimization problems. The following sections illustrate, for each class of hybrids belonging to the presented taxonomy, some hybridization schemes

	2	6				8	1	
3			7		8			6
4				5				7
	5		1		7		9	
		3	9		5	1		
	4		3		2		5	
1				3				2
5			2		4			9
	3	8				4	6	

Input game

7	2	6	4	9	3	8	1	5
3	1	5	7	2	8	9	4	6
4	8	9	6	5	1	2	3	7
8	5	2	1	4	7	6	9	3
6	7	3	9	8	5	1	2	4
9	4	1	3	6	2	7	5	8
1	9	4	8	3	6	5	7	2
5	6	7	2	1	4	3	8	9
2	3	8	5	7	9	4	6	1

Solution of the game

FIGURE 5.28 Illustration of the Sudoku game.

between constraint programming algorithms and metaheuristics. Some illustrative examples may also be found in Ref. [271].

5.3.2.1 Low-Level Relay Hybrids As within mathematical programming approaches, constraint programming may be used to explore large neighborhoods in S-metaheuristics (full or partial). Indeed, when the propagation tends to reduce the search space, CP is an efficient approach in modeling the expression of neighborhoods and exploring very large neighborhoods with side constraints [698]. Two different types of exploration may be applied:

- **Neighborhoods with expensive testing of feasibility:** Neighborhoods around the current solution are defined by adding side constraints to the original problem. Checking the feasibility for all side constraints by CP may be efficient. Indeed, the feasibility test of solutions may be an expensive task. The propagation algorithms of CP reduce the size of neighborhoods.
- **Large neighborhoods:** Optimizing the exploration of the neighborhood with in-lined constraint checks. For instance, the problem of searching very large neighborhoods is tackled with a constraint programming solver in the resolution of vehicle routing problems [611]. A CP model has been proposed for the neighborhood, where every feasible solution represents a neighbor. A given subset of decision variables may also be fixed [33]. A CP search has been carried out over the uninstantiated variables to solve a scheduling problem. A similar approach has been proposed in Ref. [698] for a vehicle routing problem, and in Ref. [110] for a job-shop scheduling problem.

5.3.2.2 Low-Level Teamwork Hybrids In this class of LTH hybrid between metaheuristics and CP, two main categories may be distinguished: exact search hybrid algorithms in which a metaheuristic is embedded into constraint programming and heuristic search algorithms in which constraint programming is embedded into a P-metaheuristic.

Embedding metaheuristics into constraint programming: Metaheuristics may be used to improve the search algorithm in CP. The following hybrid approaches may be applied to converge more quickly to the optimal solution or approximating "good" solutions:

- **Node improvement:** Metaheuristics may be applied to partial solutions of the tree to improve or repair the nodes of the search tree. A greedy approach may also explore a set of paths from a node of the search tree. Then, CP search continue from the improved solutions [113].
- **Discrepancy-based search algorithms:** This approach generates near-greedy paths in a search tree. This approach has been used in limited discrepancy search [369] and dynamic backtracking [318]. Look-ahead evaluation of greedy algorithms may also be used over the nodes of the search tree [113].
- **Branch ordering:** Metaheuristics may be applied to answer the following question: which child node to investigate first when diving deeper into the node. Metaheuristics may be used to give a preference to a branch that is consistent with the near-optimal solution. Indeed, the use of metaheuristics produces a better variable ordering and then will speed up the tree search. This approach has been used for solving satisfiability problems [693].

  Metaheuristics may also be considered to solve relaxed problem. At each node, the subproblem is relaxed by removing some constraints. The violated constraints in the obtained solution will form the basis for branching. For instance, this approach has been used to solve a scheduling problem [443,574].
- **Variable selection:** Metaheuristics are used for variable selection at each node of the tree. This strategy consists in reducing the list of candidates. A straightforward strategy has been used in Ref. [256].Let $v_1, v_2, ..., v_n$ be the possible branches in a decreasing order of preference (lower bound $h(v_i)$). The strategy consists in selecting the v_i branches such as $h(v_i) \leq h(v_1) + \alpha(h(v_n) - h(v_1))$, where $\alpha \in [0, 1]$ is a parameter. These branches constitute the RCL list (restricted candidate lists), whereas the other branches are not explored.
- **Branching restriction:** Metaheuristics may be used to filter the branches of the tree-search node. This hybrid scheme has been proposed to solve a scheduling problem [115].

CP can construct partial solutions that are used to define a search space for a metaheuristic. Then, the results obtained are used to refine the bounds or columns to generate in a branch and cut algorithm.

Embedding constraint programming into P-metaheuristics: Some search components of a P-metaheuristic induce optimization problems, which are solved by CP. For instance, some recombination operators such as crossover in EAs may be optimized using CP. In addition to the recombination operators, large neighborhood search algorithms based on CP can be integrated into unary operators of P-metaheuristics such as the mutation in EAs.

Some search ingredients of constraint programming algorithms can also be used in P-metaheuristics. For instance, the use of lower bounds in a P-metaheuristic can improve the search. The partial solutions (subproblems) maintained by CP may provide interesting initial solutions to metaheuristics. The evaluation of these partial solutions will guide the metaheuristics to more promising regions of the search space. The partial solution with the least-cost lower bound suggests a promising region.

CP algorithms can also be used as decoders of indirect representations carried out by metaheuristics. This strategy may be applied once the metaheuristics use indirect encoding that represent incomplete solutions of the problem. This strategy is efficient when the decoding involves complex constraints to satisfy.

5.3.2.3 High-Level Relay Hybrids In this class of hybrids, selfcontained metaheuristics are used in conjunction with CP in a pipeline manner. Metaheuristics are considered as a preprocessing or a postprocessing step for CP.

Information provided by metaheuristics: In the case where the informations are provided by metaheuristics, similar information exchanges as with mathematical programming algorithms may be used: upper bounds, incomplete solutions, subproblems, and so on.

Information provided by constraint programming: In the case where the information is provided by CP, the same information as with mathematical programming[9] may be considered: partial solutions (i.e., subproblems), optimal solutions for relaxed problems, and so on.

For instance, heuristic search-based hybrid scheme may be applied to solving some generated subproblems by CP. A subset of variables are assigned values using a complete search approach. This approach has been used for scheduling problems [586] and routing problems [698]. This hybrid scheme has also been proposed to solve satisfiability (SAT) problems, where a depth-bounded tree search is carried out and a local search procedure is applied to nodes reaching the depth-limit [349]. CP can also be applied to an incomplete formulation of the problem. For instance, all (or a set of) feasible solutions are generated by a CP strategy. Then, a metaheuristic will be applied to improve feasible solutions represented by the leaves of the CP tree.

5.3.2.4 High-Level Teamwork Hybrids Few hybrid HTH strategies combining CP and metaheuristics have been investigated. This class constitutes a promising way to develop efficient solvers and optimization algorithms. The architecture of this class of hybrids may be viewed as a set of agents implementing different strategies (CP, metaheuristics, MP) in solving the target problem, and different subproblems and relaxed problems. These agents will exchange information on the search. For an exact approach, the objective is to speed up the search for obtaining an optimal solution (efficiency). For a heuristic strategy, the objective is also to improve the quality of the obtained solutions (effectiveness). The information exchanged may include

[9] However, the duals cannot be considered.

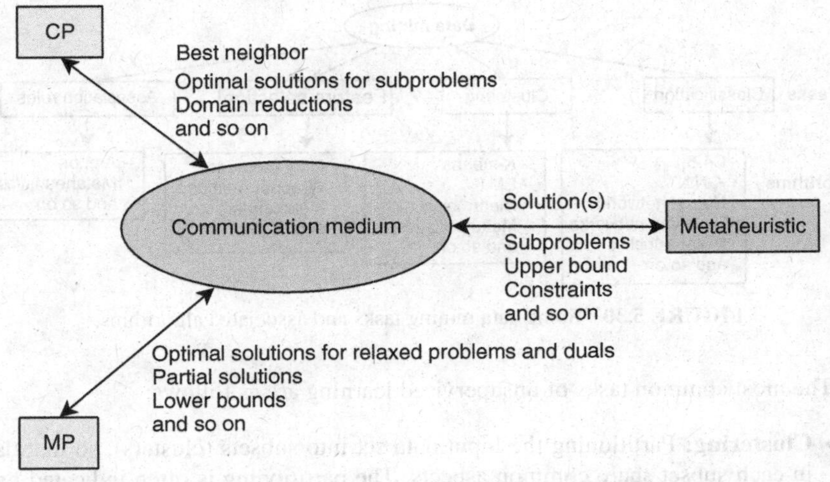

FIGURE 5.29 HTH cooperation between metaheuristics, MP, and CP strategies.

solution(s), subproblems, relaxed optimal solutions, upper bounds, lower bounds, optimal solutions for subproblems, partial solutions, and so on.(Fig. 5.29).

5.4 HYBRID METAHEURISTICS WITH MACHINE LEARNING AND DATA MINING

Combining metaheuristics with data mining and machine learning techniques represents another way to improve the efficiency and effectiveness of the optimization algorithms based on metaheuristics.

5.4.1 Data Mining Techniques

Data mining (DM), also known as knowledge discovery in databases (KDD), is the process of automatically exploring large volumes of data (e.g., instances described according to several attributes) to extract interesting knowledge (patterns). To achieve this goal, data mining uses computational techniques from statistics, machine learning, and pattern recognition.

Various data mining tasks can be used depending on the desired outcome of the model. Usually a distinction is made between supervised and unsupervised learning. Classical tasks of supervised learning are (Fig. 5.30) as follows:

- **Classification:** Examining the attributes of a given instance to assign it to a predefined category or class.
- **Classification rule learners:** Discovering a set of rules from the data that forms an accurate classifier.

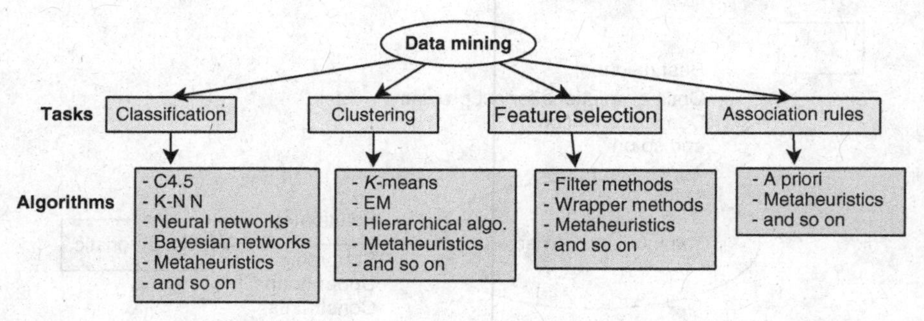

FIGURE 5.30 Some data mining tasks and associated algorithms.

The most common tasks of unsupervised learning are as follows:

- **Clustering:** Partitioning the input data set into subsets (clusters), so that data in each subset share common aspects. The partitioning is often indicated by a similarity measure implemented by a distance.
- **Association rule learners:** Discovering elements that occur in common within a given data set.

The feature selection task objective consists in reducing the number of attributes (i.e., dimensionality of the data set). Feature selection is often considered as a necessary preprocessing step to analyze data characterized by a large number of attributes. It allows to improve the accuracy of the extracted models. Two models of feature selection exist depending on whether the selection is coupled with a learning scheme or not. The first one, the *filter model*, which carries out the feature subset selection and the learning (e.g., classification, clustering) in two separate phases, uses a measure that is simple and fast to compute. The second one, the *wrapper method*, which carries out the feature subset selection and learning in the same process, engages a learning algorithm to measure the accuracy of the extracted model. From the effectiveness point of view, wrapper methods are clearly advantageous, since the features are selected by optimizing the discriminating power of the finally used learning algorithm. However, their drawback is a more significant computational cost.

Metaheuristics have been largely used to solve data mining tasks with a great success. However, using data mining techniques to improve the efficiency and effectiveness of metaheuristics, which is our concern in this chapter, is less studied. This hybridization scheme can be viewed as knowledge extraction and integration into metaheuristics. This knowledge may take different forms. Figure 5.31 describes some ways to integrate knowledge into metaheuristics.

Three criteria will be used to refine our classification [435]:

- **Time of extracting the knowledge:** Two kinds of hybridizations can be distinguished, depending on the time of extracting the used knowledge. Hybridizations that extract the knowledge before the search starts are called *off-line knowledge* strategies and combinations where the knowledge is extracted dynamically during the search are described as *online knowledge* strategies.

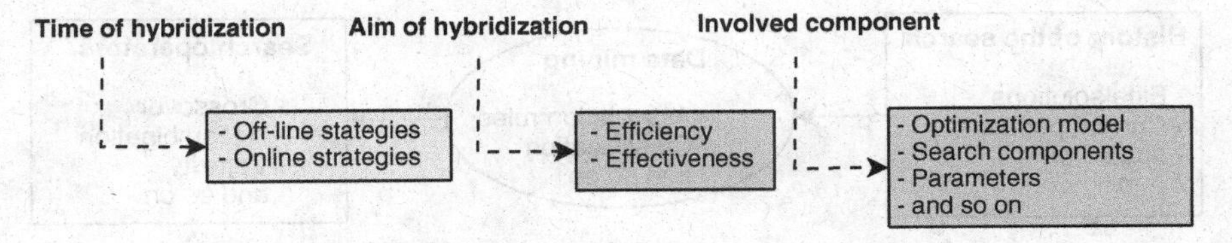

FIGURE 5.31 Some ways integrating knowledge into metaheuristics.

- **Aim of the hybridization:** Either the combination allows to improve the efficiency of the algorithm by reducing the search time, or the combination is used to improve the effectiveness of the algorithm leading to better quality of solutions. The efficiency may be carried out by approximating the objective function or reducing the size of the search space. The effectiveness may be improved by incorporating some knowledge into the search components or by updating the parameters of the metaheuristics in an adaptive way. Of course, a given hybridization may improve both criteria: efficiency and effectiveness.
- **Involved component:** As presented in previous chapters, a metaheuristic is composed of different search components. Hybridization can occur in any search component such as encoding of solutions, initialization of solutions, search variation operators (e.g., mutation, crossover, neighborhood), and so on. It may also be used to fix the parameters of the algorithm or define the optimization problem to be solved (e.g., objective function).

5.4.2 Main Schemes of Hybridization

In the following sections, some hybridization schemes between metaheuristics and data mining techniques are presented according to each class of the general taxonomy.

5.4.2.1 Low-Level Relay Hybrid In traditional S-metaheuristics, greedy or multistart strategies (e.g., GRASP algorithm) do not use any information on the search of previous iterations to initialize the next search even if the tabu search algorithm uses the concept of memory to guide the search. Hence, some knowledge may be introduced in these families of metaheuristics.

Optimization model: The extracted knowledge may be used to transform the target optimization problem. For instance, in the ART (adaptive reasoning technique) online approach, the search memory is used to learn the behavior of a greedy algorithm [606]. Some constraints are added to the problem. These constraints are generated from the noninteresting visited solutions according to the values associated with their decision variables. Similar to the tabu list strategy, these constraints are dropped after a given number of iterations.

Parameter setting: Another LRH hybrid approach provides a dynamic and adaptive setting of the parameters of a S-metaheuristic. Indeed, knowledge extracted during the search may serve to change dynamically at run time the values of some parameters such as the size of the tabu list in tabu search, the temperature in simulated annealing.

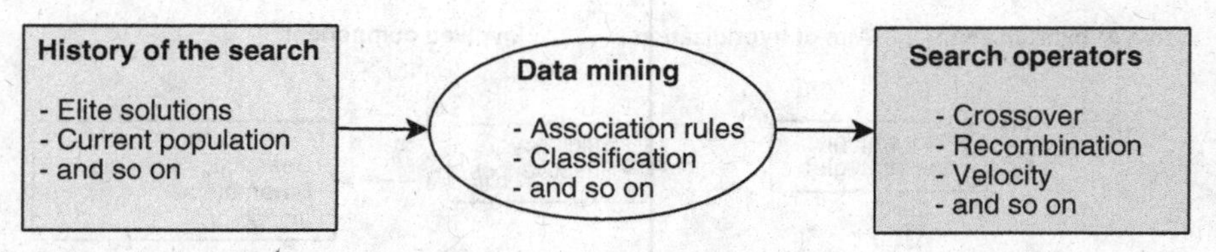

FIGURE 5.32 Extracting knowledge from the history of the search and its use into search operators.

This dynamic setting may also concern with any search component of a S-metaheuristic such as the neighborhood and the stopping criteria.

5.4.2.2 Low-Level Teamwork Hybrids

This hybrid scheme is very popular in P-metaheuristics.

Search components: A straightforward LTH hybrid approach consists in using data mining techniques in recombination operators of P-metaheuristics. In this class of hybrids, the knowledge extracted during the search is incorporated into the recombination operators for the generation of new solutions (Fig. 5.32). From a set of solutions (e.g., current population, elite solutions), some models are extracted that may be represented by classification rules, association rules, decision trees, and so on. These models (patterns) will participate in the generation of new solutions to intensify or diversify the search.

Example 5.19 Integrating knowledge into recombination operators. In this hybrid scheme, a set of decision rules describing the generated solutions are extracted. For instance, classification rules describing the best and worst individuals of the current population are extracted [549]. These rules are generated using the *AQ learning algorithm*, a general decision rule learning algorithm (Fig. 5.33). The extracted rules are incorporated

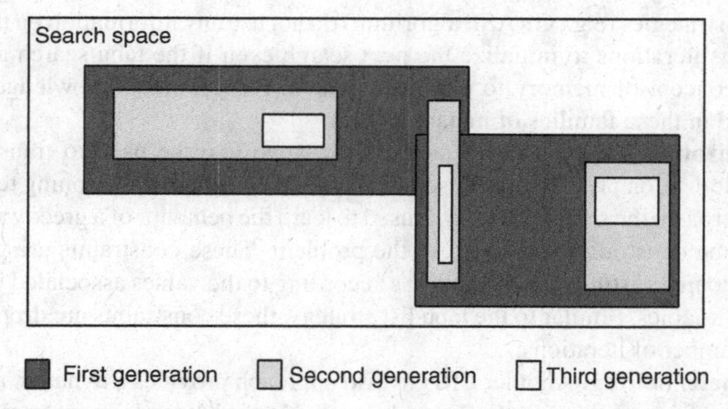

FIGURE 5.33 Reduction of the search space for the offsprings using a learnable evolution model.

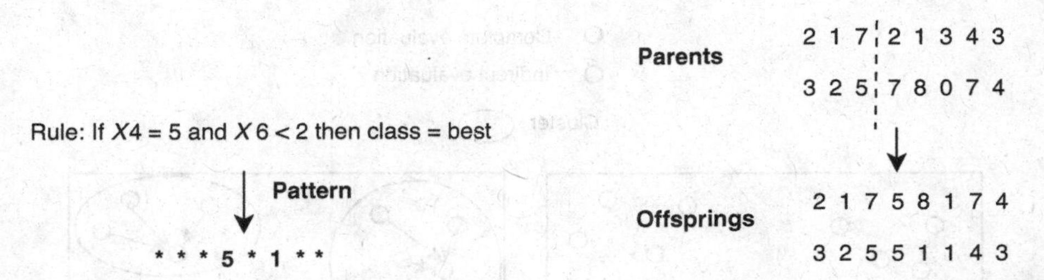

FIGURE 5.34 Crossover operator using the induced rule as a pattern. For instance, the extracted pattern (...5.1..) is included into the offsprings.

into the crossover operator of an evolutionary algorithm to reduce the search space for the offsprings (Fig. 5.34). The obtained results indicate that those learnable evolution models allow to speed up the search and improve the quality of solutions [549].

EDA (estimation of distribution algorithms) (see Section 3.4.1) can also be considered as LTH hybrids using estimated probability distributions to generate new solutions. Similarly, *cultural algorithms* use high-quality individuals to develop beliefs constraining the way in which individuals are transformed by genetic operators [653] (see Section 3.4.4). In cultural algorithms, beliefs are formed based on each entity's individual experiences. The reasoning behind this is that cultural evolution allows populations to learn and adapt at a rate faster than pure biological evolution. Importantly, the learning that takes place individually by each entity is passed on to the remainder entities of the group, allowing learning to take place at a much faster rate.

Civilized genetic algorithms constitute another LTH hybrid approach integrating concepts from machine learning [688]. They differ from Darwinian evolution as they keep information of the population to avoid doing the same errors. The knowledge is dynamically updated during the successive generations. They have been applied to binary encodings in which a preprocessing step using a genetic algorithm is carried out to obtain a diverse population.

Parameter setting: A dynamic setting of the parameters of a P-metaheuristic can be carried out by a data mining task. Any parameter of a P-metaheuristic, such as the mutation and crossover probabilities in evolutionary algorithms, the pheromone update in ant colonies, and the velocity update in particle swarm optimization, can be modified dynamically during the search. Indeed, knowledge extracted during the search may serve to change dynamically at run time the values of these parameters. For instance, the initialization of the mutation rate may be adjusted adaptively by computing the progress of the last applications of the mutation operator [386,783]. Hence, it becomes possible to determine the probabilities of application of a given operator in an adaptive manner where the more efficient is an operator, the more significant is its probability of application. Another approach could be to analyze in detail the new individuals generated by operators (in terms of quality and diversity) using clustering algorithms. This would give valuable information that can help to set the new application probabilities.

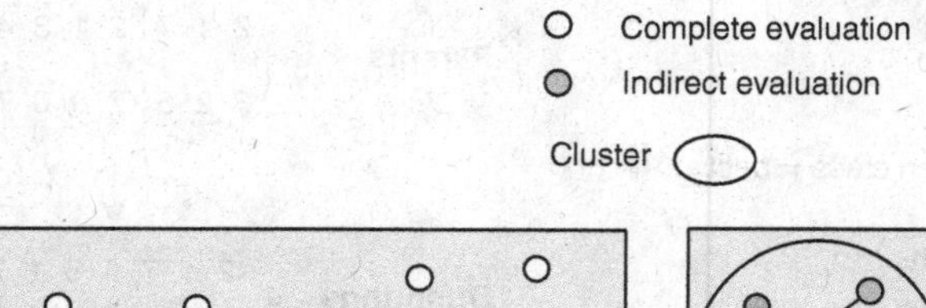

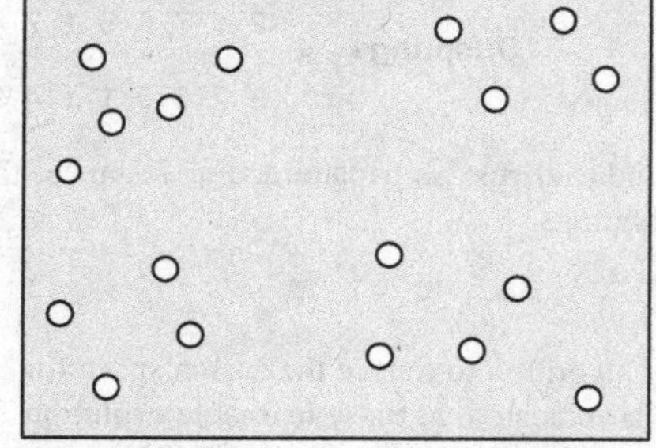

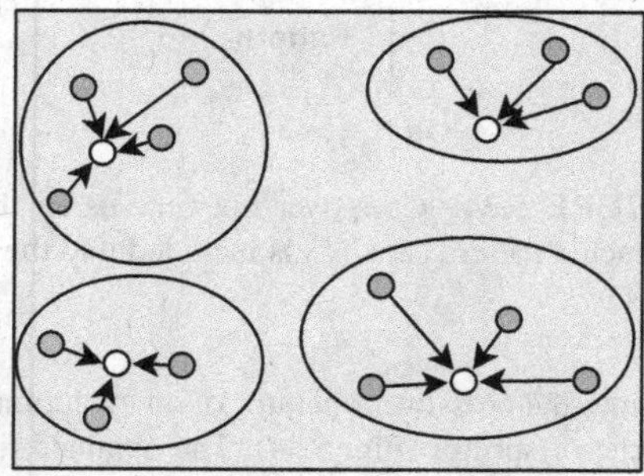

(a) Population of solutions to evaluate **(b)** Complete evaluation of representatives

FIGURE 5.35 Evaluating a solution by using the representative of its cluster (fitness imitation).

Optimization model: Many optimization problems such as engineering design problems are concerned with the expensive objective functions. In this hybrid scheme, supervised classification algorithms can be used to approximate the objective function during the search (see Section 1.4.2.5). The number of solutions to evaluate according to the real objective function can also be reduced. In this case, already evaluated solutions will represent the predefined classes. A nonevaluated solution is classified using, for example, the *k*-nearest-neighbor classification algorithm. The objective function of a given solution is then approximated using the evaluated solution of the associated class.

This process may also be carried out by clustering algorithms using *fitness imitation*. A clustering algorithm is applied to a population of solutions to be evaluated. Each cluster will have a representative solution. Only the solution that represents the cluster is evaluated [416,463,638]. Then, the objective function of other solutions of the cluster is estimated in respect to its associated representative[10] (Fig. 5.35). Different clustering techniques may be used such as *K*-means and fuzzy *c*-means.

5.4.2.3 *High-Level Relay Hybrid*

In this HRH hybrid approach, *a priori* knowledge is first extracted from the target optimization problem. Then, this knowledge is used in the metaheuristic for a more efficient search. The previously acquired knowledge may be obtained from previous experimentations, an expert landscape analysis, and so on. Many schemes may be introduced into this traditional hybrid class.

[10]This scheme is called fitness imitation or fitness inheritance.

Search components: For instance, data mining algorithms may be applied to the initialization of solutions. Instead of generating the initial solutions randomly, problem knowledge can be used to generate solutions that integrate "good" patterns.

Example 5.20 Anytime learning algorithm in dynamic optimization. A genetic algorithm has been initialized with a case-based reasoning in a tracker/target simulation with a periodically changing environment[632]. Case-based initialization (learning agent) allows the system to automatically bias the search of the GA toward relevant areas of the search space in a changing environment (dynamic optimization problem). This scheme may be seen as a general approach to continuous learning in a changing environment. The learning agent continuously tests search strategies using different initial solutions. This process allows the update of the knowledge base on the basis of the obtained results. This knowledge base generated by a simulation model will be used by any search agent.

Parameter setting: The same hybrid scheme may be used within the initialization of the parameters of any metaheuristic. As mentioned in previous chapters, a difficult part in designing metaheuristics deals with the setting of their parameters. Indeed, many parameters compose metaheuristics such as the probability of application of a given operator, the tabu list, the size of the population, or the number of iterations? An empirical approach consists in both running several times the metaheuristic with different parameter values and trying to select the best values. If the number of trials or the number of parameters is important, determining the best set of parameters may require some statistical analysis (see Section 1.6.1). This may be seen as a data mining help (Fig. 5.36).

Optimization model: Data mining techniques can also be used in decomposing the optimization problem handled by a metaheuristic. For instance, in optimization problems dealing with Euclidean distances, such as vehicle routing and the P-median

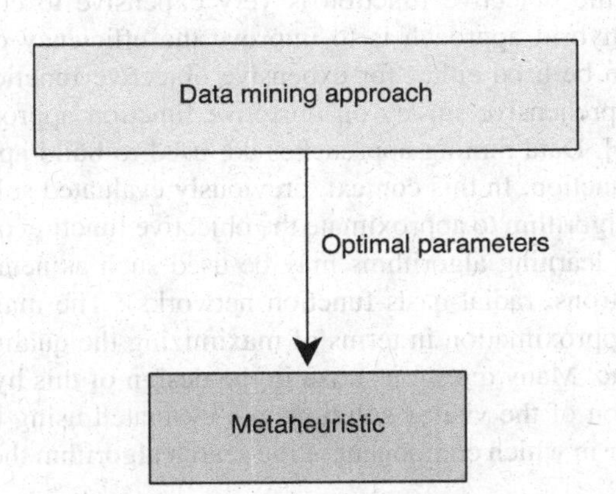

FIGURE 5.36 Setting the parameters of a metaheuristic using a data mining approach.

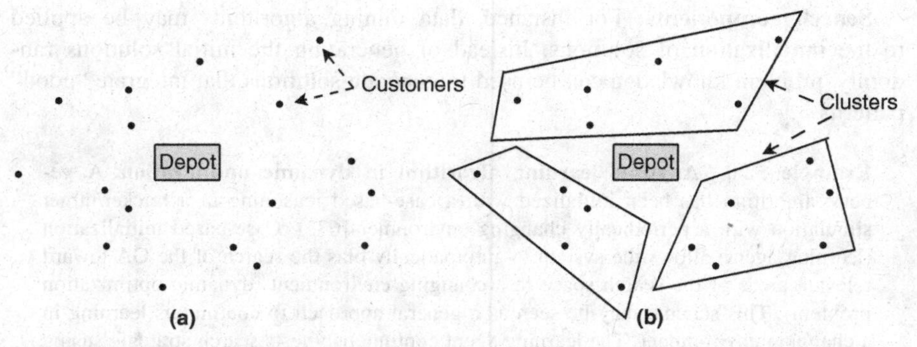

FIGURE 5.37 Decomposing an optimization problem using clustering algorithms. (a) Instance of the VRP problem. (b) Clustering the customers and then applying a TSP metaheuristic to the subproblems.

optimization problems, clustering algorithms may be used to decompose the input space into subspaces. Metaheuristics are then used to solve those subproblems associated with the subspaces. Finally, a global solution is built using partial final solutions.

> **Example 5.21 Clustering routing problems.** Some efficient techniques in solving routing problems (e.g., TSP, VRP) decompose the operational space into subspaces using clustering algorithms such as the *K*-means or the EM (expectation maximization) algorithm (Fig. 5.37). Indeed, a metaheuristic is then used to solve the different subproblems. This approach is interesting for very large problem instances.

A popular off-line hybrid scheme for expensive objective function consists in approximating the objective function of the problem. Indeed, in many complex real-life applications, the objective function is very expensive to compute. The main objective of this hybrid approach is to improve the efficiency of the search. The approximation can be used either for expensive objective functions or multimodal functions. A comprehensive survey on objective function approximations may be found in Ref.[413]. Data mining approaches are used to build approximate models of the objective function. In this context, previously evaluated solutions are learned by a data mining algorithm to approximate the objective function of other individuals (Fig. 5.38). Many learning algorithms may be used such as neural networks (e.g., multilayer perceptrons, radial-basis-function networks). The main issue here is to obtain a "good" approximation in terms of maximizing the quality and minimizing the computing time. Many questions arise in the design of this hybrid scheme such as which proportion of the visited solutions are evaluated using the approximation and at what time or in which component of the search algorithm the approximation is used.

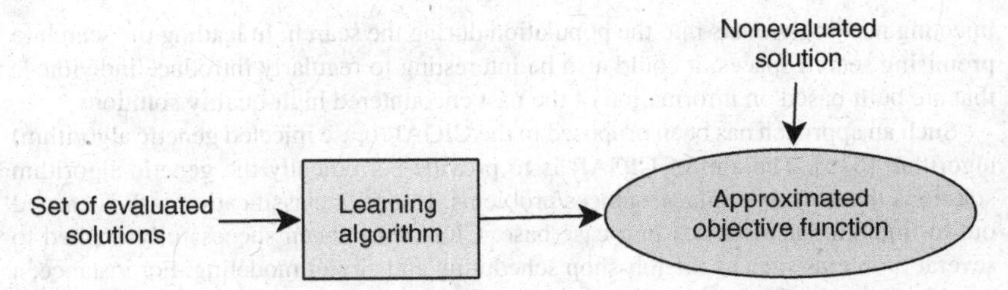

FIGURE 5.38 Data mining approach to approximate the objective function.

5.4.2.4 High-Level Teamwork Hybrid A HTH approach is a hybrid scheme in which a dynamically acquired knowledge is extracted in parallel during the search in cooperation with a metaheuristic (Fig. 5.39). Any online learning algorithms can be used to extract knowledge from informations provided by metaheuristics such as elite solutions, diversified set of good solutions, frequency memory, recency memory, and so on. From this input, the data mining agent extracts useful information to be used by metaheuristics to improve the search. Any statistical indicator for landscape analysis of a problem may also be used.

Example 5.22 Data mining in population management of a P-metaheuristic. Using the same scheme of cooperation, data mining approaches can be used to manage the population of a P-metaheuristic. Managing a population deals with the intensification and the diversification tasks of a metaheuristic. Diversification may be carried out by

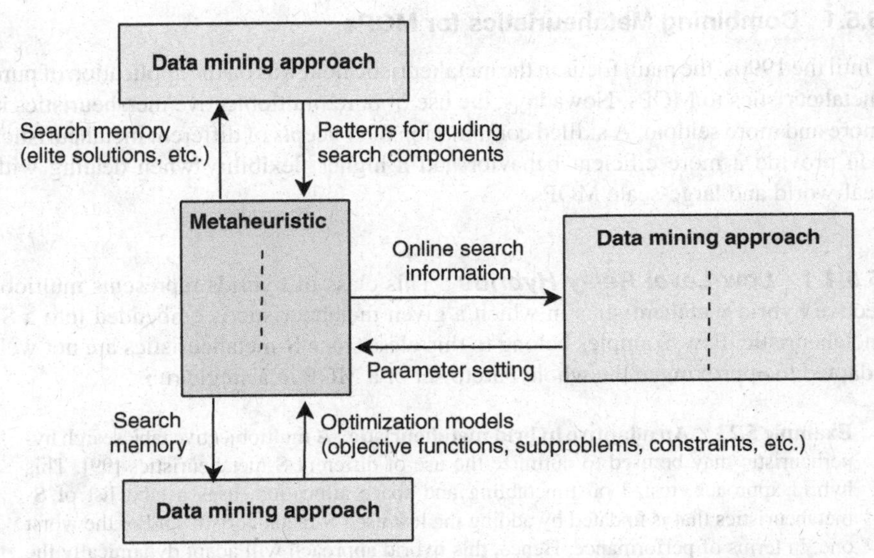

FIGURE 5.39 Online knowledge extraction and its use by a metaheuristic.

injecting new individuals into the population during the search. In leading the search to promising search spaces, it could also be interesting to regularly introduce individuals that are built based on information of the past encountered high-quality solutions.

Such an approach has been proposed in the CIGAR (case injected genetic algorithm) algorithm [516]. The aim of CIGAR is to provide periodically the genetic algorithm solutions that suit to similar instances/problems. Hence, a classification task is carried out to find similar instances in a case base. CIGAR has been successfully applied to several problems such as the job-shop scheduling and circuit modeling. For instance, a combination of a GA with the Apriori algorithm has been used to discover interesting subroutines for the oil collecting vehicle routing problem [173]. The obtained subroutes are inserted into the new individuals of the population. Another illustrative example is the combination of the GRASP heuristic with Apriori like-algorithms to extract promising patterns from elite solutions [654].

5.5 HYBRID METAHEURISTICS FOR MULTIOBJECTIVE OPTIMIZATION

The taxonomy for hybrid metaheuristics presented in this chapter holds in solving multiobjective optimization problems (MOPs). However, the design of hybrid metaheuristics for MOP needs an adaptation for the reason that in multiobjective optimization, the main goal consists in generating an approximated set of Pareto solutions whereas in monoobjective optimization, the aim is to generate a unique "good" solution.

5.5.1 Combining Metaheuristics for MOPs

Until the 1990s, the main focus in the metaheuristic field was on the application of pure metaheuristics to MOPs. Nowadays, the use of pure multiobjective metaheuristics is more and more seldom. A skilled combination of concepts of different metaheuristics can provide a more efficient behavior and a higher flexibility when dealing with real-world and large-scale MOPs.

5.5.1.1 Low-Level Relay Hybrids This class of hybrids represents multiobjective hybrid metaheuristics in which a given metaheuristic is embedded into a S-metaheuristic. Few examples belong to this class since S-metaheuristics are not well adapted to approximate the whole Pareto set of a MOP in a single run.

Example 5.23 An adaptive hybrid metaheuristic. A multiobjective tabu search hyperheuristic may be used to optimize the use of different S-metaheuristics [99]. This hybrid approach, tested on timetabling and space allocation, uses a tabu list of S-metaheuristics that is updated by adding the last used S-metaheuristic and/or the worst one, in terms of performance. Hence, this hybrid approach will adapt dynamically the search according to the performance of various S-metaheuristics. More efficient multiobjective S-metaheuristics will be more frequently used during the search.

5.5.1.2 Low-Level Teamwork Hybrids P-metaheuristics (e.g., evolutionary algorithms, scatter search, particle swarm, ant colonies) are powerful in the approximation of the whole Pareto set while S-metaheuristics are efficient in the intensification of the search around the obtained approximations. Indeed, S-metaheuristics need to be guided to solve MOPs.

Therefore, most efficient multiobjective P-metaheuristics have been coupled with S-metaheuristics such as local search, simulated annealing, and tabu search, which are powerful optimization methods in terms of exploitation of the Pareto set approximations. The two classes of metaheuristics have complementary strengths and weaknesses. Hence, LTH hybrids in which S-metaheuristics are embedded into P-metaheuristics have been applied successfully to many MOPs. Indeed, many state-of-the-art hybrid schemes are P-metaheuristics integrating S-metaheuristics.

Example 5.24 Multiobjective evolutionary local search algorithm. Many multiobjective hybrid metaheuristics proposed in the literature deal with hybridization between P-metaheuristics (e.g., evolutionary algorithms) and S-metaheuristics (e.g., local search). For instance, the well-known genetic local search[11] algorithms are popular in the multiobjective optimization community [305,404,408,755]. The basic principle consists in incorporating a local search algorithm during an evolutionary algorithm search. The local search part could not only be included by replacing the mutation operator, but it can also be added after each complete generation of the evolutionary algorithm [57]. The classical structure of a multiobjective genetic local search (MOGLS) algorithm is shown in Fig. 5.40, which depicts the relationships between the evolutionary multiobjective (EMO) component and the local search one.

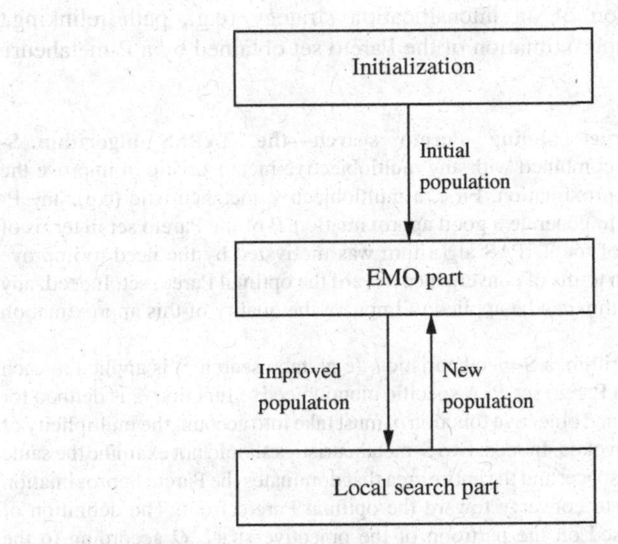

FIGURE 5.40 Generic form of multiobjective genetic local search algorithms (MOGLS).

[11] Also called *memetic*.

The local search algorithm can be applied in a given direction (i.e., weighted aggregation of the objectives) [404]. To adapt the basic local search algorithm to the multiobjective case, one may take into account the Pareto dominance relation [57]. The algorithm works with a population of nondominated solutions PO. The hybridization process consists in generating the neighborhood of each solution of the Pareto set approximation PO. The new generated nondominated neighbors are inserted into the approximation Pareto set PO. Solutions belonging to the Pareto set PO and dominated by a new introduced solution are deleted. This process is reiterated until no neighbor of any Pareto solution is inserted into the Pareto set PO. The Pareto local search(PLS) algorithm is described in Algorithm 5.2.

Algorithm 5.2 Template of the Pareto-guided local search (PLS) algorithm.

Input: an approximated Pareto set PO.
Do
$S' = PO$;
Generate the neighborhood PN_x for each solution x of S' ;
Let PO be the set of nondominated solutions of $S' \cup PN_x$;
Until PO=S' (the population has reached the local optima) ;
Output: Pareto set PO.

5.5.1.3 High-Level Relay Hybrids In HRH hybrids, self-contained multiobjective metaheuristics are executed in a sequence. A classical HRH for MOP is the application of an intensification strategy (e.g., path relinking, S-metaheuristic) on the approximation of the Pareto set obtained by a P-metaheuristic [198,437].

Example 5.25 Target aiming Pareto search—the TAPAS algorithm. S-metaheuristics can be combined with any multiobjective metaheuristic to improve the quality of a Pareto approximation. First, a multiobjective metaheuristic (e.g., any P-metaheuristic) is used to generate a good approximation P of the Pareto set in terms of diversity. The design of the TAPAS algorithm was motivated by the need to improve the approximation P in terms of convergence toward the optimal Pareto set. Indeed, any S-metaheuristic algorithm can be applied to improve the quality of this approximation [436].

In the TAPAS algorithm, a S-metaheuristic l_i (e.g., tabu search[12]) is applied to each solution s_i of the initial Pareto set P. A specific monoobjective function o_i is defined for each search l_i. The defined objective function o_i must take into account the multiplicity of the S-metaheuristics invoked. Indeed, two S-metaheuristics should not examine the same region of the objective space, and the entire area that dominates the Pareto approximation P should be explored to converge toward the optimal Pareto front. The definition of the objective o_i is based on the partition of the objective space O according to the

[12] An efficient S-metaheuristic for the target problem should be selected.

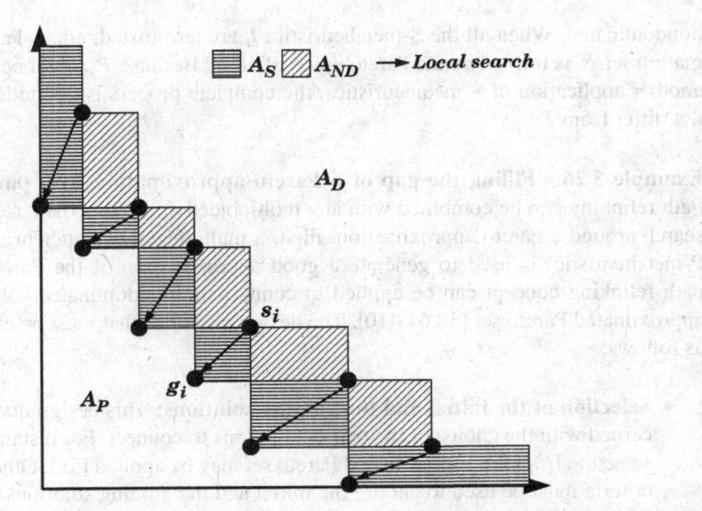

FIGURE 5.41 The hybrid TAPAS algorithm for multiobjective optimization: the goal g_i of a solution s_i is defined in function of s_i neighbors in the objective space.

approximation P (see Fig. 5.41):

$$A_D = \{s \in O / \exists s' \in P, s' \prec s\}$$
$$A_{ND} = \{s \in O / \forall s' \in P, (s' \nprec s) \text{ and } (s \nprec s')\}$$
$$A_S = \{s \in O / \nexists s' \in P, s \prec s'\}$$
$$A_P = \{s \in O / \exists s_1, s_2 \in P, (s \prec s_1) \text{ and } (s \prec s_2)\}$$

Each solution $s_i \in P$ is associated with a part A_S^i of A_S. If l_i is able to generate a feasible solution in A_S^i, then the approximation is improved according to the convergence without decreasing the diversity.

To guide the search, a goal g_i is given to each S-metaheuristic l_i, with g_i being the point that dominates all points of A_S^i. In cases where certain coordinates of g_i cannot be defined (e.g., the extremities of P), a lower bound for the missing coordinates should be used. For an objective f_m, the goal g_p is computed as follows:

$$f_m(g_p) = \arg\min_{\{f_m(s')/(s' \in P) \text{ and } (f_m(s') < f_m(s))\}} (f_m(s') - f_m(s))$$

Then, the objective o_i is stated as follows:

$$\min \left(\sum_{j=1}^{M} |f_j(s) - f_j(g_i)|^r \right)^{1/r}$$

When a S-metaheuristic l_i reaches the goal g_i or when it finds a solution that dominates g_i, it stops and produces an archive a_i, which contains all the current solutions that are nondominated. When all the S-metaheuristics l_i are terminated, a new Pareto approximation set P' is formed by the Pareto union of all a_i. Because P' might be improved by another application of S-metaheuristics, the complete process is iterated until P' does not differ from P.

Example 5.26 Filling the gap of a Pareto approximation with path relinking. Path relinking can be combined with any multiobjective metaheuristic to intensify the search around a Pareto approximation. First, a multiobjective metaheuristic (e.g., any P-metaheuristic) is used to generate a good approximation of the Pareto set. Then, path relinking concept can be applied to connect the nondominated solutions of the approximated Pareto set [58,64,410]. The design questions that must be considered are as follows:

- **Selection of the initial and the guiding solutions:** This design question is concerned with the choice of the pair of solutions to connect. For instance, a random selection from the approximated Pareto set may be applied [58]. Otherwise, some criteria must be used to choose the initial and the guiding solutions: distance between solutions (e.g., distance in the decision or the objective space), quality of the solutions (e.g., best solution according to a reference point or weighted aggregation), and so on.
- **Path generation:** Many paths may be generated between two solutions. One has to establish which path(s) has to be explored and selected. Among other concepts, a neighborhood operator and a distance measure in the decision space have to be defined. For instance, the shortest paths may be generated according to the selected neighborhood operator [58]. Let us consider x as the current solution and y as the guiding solution. The neighborhood N of x is generated with the following constraint: $\forall z \in N, \mathrm{d}(z, x) < \mathrm{d}(y, x)$. From this neighborhood, only the nondominated solutions may be selected to be potential solutions of the future paths (see Fig. 5.42). The process is iterated, until a complete path from x to y is generated. Many paths may also be considered. However, generating all possible paths may be computationally expensive. Moreover, the nondominated solutions may also be selected to participate in a Pareto local search algorithm, as shown in Fig. 5.43 [58].

5.5.1.4 High-Level Teamwork Hybrid

As already mentioned, HTH hybrid scheme involves several self-contained multiobjective metaheuristics performing a search in parallel and cooperating to find a Pareto set approximation.

Example 5.27 Cooperative multiobjective evolutionary algorithms. There is a growing interest in the design and implementation of parallel cooperative metaheuristics to solve multiobjective problems. The majority of designed parallel models in the literature are evolutionary algorithms [334,424,545,666]. In multiobjective evolutionary algorithms, the individuals are selected from the population, the Pareto archive, or both of them. In the multiobjective island model, different strategies are possible. For instance, the newcomers replace individuals selected randomly from the local population that do not belong to the local Pareto archive. Another strategy consists in ranking and grouping the individuals of the local population into Pareto fronts using the nondominance relation.

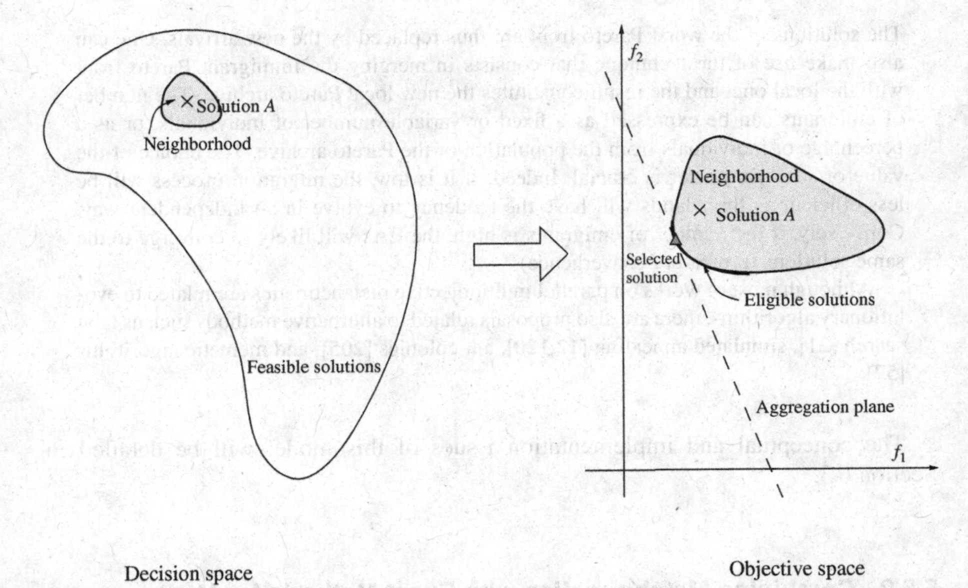

FIGURE 5.42 Path relinking algorithm filling the gap between two nondominated solutions of an approximation Pareto set: neighborhood exploration.

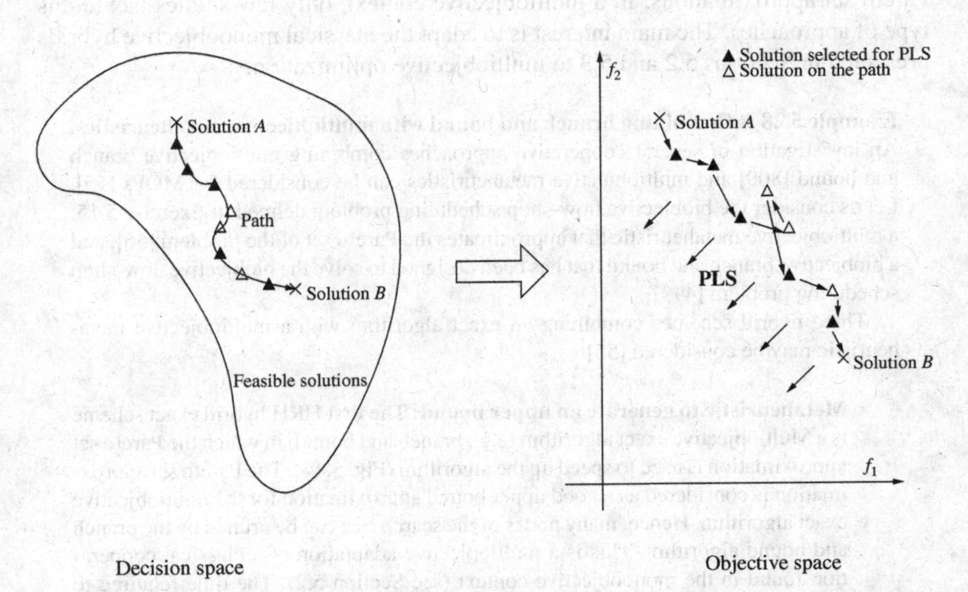

FIGURE 5.43 Path relinking algorithm combined with a Pareto local search algorithm.

The solutions of the worst Pareto front are thus replaced by the new arrivals. One can also make use of the technique that consists in merging the immigrant Pareto front with the local one, and the result constitutes the new local Pareto archive. The number of emigrants can be expressed as a fixed or variable number of individuals, or as a percentage of individuals from the population or the Pareto archive. The choice of the value of such parameter is crucial. Indeed, if it is low, the migration process will be less efficient as the islands will have the tendency to evolve in an independent way. Conversely, if the number of emigrants is high, the EAs will likely to converge to the same solutions (premature convergence).

Although most of works on parallel multiobjective metaheuristics are related to evolutionary algorithms, there are also proposals related to alternative methods such us tabu search [21], simulated annealing [12,120], ant colonies [205], and memetic algorithms [57].

The conceptual and implementation issues of this model will be detailed in Section 6.3.

5.5.2 Combining Metaheuristics with Exact Methods for MOP

Another recent popular issue is the cooperation between multiobjective metaheuristics and exact optimization algorithms. Some hybrid schemes mainly aim at providing Pareto optimal sets in shorter time, while others primarily focus on getting better Pareto set approximations. In a multiobjective context, only few studies tackle this type of approaches. The main interest is to adapt the classical monoobjective hybrids presented in Sections 5.2 and 5.3 to multiobjective optimization.

Example 5.28 Combining branch and bound with multiobjective metaheuristics. An investigation of several cooperative approaches combining multiobjective branch and bound [800] and multiobjective metaheuristics can be considered for MOPs [55]. Let us consider the biobjective flow-shop scheduling problem defined in Exercise 5.15, a multiobjective metaheuristic that approximates the Pareto set of the problem [56], and a biobjective branch and bound that has been designed to solve the biobjective flow-shop scheduling problem [499].

Three hybrid schemes combining an exact algorithm with a multiobjective metaheuristic may be considered [55]:

- **Metaheuristic to generate an upper bound:** The first HRH hybrid exact scheme is a Multiobjective exact algorithm (e.g., branch and bound) in which the Pareto set approximation is used to speed up the algorithm (Fig. 5.44). The Pareto set approximation is considered as a good upper bound approximation for the multiobjective exact algorithm. Hence, many nodes of the search tree can be pruned by the branch and bound algorithm. This is a multiobjective adaptation of a classical cooperation found in the monoobjective context (see Section 5.2). The time required to solve a given problem instance is smaller if the distance between the Pareto front approximation and the Pareto optimal front is small. If the distance is null, the exact algorithm will serve to prove the optimality of the Pareto set approximation. Even

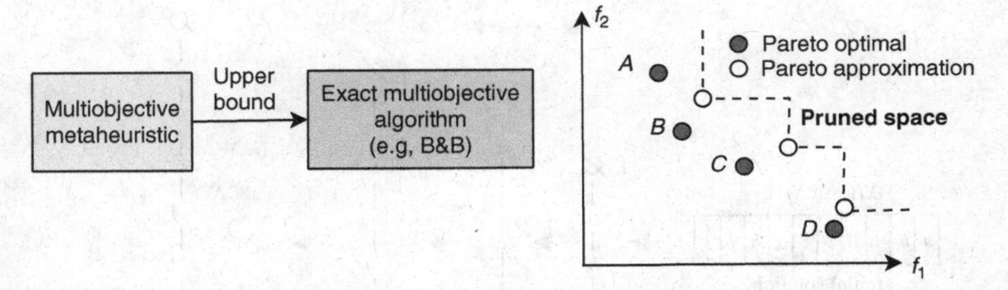

FIGURE 5.44 A HRH exact hybrid scheme in which a multiobjective metaheuristic generates an upper bound Pareto set to an exact multiobjective algorithm (e.g., branch and bound).

if this hybrid approach reduces the search time needed to find the Pareto optimal set, it does not allow to increase considerably the size of the solved instances.

- **Exact algorithm to explore very large neighborhoods:** In this hybrid heuristic approach, the exact multiobjective algorithm is used to explore large neighborhoods of a Pareto solution. The main idea is to reduce the search space explored by the exact algorithm by pruning nodes when the solution in construction is too far from the initial Pareto solution.

  Let us consider a permutation-based representation for the biobjective flow-shop scheduling problem and an insertion neighborhood operator. The exact algorithm is allowed to explore the neighborhood of the initial Pareto solution in which the solutions are within a distance less or equal to $\delta_{\max}$ (Fig. 5.45). The size of the insertion-based neighborhood is $\Theta(n^2)$, where n represents the number of jobs. Hence, the size of the search space explored by the exact algorithm is exponential and may be approximated by $\Theta(n^{2\delta_{\max}})$. Then, the distance $\delta_{\max}$ must be limited, especially for instances with large number of jobs.
- **Exact algorithm to solve subproblems:** In this hybrid heuristic approach, the exact multiobjective algorithm solve subproblems that are generated by the multiobjective metaheuristic. A given region of the decision space is explored by the

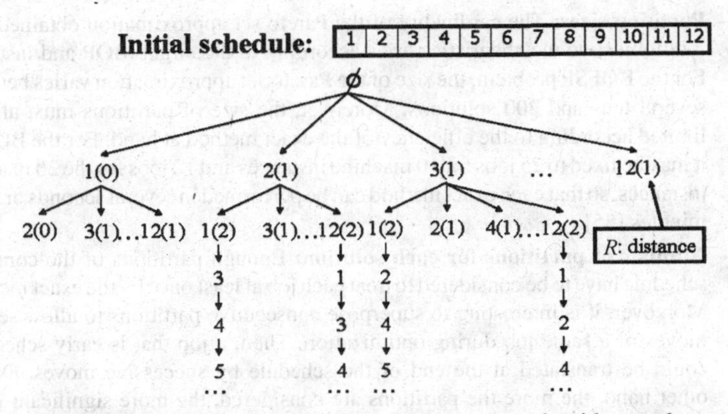

FIGURE 5.45 A hybrid heuristic scheme in which an exact algorithm explores very large neighborhoods of the multiobjective metaheuristic.

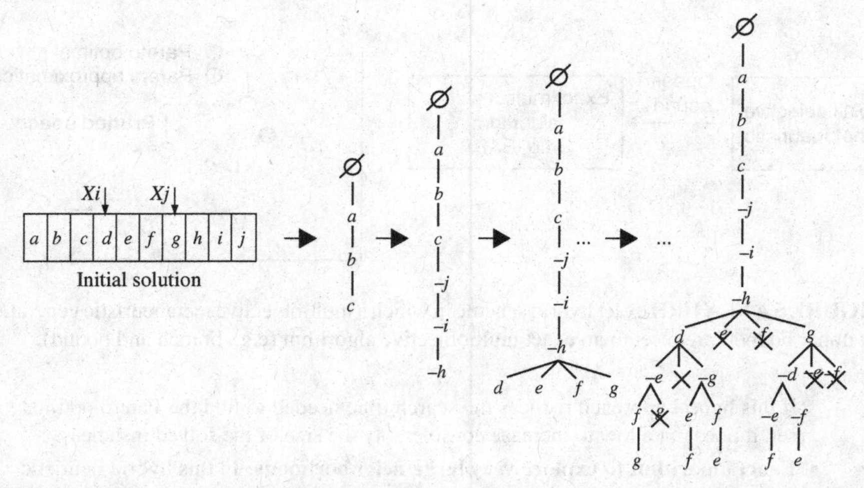

FIGURE 5.46 A hybrid heurisitic scheme in which an exact algorithm solves subproblems generated by a multiobjective metaheuristic.

exact algorithm. Figure 5.46 shows an example of such hybridization. Let us consider an initial Pareto solution composed of 10 jobs (*a*, *b*, ..., *i*, *j*), which is obtained by the multiobjective metaheuristic. Subproblems of a given size (e.g., 4) are explored by the exact algorithm (e.g., the subproblem defined by the nonfreezed jobs *d*, *e*, *f*, *g*). The first phase consists in placing the first three jobs at the beginning of the schedule. Moreover, the branch and bound algorithm places the last three jobs at the end of the schedule (a job *j* placed in queue is symbolized by $-j$). Then, the branch and bound multiobjective algorithm is applied to the remaining nonfreezed jobs to generate all Pareto solutions in this subspace.

The main parameters that have to be defined for an efficient hybrid scheme are as follows:

- **Partition sizes:** The cardinality of the Pareto set approximation obtained by a multiobjective metaheuristic varies according to the target MOP and instance. For the BOFSP problem, the size of the Pareto set approximation varies between several tens and 200 solutions. Moreover, the size of partitions must also be limited according to the efficiency of the exact method at hand. For the BOFSP, it may be fixed to 25 jobs for 10 machine instances and 12 jobs for the 20 machine instances, so that each exact method can be performed in several seconds or some minutes [55].
- **Number of partitions for each solution:** Enough partitions of the complete schedule have to be considered to treat each job at least once by the exact method. Moreover, it is interesting to superpose consecutive partitions to allow several moves of a same job during optimization. Then, a job that is early scheduled could be translated at the end of the schedule by successive moves. On the other hand, the more the partitions are considered, the more significant is the

computational time. For instance, for the BOFSP, 8 partitions for the 50 job instances, 16 partitions for the 100 job instances, and 32 partitions for the 200 job instances may be considered [55].

Example 5.29 Combining branch and cut with multiobjective metaheuristics. This example investigates the solution of a multiobjective routing problem, namely, the biobjective covering tour problem (BOCTP), by means of a hybrid HRH strategy involving a multiobjective metaheuristic and a single-objective branch and cut algorithm. The BOCTP aims to determine a minimal length tour for a subset of nodes while also minimizing the greatest distance between the nodes of another set and the nearest visited node. The BOCTP can be formally described as follows (Fig. 5.48): let $G = (V \cup W, E)$ be an undirected graph, where $V \cup W$ is the vertex set, and $E = \{(v_i, v_j)/v_i, v_j{}', V' \cup W, i < j\}$ is the edge set. Vertex v_1 is a depot, V is the set of vertices that can be visited, $T \subseteq V$ is the set of vertices that must be visited ($v_1 \in T$), and W is the set of vertices that must be covered. A distance matrix $C = (c_{ij})$, satisfying triangle inequality, is defined for E. The BOCTP consists in defining a tour for a subset of V, which contains all the vertices from T, while at the same time optimizing the following two objectives: (i) the minimization of the tour length and (ii) the minimization of the cover. The cover of a solution is defined as the greatest distance between a node $w \in W$ and the nearest visited node $v \in V$.

The BOCTP problem has been extended from the monoobjective covering tour problem (CTP). The CTP problems consists in determining a minimum length tour for a subset of V that contains all the vertices from T, and which covers every vertex w from W that is covered by the tour (i.e., w lies within a distance c from a vertex of the tour, where c is a user-defined parameter). A feasible solution for a small instance is provided in Fig. 5.47. One generic application of the CTP involves designing a tour in a network whose vertices represent points that can be visited, and from which the places that are not on the tour can be easily reached. In the biobjective covering tour problem, the constraint on the cover has been replaced by an objective in which the covering distance is minimized [438].

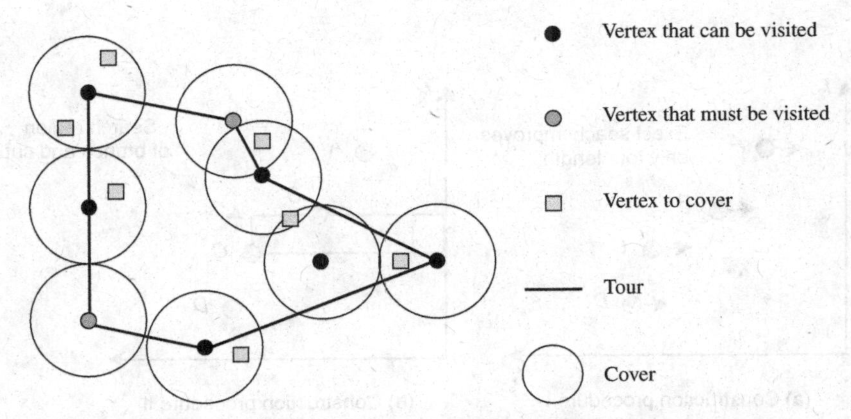

FIGURE 5.47 The covering tour problem: an example of a solution.

Let us consider a multiobjective metaheuristic to solve the BOCTP problem, which approximates the Pareto set [438], and a branch and cut algorithm to solve the monoobjective CTP problem [309]. The branch and cut algorithm may be considered as a black box optimization tool whose inputs are a subset of V, the set W, and a cover, and whose output is the optimal tour for the CTP. The branch and cut algorithm first relaxes the integrality conditions of the variables and the connectivity constraints of the integer linear programming model. Integrality is then gradually restored by means of a branch and bound mechanism. Before initiating branching at any given node of the search tree, a search is conducted for violated constraints, including the initially relaxed connectivity constraints and several other families of valid constraints. Several classes of valid inequalities have been considered such as dominance constraints, covering constraints, subtour elimination constraints, and 2-matching inequalities [309].

In the hybrid approach, the multiobjective metaheuristic generates a Pareto set approximation, which is used to build subproblems; these subproblems are then solved using the branch and cut algorithm (Fig. 5.48). Subproblem construction is a key point of the cooperative design, given that prohibitive computational times result if the subsets of V are too large. By limiting their size and giving the branch and cut algorithm access to the information extracted from the Pareto set approximation, the method makes solving the subproblems relatively easy for the branch and cut algorithm. Two procedures for building the subproblems can be considered [438]:

- **One objective improvement by an exact algorithm:** The main purpose of the first construction procedure is to improve the solutions found by the multiobjective metaheuristic in terms of the tour length objective without modifying the cover value. It accomplishes this goal by investigating the possibility that some elements

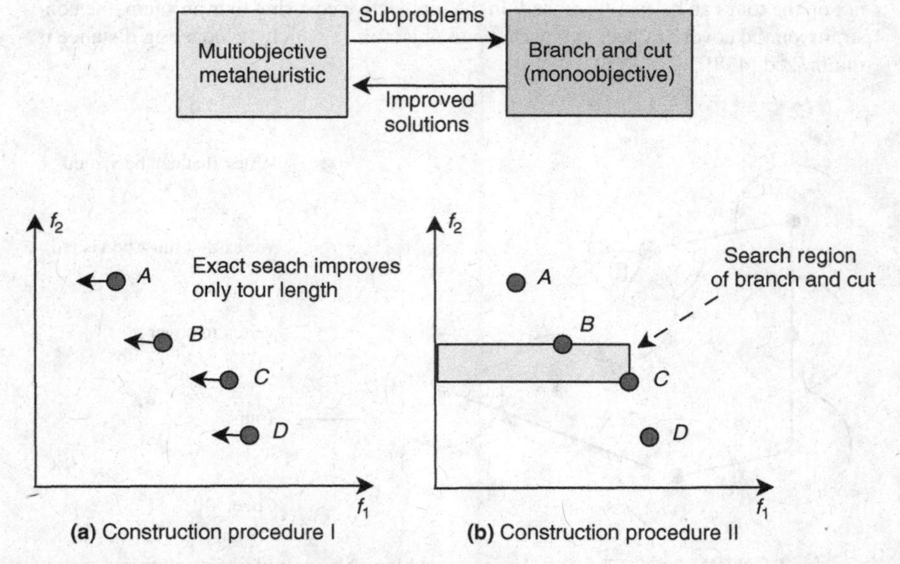

FIGURE 5.48 Combining a monoobjective branch and cut algorithm and a multiobjective metaheuristic to solve the biobjective covering tour problem.

of the set of visited vertices $\tilde{V}$ can be replaced by sets of vertices $R \subseteq V \backslash \tilde{V}$ so that the cover value $\tilde{c}$ provided by the couple (v_t, v_c) remains unchanged (Fig. 5.48a). A vertex $v_k \in \tilde{V}$ can be replaced by a set R if and only if (i) no subset of R can replace v_k; (ii) no vertex from R can provide a better cover: $\forall v_i \in R$, $c_{tc} \leq c_{ic}$; (iii) there is a vertex from $\tilde{V}$ or from R that can replace v_k for every vertex of W that can be covered by v_k. Therefore, $\forall v_l \in W \backslash \{v_c\}$, such that $c_{kl} \leq \tilde{c}$, where the following condition must be true: $\exists v_n \in R \cup (\tilde{V} \backslash \{v_k\})$, $c_{nl} \leq \tilde{c}$.

Replacing a node of $\tilde{V}$ by a subset R tends to become easier as the cardinality of R increases. However, in practice, condition (i) limits the candidate subsets. The larger the R set, the higher the cost of the test. Certainly, if the size of the set used for the branch and cut algorithm is very large, the algorithm will require much greater computational time. Therefore, in practice, the cardinality of R is limited to one or two elements.

For each solution s of the Pareto set approximation, a problem is built as follows. The set V_I of vertices that can be visited is created by the union of $\tilde{V}$ and all subsets of V with a cardinality of 1 or 2 that can replace a vertex of $\tilde{V}$. The set W of vertices that must be covered remains unchanged. Here, the parameter c is equal to the cover of s.

- **Region exploration by an exact algorithm:** In the first construction procedure, it is unlikely that all the feasible covers corresponding to Pareto optimal solutions will be identified. These unidentified solutions must always be situated between two solutions of the approximation, although not always between the same two solutions. Thus, it is reasonable to assume that new Pareto optimal solutions may be discovered by focusing searches on the area of the objective space between two neighboring solutions. The second procedure aims to build sets of vertices to potentially identify Pareto optimal solutions whose cover values were not found by the multiobjective metaheuristic. Let A and B be two neighboring solutions in the approximation sets found by the evolutionary algorithm (i.e., there are no other solutions between A and B). A (resp. B) is a solution with a cover c_A (resp. c_B) that visits the vertices of the set V_A (resp. V_B). Assuming that $c_A < c_B$, the branch and cut algorithm can be executed on a set V_{II}, built according to both V_A and V_B, with the first cover $\tilde{c}$ that is strictly smaller than c_B as a parameter (Fig. 5.48b). If $\tilde{c}$ is equal to c_A, there is no need to execute the branch and cut algorithm.

  It appears that neighboring solutions in the Pareto set have a large number of vertices in common. Thus, V_{II} contains V_A and V_B. This inclusion ensures that the branch and cut algorithm will at least be able to find the solution A, or a solution with the same cover but a better tour length in cases for which the tour on V_A is not optimal. The following process is used to complete V_{II}: for every feasible cover c, so that $c_A < c < c_B$, vertices are added to V_{II} to obtain a subset of V_{II} with c as a cover. Algorithm 5.3 provides the procedure for constructing the set V_{II}.

Algorithm 5.3 Construction of the set V_{II}.

$V_{II} = V_A \cup V_B$;
For all c so that $c_A < c < c_B$ **Do**
  For $v_l \in W$ **Do**
    $V_{II} = \cup V_{II}\{v_k \in V \backslash V_{II} / c_{kl} \leq c\}$
End For

5.5.3 Combining Metaheuristics with Data Mining for MOP

Most of the classical combinations of metaheuristics with machine learning and data mining techniques (e.g., feature selection, classification, clustering, association rules) that have been applied to monoobjective optimization (see Section 5.4) can be generalized to multiobjective optimization:

- Search operators (e.g., recombination operators in P-metaheuristics, neighborhoods in S-metaheuristics).
- Optimization models (e.g., approximation of the objectives functions, generation of subproblems, new constraints).
- Parameter setting of the metaheuristics.

Example 5.30 Search operators. Integrating knowledge into search operators is the most popular scheme in this class of hybrids. For instance, in a P-metaheuristic (e.g., evolutionary algorithm), a set of decision rules describing the best and worst individuals of the current population may be extracted. The extracted rules are incorporated into the crossover operator of an evolutionary algorithm to generate solutions sharing the characteristics of nondominated solutions and avoiding those of dominated solutions.

This principle can be applied to multiobjective optimization in the following way [434]: a set of rules that describe why some individuals dominate others (positive rules) and why some individuals are dominated by others (negative rules[13]) are extracted using the *C4.5 classifier*. Offsprings that match the positive rules and do not match the negative rules are generated. The obtained results indicate that those learnable evolution models allow to speed up the search and improve the quality of solutions.

Parameter setting: In a multiobjective metaheuristic, the efficiency of an operator may change during the execution of the algorithm: an operator may offer a better convergence at the beginning of the metaheuristic, but this convergence may be improved later with another operator. The success of an operator may also depend on the instance of the problem. This motivates the use of adaptive operator probabilities to automate the selection of efficient operators. The adaptation can be done by exploiting information gained, either implicitly or explicitly, regarding the current ability of each operator to produce solutions of better quality [783]. Other methods adjust operator probabilities based on other criteria such as the diversity of the population [158]. A classification of adaptation on the basis of the used mechanisms and the level at which adaptation operates may be found in Ref. [377].

Example 5.31 Adaptive mutation in multiobjective evolutionary algorithms. Let us consider a multiobjective evolutionary algorithm in which the choice of the mutation

[13]Negative knowledge.

operators is made dynamically during the search. The purpose is to use simultaneously several mutation operators during the EA, and to change automatically the probability selection of each operator according to its effectiveness [57]. So the algorithm more often uses the best operators than the others. Let us remark that a similar approach could be defined with other operators (e.g., crossover, neighborhoods, hybrid strategies).

Initially, the same probability is assigned to each mutation operator: $\mathrm{Mu}_1, \ldots, \mathrm{Mu}_k$. Those probabilities are equal to the same ratio $P_{\mathrm{Mu}_i} = 1/(k \cdot P_{\mathrm{Mu}})$, where k is the number of mutation operators and P_{Mu} is the global mutation probability. At each iteration, the probabilities associated with the mutation operators are updated according to their average progress. To compute the progress of the operators, each mutation Mu_i applied to the individual I is associated with a progress value:

$$\Pi(I_{\mathrm{Mu}_i}) = \begin{cases} 1 & \text{if } I \text{ is dominated by } I_{\mathrm{Mu}_i} \\ 0 & \text{if } I \text{ dominates } I_{\mathrm{Mu}_i} \\ \frac{1}{2} & \text{otherwise (noncomparable solutions)} \end{cases}$$

where I_{Mu_i} is the solution after mutation (Fig. 5.49).

At the end of each generation of the EA, an average progress $\mathrm{Progress}(\mathrm{Mu}_i)$ is assigned to each operator Mu_i. Its value is the average progress of $\Pi(I_{\mathrm{Mu}_i})$ computed with each solution modified by the mutation Mu_i:

$$\mathrm{Progress}(\mathrm{Mu}_i) = \frac{\sum \Pi(I_{\mathrm{Mu}_i})}{\|\mathrm{Mu}_i\|}$$

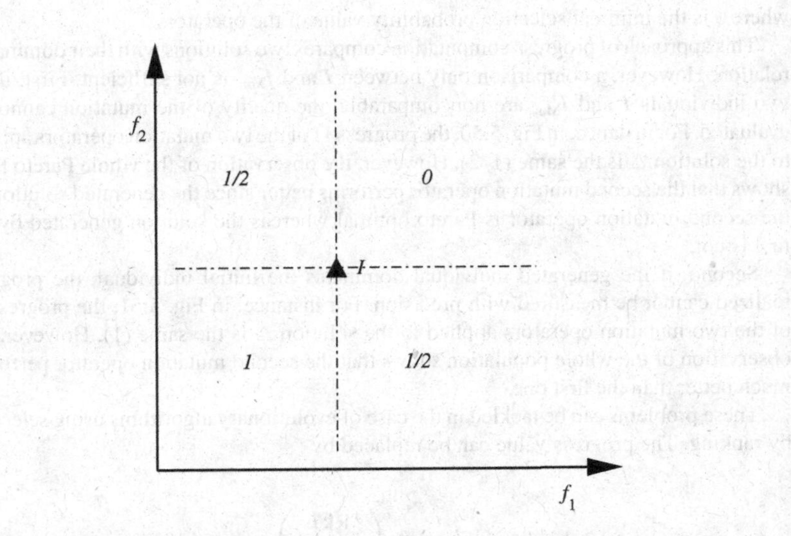

FIGURE 5.49 Progress value of $\Pi(I_{\mathrm{Mu}_i})$ for mutation operators.

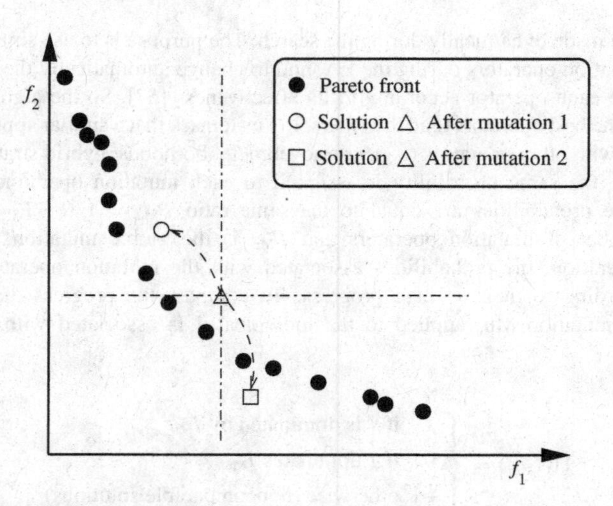

FIGURE 5.50 Evaluation of the quality of the mutation operators.

where $\|\text{Mu}_i\|$ is the number of applications of the mutation Mu_i on the population. The new selection probabilities are computed proportionally to these values:

$$P_{\text{Mu}_i} = \frac{\text{Progress}(\text{Mu}_i)}{\sum_{j=1}^{k} \text{Progress}(\text{Mu}_j)} \times (1 - k \times \delta) + \delta$$

where δ is the minimal selection probability value of the operators.

This approach of progress computation compares two solutions with their dominance relation. However, a comparison only between I and I_{Mu_i} is not sufficient. First, if the two individuals I and I_{Mu_i} are noncomparable, the quality of the mutation cannot be evaluated. For instance, in Fig. 5.50, the progress Π of the two mutation operators applied to the solution Δ is the same $(1/2)$. However, the observation of the whole Pareto front shows that the second mutation operator performs better since the generated solution by the second mutation operator is Pareto optimal whereas the solution generated by the first is not.

Second, if the generated individual dominates the initial individual, the progress realized cannot be measured with precision. For instance, in Fig. 5.51, the progress Π of the two mutation operators applied to the solution Δ is the same (1). However, the observation of the whole population shows that the second mutation operator performs much better than the first one.

These problems can be tackled in the case of evolutionary algorithms using selection by ranking. The progress value can be replaced by

$$\Pi(I_{\text{Mu}_i}) = \left(\frac{\text{Rk}I}{\text{Rk}I_{\text{Mu}_i}} \right)^{\beta}$$

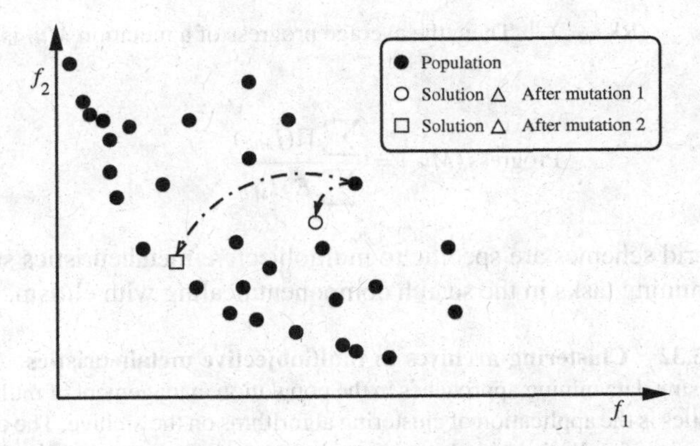

FIGURE 5.51 Computing the progress realized by different mutation operators.

where $\mathrm{Rk}I_{\mathrm{Mu}_i}$ is the rank of the solution after mutation, $\mathrm{Rk}I$ is the rank of the solution before mutation, and β is how much the progress made by mutation operators is encouraged (e.g., $\beta = 2$).

The evaluation of the progress of the mutation operators can be still improved by supporting the progresses realized on good solutions. In fact, these progresses are generally more interesting for the front progression than progresses made on bad solutions (Fig. 5.52). So an elitist factor $E_f I_{Mu_i}$ has been introduced into the last progress indicator to favor progresses made on good solutions:

$$\Pi(I_{Mu_i}) = E_f I_{Mu_i} \times \left(\frac{\mathrm{Rk}I_{Mu_i}}{\mathrm{Rk}I} \right)^{\beta}$$

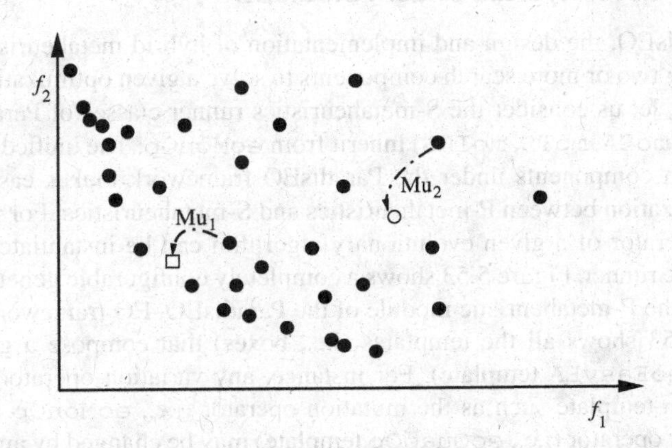

FIGURE 5.52 Progress realized by mutation operators on good quality solutions.

with $E_f I_{Mu_i} = (\text{Rk} I_{Mu_i})^{-1}$. Then, the average progress of a mutation Mu_i is defined as follows:

$$\text{Progress}\,(Mu_i) = \frac{\sum \Pi(I_{Mu_i})}{\sum E_f I_{Mu_i}} \tag{5.1}$$

Some hybrid schemes are specific to multiobjective metaheuristics such as introducing data mining tasks in the search component dealing with elitism.

Example 5.32 Clustering archives in multiobjective metaheuristics. A classical approach using data mining approaches in the population management of multiobjective metaheuristics is the application of clustering algorithms on the archive. The objective is to produce a set of well-diversified representative Pareto solutions in a bounded archive. An archive is often used to store Pareto solutions and the clustering is then performed to avoid a bias toward a certain region of the search space and to reduce the number of Pareto solutions. Such a bias would lead to an unbalanced distribution of the Pareto solutions. For instance, a hierarchical clustering can be applied using the average linkage method [848].

5.6 HYBRID METAHEURISTICS UNDER ParadisEO

The open architecture of the ParadisEO framework and its flexibility facilitates the design of hybrid metaheuristics. ParadisEO provides the most common hybridization schemes (LRH, LTH, HRH, and HTH). They can be exploited in a natural way to make cooperating metaheuristics belonging to different families of metaheuristics: monoobjective/multiobjective, homogeneous/heterogeneous, partial/global, and generalist/specialist.

5.6.1 Low-Level Hybrids Under ParadisEO

Using ParadisEO, the design and implementation of hybrid metaheuristics consists in combining two or more search components to solve a given optimization problem. For instance, let us consider the S-metaheuristics runner classes of ParadisEO–MO (e.g., `moHC`, `moSA`, `moTS`, `moILS`) inherit from `eoMonOp`. The unified architecture of the search components under the ParadisEO framework makes easier the low-level hybridization between P-metaheuristics and S-metaheuristics. For instance, the mutation operator of a given evolutionary algorithm can be instantiated by any S-metaheuristic runner. Figure 5.53 shows a completely configurable genetic algorithm available in the P-metaheuristic module of the ParadisEO–EO framework.

Figure 5.53 shows all the templates (i.e., boxes) that compose a genetic algorithm (i.e., `eoEasyEA` template). For instance, any variation operator in the `eoTransform` template such as the mutation operator (i.e., `eoMonOp` template) or the crossover operator (i.e., `eoQuadOp` template) may be changed by another search

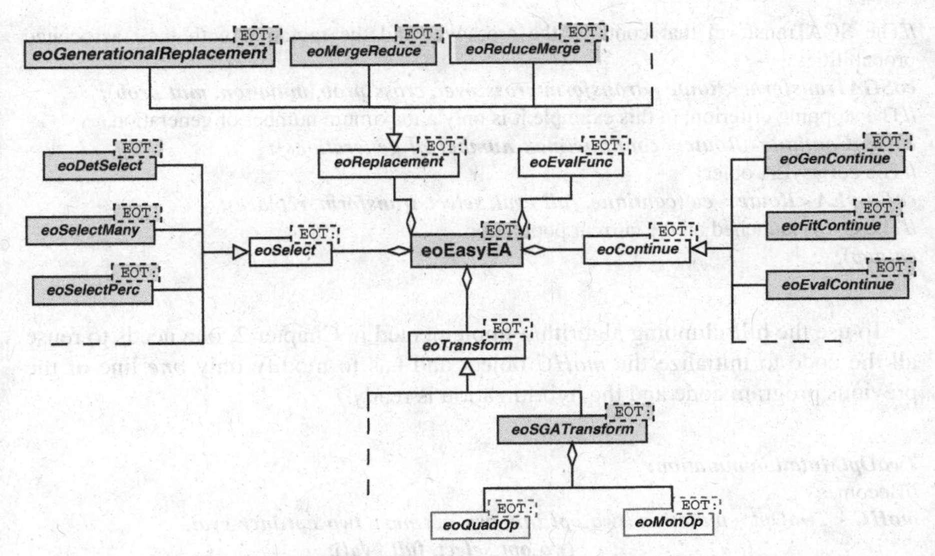

FIGURE 5.53 Diagram of an `eoEasyEA` object.

component (e.g., S-metaheuristic, exact algorithm, greedy heuristics). Figure 5.54 shows a LTH hybrid scheme in which a S-metaheuristic of the Paradiseo–MO module (i.e., `moAlgo`) has been linked to a P-metaheuristic of the ParadisEO–EO module. The S-metaheuristic template `moAlgo` replaces the mutation operator (i.e., `eoMonOp` template) of the genetic algorithm.

The following program represents a genetic algorithm implementation for the TSP:

```
...
//An eoInit that allows to generate one individual.
RouteInit route_init;
//An initial individual population that are generated thanks to an eoInit object (route_init).
eoPop<Route> pop(pop_size, route_init);
//A full evaluation method <=> eoEvalFunc.
RouteEvaluation full_eval;
//The population is evaluated.
apply<Route>(full_eval, pop);
//The selection strategy, here the individuals are selected by a determinist tournament.
eoDetTournamentSelect<Route> selectOne(number_of_selected);
eoSelectPerc<Route> select(selectOne);
//The replacement strategy.
eoPlusReplacement<Route> replace;
//The used crossover.
TwoOptCrossOver cross_over;
//The used mutation.
TwoOptMutation mutation;
```

//The SGATransform that contains the crossover and the mutation with their associated probabilities.
eoSGATransform<Route> transform(cross_over, cross_prob, mutation, mut_prob);
//The stopping criterion, in this example it is only a maximum number of generation.
eoGenContinue<Route> continue(max_number_of_generations);
//The eoEasyEA object.
eoEasyEA<Route> ea (continue, full_eval, select, transform, replace);
//The GA is launched on the current population.
ea(pop);

To use the hill-climbing algorithm implemented in Chapter 2, one needs to reuse all the code to initialize the *moHC* object and has to modify only *one* line of the previous program code and the hybridization is ready.

...
TwoOptMutation mutation;
//Becomes
moHC <TwoOpt> mutation (two_opt_init, two_opt_next, two_opt_incr_eval, two_opt_select, full_eval);

During its mutation step, an individual will be improved by a hill-climbing algorithm.

This example also illustrates that it is very easy to design and implement any low-level hybrid scheme. Indeed, any search algorithm template (e.g., S-metaheuristic, P-metaheuristic, exact algorithm, greedy heuristic) can be integrated into any

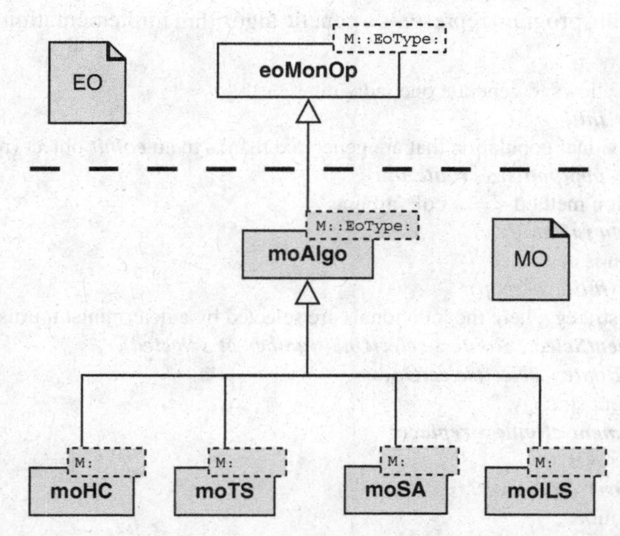

FIGURE 5.54 Diagram of the link between ParadisEO–EO and ParadisEO–MO allowing diverse LTH hybridization schemes.

component of another search algorithm template. For instance, any S-metaheuristic of the ParadisEO–MO module (`moAlgo` template) can be integrated into any P-metaheuristic of the ParadisEO–EO module (e.g. `eoMonOp`). Furthermore, one can also use several mutation mechanisms into a genetic algorithm (`eoPropCombinedMonOp` template). For instance, it can be possible to use for the mutation operator a hill-climbing algorithm half of the time and a tabu search algorithm for the rest of the time.

5.6.2 High-Level Hybrids Under ParadisEO

The HRH hybrid scheme of self-contained search components (e.g., S-metaheuristic, P-metaheuristic) is trivial to implement in the ParadisEO software framework. Indeed, this hybrid scheme corresponds to the sequential execution of the designed search components. For instance, the S-metaheuristic `MoAlgo` template (e.g., tabu search `moTS`, simulated annealing `moSA`, iterative local search `moILS`) (see Fig. 5.54) can be applied to the final population of a P-metaheuristic (e.g., evolutionary algorithm `eoEasyEA` template).

The high-level teamwork hybrid scheme is detailed in Section 6.4 dealing with parallel metaheuristics. Indeed, the design and implementation of efficient HTH hybrids need some advanced concepts from parallel and distributed computing.

5.6.3 Coupling with Exact Algorithms

There are many popular optimization solvers for solving integer programming (IP) and linear programming (LP) problems. Some of them are commercial such as CPLEX from ILOG, Xpress-MP from Dash. Others are open source such as the COIN-OR project[14]. They use a combination of branch and bound and cutting plane methods. Most of the open-source solvers are implemented in the C++ programming language using the object-oriented programming paradigm. Hence, it is natural to design and implement hybrid models between metaheuristics under ParadisEO and exact optimization algorithms from mathematical programming community under open-source C++ frameworks such as COIN-OR.

Moreover, many constraint programming solvers can be found in the literature such as ILOG Solver[15], CHIP, ECLiPSe[16], cc(FD), CLAIRE [111,112], CHOCO, and Gecode. As in mathematical programming, most of the open-source frameworks for CP are implemented in the C++ language using the object-oriented paradigm. As seen in this chapter, CP may be complemented by metaheuristic algorithms. The open architecture of the ParadisEO framework makes it easy to combine with constraint programming frameworks such as Gecode and CHOCO.

Nowadays, coupling a metaheuristic software with constraint programming and mathematical programming solvers is one of the most exciting activities in efficiently

[14] http://www.coin-or.org.

[15] www.ilog.com.

[16] http://www.icparc.ic.ac.uk/eclipse.

solving the difficult optimization problems. The actual coupling is limited in terms of designing low-level hybrid models. Hence, one of the most important perspectives is to perform a strong coupling between a software framework for metaheuristics (e.g., ParadisEO) and open-source mathematical programming and constraint programming frameworks.

5.7 CONCLUSIONS AND PERSPECTIVES

The efficient solving of complex problems must involve ideas from different paradigms: metaheuristics, mathematical programming, constraint programming, machine learning, graph theory, parallel and distributed computing, and so on. Pure metaheuristics are not generally well suited to search in high-dimensional and complex landscapes. Hybrid metaheuristics actually represent the most efficient algorithms for many classical and real-life difficult problems. This is proven by the huge number of efficient hybrid metaheuristics proposed to solve a large variety of problems.

Nowadays, combining metaheuristics is a common strategy to solve optimization problems. Hybrid algorithms will constitute competitive candidates for solving the difficult optimization problems in the coming years. As we have developed a unified view of metaheuristics, which is based on their key search components, one can say that designing a monoobjective or multiobjective metaheuristic can be reduced to select the most suited search components and combining them. This design approach is naturally a hybrid one, and it is not under the control of a single paradigm of metaheuristics[17].

A unified taxonomy, based on a hierarchical (low level versus high level, relay versus teamwork) and flat classification (homogeneous/heterogeneous, global/partial, general/specialist) has been developed to describe in terms of design and implementation the following different hybridization schemes of metaheuristics:

- **Metaheuristics:** Combining P-metaheuristics with S-metaheuristics has provided very powerful search algorithm. Pure P-metaheuristics such as evolutionary algorithms, scatter search, and ant colonies are generally not well suited to fine-tuned search in highly combinatorial spaces. P-metaheuristics are more efficient in terms of diversification (i.e., exploration) in the search space. Hence, they need to be combined with more intensification-based (i.e., exploitation-based) search algorithms, which are generally based on S-metaheuristics (e.g., local search, tabu search).
- **Mathematical programming:** In the last decade, there has been an important advance in designing efficient exact methods in the operations research

[17] Using this design approach, it is worthwhile to mention about hybrid metaheuristics as any metaheuristic will be a hybrid one!.

community (e.g., integer programming). There are many opportunities to design hybrid approaches combining metaheuristics and exact methods. Indeed, the two approaches have complementary advantages and disadvantages (e.g., efficiency and effectiveness).

- **Constraint programming:** Over the last years, interest in combining metaheuristics and constraint programming has risen considerably. The availability of high-level modeling languages and software solvers for constraint programming will lead to more hybrid approaches, which capture the most desirable features of each paradigm.
- **Data mining:** Nowadays, using metaheuristics to solve data mining and machine learning problems has become common. But the challenge is the incorporation of machine learning and data mining techniques into metaheuristics. The major interest in using machine learning and data mining techniques is to extract useful knowledge from the history of the search to improve the efficiency and the effectiveness of metaheuristics. Both positive and negative knowledge must be extracted. In fact, most of the actual works focus on only positive knowledge [557].

The main drawback of hybridization is the introduction of new parameters that define the hybrid scheme. The setting of these parameters is nontrivial. A crucial question that has to be addressed in the future is an aid for the efficient design of hybrid metaheuristics in which the automatic setting of parameters must be investigated [84,275]. Indeed, it will be interesting to guide the user to define the suitable hybrid scheme to solve a given problem. It will also be interesting to define "adaptive" cooperation mechanisms that allow to select dynamically the optimization methods according to convergence or other criteria such as diversity. Some approaches such as the COSEARCH [749] or "hyperheuristics" [98] have been proposed to deal with this problem. These approaches are dedicated to choose the right heuristic for the right operation at the right time during the search. It must be noted that these hybrid approaches operate in the heuristic space, as opposed to most implementations of metaheuristics that operate in the solution space. This principle is relatively new, although the concept of "optimizing heuristics" is not a recent one.

Using the software framework ParadisEO, it is natural to combine metaheuristics that have been developed under the framework to design S-metaheuristics (under ParadisEO–MO), P-metaheuristics (under ParadisEO–EO), and multiobjective metaheuristics (under ParadisEO–MOEO). The combining of metaheuristics with exact optimization and machine learning algorithms still remain to be done. The coupling of software frameworks dealing with the three classes of algorithms (i.e., metaheuristics, exact algorithm, and machine learning algorithm) is an important issue for the future. This enables to reduce the complexity of designing and implementing hybrid approaches and make them more and more popular.

It will also be interesting explore in depth the parallel models for hybrid methods. Parallel schemes ideally provide novel ways to design and implement hybrid algorithms by providing parallel models of the algorithms. Hence, instead of merely parallelizing and fine- tuning a sequential hybrid algorithm that has limited capabilities to be parallelized, teamwork hybrid schemes are inherently suited to parallel environments.

5.8 EXERCISES

Exercise 5.1 Greedy algorithm for population initialization. The use of a deterministic greedy approach to initialize the population of a P-metaheuristic (e.g., evolutionary algorithm) is not recommended. Indeed, the initial population must be diverse while in a deterministic greedy algorithm, the same solution is generated. Which greedy approach can be used to tackle this problem?

Exercise 5.2 Lamarckian versus Baldwin evolutions. What is the difference between the Lamarckian and the Baldwin evolutions?

Exercise 5.3 Locally optimized crossover. Some local optimization search procedure may be applied to the crossover operator. The role of the crossover operator is to generate intermediate offsprings from the parents. Among intermediate solutions, the crossover operator is blind in the sense that it will select an arbitrary one. Path generation from one parent to another may be a good strategy to recombination.

Exercise 5.4 Integrating path relinking into GRASP. Let us consider the following hybrid metaheuristic integrating the concept of path relinking into the S-metaheuristic GRASP. The GRASP algorithm maintains a set of elite solution found during the different iterations of the metaheuristic. At each iteration of the GRASP, path relinking is applied from the newly generated solution by GRASP to a given solution of the elite solutions. The target solution may be chosen randomly from the elite set [650]. To which class does this hybrid scheme belong?

Exercise 5.5 Variable neighborhood search and GRASP are complementary. Variable neighborhood search relies on the use of randomization of the local search to escape from local optima. Moreover, VNS uses different neighborhoods in the shaking and the local search procedures. The local search algorithm in GRASP stops at the first found local optima. VNS and GRASP may be considered as complementary. Propose some effective hybrid algorithms combining GRASP and VNS methods.

Exercise 5.6 Coevolutionary algorithms. To which hybrid class the predator–prey model of coevolutionary algorithms (see Section 3.4.3) belong?

Exercise 5.7 Hybrid bee colony model. Bee colony-based optimization algorithms are based on two different models: food foraging and marriage in the bee

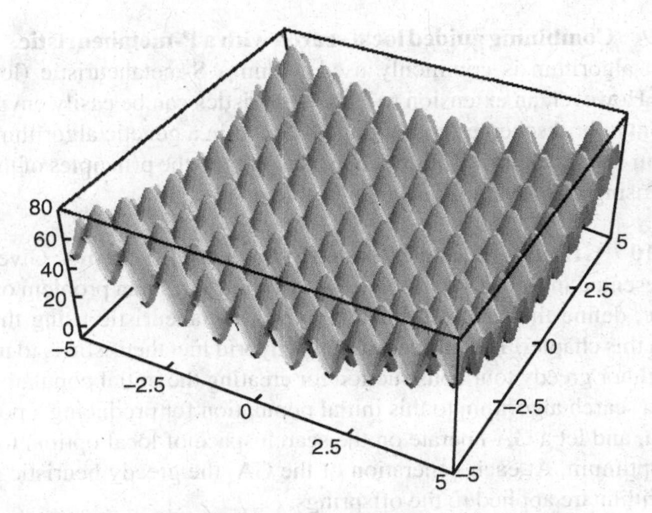

FIGURE 5.55 Rastrigin continuous function.

colony (see Section 3.7.1). Propose a HRH hybrid metaheuristic that combines the two models. Indeed, the two models are complementary and can be applied sequentially.

Exercise 5.8 Partitioning the Rastrigin function. The general form of a separable function is

$$f(x_1, ..., x_n) = \sum_{i=1}^{n} f_i(x_i)$$

The Rastrigin function is a separable function (Fig. 5.55) [774]. The Rastrigin function is a nonlinear multimodal function, which is composed of a large number of local optima (Eq. 5.1). It was first proposed by Rastrigin as a two-dimensional function [774] and has been generalized by Mühlenbein et al. in Ref.[570].

$$F(\vec{x}) = A \cdot n + \sum_{i=1}^{n} x_i^2 - A \cdot \cos(\omega \cdot x_i) \tag{5.1}$$

$$A = 10\ ;\ \omega = 2 \cdot \pi;\ x_i \in [-5.12, 5.12]$$

The landscape of the function is defined by the variables A (resp. ω), which control the amplitude (resp. frequency modulation) . Which class of hybrid algorithm is adapted to optimize such function?

Exercise 5.9 Combining guided local search with a P-metaheuristic. The guided local search algorithm is commonly used within a S-metaheuristic (local search) framework. However, an extension to P-metaheuristics can be easily envisaged. Propose different hybrid schemes combining GLS within a genetic algorithm. For some LTH problem-specific hybridization schemes, illustrate the principles of the proposed approaches using the traveling salesman problem.

Exercise 5.10 Grammar for an extended hybridization scheme. Given the metaheuristic presented in Ref.[284] to solve the traveling salesman problem on a sequential machine, define the sentence for this hybrid metaheuristic using the grammar presented in this chapter. The basic idea of this hybrid metaheuristic is to use a simple nearest-neighbor greedy tour construction for creating the initial population of a GA, apply a local search algorithm to this initial population for producing a population of local optima, and let a GA operate on the search space of local optima to determine the global optimum. At each generation of the GA, the greedy heuristic and a local search algorithm are applied to the offsprings.

Exercise 5.11 Variable neighborhood search versus mutation. The objective of this exercise is to make a parallel between variable neighborhood search method and the role of mutation in a memetic algorithm (LTH GA(LS) hybrid). In the LTH hybrid genetic algorithm, a local search procedure is applied after the mutation variation. Let us consider an optimization problem with a binary vector representation, where the neighborhood is based on complementing a bit. The shaking mechanism of VNS consists in enlarging the neighborhood by complementing k bits ($k = 1, 2, 3$, etc.), while the local search phase of the VNS is based on the same procedure as in the hybrid GA. The mutation in the hybrid GA consists in flipping with a given probability $p_{\rm m}$ each bit of the vector. Analyze the differences and the similarities between the two algorithms.

Exercise 5.12 Hybrid models for dynamic optimization. The high-level cooperative hybrid class may be considered as a good alternative to solve dynamic optimization problems. Let us consider a P-metaheuristic based on evolutionary algorithms or particle swarm optimizers. Propose a HTH model in which tracking optimal solution would be more efficient than in a pure evolutionary algorithm.

Exercise 5.13 Mixed continuous–integer optimization. Let us consider a problem in which some decision variables X are discrete and other decision variables Y are continuous. One can propose a nested hybrid approach to solve this problem. It works as follows: a continuous metaheuristic in the inner loop will optimize the problem over the decision variables X while the variables Y are fixed. In the outer loop, a discrete metaheuristic will optimize the problem over the variables Y while the variables X are fixed to the best found values in the inner loop. The search then alternate between the space of continuous variables and the space of discrete variables. What is the drawback of such a nested optimization strategy.

Exercise 5.14 Adaptive hybrid schemes. Adaptive hybridization consists in switching between the combined metaheuristics (or any search components) in a dynamic way and using the history of the search (adaptive memory). For instance, let us consider a LRH hybrid scheme between a P-metaheuristic (e.g., genetic algorithm) and a S-metaheuristic (e.g., local search). A pool of k elite solutions (best found) are memorized during the search. If $k = 1$, only the best found solution is contained in the memory. Propose an adaptive hybrid scheme using this adaptive memory. Generalize your proposal to multiobjective optimization problems. Indeed, the same approach may be used for multiobjective optimization, where the search memorizes a Pareto archive in which all generated Pareto solutions are stored.

Exercise 5.15 Path relinking the Pareto approximation. Let us consider the biobjective permutation flow-shop scheduling problem (see Section 4.2). The two handled objectives are the makespan and the total tardiness:

$$C_{\max} \quad \text{makespan (total completion time): } \max\{C_i | i \in [1 \ldots n]\}$$

$$T: \text{ total tardiness: } \sum_{i=1}^{n} [\max(0, C_i - d_i)]$$

where s_{ij} represents the time at which the task t_{ij} is scheduled and $C_i = s_{im} + p_{im}$ represents the completion time of job J_i. Using the Graham standard notation, this problem is defined as F/perm, d_i/($C_{\max}$,T). A solution of the problem is represented by a permutation of the jobs. The neighborhood operator is based on the shift (insertion) operator. In the insertion operator, a job at one position is removed and placed at another position of the permutation. The distance in the decision space between two solutions s_1 and s_2, in respect to the insertion operator, is $d_{\text{perm}} = n - s_{\max}$, where n is the number of jobs and $s_{\max}$ is the greatest shared substring between s_1 and s_2. Prove that d_{perm} is a distance and that corresponds to the minimum number of permutations required to join s_1 with s_2.

Computing the greatest shared substring between two solutions is a well-known problem in the genomics community. An example of distance between two solutions x and y obtained by computing a greatest shared substring is shown in Fig. 5.56. In this example, three inversions are necessary to link x with y—the jobs 2, 4, and 6 have to be moved to link these solutions. They correspond to the set of jobs that are not in the greatest shared substring between the two solutions. Let us remark that the greatest shared substring is not necessarily unique: the substrings "13478" and "12478" can be viewed as largest shared substrings too. Show that using a dynamic programming algorithm, the distance between any two solutions may be computed in $O(n^2)$.

Let us suppose that a good approximation of the Pareto set has been obtained by a multiobjective metaheuristic. Propose a path relinking strategy to fill the gap of the

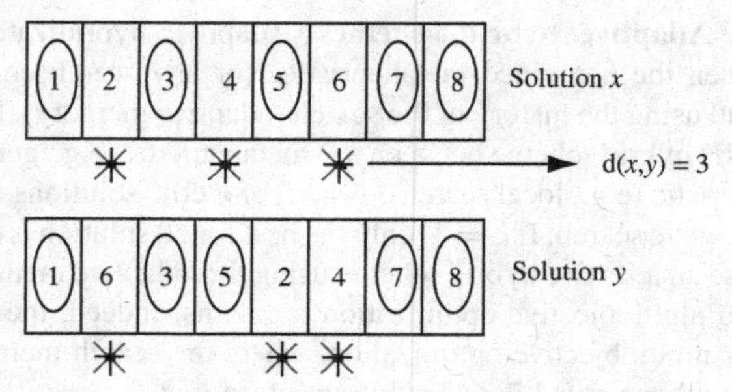

FIGURE 5.56 Distance between two solutions x and y: the greatest shared substring.

solutions belonging to the Pareto approximation. Recall that the design questions that must be considered are the selection of the initial and the guiding solutions and the path generation.

Exercise 5.16 Pareto local search. In the LTH hybrid algorithm Pareto local search presented in Algorithm 5.2, the set of nondominated solutions to store in the set P may be too large. Hence, the computational cost of the algorithm will be expensive. What are the solutions that can be applied to reduce this complexity.

Exercise 5.17 Target aiming Pareto search. In the HRH hybrid algorithm target aiming Pareto search (TAPAS) presented in Example 5.25, the set of nondominated solutions of the approximation P may be large. Hence, the computational cost of the whole S-metaheuristics to be performed will be extremely expensive. What are the solutions that can be applied to reduce the complexity of the TAPAS algorithm.

Exercise 5.18 Clustered multiobjective metaheuristics. In a multiobjective metaheuristic, different strategies have been used to deal with diversity (see Section 4.5). For instance, the NSGA-II algorithm is based on a crowding distance operator. Propose a modification of the NSGA-II algorithm in which the crowding operator is replaced by a K-means clustering algorithm. The number of generated clusters is equal to a given value k. What is the computational complexity of the proposed procedure?

Exercise 5.19 HRH hybrid under ParadisEO. In the HRH hybrid scheme, the self-contained search components (e.g., metaheuristics) are trivial to implement under the ParadisEO framework. It corresponds to the sequential execution of metaheuristics. Let us consider the already designed local search component `eoLS` and evolutionary algorithm `eoEA` for the traveling salesman problem. Implement a HRH hybrid algorithm in which the local search component is applied to the final population of the evolutionary algorithm.

Exercise 5.20 Flexibility of LTH hybrids under ParadisEO. The program example of Section 5.6.1 shows a LTH hybrid in which a hill-climbing algorithm has been integrated into an evolutionary algorithm. The mutation operator of the EA (`eoMonOp`) has been replaced by a hill-climbing algorithm (`moHC`). How can one change the hill-climbing algorithm by the other already implemented S-metaheuristics (e.g., tabu search `moTS`, simulated annealing `moSA`, iterative local search `moILS`)? Show that any search algorithm (e.g., greedy heuristic, exact algorithm) implemented outside the ParadisEO framework can be integrated into the EA algorithm.

CHAPTER 6

Parallel Metaheuristics

On one hand, optimization problems are more and more complex and their resource requirements are ever increasing. Real-life optimization problems are often NP-hard and CPU time and/or memory consuming. Although the use of metaheuristics allows to significantly reduce the computational complexity of the search process, the latter remains time consuming for many problems in diverse domains of application, where the objective function and the constraints associated with the problem are resource (e.g., CPU, memory) intensive and the size of the search space is huge. Moreover, more and more complex and resource-intensive metaheuristics are developed (e.g., hybrid metaheuristics, multiobjective metaheuristics).

On the other hand, the rapid development of technology in designing processors (e.g., multicore processors, dedicated architectures), networks (e.g., local area networks—LAN—such as Myrinet and Infiniband, wide area networks—WAN—such as optical networks), and data storage has made the use of parallel computing more and more popular (Fig. 6.1). Such architectures represent an effective strategy for the design and implementation of parallel metaheuristics. Indeed, sequential architectures are reaching physical limitation (speed of light, thermodynamics). Nowadays, even laptops and workstations are equipped with multicore processors, which represent a given class of parallel architecture. Moreover, the cost/performance ratio is constantly decreasing. The proliferation of powerful workstations and fast communication networks have shown the emergence of clusters of processors (COWs), networks of workstations (NOWs), and large-scale network of machines (grids) as platforms for high-performance computing.

Parallel and distributed computing can be used in the design and implementation of metaheuristics for the following reasons:

- **Speed up the search:** One of the main goals of parallelizing a metaheuristic is to reduce the search time. This helps designing real-time and interactive optimization methods. This is a very important aspect for some class of problems where there is hard requirements on the search time such as in dynamic optimization problems and time critical control problems such as "real-time" planning.

Metaheuristics: From Design to Implementation, by El-Ghazali Talbi

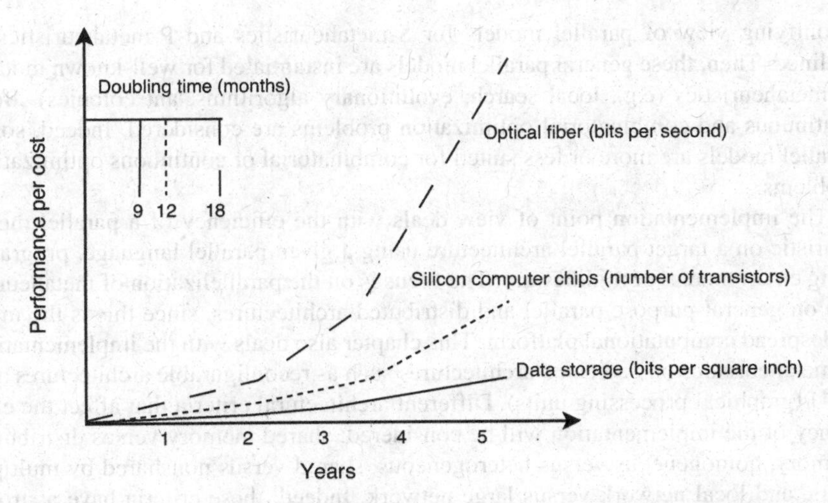

FIGURE 6.1 Performance per cost for processors, networks, and storage technologies in the last years. The performance is doubling every 9 months (resp. 12 and 18 months) for networks (resp. storage and processors).

- **Improve the quality of the obtained solutions:** Some parallel models for metaheuristics allow to improve the quality of the search. Indeed, exchanging information between cooperative metaheuristics will alter their behavior in terms of searching in the landscape associated with the problem. The main goal of a parallel cooperation between metaheuristics is to improve the quality of solutions. Both better convergence and reduced search time may happen. Let us notice that a parallel model for metaheuristics may be more effective than a sequential metaheuristic even on a single processor.
- **Improve the robustness:** A parallel metaheuristic may be more robust in terms of solving in an effective manner different optimization problems and different instances of a given problem. Robustness may also be measured in terms of the sensitivity of the metaheuristic to its parameters.
- **Solve large-scale problems:** Parallel metaheuristics allow to solve large-scale instances of complex optimization problems. A challenge here is to solve very large instances that cannot be solved by a sequential machine. Another similar challenge is to solve more accurate mathematical models associated with different optimization problems. Improving the accuracy of the mathematical models increases, in general, the size of the associated problems to be solved. Moreover, some optimization problems need the manipulation of huge databases such as data mining problems.

In this chapter, a clear difference is made between the parallel design aspect and the parallel implementation aspect of metaheuristics. From the algorithmic design point of view, the main parallel models for metaheuristics are presented.

A unifying view of parallel models for S-metaheuristics and P-metaheuristics is outlined. Then, these general parallel models are instantiated for well-known models of metaheuristics (e.g., local search, evolutionary algorithms, ant colonies). Both continuous and combinatorial optimization problems are considered. Indeed, some parallel models are more or less suited for combinatorial or continuous optimization problems.

The implementation point of view deals with the efficiency of a parallel metaheuristic on a target parallel architecture using a given parallel language, programming environment, or middleware. The focus is on the parallelization of metaheuristics on general-purpose parallel and distributed architectures, since this is the most widespread computational platform. This chapter also deals with the implementation of metaheuristics on dedicated architectures such as reconfigurable architectures and GPU (graphical processing units). Different architectural criteria that affect the efficiency of the implementation will be considered: shared memory versus distributed memory, homogeneous versus heterogeneous, shared versus nonshared by multiple users, and local network versus large network. Indeed, these criteria have a strong impact on the deployment technique employed, such as load balancing and fault tolerance. Depending on the type of parallel architecture used, different parallel and distributed languages, programming environments, and middlewares may be used, such as message passing (e.g., PVM, MPI), shared memory (e.g., multithreading, OpenMP), remote procedural call (e.g., Java RMI, RPC), high-throughput computing (e.g., Condor), and grid computing (e.g., Globus).

This chapter is organized as follows. In Section 6.1, the main parallel models for designing metaheuristics are presented. Section 6.2 deals with the implementation issues of parallel metaheuristics. In this section, the main concepts of parallel architectures and parallel programming paradigms, which interfere with the design and implementation of parallel metaheuristics, are outlined. The main performance indicators that can be used to evaluate a parallel metaheuristic in terms of efficiency are detailed. In Section 6.3, the parallel metaheuristic models and their implementation are revisited for multiobjective optimization. Finally, Section 6.4 deals with the design and implementation of the different parallel models for metaheuristics based on the software framework ParadisEO.

6.1 PARALLEL DESIGN OF METAHEURISTICS

In terms of designing parallel metaheuristics, three major parallel models are identified. They follow the following three hierarchical levels (Table 6.1):

- **Algorithmic level:** In this parallel model, independent or cooperating self-contained metaheuristics are used. It is a problem-independent interalgorithm parallelization. If the different metaheuristics are independent, the search will be equivalent to the sequential execution of the metaheuristics in terms of the quality of solutions. However, the cooperative model will alter the behavior of the metaheuristics and enable the improvement of the quality of solutions.

TABLE 6.1 Parallel Models of Metaheuristics

Parallel Model	Problem Dependency	Behavior	Granularity	Goal
Algorithmic level	Independent	Altered	Metaheuristic	Effectiveness
Iteration level	Independent	Nonaltered	Iteration	Efficiency
Solution level	Dependent	Nonaltered	Solution	Efficiency

- **Iteration level:** In this model, each iteration of a metaheuristic is parallelized. It is a problem-independent intraalgorithm parallelization. The behavior of the metaheuristic is not altered. The main objective is to speed up the algorithm by reducing the search time. Indeed, the iteration cycle of metaheuristics on large neighborhoods for S-metaheuristics or large populations for P-metaheuristics requires a large amount of computational resources, especially for real-world problems.
- **Solution level:** In this model, the parallelization process handles a single solution of the search space. It is a problem-dependent intraalgorithm parallelization. In general, evaluating the objective function(s) or constraints for a generated solution is frequently the most costly operation in metaheuristics. In this model, the behavior of the metaheuristic is not altered. The objective is mainly the speed up of the search.

In the following sections, the different parallel models are detailed and analyzed in terms of algorithmic design.

6.1.1 Algorithmic-Level Parallel Model

In this model, many self-contained metaheuristic algorithms are launched in parallel. They may or may not cooperate to solve the target optimization problem.

6.1.1.1 Independent Algorithmic-Level Parallel Model

In the *independent* algorithmic-level parallel model, the different metaheuristics are executed without any cooperation. The different metaheuristics may be initialized with different solutions for S-metaheuristics or with different populations for P-metaheuristics. In addition to the initial solution or initial population, different parameter settings may be used for the metaheuristics, such as the size of tabu list for tabu search, transition probabilities for ant colonies, mutation and crossover probabilities for evolutionary algorithms, and so on. Moreover, each search component of a metaheuristic may be designed differently: encoding, search operators (e.g., variation operators, neighborhood), objective function, constraints, stopping criteria, and so on.

This parallel model is straightforward to design and implement. The master/worker paradigm is well suited to this model. A worker implements a metaheuristic. The master defines the different parameters to be used by the workers and determines

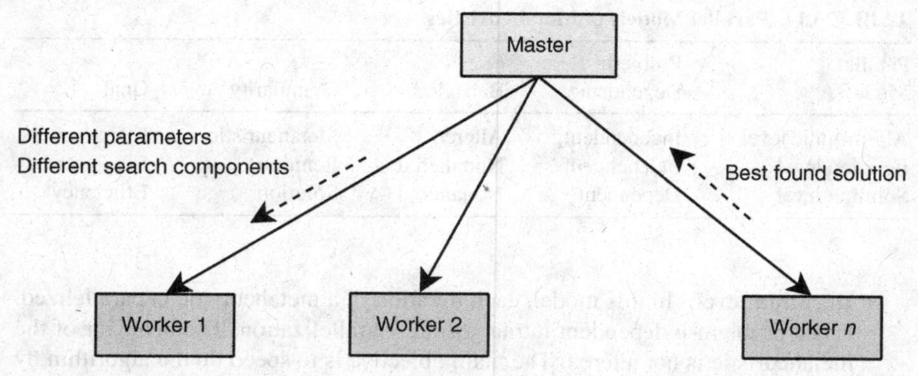

FIGURE 6.2 The parallel independent algorithmic-level model for metaheuristics.

the best found solution from those obtained by the different workers (Fig. 6.2). In addition to speeding up the algorithm, this parallel model enables to improve its robustness.

This model raises particularly the following question: Is it equivalent to execute k metaheuristics during a time t than executing a single metaheuristic during $k \cdot t$? The answer depends on the landscape properties of the problem (e.g., presence of multiple basins of attraction, distribution of the local optima, fitness distance correlation).

Example 6.1 Multistart model. Historically, the parallel independent model has been largely used for S-metaheuristics (e.g., local search, tabu search, simulated annealing) [19,162,758]. The well-known multistart local search, in which different local search algorithms are launched using diverse initial solutions, is an instantiation of this model. Different parameters of the S-metaheuristic may also be used into the parallel algorithms (e.g., size of the tabu list in tabu search). The generalization of the multistart model for P-metaheuristics using different initial populations is straightforward.

Let $P_k(t)$ be the probability of not having found a given target objective value in t time units with k independent search algorithms. If $P_1(t) = e^{(-t/\lambda)}$ with $\lambda \in \mathbb{R}^+$, which corresponds to an exponential distribution, then $P_k(t) = e^{(-kt/\lambda)}$ [259,701,798]. It implies that the probability $1 - e^{(-kt/\lambda)}$ of finding a target objective value in time $k \cdot t$ with a sequential algorithm is equal to the probability of finding a solution at least as good as the target objective value in time t using k parallel independent processes. Many pairs of optimization problems and metaheuristics fit the exponential distribution (e.g., quadratic assignment problem with tabu search [738]) or the two-parameter exponential distribution (e.g., maximum independent set, quadratic assignment problem, graph planarization, maximum weighted satisfiability, maximum covering with GRASP [20]). In a two-parameter exponential distribution, the probability to find a given objective value is $1 - e^{(-k(t-\mu)/\lambda)}$. If $\mu = 0$ or $k\mu \ll \lambda$, the two-parameter exponential distribution is more or less equivalent to the exponential distribution.

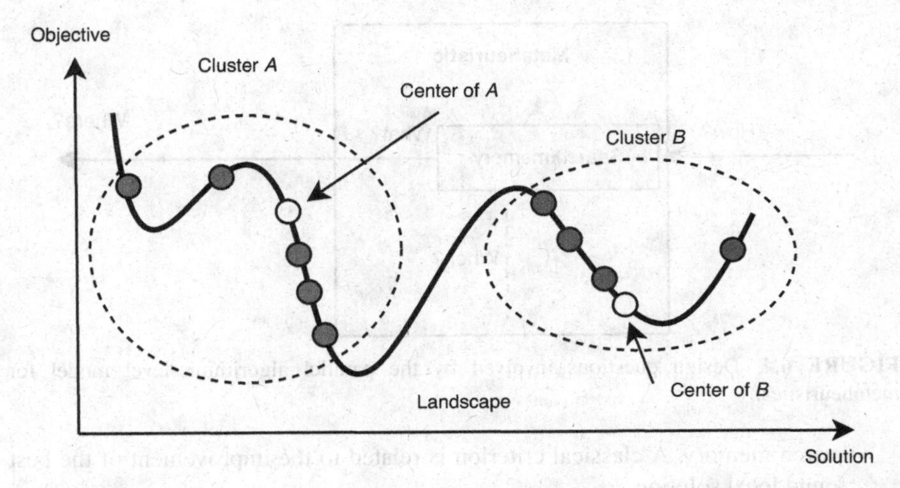

FIGURE 6.3 Parallel noncooperative models of particle swarm optimizers involving the clustering of particles.

Example 6.2 Independent algorithmic-level parallel model for particle swarm optimization. Some parallel algorithmic-level models for P-metaheuristics may be noncooperative. For instance, in a parallel particle swarm optimizer, some subswarms can be formed to search in parallel to optimize a continuous problem [456]. A standard k-means clustering method intends to divide the swarm into several clusters of particles (Fig. 6.3). Each subswarm represents a partition of the search space. Each particle i of a given subswarm uses the center of the cluster instead of its personal best position to update its velocity.

6.1.1.2 *Cooperative Algorithmic-Level Parallel Model*

In the *cooperative* model for parallel metaheuristics, the different algorithms are exchanging information related to the search with the intent to compute better and more robust solutions. The different criteria presented in Section 5.1.1 for high-level teamwork hybrid (HTH) metaheuristics also hold for the algorithmic-level parallel models.

In designing a parallel cooperative model for any metaheuristic, the same design questions need to be answered (see Fig. 6.4):

- **The exchange decision criterion (when?):** The exchange of information between the metaheuristics can be decided either in a *blind* (periodic or probabilistic) way or according to an *intelligent* adaptive criterion. Periodic exchange occurs in each algorithm after a fixed number of iterations; this type of communication is synchronous. Probabilistic exchange consists in performing a communication operation after each iteration with a given probability. Conversely, adaptive exchanges are guided by some run-time characteristics of the search. For instance, it may depend on the evolution of the quality of the solutions or the

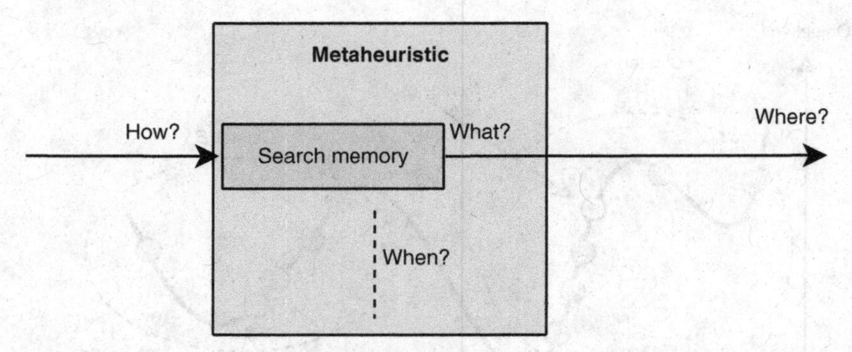

FIGURE 6.4 Design questions involved by the parallel algorithmic-level model for metaheuristics.

search memory. A classical criterion is related to the improvement of the best found local solution.

- **The exchange topology (where?):** The communication exchange topology indicates for each metaheuristic its neighbor(s) regarding the exchange of information, that is, the source/destination algorithm(s) of the information (Fig. 6.5). Several works have been dedicated to the study of the impact of the topology on the quality of the provided results, and they show that cyclic graphs are better [66,147]. The ring, mesh, and hypercube regular topologies are often used. The ring topology may be directional (i.e., directed graph) or bidirectional

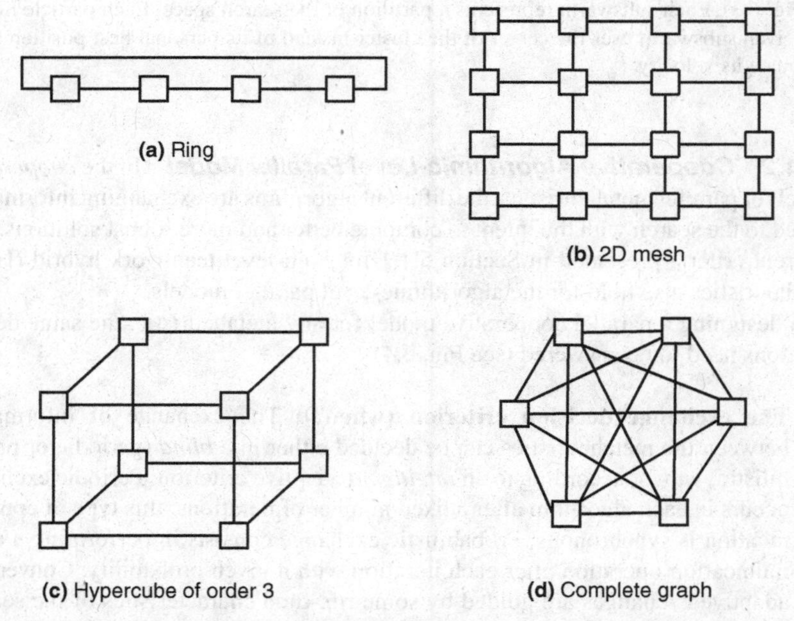

FIGURE 6.5 Some classical regular topologies for exchanging information.

TABLE 6.2 Main Characteristics of Exchange Topologies

Topology	Node Degree	Diameter	Number of Links
Linear array	2	$N-1$	$N-1$
Ring	2	$\frac{N}{2}$	N
2D Mesh	4	$2(\sqrt{N}-1)$	$2(N-\sqrt{N})$
Binary tree	3	$2(\text{Log}(N)-1)$	$N-1$
Torus	4	$2\left(\frac{\sqrt{N}}{2}\right)$	$2N$
Hypercube	$\text{Log}(N)$	$\text{Log}(N)$	$\frac{N \cdot \text{Log}(N)}{2}$
Complete graph	$N-1$	1	$\frac{N(N-1)}{2}$

N represents the number of metaheuristics involved.

(i.e.,undirected graph). In a hypercube of order k, there are 2^k nodes, and each node has k neighbors. A complete graph or a random one can also be used. In a complete graph, every node is connected to all other nodes, while in a random graph, a node sends its information to a randomly selected subset of nodes. Different strategies may be used to determine random neighbors, for example, each node has exactly one neighbor that is chosen with equal probability.

A topology is characterized by many parameters such as the degree of maximal node and the diameter of the corresponding graph. Table 6.2 shows these values for different classical topologies. The larger is the degree of nodes, the less important is the diameter of the graph, and more intensive is the information exchanged. Hence, a small diameter of the topology will increase the information exchanged between metaheuristics and then the probability of premature convergence occurrence. It is always the same involved trade-off between the exploration of the search space (less communication and good diversification) and the exploitation of the global search information (more communication and good intensification).

- **The information exchanged (what?):** This parameter specifies the information to be exchanged between the metaheuristics. In general, it may be composed of
  - **Solutions:** This information deals with a selection of the generated and stored solutions during the search. In general, it contains elite solutions that have been found, such as the best solution at the current iteration, local best solutions, global best solution, neighborhood best solution, best diversified solutions, and randomly selected solutions. The quality of the solutions must also be sent so that the evaluation of the solutions is not recomputed in the destination metaheuristics. For S-metaheuristics such as local search, the information exchanged is generally the best found solution. For P-metaheuristics, the number of solutions to exchange may be an absolute value or a given percentage of the population. Any selection mechanism can be used to select the solutions.

TABLE 6.3 Exchanged Information While Partitioning the Population of Some P-Metaheuristics

Metaheuristic	Search Memory
Evolutionary algorithms	Population of individuals
Ant colonies	Pheromone matrix
Particle swarm optimization	Population of particles
Scatter search	Reference set, population of solutions
Estimation of distribution algorithms	Probabilistic model

The most used selection strategy consists in selecting the best solutions for a given criteria (e.g., objective function of the problem, diversity, age) or random ones.

- **Search memory:** This information deals with any element of the search memory that is associated with the involved metaheuristic (Table 6.3). For tabu search, the information exchanged may be the short-term or long-term memories. For ant colonies (resp. estimation distribution algorithms), the information may be related to the pheromone trails (resp. the probability model).

- **The integration policy (how?):** Similar to the information exchange policy, the integration policy deals with the usage of the received information. In general, there is a local copy of the received information. The local variables are updated using the received ones. For instance, the best found solution is simply updated by the global best between the local best solution and the neighboring best solution. For P-metaheuristics, any replacement strategy may be applied to the local population by the set of received solutions. For example, an elitist replacement will integrate the received k solutions by replacing the k worst solutions of the local population. In ant colonies, the local and the neighboring pheromone matrices may be aggregated in a linear manner.

In the following sections, some instantiations of this parallel model for some specific metaheuristics are presented. For more illustrative examples and references, the reader may refer to Ref. [24].

Example 6.3 Algorithmic-level parallel models for evolutionary algorithms. Historically, the cooperative parallel model has been largely used in P-metaheuristics and especially in evolutionary algorithms. In sequential genetic algorithms[1], the selection takes place globally. Any individual can potentially reproduce with any other individual of the population. Among the most widely known parallel algorithmic-level models for evolutionary algorithms are the island model and the cellular model. In the well-known island model[2] for genetic algorithms, the population is decomposed into several subpopulations distributed among different nodes (Fig. 6.6). Each node is

[1] The sequential model is known as the panmictic genetic algorithm.

[2] Also known as the migration model, distributed model, multideme EA, or coarse-grain EA.

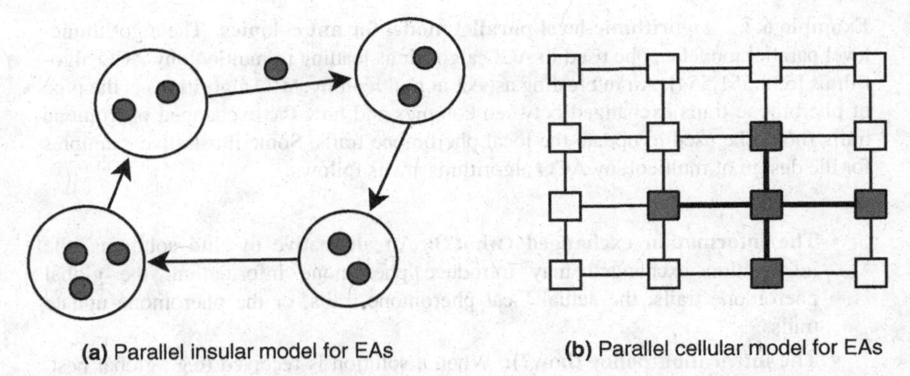

(a) Parallel insular model for EAs
(b) Parallel cellular model for EAs

FIGURE 6.6 The traditional parallel island and cellular models for evolutionary algorithms.

responsible for the evolution of one subpopulation. It executes all the steps of a classical EA from the selection to the replacement of the subpopulation. Each island may use different parameter values and different strategies for any search component such as selection, replacement, variation operators (mutation, crossover), and encodings. After a given number of generations (synchronous exchange) or when a condition holds (asynchronous exchange), the migration process is activated. Then, exchanges of some selected individuals between subpopulations are realized, and received individuals are integrated into the local subpopulation. The selection policy of emigrants indicates for each island in a *deterministic* or *stochastic* way the individuals to be migrated. The stochastic or random policy does not guarantee that the best individuals will be selected, but its associated computation cost is lower. The deterministic strategy (wheel, rank, tournament, or uniform sampling) allows the selection of the best individuals. The number of emigrants can be expressed as a fixed or variable number of individuals, or as a percentage of individuals from the population. The choice of the value of such parameter is crucial. Indeed, if the number of emigrants is low, the migration process will be less efficient as the islands will have the tendency to evolve in an independent way. Conversely, if the number of emigrants is high, the EAs are likely to converge to the same solutions. In EAs, the replacement/integration policy of immigrants indicates in a stochastic or deterministic way the local individuals to be replaced by the newcomers. The objective of the model is to delay the global convergence and encourage diversity.

The other well-known parallel model for EAs, the cellular model[3], may be seen as a special case of the island model where an island is composed of a single individual. Traditionally, an individual is assigned to a cell of a grid. The selection occurs in the neighborhood of the individual [713]. Hence, the selection pressure is less important than in sequential EAs. The overlapped small neighborhood in cellular EAs help in exploring the search space because a slow diffusion of solutions through the population provides a kind of exploration, while exploitation takes place within each neighborhood. Cellular models applied to complex problems can have a higher convergence probability than panmictic EAs.

[3] Also known as the diffusion or fine-grain model.

Example 6.4 Algorithmic-level parallel model for ant colonies. The algorithmic-level parallel model can be used in ACO algorithms leading to multicolony ACO algorithms [538,551,554]. An interesting aspect in multicolony ACO algorithms is the type of pheromone trails exchanged between colonies and how the exchanged pheromone trails should be used to update the local pheromone trails. Some illustrative examples for the design of multicolony ACO algorithms are as follows:

- **The information exchanged (what?):** An alternative to elite solutions, the information exchanged may introduce pheromone information: the global pheromone trails, the actual local pheromone trails, or the pheromone update trails.
- **The integration policy (how?):** When a solution is received (e.g., global best, local best), it is added to the pool of local elite solutions. The whole set of solutions will participate in updating the pheromone trails as local solutions. For instance, the global best solution of all subcolonies may be exchanged by the colonies, and each subcolony will update its pheromone trails according to the global best solution [553]. If the received information is a pheromone trail, it will be used to update the local pheromone trails. For instance, the new pheromone trail can be a weighted sum of the pheromone trails (the old local and the received ones):

$$\tau_r^{ij} = \sum_{k=1}^{\mathrm{NC}} \tau_k^{ij}$$

  where τ_r^{ij} is the local pheromone trail, NC is the number of neighbor colonies, and τ_k^{ij} is the pheromone trail received from the colony k.
- **The exchange decision criterion (when?):** In addition to classical blind or "intelligent" adaptive conditions related to the improvement of solutions, the pheromone trails update values can initiate an information exchange.

A *heterogeneous strategy* is a parallel model in which the search components have different features. One can distinguish various levels of heterogeneity according to the source of the heterogeneity:

- **Parameter level:** The same metaheuristic is involved in the parallel model, but various parameter configurations are used [162,378,773,797].
- **Search level:** At this level the heterogeneity is introduced by using different search components (e.g., different mutation and crossover operators in EAs, different neighborhoods in S-metaheuristics, encodings) [9,23,292].
- **Optimization model level:** At this level each metaheuristic optimizes a different problem by using, for instance, different objective functions and/or constraints (e.g., approximations with various accuracies) [509].
- **Algorithm level:** This is the most general class in which different metaheuristics are involved in the parallel model [496,631].

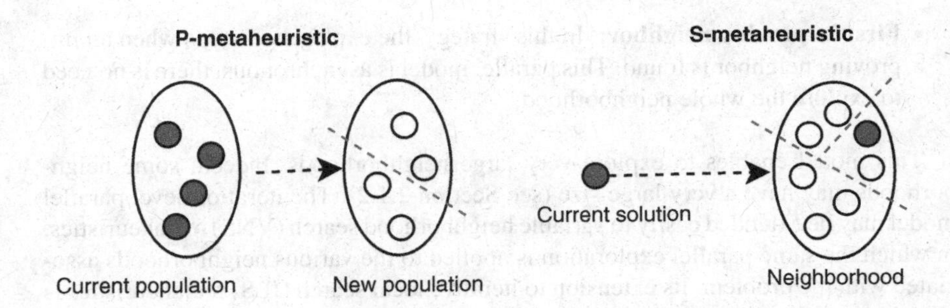

FIGURE 6.7 Iteration-level parallel model for metaheuristics: parallel handling of a population in P-metaheuristics or a neighborhood in S-metaheuristics.

6.1.2 Iteration-Level Parallel Model

Most of the metaheuristics are iterative methods. In this parallel model, the focus is on the parallelization of each iteration of metaheuristics. The iteration-level parallel model is generally based on the distribution of the handled solutions. Indeed, the most resource-consuming part in a metaheuristic is the evaluation of the generated solutions. Our concerns in this model are only search mechanisms that are problem-independent operations, such as the generation and evaluation of the neighborhood[4] (or candidates solutions) in S-metaheuristics and the generation of successive populations in P-metaheuristics. Any *search operator* of a metaheuristic that is not specific to the tackled optimization problem is concerned with the iteration-level parallel model. This model keeps the sequence of the original algorithm, and hence the behavior of the metaheuristics is not altered.

6.1.2.1 Iteration-Level Model for S-Metaheuristics In deterministic S-metaheuristics (e.g., local search, tabu search, variable neighborhood search), the generation and evaluation of the neighborhood (or candidate solutions) can be done in parallel. Indeed, this step is the most computation intensive of a S-metaheuristic. Most of the objective functions and constraints of real-life optimization problems deal with nonlinear components or even complex simulation to be performed.

In this parallel model, the neighborhood is decomposed into different partitions that are generally of equal size (Fig. 6.7). The maximum number of partitions will be equal to the size of the neighborhood. The partitions are generated and then evaluated in a parallel independent way. Following the selection strategies of local search heuristics, this parallel model is more or less synchronous:

- **Best improving neighbor:** In this case, all partitions have to be explored to find the best neighbor. This model is synchronous, one has to wait for the termination of the exploration of all partitions.

[4] Also called parallel move model.

- **First improving neighbor:** In this strategy, the exploration stops when an improving neighbor is found. This parallel model is asynchronous, there is no need to explore the whole neighborhood.

This model enables to explore very large neighborhoods. Indeed, some neighborhoods may have a very large size (see Section 2.1.2). The iteration-level parallel model may be extended easily to variable neighborhood search (VNS) metaheuristics, in which the same parallel exploration is applied to the various neighborhoods associated with the problem. Its extension to iterative local search (ILS) metaheuristics is straightforward as the iteration-level parallel model could be used at each iteration of the ILS metaheuristic.

Applied to probabilistic S-metaheuristics such as simulated annealing where only one candidate solution is evaluated at each iteration, this model needs to be rethought. Indeed, it is not easy to adapt this parallel model to simulated annealing due to its sequential nature. If different moves are evaluated in parallel, the model suffers from inconsistency due to the fact that many moves may be accepted. Theoretically, the solutions generated at a given temperature do not have to be successive. One has to divide the Markov chain into subchains carried out in parallel [41]. Two major approaches are usually used to manage the inconsistency:

- The evaluation of moves is performed in parallel and only noninteracting moves are accepted [354,665]. This strategy can be viewed as a domain decomposition approach. This strategy allows to preserve the convergence property of the sequential algorithm [354,482]. The difficulty of the approach is the determination of the noninteractive moves.
- The second approach consists in evaluating and accepting in parallel multiple interacting moves. Some errors in the calculation of the objective functions are allowed. Errors are corrected after a fixed number of moves. This may be done after each temperature by performing a synchronization between the parallel moves [354]. However, this strategy affects the convergence properties of the parallel algorithm compared to the sequential algorithm. Moreover, the efficiency of the algorithm may be affected by the synchronization cost [354].

Example 6.5 Iteration-level parallel model for GRASP. The traditional GRASP metaheuristic in which the iterations are independent fits very well with the iteration-level parallel model. The model will be based on parallelizing the different iterations; each algorithm is associated with an iteration. The number of parallel independent algorithms will be equal to the maximum number of iterations in GRASP. At the end of all algorithms, a cooperation is carried out to compute the best found solution.

6.1.2.2 Iteration-Level Model for P-Metaheuristics

Parallel iteration-level models arise naturally when dealing with P-metaheuristics, since each element belonging to the population (e.g., individuals in EAs and EDAs, ants in ACO, particles in PSO, solutions in SS) is an independent unit. The iteration-level parallel

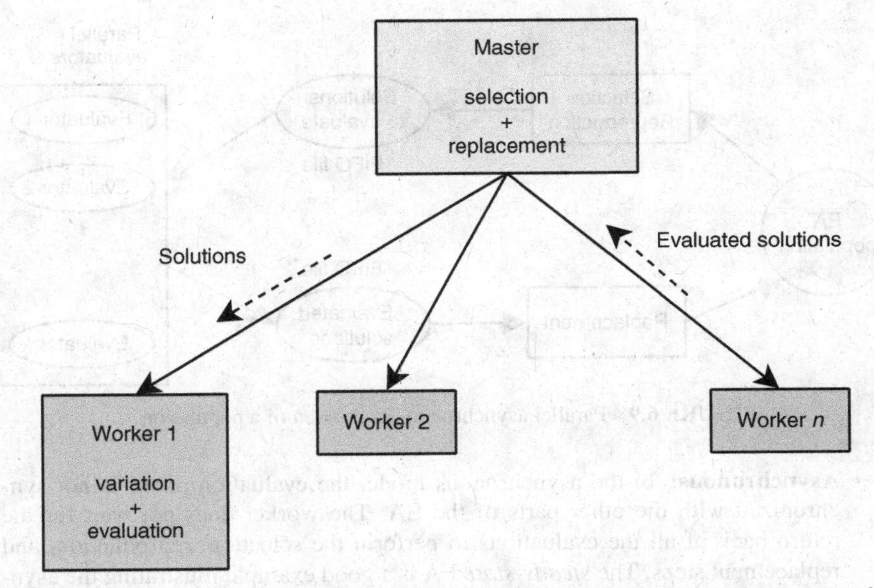

FIGURE 6.8 Iteration-level parallel model for evolutionary P-metaheuristics (e.g., evolutionary algorithms, scatter search, differential evolution).

model in P-metaheuristics involves the distribution of the population (Fig. 6.7). The operations commonly applied to each of the population elements are performed in parallel.

In evolutionary algorithms, the population of individuals can be decomposed and handled in parallel. In the beginning of the parallelization of EAs, the well-known *master–worker* (also known as *global parallelization*) method was used. In this way a master performs the selection operations and the replacement (Fig. 6.8). The selection and replacement are generally sequential procedures, as they require a global management of the population. The associated workers perform the recombination, mutation, and the evaluation of the objective function. The master sends the partitions (subpopulation) to the workers. The workers return back newly evaluated solutions to the master.

According to the order in which the evaluation phase is performed in comparison with the other parts of the EA, two modes can be distinguished:

- **Synchronous:** In the synchronous mode, the worker manages the evolution process and performs in a serial way the different steps of selection and replacement. At each iteration, the master distributes the set of newly generated solutions among the workers and waits for the results to be returned back. After the results are collected, the evolution process is restarted. The model does not change the behavior of the EA compared to a sequential model. The synchronous execution of the model is always synchronized with the return back of the last evaluated solution.

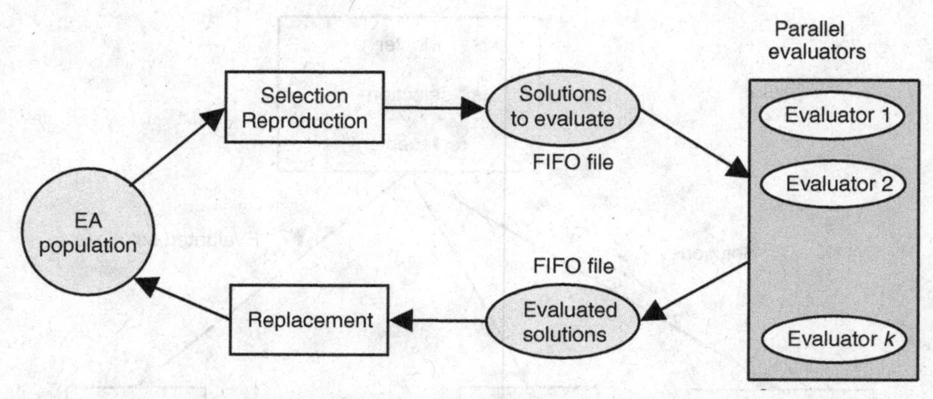

FIGURE 6.9 Parallel asynchronous evaluation of a population.

- **Asynchronous:** In the asynchronous mode, the evaluation phase is not synchronized with the other parts of the EA. The worker does not wait for the return back of all the evaluations to perform the selection, reproduction, and replacement steps. The *steady-state* EA is a good example illustrating the asynchronous model and its several advantages. In the asynchronous model applied to a steady-state EA, the recombination and the evaluation steps may be done concurrently. The master manages the evolution engine and two queues of individuals, each one with a given fixed size: individuals to be evaluated, and awaiting solutions being evaluated. The first ones wait for a free evaluating node. When the queue is full, the process blocks. The second ones are assimilated into the population as soon as possible (Fig. 6.9). The reproduced individuals are stored in a FIFO data structure, which represents the individuals to be evaluated. The EA continues its execution in an asynchronous manner, without waiting for the results of the evaluation phase. The selection and reproduction phase are carried out until the number of nonevaluated individuals equals the size of the data structure. Each evaluator agent picks an individual from the data structure, evaluates it, and stores the results into another data structure storing the evaluated individuals. The order of evaluation defined by the selection phase may not be the same as in the replacement phase. The replacement phase consists in receiving, in a synchronous manner, the results of the evaluated individual and applying a given replacement strategy of the current population.

Example 6.6 Iteration-level parallel model for scatter search. A parallel model for scatter search is obtained by parallelizing the combination and evaluation of solutions. The set of possible combinations is divided among a set of workers and solved in parallel [297]. Parallelizing the combination of solutions follows the same principle of the reproduction operator in EAs. This process may also be applied to the improvement procedure level, where the different improvement procedures are carried out in parallel for the different solutions (multistart algorithmic-level parallel model). Moreover, the iteration-level parallel model may be applied to each improvement

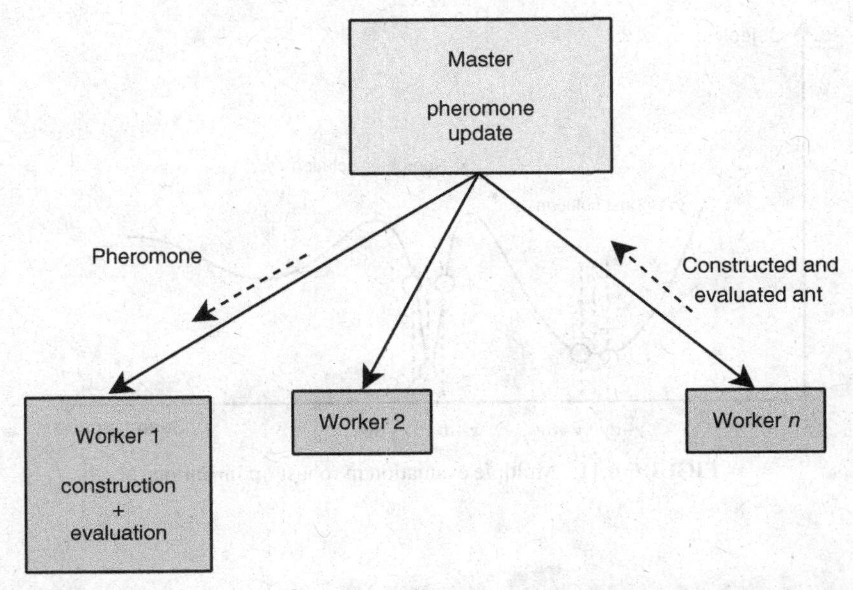

FIGURE 6.10 Iteration-level parallel model for blackboard-based P-metaheuristics (e.g. ant colonies).

procedure in a hierarchical manner. This occurs by evaluating the neighborhood in parallel.

In some P-metaheuristics (e.g., blackboard-based P-metaheuristics), some information must be shared. For instance, in ant colony optimization (ACO), the pheromone matrix must be shared by all ants. The master has to broadcast the pheromone trails to each worker. Each worker handles an ant process. It receives the pheromone trails, constructs a complete solution, and evaluates it. Finally, each worker sends back to the master the constructed and evaluated solution. When the master receives all the constructed solutions, it updates the pheromone trails [214,630,634,756] (Fig. 6.10).

Example 6.7 Iteration-level parallel model for estimation distribution algorithms. In estimation distribution algorithms, the computation cost is largely determined by the estimation of the probability model. There are three possible levels at which EDA can be parallelized:

- **Learning level:** The goal of this iteration-level parallel model is to reduce the time necessary to learn the probability distribution. Some score metrics (such as BDe and BIC) are easier to decompose. In most of the cases, the algorithms try to reduce the time required to learn the probability distribution [511,520,539,589]. In general, these learning algorithms use a scoring and search procedures that define

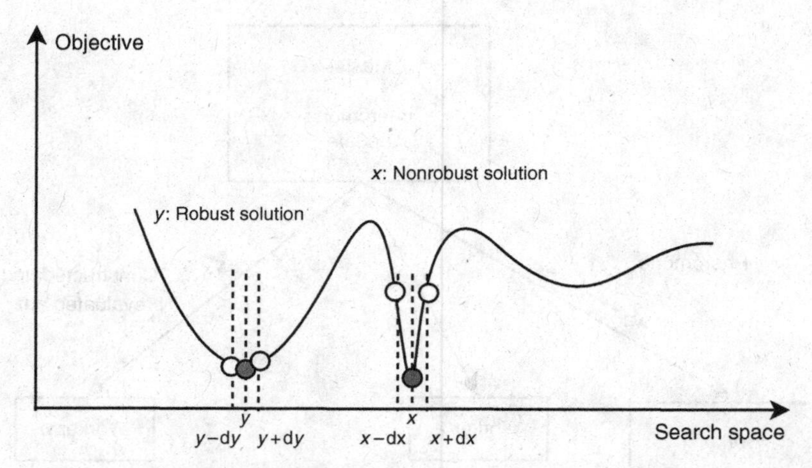

FIGURE 6.11 Multiple evaluation in robust optimization.

a metric that measures the goodness of every candidate Bayesian network with respect to a database of cases.

- **Sampling level:** According to the probabilistic model, the sampling of new individuals may be performed in parallel [540,589,590].
- **Evaluation level:** This is the classical level for all P-metaheuristics in which the evaluation of the individuals is carried out in parallel [13].

The iteration-level parallel model is also useful in optimization problems with uncertainty (stochastic optimization), where a multiple evaluation of solutions is needed. Due to the uncertainty of data, different values of the objectives may be obtained at different evaluations. For instance, an aggregation function (e.g., computing the mean value) is applied to a given number of evaluations. An example of nondeterministic objective function is the Monte Carlo procedure, where a given number s of different evaluations must be realized on a single solution. The objective function is the average over the s values.

In robust optimization, the evaluation of a given solution needs to compute the objective function in the neighborhood of the solution (see Fig. 6.11). Indeed, a robust solution must have objective values that are not sensitive to the values of the decision variables. For some optimization problems such as engineering design, the robustness issue is very important.

6.1.3 Solution-Level Parallel Model

In this model, problem-dependent operations performed on solutions are parallelized. In general, the interest here is the parallelization of the evaluation of a single

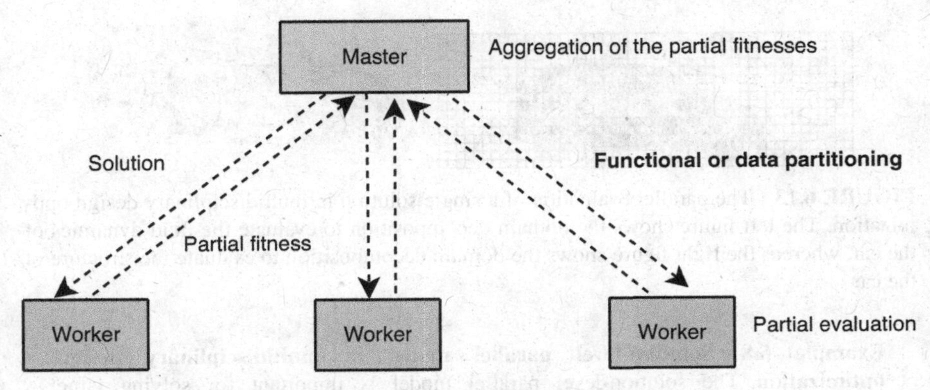

FIGURE 6.12 Parallel evaluation of a single solution.

solution[5] (objective and/or constraints) (Fig. 6.12). This model is particularly interesting when the objective function or the constraints are time and/or memory consuming and/or input/output intensive. Indeed, most of real-life optimization problems need the intensive calculation of the objectives and/or the access to large input files or databases.

Two different solution-level parallel models may be carried out:

- **Functional decomposition:** In function-oriented parallelization, the objective function(s) and/or constraints are partitioned into different partial functions. The objective function(s) or the constraints are viewed as the aggregation of some partial functions. Each partial function is evaluated in parallel. Then, a reduction operation is performed on the results returned back by the computed partial functions. By definition, this model is synchronous, so one has to wait for the termination of all workers calculating the partial functions.
- **Data partitioning:** For some problems, the objective function may require the access to a huge database that could not be managed on a single machine. Due to a memory requirement constraint, the database is distributed among different sites, and data parallelism is exploited in the evaluation of the objective function. In data-oriented parallelization, the same identical function is computed on different partitions of the input data of the problem. The data are then partitioned or duplicated over different workers.

In the solution-level parallel model, the maximum number of parallel operations will be equal to the number of partial functions or the number of data partitions. A hybrid model can also be used in which a functional decomposition and a data partitioning are combined.

[5]Also called acceleration move parallel model.

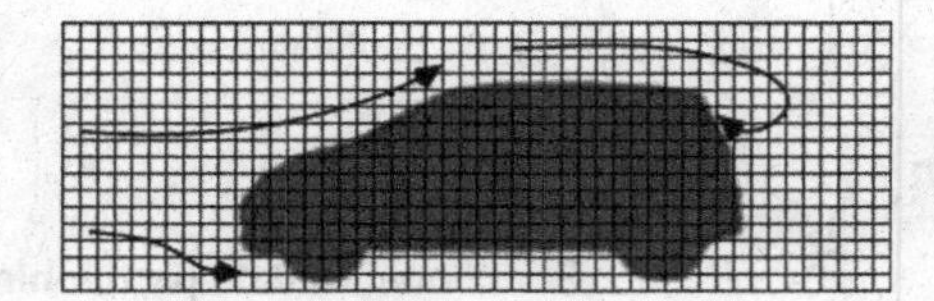

FIGURE 6.13 The parallel evaluation of a single solution in multidisciplinary design optimization. The left figure shows the domain decomposition to evaluate the fluid dynamics of the car, whereas the right figure shows the domain decomposition to evaluate the structure of the car.

Example 6.8 Solution-level parallel model in multidisciplinary design optimization. The solution-level parallel model is important for solving large and complex real-world problems arising in multidisciplinary design optimization (MDO) problems. In MDO, many engineering domains with different models are involved in the design of a given system. Different disciplines and then different solvers are used to optimize this class of problems.

For instance, in designing a car, on one hand one has to optimize the airflow around the car using computational fluid dynamics (CFD) solvers. On the other hand, one has to optimize the toughness of material using finite element (FEM) solvers (Fig. 6.13). A hybrid model combining a functional decomposition and data partitioning can be used. The functional decomposition concerns with the various solvers issued from different domains. In each solver (e.g., structure, fluid dynamics), a data decomposition can be performed on the data (Fig. 6.13).

6.1.4 Hierarchical Combination of the Parallel Models

The three presented models for parallel metaheuristics may be used in conjunction within a hierarchical structure (Fig. 6.14). The parallelism degree associated with this hybrid model is very important. Indeed, this hybrid model is very scalable; the degree of concurrency is $k \cdot m \cdot n$, where k is the number of metaheuristics used, m is the size of the population or the neighborhood, and n is the number of partitions or tasks associated with the evaluation of a single solution. For instance, if $k = 100$, $m = 50$, and $n = 20$, the degree of concurrency will be equal to 100, 000!

6.2 PARALLEL IMPLEMENTATION OF METAHEURISTICS

Parallel implementation of metaheuristics deals with the efficient mapping of a parallel model of metaheuristics on a given parallel architecture (Fig. 6.15). The main concepts of parallel architectures and parallel programming models, which interfere with the implementation of parallel metaheuristics, are then presented. The main performance indicators that can be used to evaluate a parallel metaheuristic in terms of efficiency are also outlined.

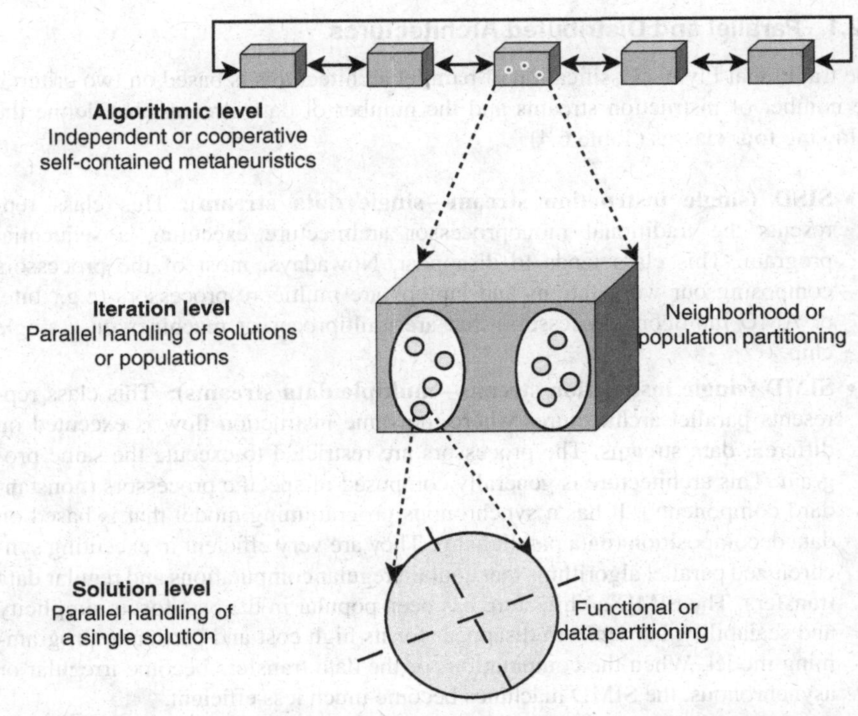

FIGURE 6.14 Combination of the three parallel hierarchical models of metaheuristics.

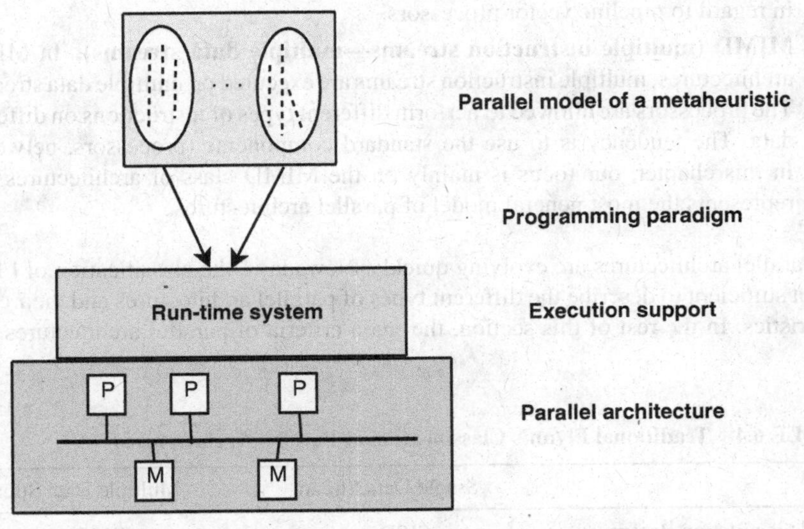

FIGURE 6.15 Parallel implementation of metaheuristics: mapping a parallel model of a metaheuristic on a given target parallel architecture.

6.2.1 Parallel and Distributed Architectures

The traditional Flynn classification of parallel architectures is based on two criteria: the number of instruction streams and the number of data streams that define the following four classes (Table 6.4):

- **SISD (single instruction stream—single data stream):** This class represents the traditional monoprocessor architecture executing a sequential program. This class tends to disappear. Nowadays, most of the processors composing our workstations and laptops are multicore processors (e.g., Intel or AMD multicore processors) that are multiprocessor machines on a single chip.
- **SIMD (single instruction stream—multiple data streams):** This class represents parallel architectures where the same instruction flow is executed on different data streams. The processors are restricted to execute the same program. This architecture is generally composed of specific processors (nonstandard components). It has a synchronous programming model that is based on data decomposition (data parallelism). They are very efficient in executing synchronized parallel algorithms that contain regular computations and regular data transfers. The SIMD architecture has been popular in the past for its simplicity and scalability, but tends to disappear for its high cost and particular programming model. When the computations or the data transfers become irregular or asynchronous, the SIMD machines become much less efficient.
- **MISD (multiple instruction streams—single data stream):** In MISD architectures, multiple instruction streams are executed on a single data stream. This class does not exist in practice. Sometimes this class of architecture is considered in regard to pipeline vector processors.
- **MIMD (multiple instruction streams—multiple data streams):** In MIMD architectures, multiple instruction streams are executed on multiple data streams. The processors are allowed to perform different types of instructions on different data. The tendency is to use the standard components (processors, network). In this chapter, our focus is mainly on the MIMD class of architectures that represents the most general model of parallel architectures.

Parallel architectures are evolving quickly. Nowadays, the classification of Flynn is not sufficient to describe the different types of parallel architectures and their characteristics. In the rest of this section, the main criteria of parallel architectures that

TABLE 6.4 Traditional Flynn's Classification of Parallel Architectures

	Single Data Stream	Multiple Data Streams
Single instruction stream	SISD	SIMD
Multiple instruction stream	MISD	MIMD

will have an impact on the implementation of parallel metaheuristics are described: memory sharing, homogeneity of resources, resource sharing by multiple users, scalability, and volatility (Fig. 6.22). These criteria will be used to analyze the different parallel models and their efficient implementation. A guideline is given for the efficient implementation of each parallel model of metaheuristics according to each class of parallel architectures.

Shared memory/distributed memory architectures: The development of parallel architectures is dominated by two types of architectures: shared memory architectures and distributed memory architectures. In shared memory parallel architectures, the processors are connected by a shared memory (Fig. 6.16a). There are different interconnection schemes for the network (e.g., bus, crossbar, multistage crossbar). This architecture is easy to program. The conventional operating systems and programming paradigms of sequential programming can be used. There is only one address space for data exchange, but the programmer must take care of synchronization in memory access, such as the mutual exclusion in critical sections. This type of architecture has a poor scalability (from 2 to 128 processors in current technologies) and a higher cost. When the number of processors increases, the time overhead to transfer data becomes too high. Indeed, the more the number of processors is, the more the access to the network is, and then more the memory bandwidth is needed to solve the memory contention problem. Examples of such shared memory architectures are SMP (symmetric multiprocessor) machines, also known as CC-UMA (cache coherent uniform memory access), and multicore processors such as the Intel and AMD dual-core or quadri-core processors.

In distributed memory architectures, each processor has its own memory (Fig. 6.16b). The processors are connected by a given interconnection network using different topologies (e.g., hypercube, 2D or 3D torus, fat tree, multistage crossbars) (Fig. 6.17). This architecture is harder to program; data and/or tasks have to be explicitly distributed to processors. Exchanging information is also explicitly handled using message passing between nodes (synchronous or asynchronous communications). The cost of communication is not negligible and must be minimized to design

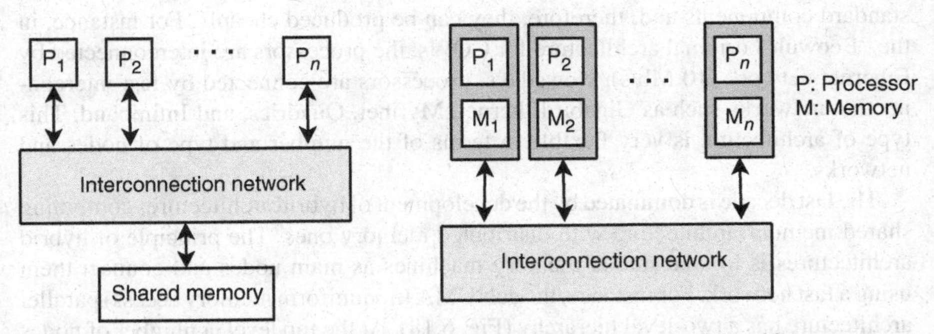

FIGURE 6.16 Shared memory versus distributed memory architectures.

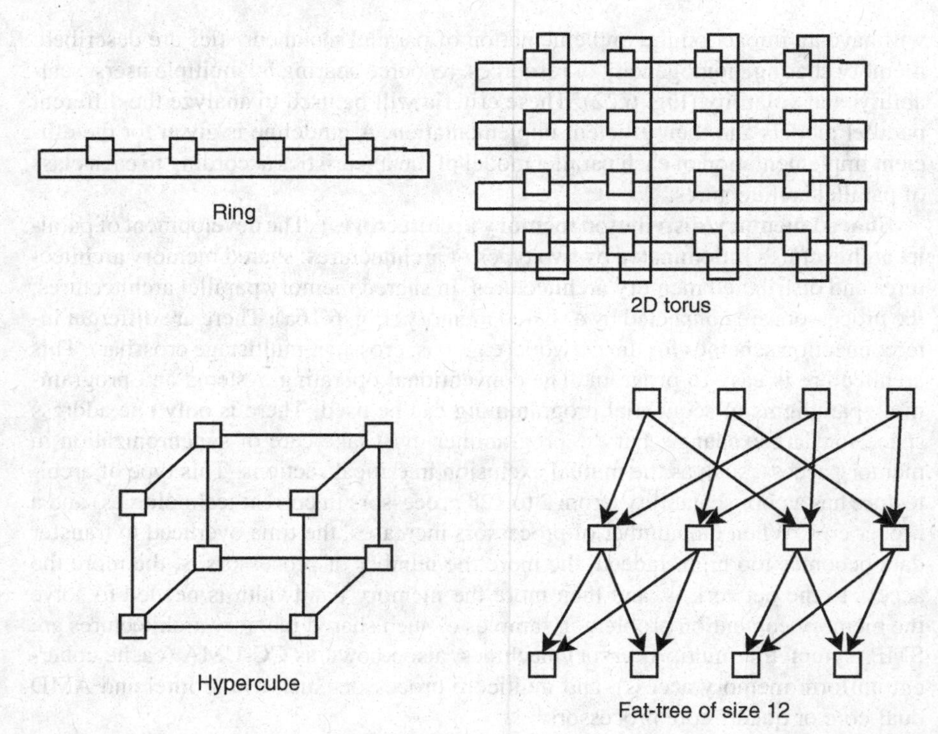

FIGURE 6.17 Traditional interconnection networks for distributed memory parallel architectures. Torus are periodic meshes. Fat trees have the best diameter.

an efficient parallel metaheuristic. However, this architecture has a good scalability in terms of the number of processors.

In recent years, clusters of processors (COWs) became one of the most popular parallel distributed memory architectures. A good ratio between cost and performance is obtained with this class of architectures. Indeed, the nodes of the machine are standard components and, therefore, they can be produced cheaply. For instance, in the "Beowulf" original architecture for COWs, the processors are interconnected by Ethernet network (10 Mb/s). Nowadays, processors are connected by fast interconnection networks such as Gigabit Ethernet, Myrinet, Quadrics, and Infiniband. This type of architecture is very flexible in terms of the number and type of nodes and networks.

The last decade is dominated by the development of hybrid architectures combining shared memory architecture with distributed memory ones. The principle of hybrid architectures is to take shared memory machines as main nodes and connect them using a fast network. For instance, the ccNUMA (nonuniform memory access) parallel architecture has a two-level hierarchy (Fig. 6.18). At the top level, a number of nodes are interconnected via a distributed memory architecture. At the lower level, each node is composed of a SMP machine. Hence, processors within one node can communicate

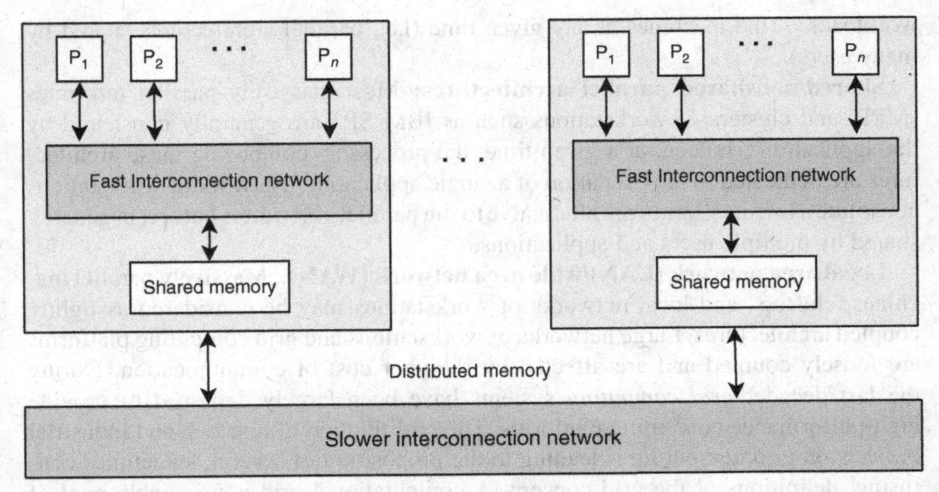

FIGURE 6.18 ccNUMA architectures combining shared and distributed memory architectures represent actually the most powerful machines (e.g., Earth Simulator, Cray X1, SGI Origin2000).

very fast with their shared memory. SMPs are connected through a less costly network with poorer performance. Hence, processors of different nodes have to communicate through a slower network. CLUMPS that are clusters of SMP machines are another example of hybrid architectures.

Homogeneous/Heterogeneous parallel architectures: Parallel architectures may be characterized by the homogeneity of the used processors, communication networks, operating systems, and so on. For instance, COWs are, in general, homogeneous parallel architectures.

The proliferation of powerful workstations and fast communication networks have shown the emergence of heterogeneous network of workstations (NOWs) as platforms for high-performance computing. This type of architecture is present in any laboratory, company, campus, institution, and so on. These parallel platforms are generally composed of an important number of owned heterogeneous workstations shared by many users. A load analysis of these platforms during long periods of time showed that only a few percentage of the available power is used. Then, they have a substantial amount of idle time (around 90% in education networks). A workstation belongs to an owner who does not tolerate external applications degrading the performance of his machine. The personal character of workstations must be taken into account. The faulty nature of workstations increases considerably the failure frequency of NOWs. If the failure rate of one node is q, the failure rate of a NOW of n workstations is at least $n \cdot q$, considering the network failures. Therefore, the performance of the NOW decreases and users can suffer from losses of their computation, especially for long running applications such as solving large optimization problems. Performance in NOWs is limited by the high-communication latencies and the different workloads of the machines at any given time (i.e., parallel architectures shared by many users).

Shared/nonshared parallel architectures: Most massively parallel machines (MPP) and clusters of workstations such as IBM SP3 are generally nonshared by the applications. Indeed, at a given time, the processors composing these architectures are dedicated to the execution of a single application. Network of workstations constitute a low-cost hardware alternative to run parallel algorithms but are, in general, shared by multiple users and applications.

Local area network (LAN)/wide area network (WAN): Massively parallel machines, clusters, and local networks of workstations may be considered as tightly coupled architectures. Large networks of workstations and grid computing platforms are loosely coupled and are affected by a higher cost of communication. During the last decade, *grid computing* systems have been largely deployed to provide high-performance computing platforms. The proliferation of research and industrial projects on grid computing is leading to the proposition of several, sometimes confusing, definitions of the grid concept. A computational grid is a scalable pool of heterogeneous and dynamic resources geographically distributed across multiple administrative domains and owned by different organizations [281]. The characteristics of such environment may have a great impact on the design of grid-enabled parallel metaheuristics.

The characteristics of grids could be summarized as follows:

- *The grid includes multiple autonomous administrative domains.* The resources are managed in different administrative domains (universities, labs, companies, etc.). The users and providers of resources are clearly identified. This allows to reduce the complexity of the security issue. However, the firewall traversal remains a critical problem to deal with. In global computing middlewares based on large-scale cycle stealing, the problem is solved in a natural way as communications are initiated from "inside the domains."
- *The grid is heterogeneous.* The heterogeneity in a grid is intensified by its large number of resources belonging to different administrative domains. This heterogeneity of resources is due to multiple hardware vendors, different network protocols, different operating systems, and so on. The emergence of data exchange standards and Java-based technologies such as RMI allows to deal with the heterogeneity issue.
- *The grid has a large scale.* The grid has a large number of resources growing from hundreds of integrated resources to millions of PCs. The design of efficient and scalable grid applications has to take into account the communication delays.

Two types of grids may be distinguished:

- **High-performance computing grid:** This grid interconnects supercomputers or clusters via a dedicated high-speed network. In general, this type of grid is nonshared by multiple users (at the level of processors). Figure 6.19 shows the

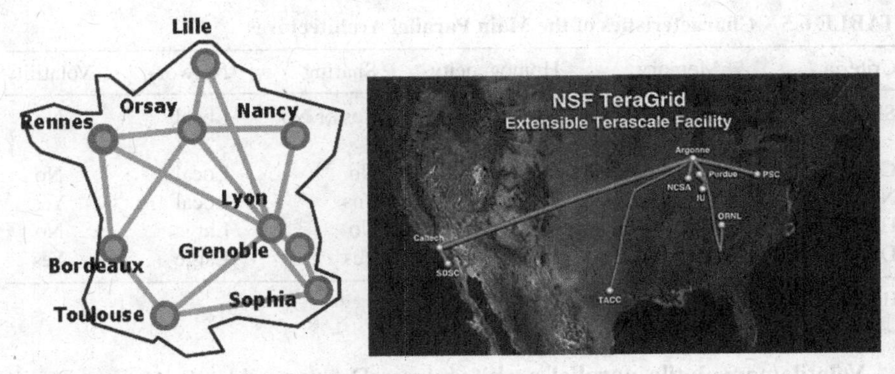

FIGURE 6.19 Examples of high-performance computing grids: Grid'5000 (http://www.grid5000.fr) and Tera Grid platforms (http://www.teragrid.org).

architecture of GRID'5000 and Tera Grid that represent such high-performance computing grids.

- **Desktop grid:** This class of grids is composed of numerous owned workstations connected via nondedicated network such as the Internet. This grid is volatile and shared by multiple users and applications. Figure 6.20 shows an example of such a desktop grid: the PlanetLab platform.

Peer-to-peer networks have been developed in parallel to grid computing technologies. Peer-to-peer infrastructures have been focused on sharing data and are increasingly popular for sharing computation.

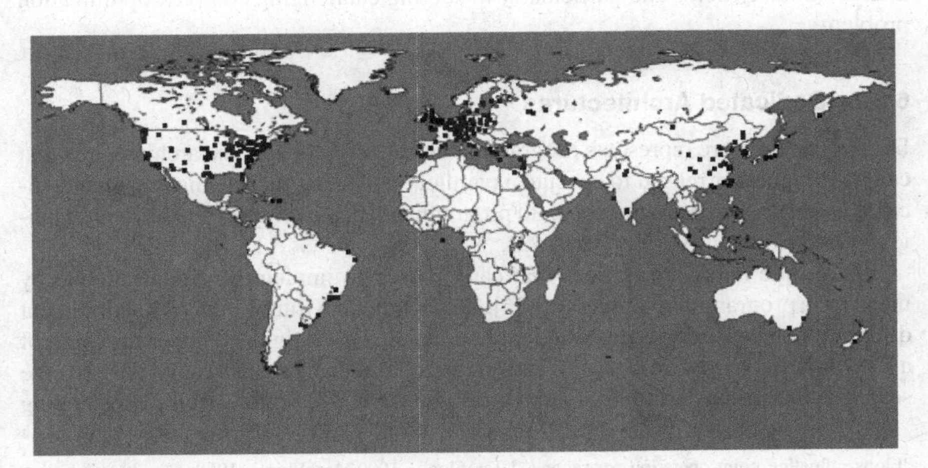

FIGURE 6.20 An example of desktop grids: PlanetLab platform (http://www.planet-lab.org/). In October 2008, PlanetLab was composed of 914 nodes at 473 sites.

TABLE 6.5 Characteristics of the Main Parallel Architectures

Criteria	Memory	Homogeneity	Sharing	Network	Volatility
SMP multicore	Shared	Hom	Yes or No	Local	No
COW	Distributed	Hom or Het	No	Local	No
NOW	Distributed	Het	Yes	Local	Yes
HPC grid	Distributed	Het	No	Large	No
Desktop grid	Distributed	Het	Yes	Large	Yes

Hom, homogeneous; Het, Heterogeneous.

Volatile/nonvolatile parallel architectures: Desktop grids are an example of volatile parallel architectures. In a volatile parallel architecture, there is a dynamic temporal and spatial availability of resources. In a desktop grid or a large network of shared workstations, volatility is not an exception but a rule. Due to the large-scale nature of the grid, the probability of resource failing is high. For instance, desktop grids have a faulty nature (e.g., reboot, shutdown, failure). Such a characteristic highlights some issues such as dynamic resource discovery and fault tolerance.

Table 6.5 recapitulates the characteristics of the main parallel architectures according to the presented criteria. These criteria will be used to analyze the efficient implementation of the different parallel models of metaheuristics.

A source for efficient and up-to-date information on the 500 most worldwide powerful machines can be found at `www.top500.org`. The top 10 machines head toward 100 Tflops[6]. Figure 6.21 illustrates the trend in terms of architectures in the past 15 years. The trend shows that clusters and grid systems (constellation) such as desktop grids aggregating standard and small machines will attract increasing interest in many fields and particularly in solving challenging complex optimization problems.

6.2.2 Dedicated Architectures

Dedicated hardware represents programmable hardware or specific architectures that can be designed or reused to execute a parallel metaheuristic. The most known dedicated hardware is represented by field programmable gate arrays (FPGAs) and graphical processing unit (GPU) (Fig. 6.22).

FPGAs are hardware devices that can be used to implement digital circuits by means of a programming process[7] [836]. The use of the Xilinx's FPGAs to implement different metaheuristics is more and more popular. The design and the prototyping of a FPGA-based hardware board to execute parallel metaheuristics may restrict some search components and tuning parameters. However, for some specific challenging

[6]Flops = floating point operation per second. 1 TeraFlop = 1000 MegaFlop = 1000,000,000 = 1 billion operation per second.

[7]Do not make an amalgam with evolvable hardware where the architecture is reconfigured using evolutionary algorithms.

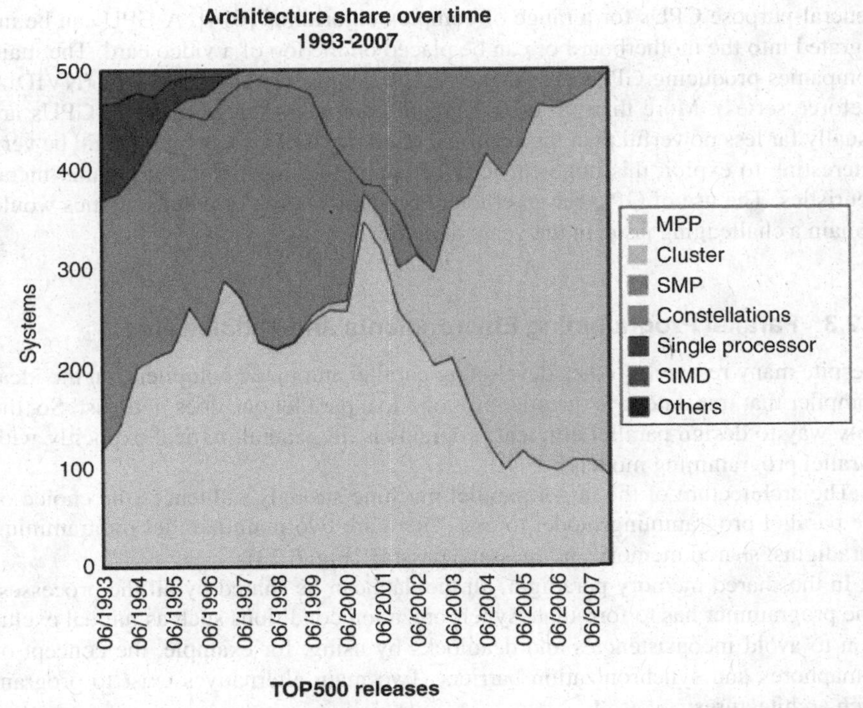

FIGURE 6.21 Architecture evolution for the 500 most powerful machines in the world (www.top500.org).

optimization problems with a high use rate such as in bioinformatics, dedicated hardware may be a good alternative.

GPU is a dedicated graphics rendering device for a workstation, personal computer, or game console. Recent GPUs are very efficient at manipulating computer graphics, and their parallel SIMD structure makes them more efficient than

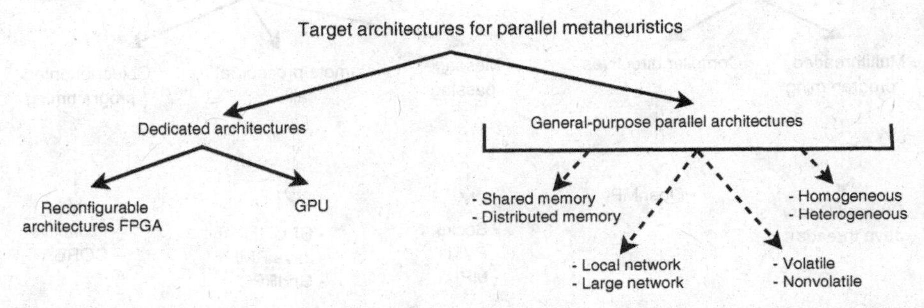

FIGURE 6.22 Hierarchical and flat classification of target parallel architectures for metaheuristics.

general-purpose CPUs for a range of complex algorithms [614]. A GPU can be integrated into the motherboard or can be placed on the top of a video card. The main companies producing GPUs are AMD (ATI Radeon series) and NVIDIA (NVIDIA Geforce series). More than 90% of personal computers integrated with GPUs are usually far less powerful than their add-in counterparts. This is why it would be very interesting to exploit this huge capacity of computing to implement parallel metaheuristics. The use of GPU for an efficient implementation of metaheuristics would remain a challenging issue in the years to come.

6.2.3 Parallel Programming Environments and Middlewares

Despite many research studies developing parallel automatic compilers, an the ideal compiler that translates a sequential program to a parallel one does not exist. So, the only way to design parallel efficient programs is, in general, to deal explicitly with parallel programming models.

The architecture of the target parallel machine strongly influences the choice of the parallel programming model to use. There are two main parallel programming paradigms: shared memory and message passing (Fig. 6.23).

In the shared memory paradigm, all the data can be shared by all the processes. The programmer has to formulate synchronization conditions such as mutual exclusion to avoid inconsistencies and deadlocks by using, for example, the concept of semaphores and synchronization barriers. Two main alternatives exist to program such architectures:

- **Multithreading:** A thread may be viewed as a lightweight process (Fig. 6.24). Different threads of the same process share some resources and the same address

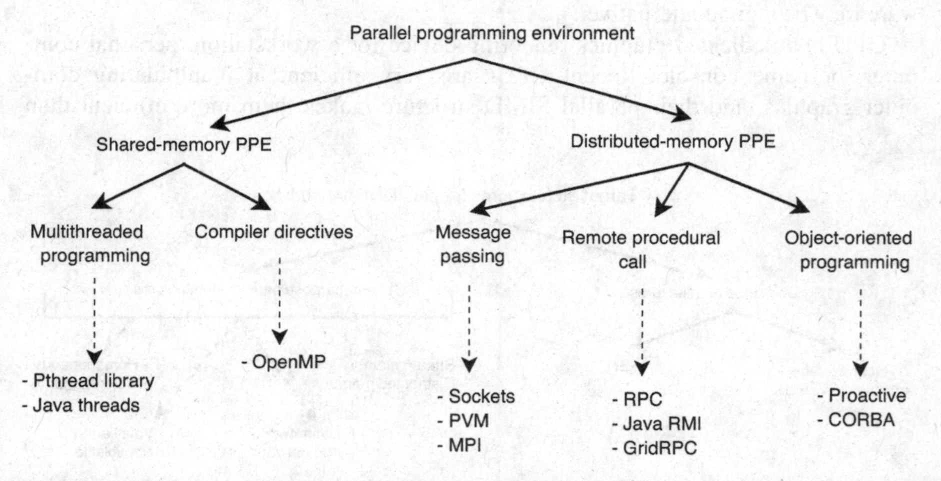

FIGURE 6.23 Main parallel programming languages, programming environments and middlewares.

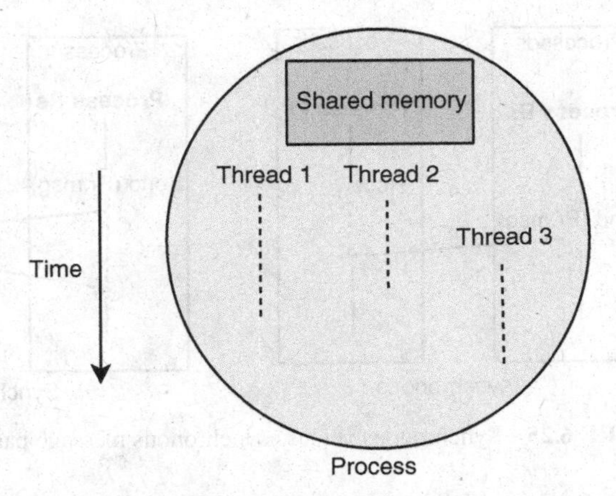

FIGURE 6.24 Multithreading: a process composed of three threads running in parallel and sharing the memory.

space. The main advantages of multithreading are the fast context switch, the low resource usage, and the possible recovery between communication and computation. On a single processor architecture, multithreading is implemented by time slicing where the processor switches between different threads. In multiprocessors or multicore systems, each thread can be executed on a different processor or core.

Multithreaded programming may be used within libraries such as the standard Pthreads library [102] or programming languages such as Java threads [401]. Nowadays, multithreaded programming has been introduced in most operating systems within the standard Pthreads library (Linux-based operating systems) or a proprietary library such as in the Solaris operating system or the Microsoft family (Windows XP, Vista). Multithreading has also been introduced in programming languages such as Java. The advantage in using Java threads is the portability aspect, but less efficiency will be obtained compared to the use of the Pthreads library binded with the C language.

- **Compiler directives:** One of the standard shared memory paradigms is OpenMP[8] (open multiprocessing). It represents a set of compiler directives (*pragma*—pragmatic information) interfaced with the languages Fortran, C, and C++ on Linux and Microsoft Windows platforms [122]. These directives are integrated into a sequential program to specify which sections of the program to be parallelized by the compiler. In addition to the compiler directives, OpenMP libraries are composed of routines and environmental variables that influence the parallel execution of the program.

[8]`www.openmp.org`.

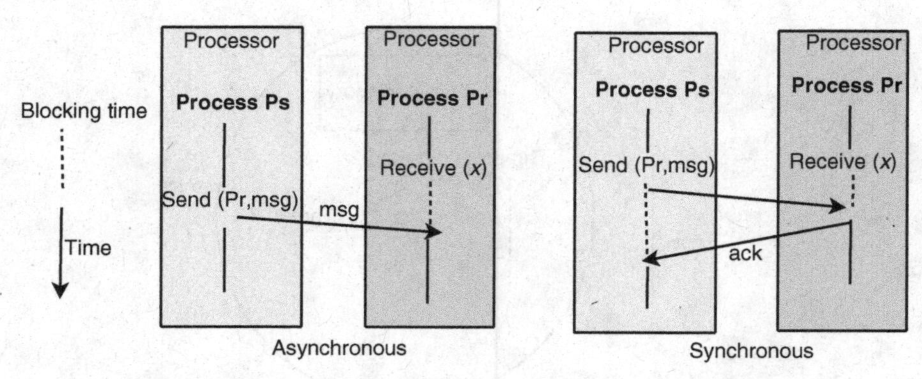

FIGURE 6.25 Synchronous versus asynchronous message passing.

Distributed memory parallel programming environments are mainly based on the following three paradigms:

- **Message passing:** Message passing is probably the most widely used paradigm to program parallel architectures. In the message passing paradigm, processes (or threads) of a given parallel program communicate by exchanging messages in a synchronous or asynchronous way (Fig. 6.25). The well-known programming environments based on message passing are sockets, PVM (parallel virtual machine), and MPI (message passing interface).

  Sockets represent a low-level application interface (API) that implement interprocess communication. They are based on TCP/UDP transport protocols and are error prone. Sockets are interfaced with the C and Java languages and are also available in the .NET platform.

  PVM and MPI are standard communication libraries. They enable portable communication in heterogeneous architectures. MPI-2 is now the *de facto* standard. It provides a set of routines for point-to-point communication, group communication, and management of groups that can be interfaced with the C, C++, and the Fortran languages. Different implementations of the MPI standard API such as MPICH[9] and LAM-MPI[10] are available.
- **Remote procedure call:** Remote procedure call (RPC) represents a traditional way of programming parallel and distributed architectures. It allows a program to cause a procedure to execute on another processor. In RPC, the programmer does not explicitly specify the details for the remote call and interaction. Hence, the programmer will have the same program code whether the procedure is local or remote to the calling program (Fig. 6.26).
- **Object-oriented models:** As in sequential programming, parallel object-oriented programming is a natural evolution of RPC. A classical example of such

[9]http://www.mcs.anl.gov/mpi/mpich.
[10]http://www.mpi.nd.edu/lam.

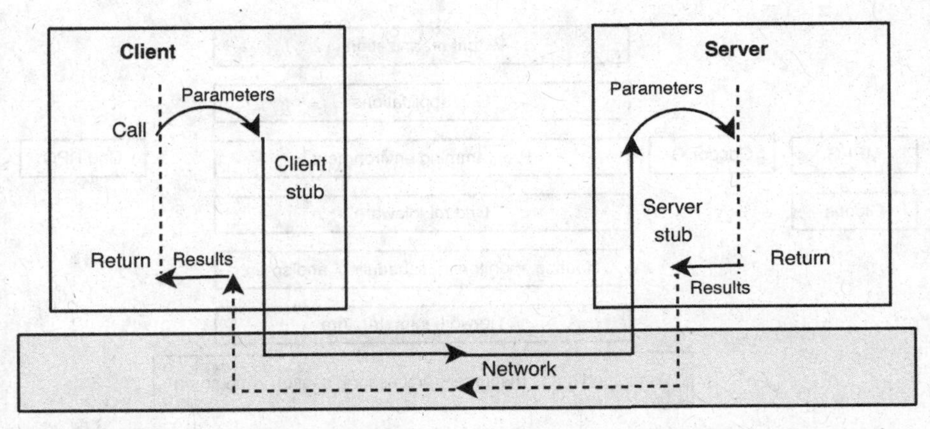

FIGURE 6.26 Using RPC to implement the client–server model in distributed computing. A client sends a request to a remote server to execute a specific procedure. In asynchronous RPC, the client continues to execute, whereas in synchronous RPC, the client blocks until the termination of the remote procedure and the reception of the results. The interface description language (IDL) is a standard contact mechanism that allows the servers to be accessed by different clients.

a model is Java RMI (remote method invocation). Java RMI concept is based on the classical object method invocation in object-oriented programming. It allows a method invocation of any JVM (Java virtual machine). The portability is paid by a cost in terms of execution efficiency. Other object-oriented middlewares based on distributed objects are Corba and Proactive.

Recent development in this area was made in *mixed-mode programming models*. The idea is to use shared memory programming paradigms inside the nodes in which the memory is shared and message passing programming models between the nodes in which the memory is distributed. For instance, mixing multithreading and MPI programming is a traditional way to implement hybrid parallel programs.

In the last decade, a great work has been carried out on the development of grid middlewares. Figure 6.27 illustrates the architecture of grid middlewares. The middleware components address the issues related to remote access, resource management, security, resource discovery, and so forth. The Globus[11] toolkit represents the *de facto* standard grid middleware. It supports the development of distributed service-oriented computing applications [711].

As in parallel programming environments, grid computing environments are based on the same paradigms:

- **Message passing:** The most used grid programming environments are Condor and MPICH-G. Condor[12] is a resource management system for high-throughput

[11]www.globus.org.
[12]http://www.cs.wisc.edu/condor.

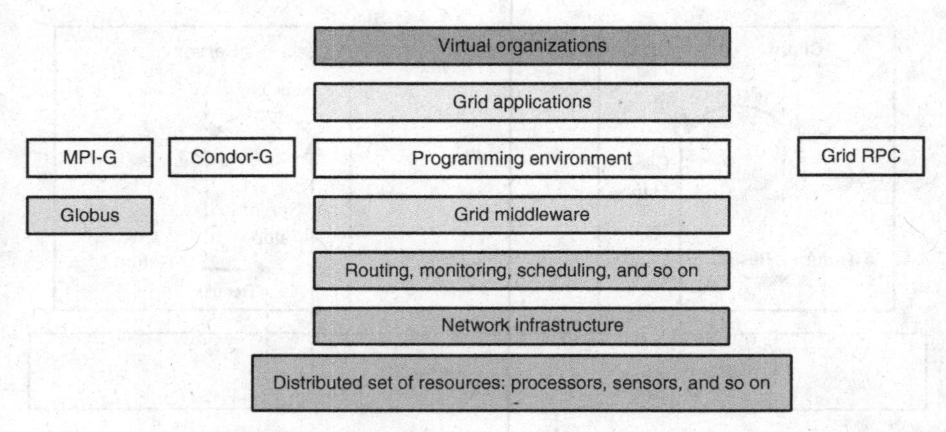

FIGURE 6.27 Architecture of grid middlewares.

computing. It deals with heterogeneous computing within multiuser shared resources. It allows to manage shared and volatile resources by deciding their availability, using both the average CPU load and the information about the recent use of some peripherals such as the keyboard and mouse. An environment including such resources is said adaptive since tasks are scheduled among idle resources and dynamically migrated when some resources get used or failed. In addition, Condor uses some sophisticated techniques like matchmaking and checkpointing [767]. These techniques allow to associate job requirements and policies on resource owners, to periodically save the state of running jobs, and to restart them using this state after their failure. Condor is implemented on PVM and MPI. It has been interfaced with Globus within Condor-G. Flocking and Condor pool have been recently integrated for a more efficient scalability.

The MPICH-G2[13] message passing library has been implemented using the services of the Globus toolkit [449]. It is grid-enabled implementation of the MPI standard.

- **Remote procedure call:** Grid RPC is a grid-enabled implementation of RPC. Its main advantage is the simplicity of use. Netsolve, Ninf-G, and Diet represent such a model implementation.
- **Object-oriented model:** Legion and Proactive are representatives of grid computing middlewares based on object-oriented concepts. The future trend is to combine grid computing technologies and Web services. This has been specified in the OGSA standard (open grid services architecture).

It is not easy to propose a guideline on which environment to use in programming a parallel metaheuristic. It will depend on the target architecture, the parallel model of

[13] http://www3.niu.edu/mpi/.

TABLE 6.6 Parallel Programming Environments for Different Parallel Architectures

Architecture	Examples of Suitable Programming Environment
SMP multicore	Multithreading library within an operating system (e.g., Pthreads) Multithreading within languages: Java OpenMP interfaced with C, C++, or Fortran
COW	Message passing library: MPI interfaced with C, C++, Fortran
Hybrid ccNUMA	MPI or hybrid models: MPI/OpenMP, MPI/multithreading
NOW	Message passing library: MPI interfaced with C, C++, Fortran Condor or object models (JavaRMI)
HPC grid	MPICH-G (Globus) or GridRPC models (Netsolve, Diet)
Desktop grid	Condor-G or object models (Proactive)

metaheuristics, and the user preferences. Some languages are more system oriented, such as C and C++. More portability is obtained with Java but at the cost of less efficiency. This trade-off represents the classical efficiency/portability compromise. A Fortran programmer will be more comfortable with OpenMP. RPC models are more adapted to implement services. Condor represents an efficient and easy way to implement parallel programs on shared and volatile distributed architectures such as large networks of heterogeneous workstations and desktop grids, where fault tolerance is ensured by a checkpoint/recovery mechanism. The use of MPI-G within Globus is more or less adapted to high-performance computing grids. However, the user has to deal with complex mechanisms such as dynamic load balancing and fault tolerance. Table 6.6 gives a guideline depending on the target parallel architecture.

6.2.4 Performance Evaluation

For sequential algorithms, the main performance measure is the execution time as a function of the input size. In parallel algorithms, this measure also depends on the number of processors and the characteristics of the parallel architecture. Hence, some classical performance indicators have been introduced to evaluate the scalability of parallel algorithms such as the speedup and the efficiency [487]. The scalability of a parallel algorithms measures its ability to achieve performance proportional to the number of processors.

The speedup S_N is defined as the time T_1 it takes to complete a program with one processor divided by the time T_N it takes to complete the same program with N processors.

$$S_N = \frac{T_1}{T_N}$$

One can use the *wall clock time* instead of the *CPU time*. The CPU time is the time a processor spends in the execution of the program, and the wall clock time is the time

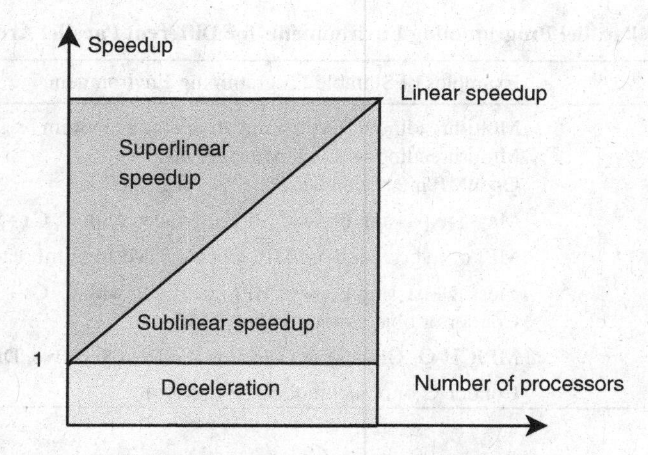

FIGURE 6.28 Speedup of a parallel program.

of the whole program including the input and output. Conceptually, the speedup is defined as the gain achieved by parallelizing a program. The larger the speedup, the greater the gain (Fig. 6.28). If $S_N > N$ (resp. $S_N = N$), a superlinear (resp. linear) speedup is obtained. Mostly, a sublinear speedup $S_N < N$ is obtained. This is due to the overhead of communication and synchronization costs. The case $S_N < 1$ means that the sequential time is smaller than the parallel time, which is the worst case. This will be possible if the communication cost is much higher than the execution cost.

The efficiency E_N using N processors is defined as the speedup S_N divided by the number of processors N.

$$E_N = \frac{S_N}{N}$$

Conceptually, the efficiency can be defined as how well are N processors used when the program is computed in parallel. An efficiency of 100% means that all of the processors are being fully used all the time. For some large real-life applications, it is impossible to have the sequential time as the sequential execution of the algorithm cannot be performed. Then, the incremental efficiency E_{N-M} may be used to evaluate the efficiency extending the number of processors from N to M processors.

$$E_{N-M} = \frac{N \cdot E_N}{M \cdot E_M}$$

Different definitions of the speedup may be used depending on the definition of the sequential time reference T_1. Asking what is the best measure is useless; there is no global dominance between the different measures. The choice of a given definition depends on the objective of the performance evaluation analysis. Then, it is important to specify clearly the choice and the objective of the analysis.

The *absolute speedup* is used when the sequential time T_1 corresponds to the best known sequential time to solve the problem. Unlike other scientific domains such as numerical algebra where for some operations the best known sequential algorithm is known, in metaheuristic search it is difficult to identify the best known sequential algorithm. So, the absolute speedup is rarely used. The *relative speedup* is used when the sequential time T_1 corresponds to the parallel program executed on a single processor.

Moreover, different stopping conditions may be used.

- **Fixed number of iterations:** This condition is the most used to evaluate the efficiency of a parallel metaheuristic. Using this definition, a superlinear speedup is possible $S_N > N$. This is due to the characteristics of the parallel architecture where there are more resources (e.g., size of main memory and cache) than in a single processor (Fig. 6.29a). For instance, the search memory of a metaheuristic executed on a single processor may be larger than the main memory of a single processor and then some swapping will be carried out in the cache that represents an overhead in the sequential time. When using a parallel architecture, the whole memory of the metaheuristic will fit in the main memory of its processors, and then the memory swapping overhead will not occur.
- **Convergence to a solution with a given quality:** This definition is interesting to evaluate the effectiveness of a parallel metaheuristic. It is only valid for parallel models of metaheuristics based on the algorithmic level that alter the behavior of the sequential metaheuristic. A superlinear speedup is possible and is due to the characteristics of the parallel search (Fig. 6.29b). Indeed, the order of searching different regions of the search space is not the same as in sequential search. This is similar to the superlinear speedups obtained in exact search algorithms such as branch and bound[14] [748].

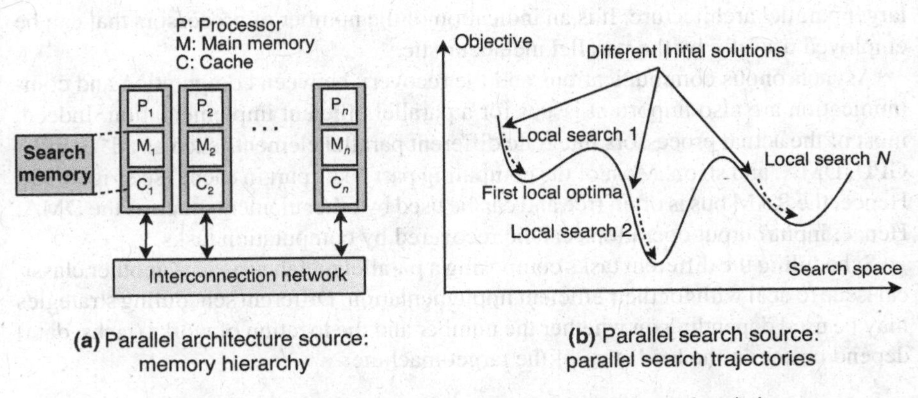

(a) Parallel architecture source: memory hierarchy

(b) Parallel search source: parallel search trajectories

FIGURE 6.29 Superlinear speedups for a parallel metaheuristic.

[14]This phenomenon is called speedup anomaly.

For stochastic metaheuristics such as evolutionary algorithms and when the stopping condition is based on the quality of the solution, one cannot use the speedup metric as defined previously. The original definition may be extended to the average speedup:

$$S_N = \frac{E(T_1)}{E(T_N)}$$

The same *seed* for the generation of random numbers must be used for a more fair experimental performance evaluation.

The speedup metric has to be reformulated for heterogeneous architectures. The efficiency metric may be used for this class of architectures. Moreover, it can be used for shared parallel machines with multiple users.

6.2.5 Main Properties of Parallel Metaheuristics

This section deals with the main properties of parallel metaheuristics that must be taken into account for an efficient implementation. The design aspects have been outlined in Section 6.1.

The performance of a parallel metaheuristic on a given parallel architecture mainly depends on its *granularity*. The granularity of a parallel program is the amount of computation performed between two communications. It computes the ratio between the computation time and the communication time. The three parallel models presented in Section 6.1 (algorithmic level, iteration level, solution level) have a decreasing granularity from coarse grained to fine grained. The granularity indicator has an important impact on the speedup. The larger is the granularity, the better is the obtained speedup.

The *degree of concurrency* of a parallel metaheuristic is represented by the maximum number of parallel processes at any time. This measure is independent from the target parallel architecture. It is an indication of the number of processors that can be employed usefully by the parallel metaheuristic.

Asynchronous communications and the recovery between computation and communication are also important issues for a parallel efficient implementation. Indeed, most of the actual processors integrate different parallel elements such as ALU, FPU, GPU, DMA, and so on. Most of the computing part takes part in cache (see Fig. 6.30). Hence, the RAM bus is often free and can be used by other elements such as the DMA. Hence, input/output operations can be recovered by computation tasks.

Scheduling the different tasks composing a parallel metaheuristic is another classical issue to deal with for their efficient implementation. Different scheduling strategies may be used depending on whether the number and the location of works (tasks, data) depend or not on the load state of the target machine:

- **Static scheduling:** This class represents parallel metaheuristics in which both the number of tasks of the application and the location of work (tasks, data) are generated at compile time. Static scheduling is useful for homogeneous and

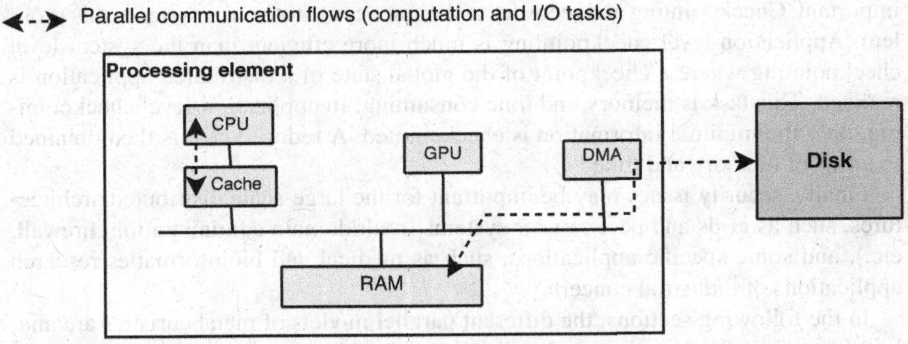

FIGURE 6.30 Recovery between computations and communications.

nonshared and nonvolatile heterogeneous parallel architectures. Indeed, when there are noticeable load or power differences between processors, the search time of an iteration is derived from the maximum execution time over all processors, presumably on the most highly loaded processor or the least powerful processor. A significant number of tasks are often idle, waiting for other tasks to complete their work.

- **Dynamic scheduling:** This class represents parallel metaheuristics for which the number of tasks is fixed at compile time, but the location of work is determined and/or changed at run time. The tasks are dynamically scheduled on the different processors of the parallel architecture. Dynamic load balancing is important for shared (multiuser) architectures, where the load of a given processor cannot be determined at compile time. Dynamic scheduling is also important for *irregular* parallel metaheuristics in which the execution time cannot be predicted at compile time and varies during the search. For instance, this happens when the evaluation cost of the objective function depends on the solution. Many dynamic load balancing strategies may be applied. For instance, during the search, each time a processor finishes its work, it proceeds to a work demand. The degree of parallelism of this class of scheduling algorithms is not related to load variations in the target machine. When the number of tasks exceeds the number of idle nodes, multiple tasks are assigned to the same node. Moreover, when there are more idle nodes than tasks, some of them would not be used.
- **Adaptive scheduling:** Parallel adaptive algorithms are parallel computations with a dynamically changing set of tasks. Tasks may be created or killed as a function of the load state of the parallel machine. A task is created automatically when a node becomes idle. When a node becomes busy, the task is killed. Adaptive load balancing is important for volatile architectures such as desktop grids.

For some parallel and distributed architectures such as shared networks of workstations and grids, fault tolerance is an important issue. Indeed, in volatile shared architectures and large-scale parallel architectures, the fault probability is relatively important. Checkpointing and recovery techniques constitute one answer to this problem. Application-level checkpointing is much more efficient than the system-level checkpointing where a checkpoint of the global state of a distributed application is realized. This task is memory and time consuming. In application-level checkpointing, only the minimal information is checkpointed. A reduced cost is then obtained in terms of memory and time.

Finally, security issues may be important for the large-scale distributed architectures, such as grids and peer-to-peer systems (multidomain administration, firewall, etc.), and some specific applications, such as medical and bioinformatics research applications of industrial concern.

In the following sections, the different parallel models of metaheuristics are analyzed successively according to the above-mentioned properties.

6.2.6 Algorithmic-Level Parallel Model

Granularity: The algorithmic-level parallel model has the largest granularity. Indeed, exchanging the information is, in general, much less costly than the computation time of a metaheuristic. There is a relatively low communication requirements for this model. The more significant the frequency of exchange and the size of exchanged information, the smaller the granularity. This parallel model is most suited to the large-scale distributed architectures over Internet such as grids. Moreover, the trivial model with independent algorithms is convenient for low-speed networks of workstations over intranet. This model is embarrassingly parallel. Indeed, as there is no essential dependency and communication between the algorithms, the speedup is generally linear for this parallel model.

For an efficient implementation, the frequency of exchange (resp. the size of the exchanged data) must be correlated to the latency (resp. bandwidth) of the communication network of the parallel architecture. To optimize the communication between processors, the exchange topology can be specified according to the interconnection network of the parallel architecture. The specification of the different parameters associated with the blind or intelligent migration decision criterion (migration frequency/probability and improvement threshold) is particularly crucial on a computational grid. Indeed, due to the heterogeneous nature of this latter, these parameters must be specified for each metaheuristic in accordance with the machine it is hosted on.

Scalability: The degree of concurrency of the algorithmic-level parallel model is limited by the number of metaheuristics involved in solving the problem. In theory, there is no limit. However, in practice, it is limited by the owned resources of the target parallel architectures and also by the effectiveness aspect of using a large number of metaheuristics.

Synchronous/asynchronous communications: The implementation of the algorithmic-level model is either *asynchronous* or *synchronous*. The asynchronous mode associates with each metaheuristic an exchange decision criterion that is evaluated at each iteration of the metaheuristic from the state of its memory. If the criterion is satisfied, the metaheuristic communicates with its neighbors. The exchange requests are managed by the destination metaheuristics within an undetermined delay.

The reception and integration of the received information is thus performed during the next iterations. However, in a computational grid context, due to the material and/or software heterogeneity issue, the metaheuristics could be at different evolution stages leading to the *noneffect* and/or *supersolution* problem. For instance, the arrival of poor solutions at a very advanced stage will not bring any contribution as these solutions will likely not be integrated. In the opposite situation, the cooperation will lead to a premature convergence. From another point of view, as it is nonblocking, the model is more efficient and fault tolerant to such a degree the threshold of wasted exchanges is not exceeded. In the synchronous mode, the metaheuristics perform a synchronization operation at a predefined iteration by exchanging some data. Such operation guarantees that the metaheuristics are at the same evolution stage, and so prevents the noneffect and supersolution quoted below. However, in heterogeneous parallel architectures, the synchronous mode is less efficient in terms of consumed CPU time. Indeed, the evolution process is often hanging on powerful machines waiting the less powerful ones to complete their computation. On the other hand, the synchronous model is not fault tolerant as wasting a metaheuristic implies the blocking of the whole model in a volatile environment. Then, the synchronous mode is globally more complex and less efficient on a computational grid.

Asynchronous communication is more efficient than synchronous communication for shared architectures such as NOWs and desktop grids (e.g., multiple users, multiple applications). Indeed, as the load of networks and processors is not homogeneous, the use of synchronous communication will degrade the performances of the whole system. The least powerful machine will determine the performance.

On a volatile computational grid, it is difficult to efficiently maintain topologies such as rings and torus. Indeed, the disappearance of a given node (i.e., metaheuristic(s)) requires a dynamic reconfiguration of the topology. Such reconfiguration is costly and makes the migration process inefficient. Designing a cooperation between a set of metaheuristics without any topology may be considered. For instance, a communication scheme in which the target metaheuristic is randomly selected is more efficient for volatile architecture such as desktop grids. Many experimental results show that such topology allows a significant improvement in the robustness and quality of solutions. The random topology is therefore thinkable and even commendable in a computational grid context.

Scheduling: Concerning the scheduling aspect, in the algorithmic-level parallel model, the tasks correspond to metaheuristics. Hence, the different scheduling strategies will differ as follows:

- **Static scheduling:** The number of metaheuristics is constant and correlated to the number of processors of the parallel machine. A static mapping between the metaheuristics and the processors is realized. The localization of metaheuristics will not change during the search.
- **Dynamic scheduling:** Metaheuristics are dynamically scheduled on the different processors of the parallel architecture. Hence, the migration of metaheuristics during the search between different machines may happen.

TABLE 6.7 Checkpoint Information for Some Metaheuristics in the Algorithmic-Level Parallel Model

Metaheuristic	Checkpoint Content
Local search	Current solution
Simulated annealing	Current solution, cooling schedule
Tabu search	Current solution, iteration, tabu list, medium- and long-term memories
Evolutionary algorithms	Population, generation
Ant colonies	Pheromone trails, iteration
Particle swarm	Population, iteration
Estimation distribution algorithms	Probabilistic model, generation
Scatter search	Reference set, population, iteration

The iteration (i.e, generation) is memorized if it is used in the stopping criteria. Otherwise, any information used in the stopping criteria must be checkpointed. Moreover, for any metaheuristic, the elite solutions found (e.g., best found solutions) are among the checkpointed data.

- **Adaptive scheduling:** The number of metaheuristics involved in the search will vary dynamically. For example, when a machine becomes idle, a new metaheuristic is launched to perform a new search. When a machine becomes busy or faulty, the associated metaheuristic is stopped.

Fault tolerance: The memory state of the algorithmic-level parallel model required for the checkpointing mechanism is composed of the memory of each metaheuristic and the information being migrated. Table 6.7 summarizes the main information to deal with in checkpointing different metaheuristics. For stochastic metaheuristics, one has to note that in an asynchronous mode, such memory may not be critical.

Example 6.9 GRASP in a homogeneous nonshared parallel machine. As mentioned in Example 6.5, a straightforward parallel model for GRASP is based on parallelizing the different iterations. Let us suppose that the different iterations have more or less the same computational time. The granularity of a parallel implementation is related to the number of iterations carried out by a process. For a homogeneous nonshared parallel machine such as a reserved cluster, a static load balancing strategy may be used by fixing the granularity to *max–iterations*/p where `max-iterations` is the maximum number of iterations for the GRASP metaheuristic and p is the number of processors of the cluster. Hence, each process will perform *max–iterations*/p iterations. The same solution holds for the multistart local search model. .

6.2.7 Iteration-Level Parallel Model

Granularity: A medium granularity is associated with the iteration-level parallel model. The ratio between the evaluation of a partition and the communication cost of a partition determines the granularity. This parallel model is efficient if the evaluation of a solution is time consuming and/or there are a large number of candidate solutions to evaluate. In S-metaheuristics, it will depend on the number of neighbors in each partition, while in P-metaheuristics, it will depend on the number of solutions (e.g., individuals, ants, particles) in each subpopulation.

Scalability: The degree of concurrency of this model is limited by the size of the neighborhood for S-metaheuristics and the size of the population for P-metaheuristics. The use of very large neighborhoods and large populations will increase the scalability of this parallel model.

Synchronous/asynchronous communications: Introducing asynchronism in the iteration-level parallel model will increase the efficiency of parallel metaheuristics. In the iteration-level parallel model, asynchronous communications are related to the asynchronous evaluation of partitions and construction of solutions. Unfortunately, this model is more or less synchronous. Asynchronous evaluation is more efficient for heterogeneous or shared or volatile parallel architectures. Moreover, asynchronism is necessary for optimization problems where the computation cost of the objective function (and constraints) depends on the solution. Different solutions may have different evaluation costs.

For S-metaheuristics, asynchronism may be introduced by using the best improving strategy for selecting the neighbor. Indeed, in the best improving strategy of selection, a parallel synchronous scheme must be applied. One has to wait the termination of the evaluation of the whole neighborhood to determine the best neighbor. In P-metaheuristics, asynchronism may be introduced by relaxing the synchronization constraints. For instance, in evolutionary algorithms, the steady-state algorithms may be used in the reproduction phase.

The two main advantages of the asynchronous model over the synchronous model are the fault tolerance of the asynchronous model and the robustness in case of the fitness computation that can take very different computations time. Although some time-out detection can be used to address the former issue, the latter one can be partially overcome if the grain is set to very small values, as individuals will be sent out for evaluations upon request of the workers. Therefore, the model is blocking and thus less efficient on an heterogeneous computational grid. Moreover, as the model is not fault tolerant, the disappearance of an evaluating agent requires the redistribution of its individuals to other agents. As a consequence, it is essential to store all the solutions not yet evaluated. From another point of view, the scalability of the model is limited to the size of the population.

Scheduling: In the iteration-level parallel model, tasks correspond to the construction/evaluation of a set of solutions. Hence, the different scheduling strategies will differ as follows:

- **Static scheduling:** Here, a static partitioning of the neighborhood or the population is applied. For instance, the neighborhood or the population is decomposed into equal-size partitions, depending on the number of processors of the parallel homogeneous nonshared machine. A static mapping between the partitions and the processors is realized. For a heterogeneous nonshared machine, the size of each partition must be initialized according to the performance of the processors.

The static scheduling strategy is not efficient for variable computational costs of equal partitions. This happens for optimization problems where different costs are associated with the evaluation of solutions. For instance, in genetic programming, individuals may widely vary in size and complexity. This makes a static scheduling of the parallel evaluation of the individuals not efficient [274,441].

- **Dynamic scheduling:** A static partitioning is applied but a dynamic migration of tasks can be carried out depending on the varying load of processors. The number of tasks generated may be equal to the size of the neighborhood or the population. Many tasks may be mapped on the same processor. Hence, more flexibility is obtained for the scheduling algorithm. If the first improving strategy is used to select a neighbor in S-metaheuristics, a dynamic scheduling scheme is more efficient as there is a large variability in exploring the different partitions. For instance, the approach based on the master–workers cycle stealing may be applied. To each worker is first allocated a small number of solutions. Once it has performed its iterations, the worker requests the master for additional solutions. All the workers are stopped once the final result is returned. Faster and less-loaded processors handle more solutions than the others. This approach allows to reduce the execution time compared to the static one.
- **Adaptive scheduling:** The objective of this model is to adapt the number of partitions generated to the load of the target architecture. More efficient scheduling strategies are obtained for shared, volatile, and heterogeneous parallel architectures such as desktop grids.

Fault tolerance: The memory of the iteration-level parallel model required for the checkpointing mechanism is composed of the different partitions. For S-metaheuristics, the partitions are composed of a set of neighbors with their associated objective values. For P-metaheuristics, the partitions are composed of a set of (partial) solutions and their associated objective values.

Example 6.10 Asynchronous evaluation in a steady-state evolutionary algorithm. The asynchronous model of evaluating the individuals (see Section 6.1.2) is more efficient than the synchronous one in terms of scheduling flexibility and fault tolerance. This model is more efficient on a heterogeneous and shared machines. Moreover, it is a fault-tolerant model. A fault of an evaluator processors does not affect the parallel program. This is an important aspect in heterogeneous networks of owned workstations and desktop grids, where the probability to have a fault is relatively important. It is naturally nonblocking and fault tolerant. The threshold of wasted evaluations is not exceeded because no control is performed on the solutions sent for evaluation. In addition, the asynchronous mode is well adapted in terms of efficiency to applications with an irregular evaluation cost of the objective function. Furthermore, it is not necessary to store the solutions evaluated by the workers, and the memory usage is thus optimized. On the other hand, the degree of concurrency is not limited by the size of the population.

6.2.8 Solution-Level Parallel Model

Granularity: This parallel model has a fine granularity. There is a relatively high communication requirements for this model. In the functional decomposition parallel model, the granularity will depend on the ratio between the evaluation cost of the subfunctions and the communication cost of a solution. In the data decomposition parallel model, it depends on the ratio between the evaluation of a data partition and its communication cost.

The fine granularity of this model makes it less suitable for large-scale distributed architectures where the communication cost (in terms of latency and/or bandwidth) is relatively important, such as in grid computing systems. Indeed, its implementation is often restricted to clusters or network of workstations or shared memory machines.

Scalability: The degree of concurrency of this parallel model is limited by the number of subfunctions or data partitions. Although its scalability is limited, the use of the solution-level parallel model in conjunction with the two other parallel models enables to extend the scalability of a parallel metaheuristic.

Synchronous/asynchronous communications: The implementation of the solution-level parallel model is always synchronous following a master–workers paradigm. Indeed, the master must wait for all partial results to compute the global value of the objective function. The execution time T will be bounded by the maximum time T_i of the different tasks. An exception occurs for hard-constrained optimization problems, where feasibility of the solution is first tested. The master terminates the computations as soon as a given task detects that the solution does not satisfy a given hard constraint. Due to its heavy synchronization steps, this parallel model is worth applying to problems in which the calculations required at each iteration are time consuming. The relative speedup may be approximated as follows:

$$S_n = \frac{T}{\alpha + T/n}$$

where α is the communication cost.

Scheduling: In the solution-level parallel model, tasks correspond to subfunctions in the functional decomposition and to data partitions in the data decomposition model. Hence, the different scheduling strategies will differ as follows:

- **Static scheduling:** Usually, the subfunctions or data are decomposed into equal-size partitions, depending on the number of processors of the parallel machine. A static mapping between the subfunctions (or data partitions) and the processors is applied. As for the other parallel models, this static scheme is efficient for parallel homogeneous nonshared machine. For a heterogeneous nonshared machine, the size of each partition in terms of subfunctions or data must be initialized according to the performance of the processors.
- **Dynamic scheduling:** Dynamic load balancing will be necessary for shared parallel architectures or variable costs for the associated subfunctions or data partitions. Dynamic load balancing may be easily achieved by evenly distributing at run time the subfunctions or the data among the processors. In optimization problems, where the computing cost of the subfunctions is unpredictable, dynamic load balancing is necessary. Indeed, a static scheduling cannot be efficient because there is no appropriate estimation of the task costs (i.e., unpredictable cost).

TABLE 6.8 Efficient Implementation of Parallel Metaheuristics According to Some Performance Metrics and Used Strategies

Property	Algorithmic Level	Iteration Level	Solution Level
Granularity	Coarse (frequency of exchange, size of information)	Medium (No. of solutions per partition)	Fine (Eval. subfunctions, eval. data partitions)
Scalability	Number of metaheuristics	Neighborhood size, population size	No. of subfunctions, No. of data partitions
Asynchronism	High (information exchange)	Moderate (evaluation of solutions)	Exceptional (feasibility test)
Scheduling and fault tolerance	Metaheuristic	Solution(s)	Partial solution(s)

- **Adaptive scheduling:** In adaptive scheduling, the number of subfunctions or data partitions generated is adapted to the load of the target architecture. More efficient scheduling strategies are obtained for shared, volatile, and heterogeneous parallel architectures such as desktop grids.

Fault tolerance: The memory of the solution-level parallel model required for the checkpointing mechanism is straightforward. It is composed of the solution and its partial objective values calculation.

Depending on the target parallel architecture, Table 6.8 presents a general guideline for the efficient implementation of the different parallel models of metaheuristics. For each parallel model (algorithmic level, iteration level, solution level), the table shows its characteristics according to the outlined criteria (granularity, scalability, asynchronism, scheduling, and fault tolerance).

6.3 PARALLEL METAHEURISTICS FOR MULTIOBJECTIVE OPTIMIZATION

More and more applications are concerned with parallel multiobjective optimization in different domains such as in engineering and life sciences. In addition to the classical motivations of designing parallel metaheuristics, interactive decision-making approaches need real-time solving of MOPs. When trying to solve real-world problems, multiobjective metaheuristics may not be powerful enough to provide a good approximation of the Pareto set in a reasonable time. Let us consider a MOP whose function evaluation requires 1 min; then, to carry out 25,000 evaluations (a typical value in many experiments), around 17 days of computing time is necessary. This becomes worse if one considers that for the evaluation of a metaheuristic when solving the problem, a minimum of 30 independent runs have to be performed. In this situation, parallelism must be considered to tackle these kinds of MOPs.

As mentioned in Chapter 4, optimal solution of a MOP is not a single solution but a set of solutions, known as the set of Pareto optimal solutions. This characteristic has a large impact on the adaptation of parallel models for metaheuristics in solving MOP. The following sections revisit the design and implementation aspects of the different parallel models of multiobjective metaheuristics. Hence, the focus is only on specific aspects of MOPs. All presented aspects of parallel models for monoobjective optimization can be useful for MOPs.

6.3.1 Algorithmic-Level Parallel Model for MOP

Besides the search for speedup, improvements in the solution quality should also be sought in the algorithmic-level parallel model. Although the latter is likely to be the most important contribution of parallelism to metaheuristics [166], few of such parallel search models have been especially designed for multiobjective optimization until recently [790].

P-metaheuristics are easier to adapt for MOP as they work on a population of solutions. Hence, this model has been mostly used for P-metaheuristics. In general, an archive is maintained in parallel to the current population. This archive contains all Pareto optimal solutions generated during the search.

In designing an algorithmic-level parallel metaheuristic for MOPs, the same questions arise (Fig. 6.4). Some answers are specific to MOPs.

- **The exchange decision criterion (when?):** Only the "intelligent" adaptive criteria are considered here. Adaptive exchanges are guided by some characteristics of the multiobjective search. For instance, it may depend on the evolution of the quality of the Pareto set instead of a single solution in monoobjective optimization. A classical criterion is related to the update of the archive, which means that a new Pareto solution is found.
- **The exchange topology (where?):** Multiobjective optimization has no specific impact on this issue.
- **The information exchanged (what?):** This parameter will be specific to MOPs. In general, the information exchanged is composed of the following:
  - Pareto solutions: This information deals with any selection strategy of the generated Pareto solutions during the search. In general, it contains solutions from the current population and/or the archive. The number of Pareto optimal solutions may be an absolute value or a percentage of the sets.
  - Search memory: This information deals with a search memory of a metaheuristic excluding the Pareto optimal solutions as in monoobjective optimization.

  The size of the data exchanged (for instance, the number of Pareto solutions) will influence the granularity of the model. If the number of Pareto solutions is high, the communication cost will be exorbitant particularly on a large-scale parallel architectures such as grids.

- **The integration policy (how?):** The local copies of the information received are generally updated using the received ones. The Pareto solutions received will serve to update the local Pareto archive. For the current population, any replacement strategy can be used (e.g., random, elitist).

The different metaheuristics involved in the cooperation may evaluate different subsets of objective functions [510] (Fig. 6.31). For instance, each metaheuristic may handle a single objective. Another approach consists in using a different aggregation weights in each metaheuristic or different constraints [721].

Each metaheuristic may also represent a different partition of the decision space or the objective space [566,753]. By this way, each metaheuristic is destined to find a particular portion of the Pareto optimal front.

Another main issue in the development of parallel metaheuristics for MOPs is how the Pareto set is built during the optimization process. Two different approaches may be considered (Fig. 6.31):

- **Centralized Pareto front:** The front is a centralized data structure of the algorithm that is built by the metaheuristics during the whole computation. This way, the new nondominated solutions in the Pareto optimal set are global Pareto optima [57,145,191].
- **Distributed Pareto front:** The Pareto front is distributed among the metaheuristics so that the algorithm works with local nondominated solutions that must be somehow combined at the end of their work [227,603,666]. No pure centralized approach has been found clearly motivated by efficiency issues [577]. All the

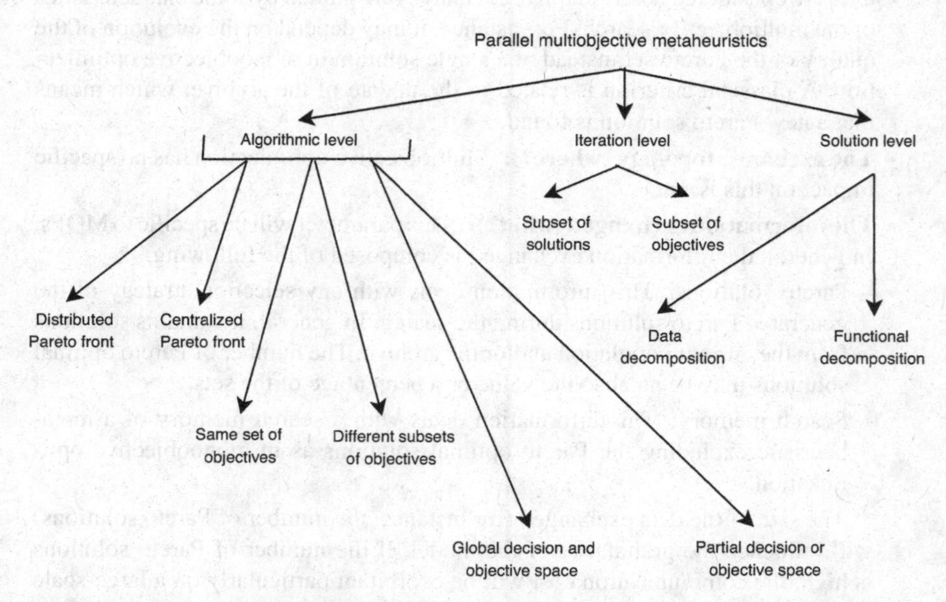

FIGURE 6.31 Classification of parallel metaheuristics for multiobjective optimization.

found centralized approaches are combined with distributed phases where local nondominated solutions are considered. After each distributed phase, a single optimal Pareto front is built by using these local Pareto optima. Then, the new Pareto front is again distributed for local computation, and so on.

6.3.2 Iteration-Level Parallel Model for MOP

The evaluation step of a multiobjective metaheuristic is generally the most time consuming. Therefore, to speed up the search, the iteration-level parallel model distributes the evaluation of solutions. This type of parallel approach is aimed at speeding up the computations and the basic behavior of the underlying algorithms is not altered. It is the easiest and the most widely used parallel model in multiobjective optimization because of the MOPs that are usually solved in this field. Indeed, many MOPs are complex in terms of the objective functions. For instance, some engineering design applications integrate solvers dealing with different disciplines: computational fluid dynamics, computational electromagnetics (CEM), or finite element methods. Other real-life applications deal with complex simulators. A particularly efficient execution is often obtained when the ratio between communication and computation is high. Otherwise, most of the time can be wasted in communications, leading to a poor parallel algorithm.

In the multiobjective context of metaheuristics, the iteration-level parallel model generally consists in distributing the set of solutions (population or neighborhood) among the different workers. Each worker evaluates the vector of all the objective functions on the associated solutions [666], or a given objective for all the solutions, or a hybrid strategy (Fig. 6.32).

Moreover, ranking methods are used to assign a fitness to each solution of a population. These ranking methods are computation intensive and may be parallelized. Updating the archives at each iteration is also a time-consuming task.

Example 6.11 Parallel cone dominance ranking. The cone dominance concept facilitates the parallelization of the fitness assignment procedure. Indeed, each process will use a different nonoverlapping cone, so that the Pareto optimality of each process is different from the other ones.

6.3.3 Solution-Level Parallel Model for MOP

The main objective of the solution-level parallel model for MOP is to speed up the search by parallelizing the treatments dealing with single solutions (e.g., objective evaluation, constraint satisfaction). Indeed, the evaluation of multiple objective functions in MOPs is the most time-consuming part in a metaheuristic. Therefore, several algorithms try to reduce this time by means of parallelizing the calculation of the fitness evaluation [715,721,737]. The classical approaches must be adapted to multiobjective optimization (Fig. 6.31):

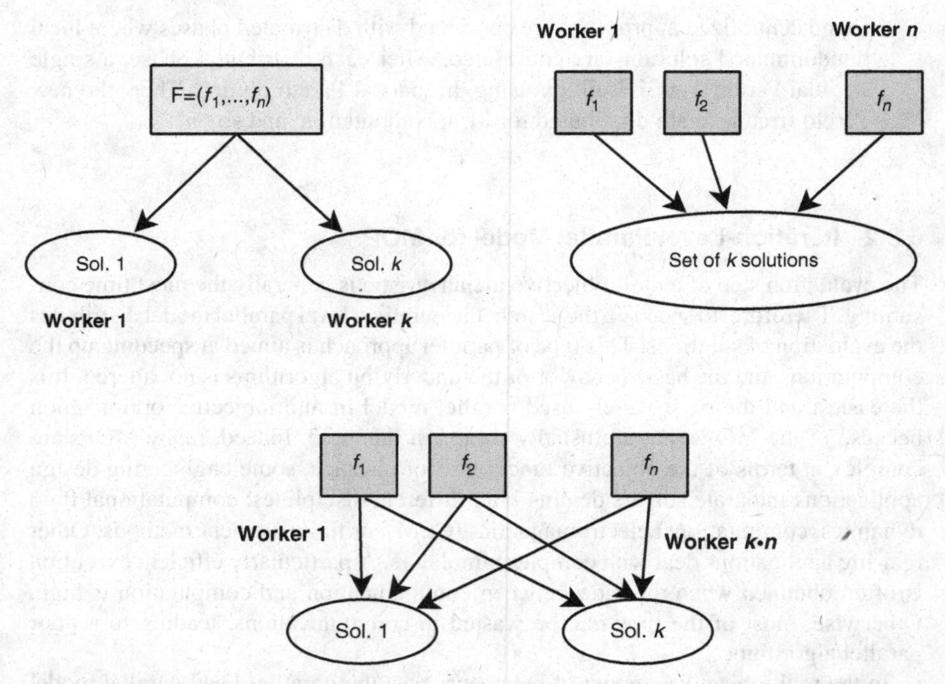

FIGURE 6.32 The iteration-level parallel model in multiobjective metaheuristics.

- **Functional decomposition:** This approach consists in distributing the different objective functions among the workers, and each of them computes the value of its assigned function on each solution. The master will then aggregate the partial results for all the solutions. Such approach allows a degree of concurrency and the scalability is limited to the number of objective functions, meaning often 2 or 3. Moreover, each objective function may be decomposed into several subfunctions. Then, the degree of concurrency will be equal to the number of subfunctions.
- **Data decomposition:** For each data partition of the problem (database, geographical area, structure, and so on), all the objectives of the problem are evaluated and returned to the master. The master will aggregate the different results.

Example 6.12 Multidisciplinary design optimization. In multidisciplinary design optimization, many engineering domains with different models are used to design a structure. For example, in designing a car, one has to optimize the airflow around the car and the toughness of materials. The former objective is based on a computational fluid dynamics solver, whereas the latter objective is based on finite element methods solver. Moreover, the structure representing a car may also be decomposed into many substructures. Each substructure will be handled in parallel (Fig. 6.33).

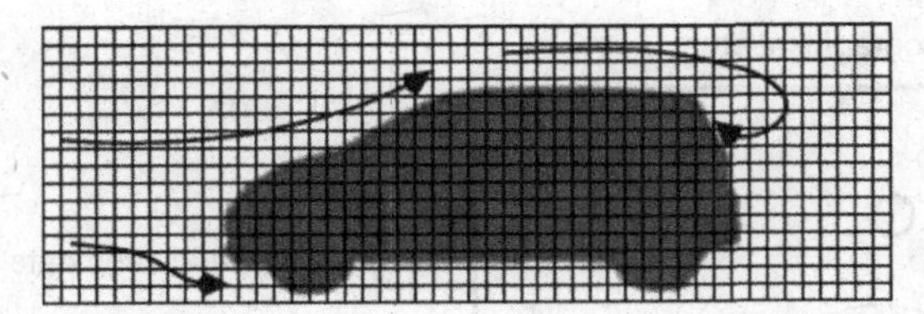

FIGURE 6.33 The solution-level parallel model in multidisciplinary design optimization. Different solvers are used within different partitions of the structure.

In the multiobjective context, the scalability of this model is limited by the number of objectives and the number of subfunctions per objective. It is then more important than in the monoobjective case. The scalability could be improved again if the different objective functions are simultaneously parallelized.

6.3.4 Hierarchical Parallel Model for MOP

As for monoobjective optimization, the three parallel models are complementary and can then be combined into a single hierarchical model.

Example 6.13 Parallel multiobjective network design. The design of large networks (e.g., telecommunication, transportation) is complex, with a great impact on the quality of service (QoS) and the cost of the network. For instance, the optimal design of radio cellular mobile networks (GSM, GPRS, UMTS, Wimax) is a challenging application for telecommunication companies. This problem can be defined as a positioning and configuration of a set of antennas on a given geographical area to fulfill two classes of objectives (Fig. 6.34):

- **Cost of the network:** This will be related to the number of antennas to minimize, their localization, and their configuration.
- **Quality of service:** This class may integrate many objectives such as minimizing the interferences and maximizing the handled traffic.

and satisfy some constraints such as the covering of the whole geographical area and the handover mobility. The antenna positioning problems deals with finding a set of sites for antennas from a set of predefined candidate sites, and setting up the configuration of different parameters of the antennas (e.g., tilt, azimuth, power).

In addition to the NP-completeness of the problem and the huge number of solutions in the search space, the other difficulty of this multiobjective problem is the high computational cost required to evaluate the objective functions and the constraints. A high memory is also needed. In fact, each evaluation needs the simulation of the whole network using complex wave propagation models. A more extensive analytical and technical formulation may be found in Ref. [752].

Hence, the following parallel hierarchical model (Fig. 6.35) can be designed to solve this complex multiobjective network design problem to exploit the characteristics of each model:

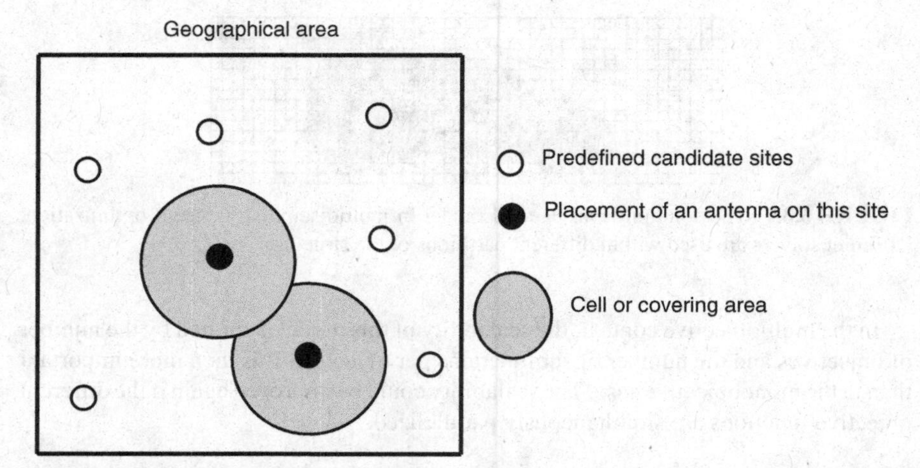

FIGURE 6.34 Network design problem: placement and configuration of antennas on a given geographical area. A cell associated with an antenna is defined as its covering area. The handover mobility constraint deals with the communication continuity when a mobile is moving toward a new cell (cell switching).

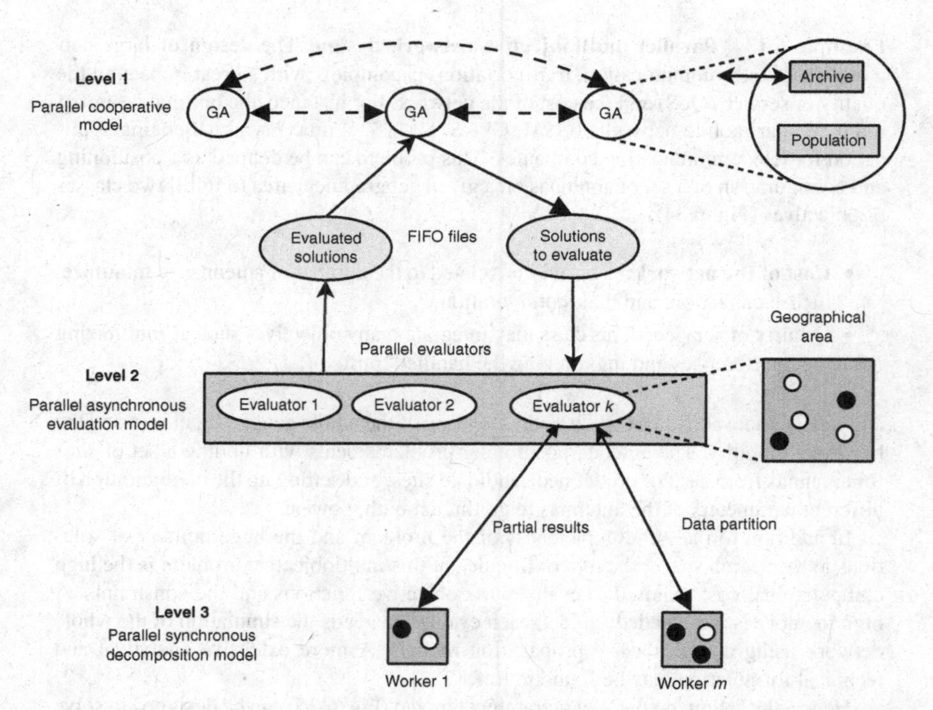

FIGURE 6.35 Parallel hierarchical model for multiobjective network design: conjunction use of the three complementary parallel models.

- **Algorithmic-level parallel model:** At this highest level, a parallel self-contained cooperative model based on evolutionary algorithms (island model) is designed. Each island represents a multiobjective Pareto approach based on a genetic algorithm. The islands are organized in a topology based on a bidirectional ring. The Pareto archive of each island is communicated to its neighbors. This Pareto archive represents all the generated Pareto solutions during the search. Each Pareto archive participates in the selection phase of the local island (elitism). The cooperation between the islands is asynchronous, that is, when the migration criteria occur for a given island, it sends the new Pareto archive to its neighbors. The migration criteria are based on the number of updates of the local archive. If this number is greater than a given threshold, a migration is carried out. When receiving an archive from a neighbor, an island will update its local archive. The Pareto solutions of the union of the two archives (local and neighbor) represent the new archive.

  The impact of cooperation in terms of effectiveness can be shown by comparing the presented model and the one without cooperation between islands. This model scales very well in terms of the efficiency. Good speedups are obtained on diverse parallel architectures: clusters, networks of heterogeneous workstations, clusters of shared-memory machines, and a desktop grid. This is due to the large granularity of this parallel model. However, increasing the number of islands will not systematically improve the quality of the obtained Pareto front.
- **Iteration-level parallel model:** At this intermediate level, a parallel asynchronous evaluation model for a steady-state evolutionary algorithm is designed. Then, the evaluation and the reproduction steps of a GA are carried out in a parallel asynchronous manner by different workers. This model is asynchronous in the sense that the order of evaluation defined by the selection phase may not be the same as in the replacement phase. Indeed, the evaluation cost depends on the characteristics of an individual (e.g., number of active sites) and also on the load and speed of the processor that handle the evaluation process.

  The obtained speedups show that this model is efficient when running on a cluster and a local network of workstations. The asynchronous characteristic of this parallel model makes it efficient even on an heterogeneous shared network of workstations and a desktop grid. Moreover, it is a fault-tolerant model. A fault of an evaluator processor does not affect the parallel program. This is an important issue for heterogeneous network of workstations and desktop grids where the probability to have a fault is relatively important.
- **Solution-level parallel model:** A parallel synchronous decomposition model can be used. The geographical area is decomposed into equal partitions. All objectives and constraints are evaluated on their associated partitions. The implementation is based on a master/worker paradigm. The master communicates its data partition to each worker. The number of partitions equals the number of used processors. Each worker computes the partial functions of the objectives and constraints on the associated geographical area and then the partial results are returned to the master. The master receives all the partial results and then aggregates them to obtain the whole evaluation of a network.

  The obtained speedups of this parallel model depend on the number of processors. For a small[15] number of processors $(1 \ldots k)$, the speedup is quasi-linear. A

[15]For this application, $k = 8$.

degradation[16] of the speedup has been shown from m processors for a cluster and from n for networks of workstations with a lower speed communication network. As the number of partitions depends on the number of processors, the granularity of the model decreases with the number of processors. Hence, the experiments show that this model is not scalable in terms of the number of processors. The Larger the instance, the better the scalability of this model. The more significant the bandwidth of the communication network, the better the scalability of this model. Let us notice that a superlinear speedup of the global parallel model has been obtained on a cluster of processors. This is due to the use of the different hierarchies of the memory (cache, etc.) and the large memory needed by the application, which is very limited for a sequential processor.

6.4 PARALLEL METAHEURISTICS UNDER ParadisEO

This section illustrates the use of ParadisEO to design and implement parallel and distributed models for metaheuristics. ParadisEO–PEO is the module in charge of parallel and distributed implementation of metaheuristics. Some illustrations are given for evolutionary algorithms, particle swarm optimization, and local search.

6.4.1 Parallel Frameworks for Metaheuristics

Designing generic software frameworks to deal with the design and efficient *transparent* implementation of parallel and distributed metaheuristics is an important challenge. Indeed, efficient implementation of parallel metaheuristics is a complex task that depends on the type of the parallel architecture used. In designing a software framework for parallel metaheuristics, one has to keep in mind the following important properties: portability, efficiency, easy use, and flexibility in terms of parallel architectures and models.

Several white box frameworks for the reusable design of parallel metaheuristics have been proposed and are available on the Web. Some of them are restricted to only parallel and distributed evolutionary algorithms. The most important of them are DREAM (Distributed Resource Evolutionary Algorithm Machine) [35], ECJ (Java Evolutionary Computation) [819], JDEAL (Java Distributed Evolutionary Algorithms Library)[17] and Distributed BEAGLE (Distributed Beagle Engine Advanced Genetic Learning Environment) [291]. These frameworks are reusable as they are based on a clear object-oriented conceptual separation. They are also portable as they are developed in Java except the last system, which is programmed in C++. However, they are limited regarding the parallel distributed models. Indeed, in DREAM and ECJ, only the island model is implemented using Java threads and TCP/IP sockets. DREAM is particularly deployable on peer-to-peer platforms. Furthermore, JDEAL provides

[16]For this application and the target architectures, $m = 32$ and $n = 16$.
[17]http://www.laseeb.org/sw/JDEAL.

only the master–worker model (iteration-level parallel model) using TCP/IP sockets. The latter implements also the synchronous migration-based island model, but deployable on only one processor.

For S-metaheuristics, most of the existing software frameworks [301,550] do not allow parallel distributed implementations. Those enabling parallelism and distribution are often dedicated to only one solution method. For instance, Ref. [79] provides parallel skeletons for the tabu search method. Two skeletons are provided and implemented in C++/MPI: independent runs (multiStart) model with search strategies and a master–slave model with neighborhood partition. The two models can be exploited by the user in a transparent way.

Few frameworks available on the Web are devoted to both S-metaheuristics and P-metaheuristics and their hybridization. MALLBA [22], MAFRA (Java mimetic algorithms framework) [481], and ParadisEO are good examples of such frameworks. MAFRA is developed in Java using design patterns [293]. It is strongly hybridization oriented, but it is very limited regarding parallelism and distribution. MALLBA and ParadisEO have numerous similarities. They are C++/MPI open-source frameworks. They provide all the previously presented distributed models and different hybridization mechanisms. However, they are quite different as ParadisEO is more flexible, thanks to the finer granularity of its classes. Moreover, ParadisEO provides also the PVM-based communication layer and Pthreads-based multithreading. On the other hand, MALLBA is deployable on wide area networks [22]. Communications are based on *NetStream*, an *ad hoc* flexible and OOP message passing service upon MPI. Furthermore, MALLBA allows the hybridization of metaheuristics with exact methods.

ParadisEO–PEO offers transparent implementation of the different parallel models on different architectures using suitable programming environments. The following sections show how could these parallel models be designed by the user in a transparent way, one has just to instantiate their associated provided classes. ParadisEO–PEO offers the easy implementation of the three main parallel models. The algorithmic-level parallel model allows several optimization algorithms to cooperate and exchange any kind of data. The iteration-level parallel model proposes to parallelize and distribute a set of identical operations. In the solution-level parallel model, any calculation block specific to the optimization problem can be divided into smaller units to speed up the treatment and gain efficiency. The goal of this section is to present how anyone could effectively use these models with ParadisEO–PEO to tackle any optimization problem. The power of the implementation is so important that, in fact, the optimization problem is just an example that can be extended to any algorithm. Consequently, the most generic example for each of the three levels are outlined.

6.4.2 Design of Algorithmic-Level Parallel Models

The algorithmic-level parallel model for metaheuristics is quite easy to design and implement. Let us consider the following problems:

- An application requires three identical optimization algorithms that cooperate. For instance, three metaheuristics need to exchange some solutions to increase the quality of the obtained solutions.
- The implementation must be distributed. For instance, a user has three available machines and he wants to deploy one metaheuristic per machine.
- The metaheuristics exchange the same kind of data.
- The three algorithms can send their data to each other. They can receive some data from each other.

Within ParadisEO–PEO, there exist all the necessary software components to quickly design and implement such a specification. The following design questions and their answers are sufficient to specify what this user should do.

6.4.2.1 Algorithms and Transferred Data (What?) The optimization algorithms could be considered as black or white boxes. That means each optimization algorithm can be any kind of C++ structure or any program embedded into a C++ structure. No heritage is imposed, the algorithms can be defined using functions, structures, or classes.

The code to be launched in parallel must be enclosed within a function operator having only one or no parameter. This operator specifies the behavior of the algorithm and it can be whatever the user wants. In addition, there are no restrictions for the transferred data, but the algorithms have to send and receive the same single type of data. For instance, it could be a population of solutions stored in a standard vector, a component, a primitive type, and so on.

Solutions exchange (selection policy): In ParadisEO, population-based metaheuristics such as EA and PSO algorithms deal with solutions that compose the population (individuals for evolutionary algorithms, particles for swarm optimization), and the transferred data may correspond to some of these solutions. Hence, a large set of ready-to-use strategies are implemented for the selection of the migrants. It is just an application of the generic transfer but set up in the specific case where EAs or PSO algorithms cooperate. It uses all the templates inheriting from the primitive `eoSelect`, the same as the one used in ParadisEO–EO to design evolutionary algorithms. Different selection strategies in Paradiseo–EO are used, for instance, to select the parents undergoing variation operators (e.g., roulette wheel, ranking, stochastic or deterministic tournaments, uniform sampling). The flexibility of the library makes it easy to reuse these policies for emigrants selection.

6.4.2.2 Transfer Control (When?) Even if there are several well-known checkpointing operations allowing to control the data transfer, the algorithms involved must have the possibility to specifically plan the exchanges with the other instances. The transfer control highly depends on the involved parallel model. Any entity aiming to start and control a transfer between cooperating programs necessarily needs to be highly flexible. Under ParadisEO–PEO, two classes `peoAsyncDataTransfer`

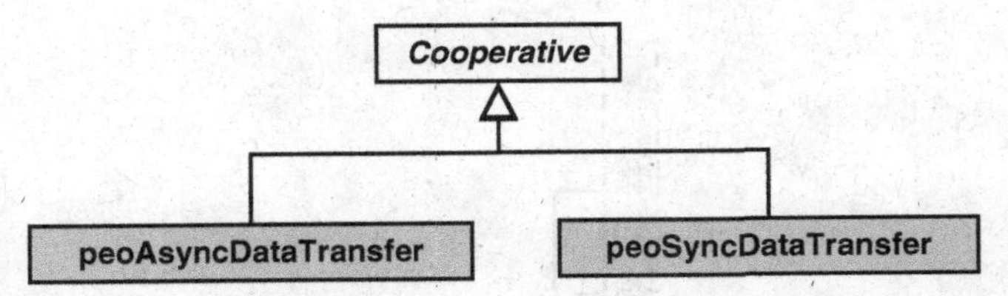

FIGURE 6.36 UML diagram of the data transfer dedicated components available within ParadisEO–PEO.

and `peoSyncDataTransfer` ensure, respectively, the asynchronous and synchronous data transfers (Fig. 6.36). They are viewed as cooperative components and can be launched anytime it is necessary in any execution state. Obviously, each of the algorithms must embed one of these two classes. It just has to call it each time it needs to send and receive data.

ParadisEO–PEO proposes many mechanisms for the exchange decision criteria, in case of the algorithms involved are metaheuristics directly implemented with ParadisEO's components. The primitives `peoAsyncIslandMig` and `peoSyncIslandMig` propose, respectively, the asynchronous and synchronous exchanges (Fig. 6.37). The exchanges can be applied to any metaheuristic and are launched at each iteration. They are embedded into the checkpointing component `eoCheckpoint`. These templates take either a migration frequency (synchronous exchange) or a continuator object inheriting from the basic `eoContinue` (asynchronous). The asynchronous continuation criteria can be periodic (e.g., time based, generation number, manually controlled), or probabilistic (e.g., fitness improvement, steady fitness). As in the rest of ParadisEO, all the quoted migration criteria are predefined as classes. Hence, the user can either easily use them directly or combine them as building blocks to design specific criteria.

6.4.2.3 Exchange Topology (Where?) The way several parallelized or distributed entities cooperate all together is defined by a communication topology. It aims to fully describe, from a high level, the entities that can send information to others. It appears clearly that this concept is essential for any distributed architecture as it gives the intrinsic communication behavior. ParadisEO–PEO proposes many topologies, all inheriting from the abstract class `topology`. The user just has to choose one of them (Fig. 6.38):

- Star topology that corresponds to `StarTopology`.
- Ring topology that corresponds to `RingTopology`.
- Complete topology that corresponds to `CompleteTopology`. Each entity cooperates with each other.
- Random topology that corresponds to `RandomTopology`. For technical constraints, it is only usable with the synchronous transfers.

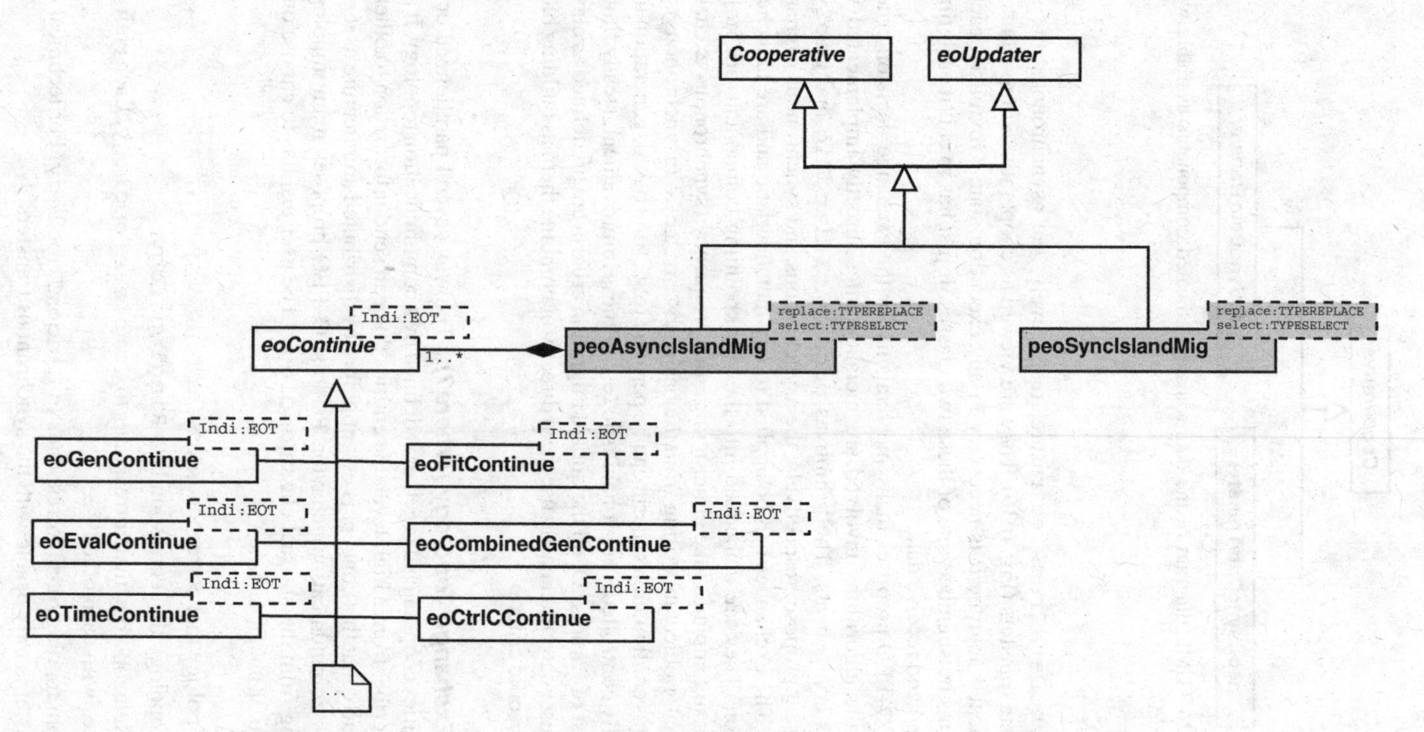

FIGURE 6.37 UML diagram for information exchange components within ParadisEO–PEO.

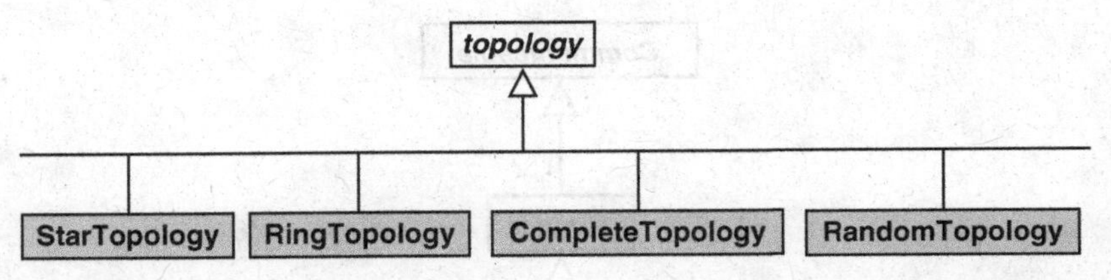

FIGURE 6.38 UML diagram of the communication topologies available within ParadisEO–PEO.

The topology can also be freely extended. Regarding the implementation, the topology must be passed to the data transfer component. Furthermore, once the communication structure is set, an important point must be raised: How the received data are effectively aggregated by the algorithms? That means, how does an algorithm treat the data arriving at the same moment from the other algorithms? In general, there is a local copy of the received information. The data transfer component cannot be constructed without the aggregation definition. ParadisEO–PEO allows the user define this aggregation by any structure, class, or template. The aggregations can also be different for the cooperating algorithms.

6.4.2.4 *Replacement Strategy (How?)* This integration policy is really facilitated within ParadisEO–PEO when P-metaheuristics (e.g., EAs, PSOs) are involved for the algorithmic-level model. For this case, the following templates (`peoAsyncIslandMig` and `peoSyncIslandMig`) can be used. Both of them expect a replacement strategy for the migrant information that arrive in the target population. It aims to answer the design question: "How are the received solutions integrated into the local population?" Similarly, with the selection strategy, designing the replacement strategy is straightforward. The user can choose one of the templates extending `eoReplacement` of the ParadisEO–EO module. The replacement strategies that can be used include, for instance, tournaments, EP-like stochastic replacement, elitist, and pure random replacement.

At this step, all design questions have been tackled. Nevertheless, the implementation aspects have not been explained. They can be completely transparent for the final user. The way the resources are distributed between the algorithms, which are all processes in terms of operating system, must be described in a short XML (eXtended Modeling Language) file.

6.4.2.5 *Parallel Implementation* The last required step wraps the sequential algorithms inside parallel programming environments and assigns the control of the parallel components to these parallel environments. Within ParadisEO–PEO, this is completely transparent. The class `peoWrapper` ensures the wrapping (Fig. 6.39). The wrapper inherits from the abstract base-class `Runner` and takes an algorithm and its parameters to make it parallel. No additional code or configuration is required for ParadisEO–PEO.

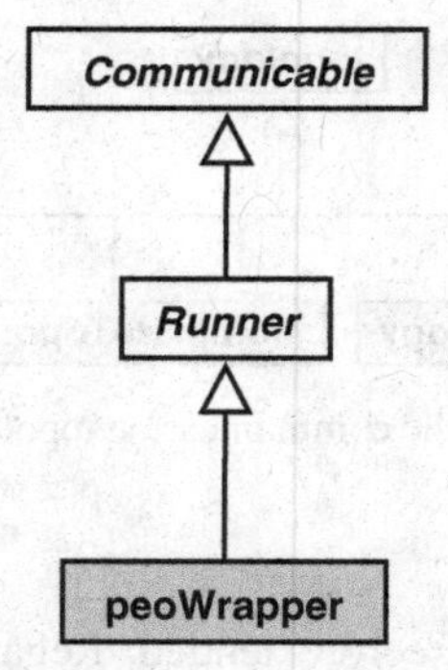

FIGURE 6.39 UML diagram of the parallel wrapper of ParadisEO–PEO.

6.4.2.6 A Generic Example In this section, a short generic example illustrating the previous concepts using ParadisEO–PEO is presented. Three identical algorithms synchronously exchange an integer value over a ring topology. Below is the C++ basic structure of the algorithm:

```
struct Algorithm {

  Algorithm( TYPE& buf, peoSyncDataTransfer& extDataTransfer )
   : transferBuffer( extTransferBuffer ), dataTransfer
    ( extDataTransfer ) {
  }

  // the algorithm uses its own vector of data.
  // ``operator'' that performs the main treatment.
  void operator()( std::vector< TYPE >& data ) {

    /* ...... problem specific treatment .....   */

    // launch the transfer
    dataTransfer();
  }

  TYPE& buf; // the data that will be transferred have the
             generic type "TYPE"
  peoSyncDataTransfer& dataTransfer;
};
```

The aggregation component:

```
struct Aggregation {
  void operator()( TYPE& currentValue, TYPE& receivedValue ) {
   // aggregation
  }
};
```

The three algorithms use a complete topology:

```
CompleteTopology topology;
```

The data transfer can be specified using

```
peoSyncDataTransfer syncTransferA( transferBufferA, topology,
  aggregation );
peoSyncDataTransfer syncTransferB( transferBufferB, topology,
  aggregation );
peoSyncDataTransfer syncTransferC( transferBufferC, topology,
  aggregation );
```

Then, the sequential algorithms are wrapped to become parallel:

```
Algorithm A (transferBufferA, syncTransferA);
Algorithm B (transferBufferB, syncTransferB);
Algorithm C (transferBufferC, syncTransferC);

peoWrapper parallelA( A, dataA ); syncTransferA.setOwner
  ( parallelA );
peoWrapper parallelB( B, dataB ); syncTransferB.setOwner
  ( parallelB );
peoWrapper parallelC( C, dataC ); syncTransferC.setOwner
  ( parallelC );
```

The execution is easily launched using

```
peo :: run();
peo :: finalize();
```

The previous lines are sufficient to underline the power of ParadisEO–PEO in terms of flexibility and components reuse; for instance, changing the topology amounts replacing the `CompleteTopology` by `RingTopology` or any other.

6.4.2.7 Island Model of EAs Within ParadisEO Here is a summary of the code where two evolutionary algorithms synchronously exchange individuals according to a ring topology. The first island (EA $n1$) is defined as follows:

```
// Individual definition: a vector of real, fitness also real
typedef eoReal<double> Indi;
// EA n1 defined as eaAlg1
// ... //
// Migrants selection strategy n1
eoRandomSelect<Indi> mig_select_one;
eoSelector <Indi, eoPop<Indi> > mig_select (mig_select_one,
   MIG_SIZE,pop);
// Integration policy n1
```

```
eoPlusReplacement<Indi> replace;
eoReplace <Indi, eoPop<Indi> > mig_replace (replace,pop);
// Synchronous exchange from the EA n1
peoSyncIslandMig<eoPop<Indi>, eoPop<Indi> > mig1(MIG_FREQ,
                mig_select,mig_replace,topology);
// add the EA1's migrations to the checkpointing operation
checkpoint.add(mig1);
// the sequential EA n1 (some of the components used are not
   detailed here)
eoEasyEA< Indi > eaAlg1( checkpoint, eval, select, transform,
replace );
// transform the sequential EA to a parallelized one
peoWrapper parallelEA1( eaAlg1, pop);
// the migrations belong to the parallel EA n1
mig1.setOwner(parallelEA1);
```

A similar configuration is defined for the other island (EA *n*2):

```
// EA n2 defined as eaAlg2
// ... //
// Migrants selection strategy n2
eoRandomSelect<Indi> mig_select_one2;
eoSelector <Indi, eoPop<Indi> > mig_select2 (mig_select_one2,
  MIG_SIZE,pop);
// Integration policy n2
eoPlusReplacement<Indi> replace2;
eoReplace <Indi, eoPop<Indi> > mig_replace2 (replace2,pop);
// Synchronous exchange from the EA n2
peoSyncIslandMig<eoPop<Indi>, eoPop<Indi> > mig2(MIG_FREQ,
  mig_select2, mig_replace2,topology);
// add the EA2's migrations to the same checkpointing
operation checkpoint.add(mig2);
// the sequential EA n2 (some of the components used are not
   detailed)
eoEasyEA< Indi > eaAlg2( checkpoint, eval, select, transform,
replace );
// transform the sequential EA to a parallelized one
peoWrapper parallelEA2( eaAlg2, pop);
// the migrations belong to the parallel EA n2
mig.setOwner(parallelEA2);
```

The model is launched by simply adding

```
peo :: run();
peo :: finalize();
```

6.4.3 Design of Iteration-Level Parallel Models

In this section, the way the iteration-level parallel model is designed and implemented within ParadisEO–PEO is studied. This parallel model is concerned with the generic aspects referred to the parallelization of a single iteration of the metaheuristics. Generally, the operation units to parallelize are more or less independent. The behavior of the algorithm is not altered but its execution can be highly accelerated.

6.4.3.1 The Generic Multistart Paradigm Basically, in terms of implementation, a `multi-start` primitive applies the same calculation or operation to a set of entities having the same type (Fig. 6.40). With such a definition, the paradigm has no limit as it allows any program, repeating the same treatment on a set of units, to be executed much faster. The following are the design questions one has to answer to implement a multistart parallel model:

- What is the sequential algorithm that performs the multistart? In other words, what is the algorithm that treats the units in an independent and parallel manner?
- What are the data the multistart is applied to and what is the associated operation unit?
- Once they have been performed, how are the treatment units replaced or integrated into the main algorithm?

What is the sequential algorithm that performs the multistart? When using ParadisEO–PEO, any C++ code could take advantage of the multistart paradigm. The implementation is completely generic and the low-level mechanisms are transparent for the final user. The algorithm (structure, class, template, and so on) must simply embed an instantiation of the `peoMultiStart` template. It is a communicable service in ParadisEO–PEO. The only constraint is that the core of the algorithm must be contained or encapsulated into the `operator()`. The `peoMultiStart` template can be applied to any set of data having an iterator (in C++ terms). For instance, it can perform the same treatment on each element contained in a standard

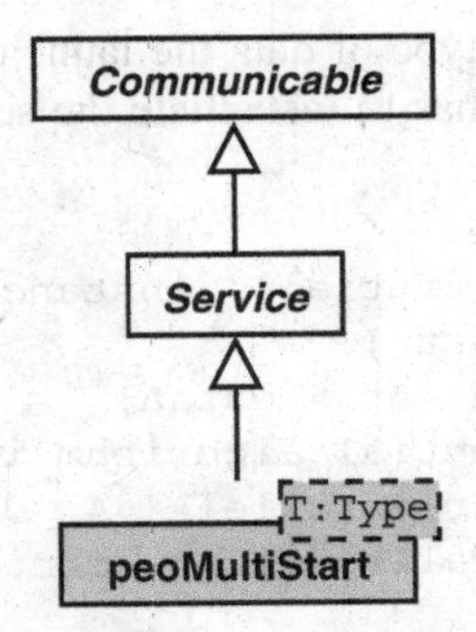

FIGURE 6.40 UML diagram of the multistart component available within ParadisEO–PEO.

vector. The following is an example of a generic structure using a `peoMultiStart`:

```
struct Algorithm {
  // a multiStart is expected to build the structure
  Algorithm( peoMultiStart< unsigned int >& extMultiStart )
    : multiStart( extMultiStart ) {}

  void operator()( std::vector< unsigned int >& data ) {
    // .... do any operation here ....
    // launch the multi-start using the data vector received
       as an argument
    multiStart( data );
  }

  peoMultiStart< unsigned int >& multiStart;
};
```

What are the data the multistart is applied to and what is the associated operation unit? The multistart cuts out a set of data, launches the operation unit using the master–slave paradigm on each data, gets back the results, and replaces the values. ParadisEO–PEO exactly gives the possibility of such generality. The operation unit can be any class, structure, or template implementing the `operator ()`. The following is a simple example where the parallelized treatment consists in putting a value squared.

```
// MultiStartAlg is the structure acting on each operation
unit struct MultiStartAlg {
void operator()( unsigned int& value ) {
    value *= value;
}
};
```

The multistart itself, embedding the previous structure, is specified by

```
peoMultiStart< unsigned int > multiStart( multiStartAlg );
```

The template specifies the type of data the launched algorithm will act on. The rest is quite simple. The user has to instantiate the sequential algorithm to make it parallel:

```
// creating the ''sequential'' instance of the algorithm
Algorithm A( multiStart );
std::vector< unsigned int > dataA;
// wrapping the sequential algorithm inside a parallel
environment peoWrapper parallelA( A, dataA );
// setOwner - the parallel environment controls the parallel
   component
multiStart.setOwner( parallelA );
```

Once they have been performed, how are the treatment units replaced or integrated into the main algorithm? For most of the cases, the transformed units are directly replaced by reference.

6.4.3.2 *Use of the Iteration-Level Model* There exist several common applications using the multistart paradigm, such as the generation and evaluation of the neighborhood in S-metaheuristics and the generation of successive populations in P-metaheuristics. Both can take advantage of the iteration-level model as it does not alter their behavior. For P-metaheuristics in general, the evaluation is by far the most costly step. Each member of the population is an independent unit and the evaluation can be easily performed in parallel. In ParadisEO–PEO, the parallel evaluation of a population in P-metaheuristics is directly integrated. One does not need to implement it as the template `peoPopEval` is already available (Fig. 6.41).

If a sequential EA is implemented, the user just has to replace

```
// the eval object acts on Indi (a vector of doubles) and
   return a double
eoEvalFuncPtr<Indi, double, const vector<double>& > plainEval
   ( real_value );
```

by

```
peoEvalFunc<Indi> plainEval(f);
peoPopEval <Indi> eval(plainEval);
```

and transform the sequential EA into a parallel one:

```
// pop is the population and ea the EA not detailed here
peoWrapper parallelEA( ea, pop);
eval.setOwner(parallelEA);
```

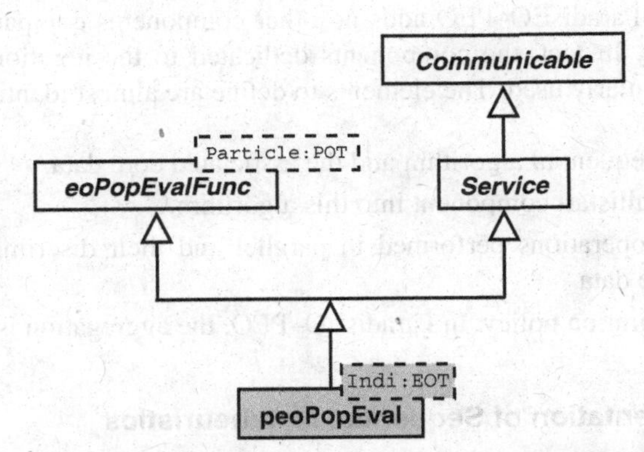

FIGURE 6.41 UML diagram of the peoPopEval template dedicated to the parallel evaluation of the population within ParadisEO.

Moreover, for neighborhood exploration, the same strategy is provided. For instance, if an EA deals with a population and if it needs to explore the neighborhood of all the individuals, the implementation with ParadisEO–PEO is straightforward. All the necessary components have been previously exposed.

```
// Initialization of a Hill-Climbing algorithm.
// The move is typed as a ``TwoOpt''
  TwoOptInit pmx_two_opt_init;
  TwoOptNext pmx_two_opt_next;
  TwoOptIncrEval pmx_two_opt_incr_eval;
  moBestImprSelect <TwoOpt> pmx_two_opt_move_select;
  moHC <TwoOpt> hc (pmx_two_opt_init, pmx_two_opt_next, pmx_
     two_opt_incr_eval, pmx_two_opt_move_select, full_eval);

  // Apply the local search on all the individuals (route) of
     a given population
  peoMultiStart <Route> initParallelHC (hc);
  peoWrapper parallelHC (initParallelHC, pop);
  initParallelHC.setOwner(parallelHC);
  peo :: run( );
  peo :: finalize( );
```

Finally, for EAs implemented with ParadisEO, the crossover and the mutation can be automatically performed in parallel. The template `peoTransform` exploits the same mechanisms. All the other operators applied to a whole population can be coded using the generic techniques already described.

6.4.4 Design of Solution-Level Parallel Models

In this model, problem-dependent operations are parallelized. The two models that may be carried out are a functional decomposition and a data decomposition. For the two aspects, ParadisEO–PEO adds no other components compared to the ones described before. In fact, the components dedicated to the iteration-level parallel model can be similarly used. The elements to define are almost identical:

- Define the sequential algorithm and the associated core data.
- Embed a multistart component into this algorithm.
- Define the operations performed in parallel and their discrimination criteria linked to the data.
- Set the integration policy. In ParadisEO–PEO, the aggregation is used.

6.4.5 Implementation of Sequential Metaheuristics

To implement a parallel metaheuristic, the first step consists in implementing a sequential algorithm, such as

- A sequential EA that is mainly composed of a reproduction class (`eoBreed`), an evaluation function (`eoPopEvalFunction`), a replacement class (`eoReplacement`), and a continuator class (`eoContinue`). Note that all the classes use a template parameter `Evolving Object Type` or `EOT` that defines the type of the individuals of the EA population. It must be instantiated by the user.
- A sequential PSO that is composed of a velocity class (`eoVelocity`), a topology class (`eoTopoloy`), a flight class (`eoFlight`), an evaluation function (`eoPopEval-Function`), and a continuator class (`eoContinue`). Note that all these classes use a template parameter `Particle Object Type` or `POT` that defines the type of the individuals of the PSO population. It must also be instantiated by the user.
- A sequential LS that is composed of generic classes and other classes specific to each local search method. Generic classes include `eoMoveInit` that allows to initialize a given movement, `eoNextMove` that enables the exploration of the neighborhood, and `eoMoveIncrEval` that computes the fitness value of a solution if a given movement is applied. Note that all the classes use a template parameter `Move Type` or `MOVET` that defines the movement type to be instantiated by the programmer.

To return the parallel algorithm, the algorithm has to be "wrapped," thanks to the component `peoWrapper` (Fig. 6.42). The execution of parallel components can be carried out inside the algorithm itself.

6.4.6 Implementation of Parallel and Distributed Algorithms

Different classes within ParadisEO–PEO (Fig. 6.43) allow to define the various models of parallelism:

- `peoPopEval`: The class `peoPopEval` inherits classes `Service` and `eoPopEvalFunc` (Fig. 6.44). It allows to manage automatically the stake in the pack of the data to send.

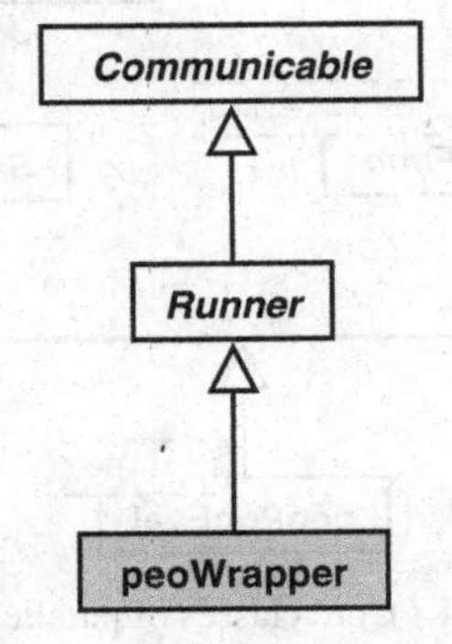

FIGURE 6.42 Core classes of wrapper.

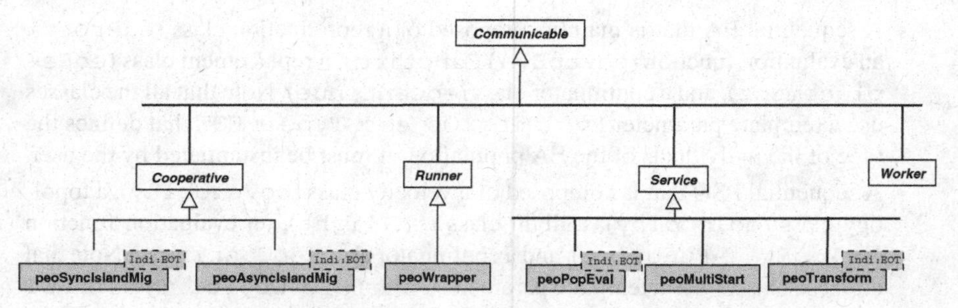

FIGURE 6.43 Core classes of ParadisEO–PEO.

- peoTransform: To make a parallel and distributed transformation, the ParadisEO framework gives the possibility of defining a peoTransform object (Fig. 6.45). This object allows, once incorporated into an algorithm, to perform a parallel and distributed operation of generating new solutions (e.g., reproduction of individuals in an EA using mutation and crossover operators).
- peoSyncIsland and peoAsyncIsland: The ParadisEO–PEO offers the required components for building in an easy manner a ring of evolutionary algorithms or/and particle swarm optimizers that exchange individuals across periodic migrations. Thus, insular models may be envisaged by grouping multiple algorithms as being part of the same topology.
- peoSyncIslandMigration and peoAsyncIslandMigration: These classes offer the support for synchronous and asynchronous migrations (Fig. 6.46).

Let us consider the following scenario in which the migration should occur every 10 generations. Moreover, one would like to have the control on selecting the individuals to exchange as well as on replacing the current individuals with

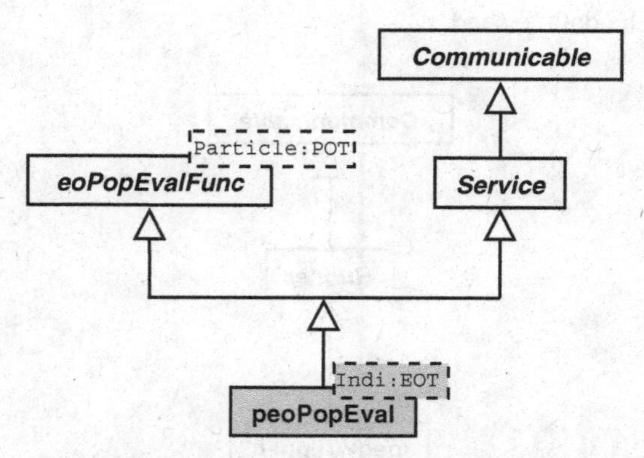

FIGURE 6.44 Core classes of parallel evaluation.

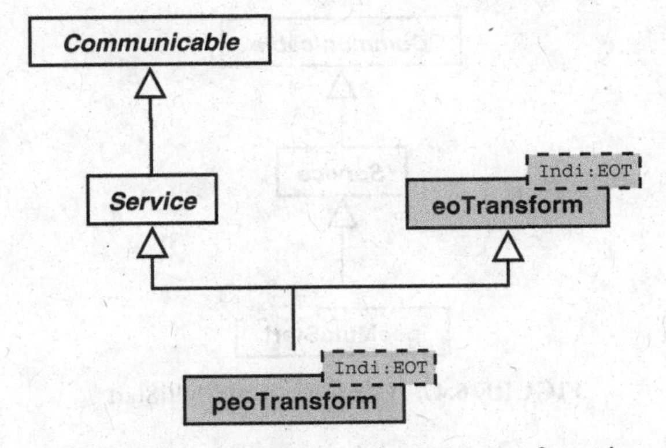

FIGURE 6.45 Core classes of parallel transformation.

the immigrant ones. In other words, constructing an insular migration model consists in

- Having a ring topological model including several evolutionary algorithms and particle swarm optimizers.
- Defining the migration frequency as well as the size of the migration.
- Selecting the emigrant individuals and integrating the immigrant ones.

- `peoMultiStart`: The class `peoMultiStart` inherits from the class Service (Fig. 6.47). It has a leading part in managing the launch of several algorithms at the same time. This class is often used to realize a hybridization between a metaheuristic and a local search.

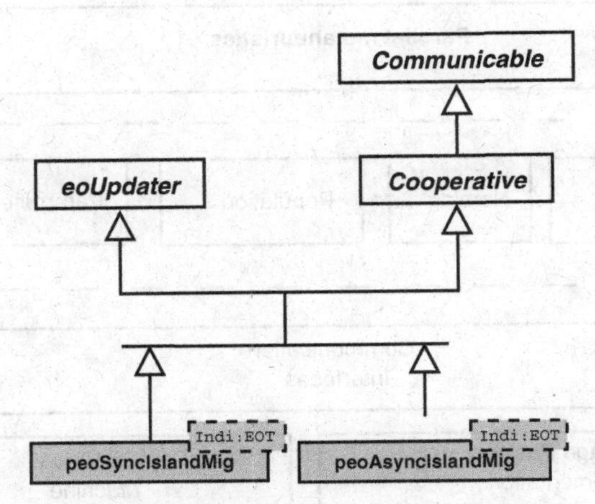

FIGURE 6.46 Core classes of island model.

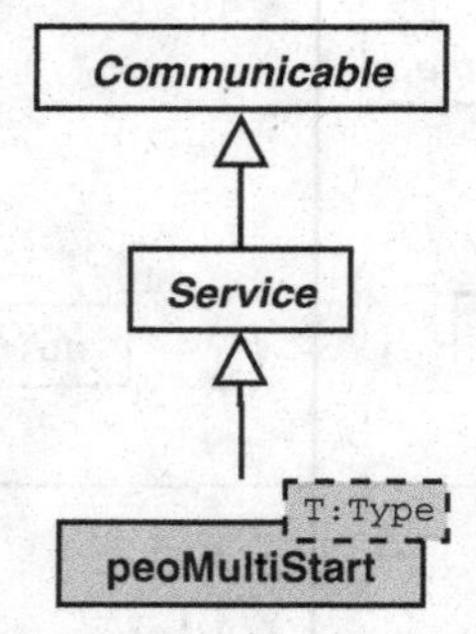

FIGURE 6.47 Core classes of MultiStart.

6.4.7 Deployment of ParadisEO–PEO

ParadisEO offers transparency in the sense that the user does not have to explicitly deal with parallel programming. One has just to instantiate the needed ParadisEO components. The implementation is portable on distributed-memory machines as well as on shared-memory multiprocessors. The user has not to manage the communications and thread-based concurrency. Moreover, the same parallel design (i.e., the same program) is portable over different architectures. Hence, ParadisEO–PEO has been implemented on different parallel programming environments and middlewares (MPI, Pthreads, Condor, Globus) that are adapted to different target architectures (shared and distributed memory, cluster and network of workstations, desktop and high-performance grid computing platforms) (Fig. 6.49).

The deployment of the presented parallel/distributed models is transparent for the user. In ParadisEO, as illustrated in Fig. 6.48, the communication scheme is composed of a communication interface that is based on message passing over a virtual machine.

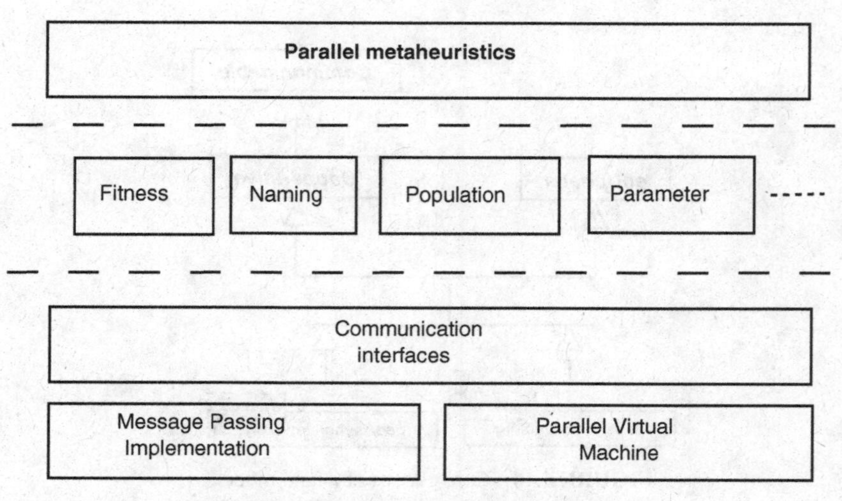

FIGURE 6.48 ParadisEO communication layers.

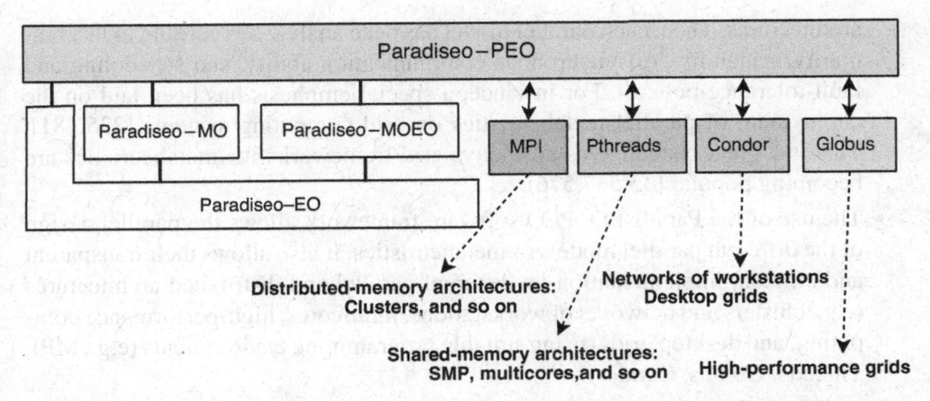

FIGURE 6.49 ParadisEO–PEO implementation under different parallel programming environments and middlewares.

6.5 CONCLUSIONS AND PERSPECTIVES

On one hand, optimization problems are more and more complex and their requirements are ever increasing. On the other hand, the rapid development of technology in designing processors (e.g., multicore, GPU, FPGA), networks (e.g., Infiniband, optical networks), and data storage has made the use of parallel computing more and more popular. Moreover, the cost/performance ratio in parallel computing systems is constantly decreasing.

Parallel and distributed computing can be used in the design and implementation of metaheuristics to speed up the search, to improve the quality of the obtained solutions, to improve the robustness, and to solve large-scale problems.

The clear separation between parallel design and parallel implementation aspects of metaheuristics is important to analyze parallel (multiobjective) metaheuristics. The key points of this chapter can be summarized as follows:

- In terms of parallel design, the different parallel models for monoobjective and multiobjective metaheuristics have been unified. Three hierarchical parallel models have been extracted: algorithmic-level, iteration-level, and solution-level parallel models. Hence, the same parallel models may be instantiated to different S-metaheuristics, P-metaheuristics, and multiobjective metaheuristics in a unified manner.
- In terms of parallel implementation, the question of an efficient mapping of a parallel model of metaheuristics on a given parallel architecture and programming environment (i.e., language, library, middleware) is handled. The focus is on the key criteria of parallel architectures that influence the efficient implementation of parallel metaheuristics: shared memory versus distributed memory, homogeneous versus heterogeneous, shared versus nonshared, local area network versus wide area network, and volatile versus nonvolatile

architectures. Then, each parallel model has been analyzed according to its granularity, scalability, (a)synchronous communication ability, and scheduling and fault-tolerance policies. For instance, a special emphasis has been laid on the deployment of parallel metaheuristics on grid computing systems [235,281]. This is a great challenge as nowadays grid frameworks for metaheuristics are becoming popular [35,537,576].

- The use of the ParadisEO–PEO software framework allows the parallel design of the different parallel models of metaheuristics. It also allows their transparent and efficient implementation on different parallel and distributed architectures (e.g., clusters and networks of workstations, multicores, high-performance computing, and desktop grids) using suitable programming environments (e.g., MPI, Threads, Globus, Condor).

One of the challenges in the coming years is to achieve Petascale performance. The emergence of multicore chips and many-core chips (i.e., GPU) technologies will speed up the achievement of this goal. In terms of programming models, cloud computing and peer-to-peer (P2P) computing will become an important alternative to traditional high-performance computing for the development of large-scale metaheuristics that harness massive computational resources. This is a great challenge as nowadays cloud and P2P-enabled frameworks for parallel metaheuristics are just emerging. A pure peer-to-peer computing system does not have the notion of clients or servers but only equal peer nodes that simultaneously function as both clients and servers to the other nodes on the network. Cloud computing is generally made available on the Internet (i.e., IP availability). Users of the cloud have access to the resources that are owned and operated by a third party on a consolidated basis. They are concerned with services it can perform rather than the underlying technologies used to perform the requested function.

In the future design of high-performance computers, the ratio between power and performance will be increasingly important. The power represents the electrical power consumption of the computer. An excess in power consumption uses unnecessary energy, generates waste heat, and decreases reliability. Very few vendors of high-performance architecture publicize the power consumption data compared to the performance data[18].

In terms of target optimization problems, parallel metaheuristics constitute unavoidable approaches to solve the large-scale real-life challenging problems (e.g., engineering design, drug design) [757]. They are also one of the important alternatives to solve dynamic and robust optimization problems, in which the complexities in terms of time and quality are more difficult to handle by traditional sequential approaches. Moreover, parallel models for optimization problems with uncertainty have to be deeply investigated.

[18]The Web site `www.green500.org` rank the top500 machines using the number of megaflops they produce for each watt of power and serve as complementary to the `www.top500.org` site.

6.6 EXERCISES

Exercise 6.1 Independent multistart search for S-metaheuristics. In heterogeneous independent multistart parallel models for S-metaheuristics, one can use different parameter settings or various search components. Propose such parallel models for tabu search, simulated annealing, and variable neighborhood search.

Exercise 6.2 Algorithmic-level parallel model for P-metaheuristics. In designing a parallel cooperative model for a metaheuristic, one has to answer the following design questions: the exchange decision criterion (when?), the exchange topology (where?), the information exchanged (what?), and the integration policy (how?). Propose such parallel models for scatter search algorithms and estimation distribution algorithms. Enumerate some alternatives for every design question.

Exercise 6.3 Algorithmic-level design for evolutionary algorithms and scatter search. Is there any difference in the design of an algorithmic-level parallel model for evolutionary algorithms and scatter search? Which design answers can be reused from each metaheuristic?

Exercise 6.4 Dynamic load balancing for an algorithmic-level parallel independent model. A straightforward parallel model for the multistart local search is based on parallelizing the different searches. For a heterogeneous or nonshared parallel machine such as a network of heterogeneous workstations, a static load balancing strategy will not be effective. Let us consider a parallel model that is based on the master/workers paradigm, in which the master distributes the work and the workers realize the different searches. Propose a simple dynamic load balancing algorithm to schedule the different searches on the processors. Let us suppose k searches and n processors with $k \gg n$. A minimal granularity m can be defined as $m = (k/q)$, where $q \ll n$. It defines the minimum number of local searches a processor will handle.

Exercise 6.5 Adaptive topology of communication. In the algorithmic-level parallel model, only static topologies of communication between metaheuristics (e.g., ring, mesh, hypercube, complete graph) have been outlined. An adaptive topology may be seen as a dynamic graph where the set of edges or nodes is updated during the search. What are the advantages of using such adaptive topologies? What are the events that can be used that cause the changes?

Exercise 6.6 Algorithmic-level parallel model for ACO. Our goal is to adapt the well-known island model of evolutionary algorithms to ant colony optimization (ACO) algorithms. Given a set of ant colonies connected by a given topology, which strategies can be applied to exchanged information between the colonies. For each type of information exchange, specify the integration procedure of the information received in the destination colony.

Exercise 6.7 Irregular parallel metaheuristics. Dynamic load balancing is an important issue for irregular parallel metaheuristics in which the execution time cannot be predicted at compile time and it varies over the iterations. Give some search components of metaheuristics (e.g., S-metaheuristics, P-metaheuristics) and optimization problems that can generate this irregularity.

Exercise 6.8 Adaptive scheduling for a parallel GRASP. As mentioned in Example 6.5, a parallel straightforward model for the GRASP metaheuristic is based on parallelizing the different iterations. For a heterogeneous and volatile parallel machine such as a desktop grid, a static load balancing strategy will not be effective. Let us consider a parallel model that is based on the master/workers paradigm, in which the master distributes the work and the workers realize the different iterations. Propose a simple adaptive load balancing algorithm to schedule the different iterations of the GRASP metaheuristic on the processors of a desktop grid. Let us suppose k iterations and n processors with $k \gg n$. A minimal granularity m can be defined as $m = (k/q)$, where $q \ll n$. It defines the minimum number of local searches a processor will handle on a large network based architecture.

Exercise 6.9 Parallel genetic programming. In genetic programming, the individuals may vary widely in size. Hence, the complexity of computing their objective function may vary. What is the impact on the parallel implementation of the three parallel models (algorithmic level, iteration level, solution level) on a homogeneous cluster of processors. Analyze each situation and propose some solutions for each parallel model.

Exercise 6.10 Parallel models for bee colony optimization. Bee-colony-based optimization algorithms are mainly based on two different models: food foraging and marriage in the bee colony. They are intrinsically parallel models in which independent agents cooperate for food foraging and compete for queen's marriage. Indeed, the bee colony has a decentralized system to collect the food. In comparison to ant colony algorithms, it will be relatively easier to treat each bee forager as an independent agent since the issue of sharing information (e.g., pheromones) does not occur. Design some parallel models for bee algorithms that are inspired by food foraging and/or marriage in the bee colony.

Exercise 6.11 Parallel models in minmax problems. Minmax continuous optimization problems initiated by Von Neumann have the form

$$\min_{x \in X}\{\max_{y \in Y}\{f(x, y)\}\}$$

where $X \subseteq R^n$ and $Y \subseteq R^n$, and $f(x, y)$ is a function defined on the product of the two sets X and Y. Minmax problems play an important role in many domains such as game theory and optimization [226]. The problem may be stated as follows:

$$\min\{g(x) : x \in X\}$$

where

$$g(x) = \max\{f(x, y) : y \in Y\}$$

Propose a parallel hierarchical nested model to solve this class of important problems.

Exercise 6.12 Implementation of the hierarchical parallel model. Our goal is to use the three models of parallel metaheuristics in conjunction in a hierarchical way. The degree of concurrency of this model is $c = k \times m \times n$, where k is the number of metaheuristics used, m is the size of the population or the neighborhood, and n is the number of partitions or tasks associated with the evaluation of a single solution. Given a cluster of N processors that is, in general, much less than the degree of concurrency c, propose a partitioning–scheduling algorithm that maps the parallel model on the parallel architecture.

Exercise 6.13 Parallel path relinking. Let us consider the hybrid path relinking strategy presented in Example 5.26 to solve a multiobjective optimization problem. Propose a parallel model for this hybrid scheme.

Exercise 6.14 Parallel Pareto local search. Let us consider the hybrid Pareto local search algorithm presented in Algorithm 5.2 to solve a multiobjective optimization problem. Propose a parallel model for this hybrid scheme.

Exercise 6.15 Parallel target aiming Pareto search. Let us consider the HRH hybrid algorithm target aiming Pareto search (TAPAS) presented in Example 5.25 to solve multiobjective optimization problems. Design and implement a parallel model for this hybrid metaheuristic. Consider different parallel architectures to implement this parallel model.

Exercise 6.16 Flexibility of the algorithmic-level parallel model under ParadisEO. Given an algorithmic-level parallel model developed under ParadisEO–MO to solve an optimization problem (see Section 6.4.2 or many examples on the Web site on the framework), what the user has to perform if he wants to

- Transform the communication topology.
- Modify the replacement strategy.
- Change the information to be exchanged.
- Update the migration criterion in case of an asynchronous exchange.
- Change the frequency of exchange in case of a synchronous exchange.

Exercise 6.17 Heterogeneous algorithmic-level parallel model. Let us notice that already implemented particle swarm optimization algorithms and evolutionary algorithms are available under ParadisEO. Our objective is to design a heterogeneous parallel model in which two particle swarm optimizers cooperate with an evolutionary

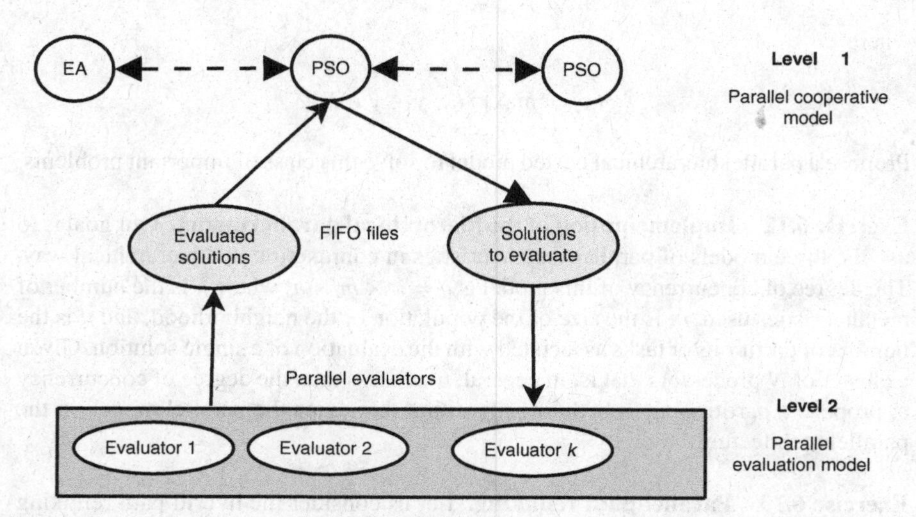

FIGURE 6.50 Cooperation between two PSO algorithms and an EA using the algorithmic-level parallel model.

algorithm (Fig. 6.50). For instance, the algorithms exchange their best solutions using a linear topology.

It is also possible to combine the algorithmic-level parallel model with the iteration-level parallel model. In each P-metaheuristic (PSO, EA), the solutions (individuals in EA and particles in PSO) are evaluated in parallel. Design and implement such a parallel hybrid model under ParadisEO–PEO.

APPENDIX

UML and C++

A.1 A BRIEF OVERVIEW OF UML NOTATIONS

In this section, a brief description of the UML notation is presented [86]. The focus is only on the diagrams and notations that are used in this book. UML stands for Unified Modeling Language. Today, it is accepted by the Object Management Group (OMG[1]) as the standard for modeling object-oriented programs. UML defines nine types of diagrams. In this book, only *class diagrams* have been used.

Class diagrams are the backbone of UML. They describe the static structure of our framework. The goal of a class diagram is to define the classes within a model and their relationships. In an object-oriented program, classes are defined by their attributes (member variables), their operations (member functions), and their relationships with other classes.

Let us give an overview of the main diagrams used: classes and active classes, composition and aggregation, generalization, and templates and template parameters.

- **Classes and active classes:** The classes designate an abstraction of entities with common characteristics. They are illustrated in Fig. A.1a with rectangles divided into compartments. The partitions contain the class name (centered, bold, and capitalized), the list of attributes, and the list of operations. To make the figures readable, only the first partition is represented. Active classes shown in Fig. A.1b allow to initiate and control the flow of activity, while passive classes store data and serve other classes.
- **Composition and aggregation:** An aggregation relationship is an ownership between *Class A*, the whole (or aggregate), and *Class B*, its part. *Class A* plays a more important role than *Class B*, but the two classes are not dependent on each other. Aggregation is illustrated in Fig. A.1c by a hollow diamond that points toward the whole class.

[1]http://www.uml.org/.

Metaheuristics: From Design to Implementation, by El-Ghazali Talbi

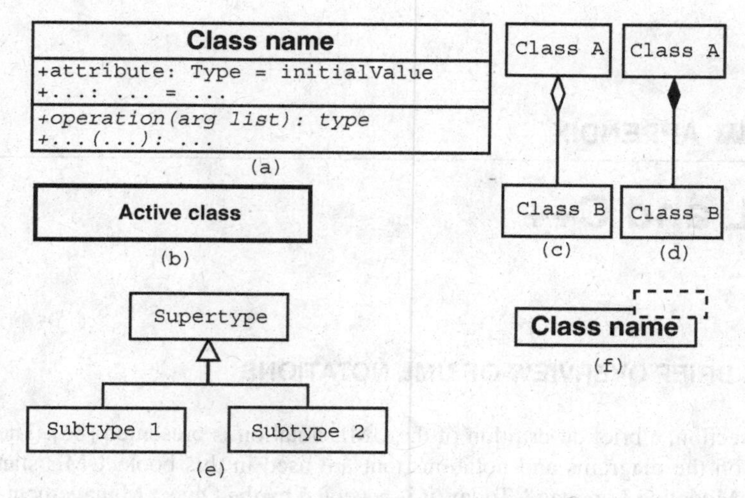

FIGURE A.1 Basic UML class diagram symbols and notations.

Composition is a special type of aggregation that denotes a strong ownership between *Class A* and *Class B*. It is illustrated in Fig. A.1d by a filled diamond that points toward the whole class. For instance, each instance of type `Population` that represents a population of solutions will contain an instance of type `Individual` that represents a single solution.

- **Generalization:** Generalization is another name of inheritance ("is a" relationship). This is represented by Fig. A.1e. Let us notice that it is possible to have multiple inheritance relationships.
- **Templates and template parameters:** Templates are generic classes that are represented by dashed rectangles. When they serve as parameters for a given class, they are represented at the top-right corner of that class (see Fig. A.1f).

For a more detailed presentation of the UML notation, the reader can refer to Ref. [86].

A.2 A BRIEF OVERVIEW OF THE C++ TEMPLATE CONCEPT

Many important concepts are introduced in object-oriented programming such as abstraction, encapsulation, inheritance, and polymorphism. Those concepts allow a better understanding of the requirements of an application, a better quality design, reusable code, and a more easy maintainable software.

The most important object-oriented programming concept used in the ParadisEO framework is the *template* paradigm. This allows a more efficient reuse of the code than in standard classes.

Templates constitute extension of the class concept. They provide the same set of functionalities as classes but can operate on multiple data types (i.e., generic types).

Hence, only one template class with multiple data types is required instead of defining a class for each data type. Using templates, a data type is passed as a parameter.

For instance, consider the encoding part of a metaheuristic. The representation (or encoding) will be defined in a template. In a standard class, each class will be restricted to a given representation (e.g., permutation, binary vector, tree, and real-values vector). Using templates, only one template will be used to operate on various representations. In addition to the compactness of the code, this will improve the ease of use of the software and its flexibility. Moreover, templates are of great utility when combined with *multiple inheritance* and *operator overloading*.

There are two kinds of templates: *function templates* and *class templates*. A function template behaves like a function that can accept arguments of many types. The algorithm A.1 below shows a function template that computes the maximum of two elements of unknown types. For instance, this function template is useful to compare two solutions (e.g., individuals) into metaheuristics.

Algorithm A.1 Function template.

```
template <typename T>
const T& maximum(const T& x, const T& y)
{
  if (y > x)
    return y ;
  else
    return x ;
}
```

The user can use the same function for many different data types. The type to be compared is given to the template:

```
maximum<int>(4, 8) ; // for integers
maximum<double>(4.0, 8.0) ; // for doubles
```

A class template defines a set of generic functions that operate on the type specified for each instance of the class (i.e., the parameter between the angle brackets, as shown in the following algorithm A.2).

Algorithm A.2 Class template.

```
template <class T>
class multiply {
  T result ;
 public:
  multiply (T first, T second)
  {
   result = first * second ;
  }
};
```

The defined class serves to multiply two elements of any valid type. For instance, if one wanted to declare an object of this class to multiply two integers of type `int` with the values `110` and `27`, one would write

```
multiply<int> myobject (110, 27) ;
```

The same class can also be used to create an object to multiply any other type, for instance, two elements of type `double`:

```
multiply<double> myfloats (5.2, 4.54) ;
```

The compiler will generate the appropriate function code at compile time for the parameter type that appears between the brackets. For a comprehensive presentation of the C++ language and templates, the reader may refer to `http://www.cplusplus.com/`.

References

1. E. H. L. Aarts and J. Korst. *Simulated Annealing and Boltzmann Machines*. Wiley, 1989.
2. E. H. L. Aarts and R. J. M. Van Laarhoven. *Simulated Annealing: Theory and Applications*. Reidel, Dordrecht, 1987.
3. E. H. L. Aarts and J. K. Lenstra. *Local Search in Combinatorial Optimization*. Wiley, 1997.
4. H. A. Abbas. Marriage in honey bees optimization: A haplometrosis polygynous swarming approach. In *CEC'2001 Congress on Evolutionary Computation*, Seoul, Korea, 2001, pp. 207–214.
5. F. Abbattista, N. Abbattista, and L. Caponetti. An evolutionary and cooperative agent model for optimization. In *IEEE International Conference on Evolutionary Computation (ICEC'95)*, Perth, Australia, Dec 1995, pp. 668–671.
6. F. Ben Abdelaziz, S. Krichen, and J. Chaouachi. A hybrid heuristic for multi-objective knapsack problems. In *Meta-Heuristics: Advances and Trends in Local Search Paradigms for Optimization*. Kluwer Academic Publishers, 1999, pp. 205–212.
7. D. Abramson, P. Logothetis, A. Postula, and M. Randall. Application specific computers for combinatorial optimisation. In *Australian Computer Architecture Workshop*, Sydney, Australia, Feb 1997.
8. D. A. Abramson. A very high speed architecture to support simulated annealing. *IEEE Computer*, 25:27–34, 1992.
9. P. Adamidis and V. Petridis. Co-operating populations with different evolution behaviours. In *3rd IEEE Conference on Evolutionary Computation*, Nagoya, Japan, May 1996. IEEE Press, 1996, pp. 188–191.
10. J. Adams, E. D. Rothman, W. E. Kerr, and Z. L. Paulino. Estimation of the number of sex alleles and queen matings from diploid male frequencies in a population of *Apis mellifera*. *Genetics*, 86:583–596, 1972.
11. C. C. Aggarwal, J. B. Orlin, and R. P. Tai. An optimized crossover for the maximum independent set. *Operations Research*, 45:226–234, 1997.
12. D. K. Agrafiotis. Multiobjective optimization of combinatorial libraries. Technical Report, *IBM Journal of Research and Development*, 2001.

---

13. C. W. Ahn, D. E. Goldberg, and R. S. Ramakrishna. Multiple-deme parallel estimation of distribution algorithms: Basic framework and application. Technical Report 2003016, University of Illinois, USA, 2003.

14. R. K. Ahuja, O. Ergun, J. B. Orlin, and A. P. Punnen. A survey of very large scale neighborhood search techniques. *Discrete Applied Mathematics*, 123:75–102, 2002.

15. R. K. Ahuja, J. B. Orlin, and D. Sharma. Very large-scale neighborhood search. *International Transactions in Operational Research*, 7:301–317, 2000.

16. R. K. Ahuja, J. B. Orlin, and D. Sharma. New neighborhood search structures for the capacitated minimum spanning tree problem. Research Report 99-2, Department of Industrial, Systems Engineering, University of Florida, 1999.

17. U. Aicklein, P. Bentley, S. Cayser, K. Jungwon, and J. McLeod. Danger theory: The link between AIS and IDS. In *ICARIS International Conference on Artificial Immune Systems*, LNCS Vol. 2787. Springer, 2003, pp. 147–155.

18. R. M. Aiex, S. Binato, and R. S. Ramakrishna. Parallel GRASP with path relinking for job shop scheduling. *Parallel Computing*, 29:393–430, 2003.

19. R. M. Aiex, S. L. Martins, C. C. Ribeiro, and N. R. Rodriguez. Cooperation multi-thread parallel tabu search with an application to circuit partitioning. In *Solving Irregularly Structured Problems in Parallel*, LNCS Vol. 1457 Springer, 1998, pp. 310–331.

20. R. M. Aiex, M. G. C. Resende, and C. C. Ribeiro. Probability distribution of solution time in GRASP: An experimental investigation. *Journal of Heuristics*, 8(3):343–373, 2002.

21. A. Al-Yamani, S. Sait, and H. Youssef. Parallelizing tabu search on a cluster of heterogeneous workstations. *Journal of Heuristics*, 8(3):277–304, 2002.

22. E. Alba, F. Almeida, M. Blesa, C. Cotta, M. Díaz, I. Dorta, J. Gabarró, J. González, C. León, L. Moreno, J. Petit, J. Roda, A. Rojas, and F. Xhafa. MALLBA: A library of skeletons for combinatorial optimisation. In B. Monien and R. Feldman, editors, *Euro-Par 2002 Parallel Processing Conference*, LNCS Vol. 2400. Springer, Berlin, 2002, pp. 927–932.

23. E. Alba, F. Luna, A. J. Nebro, and J. M. Troya. Parallel heterogeneous genetic algorithms for continuous optimization. *Parallel Computing*, 30:699–719, 2004.

24. E. Alba, E.-G. Talbi, G. Luque, and N. Melab. Metaheuristics and parallelism. In *Parallel Metaheuristics*. Wiley, 2005.

25. M. M. Ali, A. Torn, and S. Viitanen. A direct search variant of the simulated annealing algorithm for optimization involving continuous variables. *Computers and Operations Research*, 29:87–102, 2002.

26. D. J. Aloise, D. Aloise, C. T. M. Rocha, C. C. Ribeiro, J. C. Ribeiro Filho, and L. S. S. Moura. Scheduling workover rigs for onshore oil production. *Discrete Applied Mathematics*, 154(5):695–702, 2006.

27. L. Altenberg. Fitness distance correlation analysis: An instructive counterexample. In T. Bäck, editor, *7th International Conference on Genetic Algorithms*. Morgan Kaufmann, 1997, pp. 57–64.

28. I. Althofer and K.-U. Koschnick. On the convergence of threshold accepting. *Applied Mathematics and Optimization*, 24:183–195, 1991.

29. E. Angel and V. Zissimopoulos. Autocorrelation coefficient for the graph bipartitioning problem. *Theoretical Computer Science*, 191(1–2):229–243, 1998.

30. E. Angel and V. Zissimopoulos. On the landscape ruggedness of the quadratic assignment problem. *Theoretical Computer Science*, 263:159–172, 2001.

31. G. Appa, L. Pitsoulis, and H. P. Williams. *Handbook on Modeling for Discrete Optimization*. Springer, 2006.

32. D. Applegate, R. Bixby, and V. Chvatal. On the solution of traveling salesman problems. *Documenta Mathematica*, 3:645–656, 1998.

33. D. Applegate and W. Cook. A computational study of the job-shop scheduling problem. *ORSA Journal on Computing*, 3:149–156, 1991.

34. K. Apt. *Principles of Constraint Programming*. Cambridge University Press, 2003.

35. M. G. Arenas, P. Collet, A. E. Eiben, M. Jelasity, J. J. Merelo, B. Paechter, M. Preuss, and M. Schoenauer. A framework for distributed evolutionary algorithms. In *Proceedings of the Parallel Problem Solving from Nature Conference (PPSN VII)*, Sept 2002, LNCS Vol. 2439. Springer, 2002, pp. 665–675.

36. J. Arthur and J. Frendewey. Generating traveling salesmen problems with known optimal tours. *Journal of the Operational Research Society*, 39(2):153–159, 1988.

37. M. J. Atallah. *Handbook of Algorithms and Theory of Computing*. CRC Press, 1999.

38. J. B. Atkinson. A greedy look-ahead heuristic for combinatorial optimization: An application to vehicle scheduling with time windows. *Journal of the Operational Research Society*, 45:673–684, 1994.

39. P. Augerat, J. M. Belenguer, E. Benavent, A. Corberan, and D. Naddef. Separating capacity constraints in the CVRP using tabu search. *European Journal of Operational Research*, 106(2):546–557, 1998.

40. R. Axelrod and W. D. Hamilton. The evolution of cooperation. *Science*, 211:1390–1396, 1997.

41. R. Azencott. *Simulated Annealing: Parallelization Techniques*. Wiley, New York, 1992.

42. V. Bachelet, P. Preux, and E.-G. Talbi. The landscape of the quadratic assignment problem and local search methods. In *10th Meeting of the European Chapter on Combinatorial Optimization*, Tenerife, Canary Islands, Spain, May 1997.

43. T. Bäck. *Evolutionary Computation in Theory and Practice*. Oxford University Press, Oxford, UK, 1996.

44. T. Bäck, D. B. Fogel, and T. Michalewicz. *Evolutionary Computation: Basic Algorithms and Operators*. Institute of Physics Publishing, 2000.

45. T. Bäck, D. B. Fogel, and Z. Michalewicz, editors. *Handbook of Evolutionary Computation*. Oxford University Press, 1997.

46. E. Balas and W. Niehaus. Optimized crossover-based genetic algorithms for the maximum cardinality and maximum weight clique problems. *Journal of Heuristics*, 4(2):107–122, 1998.

47. S. Baluja. Population based incremental learning: A method for integrating genetic search based function optimization and competitive learning. Technical Report CMU-CS-94-163, Carnegie Mellon University, Pittsburgh, PA, 1994.

48. S. Baluja and R. Caruana. Removing the genetics from the standard genetic algorithm. In A. Prieditis et al., editor, *International Conference on Machine Learning*. Morgan Kaufmann, San Mateo, CA, 1995, pp. 38–46.

49. B. Baran and M. Schaerer. A multiobjective ant colony system for vehicle routing problem with time windows. In M. H. Hamza, editor, *21st IASTED International Conference on Applied Informatics*, Innsbruck, Austria. Acta Press, 2003, pp. 97–102.

50. C. Barnhart, E. L. Johnson, G. L. Nemhauser, M. W. P. Savelsbergh, and P. H. Vance. Branch-and-price: Column generation for huge integer programs. *Operations Research*, 46:316–329, 1998.

51. B. S. Barr, B. L. Golden, J. P. Kelly, M. G. C. Resende, and W. R. Stewart. Designing and reporting on computational experiments with heuristic methods. *Journal of Heuristics*, 46:9–32, 1995.

52. J.-F. M. Barthelemy and R. T. Haftka. Approximation concepts for optimum structural design: A review. *Structural Optimization*, 5:129–144, 1993.

53. T. Bartz-Beielstein. *Experimental Research in Evolutionary Computation*. Springer, 2006.

54. M. Basseur and E. K. Burke. Indicator-based multi-objective local search. In *CEC'2007 Congress on Evolutionary Computation*, Singapore, 2007, pp. 3100–3107.

55. M. Basseur, J. Lemesre, C. Dhaenens, and E.-G. Talbi. Cooperation between branch and bound and evolutionary approaches to solve a biobjective flow shop problem. In *Workshop on Experimental Algorithms (WEA'04)*, LNCS Vol. 3059. Springer, 2004, pp. 72–86.

56. M. Basseur, F. Seynhaeve, and E.-G. Talbi. Design of multi-objective evolutionary algorithms: Application to the flow-shop scheduling problem. In *Congress on Evolutionary Computation (CEC'02)*, Honolulu, HI, May 2002, pp. 1151–1156.

57. M. Basseur, F. Seynhaeve, and E.-G. Talbi. Adaptive mechanisms for multi-objective evolutionary algorithms. In *Congress on Engineering in System Application (CESA'03)*, Lille, France, 2003, pp. 72–86.

58. M. Basseur, F. Seynhaeve, and E.-G. Talbi. Path relinking in Pareto multi-objective genetic algorithms. In C. A. Coello Coello, A. H. Aguirre, and E. Zitzler, editors, *Evolutionary Multi-Criterion Optimization, (EMO'2005)*, LNCS Vol. 3410, Guanajuato, Mexico. Springer, 2005, pp. 120–134.

59. R. Battiti and G. Tecchiolli. The reactive tabu search. *ORSA Journal on Computing*, 6:126–140, 1994.

60. E. B. Baum. Iterated descent: A better algorithm for local search in combinatorial optimization problems. Technical Report 164-30, Crellin Laboratory, California Institute of Technology, Pasadena, CA, 1986.

61. U. Baumgartner, C. Magele, and W. Renhart. Pareto optimality and particle swarm optimization. *IEEE Transactions on Magnetics*, 40(2):1172–1175, 2004.

62. J. C. Bean. Genetic algorithm and random keys for sequencing and optimization. *ORSA Journal on Computing*, 6:154–160, 1994.

63. J. E. Beasley. OR-Library: Distributing test problems by electronic mail. *Journal of the Operational Research Society*, 41(11):1069–1072, 1990.

64. R. P. Beausoleil. Multiple criteria scatter search. In *4th Metaheuristics International Conference (MIC'01)*, Porto, Portugal, 2001, pp. 539–544.

65. R. P. Beausoleil. Moss: Multiobjective scatter search applied to non-linear multiple criteria optimization. *European Journal of Operational Research*, 169(2):426–449, 2006.

66. T. Belding. The distributed genetic algorithm revisited. In D. Eshelmann, editor, *6th International Conference on Genetic Algorithms*, Morgan Kaufmann, San Mateo, CA, 1995.

67. R. K. Belew, J. McInerny, and N. N. Schraudolph. Evolving networks: Using genetic algorithms with connectionist learning. In C. G. Langton, C. Taylor, J. D. Doyne Farmer, and S. Rasmussen, editors, *2nd Conference on Artificial Life*. Addison-Wesley, USA, 1991, pp. 511–548.

68. R. Bellman. *Dynamic Programming*. Princeton University Press, Princeton, NJ, 1957.

69. J. F. Benders. Partitioning procedures for solving mixed-variables programming problems. *Numerische Mathematik*, 4:238–252, 1962.

70. H. Bersini and F. J. Varela. Hints for adaptive problem solving gleaned from immune networks. In *Parallel Problem Solving from Nature*, Dortmund, Germany, LNCS Vol. 496. Springer, 1990, pp. 343–354.

71. D. P. Bertsekas. *Network Optimization: Continuous and Discrete Models*. Athena Scientific, Belmont, MA, 1998.

72. D. P. Bertsekas. *Nonlinear Programming*. Athena Scientific, Belmont, MA, 2004.

73. H.-G. Beyer. *The Theory of Evolution Strategies*. Springer, 2001.

74. H.-G. Beyer and B. Sendhoff. Robust optimization: A comprehensive survey. *Computer Methods in Applied Mechanics and Engineering*, 196(33):3190–3218, 2007.

75. G. Bilchev and I. C. Parmee. The ant colony metaphor for searching continuous design spaces. In *Selected Papers from AISB Workshop on Evolutionary Computing*, London, UK, LNCS Vol. 993. Springer, 1995, pp. 25–39.

76. M. Birattari, T. Stutzle, L. Paquete, and K. Varrentrapp. A racing algorithm for configuring metaheuristics. In W. B. Langdon et al., editors, *Proceedings of the Genetic and Evolutionary Computation Conference (GECCO'2002)*, Morgan Kaufmann, San Francisco, CA, 2002, pp. 11–18.

77. S. Bitam, M. Batouche, and E.-G. Talbi. A taxonomy of artificial honeybee colony optimization. In E.-G. Talbi and K. Mellouli, editors, *META'08 International Conference on Metaheuristics and Nature Inspired Computing*, Hammamet, Tunisia, Oct 2008.

78. J. L. Blanton and R. L. Wainwright. Multiple vehicle routing with time and capacity constraints using genetic algorithms. In S. Forrest, editor, *5th International Conference on Genetic Algorithms*. Morgan Kaufmann, San Mateo, CA, 1993, pp. 452–459.

79. M. J. Blesa, L. Hernandez, and F. Xhafa. Parallel skeletons for tabu search method. In *8th International Conference on Parallel and Distributed Systems*, Korea. IEEE Computer Society Press, 2001, pp. 23–28.

80. S. Bleuler, M. Brack, L. Thiele, and E. Zitzler. Multiobjective genetic programming: Reducing bloat by using SPEA2. In *Congress on Evolutionary Computation (CEC'01)*, IEEE, Piscataway, NJ, 2001, pp. 536–543.

81. S. Bleuler, M. Laumanns, L. Thiele, and E. Zitzler. PISA: A platform and programming language independent interface for search algorithms. In *EMO'03 Conference on Evolutionary Multi-Criterion Optimization*, Faro, Portugal, 2003, pp. 494–508.

82. C. Blum and D. Merkle. *Swarm Intelligence: Introduction and Applications*. Springer, 2008.

83. K. D. Boese. *Models for iterative global optimization*. PhD thesis, University of California, Los Angeles, CA, 1996.

84. K. D. Boese, A. B. Kahng, and S. Muddu. New adaptive multi-start techniques for combinatorial global optimizations. *Operations Research Letters*, 16(2):101–113, 1994.

85. E. Bonabeau, M. Dorigo, and G. Theraulaz. *Swarm Intelligence: From Natural to Artificial Systems*. Oxford University Press, 1999.

86. G. Booch, J. Rumbaugh, and I. Jacobson. *The Unified Modeling Language User Guide*. Addison-Wesley Professional, 1999.

87. R. Bowerman, B. Hall, and P. Calamai. A multi-objective optimization approach to urban school bus routing: Formulation and solution method. *Transportation Research Part A*, 29:123–197, 1995.

88. G. Box, J. S. Hunter, and W. G. Hunter. *Statistics for Experimenters: Design, Innovation, and Discovery*. Wiley, 2005.

89. G. E. P. Box and J. M. Jenkins. *Time Series Analysis, Forecasting and Control*. Holden Day, 1970.

90. G. E. P. Box and K. N. Wilson. On the experimental attainment of optimum conditions. *Journal of the Royal Statistical Society*, 13(1):1–45, 1951.

91. J. Branke. *Evolutionary Optimization in Dynamic Environments*. Kluwer, 2001.

92. H. Braun. On solving traveling salesman problems by genetic algorithms. In H.-P. Schwefel and R. Manner, editors, *Parallel Problem Solving from Nature*, Dortmund, Germany, Oct 1990, LNCS Vol. 496. Springer, 1990, pp. 129–133.

93. P. Briest, D. Brockhoff, and B. Degener. Experimental supplements to the theoretical analysis of evolutionary algorithms on problems from combinatorial optimization. In X. Yao et al., editors, *PPSN VIII—Parallel Problem Solving from Nature*, LNCS Vol. 3242. Springer, 2002, pp. 21–30.

94. T. Brueggemann and L. Hurink. Two very large-scale neighborhoods for single machine scheduling. *OR Spectrum*, 29(3):513–533, 2007.

95. B. Bullnheimer, R. F. Hartl, and C. A. Strauss. New rank based version of the ant system: A computational study. *Central European Journal for Operations Research and Economics*, 7(1):25–38, 1999.

96. R. E. Burkard, S. Karisch, and F. Rendl. QAPLIB: A quadratic assignment problem library. *European Journal of Operational Research*, 55:115–119, 1991.

97. E. K. Burke, P. I. Cowling, and R. Keuthen. Effective local and guided variable neighborhood search methods for the asymmetric traveling salesman problem. In *Evo Workshop*, LNCS Vol. 2037. Springer, 2001, pp. 203–312.

98. E. K. Burke, G. Kendall, J. Newall, E. Hart, P. Ross, and S. Schulemburg. Hyper-heuristics: An emerging direction in modern search technology. In *Handbook of Metaheuristics*. Kluwer Academic Publishers, 2003.

99. E. K. Burke, J. D. Landa Silva, and E. Soubeiga. Hyperheuristic approaches for multiobjective optimisation. In *5th Metaheuristics International Conference (MIC'2003)*, Kyoto, Japan, Aug 2003.

100. F. M. Burnet. *The Clonal Selection Theory of Acquired Immunity*. University Press, Cambridge, 1959.

101. K. Burnham and D. Anderson. *Model Selection and Multimodel Inference*. Springer, 2002.

102. D. R. Butenhof. *Programming with POSIX Threads*. Addison-Wesley, 1997.

103. G. T. Pulido, C. A. C. Coello, and M. S. Lechuga. Handling multiple objectives with particle swarm optimization. *IEEE Transactions on Evolutionary Computation*, 8(3):256–279, 2004.

104. C. Caldwell and V. S. Johnston. Tracking a criminal suspect through face-space with a genetic algorithm. In *4th International Conference on Genetic Algorithm*. Morgan Kaufmann, 1991, pp. 416–442.

105. S. Camazine, N. R. Franks, and J.-L. Deneubourg. *Self-Organization in Biological Systems. Princeton Studies in Complexity*. Princeton University Press, Princeton, NJ, 2001.

106. X. Cao, H. Qiao, and Y. Xu. Negative selection based immune optimization. *Advances in Engineering Software*, 38(10):649–656, 2007.

107. M. F. Cardoso, R. L. Salcedo, and S. F. Azevedo. Non-equilibrium simulated annealing: A faster approach to combinatorial minimization. *Industrial Engineering Chemical Research*, 33:1908–1918, 1994.

108. G. Di Caro and M. Dorigo. Antnet: Distributed stigmergetic control for communication networks. *Journal of Artificial Intelligence Research*, 9:317–365, 1998.

109. R. L. Carraway, T. L. Morin, and H. Moskowitz. Generalized dynamic programming for multicriteria optimization. *European Journal of Operational Research*, 44:95–104, 1990.

110. Y. Caseau and F. Laburthe. Disjunctive scheduling with task intervals. Technical Report LIENS-95-25, Ecole Normale Supérieure de Paris, France, 1995.

111. Y. Caseau and F. Laburthe. Claire: A brief overview. Technical Report, LIENS 96-15, 1996.

112. Y. Caseau and F. Laburthe. Claire: Combining objects and rules for problem solving. In M. Chakravarty, Y. Guo, and T. Ida, editors, *Proceedings of the JICSLP'96 Workshop on Multi-Paradigm Logic Programming*, TU Berlin, 1996, pp. 105–114.

113. Y. Caseau and F. Laburthe. Heuristics for large constrained routing problems. *Journal of Heuristics*, 5:281–303, 1999.

114. V. Cerny. A thermodynamical approach to the traveling salesman problem: An efficient simulation algorithm. *Journal of Optimization Theory and Applications*, 45:41–51, 1985.

115. A. Cesta, G. Cortellessa, A. Oddi, N. Policella, and A. Susi. A constraint-based architecture for flexible support to activity scheduling. *Lecture Notes in Computer Science*, 2175:369–390, 2001.

116. A. Chabrier, E. Danna, and C. Le Pape. Coopération entre génération de colonnes sans cycle et recherche locale appliquée au routage de véhicules. In *Huitièmes Journées Nationales sur la résolution de Problèmes NP-Complets JNPC'2002*, Nice, France, May 2002.

117. J. M. Chambers, W. S. Cleveland, B. Kleiner, and P. A. Tukey. *Graphical Methods for Data Analysis*. Wadsworth, Belmont, CA, 1983.

118. S. Chanas and P. Kobylanski. A new heuristic algorithm solving the linear ordering problem. *Computational Optimization and Applications*, 6:191–205, 1996.

119. M. Chandrasekaran, P. Asokan, S. Kumanan, T. Balamurugan, and S. Nickolas. Solving job shop scheduling problems using artificial immune system. *International Journal of Advanced Manufacturing Technology*, 31(5):580–593, 2006.

120. C. S. Chang and J. S. Huang. Optimal multiobjective SVC planning for voltage stability enhancement. *IEE Proceedings on Generation, Transmission and Distribution*, 145(2):203–209, 1998.

121. V. Chankong and Y. Y. Haimes. *Multiobjective Decision Making: Theory and Methodology*. Elsevier, New York, 1983.

122. B. Chapman, G. Jost, R. VanderPas, and D. J. Kuck. *Using OpenMP: Portable Shared Memory Parallel Programming*. MIT Press, 2007.

123. A. Charnes and W. W. Cooper. Goal programming and multiple objective optimization. *European Journal of Operational Research*, 1(1):39–45, 1977.

124. I. Charon and O. Hudry. The noising method: A new method for combinatorial optimization. *Operations Research Letters*, 14:133–137, 1993.

125. I. Charon and O. Hudry. Noising methods for a clique partitioning problem. *Discrete Applied Mathematics*, 154:754–769, 2006.

126. P. Cheeseman, B. Kanefsky, and W. M. Taylor. Where the really hard problems. In *12th IJCAI International Joint Conference on Artificial Intelligence*, 1991, pp. 331–337.

127. R. Chelouah and P. Siarry. A hybrid method combining continuous tabu search and Nelder–Mead simplex algorithms for the global optimization of multiminima functions. *European Journal of Operational Research*, 161(3):636–654, 2004.

128. H. Chen and N. S. Flann. Parallel simulated annealing and genetic algorithms: A space of hybrid methods. In Y. Davidor, H.-P. Schwefel, and R. Manner, editors, *3rd Conference on Parallel Problem Solving from Nature*, Jerusalem, Israel, Oct 1994. Springer, 1994, pp. 428–436.

129. Y. L. Chen and C. C. Liu. Multiobjective VAR planning using the goal-attainment method. In *IEEE Proceedings on Generation, Transmission and Distribution*, Vol. 141, May 1994, pp. 227–232.

130. A. J. Chipperfield, J. F. Whidborne, and P. J. Fleming. Evolutionary algorithms and simulated annealing for MCDM. In *Multicriteria Decision Making: Advances in MCDM Models, Algorithms, Theory, and Applications*. Kluwer Academic Publishing, Boston, MA, 1999.

131. D. M. Chitty and M. L. Hernandez. A hybrid ant colony optimisation technique for dynamic vehicle routing. In K. Deb et al., editors, *GECCO'2004*, LNCS Vol. 3102. Springer, 2004, pp. 48–59.

132. C. S. Chong, M. Y. H. Low, A. I. Sivakumar, and K. L. Gay. A bee colony optimization algorithm to job shop scheduling. In *Winter Simulation Conference*, Monterey, CA, Dec 2006, pp. 1954–1961.

133. C.-K. Chow and H.-T. Tsui. Autonomous agent response learning by a multi-species particle swarm optimization. In *Congress on Evolutionary Computation (CEC'04)*, Portland, OR. IEEE Press, 2004, pp. 778–785.

134. P. C. Chu. *A genetic algorithm approach for combinatorial optimization problems*. PhD thesis, University of London, London, UK, 1997.

135. V. Chvatal. A greedy heuristic for the set covering problem. *Mathematics of Operations Research*, 4(3):233–235, 1979.

136. S. H. Clearwater, T. Hogg, and B. A. Huberman. Cooperative problem solving. In B. A. Huberman, editor, *Computation: The Micro and the Macro View*. World Scientific, 1992, pp. 33–70.

137. S. H. Clearwater, B. A. Huberman, and T. Hogg. Cooperative solution of constraint satisfaction problems. *Science*, 254:1181–1183, 1991.

138. M. Clerc. The swarm and the queen: Towards a deterministic and adaptive particle swarm optimization. In *IEEE Congress on Evolutionary Computation (CEC'99)*, Washington, DC, 1999, pp. 1951–1957.

139. M. Clerc and J. Kennedy. The particle swarm: Explosion, stability, and convergence in a multidimensional complex space. *IEEE Transactions on Evolutionary Computation*, 6(1):58–73, 2002.

140. C. A. Coello and N. C. Cortés. Solving multiobjective optimization problems using an artificial immune system. *Genetic Programming and Evolvable Machines*, 6(2):163–190, 2005.

141. C. A. C. Coello. Using the min-max method to solve multiobjective optimization problems with genetic algorithms. In *IBERAMIA'98*, Springer, 1998.

142. C. A. C. Coello. An updated survey of GA-based multiobjective optimization techniques. *ACM Computing Surveys*, 32:109–143, 2000.

143. C. A. C. Coello and A. D. Christiansen. An approach to multiobjective optimization using genetic algorithms. In C. H. Dagli et al., editors, *Intelligent Engineering Systems Through Artificial Neural Networks*, Vol. 5 of *Fuzzy Logic and Evolutionary Programming*. ASME Press, St. Louis, MO, 1995, pp. 411–416.

144. C. A. C. Coello, D. A. Van Veldhuizen, and G. B. Lamont. *Evolutionary Algorithms for Solving Multi-Objective Optimization Problems.* Kluwer Academic Publishers, 2002.

145. C. A. Coello and M. Reyes. A study of the parallelization of a coevolutionary multi-objective evolutionary algorithm. In *MICAI'2004*, LNAI Vol. 2972, 2004, pp. 688–697.

146. P. R. Cohen. *Empirical Methods for Artificial Intelligence*. MIT Press, Cambridge, 1995.

147. J. Cohoon, S. Hedge, W. Martin, and D. Richards. Punctuated equilibria: A parallel genetic algorithm. In J. J. Grefenstette, editor, 2nd International Conference *on Genetic Algorithms*, July 1987. MIT, Cambridge, MA, 1987, pp. 148–154.

148. J. P. Cohoon, W. N. Martin, and D. S. Richards. Genetic algorithms and punctuated equilibria. In H.-P. Schwefel and R. Manner, editors, *Parallel Problem Solving from Nature*, Dortmund, Germany, Oct 1990, LNCS Vol. 496. Springer, 1990, pp. 134–141.

149. J. P. Cohoon, W. N. Martin, and D. S. Richards. A multi-population genetic algorithm for solving the *k*-partition problem on hypercubes. In R. K. Belew and L. B. Booker, editors, *4th International Conference on Genetic Algorithms*, Morgan Kaufmann, San Mateo, CA, 1991, pp. 244–248.

150. R. K. Congram. *Polynomially searchable exponential neighborhoods for sequencing problems in combinatorial optimization.* PhD thesis, Faculty of Mathematical Studies, University of Southampton, UK, 2000.

151. S. Cook and D. Mitchell. Finding hard instances of the satisfiability problem: A survey. In *Satisfiability Problems: Theory and Applications*. American Mathematical Society, 1997.

152. W. Cook and P. Seymour. Tour merging via branch-decomposition. *INFORMS Journal on Computing*, 15(3):233–248, 2003.

153. A. Corberán, E. Fernández, M. Laguna, and R. Martí. Heuristic solutions to the problem of routing school buses with multiple objectives. *Journal of the Operational Research Society*, 53(4):427–435, 2002.

154. O. Cordon, I. Fernandez, F. Herrera, and L. Moreno. A new ACO model integrating evolutionary algorithms concepts: The best-worst ant system. In *2nd International Workshop on Ant Algorithms*, Brussels, Belgium, 2000, pp. 22–29.

155. D. Corne, M. Dorigo, and F. Glover. *New Ideas in Optimization*. McGraw-Hill, 1999.

156. D. W. Corne, J. D. Knowles, and M. J. Oates. The Pareto envelope-based selection algorithm for multiobjective optimization. In M. Schoenauer, K. Deb, G. Rudolph, X. Yao, E. Lutton, J. J. Merelo, and H.-P. Schwefel, editors, *Proceedings of Parallel Problem Solving from Nature VI*, LNCS Vol. 1917. Springer, 2000, pp. 839–848.

157. G. Cornuejols, D. Naddef, and W. R. Pulleyblank. Halin graphs and the traveling salesman problem. *Mathematical Programming*, 26:287–294, 1983.

158. J. Coyne and R. Paton. Genetic algorithms and directed adaptation. In *Workshop on Evolutionary Computing*, Leeds, UK, LNCS Vol. 865. Springer, 1994, pp. 103–114.

159. M. Goodchild and C. P. Keller. The multiobjective vending problem: A generalization of the traveling salesman problem. *Environment and Planning B: Planning and Design*, 15:447–460, 1988.

160. T. G. Crainic, A. T. Nguyen, and M. Gendreau. Cooperative multi-thread parallel tabu search with evolutionary adaptive memory. *2nd International Conference on Metaheuristics*, Sophia Antipolis, France, July 1997.

161. T. G. Crainic, M. Toulouse, and M. Gendreau. Synchronous tabu search parallelization strategies for multi-commodity location-allocation with balancing requirements. *OR Spektrum*, 17:113–123, 1995.

162. T. G. Crainic and M. Gendreau. Cooperative parallel tabu search for capacitated network design. *Journal of Heuristics*, 8:601–627, 2002.

163. T. G. Crainic and M. Toulouse. Parallel strategies for metaheuristics. In F. W. Glover and G. A. Kochenberger, editors, *Handbook of Metaheuristics*. Springer, 2003, pp. 475–513.

164. N. Cressie. *Statistics for Spatial Data*. Wiley, 1993.

165. M. Creutz. Microcanonical Monte Carlo simulation. *Physical Review Letters*, 50:1411–1414, 1983.

166. V.-D. Cung, S. L. Martins, C. C. Ribeiro, and C. Roucairol. Strategies for the parallel implementation of metaheuristics. In C. C. Ribeiro and P. Hansen, editors, *Essays and Surveys in Metaheuristics*. Kluwer, 2003, pp. 263–308.

167. V.-D. Cung, T. Mautor, P. Michelon, and A. Tavares. A scatter search based approach for the quadratic assignment problem. In *IEEE International Conference on Evolutionary Computation (ICEC'97)*, Indianapolis, IN, April 1997.

168. V.-D. Cung, T. Mautor, P. Michelon, and A. Tavares. Recherche dispersée parallèle. In *Deuxième Congrés de la Société Francaise de Recherche Opérationnelle et d'Aide à la décision ROADEF'99*, Autrans, France, Jan 1999.

169. J. R. Current and D. A. Schilling. The median tour and maximal covering tour problems: Formulations and heuristics. *European Journal of Operational Research*, 73:114–126, 1994.

170. V. Cutello and G. Nicosia. An immunological approach to combinatorial optimization problems. In *Advances in Artificial Intelligence IBERAMIA'2002*, LNCS Vol. 2527. Springer, 2002, pp. 361–370.

171. V. Cutello and G. Nicosia. The clonal selection principle for *in silico* and *in vitro* computing. In *Recent Developments in Biologically Inspired Computing*. Idea Group Publishing, 2004, pp. 104–146.

172. G. Dahl, K. Jornsten, and A. Lokketangen. A tabu search approach to the channel minimization problem. In G. Liu, K.-H. Phua, J. Ma, J. Xu, F. Gu, and C. He, editors, *Optimization—Techniques and Applications (ICOTA'95)*, Chengdu, China, Vol. 1, World Scientific, 1995, pp. 369–377.

173. F. L. Dalboni, L. S. Ochi, and L. M. D. Drummond. On improving evolutionary algorithms by using data mining for the oil collector vehicle routing problem. In *International Network Optimization Conference (INOC'2003)*, Paris, France, Oct 2003.

174. G. B. Dantzig. Maximization of a linear function of variables subject to linear inequalities. In *Activity Analysis of Production and Allocation*. Wiley, 1951.

175. P. Darwen and X. Yao. On evolving robust strategies for iterated prisoner's dilemma. In *Progress in Evolutionary Computation*, LNAI Vol. 956. Springer, 1995, pp. 276–292.

176. C. Darwin. *On the Origin of Species by Means of Natural Selection*. John Murray, London, 1859.
177. I. Das and J. E. Dennis. A closer look at drawbacks of minimizing weighted sums of objectives for Pareto set generation in multicriteria optimization problems. *Structural Optimization*, 14(1):63–69, 1997.
178. D. Dasgupta. *Artificial Immune Systems and Their Applications*. Springer, 1999.
179. D. Dasgupta and M. Michalewicz. *Evolutionary Algorithms in Engineering Applications*. Springer, 1997.
180. Y. Davidor. Epistasis variance: A viewpoint on GA-hardness. In *Workshop on the Foundations of Genetic Algorithms and Classifier (FOGA'1)*. Morgan Kaufmann, San Mateo, CA, 1991, pp. 23–35.
181. L. Davis. Job-shop scheduling with genetic algorithms. In J. J. Grefenstette, editor, *International Conference on Genetic Algorithms and Their Applications*, Pittsburgh, PA, 1985, pp. 136–140.
182. R. Dawkins. *The Selfish Gene*. Oxford University Press, 1976.
183. R. Dawkins. *The Blind Watchmaker*. Longman, 1986.
184. L. N. de Castro. *Fundamentals of Natural Computing*. Chapman & Hall/CRC, 2006.
185. L. N. de Castro and J. I. Timmis. *Artificial Immune Systems: A New Computational Intelligence Approach*. Springer, 2002.
186. L. N. de Castro and F. J. Von. Zuben. The clonal selection algorithm with engineering applications. In *Workshop on Artificial Immune Systems and Their Applications (GECCO'00)*, Las Vegas, NV, 2000, pp. 36–37.
187. L. N. de Castro and F. J. Von. Zuben. aiNET: An artificial immune network for data analysis. In *Data Mining: A Heuristic Approach*. Idea Group Publishing, 2001, pp. 231–259.
188. L. N. de Castro and F. J. Von. Zuben. Learning and optimization using the clonal selection principle. *IEEE Transactions on Evolutionary Computation*, 6(3):239–251, 2002.
189. E. D. de Jong, R. A. Watson, and J. B. Pollack. Reducing bloat and promoting diversity using multi-objective methods. In L. Spector, E. D. Goodman, A. Wu, W. B. Langdon, H.-M. Voigt, M. Gen, S. Sen, M. Dorigo, S. Pezeshk, M. H. Garzon, and E. Burke, editors, *Genetic and Evolutionary Computation Conference (GECCO'01)*. Morgan Kaufmann, San Francisco, CA, 2001, pp. 11–18.
190. M. C. de Souza, C. Duhamel, and C. C. Ribeiro. A GRASP heuristic for the capacitated minimum spanning tree problem using a memory-based local search strategy. In *Metaheuristics: Computer Decision-Making*. Kluwer Academic Publishers, 2004, pp. 627–657.
191. F. de Toro, J. Ortega, E. Ros, S. Mota, B. Paechter, and J. M. Martín. PSFGA: Parallel processing and evolutionary computation for multiobjective optimisation. *Parallel Computing*, 30(5–6):721–739, 2004.
192. A. Dean and D. Voss. *Design and Analysis of Algorithms*. Springer, 1999.
193. K. Deb. Multi-objective genetic algorithms: Problem difficulties and construction of test problems. Technical Report CI-49-98, Department of Computer Science, University of Dortmund, Dortmund, Germany, 1998.
194. K. Deb. Multi-objective genetic algorithms: Problem difficulties and construction of test problems. *Evolutionary Computation Journal*, 7(3):201–230, 1999.

195. K. Deb. *Multi-Objective Optimization Using Evolutionary Algorithms*. John Wiley & Sons, 2001.

196. K. Deb and R. B. Agrawal. Simulated binary crossover for continuous search space. *Complex Systems*, 9:115–148, 1995.

197. K. Deb, S. Agrawal, A. Pratab, and T. Meyarivan. A fast elitist non-dominated sorting genetic algorithm for multi-objective optimization: NSGA-II. In *Proceedings of the Parallel Problem Solving from Nature VI Conference*, 2000, pp. 849–858.

198. K. Deb and T. Goel. A hybrid multi-objective evolutionary approach to engineering shape design. In E. Zitzler, K. Deb, L. Thiele, C. Coello Coello, and D. Corne, editors, *1st International Conference on Evolutionary Multi-Criterion Optimization*, Zurich, Switzerland, LNCS Vol. 1993, 2001, pp. 385–399.

199. K. Deb and D. Joshi. A computationally efficient evolutionary algorithm for real parameter optimization. Technical Report 003, KanGal, 2002.

200. K. Deb, A. Pratap, S. Agarwal, and T. Meyarivan. A fast and elitist multiobjective genetic algorithm: NSGA-II. *IEEE Transactions on Evolutionary Computation*, 6(2):182–197, 2002.

201. K. Deb, A. Sinha, and S. Kukkonen. Multi-objective test problems, linkages and evolutionary methodologies. *Genetic and Evolutionary Computation Conference (GECCO'2006)*. ACM, New York, 2006, pp. 1141–1148.

202. K. Deb, L. Thiele, M. Laumanns, and E. Zitzler. Scalable test problems for evolutionary multi-objective optimization. In *Evolutionary Multiobjective Optimization*. Springer, 2005, pp. 105–145.

203. V. Deineko and G. J. Woeginger. A study of exponential neighborhoods for the traveling salesman problem and the quadratic assignment problem. *Mathematical Programming*, 87(3):519–542, 2000.

204. A. Dekkers and E. Aarts. Global optimization and simulated annealing. *Mathematical Programming*, 50:367–393, 1991.

205. P. Delisle, M. Krajecki, M. Gravel, and C. Gagné. Parallel implementation of an ant colony optimization metaheuristic with OpenMP. In *3rd European Workshop on OpenMP (EWOMP'01)*, 2001, pp. 8–12.

206. M. DellAmico, F. Maffioli, and P. Varbrand. On prize-collecting tours and the asymmetric travelling salesman problem. *International Transactions in Operational Research*, 2:297–308, 1995.

207. R. deNeufville and M. McCord. Unreliable measurements of utility: Significant problems for decision analysis. In J. P. Brans, editor, *Operational Research*, North-Holland, 1984, pp. 464–476.

208. J. Dennis and V. Torczon. Managing approximate models in optimization. In *Multidisciplinary Design Optimization: State-of-the-Art*. SIAM, 1997, pp. 330–347.

209. U. Derigs. Using confidence limits for the global optimal in combinatorial optimization. *Operations Research*, 33:1024–1049, 1985.

210. P. J. Diggle. *Statistical Analysis of Spatial Point Patterns*. Academic Press, 1983.

211. E. W. Dijkstra. A note on two problems in connection with graphs. *Numerische Mathematik*, 1:269–271, 1959.

212. I. Dimitrescu and T. Stutzle. Combinations of local search and exact algorithms. In *Evo Workshops*, 2003, pp. 211–223.

213. K. Doerner, W. J. Gutjahr, R. Hartl, C. Strauss, and C. Stummer. Pareto ant colony optimization: A metaheuristic approach to multiobjective portfolio selection. *Annals of Operations Research*, 131:79–99, 2004.

214. K. F. Doerner, R. F. Hartl, G. Kiechle, M. Lucka, and M. Reimann. Parallel ant systems for the capacitated VRP. In J. Gottlieb and G. R. Raidl, editors, *EvoCOP'04*. Springer, 2004, pp. 72–83.

215. M. Dorigo. *Optimization, learning and natural algorithms*. PhD thesis, Politecnico di Milano, Italy, 1992.

216. M. Dorigo and C. Blum. Ant colony optimization theory: A survey. *Theoretical Computer Science*, 344:243–278, 2005.

217. M. Dorigo and L. Gambardella. Ant colony system: A cooperative learning approach to the traveling salesman problem. *IEEE Transactions on Evolutionary Computation*, 1(53–66), 1997.

218. M. Dorigo, V. Maniezzo, and A. Colorni. The ant system: Optimization by a colony of cooperating agents. *IEEE Transactions on Systems, Man, and Cybernetics*, 1(26):29–41, 1996.

219. M. Dorigo and T. Stutzle. The ant colony optimization metaheuristic: Algorithms, applications and advances. In *Handbook of Metaheuristics*. Kluwer Academic Publishers, 2002, pp. 251–285.

220. U. Dorndorf and E. Pesch. Fast clustering algorithms. *ORSA Journal of Computing*, 6:141–153, 1994.

221. K. A. Dowsland. Nurse scheduling with tabu search and strategic oscillation. *European Journal of Operational Research*, 106:393–407, 1998.

222. K. A. Dowsland, E. A. Herbert, and G. Kendall. Using tree search bounds to enhance a genetic algorithm approach to two rectangle packing problems. *European Journal of Operational Research*, 168(2):390–402, 2006.

223. K. A. Dowsland and J. M. Thomson. Solving a nurse scheduling problem with knapsacks, networks and tabu search. *Journal of Operational Research Society*, 51:825–833, 2000.

224. J. Dréo and P. Siarry. A new ant colony algorithm using the heterarchical concept aimed at optimization of multiminima continuous functions. In M. Dorigo, G. Di Caro, and M. Sampels, editors, *3rd International Workshop on Ant Algorithms (ANTS'2002)*, LNCS Vol. 2463. Springer, 2002, pp. 216–221.

225. M. Dror and L. Levy. A vehicle routing improvement algorithm comparisons of a greedy and a matching implementation for inventory routing. *Computers and Operations Research*, 13:33–45, 1986.

226. D. Z. Du and P. M. Pardalos. *Minimax and Applications*. Kluwer Academic Publishers, 1995.

227. S. Duarte and B. Barán. Multiobjective network design optimisation using parallel evolutionary algorithms. In *XXVII Conferencia Latinoamericana de Informática CLEI'2001*, 2001.

228. G. Duech and T. Scheuer. Threshold accepting: A general purpose optimization algorithm appearing superior to simulated annealing. *Journal of Computational Physics*, 90:161–175, 1990.

229. G. Dueck. New optimization heuristics: The great deluge algorithm and the record-to-record travel. *Journal of Computational Physics*, 104(1):86–92, 1993.

230. A. E. Dunlop and B. W. Kernighan. A procedure for placement of standard cell VLSI circuits. *IEEE Transactions on Computer-Aided Design*, 4:92–98, 1989.

231. W. H. Durham. *Coevolution: Genes, Culture, and Human Diversity*. Stanford University Press, Stanford, CA, 1994.

232. D. Duvivier, P. Preux, and E.-G. Talbi. Climbing up NP-hard hills. In H.-M. Voigt, W. Ebeling, I. Rechenberg, and H.-P. Schwefel, editors, *4th International Conference on Parallel Problem Solving from Nature (PPSN'96)*, LNCS Vol. 1141. Springer, Berlin, 1996, pp. 574–583.

233. M. Laumanns C. M. Fonseca E. Zitzler, L. Thiele and V. Grunert da Fonseca. Performance assessment of multiobjective optimizers: An analysis and review. *IEEE Transactions on Evolutionary Computation*, 7(2):117–132, 2003.

234. D. Eby, R. Averill, W. Punch, and E. Goodman. Evaluation of injection island model GA performance on flywheel design optimization. In *International Conference on Adaptive Computing in Design and Manufacturing*, Devon, UK. Springer, 1998, pp. 121–136.

235. A. Oram, editor. *Peer-to-Peer: Harnessing the Power of Disruptive Technologies*. O'Reilly & Associates, 2001.

236. F. Y. Edgeworth. *Mathematical Psychics: An Essay on the Application of Mathematics to the Moral Sciences*. C. Kegan Paul and Co., London, 1881.

237. J. Edmonds. Matroids and the greedy algorithm. *Mathematical Programming*, 1(1):127–136, 1971.

238. M. Ehrgott. *Multicriteria Optimization*. Springer, 2005.

239. M. Ehrgott and K. Klamroth. Non-connected efficiency graphs in multiple criteria combinatorial optimization. In R. Caballero, F. Ruiz, and R. E. Steuer, editors, *2nd International Conference on Multi-Objective Programming and Goal Programming*, Torremolinos, Spain, May 1996. Springer, 1996, pp. 140–150.

240. A. E. Eiben and J. E. Smith. *Introduction to Evolutionary Computing*. Springer, 2003.

241. N. El-Sherbeny. *Resolution of a vehicle routing problem with multi-objective simulated annealing method*. PhD thesis, Faculté Polytechnique de Mons, Mons, Belgium, 2001.

242. T. A. Ely, W. A. Crossley, and E. A. Williams. Satellite constellation design for zonal coverage using genetic algorithms. Technical Report AAS-98-128, American Astronautical Society, San Diego, CA, Feb 1998.

243. M. Emmerich and R. Hosenberg. TEA: A toolbox for the design of parallel evolutionary algorithms in C++. Technical Report CI-206/01, University of Dortmund, Germany, 2001.

244. A. P. Engelbrecht. *Computational Intelligence: An Introduction*. Wiley, 2002.

245. R. S. Engelmore and A. Morgan. *Blackboard Systems*. Addison-Wesley, 1988.

246. L. R. Esau and K. C. Williams. On teleprocessing system design. *IBM Systems Journal*, 5:142–147, 1966.

247. H. Eskandari, C. D. Geiger, and G. B. Lamont. FASTPGA: A dynamic population sizing approach for solving expensive multiobjective optimization problems. In *EMO'07 Evolutionary Multi-Criterion Optimization Conference*, LNCS Vol. 4403. Springer, 2007, pp. 141–155.

248. R. Fahrion and M. Wrede. On a principle of chain exchange for vehicle routing problems. *Journal of Operational Research Society*, 41(9):821–827, 1990.

249. I. De Falco, R. Del Balio, and E. Tarantino. An analysis of parallel heuristics for task allocation in multicomputers. *Computing*, 59(3):259–275, 1997.
250. I. De Falco, R. Del Balio, E. Tarantino, and R. Vaccaro. Improving search by incorporating evolution principles in parallel tabu search. In *IEEE Conference on Evolutionary Computation*, 1994, pp. 823–828.
251. E. Falkenauer. *Genetic Algorithms and Grouping Problems*. Wiley, 1998.
252. M. Farina, K. Deb, and P. Amato. Dynamic multi-objective optimization problems: Test cases, approximations, and applications. *IEEE Transactions on Evolutionary Computation*, 8(5):425–442, 2004.
253. J. D. Farmer, N. Packard, and A. Perelson. The immune system, adaptation and machine learning. *Physica D*, 2:187–204, 1986.
254. A. Federgruen and M. Tzur. Time-partitioning heuristics: Application to one warehouse, multi-item, multi-retailer lot-sizing problems. *Naval Research Logistics*, 46:463–486, 1999.
255. T. A. Feo and M. G. C. Resende. A probabilistic heuristic for a computationally difficult set covering problem. *Operations Research Letters*, 8:67–71, 1989.
256. T. A. Feo and M. G. C. Resende. Greedy randomized adaptive search procedures. *Journal of Global Optimization*, 6:109–133, 1995.
257. T. A. Feo, M. G. C. Resende, and S. H. Smith. A greedy randomized adaptive search procedure for maximum independent set. *Operations Research*, 42:860–878, 1994.
258. T. A. Feo, K. Venkatraman, and J. F. Bard. A GRASP for a difficult single machine scheduling problem. *Computers and Operations Research*, 18:635–643, 1991.
259. A. G. Ferreira and J. Zerovnik. Bounding the probability of success of stochastic methods for global optimization. *Computers and Mathematics with Applications*, 25:1–8, 1993.
260. F. F. Ferreira and J. F. Fontanari. Probabilistic analysis of the number partitioning problem. *Journal of Physics A: Mathematical and General*, 31(15):3417–3428, 1998.
261. G. R. Filho and L. A. N. Lorena. Constructive genetic algorithm and column generation: An application to graph coloring. In *APORS'2000 Conference of the Association of the Asian-Pacific Operations Research Societies Within IFORS*, 2000.
262. A. Fink, S. Voss, and D. Woodruff. Building reusable software components for heuristic search. In P. Kall and H.-J. Luthi, editors, *Operations Research Proceedings*, Springer, Berlin, 1999, pp. 210–219.
263. M. Fischetti and A. Lodi. Local branching. *Mathematical Programming B*, 98:23–47, 2003.
264. P. C. Fishburn. Lexicographic orders, utilities and decision rules: A survey. *Management Science*, 20(11):1442–1471, 1974.
265. M. L. Fisher. An application oriented guide to Lagrangian relaxation. *Interfaces*, 15:399–404, 1985.
266. W. Fisher. *The Design of Experiments*. Oliver and Boyd, Edinburgh, 1935.
267. M. A. Fleischer and S. H. Jacobson. Information theory and the finite-time behavior of the simulated annealing algorithm: Experimental results. *INFORMS Journal of Computing*, 11:35–43, 1999.
268. P. J. Fleming and R. C. Purshouse. Evolutionary algorithms in control systems engineering: A survey. *Control Engineering Practice*, 10:1223–1241, 2002.

269. C. Fleurent and J. A. Ferland. Genetic hybrids for the quadratic assignment problem. In *DIMACS Series in Discrete Mathematics and Theoretical Computer Science*, Vol. 16, AMS, Providence, RI, 1994, pp. 173–188.

270. C. Fleurent and J. A. Ferland. Genetic and hybrid algorithms for graph coloring. *Annals of Operations Research*, 63(3):437–461, 1996.

271. F. Focacci, F. Laburthe, and A. Lodi. Local search and constraint programming. In *Handbook of Metaheuristics. International Series in Operations Research and Management Science*. Kluwer Academic Publishers, Norwell, MA, 2002.

272. L. J. Fogel. Toward inductive inference automata. In *Proceedings of the International Federation for Information Processing Congress*, Munich, 1962, pp. 395–399.

273. L. J. Fogel, A. J. Owens, and M. J. Walsh. *Artificial Intelligence Through Simulated Evolution*. Wiley, 1966.

274. G. Folino, C. Pizzuti, and G. Spezzano. CAGE: A tool for parallel genetic programming applications. In J. F. Miller, M. Tomassini, P. L. Lanzi, C. Ryan, A. G. B. Tettamanzi, and W. B. Langdon, editors, *Proceedings of EuroGP'2001*, Italy, LNCS Vol. 2038. Springer, 2001, pp. 64–73.

275. C. Fonlupt, D. Robillard, P. Preux, and E.-G. Talbi. Fitness landscape and performance of metaheuristics. In *Meta-Heuristics—Advances and Trends in Local Search Paradigms for Optimization*. Kluwer Academic Press, 1999, pp. 255–266.

276. C. M. Fonseca and P. J. Fleming. Genetic algorithms for multiobjective optimization: Formulation, discussion and generalization. In S. Forrest, editor, *Proceedings of the 5th International Conference on Genetic Algorithms*, Morgan Kaufmann, San Mateo, CA, 1993, pp. 416–423.

277. C. M. Fonseca and P. J. Fleming. An overview of evolutionary algorithms in multiobjective optimization. *Evolutionary Computation*, 3(1):1–16, 1995.

278. C. M. Fonseca and P. J. Fleming. An overview of evolutionary algorithms in multiobjective optimization. *Evolutionary Computation*, 3(1):1–16, 1995.

279. S. Forrest, B. Javornik, R. E. Smith, and A. S. Perelson. Using genetic algorithms to explore pattern recognition in the immune system. *Evolutionary Computation*, 1(3):191–211, 1993.

280. S. Forrest, A. S. Perelson, L. Allen, R., and Cherukuri. Self-nonself discrimination in a computer. In *IEEE Symposium on Research in Security and Privacy*, Los Alamos, CA. IEEE Press, 1994.

281. I. Foster and C. Kesselman, editors. *The Grid: Blueprint for a New Computing Infrastructure*. Morgan Kaufmann, San Francisco, CA, 1999.

282. M. P. Fourman. Compaction of symbolic layout using genetic algorithms. In J. J. Grefenstette, editor, *International Conference on Genetic Algorithms and Their Applications*, Pittsburgh, PA, 1985, pp. 141–153.

283. A. Frangioni, E. Necciari, and M. G. Scutella. A multi-exchange neighborhood for minimum makespan parallel machine scheduling problems. *Journal of Combinatorial Optimization*, 8(2):195–220, 2004.

284. B. Freisleben and P. Merz. A genetic local search algorithm for solving symmetric and asymmetric traveling salesman problems. In *IEEE International Conference on Evolutionary Computation (ICEC'96)*, Nagoya, Japan, May 1996, pp. 616–621.

285. C. Friden, A. Hertz, and D. De Werra. Tabaris: An exact algorithm based on tabu search for finding a maximum independent set in a graph. *Computers and Operations Research*, 17:437–445, 1990.

286. T. L. Friesz, G. Anandalingam, N. J. Mehta, K. Nam, S. J. Shah, and R. L. Tobin. The multiobjective equilibrium network design problem revisited: A simulated annealing approach. *European Journal of Operational Research*, 65:44–57, 1993.

287. T. Fruhwirth and S. Abdennadher. *Essentials of Constraint Programming*. Springer, 2003.

288. M. Fu. Optimization for simulation: Theory vs. practice. *INFORMS Journal on Computing*, 14:192–215, 2002.

289. K. Fujita, N. Hirokawa, S. Akagi, S. Kimatura, and H. Yokohata. Multi-objective optimal design of automotive engine using genetic algorithm. In *Design Engineering Technical Conferences (DETC'98)*, Atlanta, GA, Sept 1998, pp. 1–11.

290. C. Gagné and M. Parizeau. Genericity in evolutionary computation software tools: Principles and case study. *International Journal on Artificial Intelligence Tools*, 15(2):173–194, 2006.

291. C. Gagné, M. Parizeau, and M. Dubreuil. Distributed BEAGLE: An environment for parallel and distributed evolutionary computations. In *Proceedings of the 17th Annual International Symposium on High Performance Computing Systems and Applications (HPCS'03)*, Sherbrooke, Canada, May 2003.

292. L. M. Gambardella, E. Taillard, and G. Agazzi. MACS-VRPTW: A multiple ant colony system for vehicle routing problems with time windows. In *New Ideas in Optimization*. McGraw-Hill Ltd., Maidenhead, UK, 1999, pp. 63–76.

293. E. Gamma, R. Helm, R. Johnson, and J. Vlissides. *Design Patterns, Elements of Reusable Object-Oriented Software*. Addison-Wesley, 1994.

294. X. Gandibleux, N. Mezdaoui, and A. Freville. A tabu search procedure to solve multi-objective combinatorial optimization problems. In R. Caballero, F. Ruiz, and R. Steuer, editors, *2nd International Conference on Multi-Objective Programming and Goal Programming (MOPGP'96)*, Torremolinos, Spain, May 1996. Springer, 1996, pp. 291–300.

295. B. Gao, T.-Y. Liu, G. Feng, T. Qin, Q.-S. Cheng, and W.-Y. Ma. Hierarchical taxonomy preparation for text categorization using consistent bipartite spectral graph copartitioning. *IEEE Transactions on Knowledge and Data Engineering*, 17(9):1263–1273, 2005.

296. X.-Z. Gao, S. J. Ovaska, and X. Wang. A GA-based negative selection algorithm. *International Journal on Innovative Computing Information and Control*, 4(4):971–979, 2008.

297. F. Garcia-Lopez, B. Melian-Batista, J. A. Moreno-Perez, and J. M. Moreno-Vega. Parallelization of the scatter search for the *p*-median problem. *Parallel Computing*, 29:575–589, 2003.

298. C. Garcia-Martinez, O. Cordon, and F. Herrera. A taxonomy and empirical analysis of multiple objective ant colony optimization algorithms for the bi-criteria TSP. *European Journal of Operational Research*, 180:116–148, 2007.

299. M. Garey and D. Johnson. *Computers and Intractability: A Guide to the Theory on NP-Completeness*. W. H. Freeman and Co. Publishers, New York, 1979.

300. B. Gartner and J. Matousek. *Understanding and Using Linear Programming*. Springer, 2006.

301. L. Di Gaspero and A. Schaerf. EasyLocal++: An object-oriented framework for the design of local search algorithms and metaheuristics. In *MIC'2001 4th Metaheuristics International Conference*, Porto, Portugal, July 2001, pp. 287–292.

302. M. J. Geiger. Genetic algorithms for multiple objective vehicle routing. In *MIC'01 Metaheuristic International Conference*, 2001, pp. 348–353.

303. S. Geman and D. Geman. Stochastic relaxation, Gibbs distributions, and the Bayesian restoration of images. *IEEE Transactions on Pattern Analysis and Machine Intelligence*, 6:721–741, 1984.

304. M. Gen and R. Cheng. A survey of penalty techniques in genetic algorithms. In T. Fukuda and T. Furuhashi, editors, *International Conference on Evolutionary Computation*, Nagoya, Japan, 1996, pp. 804–809.

305. M. Gen and L. Lin. Multiobjective hybrid genetic algorithm for bicriteria network design problem. In *8th Asia Pacific Symposium on Intelligent and Evolutionary Systems*, Cairns, Australia, Dec 2004, pp. 73–82.

306. M. Gendreau. An introduction to tabu search. In *Handbook of Metaheuristics*. Kluwer, 2002, pp. 37–54.

307. M. Gendreau, F. Guertin, J. Y. Potvin, and R. Seguin. Neighborhood search heuristics for a dynamic vehicle dispatching problem with pick-ups and deliveries. Technical Report CRT-98-10, Centre de Recherche sur les Transports, Montreal, Canada, 1998.

308. M. Gendreau, A. Hertz, and G. Laporte. A tabu search heuristic for the vehicle routing problem. *Management Science*, 40:1276–1290, 1994.

309. M. Gendreau, G. Laporte, and F. Semet. The covering tour problem. *Operations Research*, 45:568–576, 1997.

310. I. Gent and T. Walsh. The number partition phase transition. Technical Report RR 95-185, Department of Computer Science, University of Strathclyde, 1995.

311. I. P. Gent and T. Walsh. The hardest random SAT problems. In *18th Annual German Conference on Artificial Intelligence*, LNCS Vol. 861. Springer, 1994, pp. 355–366.

312. I. P. Gent and T. Walsh. The TSP phase transition. *Artificial Intelligence*, 88(1–2):349–358, 1996.

313. J. E. Gentle. *Random Number Generation and Monte Carlo Methods*. Springer, 1998.

314. A. Geoffrion. Proper efficiency and theory of vector maximization. *Journal of Mathematical Analysis and Applications*, 22:618–630, 1968.

315. I. Giannikos. A multiobjective goal programming model for locating treatment sites and routing hazardous wastes. *European Journal of Operational Research*, 104:333–342, 1998.

316. M. Gibbs and D. MacKey. Efficient implementation of Gaussian processes. Technical Report, Cavendish Lab, Cambridge, UK, 1997.

317. P. C. Gilmore and R. E. Gomory. A linear programming approach to the cutting stock problem. *Operations Research*, 9:849–859, 1961.

318. M. L. Ginsberg. Dynamic backtracking. *Journal of Artificial Intelligence Research*, 1:25–46, 1993.

319. F. Glover. Improved linear integer programming formulations on nonlinear integer programs. *Management Science*, 22(4):455–460, 1975.

320. F. Glover. Heuristics for integer programming using surrogate constraints. *Decision Sciences*, 8:156–166, 1977.

321. F. Glover. An improved MIP formulation for products of discrete and continuous variables. *Journal of Information and Optimization Sciences*, 5(469–471), 1984.

322. F. Glover. Future paths for integer programming and links to artificial intelligence. *Computers and Operation Research*, 13(5):533–549, 1986.

323. F. Glover. Tabu search: Part I. *ORSA Journal on Computing*, 1(3):190–206, 1989.

324. F. Glover. New ejection chain and alternating path methods for traveling salesman. *ORSA Journal on Computing*, 376–384, 1991.

325. F. Glover. Tabu search and adaptive memory programming. In *Advances, Applications and Challenges*. Kluwer, 1996, pp. 1–75.

326. F. Glover and C. McMillan. The general employee scheduling problem: An integration of MS and AI. *Computers and Operations Research*, 13(5):563–573, 1986.

327. D. Goldberg. Simple genetic algorithms and the minimal deceptive problem. In *Genetic Algorithms and Simulated Annealing*. Morgan Kaufmann, San Mateo, CA, 1987, pp. 74–88.

328. D. E. Goldberg. *Genetic Algorithms in Search, Optimization, and Machine Learning*. Addison-Wesley, 1989.

329. D. E. Goldberg, D. E. Korb, and K. Deb. Messy genetic algorithms: Motivation, analysis and first results. *Complex Systems*, 3:493–530, 1989.

330. D. E. Goldberg and R. Lingle. Alleles, loci, and the traveling salesman problem. In J. J. Grefenstette, editor, *1st International Conference on Genetic Algorithms and Their Applications*. Lawrence Erlbaum Associates, 1985, pp. 154–159.

331. D. E. Goldberg and J. Richardson. Genetic algorithms with sharing for multimodal function optimization. In *2nd International Conference on Genetic Algorithms (ICGA'2)*. Lawrence Erlbaum, Hillsdale, NJ, 1987, pp. 41–49.

332. D. E. Goldberg and R. E. Smith. Nonstationary function optimization using genetic algorithms with dominance and diploidy. In J. J. Grefenstette, editor, *2nd International Conference on Genetic Algorithms*, Cambridge, MA, 1987, pp. 59–68.

333. B. Golden, J. Pepper, and T. Vossen. Using genetic algorithms for setting parameter values in heuristic search. *Intelligent Engineering Systems Through Artificial Neural Networks*, 1:9–32, 1998.

334. I. E. Golovkin, S. J. Louis, and R. C. Mancini. Parallel implementation of niched Pareto genetic algorithm code for X-ray plasma spectroscopy. In *Congress on Evolutionary Computation (CEC'02)*, 2002, pp. 1820–1824.

335. R. E. Gomory. Outline of an algorithm for integer solutions to linear programs. *Bulletin AMS*, 64:275–278, 1958.

336. F. Gonzalez and D. Dasgupta. Anomaly detection using real-valued negative selection. *Genetic Programming and Evolvable Machines*, 4(4):383–403, 2003.

337. P. Good. *Permutation test: A Practical Guide to Resampling Methods for Testing Hypothesis*. Springer, 1994.

338. S. Goss, S. Aron, J. L. Deneubourg, and J. M. Pasteels. Self-organized shortcuts in the Argentine ant. *Naturwissenschaften*, 76:579–581, 1989.

339. D. R. Greening. Parallel simulated annealing techniques. *Physica D*, 42:293–306, 1990.

340. J. J. Grefenstette. Incorporating problem specific knowledge into genetic algorithms. In L. Davis, editor, *Genetic Algorithms and Simulated Annealing, Research Notes in Artificial Intelligence*, Morgan Kaufmann, San Mateo, CA, 1987, pp. 42–60.

341. D. Grierson and W. Pak. Optimal sizing, geometrical and topological design using a genetic algorithm. *Structural Optimization*, 6(3):151–159, 1993.

342. M. Grotschel, M. Junger, and G. Reinelt. A cutting plane algorithm for the linear ordering problem. *Operations Research*, 32(6):1195–1220, 1985.

343. J. Gu and X. Huang. Efficient local search with search space smoothing: A case study of the traveling salesman problem. *IEEE Transactions on Systems Man and Cybernetics*, 24(5):728–735, 1994.

344. G. Gutin and P. Punnen. *The Traveling Salesman Problem and its Variations*. Kluwer Academic Publishers, 2002.

345. G. M. Gutin. On the efficiency of a local algorithm for solving the traveling salesman problem. *Automation and Remote Control*, 11(2):1514–1519, 1988.

346. G. M. Gutin. Exponential neighborhood local search for the traveling salesman problem. *Computers and Operations Research*, 26(4):313–320, 1999.

347. G. M. Gutin and A. Yeo. Small diameter neighborhood graphs for the traveling salesman problem. *Computers and Operations Research*, 26:321–327, 1999.

348. W. J. Gutjahr. ACO algorithms with guaranteed convergence to the optimal solution. *Information Processing Letters*, 82:145–153, 2002.

349. D. Habet, C. M. Li, L. Devendeville, and M. Vasquez. A hybrid approach for SAT. In *CP'2003 Principles and Practice of Constraint Programming*, Ithaca, NY, LNCS No. 2470. Springer, 2002, pp. 172–184.

350. A. B. Hadj-Alouane and J. C. Bean. A genetic algorithm for the multiple-choice integer program. *Operations Research*, 45(1):92–101, 1997.

351. Y. Y. Haimes, L. S. Lasdon, and D. A. Wismer. On a bicriterion formulation of the problems of integrated system identification and system optimization. *IEEE Transactions on Systems, Man and Cybernetics*, 1:296–297, 1971.

352. B. Hajek and G. Sasaki. Simulated annealing: To cool or not. *Systems and Control Letters*, 12:443–447, 1989.

353. P. Hajela and C. Y. Lin. Genetic search strategies in multicriterion optimal design. *Structural Optimization*, 4:99–107, 1992.

354. A. M. Haldar, A. Nayak, A. Choudhary, and P. Banerjee. Parallel algorithms for FPGA placement. *Proceedings of the Great Lakes Symposium on VLSI*, 2000, pp. 86–94.

355. D. Halhal, G. A. Walters, D. Ouazar, and D. A. Savic. Water network rehabilitation with a structured messy genetic algorithm. *Journal of Water Resources Planning and Management*, 123(3):137–146, 1997.

356. K.-H. Han and J.-H. Kim. Quantum-inspired evolutionary algorithm for a class of combinatorial optimization. *IEEE Transactions on Evolutionary Computation*, 6(6):580–593, 2002.

357. J. Handl, D. B. Kell, and J. Knowles. Multi-objective optimization in bioinformatics and computational biology. *IEEE Transactions on Evolutionary Computation*, 5(2):1–59, 2006.

358. M. P. Hansen. Tabu search in multiobjective optimisation: MOTS. In *Proceedings of the 13th International Conference on Multiple Criteria Decision Making (MCDM'97)*, Cape Town, South Africa, 1997.

359. M. P. Hansen. Use of substitute scalarizing functions to guide local search based heuristic: The case of the moTSP. *Journal of Heuristics*, 6:419–431, 2000.

360. M. P. Hansen and A. Jaskiewicz. Evaluating the quality of approximations to the non-dominated set. Technical Report IMM-REP-1998-7, Technical University of Denmark, March 1998.

361. N. Hansen and S. Kern. Evaluating the CMA evolution strategy on multimodal test functions. In X. Yao et al, editors, *Parallel Problem Solving from Nature - (PPSN VIII)*. Springer, 2004, pp. 282–291.

362. N. Hansen, S. D. Muller, and P. Koumoutsakos. Reducing the time complexity of the derandomized evolution strategy with covariance matrix adaptation (CMA-ES). *Evolutionary Computation*, 11(1):1–18, 2003.

363. N. Hansen and A. Ostermeier. Adapting arbitrary normal mutation distributions in evolution strategies: The covariance matrix adaptation. In *IEEE Conference on Evolutionary Computation (ICEC'96)*, 1996, pp. 312–317.

364. P. Hansen. The steepest ascent mildest descent heuristic for combinatorial programming. In *Congress on Numerical Methods in Combinatorial Optimization*, Capri, Italy, 1986.

365. P. Hansen, M. Mladenovic, and D. Perez-Britos. Variable neighborhood decomposition search. *Journal of Heuristics*, 7(4):330–350, 2001.

366. P. Hansen and N. Mladenovic. Variable neighborhood search. In *Search Methodologies*. Springer, 2005, pp. 211–238.

367. J. P. Hart and A. W. Shogan. Semi-greedy heuristics: An empirical study. *Operations Research Letters*, 6(3):107–114, 1987.

368. W. E. Hart. *Adaptive Global Optimization with Local Search*. PhD thesis, University of California, San Diego, CA, 1994.

369. W. D. Harvey and M. L. Ginsberg. Limited discrepancy search. In *IJCAI International Joint Conference on Artificial Intelligence*. Morgan Kaufmann, 1997, pp. 607–613.

370. S. Helbig and D. Pateva. On several concepts for epsilon-efficiency. *OR Spectrum*, 16(3):179–186, 1994.

371. M. Held and R. M. Karp. The traveling-salesman problem and minimum spanning trees. *Operations Research*, 18:1138–1162, 1970.

372. M. Herdy. Evolutionary optimisation based on subjective selection: Evolving blends of coffee. In *5th European Congress on Intelligent Techniques and Soft Computing (EUFIT'97)*, 1997, pp. 640–644.

373. A. Hertz, B. Jaumard, C. C. Ribeiro, and W. P. Formosinho Filho. A multicriteria tabu search approach to cell formation problems in group technology with multiple objectives. *RAIRO Recherche Opérationnelle/Operations Research*, 28(3):303–328, 1994.

374. A. Hertz and M. Widmer. La méthode tabou appliquée aux problèmes d'ordonnancement. *Automatique, Productique, Informatique Industrielle*, 29(4):353–378, 1995.

375. W. D. Hillis. Co-evolving parasites improve simulated evolution as an optimization procedure. *Physica D*, 42(1):228–234, 1990.

376. K. S. Hindi, K. Fleszar, and C. Charalambous. An effective heuristic for the CLSP with setup times. *Journal of the Operations Research Society*, 54:490–498, 2003.

377. R. Hinterding, Z. Michalewicz, and A.-E. Eiben. Adaptation in evolutionary computation: A survey. In *Proceedings of the IEEE Conference on Evolutionary Computation*, Indianapolis, IN, April 1997, pp. 65–69.

378. T. Hiroyasu, M. Miki, and M. Negami. Distributed genetic algorithms with randomized migration rate. In *Proceedings of the IEEE Conference of Systems, Man and Cybernetics*, Vol. 1. IEEE Press, 1999, pp. 689–694.

379. S. L. Ho, Y. Shiyou, N. Guangzheng, E. W. C. Lo, and H. C. Wong. A particle swarm optimization based method for multiobjective design optimizations. *IEEE Transactions on Magnetics*, 41(5):1756–1759, 2005.

380. D. S. Hochbaum. *Approximation Algorithms for NP-Hard Problems*. International Thomson Publishing, 1996.

381. S. A. Hofmeyr and S. Forrest. Architecture for an artificial immune system. *Evolutionary Computation*, 7(1):45–68, 2000.

382. T. Hogg and C. Williams. Solving the really hard problems with cooperative search. In *11th Conference on Artificial Intelligence (AAAI'93)*. AAAI Press, 1993, pp. 231–236.

383. J. H. Holland. Outline for a logical theory of adaptive systems. *Journal of the ACM*, 3:297–314, 1962.

384. J. H. Holland. *Adaptation in Natural and Artificial Systems*. University of Michigan Press, Ann Arbor, MI, 1975.

385. S.-C. Hong and Y.-B. Park. A heuristic for a bi-objective vehicle routing with time window constraints. *International Journal of Production Economics*, 62:249–258, 1999.

386. T.-P. Hong, H.-S. Wang, and W.-C. Chen. Simultaneous applying multiple mutation operators in genetic algorithm. *Journal of Heuristics*, 6(4):439–455, 2000.

387. W. Hordijk. A measure of landscapes. *Evolutionary Computation*, 4(4):335–360, 1996.

388. J. Horn and N. Nafpliotis. Multiobjective optimization using the niched Pareto genetic algorithm. IlliGAL Report 93005, Illinois Genetic Algorithm Laboratory, University of Illinois at Urbana-Champaign, Illinois, USA, 1993.

389. J. Horn, N. Nafpliotis, and D. E. Goldberg. A niched Pareto genetic algorithm for multiobjective optimization. In *Proceeding of the 1st IEEE Conference on Evolutionary Computation, IEEE World Congress on Computational Intelligence*, Vol. 1, 1994, pp. 82–87.

390. T. C. Hu, A. B. Kahng, and C.-W. A. Tsao. Old bachelor acceptance: A new class of nonmonotone threshold accepting methods. *ORSA Journal on Computing*, 7(4):417–425, 1995.

391. X. Hu, C. Eberhart, and Y. Shi. Particle swarm with extended memory for multiobjective optimization. In *IEEE Swarm Intelligence Symposium*, Indianapolis, IN, 2003, pp. 193–197.

392. M. D. Huang, F. Romeo, and A. L. Sangiovanni-Vincentelli. An efficient general cooling schedule for simulated annealing. In *IEEE International Conference on Computer-Aided Design*, Santa Clara, CA, 1986, pp. 381–384.

393. S. Huband, L. Barone, L. While, and P. Hingston. A scalable multi-objective test problem toolkit. In *Evolutionary Multi-Criterion Optimization (EMO-2005)*, LNCS Vol. 3410. Springer, 2005, pp. 280–295.

394. B. A. Huberman. The performance of cooperative processes. *Physica D*, 42:38–47, 1990.

395. J. Hunt and D. Cooke. An adaptive and distributed learning mechanism system based on the immune system. In *IEEE International Conference on Systems, Man and Cybernetics*, 1995, pp. 2494–2499.

396. J. Hurink. An exponential neighborhood for a one-machine batching problem. *OR Spektrum*, 21:461–476, 1999.

397. P. Husbands and F. Mill. Simulated co-evolution as the mechanism for emergent planning and scheduling. In R. Belew and K. Booker, editors, *4th International Conference on Genetic Algorithms,* San Diego, CA, July 1991. Morgan Kaufmann, 1991, pp. 264–270.

398. P. Husbands, F. Mill, and S. Warrington. Genetic algorithms, production plan optimisation and scheduling. In H.-P. Schewefel and R. Manner, editors, *Parallel Problem Solving from Nature,* Dortmund, Germany, Oct 1990, LNCS Vol. 496. Springer, 1990, pp. 80–84.

399. C.-L. Hwang and M.-J. Lin. *Group Decision Making Under Multiple Criteria: Methods and Applications.* Springer, 1987.

400. C. L. Hwang and A. S. M. Masud. Multiple objective decision making—methods and applications: A state-of-the-art survey. In *Lectures Notes in Economics and Mathematical Systems,* Vol. 164. Springer, Berlin, 1979.

401. P. Hyde. *Java Thread Programming.* Sams, 1999.

402. L. Ingber. Adaptive simulated annealing. *Control and Cybernetics,* 25(1):33–54, 1996.

403. S. Iredi, D. Merkle, and M. Middendorf. Bi-criterion optimization with multi colony ant algorithms. In *Conference on Evolutionary Multi-Criterion Optimization (EMO'01),* LNCS 1993, 2001, pp. 358–372.

404. H. Ishibuchi and T. Murata. A multi-objective genetic local search algorithm and its application to flowshop scheduling. *IEEE Transactions on Systems, Man, and Cybernetics—Part C: Applications and Reviews,* 28(3):392–403, 1998.

405. H. Ishibuchi, N. Tsukamoto, and Y. Nojima. Behavior of evolutionary many-objective optimization. In *10th International Conference on Computer Modeling and Simulation, (UKSIM'2008),* 2008, pp. 266–271.

406. C. A. R. Jahuira and E. Cuadros-Vargas. Solving the TSP by mixing GAs with minimal spanning trees. In *1st International Conference of the Peruvian Computer Society,* Lima, Peru, 2003, pp. 123–132.

407. W. Jakob, M. Gorges-Schleuter, and C. Blume. Application of genetic algorithms to task planning and learning. In R. Manner and B. Manderick, editors, *Parallel Problem Solving from Nature (PPSN'2),* North-Holland, Amsterdam, 1992, pp. 291–300.

408. A. Jaszkiewicz. Genetic local search for multiple objective combinatorial optimization. Technical Report RA-014/98, Institute of Computing Science, Poznan University of Technology, 1998.

409. A. Jaszkiewicz. Genetic local search for multi-objective combinatorial optimization. *European Journal of Operational Research,* 137:50–71, 2002.

410. J. Jaszkiewicz. Path relinking for multiple objective combinatorial optimization: TSP case study. In *16th Mini-EURO Conference and 10th Meeting of EWGT (Euro Working Group Transportation),* 2005.

411. M. T. Jensen. Guiding single-objective optimization using multi-objective methods. In *Applications of Evolutionary Computation.* Springer, 2003, pp. 268–279.

412. N. K. Jerne. Toward a network theory of the immune system. In *Annales d'Immunologic (Institute Pasteur),* Paris, France, 1974, pp. 373–389.

413. Y. Jin. A comprehensive survey of fitness approximation in evolutionary computation. *Soft Computing,* 9(1):3–12, 2005.

414. Y. Jin and J. Branke. Evolutionary optimization in uncertain environments—a survey. *IEEE Transactions on Evolutionary Computation,* 9(3):303–317, 2005.

415. Y. Jin and B. Sendhoff. Trade-off between performance and robustness: An evolutionary multiobjective approach. In *Evolutionary Multicriterion Optimization (EMO'03)*, LNCS Vol. 2632. Springer, 2003, pp. 237–251.

416. Y. Jin and B. Sendhoff. Reducing fitness evaluations using clustering techniques and neural network ensembles. In *Genetic and Evolutionary Computation (GECCO'2004)*, LNCS Vol. 3102. Springer, 2004, pp. 688–699.

417. P. Jog, J. Y. Suh, and D. Van Gucht. The effects of population size, heuristic crossover and local improvement on a genetic algorithm for the traveling salesman problem. In *3rd International Conference Genetic Algorithms*. Morgan Kaufmann, USA, 1989.

418. D. S. Johnson. Local optimization and the travelling salesman problem. In *17th Colloquium on Automata, Languages and Programming*, LNCS Vol. 443. Springer, Berlin, 1990, pp. 446–461.

419. D. S. Johnson. A theoretician's guide to the experimental analysis of algorithms. In M. H. Goldwasser, D. S. Johnson, and C. C. McGeoch, editors, *Data Structures, Near Neighbor Searches, and Methodology: Fifth and Sixth DIMACS Implementation Challenges*. American Mathematical Society, Providence, RI, 2002, pp. 215–250. .

420. D. S. Johnson, C. R. Aragon, L. A. McGeoch, and C. Schevon. Optimization by simulated annealing: An experimental evaluation. Part I. Graph partitioning. *Operations Research*, 37:865–892, 1989.

421. D. S. Johnson and L. A. McGeoch. The travelling salesman problem: A case study in local optimization. In *Local Search in Combinatorial Optimization*. Wiley, 1997, pp. 215–310.

422. R. Johnson and B. Foote. Designing reusable classes. *Journal of Object-Oriented Programming*, 1(2):22–35, 1988.

423. J. Joines and C. Houck. On the use of non-stationary penalty functions to solve nonlinear constrained optimization problems with genetic algorithms. In D. Fogel, editor, *1st IEEE Conference on Evolutionary Computation*. IEEE Press, 1994, pp. 579–584.

424. B. R. Jones, W. A. Crossley, and A. S. Lyrintzis. Aerodynamic and aeroacoustic optimization of airfoils via parallel genetic algorithm. *Journal of Aircraft*, 37(6):1088–1098, 2000.

425. G. Jones, R. D. Brown, D. E. Clark, P. Willett, and R. C. Glen. Searching databases of two-dimensional and three-dimensional chemical structures using genetic algorithms. In S. Forrest, editor, *5th International Conference on Genetic Algorithms*, Morgan Kaufmann, San Mateo, CA, 1993, pp. 597–602.

426. M. Jones. *A object-oriented framework for the implementation of search techniques*. PhD thesis, University of East Anglia, 2000.

427. M. Jones, G. McKeown, and V. Rayward-Smith. Templar: A object-oriented framework for distributed combinatorial optimization. In *Proceedings of the UNICOM Seminar on Modern Heuristics for Decision Support*, Brunel University, UK, 1998.

428. T. Jones. *Evolutionary algorithms, fitness landscapes and search*. PhD thesis, University of New Mexico, Albuquerque, NM, May 1995.

429. T. Jones and S. Forrest. Fitness distance correlation as a measure of problem difficulty for genetic algorithms. In *Proceedings of the 6th International Conference on Genetic Algorithms*. Morgan Kaufmann, San Francisco, CA, 1995, pp. 184–192.

430. K. A. De Jong. *An analysis of the behavior of a class of genetic adaptive systems*. PhD thesis, Ann Arbor, University of Michigan, 1975.

431. K. A. De Jong. Genetic algorithms: A 10 year perspective. In *International Conference on Genetic Algorithms*, 1985, pp. 169–177.

432. K. De Jong and W. M. Spears. Using genetic algorithms to solve NP-complete problems. In J. D. Schaffer, editor, *3rd International Conference on Genetic Algorithms*. Morgan Kaufmann, 1989, pp. 124–132.

433. L. Jourdan, M. Basseur, and E.-G. Talbi. Hybridizing exact methods and metaheuristics: A taxonomy. *European Journal of Operational Research*, 2009.

434. L. Jourdan, D. Corne, D. A. Savic, and G. A. Walters. Preliminary investigation of the learnable evolution model for faster/better multiobjective water systems design. In *International Conference on Evolutionary Multi-Criterion Optimization (EMO'05)*, LNCS Vol. 3410. Springer, 2005, pp. 841–855.

435. L. Jourdan, C. Dhaenens, and E.-G. Talbi. Using data mining techniques to help metaheuristics: A short survey. In *Hybrid Metaheuristics (HM'2006)*, Gran Canaria, Spain, LNCS Vol. 4030, 2006, pp. 57–69.

436. N. Jozefowiez. *Modélisation et résolution approchée de problèmes de tournées multi-objectif*. PhD thesis, University of Lille, Lille, France, 2004.

437. N. Jozefowiez, F. Semet, and E.-G. Talbi. Parallel and hybrid models for multi-objective optimization: Application to the vehicle routing problem. In J. Guervos, P. Adamidis, H.-G. Beyer, J.-L. Fernández-Villacanas, and H.-P. Schwefel, editors, *Parallel Problem Solving from Nature (PPSN VII)*, Granada, Spain, LNCS Vol. 2439. Springer-Verlag, 2000. pp. 271–280.

438. N. Jozefowiez, F. Semet, and E.-G. Talbi. The bi-objective covering tour problem. *Computers and Operations Research*, 34:1929–1942, 2007.

439. N. Jozefowiez, F. Semet, and E.-G. Talbi. Multi-objective vehicle routing problems. *European Journal of Operational Research*, 189(2):293–309, 2008.

440. M. Juenger, G. Reinelt, and S. Thienel. Practical problem solving with cutting plane algorithms in combinatorial optimization. In *DIMACS Series in Discrete Mathematics and Theoretical Computer Science*, Vol. 20. AMS, Providence, RI, 1995, pp. 111–152.

441. H. Juille and J. B. Pollack. Massively parallel genetic programming. In P. J. Angeline and K. E. Kinnear Jr., editors, *Advances in Genetic Programming 2*. MIT Press, Cambridge, MA, 1996, pp. 339–358.

442. P. Kall and J. Mayer. *Stochastic Linear Programming: Models, Theory, and Computation*. Springer, 2005.

443. O. Kamarainen and H. E. Sakkout. Local probing applied to scheduling. In *CP'2002 International Conference on Principles and Practice of Constraint Programming*, 2002, pp. 155–171.

444. N. K. Kamarkar. A new polynomial-time algorithm for linear programming. *Combinatorica*, 4:373–395, 1984.

445. D. Karaboga. An idea based on honey bee swarm for numerical optimization. Technical Report TR-06, Erciyes University, Kayseri, Turkey, Oct 2005.

446. D. Karaboga and B. Basturk. On the performance of artificial bee colony (ABC) algorithm. *Applied Soft Computing*, 8(1):687–697, 2008.

447. E. K. Karasakal and M. Köksalan. A simulated annealing approach to bicriteria scheduling problems on a single machine. *Journal of Heuristics*, 6(3):311–327, 2000.

448. H. Kargupta and D. E. Goldberg. Search, blackbox optimization, and sample complexity. In R. K. Belew and M. D. Vose, editors, *4th Workshop on Foundations of Genetic Algorithms (FOGA)*, San Diego, CA. Morgan Kaufmann. 1996, pp. 291–324.

449. N. Karonis, B. Toonen, and I. Foster. MPICH-G2: A grid-enabled implementation of the message passing interface. *Journal of Parallel and Distributed Computing*, 63(5):551–563, 2003.

450. R. M. Karp. Probabilistic analysis of partitioning algorithms for the traveling salesman problem in the plane. *Mathematics of Operations Research*, 2:209–224, 1977.

451. S. A. Kauffman. Adaptation on rugged fitness landscapes. In D. L. Stein, editor, *Santa Fe Institute Studies in the Sciences of Complexity*, Vol. 1 of *Lectures in Complex Systems*. Addison-Wesley, 1988, pp. 619–712.

452. S. A. Kauffman. *The Origins of Order: Self-Organization and Selection in Evolution*. Oxford University Press, 1993.

453. M. Keijzer, J. Merelo, G. Romero, and M. Schoenauer. Evolving objects: A general purpose evolutionary computation library. In *Proceedings of the 5th International Conference on Artificial Evolution (EA'01)*, Le Creusot, France, 2001, pp. 231–244.

454. J. Kelsey and J. Timmis. Immune inspired somatic contiguous hypermutation for function optimization. In E. Cantu Paz, editor, *GECCO Genetic and Evolutionary Computation Conference*, LNCS Vol. 2723. Springer, 2003, pp. 207–218.

455. J. Kennedy. The behavior of particles. In V. W. Porto, N. Saravanan, and D. Waagen, editors, *International Conference on Evolutionary Programming VII*, San Diego, CA, LNCS Vol. 1447. Springer, 1998, pp. 581–589.

456. J. Kennedy. Stereotyping: Improving particle swarm performance with cluster analysis. In *International Conference on Evolutionary Computation*, 2000, pp. 1507–1512.

457. J. Kennedy and R. C. Eberhart. Particle swarm optimization. In *IEEE International Conference on Neural Networks*, Perth, Australia, 1995, pp. 1942–1948.

458. J. Kennedy and R. C. Eberhart. A discrete binary version of the particle swarm algorithm. In *IEEE International Conference Systems, Man and Cybernetic*, Oct 1997, pp. 4104–4108.

459. J. Kennedy and R. C. Eberhart. *Swarm Intelligence*. Morgan Kaufmann, San Francisco, CA, 2001.

460. M. Khabzaoui, C. Dhaenens, and E.-G. Talbi. A multicriteria genetic algorithm to analyze DNA microarray data. In *CEC'2004, Congress on Evolutionary Computation*, Portland, OR, 2004, pp. 1874–1881.

461. B. N. Khoury, P. M. Paradalos, and D. Z. Zhu. A test problem generator for the Steiner problem in graphs. *ACM Transactions on Mathematical Software*, 19:509–522, 1993.

462. H. Kim, Y. Hayashi, and K. Nara. The performance of hybridized algorithm of genetic algorithm simulated annealing and tabu search for thermal unit maintenance scheduling. In *2nd IEEE Conference on Evolutionary Computation (ICEC'95)*, Perth, Australia, Dec 1995, pp. 114–119.

463. H.-S. Kim and S.-B. Cho. An efficient genetic algorithm with less fitness evaluation by clustering. In *Congress on Evolutionary Computation (CEC'01)*, IEEE Press, 2001, pp. 887–894.

464. S. Kirkpatrick, C. D. Gelatt, and M. P. Vecchi. Optimization by simulated annealing. *Science*, 220(4598):671–680, 1983.

465. S. Kirkpatrick and G. Toulouse. Configuration space analysis of the travelling salesman problem. *Journal de Physique*, 46:1277–1292, 1985.

466. J. Klockgether and H.-P. Schwefel. Two-phase nozzle and hollow core jet experiments. In D. Elliot, editor, *11th Symposium on Engineering Aspects of Magnetohydrodynamics*, California Institute of Technology, Pasadena, CA, 1977, pp. 141–148.

467. J. D. Knowles and D. Corne. Approximating the nondominated front using the Pareto archived evolution strategy. *Evolutionary Computation*, 8(2):149–172, 2000.

468. J. D. Knowles and D. W. Corne. On metrics for comparing non-dominated sets. *Congress on Evolutionary Computation (CEC'2002)*, Vol. 1. IEEE Service Center, Piscataway, NJ, May 2002, pp. 711–716.

469. J. D. Knowles and D. W. Corne. Bounded Pareto archiving: theory and practice. In *Metaheuristics for Multi-Objective Optimization*, Vol. 535 of *Lecture Notes in Economics and Mathematical Systems*. Springer, 2004.

470. J. D. Knowles, R. A. Watson, and D. W. Corne. Reducing local optima in single-objective problems by multi-objectivization. In *1st International Conference on Evolutionary Multi-Criterion Optimization*, Zurich, Switzerland. Springer, 2001, pp. 269–283.

471. D. Knuth. *The Art of Computer Programming*. Addison-Wesley, 1981.

472. T. Koopmans. Analysis and production as an efficient combination of activities. In *Activity Analysis of Production and Allocation*. Wiley, New York, 1951, pp. 33–97.

473. R. Korf, Depth-first iterative-deepening: An optimal admissible tree search, *Artificial Intelligence*, 27(1):97–109, 1985.

474. R. E. Korf. From approximate to optimal solutions: A case study of number partitioning. In C. S. Mellish, editor, *14th IJCAI International Joint Conference on Artificial Intelligence*. Morgan Kauffman, 1995, pp. 266–272.

475. P. Korhonen and J. Laakso. A visual interactive method for solving the multiple criteria problem. *European Journal of Operational Research*, 24:277–287, 1986.

476. A. Kosorukoff. Human-based genetic algorithm. *IEEE Transactions on Systems, Man, and Cybernetics*, 5:3464–3469, 2001.

477. K. Kostikas and C. Fragakis. Genetic programming applied to mixed integer programming. In M. Keijzer et al., editors, *EuroGP Conference on Genetic Programming*, LNCS Vol. 3003. Springer, 2004, pp. 113–124.

478. C. Koulamas, S. R. Anthony, and R. Jaen. A survey of simulated annealing application to operations-research problems. *OMEGA International Journal of Management*, 22:41–56, 1994.

479. J. Koza and D. Andre. Parallel genetic programming on a network of transputers. Technical Report CS-TR-95-1542, Stanford University, 1995.

480. J. R. Koza. *Genetic Programming*. MIT Press, Cambridge, MA, 1992.

481. N. Krasnogor and J. Smith. MAFRA: A Java memetic algorithms framework. In A. A. Freitas, W. Hart, N. Krasnogor, and J. Smith, editors, *Data Mining with Evolutionary Algorithms*, Las Vegas, NV, 2000, pp. 125–131.

482. S. A. Kravitz and R. A. Rutenbar. Placement by simulated annealing on a multiprocessor. *IEEE Transactions in Computer-Aided Design*, 6:534–549, 1987.

483. B. Krishnamurthy. Constructing test cases for partitioning heuristics. *IEEE Transactions on Computers*, 36(9):1112–1114, 1987.

484. M. Krueger. *Méthodes d'analyse d'algorithmes d'optimisation stochastiques à l'aide d'algorithmes génétiques*. PhD thesis, Ecole Nationale Supèrieure des Télécommunications, Paris, France, Dec 1993.

485. H. Kuhn and A. Tucker. Nonlinear programming. In J. Neyman, editor, *2nd Berkeley Symposium on Mathematical Statistics and Probability*, University of California, Berkeley, CA, 1951, pp. 481–492.

486. S. Kukkonen and K. Deb. A fast and effective method for pruning of non-dominated solutions in many-objective problems. Technical Report 4, Indian Institute of Technology, Kanpur, India, 2006.

487. V. Kumar, A. Grama, A. Gupta, and G. Karypis. *Introduction to Parallel Computing: Design and Analysis of Algorithms*. Addison-Wesley, 1994.

488. F. Kursawe. A variant of evolution strategies for vector optimization. In H.-P. Schwefel and R. Männer, editors, *Parallel Problem Solving from Nature*. Springer, 1991, pp. 193–197.

489. P. J. M. Van Laarhoven and E. H. L. Aarts. *Simulated Annealing: Theory and Applications*. Reidel, Dordrecht, 1987.

490. P. Lacomme, C. Prins, and M. Sevaux. A genetic algorithm for a biobjective capacitated arc routing problem. *Computers and Operations Research*, 33:3473–3493, 2006.

491. M. Laguna and R. Marti. *Scatter Search: Methodology and Implementations in C*. Kluwer Academic Publishers, Boston, MA, 2003.

492. H. H. Laidlaw and R. E. Page. Mating designs. In *Bee Genetic and Breeding*. Academic Press, 1986, pp. 323–341.

493. W. B. Langdon and R. Poli. *Foundations of Genetic Programming*. Springer, 2002.

494. M. Laumanns, L. Thiele, K. Deb, and E. Zitzler. Combining convergence and diversity in evolutionary multi-objective optimization. *Evolutionary Computation*, 10(3):263–282, 2002.

495. M. Laumanns, L. Thiele, and E. Zitzler. An adaptive scheme to generate the Pareto front based on the epsilon-constraint method. Technical Report TIK-report 199, Computer Engineering and Networks Laboratory (TIK), Swiss Federal Institute of Technology (ETH) Zurich, 2004.

496. A. Le Bouthillier and T. G. Crainic. Co-operative parallel meta-heuristic for vehicle routing problems with time windows. *Computers and Operation Research*, 32(7):685–1708, 2005.

497. T.-R. Lee and J.-H. Ueng. A study of vehicle routing problem with load balancing. *International Journal of Physical Distribution and Logistics Management*, 29:646–648, 1998.

498. J. Lemesre, C. Dhaenens, and E.-G. Talbi. Méthode parallèle par partitions: Passage d'une méthode exacte bi-objectif à une méthode exacte multi-objectif. In *ROADEF'06 Proceedings*, 2006.

499. J. Lemesre, C. Dhaenens, and E.-G. Talbi. An exact parallel method for a bi-objective permutation flowshop problem. *European Journal of Operational Research (EJOR)*, 177(3):1641–1655, 2007.

500. J. Lemesre, C. Dhaenens, and E.-G. Talbi. Parallel partitioning method (PPM): A new exact method to solve bi-objective problems. *Computers and Operational Research*, 34(8):2450–2462, 2007.

501. J. R. Levenick. Inserting introns improves genetic algorithm success rate: Taking a cue from biology. In R. K. Belew and L. B. Booker, editors, *4th International Conference on Genetic Algorithms*, San Diego, CA, 1991, pp. 123–127.

502. D. Levine. *A parallel genetic algorithm for the set partitioning problem*. PhD thesis, Argonne National Laboratory, Illinois Institute of Technology, Argonne, USA, May 1994.

503. W. Li. Finding Pareto-optimal set by merging attractors for a bi-objective traveling salesman problem. In C. A. Coello, A.H. Aguirre, and E. Zitzler, editors, *EMO'2005 International Conference on Evolutionary Multi-Criterion Optimization*, Guanajanto, Mexico, LNCS Vol. 3410. Springer, 2005, pp. 797–810.

504. X. Li. A non-dominated sorting particle swarm optimizer for multiobjective optimization. In *Genetic and Evolutionary Computation Conference (GECCO'2003)*, LNCS Vol. 2723. Springer, 2003, pp. 37–48.

505. K.-H. Liang, X. Yao, and C. Newton. Combining landscape approximation and local search in global optimization. In *CEC'1999 Congress on Evolutionary Computation*, 1999, pp. 1514–1520.

506. A. Liefooghe, M. Basseur, L. Jourdan, and E.-G. Talbi. Combinatorial optimization of stochastic multi-objective problems: An application to the flow-shop scheduling problem. In *EMO'2007 Evolutionary Multi-Criterion Optimization*, LNCS Vol. 4403. Springer, 2007, pp. 457–471.

507. F. T. Lin, C. Y. Kao, and C. C. Hsu. Incorporating genetic algorithms into simulated annealing. *Proceedings of the 4th International Symposium on AI*, 1991, pp. 290–297.

508. S. Lin and B. Kernighan. An effective heuristic algorithm for the traveling salesman problem. *Operations Research*, 21:498–516, 1973.

509. S.-L. Lin, W. F. Punch, and E. D. Goodman. Coarse-grain parallel genetic algorithms: Categorization and new approach. In *6th IEEE Symposium on Parallel and Distributed Processing*, 1994, pp. 28–37.

510. D. A. Linkens and H. O. Nyongesa. A distributed genetic algorithm for multivariable fuzzy control. In *IEE Colloquium on Genetic Algorithms for Control Systems Engineering*, 1993, pp. 9/1–9/3.

511. F. G. Lobo, C. F. Lima, and H. Mártires. An architecture for massively parallelization of the compact genetic algorithm. In *Proceedings of the Genetic and Evolutionary Computation Conference (GECCO'2004)*, LNCS Vol. 3103. Springer, 2004, pp. 412–413.

512. M. Locatelli. Simulated annealing algorithms for continuous global optimization: Convergence conditions. *Journal of Optimization Theory and Applications*, 29(1):87–102, 2000.

513. W. L. Loh. On Latin hypercube sampling. *Annals of Statistics*, 33(6):2058–2080, 2005.

514. D. H. Loughlin. *Genetic algorithm-based optimization in the development of tropospheric ozone control strategies*. PhD thesis, North Carolina State University, Raleigh, NC, 1998.

515. D. H. Loughlin and S. Ranjithan. The neighborhood constraint method: A genetic algorithm-based multiobjective optimization technique. In T. Bäck, editor, *7th International Conference on Genetic Algorithms (ICGA'97)*, July 1997. Morgan Kaufmann, San Mateo, CA, 1997, pp. 666–673.

516. S. J. Louis. Genetic learning from experiences. In *Congress on Evolutionary Computations (CEC'2003)*, Australia, 2003, pp. 2118–2125.

517. H. R. Lourenco. Job-shop scheduling: Computational study of local search and large-step optimization methods. *European Journal of Operational Research*, 83:347–367, 1995.

518. H. R. Lourenco, O. Martin, and T. Stutzle. Iterated local search. In *Handbook of Metaheuristics*. Vol. 57 of *Operations Research and Management Science*. Kluwer Academic Publishers, 2002, pp. 321–353.

519. J. A. Lozano, P. Larrañaga, I. Inza, and E. Bengoetxea. *Towards a New Evolutionary Computation. Advances in Estimation of Distribution Algorithms*. Springer, 2006.

520. J. A. Lozano, R. Sagarna, and P. Larrañaga. Parallel estimation of distribution algorithms. In P. Larrañaga and J. A. Lozano, editors, *Estimation of Distribution Algorithms. A New Tool for Evolutionary Computation*. Kluwer Academic Publishers, 2001.

521. M. Lundy and A. Mees. Convergence of an annealing algorithm. *Mathematical Programming*, 34:111–124, 1986.

522. H. Maaranen, K. Miettinen, and A. Penttinen. On initial populations of a genetic algorithm for continuous optimization problems. *Journal of Global Optimization*, 37:405–436, 2007.

523. S. MacDonald. *From design patterns to frameworks to parallel programs*. PhD thesis, Department of Computing Science, University of Alberta, 2002.

524. S. W. Mahfoud and D. E. Goldberg. Parallel recombinative simulated annealing: A genetic algorithm. *Parallel Computing*, 21:1–28, 1995.

525. B. Manderick, M. De Weger, and P. Spiessens. The genetic algorithm and the fitness landscape. In *4th International Conference on Genetic Algorithms (ICGA'4)*, July 1991. Morgan Kauffman, La Jolla, CA, 1991, pp. 143–150.

526. L. Mandow and E. Millan. Goal programming and heuristic search. In R. Caballero, F. Ruiz, and R. Steuer, editors, *2nd International Conference on Multi-Objective Programming and Goal Programming (MOPGP'96)*, Torremolinos, Spain, May 1996. Springer, 1996, pp. 48–56.

527. V. Maniezzo. Exact and approximate nondeterministic tree-search procedures for the quadratic assignment problem. *INFORMS Journal on Computing*, 11(4):358–369, 1999.

528. C. E. Mariano and E. Morales. A multiple objective ant-Q algorithm for the design of water distribution irrigation networks. In *1st International Workshop on Ant Colony Optimization (ANTS'98)*, Brussels, Belgium, 1998.

529. C. E. Mariano and E. Morales. MOAQ and ANT-Q algorithm for multiple objective optimization problems. In *Proceedings of the Genetic and Evolutionary Computation Conference*, Orlando, FL, 1999, pp. 894–901.

530. O. Maron and A. W. Moore. Hoeffding races: Accelerating model selection search for classification and function approximation. In *Advances in Neural Information Processing Systems*, Vol. 6. Morgan Kaufmann, San Francisco, CA, 1994, pp. 59–66.

531. O. Martin, S.W. Otto, and E. W. Felten. Large-step Markov chains for the traveling salesman problem. *Complex Systems*, 5(3):299–326, 1991.

532. O. C. Martin, S. W. Otto, and E. W. Felten. Large-step Markov chains for the TSP: Incorporating local search heuristics. *Operation Research Letters*, 11:219–224, 1992.

533. P. Matzinger. Tolerance, danger and the extended family. *Annual Reviews of Immunology*, 12:991–1045, 1994.

534. P. Matzinger. The danger model: A renewed sense of self. *Science*, 296:301–305, 2002.

535. T. Mautor and P. Michelon. Mimausa: A new hybrid method combining exact solution and local search. In *2nd International Conference on Metaheuristics*, Sophia-Antipolis, France, 1997.

536. M. D. Mckay, R. J. Beckman, and W. J. Conover. A comparison of three methods for the selecting values of input variables in the analysis of output from a computer code. *Technometrics*, 21(2):239–245, 1979.

537. N. Melab, S. Cahon, and E.-G. Talbi. Grid computing for parallel bioinspired algorithms. *Journal of Parallel and Distributed Computing*, 66(8):1052–1061, 2006.

538. R. Mendes, J. R. Pereira, and J. Neves. A parallel architecture for solving constraint satisfaction problems. In *Proceedings of Metaheuristics International Conference 2001*, Vol. 2, Porto, Portugal, 2001, pp. 109–114.

539. A. Mendiburu, J. A. Lozano, and J. Miguel-Alonso. Parallel estimation of distribution algorithms: New approaches. Technical Report EHU-KAT-IK-1-3, Department of Computer Architecture and Technology, University of the Basque Country, Spain, 2003.

540. A. Mendiburu, J. Miguel-Alonso, and J. A. Lozano. Implementation and performance evaluation of a parallelization of estimation of Bayesian networks algorithms. Technical Report EHU-KAT-IK-XX-04, Computer Architecture and Technology, Department of Computer Architecture and Technology, University of the Basque Country, Spain, 2004.

541. D. Merkle and M. Middendorf. Swarm intelligence. In *Search Methodologies*. Springer, 2005. pp. 401–435.

542. P. Merz. Advanced fitness landscape analysis and the performance of memetic algorithms. *Evolutionary Computation*, 12(3):303–325, 2004.

543. N. Metropolis, A. Rosenbluth, M. Rosenbluth, A. Teller, and E. Teller. Equation of state calculations by fast computing machines. *Journal of Chemical Physics*, 21:1087–1092, 1953.

544. H. Meunier. *Métaheuristiques pour l'optimisation multi-critères : Application à la conception de réseaux de radio communication mobiles*. PhD thesis, LIFL/University of Lille, Lille, France, July 1999.

545. H. Meunier, E.-G. Talbi, and P. Reininger. A multiobjective genetic algorithm for radio network optimization. In *Proceedings of the 2000 Congress on Evolutionary Computation (CEC'00)*, La Jolla, CA. IEEE Press, 2000, pp. 317–324.

546. M. Mezmaz, N. Melab, and E.-G. Talbi. A grid-enabled branch and bound algorithm for solving challenging combinatorial optimization problems. In *21st International Parallel and Distributed Processing Symposium (IPDPS'2007)*, Long Beach, CA. IEEE, 2007, pp. 1–9.

547. Z. Michalewicz and N. Attia. Evolutionary optimization of constrained problems. In *3rd Annual Conference on Evolutionary Programming*. World Scientific, 1994, pp. 98–108.

548. Z. Michalewicz, G. Nazhiyath, and M. Michalewicz. A note on usefulness of geometrical crossover for numerical optimization problems. In *5th Annual Conference on Evolutionary Programming*, San Diego, CA. MIT Press, 1996, pp. 305–312.

549. R. S. Michalski. Learnable evolution model: Evolutionary processes guided by machine learning. *Machine Learning*, 38(1):9–40, 2000.

550. L. Michel and P. Van Hentenryck. Localizer++: An open library for local search. Technical Report CS-01-02, Department of Computer Science, Brown University, 2001.

551. R. Michel and M. Middendorf. An island model based ant system with lookahead for the shortest supersequence problem. In A.E. Eiben et al., editors, *5th International Conference on Parallel Problem Solving from Nature*, LNCS Vol. 1498. Springer, 1998, pp. 692–701.

552. R. Michel and M. Middendorf. An ACO algorithm for the shortest common supersequence problem. In D. Corne, M. Dorigo, and F. Glover, editors, *New Ideas in Optimization*. McGraw-Hill, London, UK, 1999, pp. 51–61.

553. M. Middendorf, F. Reischle, and H. Schmeck. Information exchange in multi colony ant algorithms. In J. Rolim et al., editors, *15th IPDPS Workshops*, LNCS Vol. 1800. Springer, 2000, pp. 645–652.

554. M. Middendorf, F. Reischle, and H. Schmeck. Multi colony ant algorithms. *Journal of Heuristic*, 8:305–320, 2002.

555. K. Miettinen. *Nonlinear Multiobjective Optimization*. Kluwer, 1999.

556. P. Mills, E. Tsang, and J. Ford. Applying an extended guided local search to the quadratic assignment problem. *Annals of Operations Research*, 118:121–135, 2003.

557. M. Minsky. Negative expertise. *International Journal of Expert Systems*, 7(1):13–19, 1994.

558. D. Mitchell, B. Selman, and H. Levesque. Hard and easy distributions of SAT problems. In P. Rosenbloom and P. Szolovits, editors, *10th National Conference on Artificial Intelligence*, AAAI Press, Menlo Park, CA, 1992, pp. 459–465.

559. M. Mitchell. *An Introduction to Genetic Algorithms*. MIT Press, Cambridge, MA, 1996.

560. M. Mladenovic and P. Hansen. Variable neighborhood search. *Computers and Operations Research*, 24:1097–1100, 1997.

561. N. Mladenovic. A variable neighborhood algorithm—a new metaheuristic for combinatorial optimization. In *Abstracts of Papers Presented at Optimization Days*, 1995.

562. D. Montgomery. *Design and Analysis of Experiments*. Wiley, 1984.

563. A. Moraglio, C. D. Chio, and R. Poli. Geometric particle swarm optimization. In *EUROGP'07 10th European Conference on Genetic Programming*, LNCS Vol. 4445. Springer, 2007, pp. 125–136.

564. R. W. Morrison. *Designing Evolutionary Algorithms for Dynamic Environments*. Springer, 2004.

565. P. Moscato and J. F. Fontanari. Convergence and finite-time behavior of simulated annealing. *Advances in Applied Probability*, 18:747–771, 1990.

566. S. Mostaghim, J. Branke, and H. Schmeck. Multi-objective particle swarm optimization on computer grids. In *Genetic and Evolutionary Computation Conference (GECCO'07)*, London, UK. ACM, 2007, pp. 869–875.

567. S. Mostaghim and J. Teich. The role of ϵ-dominance in multi objective particle swarm optimization methods. In *Congress on Evolutionary Computation (CEC'2003)*, Canberra, Australia. IEEE Press, 2003, pp. 1764–1771.

568. H. Muhlenbein and G. Paass. From recombination of genes to the estimation of distributions. In H. M. Voight et al., editors, *International Conference on Parallel Problem Solving from Nature (PPSN'IV)*, LNCS Vol. 1141. Springer, Berlin, 1996, pp. 178–187.

569. H. Muhlenbein, M. G. Schleuter, and O. Kramer. Evolution algorithms in combinatorial optimization. *Parallel Computing*, 7:65–85, 1988.

570. H. Muhlenbein, M. Schomisch, and J. Born. The parallel genetic algorithm as function optimizer. *Parallel Computing*, 17:619–632, 1991.

571. R. Myers and D. Montgomery. *Response Surface Methodologies*. Wiley, 1995.

572. A. Nagar, S. S. Heragu, and J. Haddock. A metaheuristic algorithm for a bi-criteria scheduling problem. *Annals of Operations Research*, 63:397–414, 1995.

573. K. Nanobe and T. Ibaraki. A tabu search approach to the constrained satisfaction problem as a general problem solver. *European Journal of Operational Research*, 106:599–623, 1998.

574. A. Narayek, S. Smith, and C. Ohler. Integrating local search advice into a refinement search solver (or not). In *CP'03 Workshop on Cooperative Constraint Problem Solvers*, 2003, pp. 29–43.

575. B. Naudts and L. Kallel. A comparison of predictive measures of problem difficulty in evolutionary algorithms. *IEEE Transactions on Evolutionary Computation*, 4(1):1–15, 2000.

576. A. J. Nebro, E. Alba, and F. Luna. Multi-objective optimization using grid computing. *Soft Computing Journal*, 11(6):531–540, 2004.

577. A. J. Nebro, F. Luna, E.-G. Talbi, and E. Alba. Parallel multiobjective optimization. In E. Alba, editor, *Parallel Metaheuristics*. Wiley, 2005, pp. 371–394.

578. J. A. Nelder and R. Mead. A simplex method for function minimization. *The Computer Journal*, 7:308–313, 1964.

579. G. Nemhauser and L. Wolsey. *Integer and Combinatorial Optimization*. Wiley, 1999.

580. F. Neumann and I. Wegener. Minimum spanning trees made easier via multi-objective optimization. *Natural Computing*, 5(3):305–319, 2006.

581. H. Niederreiter. *Random Number Generation and Quasi-Monte Carlo Methods*. SIAM, Philadelphia, NJ, 1992.

582. V. Nissen. Solving the quadratic assignment problem with clues from nature. *IEEE Transactions on Neural Networks*, 5(1):66–72, 1994.

583. J. Nocedal and S. J. Wright. *Numerical Optimization*. Springer, 2006.

584. S. Nolfi and D. Floreano. Co-evolving predator and prey robots: Do arm races arise in artificial evolution? *Artificial Life*, 4(4):311–335, 1998.

585. A. Nowak, B. Szamrej, and B. Latané. From private attitude to public opinion: A dynamic theory of social impact. *Psychological Review*, 97:362–376, 1990.

586. W. Nuijten and C. Le Pape. Constraint based job scheduling with ILOG scheduler. *Journal of Heuristics*, 3:271–286, 1998.

587. V. Nwana, K. Darby-Dowman, and G. Mitra. A cooperative parallel heuristic for mixed zero-one linear programming. *European Journal of Operational Research*, 164:12–23, 2005.

588. S. Obayashi, S. Takahashi, and Y. Takeguchi. Niching and elitist models for multiobjective genetic algorithms. In *Parallel Problem Solving from Nature (PPSN'5)*, Amsterdam, Sept 1998. Springer, 1998.

589. J. Ocenásek and J. Schwarz. The parallel Bayesian optimization algorithm. In *European Symposium on Computational Intelligence*, 2000, pp. 61–67.

590. J. Ocenásek and J. Schwarz. The distributed Bayesian optimization algorithm for combinatorial optimization. In *Evolutionary Methods for Design, Optimisation and Control*, 2001, pp. 115–120.

591. T. Okabe, Y. Jin, M. Olhofer, and B. Sendhoff. On test functions for evolutionary multiobjective optimization. In *Parallel Problem Solving from Nature (PPSN VIII)*, 2004. pp. 792–802.

592. I. M. Oliver, D. J. Smith, and J. R. C. Holland. A study of permutation crossover operators on the traveling salesman problem. In J. J. Grefenstette, editor, *2nd International Conference on Genetic Algorithms*, Hillsdale, NJ, 1987, pp. 224–230.

593. B. Ombuki, B. J. Ross, and F. Hanshar. Multi-objective genetic algorithm for vehicle routing problem with time windows. *Applied Intelligence*, 24:17–30, 2006.

594. I. Ono and S. Kobayashi. A real-coded genetic algorithm for functional optimization using unimodal normal distribution crossover. In *ICGA-7, 7th International Conference on Genetic Algorithms*, 1997, pp. 246–253.

595. U.-M. O'Reilly and F. Oppacher. Hybridized crossover-based techniques for program discovery. In *IEEE International Conference on Evolutionary Computation (ICEC'95)*, Perth, Australia, Dec 1995, pp. 573–578.

596. L. Ozdamar and M. Demirhan. Experiments with new stochastic global optimization search techniques. *Computers and Operations Research*, 27(9):841–865, 2000.

597. C. H. Papadimitriou and K. Steiglitz. *Combinatorial Optimization: Algorithms and Complexity*. Prentice-Hall, New York, 1982.

598. C. H. Papadimitriou. *The complexity of combinatorial optimization problems*. Master's thesis, Princeton University, 1976.

599. J. Paredis. Co-evolutionary constraint satisfaction. In *3rd Conference on Parallel Problem Solving from Nature*. Springer, 1994, pp. 46–55.

600. V. Pareto. *Cours d'économie politique*. Rouge, Lausanne, Switzerland, 1896.

601. Y. B. Park and C. P. Koelling. An interactive computerized algorithm for multicriteria vehicle routing problems. *Computers and Industrial Engineering*, 16:477–490, 1989.

602. G. T. Parks and I. Miller. Selective breeding in a multiobjective genetic algorithm. In *Parallel Problem Solving from Nature (PPSN'5)*, Amsterdam, Sept 1998. Springer, 1998, pp. 250–259.

603. K. E. Parsopoulos, D. K. Tasoulis, N. G. Pavlidis, V. P. Plagianakos, and M. N. Vrahatis. Vector evaluated differential evolution for multiobjective optimization. In *Proceedings of the IEEE 2004 Congress on Evolutionary Computation (CEC'04)*, 2004.

604. K. E. Parsopoulos, D. K. Tasoulis, and M. N. Vrahatis. Multiobjective optimization using parallel vector evaluated particle swarm optimization. In *IASTED International Conference on Artificial Intelligence and Applications (AIA 2004)*, Innsbruck, Austria. ACTA Press, 2004, pp. 823–828.

605. K. E. Parsopoulos and M. N. Vrahatis. Particle swarm optimization method in multiobjective problems. In *ACM Symposium on Applied Computing (SAC'2002)*, Madrid, Spain. ACM Press, 2002, pp. 603–607.

606. R. Patterson, E. Rolland, and H. Pirkul. A memory adaptive reasoning technique for solving the capacitated minimum spanning tree problem. *Journal of Heuristics*, 5:159–180, 1999.

607. M. Pelikan, D. E. Goldberg, and F. Lobo. A survey of optimization by building and using probabilistic models. In *American Control Conference*, Chicago, IL, 2000.

608. M. Pelikan, D. E. Goldberg, and E. Cantu-Paz. BOA: The bayesian optimization algorithm. In W. Banzhaf et al., editors, *Proceedings of the GECCO'99 (Genetic and*

Evolutionary Computation Conference). Morgan Kaufmann, San Francisco, CA, 1999, pp. 525–532.

609. M. Pelikan, K. Sastry, and E. Cantu-Paz. *Scalable Optimization via Probabilistic Modeling: From Algorithms to Applications*. Springer, 2006.
610. J. W. Pepper, B. L. Golden, and E. A. Wasil. Solving the traveling salesman problem with annealing-based heuristics: A computational study. *IEEE Transactions on Systems, Man and Cybernetics*, 32(1):72–77, 2002.
611. G. Pesant and M. Gendreau. A view of local search in constraint programming. *Journal of Heuristics*, 5:255–279, 1999.
612. D. T. Pham and A. Ghanbarzadeh. Multi-objective optimisation using the bees algorithm. In *Innovative Production Machines and Systems (IPROMS'07) Conference*, July 2007.
613. D. T. Pham, A. Ghanbarzadeh, E. Koc, S. Otri, S. Rahim, and M. Zaidi. The bees algorithm: A novel tool for complex optimization problems. In *IPROMS'2006 Conference*, 2006, pp. 454–461.
614. M. Pharr. *GPU Gems 2: Programming Techniques for High-Performance Graphics and General-Purpose Computation*. Addison-Wesley, 2005.
615. M. G. Pilcher and R. L. Rardin. Partial polyhedral description and generation of discrete optimization problems with known optima. *Naval Research Logistics*, 39:839–358, 1992.
616. J. C. L. Pinto and F. J. Von Zuben. Fault detection algorithm for telephone systems based on the danger theory. In *ICARIS International Conference on Artificial Immune Systems*, LNCS Vol. 3627. Springer, 2003, pp. 418–431.
617. P. Pinto, T. A. Runkler, and J. M. Sousa. Wasp swarm optimization of logistic systems. In *Adaptive and Natural Computing Algorithms*, Coimbra, Portugal. Springer, 2005, pp. 264–267.
618. V. V. Podinovski. Criteria importance theory. *Mathematical Social Sciences*, 27(3):237–252, 1994.
619. G. Polya. *How to Solve It*. Princeton University Press, Princeton, NJ, 1945.
620. M. A. Potter and K. A. DeJong. A cooperative coevolutionary approach to function optimization. In Y. Davidor et al., editors, *Parallel Problem Solving from Nature (PPSN III)*, LNCS Vol. 866. Springer, Berlin, 1994, pp. 149–257.
621. C. N. Potts and S. L. Velde. Dynasearch: Iterative local improvement by dynamic programming. Technical Report TR, University of Twente, The Netherlands, 1995.
622. M. Powell. Radial basis functions for multivariable interpolation. In *Algorithms for Approximation*. Oxford University Press, 1987, pp. 143–167.
623. M. Prais and C. C. Ribeiro. Reactive GRASP: An application to a matrix decomposition problem in TDMA traffic assignment. *INFORMS Journal on Computing*, 12:164–176, 2000.
624. W. Pree, G. Pomberger, A. Schappert, and P. Sommerlad. Active guidance of framework development. *Software—Concepts and Tools*, 16(3):136, 1995.
625. S. Prestwich. Combining the scalability of local search with the pruning techniques of systematic search. *Annals of Operations Research*, 115:51–72, 2002.
626. K. Price. Genetic annealing. *Dr. Dobb's Journal*, 127–132, 1994.
627. K. V. Price, R. M. Storn, and J. A. Lampinen. *Differential evolution: A Practical Approach to Global Optimization*. Springer, 2006.

628. J. Puchinger and G. R. Raidl. Combining metaheuristics and exact algorithms in combinatorial optimization: A survey and classification. In *Artificial Intelligence and Knowledge Engineering Applications: A Bioinspired Approach*, LNCS Vol. 3562. Springer, 2005, pp. 41–53.

629. N. J. Radcliffe and P. D. Surry. Fitness variance of formae and performance prediction. In L. D. Whitley and M. D. Vose, editors, *3rd Workshop on Foundations of Genetic Algorithms*. Morgan Kaufmann, 1994, pp. 51–72.

630. M. Rahoual, R. Hadji, and V. Bachelet. Parallel ant system for the set covering problem. In M. Dorigo et al., editors, *3rd International Workshop on Ant Algorithms*, LNCS Vol. 2463. Springer, 2002, pp. 262–267.

631. D. J. Ram, T. H. Sreenivas, and K. G. Subramaniam. Parallel simulated annealing algorithms. *Journal of Parallel and Distributed Computing*, 37:207–212, 1996.

632. C. L. Ramsey and J. J. Grefenstette. Case-based initialization of genetic algorithms. In *5th International Conference on Genetic Algorithms*, 1993, pp. 81–91.

633. S. Rana and D. Whitley. Bit representation with a twist. In T. Bäck, editor, *7th International Conference on Genetic Algorithms*. Morgan Kaufmann, pp. 188–196.

634. M. Randall and A. Lewis. A parallel implementation of ant colony ptimization. *Journal of Parallel and Distributed Computing*, 62(9):1421–1432, 2002.

635. M. Randall and E. Tonkes. Intensification and diversification strategies in ant colony optimization. *Complexity International*, 9, 2002. http://life.es.edn.au/ci/sub07/randal01.

636. C. R. Raquel, J. Prospero, and C. Naval. An effective use of crowding distance in multiobjective particle swarm optimization. In *Genetic and Evolutionary Computation Conference (GECCO'05)*, Washington, DC. ACM Press, 2005, pp. 257–264.

637. R. Rardin and R. Uzsoy. Experimental evaluation of heuristic optimization algorithms: A tutorial. *Journal of Heuristics*, 7(3):261–304, 2001.

638. K. Rasheed, S. Vattam, and X. Ni. Comparison of methods for developing dynamic reduced models for design optimization. In *CEC'2002 Congress on Evolutionary Computation*, 2002, pp. 390–395.

639. T. Ray and K. M. Liew. A swarm metaphor for multiobjective design optimization. *Engineering Optimization*, 34(2):141–153, 2002.

640. B. J. Reardon. Fuzzy logic vs. niched Pareto multiobjective genetic algorithm optimization. Part 1. Schaffer's f2 problem. Technical Report LA-UR-97-3675, Los Alamos National Laboratory, New Mexico, Sept 1997.

641. B. J. Reardon. Fuzzy logic vs. niched Pareto multiobjective genetic algorithm optimization. Part 2. A simplified Born-Mayer problem. Technical Report LA-UR-97-3676, Los Alamos National Laboratory, New Mexico, Sept 1997.

642. I. Rechenberg. Cybernetic solution path of an experimental problem. Technical Report, Royal Aircraft Establishment Library Translation No. 1112, Farnborough, UK, 1965.

643. I. Rechenberg. *Evolutionstrategie: Optimierung technischer systeme nach prinzipien der biologischen evolution*. Frommann-Holzboog, 1973.

644. R. D. Reed and R. J. Marks II. *Neural Smithing*. MIT Press, 1999.

645. C. Rego and C. Roucairol. A parallel tabu search algorithm for the vehicle routing problem. In I. H. Osman and J. P. Kelly, editors, *Meta-Heuristics: Theory and Applications*, Kluwer, Norwell, MA, 1996, pp. 253–295.

646. J. Reinelt. TSPLib: The traveling salesman problem library. *ORSA Journal on Computing*, 3:376–384, 1991.

647. G. V. Rekliatis, A. Ravindrab, and K. M. Ragsdell. *Engineering Optimisation Methods and Applications*. Wiley, 1983.
648. J.-M. Renders and H. Bersini. Hybridizing genetic algorithms with hill-climbing methods for global optimization: two possible ways. In *1st IEEE International Conference on Evolutionary Computation*, 1994, pp. 312–317.
649. M. G. C. Resende and C. C. Ribeiro. Greedy randomized adaptive search procedures. In *Handbook of Metaheuristics*. Kluwer Academic Publishers, 2003, pp. 219–249.
650. M. G. C. Resende and C. C. Ribeiro. GRASP and path relinking: Recent advances and applications. In *Metaheuristics: Progress as Real Problem Solvers*. Kluwer Academic Publishers, 2005.
651. C. Reyes-Sierra and C. A. C. Coello. Multi-objective particle swarm optimizers: A survey of the state-of-the-art. *International Journal of Computational Intelligence Research*, 2:287–308, 2006.
652. R. G. Reynolds. An introduction to cultural algorithms. In A. V. Sebald and L. J. Fogel, editors, *3rd Annual Conference on Evolutionary Programming*. World Scientific, River Edge, NJ, 1994, pp. 131–139.
653. R. G. Reynolds, Z. Michalewicz, and B. Peng. Cultural algorithms: Computational modeling of how cultures learn to solve problems: An engineering example. *Cybernetics and Systems*, 36(8):753–771, 2005.
654. M. Ribeiro, A. Plastino, and S. Martins. Hybridization of GRASP metaheuristic with data mining techniques. *Journal of Mathematical Modelling and Algorithms*, 5(1):23–41, 2006.
655. R. Ribeiro and H. R. Lourenco. A multi-objective model for a multi-period distribution management problem. In *Metaheuristic International Conference (MIC'2001)*, 2001, pp. 91–101.
656. J. T. Richardson, M. R. Palmer, G. Liepins, and M. Hilliard. Some guidelines for genetic algorithms with penalty functions. In *3rd International Conference on Genetic Algorithms (ICGA'3)*, 1989, pp. 191–197.
657. T. E. Rinderer and A. M. Collins. Behavioral genetics. In *Bee Genetics and Breeding*. Academic Press, 1986, pp. 155–176.
658. B. D. Ripley. *Spatial Statistics*. Wiley, 1981.
659. B. J. Ritzel, J. W. Eheart, and S. Ranjithan. Using genetic algorithms to solve a multiple objective groundwater pollution problem. *Water Resources Research*, 30(5):1589–1603, 1994.
660. D. Roberts and R. Johnson. Evolving frameworks: A pattern language for developing object-oriented frameworks. In *Proceedings of the 3rd Conference on Pattern Languages and Programming*. Addison-Wesley, 1996.
661. R. S. Rosenberg. *Simulation of genetic populations with biochemical properties*. PhD thesis, University of Michigan, Ann Arbor, MI, 1967.
662. C. D. Rosin and R. K. Belew. New methods for competitive coevolution. *Evolutionary Computation*, 5(1):1–29, 1997.
663. K. E. Rosing and C. S. ReVelle. Heuristic concentration: Two stage solution construction. *European Journal of Operational Research*, 97(1):75–86, 1997.
664. F. Rossi, P. Van Beek, and T. Walsh. *Handbook of Constraint Programming*. Elsevier, 2006.

665. P. Roussel-Ragot and G. Dreyfus. A problem-independent parallel implementation of simulated annealing: Models and experiments. *IEEE Transactions on Computer-Aided Design*, 9:827–835, 1990.

666. J. Rowe, K. Vinsen, and N. Marvin. Parallel GAs for multiobjective functions. In *Proceedings of the 2nd Nordic Workshop on Genetic Algorithms and Their Applications (2NWGA)*, 1996, pp. 61–70.

667. B. Roy and V. Mousseau. A theoretical framework for analysing the notion of relative importance of criteria. *Journal of Multi-Criteria Decision Analysis*, 5(2):145–159, 1996.

668. R. K. Roy. *Design of Experiments Using the Taguchi Approach*. Wiley, 2001.

669. G. Rudolph. Convergence analysis of canonical genetic algorithms. *IEEE Transactions on Neural Networks*, 5(1):96–101, 1994.

670. G. Rudolph and A. Agapie. Convergence properties of some multi-objective evolutionary algorithms. In A. Zalzala and R. Eberhart, editors, *CEC'00 Congress on Evolutionary Computation*. IEEE Press, Piscataway, NJ, 2000, pp. 1010–1016.

671. D. E. Rumelhart, G. E. Hinton, and R. J. Williams. Learning representations by back-propagating errors. *Nature*, 323:533–536, 1986.

672. T. A. Runkler. Wasp swarm optimization of the *c*-means clustering model. *International Journal of Intelligent Systems*, 23(3):269–285, 2008.

673. S. Russell and P. Norvig. *Artificial Intelligence: A Modern Approach*. Prentice-Hall, 1995.

674. A. Ruszczynski and A. Shapiro. *Stochastic Programming*, Vol. 10 of *Handbook in Operations Research and Management Science*. Elsevier, 2003.

675. Y. Saab and V. Rao. Combinational optimization by stochastic evolution. *IEEE Transactions on Computer-Aided Design*, 10:525–535, 1991.

676. M. Salami and G. Cain. Genetic algorithm processor on reprogrammable architectures. In *5th Annual Conference on Evolutionary Programming (EP'96)*, San Diego, CA. MIT Press, 1996.

677. L. A. Sanchis. Generating hard and diverse test sets for NP-hard graph problems. *Discrete Applied Mathematics*, 58:35–66, 1995.

678. E. Sandgren. Multicriteria design optimization by goal programming. In *Advances in Design Optimization*. Chapman & Hall, London, 1994, pp. 225–265.

679. D. T. J. Santner, B. J. Williams, and W. Notz. *The Design and Analysis of Computer Experiments*. Springer, 2003.

680. Y. Sawaragi, H. Nakayama, and T. Tanino. *Theory of Multiobjective Optimization*. Academic Press, Orlando, FL, 1985.

681. S. Sayin and S. Karabati. A bicriteria approach to the two-machine flow shop scheduling problem. *European Journal of Operational Research*, 113:435–449, 1999.

682. J. D. Schaffer. Multiple objective optimization with vector evaluated genetic algorithms. In J. J. Grefenstette, editor, *ICGA International Conference on Genetic Algorithms*. Lawrence Erlbaum, 1985, pp. 93–100.

683. J. D. Schaffer, R. A. Caruana, L. Eshelman, and R. Das. A study of control parameters affecting online performance of genetic algorithms for function optimization. In J. D. Schaffer, editor, *3rd International Conference on Genetic Algorithms*, Morgan Kaufman, San Mateo, CA, 1989, pp. 51–60.

684. F. Schoen. Stochastic techniques for global optimization: A survey of recent techniques. *Journal of Global Optimization*, 1:207–228, 1991.

685. J. R. Schott. *Fault tolerant design using single and multicriteria genetic algorithm optimization*. PhD thesis, Department of Aeronautics and Astronautics, Massachusetts Institute of Technology, Cambridge, MA, 1995.

686. A. Schrijver. *Theory of Linear and Integer Programming*. Wiley, 1998.

687. H-P. Schwefel. Kybernetische evolution als strategie der experimentellen forschung in der strömungstechnik. Technical report, Diplomarbeit Hermann Fottinger Institut für Strömungstechnik, Technische universität, Berlin, Germany, 1965.

688. M. Sebag, M. Schoenauer, and C. Ravise. Toward civilized evolution: Developing inhibitions. In T. Bäck, editor, *7th International Conference on Genetic Algorithms*, 1997, pp. 291–298.

689. T. D. Seeley. *The Wisdom of the Hive*. Harvard University Press, Cambridge, MA, 1995.

690. T. D. Seeley and S. C. Buhrman. Group decision making in swarms of honey bees. *Behavioral Ecology and Sociobiology*, 45:19–31, 1999.

691. T. D. Seeley, P. K. Visscher, and K. M. Passino. Group decision making in honey bee swarms. *American Scientist*, 94(3):220–238, 2006.

692. M. Sefraoui and J. Periaux. A hierarchical genetic algorithm using multiple models for optimization. In *Parallel Problem Solving from Nature (PPSN'2000)*, LNCS Vol. 1917. Springer, 2000, pp. 879–888.

693. M. Sellmann and C. Ansótegui. Disco-novo-gogo: Integrating local search and complete search with restarts. In *21st National Conference on Artificial Intelligence and 18th Innovative Applications of Artificial Intelligence Conference*, Boston, MA, 2006.

694. T. Sen, M. E. Raiszadeh, and P. Dileepan. A branch and bound approach to the bicriterion scheduling problem involving total flowtime and range of lateness. *Management Science*, 34(2):254–260, 1988.

695. P. Serafini. Simulated annealing for multiple objective optimization problems. In *Proceedings of the 10th International Conference on Multiple Criteria Decision Making*, Vol. 1, Taipei, Taiwan, 1992, pp. 87–96.

696. W. Sessomboon, K. Watanabe, T. Irohara, and K. Yoshimoto. A study on multi-objective vehicle routing problem considering customer satisfaction with due-time (the creation of Pareto optimal solutions by hybrid genetic algorithm). *Trans. Jpn. Soc. Mech. Eng.*, 64:1108–1115, 1998.

697. K. Shahookar and P. Mazumder. A genetic approach to standard cell placement using meta-genetic parameter optimization. *IEEE Transactions on Computer-Aided Design*, 9(5):500–511, 1990.

698. P. Shaw. Using constraint programming and local search methods to solve vehicle routing problems. In M. Maher and J.-F. Puget, editors, *CP'98 Principle and Practice of Constraint Programming*, LNCS Vol. 1520. Springer, 1998, pp. 417–431.

699. Y. Shi and R. Eberhart. A modified particle swarm optimizer. In *IEEE International Conference on Evolutionary Computation*. IEEE Press, Piscataway, NJ, 1998, pp. 69–73.

700. J. E. Shigley. *Mechanical Engineering Design*. McGraw-Hill, 1973.

701. R. Shonkwiler and E. Van Vleck. Parallel speed-up of Monte Carlo methods for global optimization. *Journal of Complexity*, 10:64–94, 1994.

702. T. Siegfried and W. Kinzelbach. A multi-objective discrete, stochastic optimization approach to shared aquifer management: Methodology and application. *Water Resources Research*, 42(2), 2006.

703. M. R. Sierra and C. A. C. Coello. Improving PSO-based multi-objective optimization using crowding, mutation and ϵ-dominance. In *3rd International Conference on Evolutionary Multi-Criterion Optimization, (EMO'05)*, Guanajuato, Mexico, LNCS Vol. 3410, Springer, 2005, pp. 505–519.

704. B. W. Silverman. *Density Estimation for Statistics and Data Analysis*. Chapman & Hall, London, UK, 1986.

705. K. Sims. Artificial evolution for computer graphics. *Computer Graphics*, 25(4):319–328, 1991.

706. B. M. Smith. Phase transition and the mushy region in constraint satisfaction problems. In A. G. Cohn, editor, *ECAI'94 European Conference on Artificial Intelligence*, Amsterdam, The Netherlands. Wiley, 1994, pp. 100–104.

707. R. E. Snodgrass. *Anatomy of the Honey Bee*. Comstock Publishing Associates, Ithaca, NY, 1953.

708. K. Socha. ACO for continuous and mixed-variable optimization. In *International Workshop on Ant Colony Optimization and Swarm Intelligence (ANTS'04)*, Brussels, Belgium, LNCS Vol. 3172. Springer, 2004, pp. 25–36.

709. K. Socha and M. Dorigo. Ant colony optimization for continuous domains. *European Journal of Operational Research*, 2008. doi:10.1016/j.ejor.2006.06.046.

710. J. Song, J. Hu, Y. Tian, and Y. Xu. Re-optimization in dynamic vehicle routing problem based on wasp-like agent strategy. In *Intelligent Transportation Systems*. IEEE, 2005, pp. 231–236.

711. B. Sotomayor and L. Childers. *Globus Toolkit 4: Programming Java Services*. Morgan Kaufmann, 2005.

712. F. Sourd. Scheduling tasks on unrelated machines: large neighborhood improvement procedures. *Journal of Heuristics*, 7:519–531, 2001.

713. P. Spiessens and B. Manderick. A massively parallel genetic algorithm. In R. K. Belew and L. B. Booker, editors, *Proceedings of the 4th International Conference on Genetic Algorithms*. Morgan Kaufmann, 1991, pp. 279–286.

714. J. Sprave. A unified model of non-panmictic population structures in evolutionary algorithms. In *Proceedings of the 1999 Congress on Evolutionary Computation*, Vol. 2. IEEE Press, Piscataway, NJ, 1999, pp. 1384–1391.

715. N. Srinivas and K. Deb. Multiobjective optimization using non-dominated sorting in genetic algorithms. *Evolutionary Computation*, 2(3):221–248, 1995.

716. D. Srinivasan and T. H. Seow. Particle swarm inspired evolutionary algorithm (PS-EA) for multiobjective optimization problem. In *Congress on Evolutionary Computation (CEC'03)*, Canberra, Australia. IEEE Press, 2003, pp. 2292–2297.

717. P. Stadler and W. Schnabl. The landscape of the traveling salesman problem. *Physics Letter A*, 161:337–344, 1992.

718. P. F. Stadler. Towards a theory of landscapes. In R. Lopéz-Peña, R. Capovilla, R. García-Pelayo, H. Waelbroeck, and F. Zertuche, editors, *Complex Systems and Binary Networks*, Vol. 461. Springer, Berlin, 1995, pp. 77–163.

719. P. F. Stadler. Landscapes and their correlation functions. *Journal of Mathematical Chemistry*, 20:1–45, 1996.

720. W. Stadler. Application of multicriteria optimization in engineering and the sciences. In *Multiple Decision Criteria Making: Past Decade and Future Trends*. Greenwich, 1984.

721. T. J. Stanley and T. Mudge. A parallel genetic algorithm for multiobjective microprocessor design. In *Proceedings of the 6th International Conference on Genetic Algorithms*, 1995, pp. 597–604.

722. R. Steuer. *Multiple Criteria Optimization: Theory, Computation and Application*. Wiley, New York, 1986.

723. B. S. Stewart and C. C. White. Multiobjective A*. *Journal of the ACM*, 38(4):775–814, 1991.

724. R. Storn and K. Price. Differential evolution: A simple and efficient adaptive scheme for global optimization over continuous spaces. Technical Report TR-95-012, Int CS Institute, University of California, Mar 1995.

725. R. Storn and K. Price. Differential evolution: A simple evolution strategy for fast optimization. *Dr. Dobb's Journal*, 22(4):18–24, 1997.

726. T. Stutzle. *Local search algorithms for combinatorial problems: Analysis, algorithms and new applications*. PhD thesis, DISKI—Dissertationen zur Kunstliken Intelligenz., Sankt Augustin, Germany, 1999.

727. T. Stutzle and M. Dorigo. A short convergence proof for a class of ACO algorithms. *IEEE Transactions on Evolutionary Algorithms*, 6(4):358–365, 2002.

728. T. Stutzle and H. Hoos. MAX-MIN ant system. *Future Generation Computing Systems*, 16:889–914, 2000.

729. T. Stutzle and H. H. Hoos. The MAX-MIN ant system and local search for combinatorial optimization problems: Towards adaptive tools for global optimization. In *2nd International Conference on Metaheuristics*, Sophia Antipolis, France, July 1997. INRIA, 1997, pp. 191–193.

730. T. Sudkamp. *Languages and Machines: An introduction to the Theory of Computer Science*. Addison-Wesley, 2005.

731. J. Y. Suh and D. Van Gucht. Incorporating heuristic information into genetic search. In *2nd International Conference on Genetic Algorithms*. Lawrence Erlbaum Associates, USA, 1987, pp. 100–107.

732. K. A. Sullivan and S. H. Jacobson. A convergence analysis on generalized hill climbing algorithms. *IEEE Transactions of Automatic Control*, 46(8):1288–1293, 2001.

733. B. Suman and P. Kumar. A survey of simulated annealing as a tool for single and multiobjective optimization. *Journal of the Operational Research Society*, 57(10):1143–1160, 2006.

734. M. M. Syslo and A. Proskurowski. On Halin graphs. In *Graph Theory*, Vol. 1018 of *Lecture Notes in Mathematics*, Springer, 1983.

735. G. Syswerda. Schedule optimization using genetic algorithms. In *Handbook of Genetic Algorithms*. Van Nostrand Reinhold, 1991, pp. 332–349.

736. G. Syswerda and J. Palmucci. The application of genetic algorithms to resource scheduling. In R. K. Belew and L. B. Booker, editors, *4th International Conference on Genetic Algorithms (ICGA'4)*. Morgan Kaufmann, San Mateo, CA, 1991, pp. 502–508.

737. R. Szmit and A. Barak. Evolution strategies for a parallel multi-objective genetic algorithm. In D. Whitley et al., editors, *Proceedings of the Genetic and Evolutionary Computation Conference*. Morgan Kaufmann, 2000, pp. 227–234.

738. E. Taillard. Robust taboo search for the quadratic assignment problem. *Parallel Computing*, 17:443–455, 1991.

739. E. Taillard. Parallel iterative search methods for vehicle routing problem. *Networks*, 23:661–673, 1993.

740. E. Taillard. Comparison of non-deterministic iterative methods. In *MIC'2001 Metaheuristics International Conference*, Porto, Portugal, July 2001.

741. E. Taillard. Heuristic methods for large centroid clustering problems. *Journal of Heuristics*, 9(1):51–74, 2003.

742. E. Taillard and S. Voss. POPMUSIC: Partial optimization metaheuristic under special intensification conditions. In *Essays and Surveys in Metaheuristics*. Kluwer Academic Publishers, 2002, pp. 613–629.

743. E. D. Taillard and L. Gambardella. Adaptive memories for the quadratic assignment problem. Technical Report 87-97, IDSIA, Lugano, Switzerland, 1997.

744. E. D. Taillard, L. M. Gambardella, M. Gendreau, and J.-Y. Potvin. Adaptive memory programming: A unified view of metaheuristics. *European Journal of Operational Research*, 135(1):1–16, 2001.

745. H. Takagi. Interactive evolutionary computation. In *5th International Conference on Soft Computing and Information Intelligent Systems*, Iizuka, Japan. World Scientific, 1998, pp. 41–50.

746. E.-G. Talbi. Métaheuristiques pour l'optimisation combinatoire multi-objectifs. Technical Report, LIFL, University of Lille, France, 1999.

747. E.-G. Talbi. A taxonomy of hybrid metaheuristics. *Journal of Heuristics*, 8:541–564, 2002.

748. E.-G. Talbi. *Parallel Combinatorial Optimization*. Wiley, 2006.

749. E.-G. Talbi and V. Bachelet. COSEARCH: A parallel cooperative metaheuristic. *Journal of Mathematical Modelling and Algorithms*, 5(2):5–22, 2006.

750. E.-G. Talbi, C. Fonlupt, P. Preux, and D. Robillard. Paysages de problèmes d'optimisation et performances des méta-heuristiques. In *Premier Congrés de la Société Francaise de Recherche Opérationnelle et Aide à la Décision ROAD*, Paris, France, Jan 1998.

751. E.-G. Talbi, Z. Hafidi, and J.-M. Geib. A parallel adaptive tabu search approach. *Parallel Computing*, 24(14):2003–2019, 1998.

752. E.-G. Talbi and H. Meunier. Hierarchical parallel approach for GSM mobile network design. *Journal of Parallel and Distributed Computing*, 66:274–290, 2006.

753. E.-G. Talbi, S. Mostaghim, H. Ishibushi, T. Okabe, G. Rudolph, and C. C. Coello. Parallel approaches for multi-objective optimization. In *Multiobjective Optimization: Interactive and Evolutionary Approaches*, LNCS Vol. 5252. Springer, 2008, pp. 349–372.

754. E.-G. Talbi, T. Muntean, and I. Samarandache. Hybridation des algorithmes génétiques avec la recherche tabou. In *Evolution Artificielle (EA94)*, Toulouse, France, Sept 1994.

755. E.-G. Talbi, M. Rahoual, M.-H. Mabed, and C. Dhaenens. A hybrid evolutionary approach for multicriteria optimization problems: Application to the flow shop. In E. Zitzler et al., editors, *1st International Conference on Evolutionary Multi-Criterion Optimization (EMO'01)*. Zurich, Switzerland, LNCS Vol. 1993. Springer, 2001, pp. 416–428.

756. E.-G. Talbi, O. Roux, C. Fonlupt, and D. Robillard. Parallel ant colonies for combinatorial optimization problems. In J. Rolim et al., editors, *BioSP3 Workshop on Biologically Inspired Solutions to Parallel Processing Systems in IPPS/SPDP International Conference*, San Juan, Puerto Rico, Apr 1999, LNCS Vol. 1586. Springer, 1999, pp. 239–247.

757. E.-G. Talbi and A. Zomaya. *Grid Computing for Bioinformatics and Computational Biology*. Wiley, 2007.

758. E.-G. Talbi, Z. Hafidi, and J. M. Geib. A parallel adaptive tabu search approach. *Parallel Computing*, 24:2003–2019, 1996.

759. K. T. Talluri. Swapping applications in a daily airline fleet assignment. *Transportation Science*, 30(3):237–248, 1996.

760. S. Talukdar, L. Baerentzen, A. Gove, and P. De Souza. Asynchronous teams: Cooperation schemes for autonomous agents. *Journal of Heuristics*, 4(4):295–321, 1998.

761. H. Tamura, A. Hirahara, I. Hatono, and M. Umano. An approximate solution method for combinatorial optimization: Hybrid approach of genetic algorithm and Lagrangean relaxation method. *Transactions of the Society of Instrument and Control Engineering*, 130:329–336, 1994.

762. K. C. Tan, Y. H. Chew, and L. H. Lee. A hybrid multi-objective evolutionary algorithm for solving truck and trailer vehicle routing problems. *European Journal of Operational Research*, 172:855–885, 2006.

763. K. C. Tan, Y. H. Chew, and L. H. Lee. A hybrid multi-objective evolutionary algorithm for solving vehicle routing problems with time windows. *European Journal of Operational Research*, 34:115–151, 2006.

764. K. C. Tan, T. H. Lee, D. Khoo, E. F. Khor, and R. S. Kannan. MOEA toolbox for computer aided multi-objective optimization. In *CEC'2000 Congress on Evolutionary Computation*. IEEE Press, 2000, pp. 38–45.

765. R. Tanese. Parallel genetic algorithms for a hypercube. *Proceedings of the 2nd International Conference on Genetic Algorithms*, July 1987. *MIT, Cambridge, MA*, 1987, pp. 177–183.

766. A.-A. Tantar, N. Melab, and E.-G. Talbi. A parallel hybrid genetic algorithm for protein structure prediction on the computational grid. *Future Generation Computer Systems*, 23(3):398–409, 2007.

767. D. Thain, T. Tannenbaum, and M. Livny. Distributed computing in practice: The Condor experience. *Concurrency and Computation: Practice and Experience*, 17(2):323–356, 2005.

768. J. Thiel and S. Voss. Some experiences on solving multiconstraint zero-one knapsack problems with genetic algorithms. *INFOR*, 32(4):226–242, 1994.

769. P. M. Thompson and H. N. Psaraftis. Cyclic transfer algorithms for multivehicle routing and scheduling problems. *Operations Research*, 41(5):935–946, 1993.

770. J. Timmis, M. Neal, and J. Hunt. An artificial immune system for data analysis. *Biosystems*, 55(1):143–150, 2000.

771. V. T'Kindt and J.-C. Billaut. *Multicriteria Scheduling—Theory, Models and Algorithms*. Springer, 2002.

772. D. S. Todd and P. Sen. A multiple criteria genetic algorithm for container loading. In T. Bäck, editor, *7th International Conference on Genetic Algorithms (ICGA'97)*, July 1997. Morgan Kaufmann, San Mateo, CA, 1997, pp. 674–681.

773. S. Tongchim and P. Chongstitvatana. Parallel genetic algorithm with parameter adaptation. *Information Processing Letters*, 82(1):47–54, 2002.

774. A. Torn and A. Zilinskas. *Global Optimization*, LNCS Vol. 350. Springer, 1989.

775. P. Toth and D. Vigo. *The Vehicle Routing Problem. SIAM Monographs on Discrete Mathematics and Applications.* SIAM, 2002.

776. M. Toulouse, T. Crainic, and M. Gendreau. Communication issues in designing cooperative multi-thread parallel searches. In I. H. Osman and J. P. Kelly, editors, *Meta-Heuristics: Theory and Applications.* Kluwer Academic Publishers, 1996, pp. 501–522.

777. C. A. Tovey. Simulated annealing. *American Journal of Mathematical and Management Sciences*, 8:389–407, 1988.

778. S. Tsutsui. Ant colony optimisation for continuous domains with aggregation pheromones metaphor. In *5th International Conference on Recent Advances in Soft Computing (RASC-04)*, UK, Dec 2004, pp. 207–212.

779. S. Tsutsui, M. Yamamura, and T. Higuchi. Multi-parent recombination with simplex crossover in real-coded genetic algorithms. In *GECCO'99 Genetic and Evolutionary Computation Conference*, 1999, pp. 657–664.

780. E. R. Tufte. *The Visual Display of Quantitative Information*, 2nd edition. Graphics Press, Cheshire, CN, 2001.

781. J. W. Tukey. *Exploratory Data Analysis*. Addison-Wesley, Reading, MA, 1977.

782. A. M. Turing. A correction. On computable numbers, with an application to the entscheidungsproblem. *Proceedings of the London Mathematical Society, Series 2*, 43:544–546, 1938.

783. A. Tuson and P. Ross. Adapting operator settings in genetic algorithms. *Evolutionary Computation*, 6(2):161–184, 1998.

784. N. L. J. Ulder, E. H. L. Aarts, H.-J. Bandelt, P. J. M. Van Laarhoven, and E. Pesch. Genetic local search algorithms for the traveling salesman problem. In H.-P. Schewefel and R. Manner, editors, *Parallel Problem Solving from Nature*, Dortmund, Germany, Oct 1990, LNCS Vol. 496. Springer, 1990, pp. 109–116.

785. E. Ulungu, J. Teghem, P. Fortemps, and D. Tuyttens. MOSA method: A tool for solving multiobjective combinatorial optimization problems. *Journal of Multi-Criteria Decision Analysis*, 8(4):221–236, 1999.

786. E. L. Ulungu and J. Teghem. Multi-objective combinatorial optimization problems: A survey. *Journal of Multi-Criteria Decision Analysis*, 3:83–104, 1994.

787. E. L. Ulungu and J. Teghem. The two phase method: An efficient procedure to solve bi-objective combinatorial optimization problems. *Foundations of Computing and Decision Sciences*, 20:149–165, 1995.

788. E. L. Ulungu, J. Teghem, P. Fortemps, and D. Tuyttens. MOSA method: A tool for solving multi-objective combinatorial optimization problems. Technical Report, Laboratory of Mathematics and Operational Research, Faculté Polytechnique de Mons, 1998.

789. T. Unemi. Sbart 2.4: An IEC tool for creating 2D images, movies and collage. In *Genetic and Evolutionary Computational Conference (GECCO'2000)*, Las Vegas, NV, 2000, pp. 153–156.

790. D. A. van Veldhuizen, J. B. Zydallis, and G. B. Lamont. Considerations in engineering parallel multiobjective evolutionary algorithms. *IEEE Transactions on Evolutionary Computation*, 7(2):144–173, 2003.

791. V. Vapnik. *Statistical Learning Theory*. Wiley, 1998.

792. M. Vasquez and J.-K. Hao. A hybrid approach for the 0-1 multidimensional knapsack problem. In *Proceedings of the International Joint Conference on Artificial Intelligence (IJCAI)*, 2001, pp. 328–333.

793. V. Vazirani. *Approximation Algorithms*. Springer, 2003.

794. D. A. Van Veldhuizen and G. B. Lamont. Multiobjective evolutionary algorithm research: A history and analysis. Technical Report TR-98-03, Graduate School of Engineering, Air Force Institute of Technology, Wright-Patterson, USA, Dec 1998.

795. D. A. Van Veldhuizen and G. B. Lamont. On measuring multiobjective evolutionary algorithm performance. In A. Zalzala and R. Eberhart, editors, *CEC'00 Congress on Evolutionary Computation*. IEEE Press, Piscataway, NJ, 2000, pp. 204–211.

796. D. A. Van Veldhuizen, B. S. Sandlin, R. E. Marmelstein, G. B. Lamont, and A. J. Terzuoli. Finding improved wire-antenna geometries with genetic algorithms. In P. K. Chawdhry, R. Roy, and P. K. Pant, editors, *Soft Computing in Engineering Design and Manufacturing*, Springer, London, 1997, pp. 231–240.

797. R. Venkateswaran, Z. Obradović, and C. S. Raghavendra. Cooperative genetic algorithm for optimization problems in distributed computer systems. In *Proceedings of the 2nd Online Workshop on Evolutionary Computation*, 1996, pp. 49–52.

798. M. G. A. Verhoeven and E. H. L. Aarts. Parallel local search. *Journal of Heuristics*, 1(1):43–65, 1995.

799. R. Viennet. Multicriteria optimization using a genetic algorithm for determining the Pareto set. *International Journal of System Science*, 27(2):255–260, 1996.

800. M. Visée, J. Teghem, M. Pirlot, and E. L. Ulungu. Two-phases method and branch and bound procedures to solve knapsack problem. *Journal of Global Optimization*, 12:139–155, 1998.

801. H.-M. Voigt, J. Born, and I. Santibanez-Koref. Modelling and simulation of distributed evolutionary search processes for function optimization. In H.-P. Schwefel and R. Manner, editors, *Parallel Problem Solving from Nature*, Dortmund, Germany, Oct 1990, LNCS Vol. 496. Springer, 1990, pp. 373–380.

802. S. Voss. Tabu search: Applications and prospects. In *Network Optimization Problems*. World Scientific, USA, 1993, pp. 333–353.

803. S. Voss, A. Fink, and C. Duin. Looking ahead with the pilot method. *Annals of Operations Research*, 136(1):285–302, 2005.

804. S. Voss and D. L. Woodruff. *Optimization Software Class Libraries*. Kluwer, 2002.

805. C. Voudouris. Guided local search: An illustrative example in function optimization. *BT Technology Journal*, 16(3):46–50, 1998.

806. C. Voudouris, R. Dorne, D. Lesaint, and A. Liret. iOpt: A software toolkit for heuristic search methods. In *CP'01 7th International Conference on Principles and Practice of Constraint Programming*, LNCS Vol. 2239. Springer, 2001, pp. 716–729.

807. C. Voudouris and E. Tsang. Guided local search. Technical Report CSM-247, University of Essex, UK, 1995.

808. C. Voudouris and E. Tsang. Guided local search. *European Journal of Operational Research*, 113(2):469–499, 1999.

809. M. Wall. GAlib: A C++ library of genetic algorithm components. Technical Report, Mechanical Engineering Department, Massachusetts Institute of Technology, 1996.

810. L.-H. Wang, C.-Y. Kao, M. Ouh-young, and W.-C. Chen. Molecular binding: A case study of the population-based annealing genetic algorithms. In *IEEE International Conference on Evolutionary Computation (ICEC'95)*, Perth, Australia, Dec 1995, pp. 50–55.

811. A. Warburton. Approximation of Pareto optima in multiple-objective shortest-path problems. *Operations Research*, 35:70–79, 1987.

812. E. D. Weinberger. Correlated and uncorrelated fitness landscapes and how to tell the difference. *Biological Cybernetics*, 63:325–336, 1990.

813. E. D. Weinberger and P. F. Stadler. Why some fitness landscapes are fractal. *Journal of Theoretical Biology*, 163:255–275, 1993.

814. D. J. White. The set of efficient solutions for multiple-objectives shortest path problems. *Computers and Operations Research*, 9:101–107, 1982.

815. D. Whitley, K. Mathias, S. Rana, and J. Dzubera. Evaluating evolutionary algorithms. *Artificial Intelligence*, 85:245–276, 1996.

816. P. B. Wienke, C. Lucasius, and G. Kateman. Multicriteria target optimization of analytical procedures using a genetic algorithm. *Analytical Chimica Acta*, 265(2):211–225, 1992.

817. A. P. Wierzbicki. The use of reference objectives in multiobjective optimization. In *Multiple Criteria Decision Making Theory and Applications*. Springer, 1980, pp. 468–486.

818. C. P. Williams and S. H. Clearwater. *Explorations in Quantum Computing*. Springer, 1998.

819. G. C. Wilson, A. McIntyre, and M. I. Heywood. Resource review: Three open source systems for evolving programs—Lilgp, ECJ and grammatical evolution. *Genetic Programming and Evolvable Machines*, 5(19):103–105, 2004.

820. P. B. Wilson and M. D. Macleod. Low implementation cost IIR digital filter design using genetic algorithms. In *IEE/IEEE Workshop on Natural Algorithms in Signal Processing*, Chelmsford, UK, 1993, pp. 4/1–4/8.

821. S. Wilson and D. Goldberg. A critical review of classifier systems. In J. Schaffer, editor, *International Conference on Genetic Algorithms*, 1989, pp. 244–255.

822. P. Winter. Steiner problem in Halin networks. *Discrete Applied Mathematics*, 17:281–294, 1987.

823. D. W. Wolpert and W. G. Macready. No free lunch theorems for optimization. *IEEE Transactions on Evolutionary Computation*, 1(1):67–82, 1997.

824. I. Wood and T. Downs. Demon algorithms and their application to optimization problems. In *IEEE World Congress on Computational Intelligence*, 1998, pp. 1661–1666.

825. D. L. Woodruff and E. Zemel. Hashing vectors for tabu search. *Annals of Operations Research*, 41:123–137, 1993.

826. A. H. Wright. Genetic algorithms for real parameter optimization. In *Foundation of Genetic Algorithms*. Morgan Kaufmann, 1991, pp. 205–218.

827. S. Wright. The roles of mutation, inbreeding, crossbreeding, and selection in evolution. In D. F. Jones, editor, *6th International Conference on Genetics*, 1932, pp. 356–366.

828. A. S. Wu and R. K. Lindsay. Empirical studies of the genetic algorithm with noncoding segments. *Evolutionary Computation*, 3:128–148, 1995.

829. Y. Xiong, B. Golden, and E. Wasil. The colorful traveling salesman problem. In *Extending the Horizons: Advances in Computing, Optimization, and Decision Technologies, Vol. 37*. Springer, 2007, pp. 115–123.

830. F. Xue, A. C. Sanderson, and R. J. Graves. Multi-objective differential evolution—algorithm, convergence analysis, and applications. In *IEEE Congress on Evolutionary Computation (CEC'05)*, Sept 2007. IEEE Press, 2007, pp. 743–750.

831. M. Yagiura and T. Ibaraki. Metaheuristics as robust and simple optimization tools. In *IEEE International Conference on Evolutionary Computation, (ICEC'96)*, 1996, pp. 541–546.

832. M. Yagiura, T. Ibaraki, and F. Glover. An ejection chain approach for the generalized assignment problem. *INFORMS Journal on Computing*, 16(2):133–151, 2004.

833. D. Yang and S. J. Flockton. Evolutionary algorithms with a coarse-to-fine function smoothing. In *IEEE International Conference on Evolutionary Computation*, Perth, Australia. IEEE Press, 1995, pp. 657–662.

834. X. Yang and M. Gen. Evolution program for bicriteria transportation problem. In M. Gen and T. Kobayashi, editors, *16th International Conference on Computers and Industrial Engineering*, Ashikaga, Japan, 1994, pp. 451–454.

835. Y. Yonezawa and T. Kikuchi. Ecological algorithm for optimal ordering used by collective honey bee behavior. In *7th International Symposium on Micro Machine and Human Science*, Oct 1996, pp. 249–256.

836. R. Zeidman. *Designing with FPGAs and CPLDs*. CMP Books, 2002.

837. M. Zeleny. *Multiple Criteria Problem Solving*. McGraw-Hill, New York, 1982.

838. E. Zemel. Measuring the quality of approximate solutions to zero-one programming problems. *Mathematics of Operations Research*, 6:319–332, 1981.

839. Q. Zhang, J. Sun, E. Tsang, and J. Ford. Combination of guided local search and estimation of distribution algorithm for quadratic assignment problem. In *GECCO'2003 Genetic and Evolutionary Computation Conference*, Chicago, IL, 2003, pp. 42–48.

840. G. Zhou and M. Gen. Genetic algorithm approach on multi-criteria minimum spanning tree problem. *European Journal of Operational Research*, 114:141–152, 1999.

841. E. Zitzler, K. Deb, and L. Thiele. Comparison of multiobjective evolutionary algorithms: Empirical results. *Evolutionary Computation*, 8(2):173–195, 2000.

842. E. Zitzler and S. Künzli. Indicator-based selection in multiobjective search. In *Proceedings of the 8th International Conference on Parallel Problem Solving from Nature (PPSN VIII)*, Birmingham, UK, 2004, pp. 832–842.

843. E. Zitzler, M. Laumanns, and S. Bleuer. A tutorial on evolutionary multiobjective optimisation. *Workshop on Multiple Objective Metaheuristics (MOMH 2002)*, 2004.

844. E. Zitzler, M. Laumanns, and L. Thiele. SPEA2: Improving the strength Pareto evolutionary algorithm. Technical Report 103, Computer Engineering and Networks Laboratory (TIK), Swiss Federal Institute of Technology (ETH), Zurich, Switzerland, 2001.

845. E. Zitzler, M. Laumanns, and L. Thiele. SPEA2: Improving the strength Pareto evolutionary algorithm for multiobjective optimization. In *Evolutionary Methods for Design, Optimisation and Control with Application to Industrial Problems*, Barcelona, Spain, 2002, pp. 95–100.

846. E. Zitzler and L. Thiele. An evolutionary algorithm for multi-objective optimization: The Strength Pareto approach. Technical Report 43, Computer Engineering and Communication Networks Lab (TIK), Swiss Federal Institute of Technology, Zurich, Switzerland, May 1998.

847. E. Zitzler and L. Thiele. Multiobjective optimization using evolutionary algorithms: A comparative case study. In *PPSN V Parallel Problem Solving from Nature*, Amsterdam, The Netherlands, 1998, pp. 292–301.

848. E. Zitzler and L. Thiele. Multiobjective evolutionary algorithms: A comparative case study and the strength Pareto approach. *IEEE Transactions on Evolutionary Computation*, 3(4):257–271, 1999.

849. M. Zlochin and M. Dorigo. Model based search for combinatorial optimization: A comparative study. In J. Merelo et al., editors, *Parallel Problem Solving from Nature (PPSN VII)*. Springer, Berlin, 2002, pp. 651–661.

INDEX

Metaheuristics: From Design to Implementation, by El-Ghazali Talbi